LOCAL AREA NETWORK REFERENCE

Dr. Dimitris N. Chorafas

LOCAL AREA NETWORK REFERENCE

McGraw-Hill Book Company
New York St. Louis San Francisco Auckland Bogotá
Hamburg Johannesburg London Mexico Montreal
New Delhi Panama Paris São Paulo Singapore
Sydney Tokyo Toronto

Library of Congress Cataolg Card Number 89-85035

10 9 8 7 6 5 4 3 2

ISBN 0-07-010889-7

Intertext Publications/Multiscience Press, Inc.
One Lincoln Plaza
New York, NY 10023

McGraw-Hill Book Company
1221 Avenue of the Americas
New York, NY 10020

Contents

PART 1 NETWORKS—CURRENT AND COMING PERSPECTIVES 1

1 The Network as a Strategic Product 3

1.1 Introduction, 3
1.2 A Network Concept, 5
1.3 Elaborating the Conceptual Definition, 7
1.4 Architectural Requirements, 12
1.5 Responding to Security Needs, 15
1.6 Focusing on Network Services, 18

2 Goals of Multimedia Communications 23

2.1 Introduction, 23
2.2 What's the Sense of Multimedia Orientation?, 24
2.3 Able Solutions with a Multimedia Perspective, 29
2.4 Workspace Definition: From Hypercubes to LAN, 31
2.5 Prerequisites for a Response to User Requirements, 34
2.6 Background and Foreground Approaches to Technical Issues, 37
2.7 The Role of an Architecture, 40

3 Network Standards and the Normalization Effort 43

3.1 Introduction, 43
3.2 The Public Telephone Network, 45
3.3 Integrated Service Digital Network (ISDN), 50
3.4 Tariffs and Digital Circuits, 54

3.5 Open System Interconnection (ISO/OSI), 56
3.6 The IEEE 802 LAN Reference Model, 61
3.7 Multimedia versus Voice Communications, 66

4 Able Answers tro LAN Implementation 69

4.1 Introduction, 69
4.2 The Modern Sense of Manufacturing Automation, 70
4.3 Problem Solving at General Electric, 75
4.4 New Protocols to Enhance Connectivity, 79
4.5 The General Mills Experience, 82
4.6 The Approach by Northwestern Bell, 85
4.7 PC and Databases, 87

5 Organizational Solutions for Effective Communications 91

5.1 Introduction, 91
5.2 Organization and Structure, 92
5.3 Authority, Responsibility, Span of Control, 96
5.4 Projecting a New System Architecture, 98
5.5 Technical Characteristics of Network Solutions, 103
5.6 Quality Improvements and Cost Effectiveness, 106
5.7 End-User Orientation and Contributions of Artificial Intelligence Research, 109

PART 2 CHARACTERISTICS OF LOCAL AREA NETWORKS 113

6 What Is a Local Area Network? 115

6.1 Introduction, 115
6.2 The Vital Communications Link, 116
6.3 Profile of a Local Area Network—Baseband and Broadband, 119
6.4 A Bird's Eye View of LAN Protocols, 122
6.5 Classes of LAN Service, 125
6.6 LAN versus Centralized Resources, 127
6.7 Resource Sharing, 131

7 The Nodes and the Topology 135

7.1 Introduction, 135
7.2 Nodes at the Network, 136
7.3 Developing Multiprocessor Capabilities, 139
7.4 Functions of Network Control, 142
7.5 Star versus Bus versus Ring, 145
7.6 A PBX Alternative?, 149
7.7 Network Throughout, 153

8 Technical Choices for the Cabling Plant 155

8.1 Introduction, 155
8.2 Choosing the Bus, 156
8.3 Evaluating Channel Capacity, 165
8.4 Implementing Megastreams, 167
8.5 Forms of Modulation, 169
8.6 Midsplit and Subsplit, Dual Cable, and Bridges, 175

9 Bus Interface Unit and Control of the LAN 183

9.1 Introduction, 183
9.2 Functions of the BIU, 185
9.3 A Specific Example of a Bus Interface Structure, 191
9.4 An Integrated LAN Controller, 197
9.5 Solution Selling and the BIU, 201
9.6 Forward Error Protection, 207
9.7 Very High-Frequency Switch, 208

10 Protocols and Multiple Access Methods 211

10.1 Introduction, 211
10.2 Global Observance of Standard Protocols, 212
10.3 Protocols at the Data Link Level, 215
10.4 Token Passing and Carrier Sensing, 217
10.5 Multiple Access Methods, 219
10.6 Protocols Defined by IEEE 802, 222
10.7 Comparative Evaluation, 225

11 Solutions in Baseband and Broadband Environments—Internetworking 227

11.1 Introduction, 227
11.2 Cost, Benefit, and the BAB and BRB Technologies, 229
11.3 Critical Aspects of LAN Communications, 232
11.4 Prototyping and Experimentation for LAN Design, 238
11.5 Protocols for System Interconnection—Considerations on X.25, 242
11.6 Internet Protocol and Design Control, 244
11.7 Perspectives in Internetworking, 246

PART 3 LOCAL AREA NETWORKS OFFERED BY VENDORS 251

12 Network Systems Corporation's Hyperchannel 253

12.1 Introduction, 253
12.2 The Network Executive, 254
12.3 A Product Line, 259
12.4 Design Philosophy of Datapipe, 262
12.5 Exploring Interconnect Requirements, 263
12.6 High-Level Logical Supports, 265
12.7 Primitives for Networking Requirements, 269

13 Massnet Plus, by Masstor Systems Corporation 277

13.1 Introduction, 277
13.2 The Database Machine, 278
13.3 Goals of Massnet Software, 280
13.4 Establishing a Multicomputer Service with Incompatible OS, 284
13.5 Technical Solutions for Open Vendor Policy, 288
13.6 The Applications Control Environment, 291
13.7 File Exchange and Process Interconnection, 294
13.8 System Control and Administration, 298

14 IBM's Local Area Networks 303

14.1 Introduction, 303

14.2 New Life for SNA, 305
14.3 Personal Computer Networks by IBM, 308
14.4 The Cabling System, 311
14.5 Token Passing, 314
14.6 APPC and SNA, 319
14.7 Other Types of IBM-Sponsored Approaches, 324
14.8 Netview—A Means for Network Control, 329

15 Ethernet by DEC, Intel, Xerox, and Others 333

15.1 Introduction, 333
15.2 A Multivendor Environment, 334
15.3 Technical Fundamentals of the Ethernet Solution, 337
15.4 The Ethernet Packet Structure and Carrier Sensing Mechanism, 340
15.5 An Example with TI Etherseries and Thin Ethernet Software, 344
15.6 LAN Interconnecting by Digital Equipment Corporation, 348

16 A LAN Operating System 353

16.1 Introduction, 353
16.2 Meeting Design Objective with Network OS, 354
16.3 Goals in Operating System Design for LAN, 358
16.4 Supervisory Activities from Source to Destination, 362
16.5 A LAN Operating System and the Network Architecture, 366
16.6 OS Functionality for Message Handling, 368
16.7 Intratask and Intertask Communications File Exchange, 371
16.8 Silicon Nodes for a LAN, 374

PART 4 LAN SERVERS, GATEWAYS, AND DISTRIBUTED DATABASES 377

17 Concepts and Practices with LAN Servers 379

17.1 Introduction, 379
17.2 User Stations and Servers, 380
17.3 Managing Databases in a Network Environment, 384
17.4 File Servers on a LAN, 389
17.5 Goals and Functionality of Printer Servers, 393
17.6 Communications Servers, Gateways, and Organizational Prerequisites, 395
17.7 The Administrator's View of LAN Servers, 399

18 Implementing Efficient File Servers 401

18.1 Introduction, 401
18.2 Security Procedures Connect to File Server Operations: A Controlware Architecture, 402
18.3 Evaluating Approaches to File Allocation: Absolute and Relative Naming, 405
18.4 Software, Organization, and Access in File Server Environments, 408
18.5 File Servers as Systems Components Combining Databasing and Communications, 411
18.6 Contributions by the Data Dictionary, 413
18.7 Making Better Use of Query Facilities, 416

19 Choosing File Server Protocols 421

19.1 Introduction, 421
19.2 Common Characteristics of File Transfer Protocols, 422
19.3 A File Transfer Architecture, 425
19.4 Looking at a Basic Protocol Structure, 430
19.5 Data Units and Transport Protocol Services, 435
19.6 Session and Presentation Level Message Management, 442
19.7 Cooperating Transactions and Pipelining Requirements, 446

20 Communications Challenges and PC-to-Mainframe Links **451**

20.1 Introduction, 451
20.2 Links, Files, and Message Tasks, 453
20.3 Enhanced Products for Communications Links, 457
20.4 Plus and Minus in PC-to-Mainframe Connectivity, 459
20.5 Logical Differences Handicapping Efficient Solutions, 463
20.6 Overcoming Physical Differences, 466
20.7 Internetworking—Short Haul and Wide Area, 469

21 Interconnecting and Managing Distributed Databases **473**

21.1 Introduction, 473
21.2 Bridges and Gateways, 474
21.3 Subnetworking for Electronic Message Services, 480
21.4 Database Access to Serve Management Purposes, 483
21.5 Morgan Stanley and the Database Challenge, 487
21.6 Focusing on Distributed Database Design, 489
21.7 Agile User-Level Interfaces, 491

PART 5 APPLICATIONS OF LOCAL AREA NETWORKS **495**

22 Focusing Computer Technology on the End User's Needs **497**

22.1 Introduction, 497
22.2 Procedure for LAN Implementation, 498
22.3 Three Successful Applications Examples, 501
22.4 Contributions to an Information Center Orientation, 505
22.5 Programmatic Interfaces and Local Area Networks, 508
22.6 Looking into the Implementation of a New Operating System, 511
22.7 Obtaining and Holding End-User Acceptance, 514

23 Requirements and Prerequisites in Implementing the LAN **519**

23.1 Introduction, 519
23.2 An Establishment Information System, 521
23.3 Search for Solutions and the Impact of an Architecture, 524
23.4 LAN Implementation in an Office Environment, 530
23.5 WSs and LANs in Foreign Exchange—An Example of an Application, 533
23.6 Local Area Networks in Factory Installations, 537
23.7 Management's Strategic View of Networks, 541

24 Myriaprocessors—The LAN as System Integrator, **545**

24.1 Introduction, 545
24.2 Ways and Means Toward an Integrating Capability, 546
24.3 Conceptual Transition for Effective Implementation, 549
24.4 Effective Approaches to Personal Computing—A Recycling Policy, 553
24.5 Personal Computers and LANs in an Insurance Environment, 560
24.6 Supporting an SNA Gateway, 562
24.7 Instituting a Network Control Center (NCC), 565
24.8 Quality Histories to Manage Myriaprocessor Resources, 568

25 Cost and Effectiveness **571**

25.1 Introduction, 571
25.2 The Supplier Problem—How to Handle It, 572
25.3 A Computer Manufacturer's Viewpoint, 575
25.4 Economic Justification of the Way Users Look at the Problem, 577
25.5 Budgeting for the Myriaprocessor, 581
25.6 An Open Vendor Policy, 584
25.7 Making the Commodity Software Choice, 589

26 LAN Applications Where Cost Benefit Really Counts **593**

26.1 Introduction, 593
26.2 Making a Distinction Between Substitution and Innovation, 594
26.3 LAN Capacity Planning, 598
26.4 LAN Availability, 601
26.5 Cost Evaluation in a Small Business Environment, 604
26.6 A LAN Perspective Expended to Document Handling, 609
26.7 Designing Increasingly Powerful Workstations—Project Athena, 612
26.8 CASE—A Comprehensive Picture of Technological Change, 615

Index **619**

PART 1

Networks —Current and Coming Perspectives

Chapter

1

The Network as a Strategic Product

1.1 Introduction

For strategic reasons industrial, business, and financial applications are increasingly based on computers and communications. However, problems are raised by distributed real-time computing. To solve these problems, we must understand basic concepts and techniques that are applied to existing systems and those under development. We should also make substantiated decisions when choosing and developing new systems. Decisions made today will commit *our* company over the next 10 years—not only in equipment but also, if not primarily, in the systems approach we take.

As Figure 1.1 suggests, the business and information systems domains have evolved separately. Yet their integration is needed for an able response to strategic requirements. We must assess the impact of a network, align the forces we have available, and evaluate the results of their integration. We must also provide solutions for connectivity,

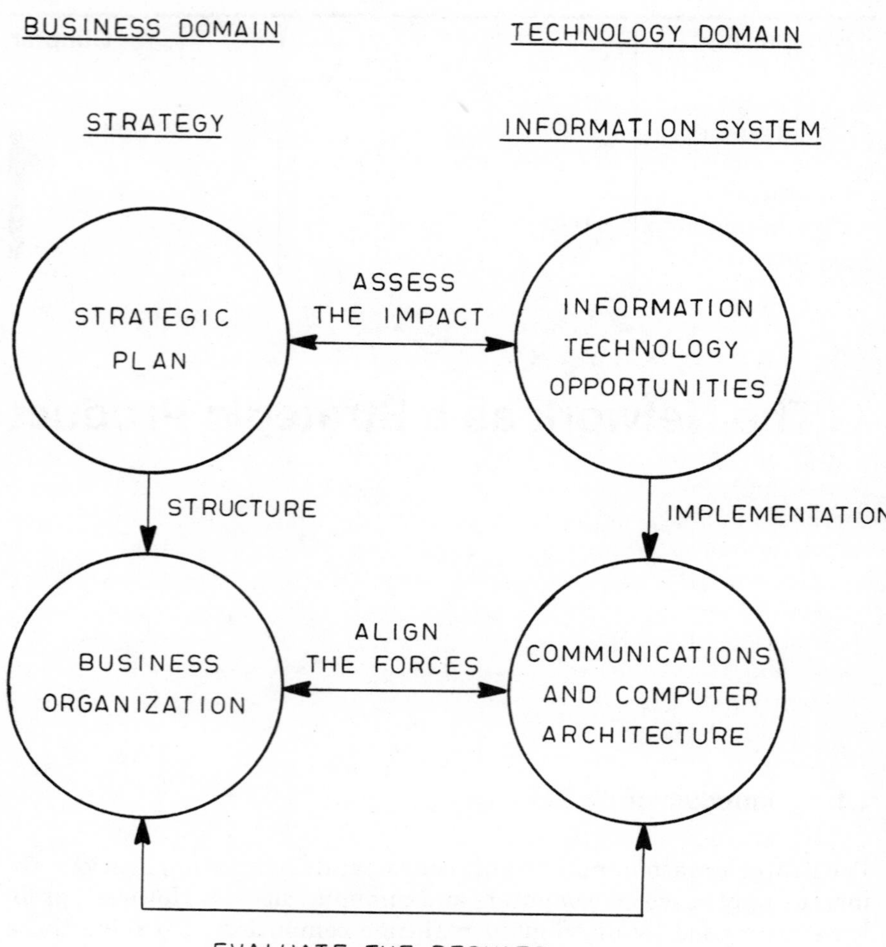

Figure 1.1 Evolution and merger of business and technological domains.

which should be in real time, and should be reliable and secure. Local area networks (LANs) are projected to fill this need.

In the term "local area networks", "networks" is the key word. It says what the construct is supposed to do: transport information—whether this information is data, text, graphics, image, or voice. Hence, prior to discussing LANs, we should look at networks and define what they are, the services they offer, and the benefits we can derive from their use.

Then we can talk about solutions in terms of topology, transmission technology, media, bandwidth allocation, protocols, and architectures.

This discussion will be supplemented by references to specific products as representative of major approaches. Particular emphasis will be given to LAN products for connecting personal computers as well as mainframes. Significant issues, such as network interconnection, network management, selection factors, and future trends, will be meaningful if we first establish the fundamentals.

1.2 A Network Concept

A network is a well-defined collection of communications services. It is a controllable structure that ties together systems and components. Increasingly, communications networks are used to draw together corporate information services. Whether in manufacturing, merchandizing, or banking, corporate information is a vital resource.

Modern networks have little to do with the crude transmission service of the past. They are intelligent carriers that provide effective information interchange among attached devices—mainframes, personal computers (PCs), telephone sets, and video presentation units. To efficiently plan the way in which technology should be used, we should first establish:

1. Why we need networks, local or long haul.
2. What the leading direction in telecommunications is.
3. What skill is necessary to exploit what technology currently offers.
4. How we should manage networks in order to get results.

Effective answers to these questions go beyond classes of traffic, physical architectures, transmission media, multiple-access protocols, message-scheduling algorithms, end-to-end connectivity, very large-scale integration (VLSI) circuits, performance evaluation, or even standardization trends in the context of distributed computing systems implemented on a real-time basis. The requirements include examination of both theoretical and practical issues as well as of industrial strategies and their impact.

Networks are fundamental to the achievement of the electronic office. The office is not a series of individual people working independ-

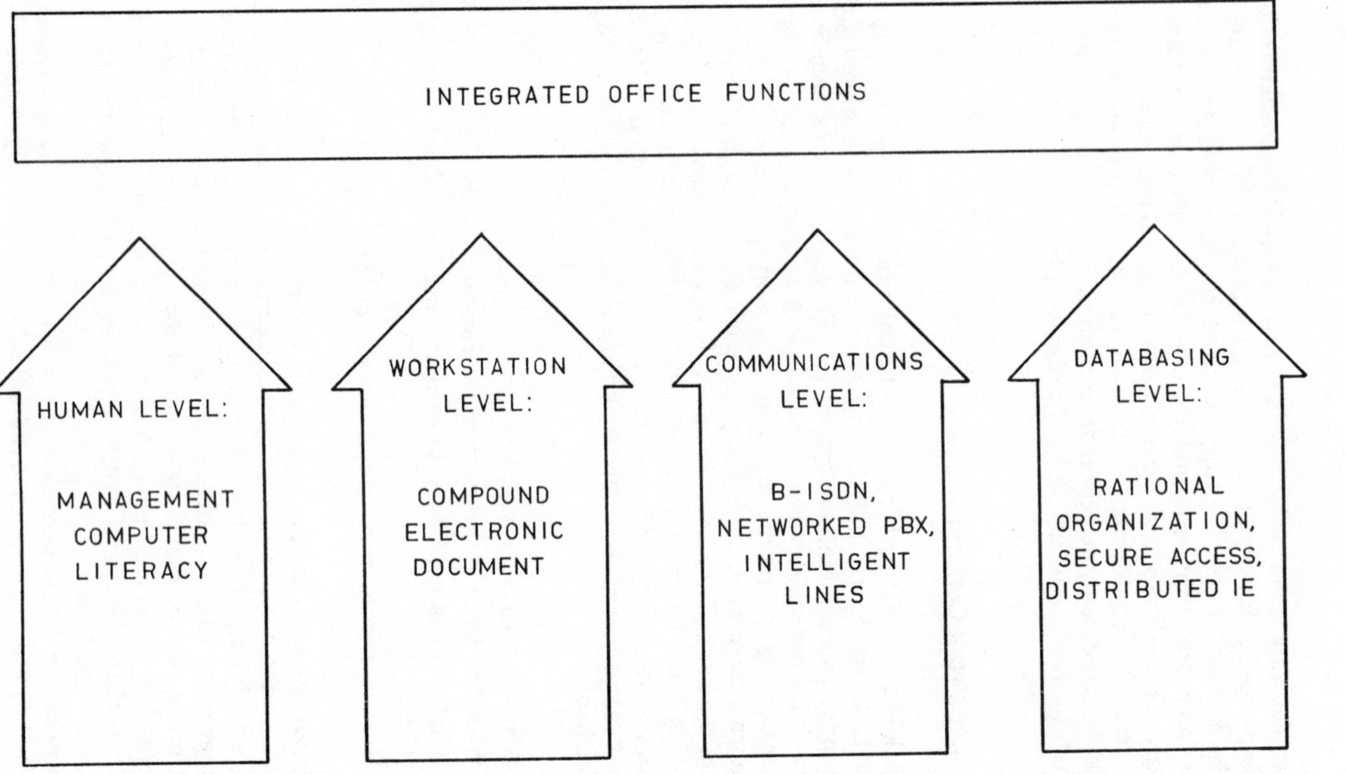

Figure 1.2 Integrated office functions include a range of references from the human to the data basing level.

ently; it is a network of staff working together to reach a common goal. Therefore, more than stand-alone machines and networks are necessary to serve the modern office. As Figure 1.2 suggests, the four basic levels that must be considered are:

1. Human, including computer literacy.
2. Workstation, also handling compound electronic documents.
3. Communications, focusing on intelligent lines.
4. Databasing, particularly secure distributed databases.

All four levels are very important. Specifically in terms of networking, the focal point should be one of understanding the telecommunications network in its fundamentals.

Figure 1.3 brings together four types of office automation projects. Their use ranges from telecommunications to databases, workstations, and end-user functions. What is important is that they have a *unified architecture* with the aim of *full integration*.

System architecture, system integration, and the implementation of artificial intelligence form an aggregate of concepts which should be taken as a whole. Our challenge is to systematically expand state-of-the-art services to enhance the prospects of future growth.* Only then can a company's substantial investments in communications and computers generate cost savings, leading to an increase in profit margins.

The right conceptual definition has a great impact on investments. Some big banks now have plans for 50,000 workstations online. One recent study suggested that by 1990/91 there will be 20 to 50 million workstations operating online in America, with another 10 to 30 million interconnected in Europe. Such massive communications requirements call for properly tuned wide area networks as well as an able choice of local networking capabilities. Today there is no way to design a computer system without thinking of telecommunications. Whatever happens at the network side reflects itself in all the software used by the host. Computers and communications are indivisible. Able solutions in one field help to support what is happening in other areas.

1.3 Elaborating the Conceptual Definition

To succeed with advanced technology, we need a concept and a perspective—not one-way streets but compositions with alternatives. Clear conceptual definitions help us escape a sad fact of modern industrial life:

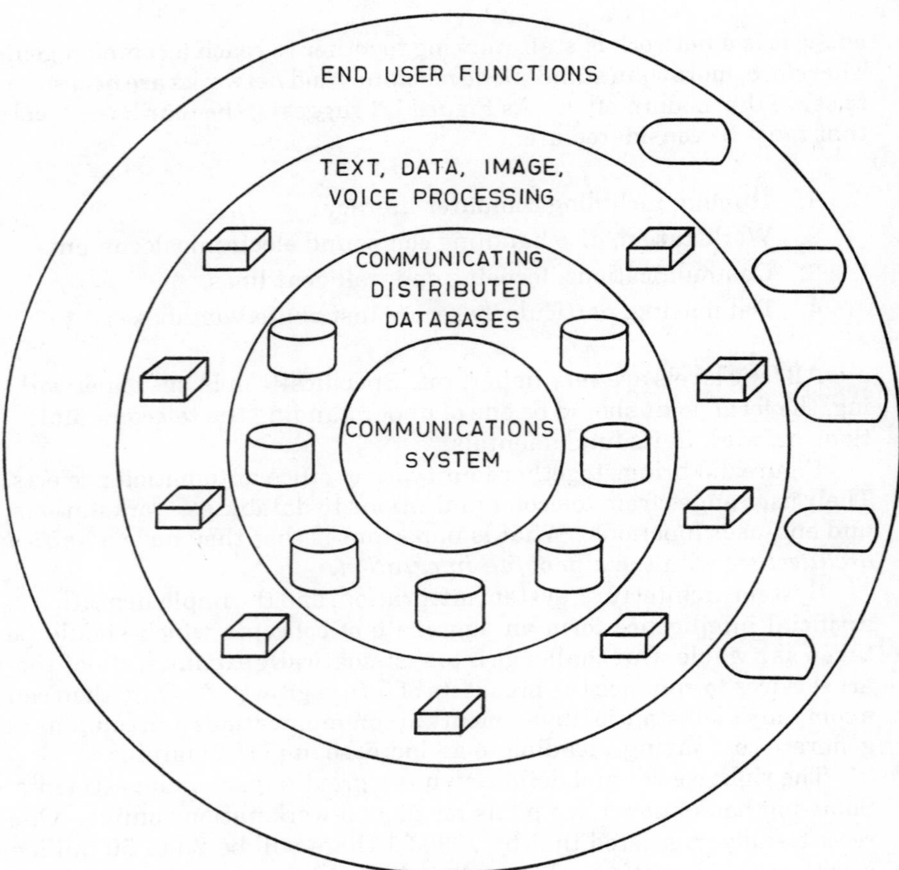

Figure 1.3 Communications is the kernel. User visibility is greater at the outer layer. The other layers must be transparent.

the higher up one climbs in an organization, the less sophisticated is the information equipment at one's disposition. Projected in the proper way, networks and workstations (WSs) aim to correct this prevailing imbalance. Our conceptual definition should include the critical factors which come into play and also reflect on critical characteristics of communications networks. The prime consideration in choosing networking solutions must be:

1. Security.
2. Reliability.

3. Performance, including multimedia.
4. Network control.
5. Flexibility and expandability.
6. Overall design and integration capability.
7. Maintainability and maintenance cost.
8. Procurement and installation cost.
9. Conservation of space, power, and other utilities.
10. Overall vendor dependability.

No network is ever built just for the sake of building it. The investments we make in one should have benefits that exceed the involved costs. As Figure 1.4 suggests, the network may serve classic computer applications as well as sophisticated user needs that expert systems make feasible.

A global implementation definition is given in Figure 1.4. Our goal should be service to management and customer satisfaction. This includes real-time availability of applications to customers. Also important at the management side are adherence to budgets and keeping up with schedules.

One way to make sure that we reach our goal is to use "metrics." Metrics can reveal strengths and weaknesses while the network is in operation. For example, when asked which network factors they currently measure, respondents to a recent study cited improved customer satisfaction, establishment of management information standards, control over exploding communications costs, fewer production errors and reruns, and increased awareness of problems. They also mentioned adherence to project schedules, sticking to project budgets, and software tools to collect quantitative as well as qualitative information and analyze it. When applied to current networks, metrics can also be instrumental in providing us with guidelines for developing new networks and in establishing performance criteria and constraints for them:

- What are the limits of current technology?
- What are the limits of the next effort?
- What should be done to meet developing requirements?
- What can be done given available resources: human, financial, technological?

---

* See also: D.N. Chorafas, *System Architecture, System Integration, and the Role of Artificial Intelligence*, McGraw-Hill, New York, 1988.

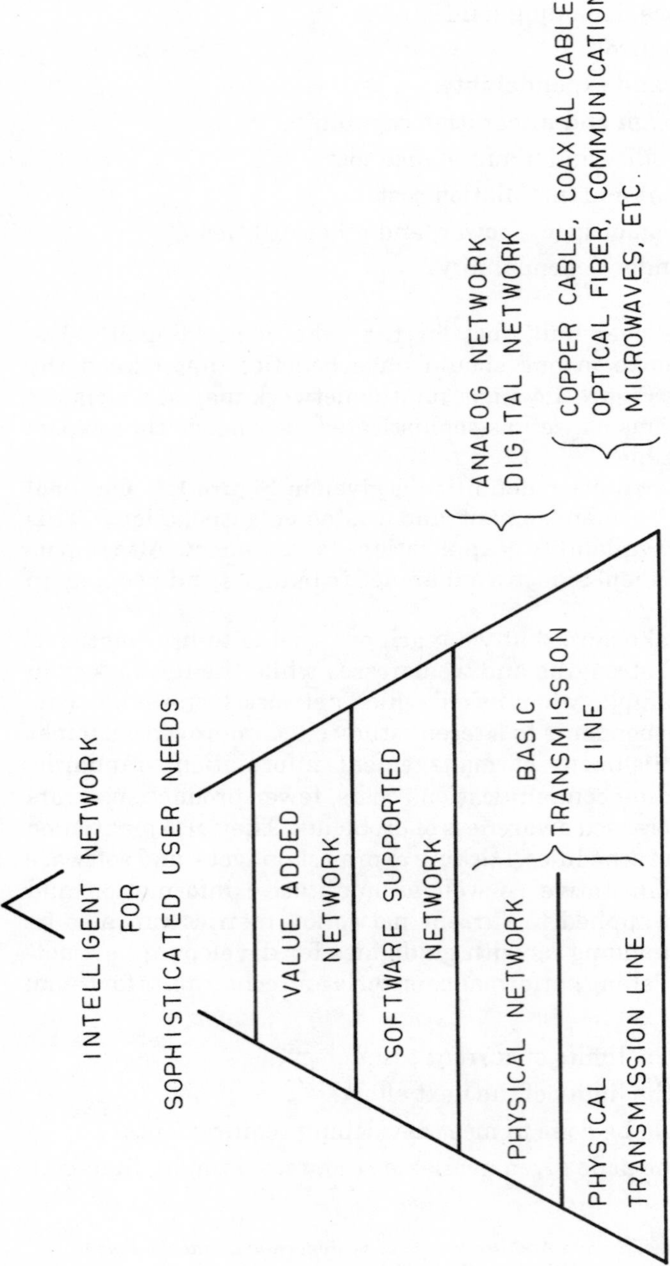

Figure 1.4 A universal network will provide the infrastructure for social and economic activities.

- What should *not* be done?

We often fail to appreciate the importance of the last query, yet its role is significant. Constraints exist with all systems. No conceptual definition can be elaborated in an able manner without properly identifying the constraints which we face in system design and those the network users will be subjected to.

Like other systems, networks fail. Therefore, we should plan for reliability. To do so in an effective manner we should look carefully at the application itself, not just at the technical side of the installation. An accident at the November 1987 Comdex Convention in Las Vegas helps exemplify this reference. To display its wares to the nearly 1,500 reporters at the show, Novel rigged up a LAN in the press room using a dozen personal computers. The installation used one file server to store the information for the PCs hooked up to it. When a reporter yanked the cord on the file server to plug it into his laptop computer, he wiped out the stories of more than a dozen journalists. The system crashed. A sound policy to follow with a network is forecasting crash points and streamlining differences in the applications part of the system. This is an opportunity to apply the rules we have learned with system engineering during the last 30 years.

The physical side of a LAN installation should be thoroughly investigated but so should the logical aspects of the projected implementation. The implementation itself should be looked at as an integral whole. Artificial intelligence can be instrumental in this effort. It can contribute both rules and a methodology to system design. Through metapredicates (second-order logic), intelligent systems will allow only nonredundant and consistent knowledge to accumulate in the knowledge bank, which is important for a running processor.

While we should pay significant attention to system perspectives, we should also consider components individually. We should describe several system solutions built from these components, emphasizing independently single-source systems, maximum dependability, expansion capability, layered solutions, sophisticated software, and the minimization of cost on a documented life-cycle basis. Our network concept must stress value-added telecommunications. Telecommunications as a straight data and voice transfer business is going to disappear. It's the added value that counts.

It should be possible to add new services at a reasonable cost. This is the sense of the transition we have witnessed during the last 5 years, as computers and communications networks developed from experimental projects into fully commercial offerings. For many companies computer networks become the infrastructure for further growth. While many problems still remain to be solved—such as those associated with flow control, congestion control, user access, and security—the need for network implementation is undeniable. At the same time, the size and costs of the network demands the acquisition of appropriate knowledge regarding its behavior. This applies to both computer components and specific telecommunications concerns.

A network concept should see to it that the foundation is provided for orderly movement of information from source of destination and that such information transfer takes place in a dependable manner.

1.4 Architectural Requirements

When we speak of networks with 200,000 attached computers, we make reference to very large systems. We are just starting to understand the sort of architecture very large systems need in order to function properly. Telecommunications systems with 5,000 and 10,000 connected computers are also large systems by today's standards. The same principle applies to them: *Big systems must be architectured.* They cannot happen in a hazardous, unplanned manner. The use of a system architecture permits a stable basis for planning and gives a common direction in the development of distributed computers and communications. This should be a pivotal point in a network concept. The freedom provided by a system architecture makes it possible for a network to be customer oriented rather than product oriented, tuning our organization's information flow to market demands. Before the system architecture can be chosen, the function of the network must be clearly defined, keeping the following points in mind:

1. Describing is not enough because describing is not defining.
2. Accuracy is important in assuring the framework for user service.
3. Completeness, simplicity, maintainability, and the ability to provide the infrastructure for systems integration are paramount.

Completeness refers to the full coverage of functionality outlined in the International Standards Organization's Open Systems Interconnection (ISO/OSI) model. It establishes one physical and six logical layers. However, the ISO/OSI layers should be enriched to include:

- Network Control Center (NCC) facilities (which account for roughly 40 percent of a network architecture's lines of code)
- A polyvalent device-independent interconnect interface to make feasible an open vendor policy

Simplicity, integration, and maintainability are vital architectural requirements.

Simplicity is reflected not only in system design but also in ease of learning and ease of use. This is valid both in an end-user sense and in terms of the work to be contributed by the computers and communications specialists. Furthermore, the level of simplicity to be established (and maintained) is heavily affected by integration policies. Such policies must be carefully outlined and closely followed thereafter. Simplicity may be difficult to establish, but it is not impossible. Modern networks will typically involve a number of links from satellite broadcasting to terrestrial and submarine connections (Figure 1.5). While these are diverse in a physical sense, we are concerned with the logical level, which is where we should pay the most attention.

Our goal should be full integration by means of *one logical network* that is able to interconnect all the logical and physical networks we had in the past—whether private or public. Our solutions must respond to requirements at service levels. Some users and some applications require both high-quality and high-capacity networking. They also call for integration, which means ease of moving between the various functions of product offerings, making different components appear similar to the user. Typically, integrated systems use identical routines and common files, independent of their software and hardware characteristics.

A successful system integration must be conceptual, logical, and physical. Actually, it takes place at different levels. Architectural references provide the overall system perspective. Communications protocols permit the exchange of information among devices attached to the network. Functional integration happens at the user's level, on a multipurpose, intelligent, communicating WS. Procedural integration includes all functions not yet automated, and channel integration refers to voice, text, data, graphics, image—with PBX as pivot point. Training is important for a knowledgeable, homogeneous implementation.

Gateways of all sorts are necessary: PC-to-mainframe, LAN, long

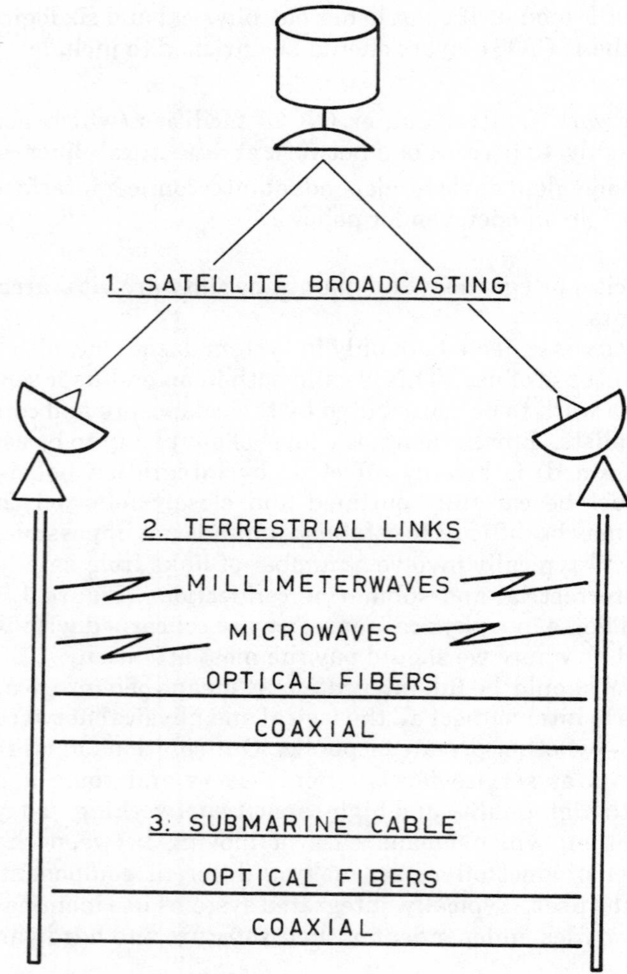

Figure 1.5 Modern networks are characterized by the use of alternative, mutually supporting paths.

haul, metropolitan area networks (MANs). Here operating system(s) act as the fundamental common ground of attached devices of attached devices; database management systems (DBMSs) manage the distributed databases including access to central resources and public databases; programming languages—also four generation languages and integrated software—play a key role for applications, decision support, and document handling. Maintainability, too, is built in at the conceptual level. Otherwise, maintainability will *not* be effective, particularly when it is needed the most. We should not assume a priori that mixed vendor systems are not maintainable. There is a whole spectrum of maintenance possibilities for these systems, particularly in major metropolitan areas.

If *our* organization is considering an open vendor policy, we should assure each vendor's dependability. We must insist on the names of long-term customers and talk a lot about their maintenance experience. There are two more observations about buying equipment:

- The service we will receive from our vendor source is directly proportional to the risk in using that source.
- The service often is inversely proportional to the source's size.

Loosely translated, little firms work harder. Many firms which have dealt with major vendors report disappointing experiences. Lack of product knowledge and an inability to bend to customer needs are typical complaints. This is not to say that big vendors are not excellent. They are. But their problems must be properly faced at the negotiating table.

In short, the networking solution incorporating a telecommunications concept must account for the implementation and the application requirements of workstations, departmental machines, and central resources. The architectural perspective is important because we are faced with a growing range of converging technologies.

We must look at the office as an intelligence machine—an extension of the human mind. The network concept should take full account of a modern organization's dependence on communicating databases, decision support, office automation, and robotics. The current and coming requirements lead to large, fairly complex aggregates of people, software, and machinery.

1.5 Responding to Security Needs*

Whenever we talk of strategic products, detail in the elaboration of a conceptual definition is always critical. Such detail is not only technical,

---

* Given its great importance to networks and to organizations as a whole, security will be discussed in several chapters.

it includes reliability, security, and cost, which help define the level of trust we can place on the network and the functionality and service it can provide. The adoption of new technologies in communications should have among its goals that of promoting the best service. Therefore, the strategic perspectives to be decided by top management are:

1. How to project client service needs in the coming years.
2. How to structure the delivery system to respond in an able manner to client requirements.
3. How to supply the management of our company with state-of-the-art decision support facilities.
4. How to implement a network of communicating databases which is competitive, cost effective, reliable, and secure.
5. How much money to invest in high technology and at which rate.

The answers to these questions are not self-evident. They require significant study and detail. Information security is an example of the range of possibilities we should consider.

It is not always properly understood that in a communications network access, integrity, and security are not individual problems—they are a collective one. Therefore, they must be faced in an integrated manner. Like any other system, security procedures have to be easy to use, yet powerful enough to provide comprehensive and flexible protection. This should be a goal in conceptual development and network design. Security, like reliability, is built at the drafting board. Our organization should be aware of the real threats to automated systems that exist today. A proper study would consider the value of information in our system, the costs of security failures (which can be high), and the steps needed to maintain cost-effective controls. We must always be aware of the current managerial and technological issues that affect today's security decisions about tomorrow's systems.

Security techniques must be applied to the design, development, testing, and operation of information systems, the whole network, the mainframes, the departmental machines, and the workstations. We must identify the appropriate security controls based on an analysis of the performance specifications and security requirements. While necessary, line encryption is no longer sufficient. The new goal is end-to-end security: workstation to workstation and workstation to mainframe. There are also functional viewpoints to be observed:

- Analytical queries and messages have different requirements.
- Messages and transactions have different sets of security and protection needs.

The right to read, write, insert, and delete must be assured in a dependable manner. Organizational hierarchy should also be accounted for in designing the protection system.

In terms of system design, the addition of a cryptography function as a means of protecting information from disclosure or deliberate modification affects the architecture in terms of selection, distribution, and verification of supported functions. It is also necessary to estimate the potential for loss in case of a security breach, which can cause a loss that ranges from relatively insignificant to catastrophic. After they have been identified as to their importance, losses can be avoided or minimized through appropriate security measures. Hence, the first key question is straightforward: "What kind of losses might be incurred through security breaches?"

The answer to this question is neither simple nor linear. As Figure 1.6 suggests, we must consider the whole span of the network, including:

- Its topology, which may cover the country or several countries
- The functional product the network offers, from R&D to manufacturing and sales
- The information types being handled—data, text, image, voice and other communications requirements

The use of online workstations and microfiles (hard disks on workstations) amplifies the need for security at the work space level. A detailed study is necessary so that public and private keys can be used in an able manner. Such study must be done within our company's own environment, and we must consider not only cryptography but also key management and efficient user authentication procedures. User identification, authentication, and authorization is a dynamic process. Beyond the direct issue of maintaining confidentiality of proprietary information, there exists a number of ethical and legal issues which force the close safeguarding of certain categories of information. Failure to assure the privacy of information can be the basis for legal action or can cause an organization (industry or financial institution) to lose its reputation.

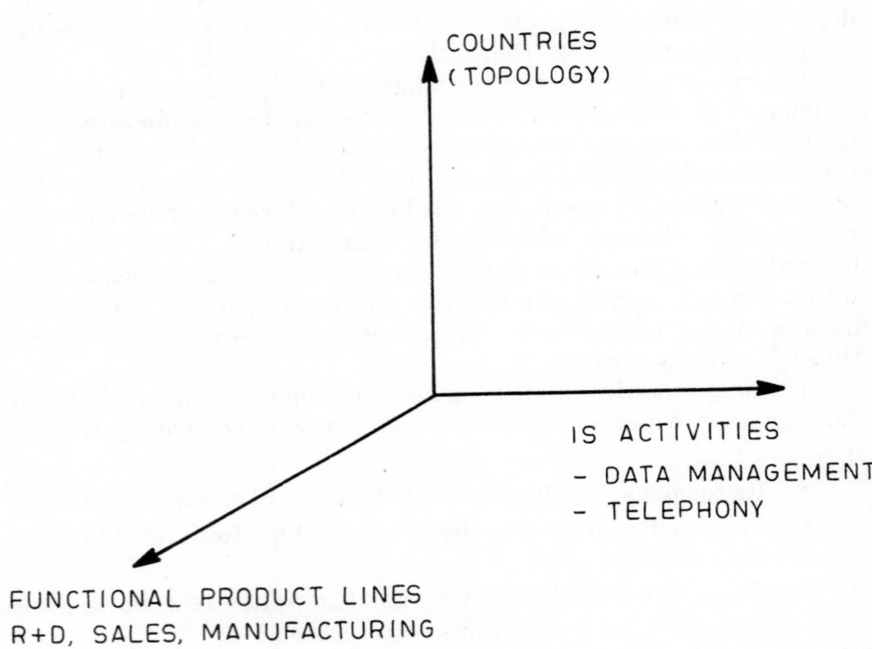

Figure 1.6 Span of a network.

All this brings attention to the fact that networking has little to do with the simple act of providing connecting lines—though such lines are part of the infrastructure. The mark of competence is in the additional levels of sophistication in network design.

1.6 Focusing on Network Services

Over the years, networks have been put in place to interconnect mainframe resources and terminals. Now the roles have changed. Companies must project computer networks first and add the usual array of processors, printers, and disk drives later on. The problem is that everyone is buying the computers first and then trying to connect them together.

The new and rational way to architect a system is to think of computers as peripherals. We must start with the network. Mainframes, departmental machines, and personal computers are elements of the system. So is software. But the commanding authority is the network:

1. For many branches of industry today, without a network there is no profit.
2. Technology-intense products and applications require a network.
3. Unless there is a universal network there are overlaps and delays.
4. Network requirements increase almost logarithmically with the work we do online.

Particular attention must be paid to the delicate balance which must now be kept between information delivery and information processing. While many companies are in search for an equilibrium between them, thanks to networks the delivery side of services has become simpler, more rapid, very accurate, and of lower cost than they used to be.

The network choices made will provoke significant changes in our firm as well as in our competition. The new delivery mechanism must reflect the fact that products and services for knowledge industries are:

1. Made the very moment they are sold to the customer.
2. Have a higher information content than any other product in the past.
3. Must move across physical and logical barriers, protected but unimpeded.

Technical solutions should be fully dynamic, reflecting the fact that, according to the best projections currently available, every 6 months something very significant will be happening that changes our mind about the way we look at the workplace and the communications means at our disposition. It is likely that this will continue to happen in some measure over the next 10 years. At the same time we no longer speak of solutions contained within a preestablished framework—such as point-to-point or multidrop lines—but of big, integrated systems. Big systems are not little systems that have outgrown their original size. Big systems are totally different in terms of design, implementation, verification, and maintenance.

Over a time frame which varies from one implementation to another, successful systems can become global, reaching 100 percent of the population. Examples are telephones and television (Figure 1.7). Other products target part of a population which is within easier reach in an economic and technical sense. Cable television is a good example of metropolitan area installations which will increasingly interest industry in the future.

A dynamic organization must be planning for communications. In the past, such planning focused merely on equipment, facilities, and costs. The new approach is to:

- Identify opportunities
- Develop strategies to exploit them
- Elaborate on the potential impact of the communications resources—both on the client base and on our own management

We must develop policies and procedures that assure uniform means of dealing with *total* corporate communications requirements; these requirements include multifunctionality in implementation, financial savings from shared communications facilities, enhanced communication between business units—even seemingly unrelated ones—and support for future applications. To face the challenges of real-time online operations, we must attack the basic issues of telecommunications with determination, providing gateways to other communications systems—both public and private—assuring 99.99 percent reliability, focusing on security, controlling costs through balanced use, and keeping ahead with technological developments. But we must also be able to implement such developments without being swamped by the costs.

On the technical side, this requires that we pay attention to the topology over which the network will span, the transmission proper (media, capacity), switching (central, regional, local), polyvalent multifunctional stations, time division and frequency division multiplexing (TDM, FDM), electrical characteristics (noise, conditioning, synchronization, regeneration, frequency spectrum), protocols (at each layer of a layered architecture), and effective interfaces (between successive lay-

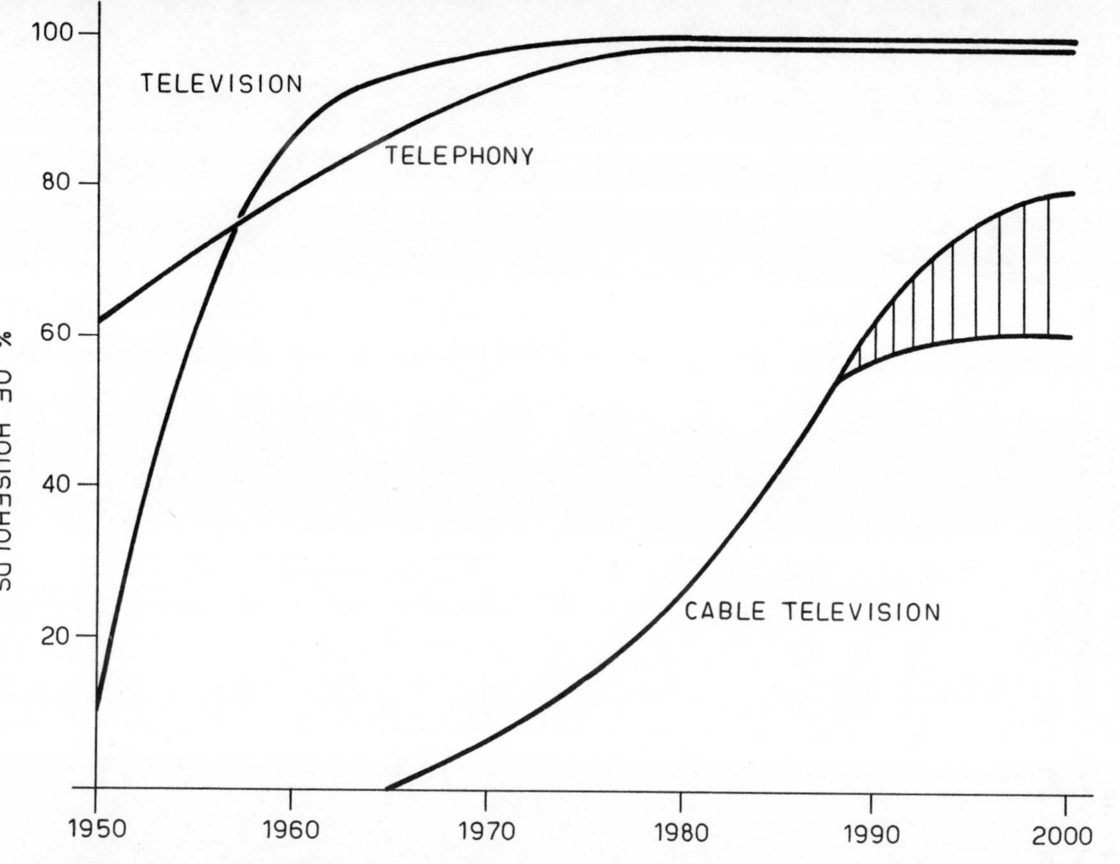

Figure 1.7 **Successful communications systems tend to become global.**

ers). The last two points are logical. They presuppose the adoption of corporate-wide system architecture which follows a layered approach. A layered approach typically follows the open system interconnection model of the International Standards Organization (ISO/OSI). We will return to this subject in Chapter 3.

Chapter

2

Goals of Multimedia Communications

2.1 Introduction

The new generation of networks is a combination of intelligent digital transmission capabilities and software-controlled switching. Such an intelligent network allows its customers to call upon voice, image, graphics, text, or data through a single-line connection. It also eliminates the need for a large number of special-purpose lines. Multimedia networks permit their users to become self-provisioning, giving them the ability to obtain a vast array of services quickly and economically. The incorporation of artificial intelligence capabilities makes the network self-healing, continually monitoring and repairing itself before the user experiences any trouble. This greatly increases the value of a network to its clients.

Current projections indicate that the world is going to be full of multifunctional terminals. Who is going to use them and for what reason? By and large, casual users are going to need them; but "casual" does not mean "trivial." In fact, even part-time use of multimedia capabilities can be very important to a company's profitability and competitiveness. Therefore, the network has to support part-time use in an efficient, easy-to-employ manner. This means total commitment to the development of technology powerful enough to connect an expanding number of information resources. It also presupposes companies determined to use that technology intelligently to provide themselves and their clients with tools to manage the pace of change and meet the dynamic challenges ahead. Networks must cope with:

- Growth
- Speed
- Multifunctionality
- Globalization
- Innovation
- Dependability of services to the end user

As we automate more and more services for more and more people, the services have to be *really* helpful. Design perspectives must assure the boundaries of functionality and install a human safety net through help functions and full problem tracking. The electronic distribution of services should not be a one-way channel or a monofunctional offering. Multimedia capabilities encourage people to use the system, see that it is appealing, provide choice and quality, and assure a competitive edge and an innovative image.

Multimedia communications are indivisible from distributed multimedia databases, although the latter depend on the former for their existence. One of the factors promoting multimedia databases is progress in large wideband optical communications. Another is progress in storage media such as optical disks. Similarly, the development of software technologies has had its impact: multiwindows, vector graphics, facsimile, and digitizers are examples.

2.2 What's the Sense of Multimedia Orientation?

The ever-increasing management demand to improve mental productivity at the end-user level is cited as a reason for multimedia orientation. The same is true of the standardization of communication protocols such as those supported by ISO/OSI, as well as the development of semantic data models and object-oriented programming languages.

User requests and technological advancements are complementary and constitute a self-feeding cycle. Research on artificial intelligence, knowledge representation, the development of engineering databases and office management systems are all influenced by multimedia solutions, which contribute to their further development. Sophisticated engineering and managerial WSs pose requirements which only AI can solve in an able manner. Even in a more classical sense of implementation, a system solution cannot and should not be one-sided; as Figure 2.1

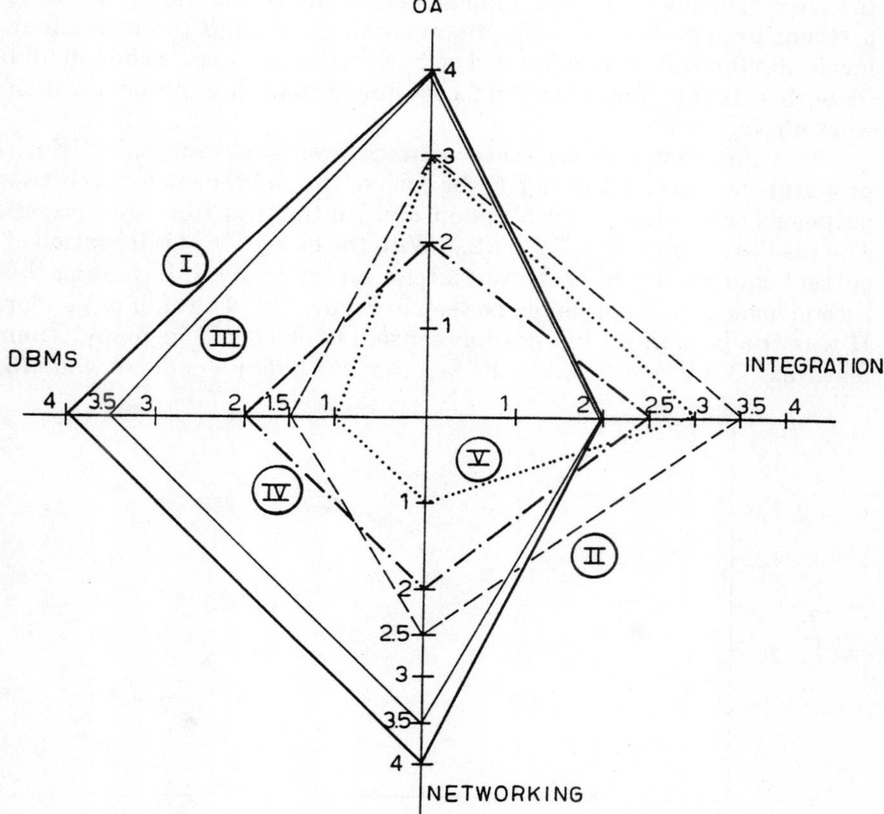

Figure 2.1 Axes of reference in the evaluation of a communications system.

suggests, there are four axes of references we should look at very carefully:

- System integration
- Networking
- DBMS
- Office automation, focusing on end-user functions

No vendor is going to provide the "best" approach to globally meet customer-specified requirements. Therefore, the user organization has to take responsibility for reaching all pertinent decisions. For example, a recent project for a leading organization considered the above four levels of reference. It also focused on how well-posed approaches should fit with existing computers and communications investments which were already made.

Five different vendors were invited to submit proposals. Each proposal was rated 1 through 5, for each of the reference levels. If two proposals came close, only 1/2 point divided the first from the second. The results are shown in Figure 2.1. With the exception of integration of current equipment, the best proposal came from Vendor I. It was also the second least expensive, as can be seen in Figure 2.2. The offer of Vendor II was the best in an integration sense, but it lacked in many other features. Quite significant is the fact that the bid by Vendor V was 173

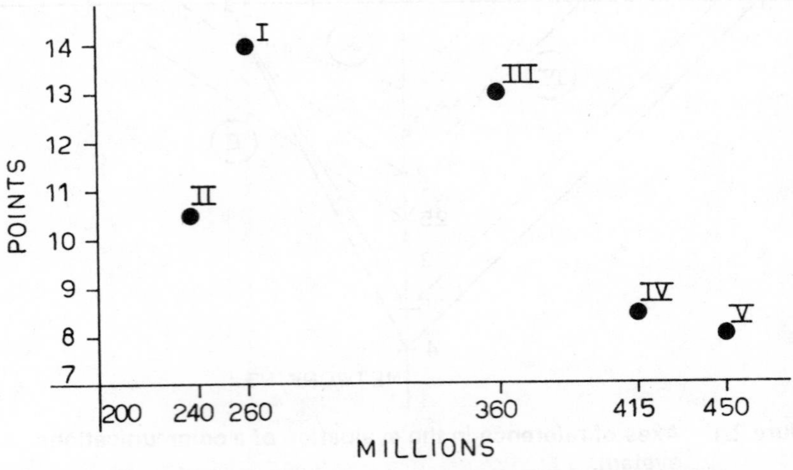

Figure 2.2 Evaluation of five vendor proposals. Performance vs. cost.

percent more expensive than that of Vendor I, yet it was by far the worst of all five proposals.

Two lessons can be derived from this experience. First, the most expensive solution is not necessarily the best one. Actually, it may be the worst possible. Second, while integration with the existing computer and communications investments is definitely one of our goals, multimedia approaches and AI are challenging this notion:

1. The change from classic DP and WP toward multimedia is so profound that much installed equipment will become obsolete.
2. Artificial intelligence constructs can be used not only to help specific tasks but also as a means of integration that is not otherwise available.

The implementation of a system architecture (see Section 2.6) can gain in many ways from object-oriented notions, which are inherent in AI. As systems grow in size and complexity, we can no longer support them through the rather simple programming approaches of the 1950s—which we still use. Eventually artificial intelligence and system integration will become indivisible. While really profound AI developments are still a few years away, now is the time to look at the forthcoming implementations and account for them. The system architecture which we are currently adopting should have an artificial intelligence backbone. Within 5 to 7 years AI will have lost its identity because DB, DC, and DP will be nothing but AI. This can be seen from the histograms in Figure 2.3. The statistics are based on a research I did during 1986/87 in Japan. They identify fields of implementation and subject areas. The research also showed:

- Significantly, the largest field of expert system usage is managerial and financial.
- The most important area of applications is analysis, consulting, and diagnosis.

While expert systems and multimedia solutions are by no means synonymous, they have several aspects in common. Multimedia WSs are inconceivable without AI support. Communications-intense applications—particularly the integration of text, data, graphics, image, and voice—require expert systems tools. The management of very large databases requires built-in intelligence, the so-called surface expert

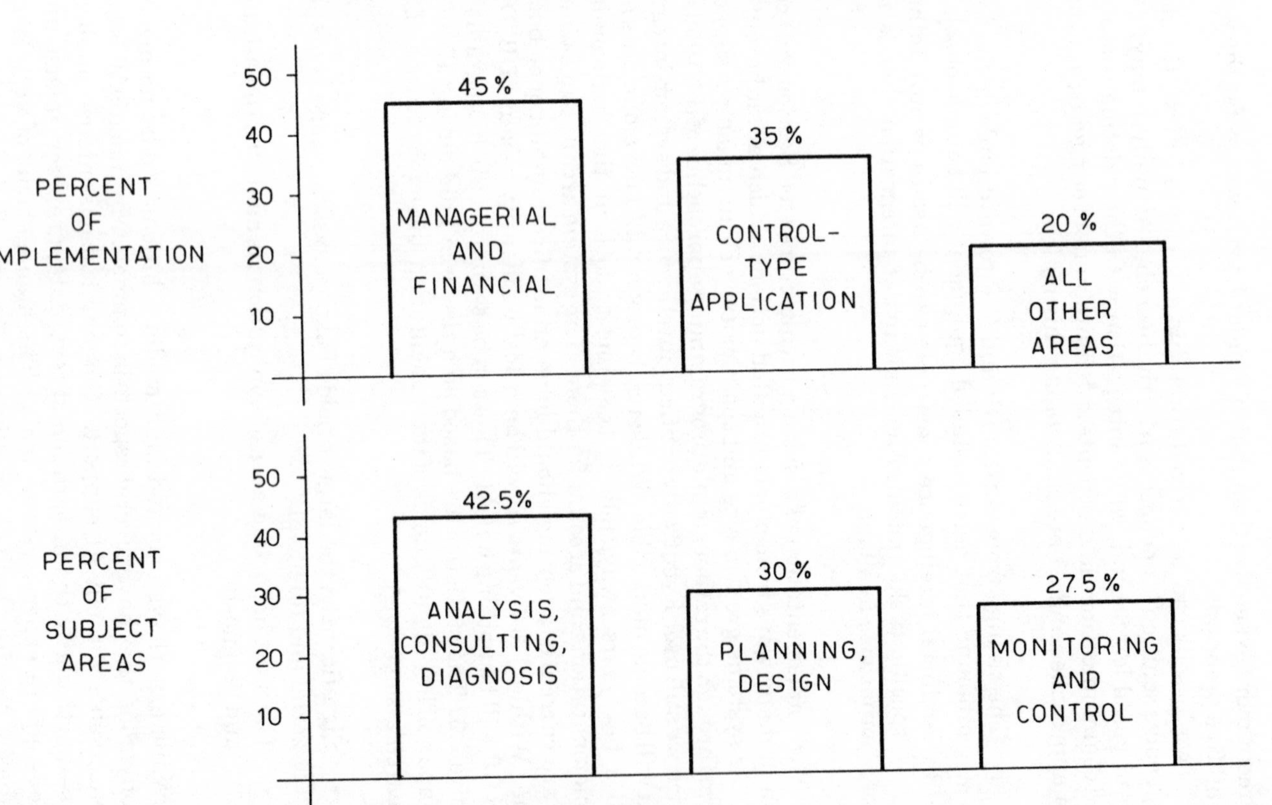

Figure 2.3 Statistics on current expert systems implementation.

systems. Eventually, deep expert systems will increasingly require multimedia support.

2.3 Able Solutions with a Multimedia Perspective

After nearly 4 decades of computer use, it is estimated that today between 70 and 75 percent of essential office functions have no computer support. The able performance of such functions requires a blending of concepts from a number of disciplines: artificial intelligence, distributed database design, multifunctional communications, human windows, and so on. Able solutions to multimedia issues address the capture, storage, retrieval, presentation, and manipulation of information in a hybrid environment. We need agile end-user interfaces to deal with multimedia entities. We must be able to support graphics and other objects, including dynamic update. We must explore the problems of synchronizing multimedia such as sound and images. Artificial intelligence approaches would enhance the user-information interface in a window-to-window communication as Figure 2.4 suggests.

Inference constructs are being studied for information analysis, fault diagnosis, and maintenance on a multimedia basis. A good example of image handling and animation is a project at the Microelectronics and Computer Development Corp. (MCC) that permits software modules to be overlaid in a three-dimensional sense for inspection and control purposes.

Distributed, cooperative, and multimedia environments are based on networks that combine end-user workstations, specialized input-output equipment, multiaccess databases, and intelligent communica-

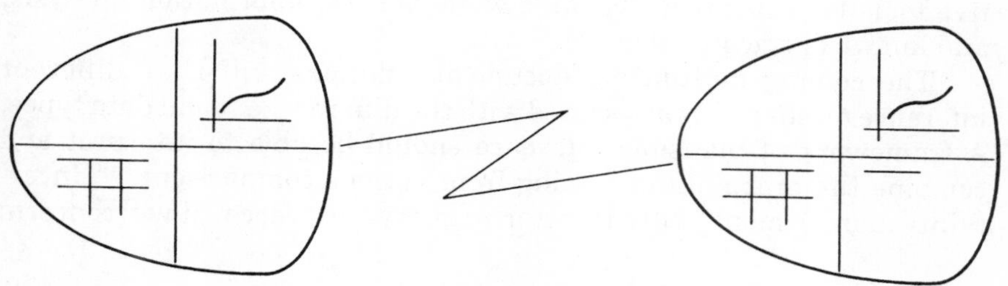

Figure 2.4 Window-to-window communication.

tions links, as well as powerful host systems. One of the challenges is to calibrate this aggregate to work in synchronization with the purpose for which it has been developed. But the greatest challenge is conceptual. Multimedia databases (MDB) are a new concept. In a physical sense, they are defined as traditional data plus information elements (IE) in the form of voice (audio), image, icons, vector graphics, text, and documents. In a logical sense, which is the more important, multimedia databases are object based with supporting data structures that are essentially text structures.

Multimedia solutions integrate documents for storage, retrieval, presentation, and exchange. They are open ended and extensible architectures featuring multimedia DBMS and managed through relational principles.

The term "hypertext" connotes information management in which multimedia information elements are stored in a network of nodes connected by links. Hypertext solutions to multimedia involve issues, systems, and applications. Among the issues are cognitive aspects of using and designing hypertext systems, supporting collaborative work, the management of complexity in large information networks, strategies for effective use of hypertext, and also copyrights, royalties, and social implications. These subjects must be part of future networking solutions.

Multimedia support systems involve database constructs, virtual memory, abstract machines, database engines, database management, distributed systems, query and search, uncertainty in search, and user interfaces. Applications include computer-aided design, management productivity tools, authoring, technical documentation, electronic publishing, electronic encyclopedias, medical and legal information, interactive tools for education, scholar's workbenches, information analysis, and knowledge acquisition.

The coming multimedia document solutions will have different inference mechanisms associated with the different text and data types. A framework of plausible inference should be able to interpret and combine the probabilities arising from various comparisons. "Uncertainty management" will characterize query and search. It will concern:

- Type of document
- Logical structure and contents
- Retrieval criteria

The retrieval process should be regarded as a form of plausible inference, plausibility being quantified by some form of probability or possibility measure. ISO's office document architecture (ISO/ODS) is based on this concept. It involves:

1. Office document models.
2. The concept of uncertainty in retrieval.

Uncertainty here is related to the query rather than the document base itself. Documents have types, logical layout, and structures. The type, layout, and structure definitions are constrained by ODA standards.

Document standards are applicable in both communicating and databasing. They help describe the range of document structures which are permitted and the relationships between logical and layout views of a document. A means for assuring the standard is also enforced. A multimedia communications network is based on these premises.

We should not close this discussion without underlining the importance of computer literacy among end users and systems specialists in a multimedia environment. The last assertion may sound funny, yet, without the mastery of expert systems the systems specialists would be computer illiterate. We must also evaluate how the use of multimedia and expert systems affects workstation chores. This leads to a discussion on cost effectiveness. AI constructs and the benefits we get from networks, to cover costs and leave a profit, are highly connected subjects. Computer literacy plays a vital role in understanding their interdependence.

2.4 Workspace Definition: From Hypercubes to LAN

The goals of multimedia solutions are just as important with local area networks as they are in a wide area perspective. The approach we are after is workstation to workstation, or end to end. Users are not interested in how this connection is done. What they are after is good functionality at an affordable cost. The user's workspace, supported through a knowledge bank (KB) and the appropriate communications channels, provides for:

- Domain knowledge
- Concurrency of access
- Distributed operations

- Security
- Reliability

Figure 2.5 exemplifies this and adds adaptive learning by the workstation as a future goal. The inference engine of a workstation is the knowledge bank's interpreter. It provides deep knowledge and consistent information.

The able performance of workstation functions cannot be limited to WS software functionality. Communications is the key, more precisely "data-level parallelism." This concept uses a single control sequence—hence, a single program—and executes it on all data simultaneously. Approaches to data-level parallelism can also be handled through local networks, but typically such networks are of a different type from what comes to mind when we think of a LAN. A good example is an aggregate of microcomputers at the nodes, know as "hypercube."

Hypercubes combine a binary number of processors in an n^3 dimension which is equal to a power of 2. Such dimension defines the communications paths:

- n^4 has four communications paths.
- n^{16}, sixteen communications paths, and so on.

A cube may consist of one, two, or four 32-node computational units. They are expected to grow as systems become more complex.

Hypercube solutions permit the whole data set to be used at once. For instance, the Connection Machine has a distinct processor for each data element. A network of 65,536 individual computers, each with 4,096 bits of cache memory, handles an equal number of messages in random pattern. There is no shared memory. Such processors are interconnected through a massive communications system:

- The router operates at 500 megabits per second (MBPS).
- The operating system supports networking.
- The languages are C and LISP.

Communication primitives in hypercube systems provide for message exchange through global broadcast (sending a message from one node to all others), global operations, and commutative arithmetic operations (such as sum or maximize) with contributions from each node. Global concatenation permits collecting messages from each node.

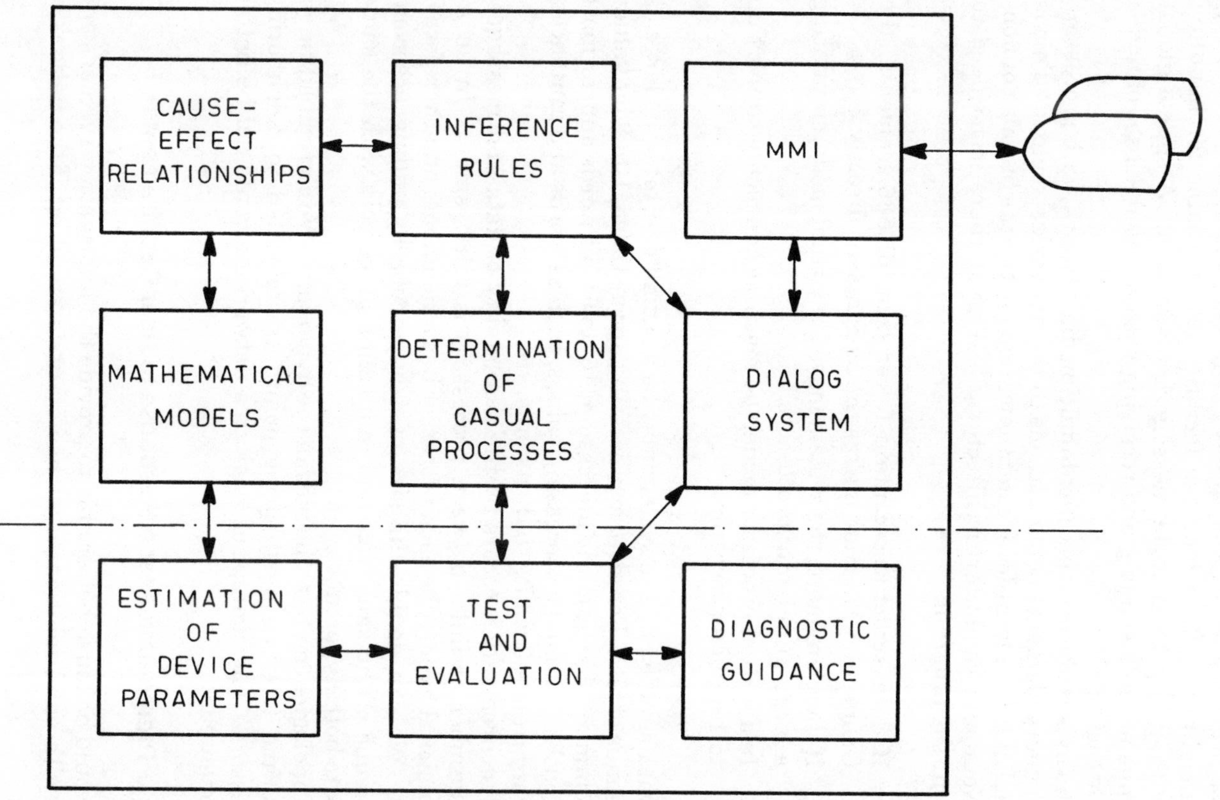

Figure 2.5 Expert knowledge bank support to the user's workplace.

Meshes provide each node with left to right or north, east, south, and west neighbors. Long message facilities are available for handling longer than say 16-kilobyte message transmission. A sparse global exchange permits sending and receiving with selected subset of nodes (narrowcasting).*

The hypercube is an excellent multimedia network, with processors and memory elements being add-ons to the network structure. This is a model of future local-level communications networks but also of non-von Neumann computer architectures. With it there is no need to segment the program:

- If data structures contain fewer than 65,536 elements, the Connection Machine makes the assignment directly.
- If there are more, the system moves in virtual mode, simulating a larger number of processors.
- In a virtual processor mode, the machine can easily support up to 1 million processors.

Data handled by the system may be as small as 1 bit or as large as thousands of bits. For picture processing, for instance, 1-to-8 bit values are common. For numeric processing, 16- to 64-bit words appear most frequently. Language processing values, such as words and sentences, can vary from a few bits to thousands.

Synchronization occurs by the availability of data and messages. The number of links between processors is fairly small. In an n-dimensional hypercube each processor has n neighbors and therefore n links. We can double the size of a hypercube by adding a second hypercube of the same size and connecting processors with the same index to both hypercubes.

Topologies can be embedded in the hypercube. We can embed rings, grids, and trees as neighboring points are allocated to neighboring processors. The concept of local area networking could not be better documented.

2.5 Prerequisites for a Response to User Requirements

We would be much better able to provide the information system's end user with valid solutions if we had an understanding of the notions of

* Such references are valid with Intel's iPSC, also a hypercube architecture.

innovative computers and communications architectures, could appreciate object-oriented programming languages and the rationale behind them, and decided to get over the software crisis created by the conventional von Neumann-type computer architecture and associated programming styles.

The cost of software development and its unreliability has increased dramatically because of ever increasing demands on the system. This has led to software that requires tremendous efforts to design, implement, debug, and maintain. The present generation of costly mainframe computers still operates along concepts of the 1950s or 1960s and end users are quite remote from the solutions which they get. Yet, a central concern of modern software engineering is the design and production of software that is comprehensible, reliable, and easy to modify and maintain in terms of both computers and communications. Ideally, we would like to offer the end user a:

1. Multimedia and multivendor structure.
2. One logical network on which to work.

One logical network should serve all requirements from top management to the professional to the clerical level. Such a network-based approach would feature an open architecture and common rules and protocol, dynamic structures and steady flow, implementation flexibility, and integration capability such as multiple OS, DBMS, and front-end processors (FEP).

A corporate-wide single logical network would assure transparent links and interfaces, interconnect to distributed databases, and use high technology to do so. *System integration will be achieved in a distributed sense*, along the lines of the structural pyramid in Figure 2.6. But without base technologies we cannot organize or manage even single-media distributed databases. Furthermore, our work in the multimedia domain should overcome the heterogeneity of media using the following key design prerequisites:

- Predict the direction of technology
- Invest to take advantage of cost-effective solutions
- Operate to enhance user satisfaction and therefore corporate profitability

The direction of technology is progress in communications at large

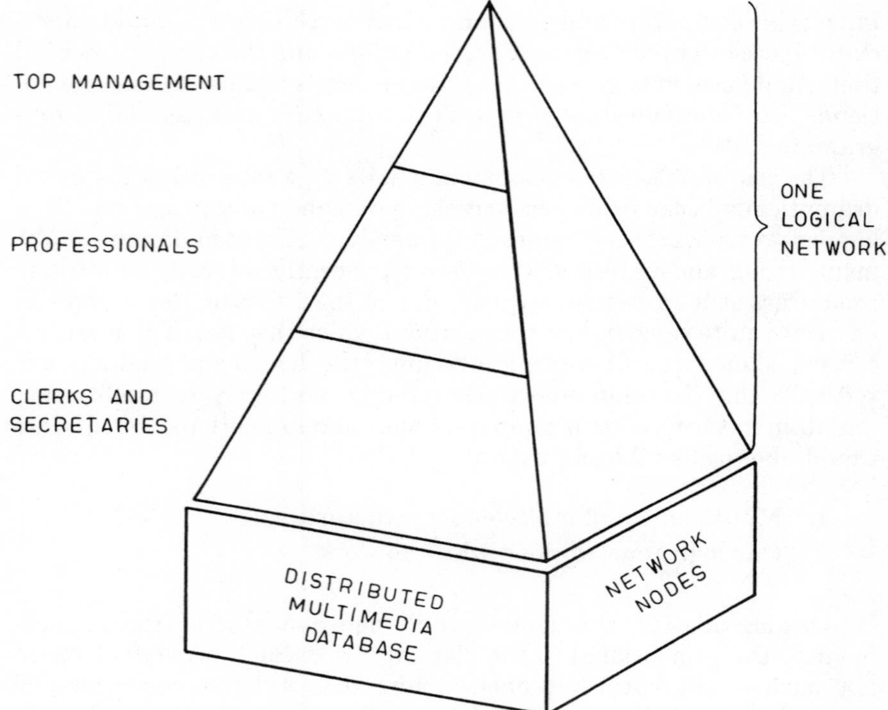

Figure 2.6 Achieving system integration in a distributed, network-oriented sense.

and especially wideband optical communication. It is also the implementation of new storage media such as optical disks. The file servers attached to the local area network offer the user a range of rear-end facilities. They should also provide free-form database access capability (idea processor). The workstation should feature fourth and fifth generation languages (4GL/5GL) and development tools for end users and system professionals—with alternatives at the level of difficulty each can handle.

We have spoken of the protected mode of operations. We must also consider the management of large databases (beyond 100 gigabytes) as well as distributed multimedia databases. This is not easily done through the DBMS alone. Existing DBMSs are *passive*. They respond only when invoked by a user. Therefore, they cannot provide effective access to diverse information types. The result is that applications suffer unacceptable errors and delays; information is manually compiled from a variety of sources; and processing primarily recognizes only limited kinds of knowledge.

This imbalance could be corrected through the now developing office document retrieval theory of ODA (see Section 2.3). Such approaches rest on AI notions. They also call for a manipulation language associated with text and data models. To help the user, query specification must assure the handling of query predicates and associated uncertainty.

Uncertainty is a very important part of retrieval. With certainty, only very limited goals can be satisfied. Partial match attributes are based on the probability of a match. They can have preferred and acceptable attributes of different levels of importance: high, medium, low. One approach is to associate quantitative references with these qualitative levels, then compute the overall score for a document. The cornerstone is plausible inference.

While the material in this section seems to primarily pertain to databases and human windows, in reality it greatly affects wide area and local networks. It is simply not possible to effectively construct a network structure and choose the protocols to apply without precise goals. Such goals must start at the end-user level and should consider all requirements: present and future; then they affect workstations, databases, and networks.

2.6 Background and Foreground Approaches to Technical Issues

The integration of voice, image, text, and data on a systems level goes beyond the transmission channel. In the background we find architected systems solutions, voice and data connectivity, protocols, code transformation, and bandwidth management. The bandwidth itself is one of the factors in the foreground. Both background and foreground factors see to it that the network is the system. This view has been promoted by the spectacular spread of computers and by the technological advances in software and telecommunications. It has been further enhanced by the increased population of computer-trained managers and professionals.

In many industries, global competition puts pressure on management to solve more complex problems within shorter time frames. Management needs systems to guide conceptual thinking, enhance analytical power, and steer toward action. Knowledge and information are a competitive force. This contrasts to the old sense of networking, which meant raw transmission of data, and leads to the ability of any user to access applications transparently over network-based services.

What's the dominant topology of interconnection? Digital Equipment Corp. gives a documented answer to this query. As of 1987, it had 75,000 license holders for DECnet. There were 115,000 Ethernet connections and 8,000 Ethernet customer locations:

- 33 percent were in the same building.
- 22 percent were in the same city or state.
- 28 percent connected different locations in one country.
- 17 percent extended beyond a single country's frontiers.

And pressure was mounting to provide customers with integrated applications at the network level. In this as in all other cases, background factors have to guarantee that information is up to date and correct, that every file contains adequate processing, and that security controls maintain confidentiality as information is transmitted.

As part of background capabilities, user-definable data dictionaries specify the files to be used, the fields to be searched, the type of information to be found in those fields, and the processing format to be used in transmitting the information elements. Data may be compressed for speedy transfer, and formats translated to be compatible with WS requirements. Among other value-added elements, protocol conversion can permit interconnecting systems under diverse protocols, multiple-link access make feasible additional functionality, and data assurance includes error detection, correction, and verification. Backup facilities improve availability and up time. Global network management supports distributed databases. End-to-end digital connectivity is based as much as possible on standards. A full range of interconnected products is made available to end users, to assure able answers to client demands within a reasonable homogeneous environment.

But while these background factors support the more sophisticated part of the network, other considerations are brought to the foreground. They mostly have to do with pipe capacity (bit streams), bit error rates (BER), and the topology of the cabling plant. Together with reliability such factors define a significant part of the visibility reaching the end-user level. Ideally there should be:

1. High network availability of 99.9 percent or better.

2. Network response time of 1 to 2 seconds or less.
3. Network data integrity that does away with changing, losing, or misdirecting messages and transactions.
4. Network integration in the global service we have been promoting.

Network integration must support, not inhibit, flexibility. Network configurations are not fixed forever. Expansions and modifications are steadily needed to satisfy user requirements and improve the service. But the network which we develop should be valid from its conception.

The stability and availability of the system should be satisfactory both in a technical and in a managerial sense. In case of any circuit trouble, disturbance to any service must be avoided through appropriate automatic recovery functions. At the WS level, response time must be steady with a design-object value of less than 1 second (subsecond speed). Design should account for the fact that each application running on the integrated network has different requirements with respect to computing power and online control procedures. Therefore, parametric solutions should be selected to match each application requirement. The influence of restructuring, alteration, or reconfiguration should be localized.

While the design of a network is not easy, installing and operating it in a dependable manner is more difficult. The real challenge is system network management, which includes:

- Problem determination
- Traffic management
- Meaningful traffic statistics
- Fast intervention to restore normal conditions

Network management should be projected at the design stage. Telecommunications engineers must be very careful in the way they study, define, secure, present, and support the network services. A strategy should be chosen in view of strengths, weaknesses, and competition. The design team itself should be small but highly knowledgeable. Keep in mind the basic systems rule: The time needed to finish a job expands by the square of the number of people put to work on it. In building the network, as well as in any other systems project, we should only be satisfied with the best tools and brains available to us.

2.7 The Role of an Architecture

The first questions we should ask are what are the goals we are after? What range of functions we would like to see supported by the system architecture? Can we define the contribution a system architecture will make to our solution? From multimedia to the supporting technical issues we have objectives, characteristics, and milestones. We have to develop a properly functioning network that is able to integrate its attached devices. A system architecture is the art of:

1. Building according to well-defined principles of proportion.
2. Making it feasible to meet functional service goals.
3. Enabling us to face future growth requirements.
4. Paving the way to incorporate change through a system whose completion may exceed the architect's lifetime.

A system architecture helps absorb and integrate new technologies (Figure 2.7). It assures a framework for design and makes feasible higher performance at a reduced cost per function. The architecture can achieve this goal if it is implemented corporate-wide and if it covers all projected functions, not only a part of them. The system architecture is of value to the user organization as a whole and to the network designers in particular. It represents a set of rules, procedures, conventions, standards, protocols, and software. It permits a variety of attached end users—persons, processes, workstations, minis and mainframes—to communicate with each other and with distributed databases. That is precisely what we need.

But while an architecture is necessary, it is not enough. Once the goal has been defined, we must describe what we are after. A properly designed system architecture should include the whole range of activities:

1. Classical functions such as monitoring, supervising, terminal management, file import and export control, and associated utilities.
2. Distributed database management requirements such as distributed data dictionary, handling of text, data, graphics, and voice, and associated manipulation language.
3. All communications perspectives including routing, virtual circuits and/or datagrams, flow control, and document interchange.

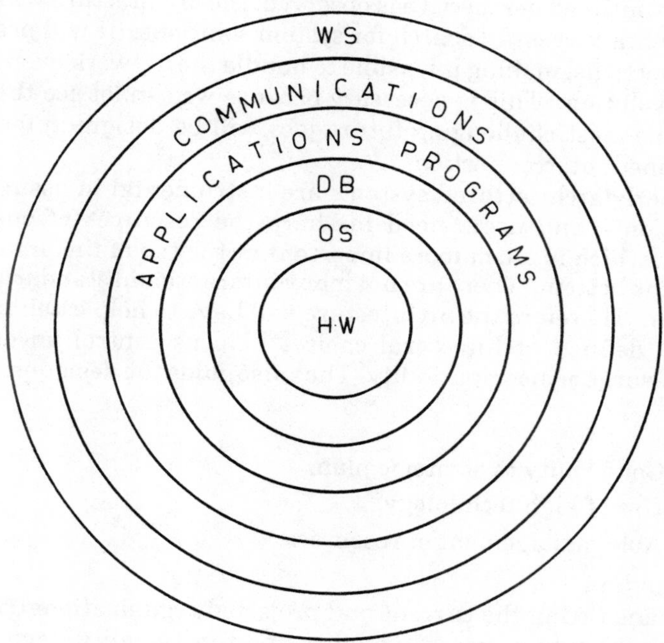

Figure 2.7 Items an architectural approach must consider.

4. Presentation functionality—from compound electronic document structures to finer programmatic interfaces and presentation level protocol(s).

Furthermore, the system architecture to be chosen should be flexible and allow for expansion. Such architectural construction is bound to be complex. Hence, the wisdom of providing higher and lower functionality options—within a *complete* systems offering.

If the outlined perspective is observed, the architecture will become the hub for a successful search for system solutions. It will provide for any connections, making it feasible to handle the network even if it is in steady evolution. This is necessary because we cannot see the future. One of the most challenging future jobs will be designing for flexible user-defined interconnection.

Properly architectured systems are instrumental in assuring user satisfaction. End users need to share the resources of one logical network, which is much more important at the top of the organization than at the bottom. There are not many international standards we can deal with. Therefore the architecture will have to help establish them. Properly defined architectural choices help us control an otherwise frequent surge of incompatibility. They also guide the designers in terms of:

1. Conformity to strategic plan.
2. Use of high technology.
3. Able management of resources.

This means fitting the current and projected organizational objectives within the chosen network structure and functionality, responding to requirements in a way which is efficient and reasonably low cost, and planning, implementing, and controlling resources and managing of events through real-time monitoring and an online quality database. The latter is supported and run by software provided by the network control center, a standard part of the better-known architectural solutions. Our goal in such implementation is overall quality of service, not just after-the-fact control action.

Chapter

3

Network Standards and the Normalization Effort

3.1 Introduction

There is a significant difference in system design between prototyping or addressing exception situations and organizing for mass processing and communications requirements. Standardization is very important in the latter case. In fact, we cannot properly handle mass transactions or large volumes of message exchanges without properly establishing norms and methods. Standardization can happen at different levels, from local area to global network, as Figure 3.1 suggests. But it will be much more successful if a global approach is taken. At the protocol level, this will mean that lower layers integrate into the higher ones. Something similar can be stated in a topological sense, though connectivity will be spatial rather than layered.

The normalization effort is steady. It is also continuously faced with new challenges. To a very significant extent normalization and stan-

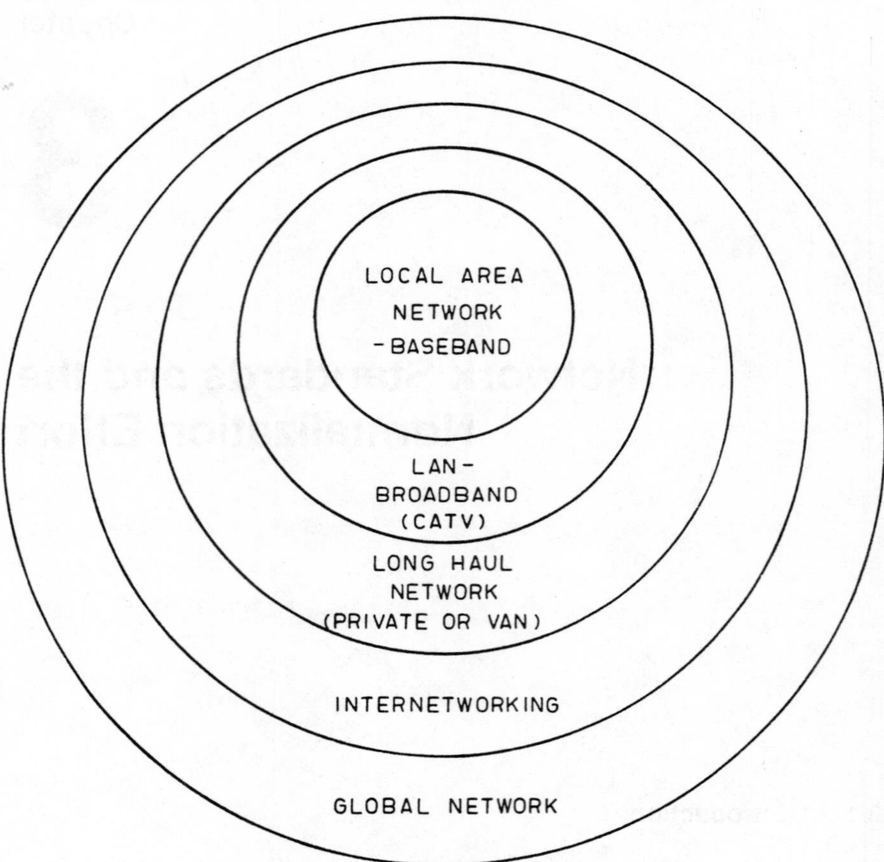

Figure 3.1 Reference levels in networking, from LAN to wide area.

dardization trail the implementation of new technological developments; they demand considerable time to establish themselves. However, once they are established, there is a tendency to follow a standard, though different vendors interpret it in their particular way, leading to a number of dialects.

For these reasons the architecture of computers and communications systems is undergoing a major revolution which is further fueled by the continuing expansion of networks. In terms of normalization the most relevant references in networking are:

1. *The ISO / OSI model and protocols for transport, session, presentation, and applications.* Its state of development will significantly influence the computing and telecommunications environments of the future. Let's, however, recall that Open Systems Interconnection is a reference model. Furthermore, its layers, protocols, and interfaces are defined but not described.
2. *The IEEE 802 local area network reference model addresses the medium, physical, and data link layers.* This model, too, is layered. It shows a correspondence to the lower layers (physical and data link) of ISO/OSI. In fact, it has been developed to be in conformance with OSI, as stipulated in the IEEE 802 functional requirements.
3. *The emergence of integrated services digital networks (ISDN) with the new channel capacities, interfaces, and protocols it introduces.* From the cabling solutions of ISDN to the higher-level references of the Manufacturing Automation Protocol (MAP) and Technical and Operations Protocol (TOP), emerging standards will play a strategic role for manufacturers and users alike. Their vocabulary will be a common language used by computing systems designers. Standardized products—or nearly so—will reach the market, creating both new constraints and opportunities for the development of local, national, and international services.

3.2 The Public Telephone Network

In the context of a wide area environment the basic infrastructure for data communications is provided by the public telephone network. While the impact of a public network on the communications patterns of business life has been gradually emerging for over 100 years, at no time has it been more visible than it is today. Therefore, it is important to understand the physical structure of such a network.

The problems with the public telephone network are many. One of the most important handicaps to development is that telecommunications authorities are both referee and player at the same time. Yet, they should realize that they cannot both participate in the market and regulate the competition. The need for this separation is evident to everybody—except the telcos themselves. In principle, a public communications network aims to meet the changing needs of both its end users and long distance company customers. Modern communications networks combine software-controlled digital switching and transmission capabilities.

The network today is far more than a series of wires, computers, and connections. It is the pathway to the information age. In terms of structure, the network can be divided into two parts, transmission and switching, each consisting of integrated elements. Transmission includes the local loop, which is mostly cable and wire pairs; the transmission paths between the customer's location; and the local central office. It is the basic consumer connection. Another crucial transmission link is the interoffice facility. This provides the transmission paths that interconnect central offices. The local central office provides the primary switching equipment for local calls. The tandem office(s) provides the routing from one central office to another. This assures the connection between users located at distant points.

It is precisely this system of transmission and switching that gave the telecommunication network its most important characteristic: a virtually universal connection between every member of society. The telecommunications industry is currently modernizing its network by providing digital switching capabilities at the local central office level. Some telephone companies have launched a strategic modernization program with the goal of providing end-to-end digital connections for each of their customers.

Network challenges must be faced within the context of an operating environment. Network developments do not occur in a vacuum. The right decisions must be made on every level. For example, it is not enough that terrestrial fiber optic loops are found to be highly reliable communications media; they are also cost effective as the price of this technology falls. It is also necessary that telecommunications companies are allowed to offer customers the full range of options that network development makes possible, thus providing the extra business to justify new investments.

Figure 3.2 shows a broad implementation perspective. High-capacity communications integrate a layered approach which has a business system as a top layer and home-oriented solutions as the lower, interconnected through transparent, public, wide area communications networks. The latter should support workstations, departmental machines, mainframes, and communicating databases.

It takes vision to make the right decisions about a digital network as well as to understand its true value to society. But it also requires a properly timed transition process for moving out of analog solutions and

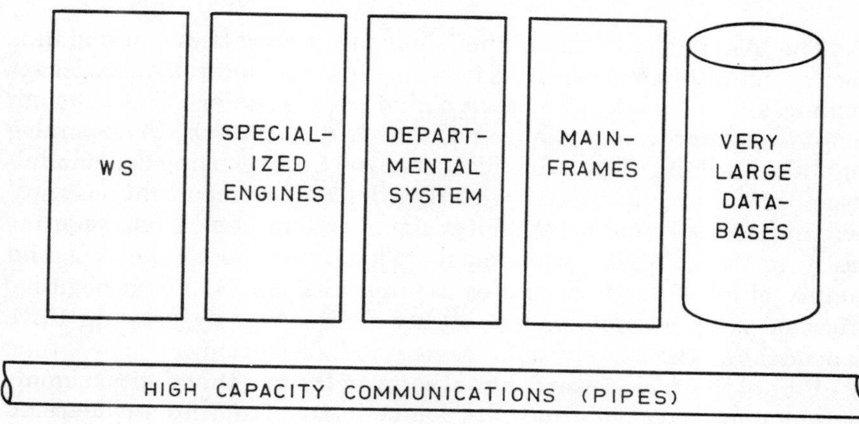

BUSINESS SYSTEM

(OFFICE AUTOMATION, FACTORY AUTOMATION, FACILITIES CONTROL, CLIENT TELECOM)

TRANSPARENT PUBLIC WIDE AREA NETWORKS

(INFRASTRUCTURE, BROADCASTING, NARROWCASTING, SPECIALIZED BUSINESS COMMUNICATIONS)

HOME SYSTEMS

(EDUCATION, ENTERTAINMENT, FACILITIES CONTROL, BUSINESS COMMUNICATIONS)

Figure 3.2 Implementation perspective: from an inhouse to a wide area system.

into a digital structure. For more than a century, telecommunications networks have been totally designed around analog transmission and voice communications. Now we say that a network should permit full access to digital capabilities. Why this change? The reasons are technological, operational, and financial.

The historical medium of the telephone, analog transmission, has been designed to carry voice and low-speed data communications. At set distances, the signal must be amplified by a repeater. Even though significant improvements have been made in the 1980s, these analog amplifiers still increase transmission noise, thus reducing dependability and worsening the bit error rate (BER). Another important technical fact is that transmission of digital signals on an analog line requires costly analog-to-digital conversion. That affects both the cost and quality of computer-to-computer communications. It has a negative effect on a critical factor in a society that is rapidly growing more dependent on the use and management of information.

Part of the drive toward digital rests on the fact that digital signals are not amplified at intermediate points; instead, they are regenerated during the transmission process to their original form. As a result, there is a significant reduction in the random noise component which is amplified by analog technology. Furthermore, digital solutions make possible direct connections between digital equipment and digital transmission and switching facilities, enabling users to obtain inexpensive access to information resources.

The move toward a fully digital system is paralleled by the deployment of microelectronic and silicon chip technology within the network. The fact that increased volumes of multimedia information can be stored in less and less space is critically important. It means more functions can be handled more efficiently. Maintenance and add-ons of modular switching units are also far easier, but there is also another side to this transformation: A network that is all it could be is now possible. A network that can live up to the intent of its planners is one that is well studied and properly implemented. However, during the early to mid 1980s, there was some concern that the switch to digital would benefit only high-volume business users. Today, we see that our society as a whole—at work and at home—benefits from this transformation. The need for access to information does not stop when we leave our office.

The drive toward digital communications is both facilitated and enhanced by the installation of software-controlled switching. Such a pattern, as a whole, reflects six basic concepts. The first regards the bottom line. By the mid 1980s, silicon chip switching technology with electronic stored program control became affordable. It also proved easier to maintain and far more powerful than its electromechanical predecessors. Through its placement in the network, business and residential customers benefited in a factual and documented manner.

Second, growing user requirements stipulated that the network had to be fast. As society increasingly relied on interactive computer systems, the speed and accuracy of communication became more critical than the basic computer capabilities. That is why telcos became leading installers of fiber optics. For instance, between 1983 and 1987, Pacific Bell spent more than $150 million to give major metropolitan area users the benefits of digital transmission.

Third, the proper transition plan is very important. The analog and digital parts of the network will coexist and interlink for more than a decade. This should be fully transparent to the business of messages and transactions—and to be so, protocols and interfaces have to be properly studied. Figure 3.3 suggests a matrix approach to the study needed for moving from an analog to a digital solution.

Fourth, the network has to be dependable and reliable. In a society

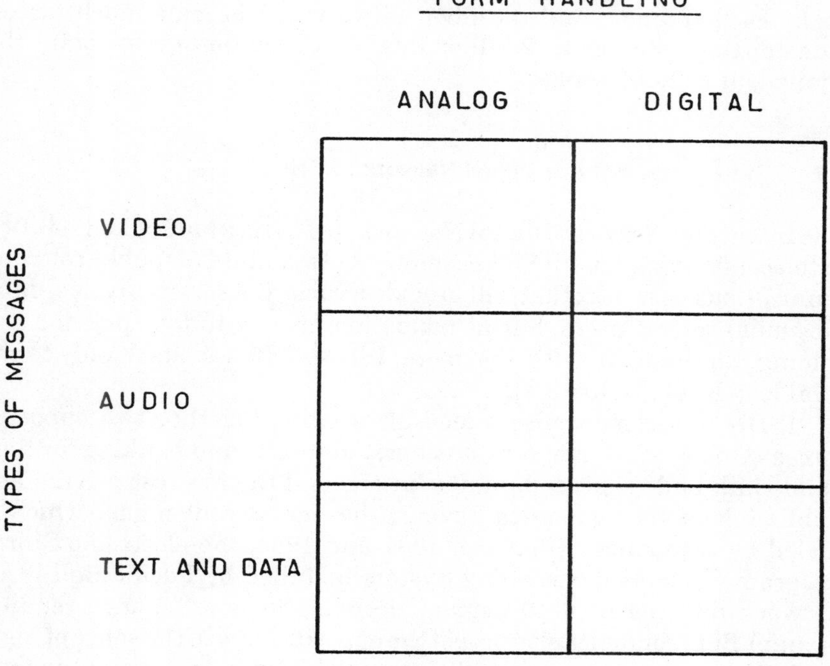

Figure 3.3 **Analog versus digital communications with different types of messages.**

based on data transmission and an information economy, error tolerances must be reduced to a minimum. Again taking Pacific Bell as an example, this is the reason why it plans to make 93 percent of the circuits between central offices digital by 1992.

Fifth, the information age network has to be versatile, flexible, and rich in features needed to meet customer's needs. That means telcos should spend millions of dollars to modernize facilities, installing computer-controlled switching. The manual design of multipoint dedicated data circuits (a process requiring complex design, installation, and repair procedures) has no place in an information society.

Sixth, the system must be architectured with full-scale integration in mind. Such an architectural solution should consider the fast-evolving network capacity—both in transmission and in switching. Even with 400 megabits per second (MBPS), which is now a relatively low rate, an optical fiber network can transmit the equivalent of 200 books each second. And the fiber network can become much faster, transmitting as much as 2 billion bits of information per second—the equivalent of 1,000 books.

3.3 Integrated Service Digital Network (ISDN)

The Integrated Services Digital Network (ISDN) is a half-baked solution in telecommunications; it is a recommended standard for public telecommunications networks that will provide a variety of services (voice, data, facsimile) to end users, but at bands too narrow to face present and coming requirements. Furthermore, ISDN addresses itself only to the local loop level (Figure 3.4).

ISDN is a compromise aimed at bringing together two opposing forces. One is the demand by business, industry, and banking for high bandwidth and reliable, digital solutions and the interest private and public telephone companies have in the digital conversion, which is fueled by economics. (Between 1981 and 1984, the electronic Stored Program Controlled Switching System installed by Pacific Bell in its network resulted in a 40 percent decrease in maintenance requirements.) But economics also propel the opposite force in the sense of high-capital investments for a fully digital solution with broadband capabilities. For many telcos—particularly those with antiquated equipment—the cost of the local loop is higher than the whole national network.

So ISDN came as a compromise to protect the telco's own interests but not those of the users. It supports three channels:

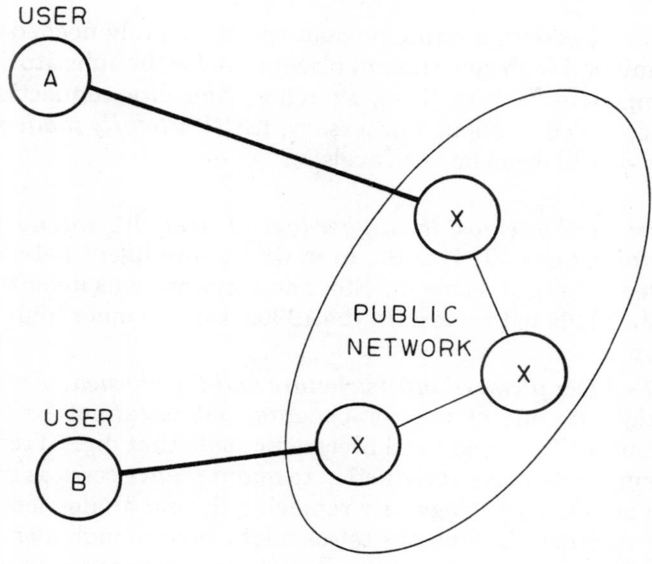

Figure 3.4 A shortcoming of ISDN. Restriction at the local loop level.

- 64 KBPS
- 64 KBPS
- 16 KBPS (signaling channel)

The first two address themselves to voice and data rather than multimedia, since multimedia would require megastreams and gigastreams, as we will see in the following section.

It is futile to make grandiose statements about ISDN—given the current level of technology. The renewal of telephone systems' cabling plants should have been done long ago. In the 1960s, with satellites showing the direction, a strategic plan was absolutely needed—on the telcos' behalf and with government blessings—for the substitution of all major components: long lines, switches, and city connections (the current loop). Today, though necessary, ISDN is *totally inadequate*. A valid plan should focus on two levels:

- *First and foremost the higher logical structure and its strategic implications.* This is the area where intelligent networks and idea databases come in. Store and forward was invented in the late 1940s with telex. In the 1990s it is no longer high technology.
- *The lower physical infrastructure and the physical plant.* ISDN might be one of the components, but it cannot be the goal. General Telephone and Electronics said that digital technology brings a 40 percent reduction to maintenance costs as compared to analog technology. By replacing the old analog loops of city center installations, the telcos might save enough money to pay for the investment—while rendering a great service to the users.

That's how a nation moves into the twenty-first century: through first-class, wideband, low-cost communications. Telecommunications will be to business and industry in the 1990s what data processing was during the last three decades.

Technically, ISDN evolved from the Integrated Digital Network (IDN) ideas, aiming to provide end-to-end digital connectivity, assuring user access through a limited set of standard multipurpose network interfaces. This was judged to be the minimum necessary to face the growth in public demand. It is also a force which will lead public networks into new technology. The fact, however, remains that ISDN is a bypass effort to provide an alternative to POTS (plain old telephone service). Taken strictly on their own, satellites are another bypass—while what is really needed is a network-wide system solution to sharing broadband resources.

In my book, *System Architecture, System Integration and the Role of Artificial Intelligence* (McGraw-Hill Book Company, New York), I explain the technical side of the deadly sins of ISDN:

1. Industry requirements projected for the mid-1990s are 2 to 3 gigabits per second, a gigastream (GBPS). This is more than 4 orders of magnitude above the combined 144 kilostream of ISDN.

2. Integrated services packet networks and metropolitan area networks, that the telcos say they will provide require both a top-down grand design and a detailed bottom-up design. By addressing itself only to the local loop and its obsolete equipment, ISDN is a patch.
3. In the hurry to get the patchwork going, the PTT forgot they will have to change switches and trunks. Eventually, this will mean double investment rather than savings on current aging plants.
4. Even the too little, too late ISDN recommendation is applicable only to a very limited topology: the local loop's connection to the city office. Without the system approach of a grand design, nobody can guarantee the recommended standard will be applied uniformly. We had that experience with X.25.
5. Bad enough in themselves, channel capacity and limited topology are only part of the picture. A much more important issue is transmission quality and dependability.

Transmission quality is expressed in bit error rate (BER). Voice quality lines range from 10^{-2} to 10^{-4} and 10^{-5}. The so-called data quality lines have a BER of 10^{-7} and 10^{-8}. All this is the old plant. what is *really* needed is 10^{-11}, 10^{-12}, or better. The old plant cannot provide it. High-quality lines and megastreams will not be necessary in another century. They are needed *now*. Gigastreams will be necessary in the 1990s. ISDN provides neither. The Swiss PTT mentioned that though it started the ISDN implementation in 1987, it will ßbe fully implemented prior to 2020.* Yet, it is already known that 64 KBPS is simply not enough.

In Switzerland today, as in the rest of Europe, about 30 percent of the network is digital. The French PTT projects that by 1990-92, 90 percent of the central network will be digitized—but not the local loop. To cover the local loop, it will be at least 2010 to 2015, and probably 2025 as in Switzerland.

Just as important is the question of tariffs. Computers and communications are a unified field. With computers, costs and prices drop by 25 percent per year for CPU, about 40 percent per year for disk storage. That's the effect of high technology. There is no high technology in ISDN to permit even remotely such cost and tariff reduction. The German PTT (Bundespost) will charge the price of two telephone calls for two channels

---

* A couple of telcos were to suggest that the switch for 144 KBPS (64 + 64 + 16) is not yet really ready. The prototypes work, but . . . . And besides, it will take at least 25 years to implement all over the country.

(of the 64-, 64-, and 16-KBPS variety). As far as voice is concerned, that is no deal. But it might have a mild effect in stimulating use of data communications.

3.4 Tariffs and Digital Circuits

Transmission of information over networks takes place on a carrier. The rate of transmission this carrier can support puts limits on the stream of communication. In the late 1950s and early 1960s the rate of transmission taking place on digital circuits increased from 50 and 70 baud to 600 baud. It became 1.2 KBPS in the mid to late 1960s, then 2.4, 4.8, 9.6, and 19.2 KBPS. With ISDN it stands at 64 KBPS. Thus we speak of kilostreams. In Section 3.2 we have also made reference to megastreams in connection with optical fibers, also suggesting the coming gigastreams. They are units of measurement in digital transmission, but in reality they tell much more than pipe capacity. Other things equal, the larger the channel the lower the cost per transmitted bit of information.

This reference to cost effectiveness is crucial. For the last 30 years or so, everybody in the computer business got accustomed to the idea that costs drop by about 25 percent per year. This was not so for communications. As a result, telecommunications was a resource to be used sparsely. This is now changing. The relatively lower cost of digital circuits allows a change in the way we look at networks. This statement is much more valid in a deregulated environment. So far, only the United States, England, and Japan had the courage to semideregulate. Theirs is no full deregulation, because full deregulation would mean:

1. Many players at the local service level.
2. Each player using high-technology solutions to bring up bandwidth, reduce bit error rate, and swamp not only costs but also prices.

This has not yet happened in the United States, Japan, and the United Kingdom, though it may. Other countries though are much worse off because they still live in a fully regulated environment. That this is totally irrational should be evident to everybody. Communications poverty strangles a post-industrial economy. This is something which has not yet become a global conscience. Let's hope it will become so.

The effects of a communications monopoly can be disastrous. Today, in Germany, a kilostream costs 36 times as much as in England; a megastream costs 107 times as much. Such outrageous prices do not allow system designers to throw lots of bandwidth at the problem and its solution. The current policies followed by telcos which feature high tariffs and low bandwidth are myopic at best. Many telecommunications authorities (particularly the PTT) are death-bound in a manner reminiscent of the steamships versus airplanes challenge. The kilostream is the steamship; the megastream, the propeller airplane; and the gigastream, the supersonic jet. Just as the death of the steamship made the classical harbors fully irrelevant, megastreams and gigastreams will make installed communications equipment obsolete overnight—hence, ISDN is a last-ditch survival effort of telco's irrelevancy to twenty-first century needs.

Change requires vision. It calls for imagination, plans, effort, resources, and the projection of a new environment which will be in steady evolution. Such an environment must focus on:

- Liberal laws
- Forward-looking policies
- Regulations adjustable to needs and technology
- Technical requirements definition
- Steady technological innovation
- Gigastreams in terms of capacity
- Affordable tariffs

There are multiple players affecting such an environment and, in turn, affected by it, they are:

- Governments
- Standards bodies
- Telecommunications firms
- Telecommunications vendors
- Computer manufacturers
- Terminals manufacturers
- Users—at the bottom layer

The users have been the least-influential group. But there is also a void in the regulations; uniform tariffs do not exist. At the same time, the large-scale system we require for communications cannot be provided by one company alone. More and more there is the need for many enterprises to work together, both on the basics and in assuring value-added services.

3.5 Open System Interconnection (ISO/OSI)

ISO is a voluntary organization in which voting is done by country. Each country is represented by its national standards body, for instance, ANSI in the United States. In turn, the national standards organization is comprised of users, manufacturers, government (NBS in the United States, and public utilities (telco, PTT). ISO develops recommended standards. For communications, there are also other international organizations making standards recommendations, for instance, CCITT, the International Telegraph and Telephone Consultative Committee. CCITT is a United Nations treaty organization. Voting is by country, the country being represented by the PTT—or, in the case of America, by the Secretary of State. Generally, non-PTT representatives can attend and comment but cannot vote.

Another multination standards organization is ECMA—the European Computer Manufacturers Association. This is an industry standards development organization. Voting is by member, mostly manufacturers. American computer vendors are participating in ECMA.

Designed by ISO, OSI is a layered structure; its seven levels of protocols perform the defined functions necessary for realization of full and meaningful communications among systems of different design and manufacture. The lower four layers of ISO/OSI provide the bit pipe for transfer of information among distributed systems. The upper three layers focus on coordination and translation of system functions so that the information reaching the destination is meaningful and can be processed. Each of the seven layers is described in the following paragraphs.

1. The lowest layer is physical. It addresses functional and procedural characteristics that activate, maintain, and deactivate the physical circuit. The OSI proposal states: "The Physical Layer provides electrical, mechanical, functional, and procedural characteristics" (that is, the physical interface with the transmission medium). Higher layers, for instance X.25 (networking), reflect on these specifications by reference to other stan-

dards. At the physical layer level, the standards (recommendations and reference models) are:

- X.21 bis adaptation to existing interfaces
- V.28/V.24: RS-232-C electrical and functional specifications
- V.35 mode
- V.10/V.11: RS-422-A/RS-423-A electrical characteristics
- X.21 physical elements

Reference models at the physical level also include active and inactive states of the OSI physical service.

2. The next layer is the data link. The object of data link is connection activation and deactivation. It specifies the link level for reliable transfer of data over the physical link, including synchronization, error detection, error recovery, and flow control. It also maps units provided by the network layer into data link protocol units for transmission over the physical link and performs error detection and recovery and notification as appropriate. (The hierarchical layered structure is described in Figure 3.5.)

   Current examples of data link layer implementations are SDLC, HDLC, and LAP-B. The high-level data link control (HDLC) is an ISO developed protocol based on line access protocol A (LAP-A). This original link access procedure has been displaced by the preferred LAP-B, which is a compatible subset of ISO's HDLC. In addition, new multilink procedures have been added. Examples of the latter are principles of character-oriented and bit-oriented operation, framing and transparency mechanisms, format structure (addressing, control, information, better error detection, and recovery), frame types (information, supervisory, unnumbered), operating scenarios, and multilink procedures.

3. The network layer focuses on routing and switching transmission paths through a telecommunication resource. The packet level of X.25 is now consistent with the OSI network layer. It provides the procedures for interaction between the subscriber and the network for establishing virtual circuits, transferring data, error recovery, and clearing calls. A great number of

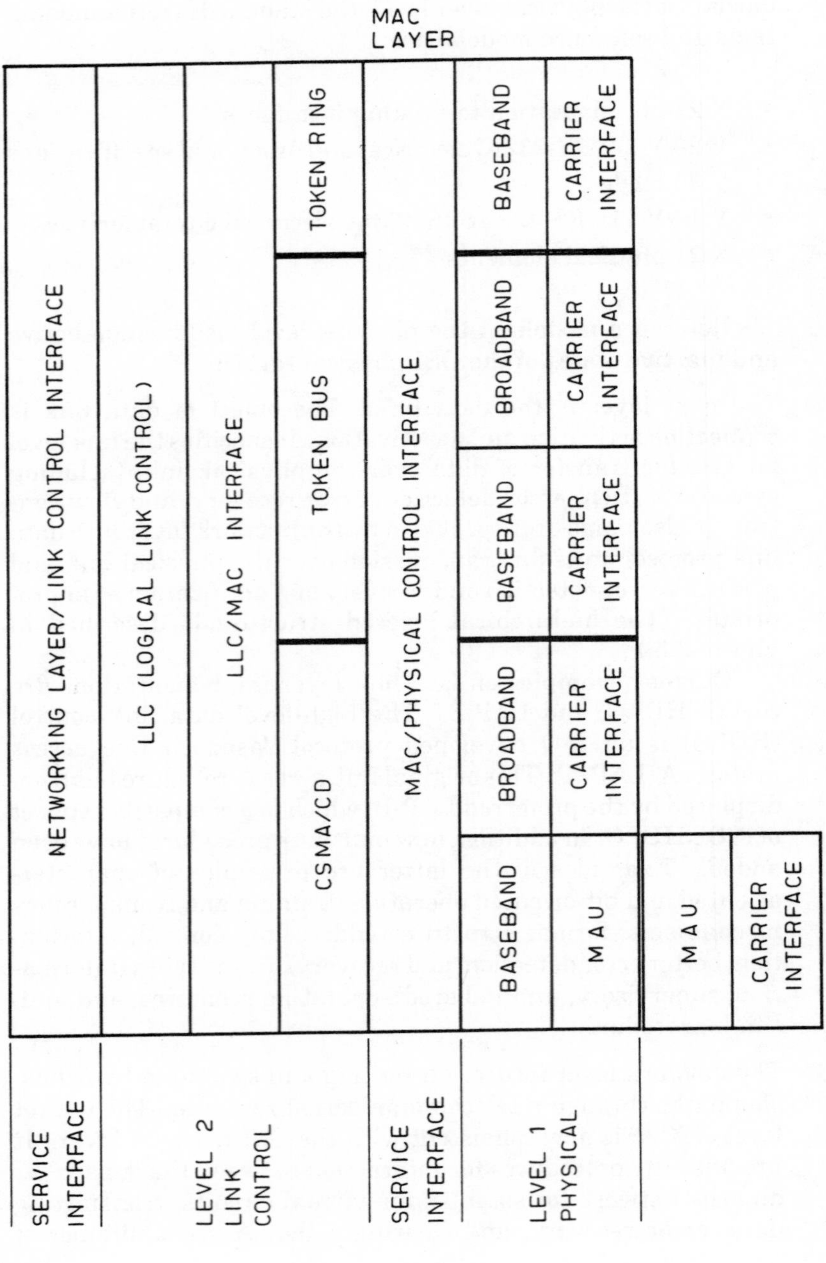

Figure 3.5 Hierarchial structure of the lower ISO/OSI layers addressed to LAN implementation.

special service features are specified to assure a comprehensive operating capability.

Important references relative to the networking level are the OSI network service definition, statistical multiplexing of logical channels, virtual calls and permanent virtual circuits, packet formats and field encoding, sequencing and acknowledgment significance for data transfer, and multiple-packet sequence integrity. Others are the handling of error conditions and recovery actions, closed user-group configurations and operation, a select facility, and conformance testing.

4. The aim of the transport layer is to provide the appropriate quality of service for the reliable transfer of information between communicating users. To assure a consistent data transfer service to the user applications, the transport layer provides additional error recovery mechanisms. For instance, X.25 reset actions can result in loss of data; the transport protocol then initiates a recovery action to retransmit any data that is identified as missing.

   Thus, transport layer goals are quality of service considerations and parameters, protocol data units and associated formats, resynchronization recovery from signalled errors, and so on. Transport should be examined within the perspective of a four-layer structure which must function in harmony while performing defined tasks. Primitive requests or responses from a layer above cause protocol actions to be initiated. In turn, protocol actions cause primitive indications or confirmations to be passed to the layer above. The operation of the four lower layers provides total transport service in the OSI environment.

5. The goal of the session layer is the management of dialogue for orderly communication between users. It provides the means needed for cooperating presentation entities to organize and synchronize their dialogue and to manage their information exchange. The session layer assures such services to the higher-up presentation layer as session-connected establishment and release, synchronization, normal and expedited data exchange, quarantine service, coarse programmatic interfaces for interaction management, exception reporting, and so on.

6. The presentation layer controls the encoding of information being transferred. As defined by OSI, its purpose is to represent

information to the communicating application-entities in a way that preserves meaning while resolving syntax differences. Data transformation and data formatting are among the functions it supports. It also supports syntax selection and the finer programmatic interfaces for interaction management.

7. The application layer interfaces with communicating users and manages the context of the communication. The OSI-defined communications process is represented to the user by this layer. Based on requests from the network user, the applications layer selects appropriate services to be supplied from lower-layer functions. Examples are functions acting on behalf of a local party to the conversation and peer functions acting on behalf of the remote party.

The following services are within the scope of the application layer acting on behalf of a particular network user, as specified by ISO/OSI: identification of intended communications partners and their availability and authenticity, establishment of authority to communicate, agreement on required privacy mechanisms, determination of cost allocation methodology, and definition of resource adequacy to provide an acceptable quality of service. Other functions include synchronization of cooperating applications, selection of dialogue discipline, establishment of error recovery responsibility, agreement on data validity commitment, and identification of data syntax constraints. Standards developed for the applications layer define the overall message-handling environment and identify the key terminology that applies at each boundary.

The user is either a person or a computer application process that originates and receives messages as communications. The message-handling system provides the total support to enable users to communicate by exchanging messages. Within this context there are a number of elements that are involved in processing the messages in transit. To handle them, the X.400 protocol specifies:

- User agent. The functional element that represents the user
- Message transfer system. The means for cooperating user agents to exchange messages
- Message transfer agent. The functions for relaying messages to their destinations

Functional layers, system types, operating protocols, and message structures are part of the definition. The relationship between a memo and an inter-personal message and the naming and addressing concepts and structure are also part of protocol definition.

There are problems with ISO/OSI. First, its layer functionality and protocols are described—not defined—though subsequent definitions such as X.25 and X.400 cover part of the gap. Second, transactional standards are not incorporated. Third, high performance is not guaranteed. Fourth, the very important network management is not included. Among other shortcomings we notice that no weight has been given to reliability, database synchronization is not included, neither channel capacity nor bit error rate are accounted for, and a migration path with standardization is not incorporated. Further, no provision is made for voice, interconnection of different OSI is not assured, and global integration is not possible.

3.6 The IEEE 802 LAN Reference Model

The IEEE Local Area Network Reference Model is a layered structure that corresponds to the ISO/OSI, particularly the link and physical layers. This local area network standard is stipulated in the IEEE 802 Functional Requirements Section 4.1.2 (version 5.3, 23 July 1981). A number of implementation areas have been considered in the work of the IEEE 802 Committee. They include LAN applications such as file transfer, file access, graphics, word processing, electronic mail, and remote database manipulation; it will eventually consider digital voice.

The object of the IEEE 802 reference model is to promote compatibility among different equipment coming from different manufacturers, with a minimum effort for implementation. Emphasis has been placed on the local network as a data communications system that allows a number of devices to communicate with each other. The reference model defines a set of interfaces and protocols for the local network.

Two reference model views are given for the IEEE 802 LAN. Figure 3.5 shows the architectural perspective and Figure 3.6 reflects an implementation view. The data link and physical layers of ISO/OSI map onto three layers in the IEEE LAN reference model:

- Logical link control (LLC)
- Media access control (MAC)

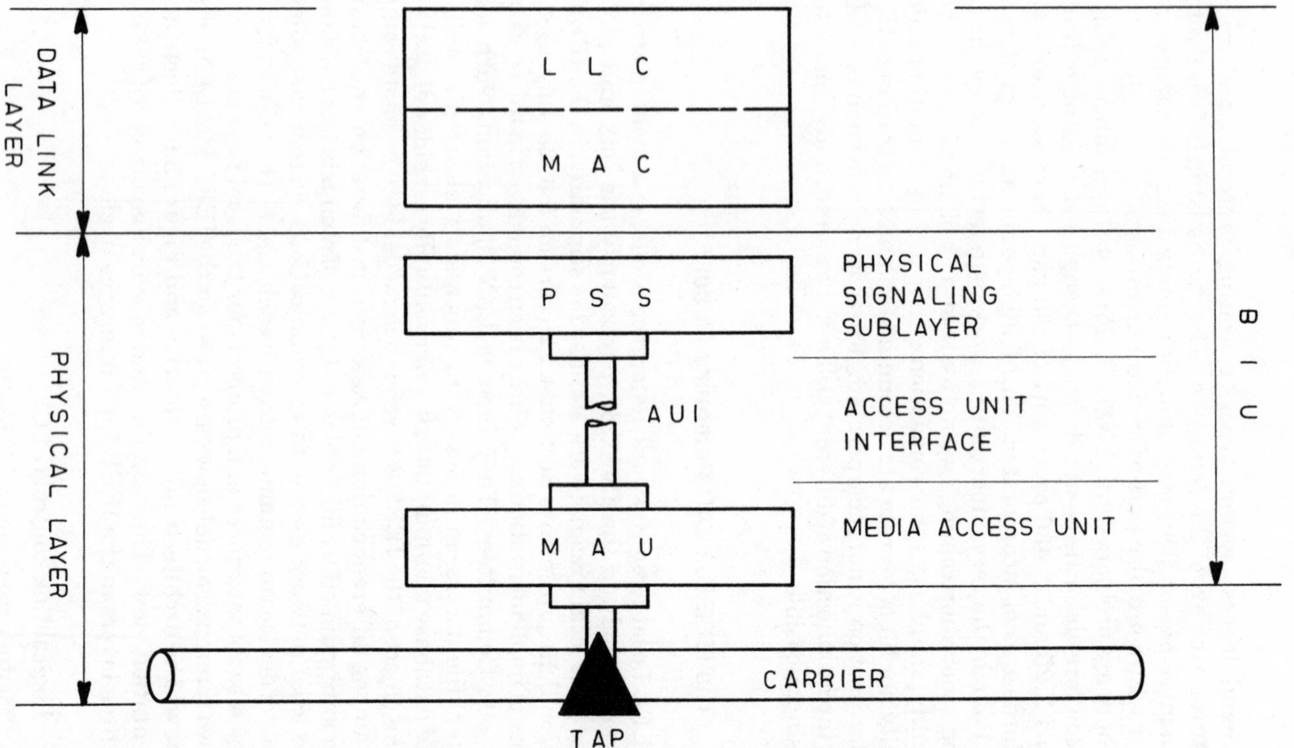

Figure 3.6 Implementation view of the lower ISO/OSI layers in a LAN environment.

- Physical layers

Service access points (SAP), for addressing end points, are also part of the construct.

The IEEE 802 local area network is a peer-to-peer communications system. No intermediate switching or routing nodes exist within the definition. Data terminal equipment (DTE) are devices that attach directly to the local network medium. The LAN enables DTE to communicate directly on the same logical link that was established on a point-to-point basis without requiring any intermediate switching node. This contrasts to wide area networks, where switching is performed at the network layer.

The logical link control layer defines procedures for establishing, maintaining, and terminating logical links, or sessions, between DTE on the local area network. The objective of these control procedures is to provide reliable data transmission from one node to another: no data should be lost or duplicated. This is commonly called "connection-oriented" service. The primary characteristics of links complying with these standards are:

- Sessions are always peer-to-peer.
- Multiple logical links can be established on one physical link.
- Groups of logical links are controlled by a higher-level entity, the service access point.

The MAC layer is concerned with norms regarding the use of transport media so that there are no conflicting transmissions which result in unintelligible data. "Soft errors" are intermittent faults that temporarily degrade the performance of the network. They are normally tolerated by error recovery procedures. Such errors are indicated by architectural inconsistencies, such as cycling redundancy checks (CRC) or timeouts, in received or repeated frames.

"Hard errors" are permanent faults that cause the LAN to stop operating within the normal protocols. When a hard failure is detected, its cause must be isolated in order to restore proper operation of the network. For instance, a ring station might have detected the transmission of a MAC frame with an all-stations address to its ring only (beaconing station). All other stations that receive the beacon MAC frame enter "beacon repeat mode." In that beacon MAC frame, the address of the nearest active upstream neighbor (NAUN) is stated.

When the beaconing station's NAUN has copied eight of these beacon MAC frames, the NAUN removes itself from the ring and tests itself. If the test is successful, the NAUN reattaches to the ring; otherwise the NAUN remains unattached. If the ring does not recover after the NAUN tests itself, the beaconing station removes itself from the ring and tests itself. If the test is successful, the beaconing station reattaches to the ring; otherwise it remains unattached.

ISO/OSI and IEEE 802 LAN have a different scope and coverage. Layers above the OSI link layer are outside the scope of the IEEE 802 standard. But they are included within its field of study to insure compatibility. A peculiarity of 802 are the so-called service access points (SAP). The IEEE LAN consists of the LLC, MAC, and physical layers. To provide support for multiple higher-level client protocols, LLC service access points (L-SAP) assure interface ports at the network-to-LLC layer boundary. A MAC service access point (MAC-SAP) provides a single interface port to a single LLC entity physical service access point (P-SAP) which provides an interface port to a single MAC entity.

Two types of link services are assured by the IEEE 802 LAN standard:

- Connectionless (type 1)
- Connection oriented (type 2)

In type 1 (connectionless) operation, frames are exchanged between LLC stations without the need for the establishment of a logical link between two LLC service access points (L-SAPS). In LLC these frames are not acknowledged, nor are there any flow control or error recovery procedures.

Another important reference is in connection to broadband frequency allocation. As we will see in the appropriate chapter, the Electronics Industry Association (EIA) proposed a frequency allocation for broadband networks incorporated into the IEEE 802 LAN reference model. At the channel capacity level for LAN, the IEEE 802 committee addressed both baseband (BAB) and broadband (BRB). The two classes of service elaborated by the 802 LAN are token passing and carrier sensing multiple access and collision detection (CSMA/CD) (Figure 3.7).

To elaborate these alternative configurations, the IEEE committee divided its work into several parallel subgroups which generated reference model documents:

1. Document 8802.1 higher-level interface standard is the overall guideline describing the relationship among the various 8802

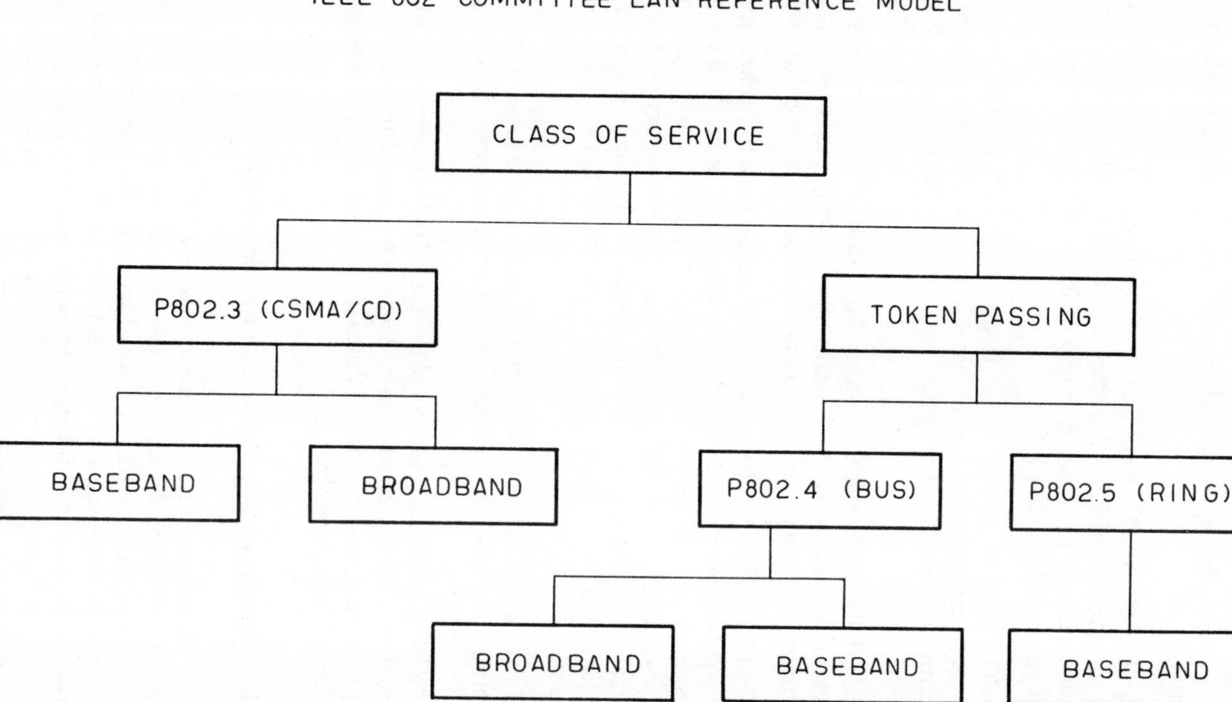

Figure 3.7 IEEE 802 committee LAN reference model.

standards and their connection to the OSI model. It also discusses the issues of internetworking and network management.

2. ISO/DIS 8802.2 logical link control standard defines the logical link control standard common to all the lower-layer access methods. It provides a single unified interface to the network layer which is above it.

3. ISO/DIS 8802.3 addresses itself to the CSMA/CD version of access control with its own specified communications media (50-ohm cable and transmission at 10 MHz). This is the CSMA/CD standard.

4. ISO/DIS 8802.4 token bus standard treats the token-passing bus version of access control with several permitted combinations of communication media, transmission speed, and modulation.

5. ISO/DIS 8802.5 token ring standard defines the token-passing ring version of 8802. It uses a token-passing method for access control and implements it using a ring architecture in the physical medium. Each station reads the message and regenerates it for the next station around the physical ring of connections. This is particularly appropriate for optical fiber connection.

6. Document 8802.6 is intended to define an access method and media suitable for a metropolitan area network (MAN).

Included within each main section of the standard are various additional options such as addressing (2-byte address or 6-byte address), line speed (1, 5, 10 MHz), and modulation methods (phase coherent, phase continuous, baseband, and broadband).

3.7 Multimedia versus Voice Communications

The idea of using geostationary earth satellites as relay stations for an international microwave telephone system was first proposed in 1945 by Arthur C. Clarke in a British technical journal. By the 1960s satellite communications were seen as an extension of the existing telephone network—a voice-oriented telecommunications system in the sky. But concepts changed with the merger of computers and communications, the ongoing deregulation of telephone service, and the advent of digital circuits, which make it feasible to share the same media for the transmission of voice and data. While the number of voice stations continues to increase, the actual number of voice endpoints grows very slowly; however, the number of DTE installations grows exponentially.

Services which might have been seen as added value on voice, for instance the videophone, have not taken off. By contrast, the bandwidth for terminals shows a steep increase. The most impressive growth started with personal computers, particularly online workstations. The bandwidth is for the end user. This reference remains valid whether we talk of satellites or of local area networks. The big demand for capacity in the coming years will be for multimedia, not just for voice. Many companies foresee giant productivity improvement *if* the end user can be given *subsecond response time.*

Multimedia solutions are taking the spotlight. There is a compound effect on this growth. The arrival of digital circuits has been paralleled by significant increase in mainframe power and in personal workstations able to sustain subsecond response time. With high bandwidth, companies move toward both windowing and facsimile communication at high rate. It is not only that in some countries voice usage declines by about 2 percent per year while data usage increases by more than 15 percent per year. It is the whole trend which is significant. We do not talk less, but we use the telephone less because of electronic mail and other message services.

Few organizations have properly perceived what the convergence of voice and data means to their business. What will people do other than talk on the line? The telcos say "picturephone," but the marketplace does not buy it. The market drives for multimedia communication that is able to transmit memos, pictures, graphs, and whole databases. Interactive multimedia exchanges would allow end users to rip windows from their own screens and send them to the other peoples' screens. This is not just a mapping problem. Neither is the solution demanding just a directory and numbering scheme. The global approach is important as is the architecture to be chosen.

We spoke of multimedia communications in Chapter 2 and emphasized what a well-rounded solution means. It is no longer an issue of nude wire or of a naked active satellite even if the wire transmits at gigabit or even terabit per second speeds. Plenty of optical fibers projects that are in laboratories at the moment are able to run at a terabit per second (TBPS) speed. Yet, while necessary, speed alone is not enough. A most significant organizational effort is necessary to complement technology. The management which is only interested in buying technology typically gets back only a small fraction of its money's worth. Intelligent management does understand that the face its corporation will present to the world during the next 10 to 15 years is going to be a communications face—and that means a great deal of preparation.

Chapter

4

Able Answers to LAN Implementation

4.1 Introduction

Change toward new and therefore lesser-known systems should be done in a factual and documented manner, bringing together both the lessons learned by the early starters and a comprehensive approach to the way LAN implementation influences the user's work. Among background factors are:

1. The rising user-information communication expectancies.
2. The users' demands for online processing and databasing.
3. The inefficiency of centralization: poor response time and long applications development.
4. The greater communications costs in front of falling processor and memory costs.
5. More end user-control—therefore greater data processing accountability.

New technologies bring new challenges. Personal computer based local area network design increasingly includes partitioned replicated databases, well-defined implementations plans, user-level evoluting applications, and a properly studied technical infrastructure, with cost effectiveness as one of the key preoccupations.

A basic premise for the future is that one WS per desk should be performing everything the office needs. This imposes the requirement for compatibility, modularity, expandability, predictability, human engineering, and wide bandwidth. At the center of the communications system is the local area network. Its usage is primarily internal to the organization. A LAN is typically installed inside the office premises or plant. Access is multipoint, which may reach a three-digit number of devices, making full use of bandwidth. Implementation of local area networks is no longer a matter of laying down a cable after the choice of token passing or CSMA has been made. That is the known and therefore easy part of the job. *The goal of instrumental LAN implementation should be an effective system-wide connectivity* assuring that the thousands of attached devices—at any part of the LAN structure—talk to each other.

Another vital part of properly architectured LAN systems is their ability to provide an increasing amount of bandwidth without interruption of ongoing operations. Business and industry experience a steadily increasing, difficult to satisfy demand for bandwidth. This is not only true for workstations but also for communicating mainframes, as the cases we will examine in this chapter will show. With this reference in mind, remember that a careful technical study is a prerequisite. It should be aimed at the definition of a global solution and protocols and connection costs. Let's always recall that *the network is owned by the user* organization. There is no public utility offering in the LAN domain. The user organization must decide on the structure, the functionality, and the topology. Significant physical choices are made in terms of wires, BIU, modems, protocols, and commodity software solutions.

4.2 The Modern Sense of Manufacturing Automation

During the last 5 years, major engineering companies have made concrete plans to achieve system integration of all their computers and communications resources and have made contractual agreements with vendors for the development of multicommunications systems software to cover end-to-end functionality. Prerequisites to a successful implementation have been:

1. The examination and definition of what system integration is all about.
2. The provision not only of a LAN solution at the IEEE 802 level but also of associated software able to cover the seventh layer of ISO/OSI and beyond.

To date, no firm has been totally successful in installing generic systems that are able to tie up all of the various aspects of an automated manufacturing process; but many expect to do so. General Electric and General Motors are two prime examples.

Leading mechanical, electrical, and electromechanical manufacturers have spent tens of millions of dollars in attempts to automate their factories and distribution networks; they have been unsuccessful because of the difficulty of achieving system integration. It is therefore no surprise that this subject is paramount in managerial thinking and in the list of technical goals. Because of basic incompatibilities in software and hardware, in most cases the result of attempts toward integration has been a vast expansion of islands of automation in which only certain aspects of the manufacturing process are under computer control. Most importantly, a number of attempts have failed to create the interconnect solution that binds the systems together.

This is a problem of systems integration. Able solutions require experience with communications and systems architecture—not just manufacturing know how. Similar problems exist in banking and other financial industries, but in a service network solutions are more homogeneous. As Figure 4.1 outlines, integration solutions in a manufacturing world must address two parts:

1. *Technological*, from engineering to fabrication and field maintenance.
2. *Commercial*, including marketing, sales distribution, and administration.

In both cases, specializing in systems integration means tackling large jobs. Systems integration possibilities involve purchasing and putting

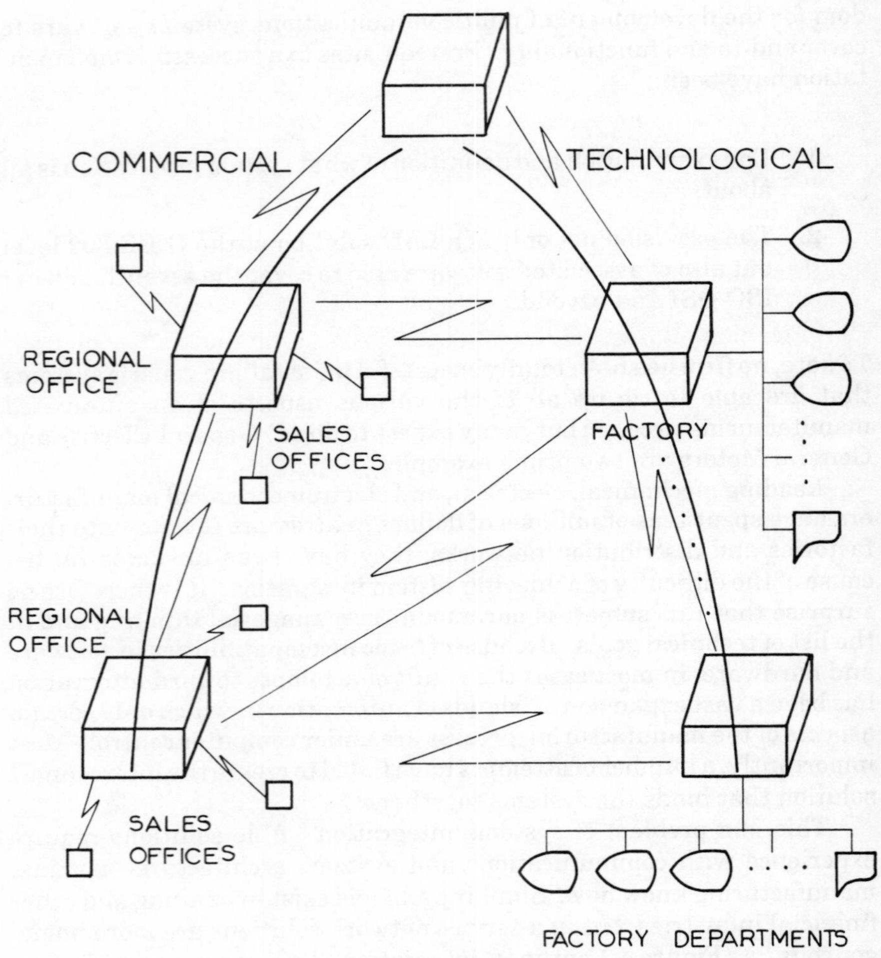

Figure 4.1 A manufacturing company has two types of networks to care about. They should be integrated.

together all of the necessary pieces of an aggregate of computers and communications. This is the antithesis of contract programming (body shop) work, which typically entails small-scale operations and has little leverage or follow-in business.

For instance, EDS is building one logical network for General

Motors—both to integrate the many physical networks in existence and to expand GM's communications capacity. System integration will greatly reduce the cost of all forms of communications. To this end, EDS has been ripping out much of AT&T's existing equipment, lines, phones, and Centrex systems and replacing them with more modern equipment, including high-capacity digital PBX. Moreover, it is gradually taking control of the pipelines that tie all of these systems together.

By circumventing the Bell System's land lines with microwave and satellite communications, EDS plans to reduce the cost of GM's communications by about 20 to 30 percent per transmission. Over time, when marginal communications costs drop and information transport speed and capacity are enhanced, a variety of new types of previously uneconomical communications will become cost justified: video, graphics output from CAD systems, and so on—providing there are radically improved productivity tools for managers and professionals.

As the electrical engineering business, and much of the electromechanical, has shifted toward electronics, excellence in system integration work represents for manufacturing firms a big opportunity to demonstrate (and further develop) their expertise. Such expertise is required for building and maintaining large-scale, truly global telecommunications systems. Fortune 1,000 companies with geographically disparate sites are prime candidates for such studies. Banks and insurance companies are also interested in the systems integration effort. All labor-intense industries have been actively shopping to automate their operations for at least 10 to 15 years. But as in manufacturing, this has been done by discreet islands with the result that installed systems don't talk to each other.

In a manufacturing industry, the discreet islands of implementation fall under five main classes. Three among them are representative of the state of the art in manufacturing automation—yet they are still not properly integrated with one another.

1. *Computer-aided design (CAD).* Many product engineers have access to computer-aided tools that enable them to design and test an item without having to manufacture it. CAD has three main benefits. It cuts development timetables, helps to improve quality, and enables engineers to work much more productively than was possible some years ago. However, CAD systems typically run on specialized, graphics-oriented computers and are not tied in with the rest of the manufacturing system. This makes it difficult for a complete range of design tools to be

deployed and creates coordination problems. The LAN approach has evident advantages but also poses demanding requirements.

2. *Manufacturing requirements planning (MRP).* This is a complex system of tracking orders, inventories, supplies, suppliers, and the factory floor. The object is facilitating efficient production scheduling. With computerized scheduling systems, zero in-process inventory (just-in-time) systems are now being installed in many plants; manufacturers are able to order parts from vendors only as the parts are required. If used properly, MRP can drastically cut the production costs through better planning, tracking, and delivery.

   As a software construct, MRP is driven by a list of components of the products being manufactured. The list is determined by the product design, specified by the engineering department. The problem is that today there are few, if any, automated links between CAD and MRP. Here again local and wide area networks can provide the link-but more is necessary to assure perfect functionality. "More" means beyond the classical LAN approaches.

3. *The automated shop floor.* A typical shop floor has computer-controlled tools and robots which cannot communicate well with each other. This incompatibility creates all sorts of barriers. System integration cannot be provided strictly at the LAN level of reference addressed by the IEEE 802 recommended standard. Much higher protocols are necessary. For this reason, GM started the effort to force hardware vendors to adopt MAP as the universal standard for allowing computers and tools to communicate.

   This problem is not only acceptance but also implementation. Though some of the necessary ideas for interconnection are in place, there is no software that can solve the islands of automation problem. True factory automation requires a tremendous amount of communication, as well as the creation and maintenance of large databases regarding:

- Suppliers and vendors
- Equipment
- Products
- Parts
- Labor

True manufacturing automation is a system integration problem, where the most important aspect in putting the pieces together is finding the correct interconnect capability.

4. *Word processing at headquarters, factories and sales offices.* Here, too, interconnection is vital not only for the existing equipment but also for that to be installed (an estimated 70 percent of important managerial and office work is still not automated). For the years to come, multimedia solutions will dominate the picture. Studies have demonstrated that 75 percent of all paper-based information in a manufacturing industry is for internal consumption. This goes up to 90 percent in banking environments.

   In this sense, making WP more efficient is a meaningless exercise. The emphasis should be to eliminate WP altogether, substituting paper with electronic mail—and integrating other presentation forms (voice, graphics) into compound electronic documents. LANs must provide support for reaching this goal and support means multimedia.

5. *The mainframe business.* The data center has typically been stuffed with a variety of incompatible mainframes, usually from different manufacturers—and even if they are from the same vendor, they have incompatible operating systems. The need for effective mainframe-to-mainframe connectivity became particularly apparent during the last decade when the online trend pushed toward interconnection. This need became greater with InfoCenter implementation and personal computing.

4.3 Problem Solving at General Electric

Even within a fully integrated distributed environment—which nobody has by any means—there is a dividing line between the central resources and those in the periphery, with workgroups and departmental engines at interfaces (Figure 4.2). But integration standards can see to it that dichotomies are transparent, both to the user and to the specialist. The following points have been learned from General Electric's early integration attempts:

1. A 10-MBPS LAN (in this case Ethernet) is not capable of interconnecting mainframes among themselves and with minis. The channel is simply *too narrow* and the protocol does not

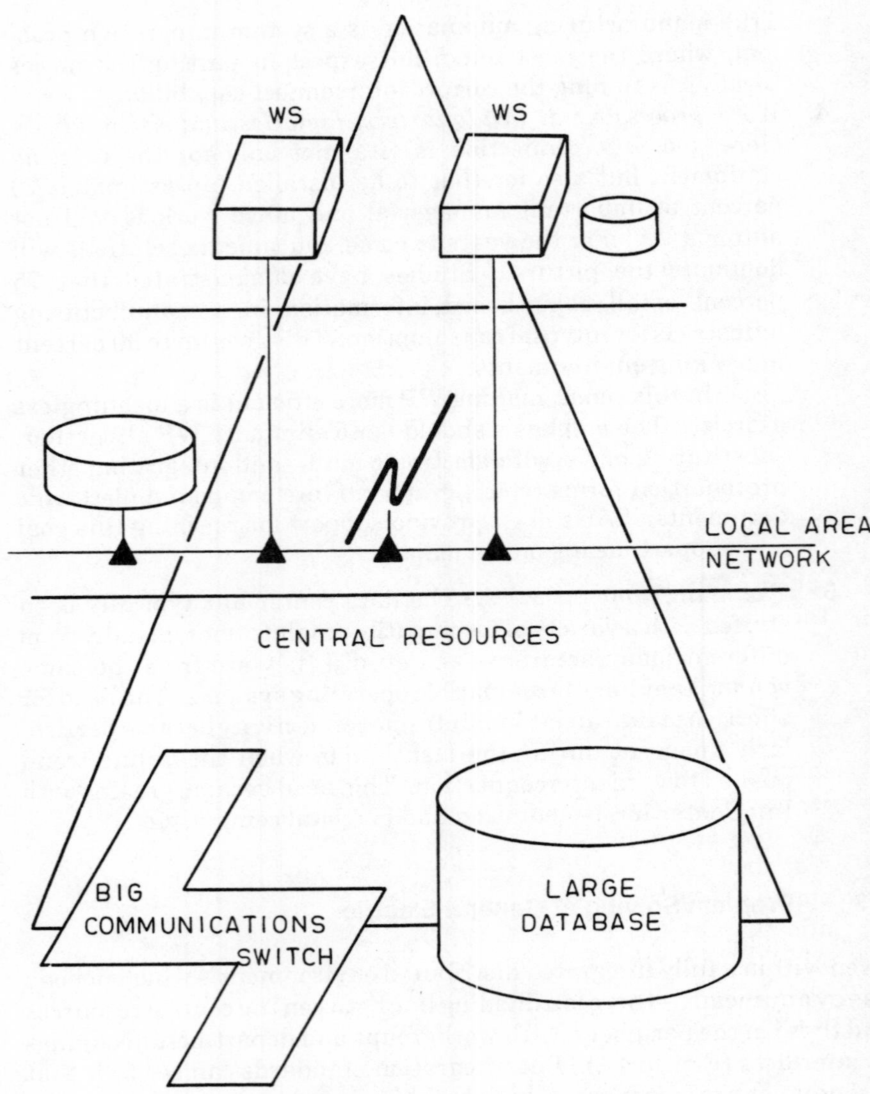

Figure 4.2 **Data processing gear should be fully distributed. Control resources should focus on databasing for backup and/or communications switching.**

respond to heavy dataflow requirements.

2. A 50-MBPS LAN capacity (offered by Hyperchannel) was found to be the minimum necessary for the job in reference. In other words 50-MBPS is not a wideband. It is a rather narrow band for interconnected mainframes, sure to be overtaken by communications requirements as applications expand, but the best available for the job in reference.

3. Standard vendor software covering the session layer and some of the presentation layer of ISO/OSI (in this case Netex) is *not enough* to assure interconnection of diverse operating systems (OS) on mainframes. All seven layers of ISO/OSI must be covered. For this reason GE contracted a tailor-made solution. (We will follow a similar case with General Mills.)

Still, the tailor-made solution did not cover all OS. In the GE environment there is also a Cray special array processor, but not on Hyperchannel; the Cray is connected directly to the IBM (Figure 4.3). Polished organizational interfaces facilitate the interconnection. Command labels are the same for all three makes of mainframes, the solution being GE proprietary.

While Massnet served better than the native Hyperchannel software, it didn't have all the needed software for linking HIS and IBM mainframes in a way that was fully transparent to the periphery. Transparency had to be the rule from the WSs at professional desks to the minis on the factory floor. For this reason a contract was given to Masstor Systems for developing software able to cover the seventh layer functionality of the ISO/OSI reference model. The Lynn factory was selected as the introduction site. It took 9 months to establish the specifications with the GE computing centers, and 30 months to develop the ACE, SCA, and associated routines—over and above the existing Massnet investment.* During this time some 300 worker-months were spent on the project.

The next stage was interconnecting computer centers through a full range of applications that included consolidation of financial reports (leading to daily cash management) and the corporate recovery facility. The latter involves the computer center in Schenectady, among other data centers. The plan is to take 16 major computer operations into the

* The definition of ACE, SCA, and other modules is given in Chapter 13.

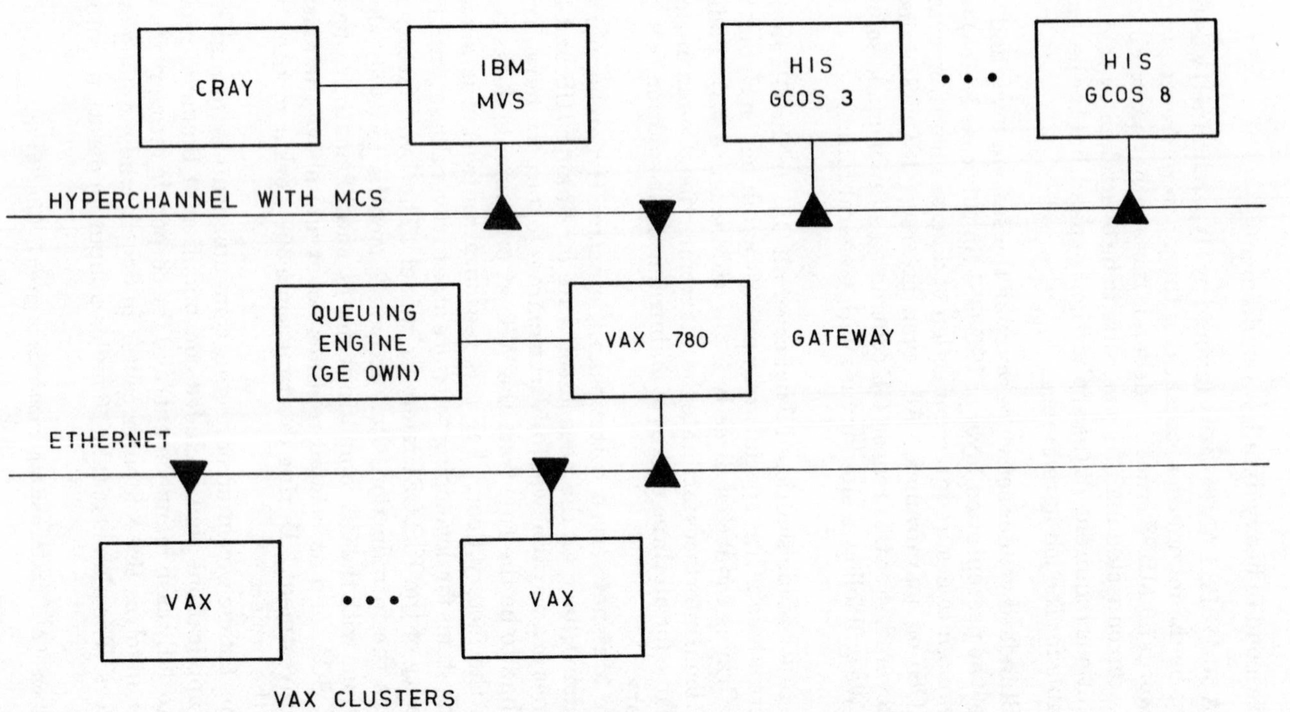

Figure 4.3 Networking mainframes and maxicomputers at General Electric.

network. The goal is running a fully distributed database on established mainframe resources. Several other organizations have or are planning to have a similar objective.

Powerful local area networks interconnecting computer resources are at the center of this approach. The quest for high performance dominates. The aim is to build a large, fast, very reliable LAN—but also to provide a system architecture able to support foolproof solutions for time-shared multiprocessed and multitasked systems. The goals have grown with experience. They moved from the peripheral device interconnect bus idea (which was good for workstations and simple servers) to backbone and tributary systems. The former link the later—as well as mainframes and robotics—into an integrated network. Work among the hooked-up computer centers in the GE orbit now stress the factory of the future and the inventory management of the future. Both are in need of interconnect capabilities and of protocol standards. American companies have embraced manufacturing automation because they perceive that, implemented correctly, it provides increased efficiency in an evermore competitive industrial environment.

Over the past few years automation has tremendously changed the entire scope of manufacturing from product design to production scheduling and the physical manufacturing process itself. Yet, as the preceding section outlined, despite all such progress only isolated pieces of the entire manufacturing puzzle are automated.

4.4 New Protocols to Enhance Connectivity

The MAP advanced by General Motors is an attempt to create a standard way of sending data around the factory. Standards are being set, but successive MAP demonstrations in Detroit prove how much work remains to be done.

Like the U.S. Department of Defense, GM has the dollars and the determination to make things happen. Unless a supplier's equipment conforms to MAP, management said, it will get little of GM's investment budgets, which is put at $100 billion for the 1990-92 time frame. How effective can this policy be?

If the LAN is to act as an integrator, it should encompass hardware and software designed for and installed at the desk of all professionals—from R&D engineers to manufacturing engineers, reliability and quality control experts, and maintenance coordinators. These professionals would typically work not only in *our* firm but also for our business partners—from suppliers to clients. It is precisely this global relationship which is very difficult to implement.

Lots of companies, particularly the larger ones, offer good examples of incompatibility. In one case, management decided computer operations had to respond to an engineering request to exchange documents between all engineering workstations. But many of the WSs were incompatible and Decmail and Mailway will not integrate even if they run on the same network. In this specific case, a tentative solution seemed to be found through third-party software and hardware. However, this made a batch file transfer activity feasible and not the interactive procedures management had put as its goal. The third-party solution provided format conversion. There was no database access, just document transfer in 2780/3780 mode with reference format DIA/DCA.

As the solution stands today, the third-party software resides on the gateway. It helps interconnect computers under IBM MVS and DEC VMS, but not on Wang. The third party also provided PC file transfer in asynchronous mode, which is hard to find. Yet, even if these solutions satisfy user requirements, they don't cover all computer equipment at this particular firm. Engineering, for example, has Apollo computers for CAD. Apollo is still self-standing. An intermediate step is hooking to VAX. Then permanent solutions must be found.

This is not an isolated reference. Most organizations are at the same crossroads. System solutions are necessary and able answers can only be found by way of integration which is polyvalent and able to address different reference levels. New higher-level protocols should address not only the communications level but also databasing. What's more, there should be the same protocols both for multimedia datacomm and for multimedia databases. A message is a file in the database, and every file should be designed as a message. Furthermore, new protocols should specialize by application area as the applications domain is rapidly expanding and formalisms cannot do all things to all situations. Figure 4.4 shows an end-user-oriented editing terminal, supporting menus, different data entry devices, online communications, and hard disk and optical disk storage. A cost-effective line discipline, graphics standards, databasing protocol, and user-friendly interactive features are necessary.

There is an unquestionable need for able, universally acceptable protocol solutions—some specialized, others generalized. The generalization need was the origin of the MAP standard. By 1980, GM had grown tired of robots, conveyors, machine tool controllers, and shop floor terminals that did not communicate with each other. Only 15 percent of

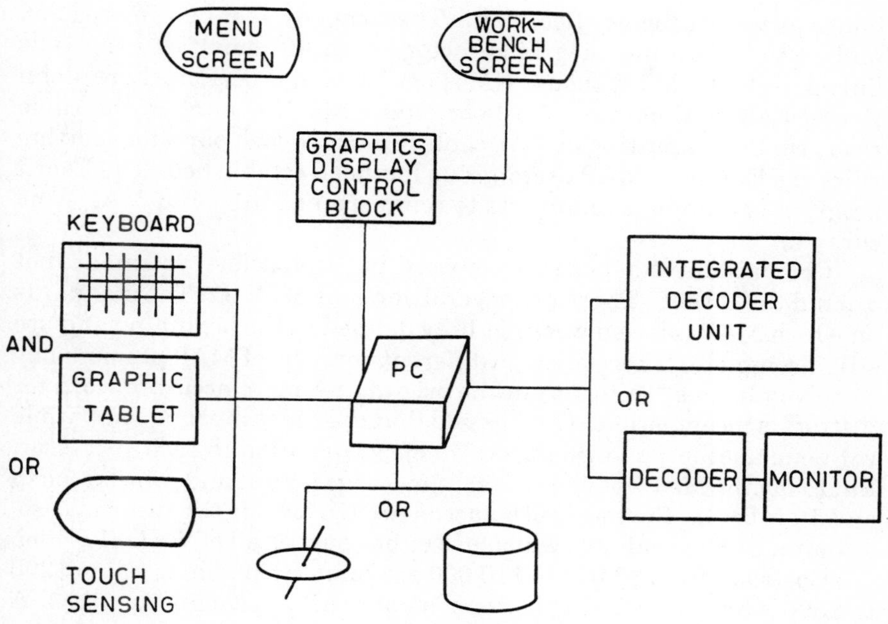

Figure 4.4 End-to-end interconnected workstations with photonics storage.

more than 60,000 different devices on GM's shop floor exchanged information beyond their own processes. This percentage was so low than an integral study demonstrated 40 percent of the investment was watered down to pay for interfaces necessary to sort out the sprawling but diverse environment. There were even incompatibilities in controlling screens and keyboards.

The basic GM idea has been to run one local area network around a factory which connects every programmable device. This then should link to factory-wide mainframe manufacturing control systems. For LAN implementation, GM used broadband, which can carry speech and image as well as factory-floor data. The company spent a rumored $50 million to set up an integrated factory with 40 manufacturing cells linked to CAD/CAM systems. GM is not alone in this effort; Ford, John Deere, Kaiser Aluminum, Du Pont, and Kodak have taken the same road. Du Pont is putting in MAP cable to make breach parts for sporting rifles. In Europe, a MAP users' group has been established. The Esprit program is funding two projects to complement MAP. But MAP is no cure-all.

Compatibility has been the key word, but compatible systems are not around the corner. There are several versions of MAP. The standards on which MAP is based were not fully defined at the beginning and are still incomplete. There are also different versions of MAP promoted by some vendors as "better" than the original. A more accurate word for "better" is incompatible. GM hassaid that upgrades must be compatible with one another, allowing users an easy transition to each successor. But today the MAP versions differ in message format and cable speed (5 and 10 MBPS). Further, such speeds are too low for the future. Also, variants will be available which use either part or all of the OSI model.

Costs are from $2,000 to $10,000 per connection, due to fall to $200 to $500 when the VLSI chip versions of MAP appear in quantity. A greater cost is that new standards can make the plan obsolete. MAP is not ready yet, even though companies which have to automate to stay in business cannot afford to wait.

4.5 The General Mills Experience

The General Mills experience is interesting for two reasons. First, they used higher-level protocols and associated software that are different from the ones specified by IEEE 802: the NSC* Netex product. Second, the standard NSC offering did not totally fit the environment, and it was adapted to the ongoing operations. This adaptation did not necessarily give the expected results. Though NSC was of help in doing the adaptation and General Mills put first-class people on this project, there were too many problems with this software change. If a user organization buys commodity software, it should use it as is. Changes in somebody else's special software are like opening Pandora's box.

Let's start with a definition of the problem. General Mills has a

* Network Systems Corporation (NSC) is the maker of Hyperchannel.

mixed mainframe environment of IBM (3983E) and Burroughs (6800). Each has many attached terminals. The mainframes are connected to Hyperchannel. Netex software is employed in this context. Connected peripherals to Hyperchannel use IBM JES. Other interconnected attachments are Hewlett-Packard minis. Each has its own terminals. The whole lot is devoted to two main applications. Eight HP minis are attached to the Hypernet. Eleven others are distributed. the HPs in the plant are connected 1:1 to an HP in headquarters.

Also attached to hyperchannel are Honeywell page printers and Kodak Computer Output to Microfiche (COM). Prior to the Hyperchannel, they were served offline through magnetic tapes. The LAN solution eliminated the handling of 700 magnetic tapes per month, a good example of data center productivity and the benefits of a LAN. At General Mills, not only productivity has been enhanced, but also performance. Delay through tape handling was 1 1/2 hours per day. Now it is 13 minutes. At the same time, doing away with manual tape handling led to the elimination of many operators.

The prime application at the level of the networked mainframes is file transfer. It uses both Netex and software written above Netex. File transfer is a computer-to-computer application, not terminal-to-terminal. Let's recall that this takes place among different types of computers running under incompatible OS. When asked if they were satisfied with the functionality of Netex or if they ever lost control of files, the company answered:

> With Netex for program-to-program communication we only write the application controlling the file level. The system allows office communication. Higher-level software sees to it that we don't care how the Hyperchannel adapter works. But at the file proper level—opening and closing and addressing files—we had to write ourselves the needed routines. They are not in Netex.

Whenever necessary, Netex gives an error code but does not say "why." It is a logical I/O but does not include diagnostics. Online diagnostics for file transfer and dataflow are not addressed by ISO/OSI. This is one of the weaknesses of the recommended standard. Note that for this implementation there was no change necessary in the application software. Conversion became transparent. General Mills used bulk file transfer on IBM and Burroughs and wrote a Pascal program to generate JCL and link networking.

Another problem to which company specialists addressed themselves was workstation interconnection to mainframes. They are equipped with IRMA. This uses a low-level (3270) protocol, which does not answer applications perspectives. For instance, today WS users need to know on which mainframe their files are. A system solution is necessary to expand beyond point-to-point connectivity toward more sophisticated implementation.

Since the corporate database is kept on mainframes, the priority General Mills gave to the Hyperchannel-Netex aggregate was mainframe oriented, aimed to provide quick movement of data to and from factories. PCs originally used a digital switch (Micom port selector) which was in place well before Hyperchannel. But integration must take place in a system-wide sense. Correctly, the company was very careful in its approach to a broadband LAN solution. One executive said, "When we started looking at Hyperchannel, we saw some companies who would write software for us. But what we wanted was something ready to test. Netex was available for IBM. Essentially it gives us logical I/O."

The way General Mills looks at the subject, Netex connect routines lead to pipes, which avoid packetizing and retries. But even if it provides support well above the levels defined in IEEE 802, it is still medium-level connectivity. General Mills looked for a way to make its multimainframe environment totally transparent, but found that takes a large amount of code. It also found that:

- The extra code would be quite complex for polyvalence.
- It would be simpler if query-only applications were supported.

Maintenance, too, was a concern since the proprietary code needed to be updated whenever the vendor came in with new features. One way to do this would be to define in menu (for the user) what is in which database, avoiding the need to write too many interfaces. General Mills decided to do what they could quickly to get it running, even though the solution was suboptimal. They felt that it was impossible to do everything at once.

That's a first-class advice. It gives you the opportunity to learn from experience. Here the change to Burroughs was done by NSC, which took about 1 year. Changes at General Mills were for interfaces to their programs, which were relatively easy. Their advice is: "Keep changes flexible. If the Hyperchannel-Netex box fails, be ready to switch to bisynchronous communication."

Another valid practice regards management control. As a matter of information systems policy, General Mills keeps audit trails on every system. It can be interrogated for quality history purposes, and was made for BSC and converted to Hyperchannel. Finally, network control functions have been implemented and give first-class results; the network software by General Mills is both following operations and reporting exceptions. Network control software is a must to any sophisticated LAN implementation.

4.6 The Approach by Northwestern Bell

Northwestern Bell has a mixed environment of mainframes: IBM, Univac, and Honeywell. The information center and transaction routines run on IBM. Programs on Univac mainframes are oriented to facility assignment, but there is no link to the information center. They were acquired because Bell Corporate Research application programs run on Univac.* The Honeywell mainframes are in different data centers, Minneapolis, Des Moines, and Omaha, and are linked to the information center. Therefore Northwestern Bell has an applications environment that is geographically distributed over three locations and is distributed over three types of computer:

- Univac handles the inventory management switchgear, lines, etc., and general equipment applications.
- Honeywell handles call recording. It is fully distributed.
- IBM handles the backoffice (accounting receivable, etc.), customer billing, and the infocenter.

Within this environment, interactive access is necessary for all online users. For instance, if a customer calls and complains about a bill, the answer requires verification of toll records, hence, the need for cross-equipment capabilities.

To reduce paper records, copies of bills are made. (If they were, they would have been on IBM where the application resides.) All customer and operational queries are channelled to the HIS original files (call

* Burroughs and Univac mainframes are marketing under the Unisys name after the merger of Burroughs and Sperry. Nevertheless they run under different incompatible OS. Since *operating systems* rather than corporate identity is the reference for interconnection, I use the original make of the machines for identification.

recording). Such an approach calls for transaction pass through, which has been implemented through Masstor Systems*. The MDX software (Massnet) runs on the IBM and Honeywell mainframes. There are also NSC programs in operation. A question about comparing Masstor to NSC got the following response: "NSC is better documented. It is also in Minneapolis, hence at easier access by the specialists." The use of Masstor and NSC is important as both concern Hyperchannel implementation. The cable, BIU, and lower-level protocols are the same. But Massnet has written its own protocols, and Netex, its own software for the higher-up layers of ISO/OSI. Thus both offer enriched LAN communications, and a comparison between them is quite meaningful.

There are currently three Hyperchannel installations at Northern Bell, each being 300 feet long. They are not interconnected among themselves. One of these Hyperchannels provides connectivity front end to front end (FEP-to-FEP) for a Honeywell DPS 8/70 and an Amdahl mainframe. A Univac mainframe is connected to the Amdahl through an internal network link. A key application running on this triple system is facility assignment. When service orders get entered into the Honeywell side, they must be pushed to the Univac box because of the application programs running on the latter. Hence, multiprocessing involving diverse OS and broadband LAN connectivity is the best solution.

The system specialists at Northwestern Bell are searching for sound approaches to these rather complex problems. They are also carefully evaluating what the mainframe vendors offer in terms of ongoing and projected requirements. Along this line of evaluation:

- They found that one of the query systems was a very archaic reactionary program. It cannot generate needed output.
- Similarly, the mainframe's input output interface was ineffectual. It has been replaced by a Massnet interface for run-time.

While these points particularly affect two of the vendors and underline the significant service offered by the Hyperchannel LAN and its software, basic routines at the IBM side also needed fixing. DNAM is an LU 6.2-based protocol converter by Bell Labs, replacing BTAM and VTAM. Its development was necessary because of Bell's own network used in the Amdahl-Univac connection.

Page Bill is one of the key applications on the same computer aggregate. Since Northwestern Bell decided to migrate from Honeywell to IBM, the new page-long telephone bill was put on the IBM side. The connection of the two mainframes is Hyperchannel with Massnet software. They have found the up time of Massnet to be quite good. At the time of our meeting, there was no operational Netex application but one was being tested. They clearly did not expect to write their own systems software.

In terms of satisfaction with Masstor Systems, it was said that in the beginning there were delays in bringing the system rapidly online, but these have been corrected. Performance is satisfactory, which is very critical. Having different hardware (Hyperchannel) and software (Masstor) vendors posed no problems; NSC runs some diagnostics; Masstor has other ones, with which Northwestern Bell is really happy. However, they have found that the current releases by different vendors below the Session and Presentation control are not supporting interactive activity. Since interactivity is a competitive advantage, all organizations have to be careful on this matter.

Further, they have not yet decided how, in an all-IBM environment, to tie the mainframes together, *but they would rather follow an SNA-compatible strategy*. This preference has an evident impact on plans for multicomputer aggregates. If a protocol shell solution is chosen to overcome diverse OS characteristics, LU 6.2 should be the prime option. This is based on the premises we discuss throughout this book. Given that network-wide, multifunctional and multimedia solutions are not available off-the-shelf, intermediate software should be provided, but solutions should point to the directions of standards-whether *de jure* or *de facto*.

4.7 PC and Databases

Effective answers to LAN implementation are no more a question of just choosing and installing one. Even if the best LAN choice is made, the result will be substandard. Effective answers require network-wide research which starts with a needs analysis and then samples networking approaches, prototyping and testing them with full service in mind. Is our company going to put micros at every desk? If so, everything we do should be part of a learning process to move us toward that goal. We should prepare for the future.

The first LANs to come around were for microcomputers. They were developed in response to demands for PC communications requirements. Figure 4.5 gives an example. But since the early 1980s, the whole

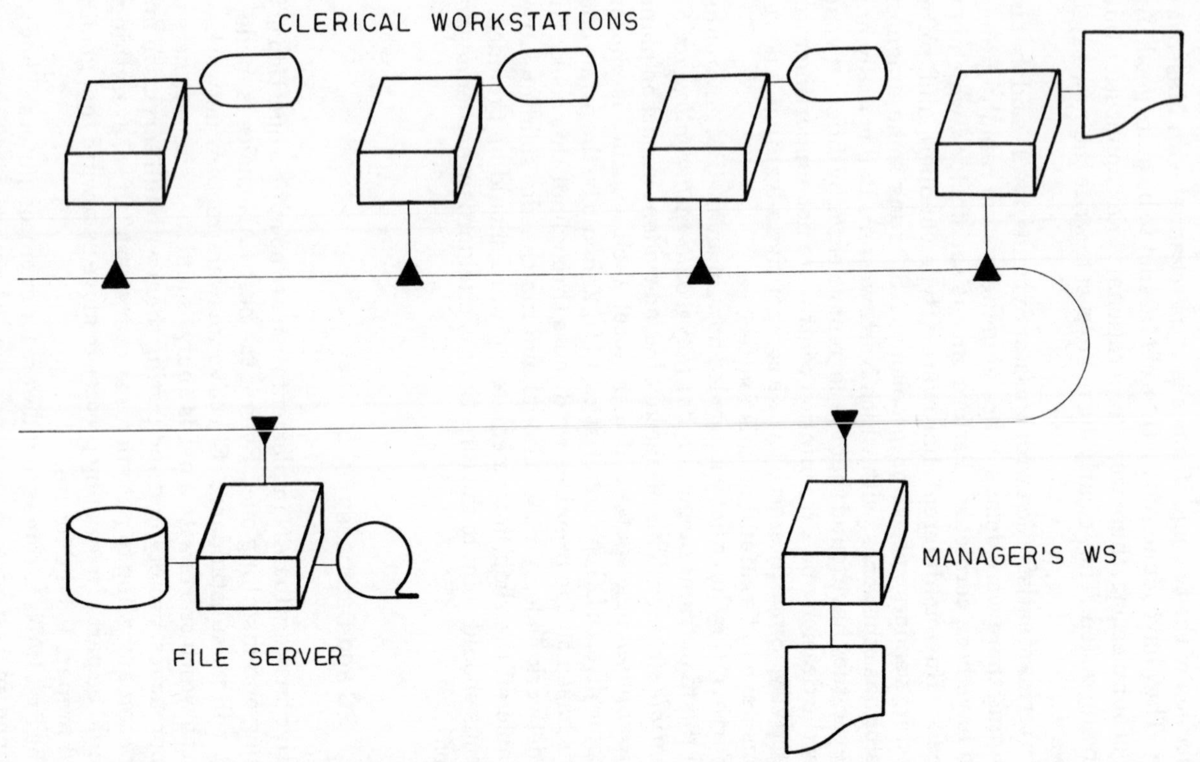

Figure 4.5 Typical LAN configuration with WSs and file server.

frame of reference has changed. LANs today are established to interconnect all information resources in a company, not just some of them. The General Motors, General Electric, General Mills, and Northwestern Bell case studies fully document this point. The trouble is that the necessary software products appealing to the top layers of ISO/OSI and beyond the seventh layer are neither available to the level of support which is necessary nor are they that generalized yet. So we have to write all the software ourselves.

There have been other problems as well. Some of the advantages many organizations expected to get right away, such as bringing down data from the host and manipulating it on micros, have not materialized. Other companies have found it necessary to move slowly because their WS users are taking longer to become attuned to online interactivity than was thought would be the case. Practically every organization using LANs has found that its own people must do a significant amount of research:

- They should require the vendor, the designer, and the installer to rephrase their jargon and provide schematics and examples until it all makes sense.
- They should also learn the subject themselves to a respectable amount of detail. Otherwise, they don't control the vendor.

Learning means taking courses, visiting successful installations, and getting and *reading* all available documentation about technical characteristics, such as the specific frequencies used for each different service offering, the frequencies they may use as they see fit, those unused portions of the bandwidth that the vendor is reserving for future use, the maximum distance they can locate terminal equipment from the trunk cable, the trunk-interface-device specifications (including number of ports, speed, process chips employed), and how many interface devices are needed.

Part and parcel of a sound, thorough organizational work is the relational database structure and its implementation. (This is discussed further in Chapter 5.) If you currently use any DBMS other than relational, forget it. It will not help you in an interactive, LAN-supported environment. it is precisely for this reason that a good part of the LAN discussion at Northwestern Bell focused on databases and database management systems (DBMS). There, they are in an evaluation stage which involves small production runs with DB2 and prototyping with DB2. The tests have focused on the potential of IBM's relational DBMS offer with applications at the records level. The goal has been to obtain *subsecond response*.

This evaluation demonstrated that DB2 is still undergoing transition. The potential for performance bottlenecks is still there. One of the limitations which have been established is that there is no integrated data dictionary yet available. But some system specialists like what they find with DB2. Said one of them: "In the DB2 arena we see new concepts and their implementation. They provide the ability to do a whole new range of applications." On a 3092 series machine, the DB2 experimentation in process was able to substain 47.2 transactions per second. There have been 14 calls per transaction in a PL/1 program. However, I subsequently saw in a DB2 interactive test with another firm that the figure drops to only five transactions per second in the case of 4381 equipment. Prudence advises benchmarking *prior to* a DBM commitment. *The choice of the proper DBMS for mainframes is an integral part in planning for successful LAN implementation.* As we will see in the chapter on file servers, the mainframe is the LAN's database—and no system solution is worth its salt unless it can guarantee subsecond response time to the online users.

Highly connected to the DBMS decision is the query language to be chosen. The SQL standard was a factor in Northwestern Bell's decision. Another factor has been the ability to spread DB2 across multiple systems. Prior to starting in-depth evaluations, company specialists looked at other vendors: Cullinet, ADR, etc. They also examined IBM's cross-system product (CSP), which came out a little better than the third parties just mentioned.

Chapter

5

Organizational Solutions for Effective Communications

5.1 Introduction

One major difference between a collection of computers and an integrated information system lies in the communication capability. Many of the automation characteristics require an effective method of passing information from one computer to another freely. As a rule, the more sophisticated the communications setup, the more easily a user will be able to access and use the facilities in a global sense without worrying about where they may be physically. And it is important that end users do not have to think about the system's communications at all. Obtaining a document from another computer should be no more difficult than pulling it from a hard disk at the WS level. It must be completely transparent and automatic. Communication between systems depends on network software to provide this transparency. At a local area level, the physical connection should be organized horizontally and vertically throughout the building. Horizontally, a local area network(s) connect(s) the computers on each floor.

The cables for feeder lines may be protected twisted pair at a one-digit megastream (1 to 10 MBPS). An order of magnitude more capacity is required of a departmental network which allows department computer users to share resources such as disk files, printers, and workstations. A workstation can run its own software or execute software running on larger computers. The user makes the choice depending on the nature of the job. To complete the communications connection, departmental LAN must be tied together through a backbone; such a network connects the individual networks, on, for example, each floor using optical fiber cables. This interconnects the departments into the corporate computers and other information systems including public databases.

The basic message, however, is that business is more than departments and computers—it is organizations. The nature of each division determines the type of information it needs to perform its function. Interconnection is successful when it considers the whole business organization, which is the vital—and often missing link—in the creation of a complete information management system. Key to executive decision making is access to the firm's accumulated knowledge. Other things equal, the more accurate the information, the more learned the decisions which can be made. This is what I call the "truth table" and it is shown in Figure 5.1.

5.2 Organization and Structure

A serious consideration of business problems involves the examination of organization and structure. "Structure" means the internal organic arrangements on which relationships between persons, functions, and the physical and logical resources of a going concern are established. Business has always been delimited in its significance by its: Organization, Environment, and Objectives. "Organization" denotes a process and relationships associated with the structure. A business organization does not come into existence spontaneously. It is the result of the creative efforts of management.

To a considerable extent, *organization means functionalization.* A function is any task that can be clearly distinguished from any other task. It denotes an activity specialized in character that is performed by an individual or group of individuals within the organization. Successful functionalization leads to a sound departmentation. In its fundamentals it involves two techniques:

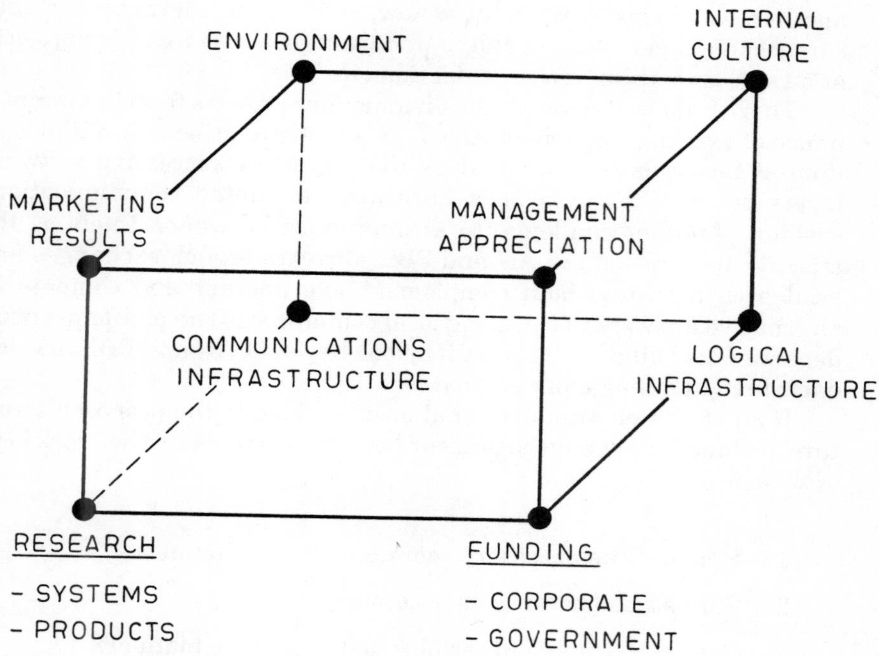

Figure 5.1 Truth Cube. Are we in control of every node and every link?

1. The ability to recognize functions by their distinctive characteristics.
2. The skill to combine functions so as to realize coordinated and efficient performance without unduly increasing the number of management levels and/or management posts.

Functions are readily distinguished from one another with respect to the know how, processes, and activities they entail. More difficult is the problem of determining a factual and documented basis for each combination of functions that are necessary for a given major project.

Figure 5.2 outlines the organization and structure of a communications department. It groups together planning, implementation, and maintenance, as well as security, quality control, and reliability. It is practice to split the available skill; planning and implementation should stay together. Every time we transfer a project from one department to another, we are losing time, know how, and money. The chart includes a project management unit able to undertake one or more major projects at a time, something few organizations include.

There is no well-defined line dividing new projects from the maintenance of existing implementations. Every installation is in full evolution—a fact greatly magnified by the impact of successive software layers on what used to be a hardware-dominated communications system. Another challenge to a communications department is the effective integration of LAN and PBX. Private branch exchanges and local area networks both complement one another and compete as alternative answers to the same local communications problems, but a department should have the skill to look beyond LAN and PBX to voice, data, text, and image integration.

If an operation organizational unit is added to the proposed structure, its functions should be to assure at all times that each network local or wide area:

1. Provides the necessary communications channels.
2. Stores and forwards as necessary.
3. Connects origin and termination in an able manner.
4. Assures uninterrupted flow of all types of information.

Operations must definitely feature and manage network control center(s) for reliability, flow control, congestion control, journaling, accountability, and operational statistics. They should make communications management aware of the need for long-, medium-, and short-term maintenance (in that order) but should not be preoccupied with it.

The other major unit to be observed in the proposed organization chart is technologies, which should have a wide state-of-the-art knowledge for design and operations and be able to assist these departments in their efforts and to perform the necessary quality control and audit on behalf of the director of communications.

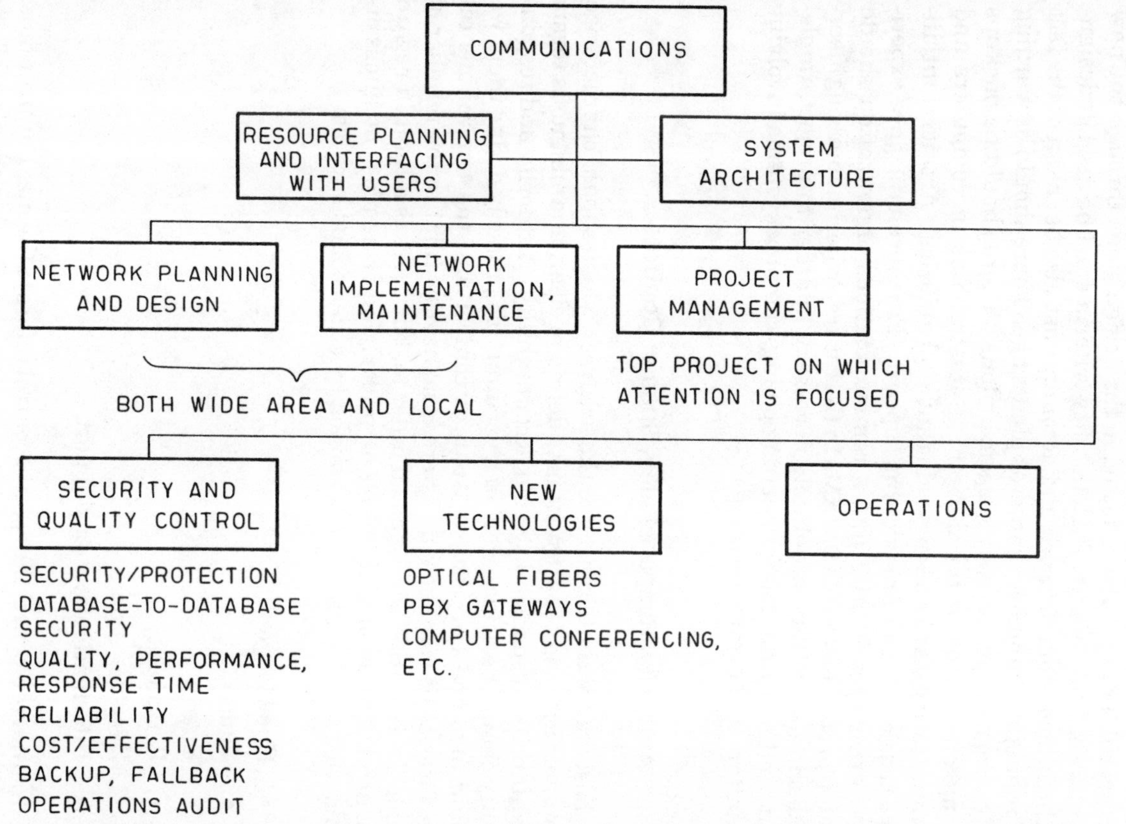

Figure 5.2 Organization and structure of a corporate telecommunications department.

Reliability is of utmost importance. In today's high-technology world, a disaster that cuts off the information resources is probable. Such probability must be reflected in the design stage through the new discipline of "risk analysis." Reliability criteria must be used in designing the information network and account must also be taken of the fact that reliability numbers change as plants age. There should be warning subsystems and emergency response plans. There should be backups and means to isolate the danger. Catastrophies in computers and communications are no longer distant probabilities. Artificial intelligence constructs can provide this support. Furthermore, since experience in this area is still thin, a communications organization should develop prototypes on CAD/CAM. In the future, experimental engineering disciplines will be absolutely necessary in order to project, implement, and maintain top functioning on big, complex systems involving computers and communications.

5.3 Authority, Responsibility, Span of Control

The best way of contributing to the accuracy which should characterize a communications department is to define in clear, unambiguous terms its authority, responsibility, and accountability. Authority and responsibility cannot be established in a vacuum. To properly define them we should examine two issues: span of control and the environmental interfaces to be established. There is no narrow limit to the number of people an executive can issue an order to, but there is a limit in regard to control. The span of control is an underlying principle of business organization. Its limits are determined by other spans such as:

- Knowledge
- Time
- Energy
- Personality
- Decision style
- Information system support

In a narrow sense, the span of control refers to the maximum number of subordinates which may be placed under the jurisdiction of one executive who is immediately superior to them. Citibank, for instance, has been successfully using information systems to enlarge their span of control. In the early 1970s it had an average 1:5 span of control; it has now reached 1:7, with a goal of 1:8. The other key ingredient for enlarging the span of control is the choice of well-trained assistants.

Within the span of control, the span of knowledge is a most important factor; it extends, affects, and modifies the levels of management; the ancient maxim that "knowledge is power" has particular force in managerial activity applicable to fields of high technology. Knowledge, time, and energy define the span of attention. The human brain is able to pay attention efficiently to relatively few items at a time. The greater the knowledge, personal energy, and time saved by information systems, the broader the span of attention of an executive. Mental productivity tools become addictive when we use them. This helps the system grow and expand in an intelligent manner. There is no substitute for the experience that comes from daily exposure to the pluses and minuses of automation.

Less definite in its nature than time and energy and more difficult to analyze than knowledge and control is the span of personality. Personality has been defined as that part of character effective in influencing other people. Decision styles vary from one person to another. There is no uniform rule on how decisions are taken, nor should there be one. This underlines the need for: flexibility, polyvalence, and multifunctionality in communications solutions. Some executives depend more on voice communications for their decision, others on graphical presentation (chartists), on text they read, or on tabulted data.

The communications network has to fit all decision styles. Whether long haul or local area, the network should fit executives, professionals, and clerical staff it serves. This task involves:

1. Determining the kind and extent of specialization of a business unit.
2. Undertaking the allocation of authority, responsibility, and accountability for the performance of such specialization work.
3. Providing the proper tools, through computers and communications, to enhance intellectual productivity.
4. Striving for coordination in the work to be done within a well-defined environmental perspective.

It is understood that the communications department is going to evolve in the environment of the other organizational units of the corporation, as well as the environment of clients and suppliers. And for them, it must provide competent solutions to end-user functions, text and data processing, secure database access, and voice communications. Solutions to these issues cannot be provided overnight, but they should be an integral part of a 5-year plan. Among critical issues on which to focus attention are perspectives in handling messages and transactions, electronic mail and computer comferencing, PC-to-mainframe linkage, network operating system, network control center, data integrity and data security, requirements for interactivity, and conditions for system integration.

All this must be examined within the perspective of each workplace (or group of homogeneous workplaces), not in a general, averaged-out sense. For instance, in a foreign exchange environment three system objectives are top most:

- Online dealer support
- Efficient backoffice automation
- Front and back office integration

In this context, communications and computer-based assistance to the dealer permits simultaneous access to databases and information providers, agile user-machine interfaces for queries, and comprehensive information presentation. It makes feasible fast dealer interactivity from deal capture and position keeping to calculation, experimentation, simulation, and exposure management.

This represents the organizational sense of blending high technology with efficient procedures to respond to dealer requirements. Able approaches will steadily look to incorporate newer tools such as expert systems capabilities for consolidation purposes and newer tools typically go beyond the basics. Provision must also be made for adaptability to changes.

5.4 Projecting a New System Architecture

It is important to properly define authority, responsibility, and span of control—the qualitative measures of a network—prior to elaborating on the quantitative aspects. Only a proper analysis of competitive forces will provide the right answer to information requirements and therefore to the nature of computers and communications solutions. Figure 5.3 underlines the importance of a competitive strategy from strategic

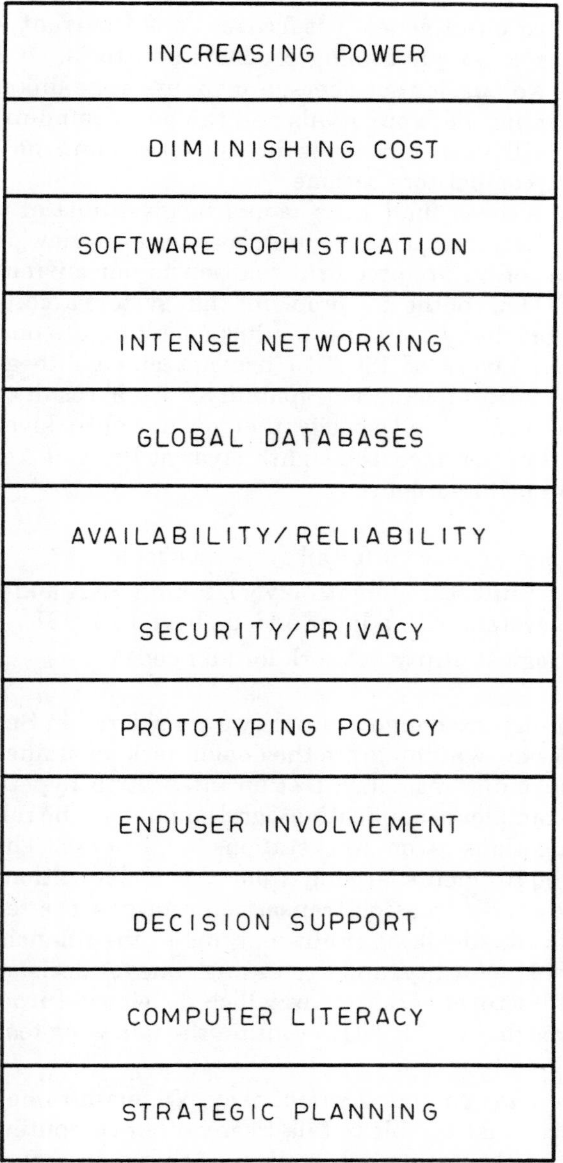

Figure 5.3 **While the layers may be similar, starting point and final goal revert themselves depending on whether we talk of system development or usage.**

planning to cost effectiveness. It focuses on our current products and services and also on our coming products and tools. It includes our customers as well as our suppliers, providing online linkage to both of them. It examines both our rivals and the new communications solutions which will keep our firms in the foreground no matter how advanced our competitors become.

Answers to these challenges cannot be given just at the level of a network architecture. They require a long-term view including the establishment of an architectural solution to our current and future requirements. One of the key problems that system architecture has to solve is that too many computer products don't talk to one another.

The seven layers of ISO/OSI are not enough to guarantee an enterprise-wide interconnect capability. As a result, leading-edge organizations design and specify their own eighth layer for system integration. For instance, the eighth layer at Bank of America (CAN) rest on the following premises:

- One center concept for all systems people
- One architecture (eighth layer), taking SNA and making it an open system with a layer added above ISO/OSI
- One logical utility network for all needs

Using the foreign exchange example we considered in Section 5.3, the systems overview will integrate the dealer desk, examine the information sources coming into play, test an integration hypothesis against real- world examples of applications, and emphasize the role of multimedia communications—from workstations to networks. This concept responds to requirements arising from the globalization of financial markets, the ever-increasing transaction routines, the resulting information overload, shrinking profit margins in the financial industries, greater market volatility, and decreasing time for decision.

The architectural perspectives which developed through CAN and similar approaches (MAP, TOP) contain the following features:

1. *Any-to-any communication.* Any WS, mainframe, or whatever device must be able to talk to any other computer resource not only on the network it is attached to but on any other network serving the organization. All applications must be able to communicate with one another without difficulty, heavy overhead, or exceptions. Even if the physical networks are different,

such difference must be transparent. The logical network must be unique. Furthermore, applications and equipment must talk the same way. This can occur if common standards are established within the organization and a distributed communications intelligence exists at all points of the communications systems.

2. *Sharing of resources*. Not only is there a need for communicating applications, mainframes, WSs, people, and so on, but we also have to look at them as vital resources. Every resource must be fully utilized, and to do so, we must tie them together and provide for access and control. We must also assure metrics to measure network management, accountability, billing, conversion procedures, and resource use. Our approach should be global, including all components in a network, which needs a layered infrared structure. Figure 5.4 suggests the nature of the top four layers (the eighth to the fifth).
3. *Network management*. Network management must be complete and involve not only planning and control activities but also significant run-time capabilities—from monitoring to reconfiguration. The network has to be managed like AT&T runs its long lines system, with links and nodes, distributed intelligence, and disaster recovery capability. A global network management facility must be assured.
4. *Long-range timetable with life-cycle perspectives*. While everyone should work in a different manner and timetables for implementation should be reasonably short, a longer range life-cycle perspective must also be followed. Leading-edge organizations actively involved in designing and implementing one logical network estimate that it will take about 10 years to complete what should be done, particularly if the orientation is not vendor specific—as should be the case.

By taking a global view at the seven layers of ISO/ISO, system architects and designers typically focus on a top-down approach, from applications toward the lower subordinate layers, not on a bottom-up approach (physical layer first) as is the case for all current network architectures that have been built. The principle is: Draw a line between network and applications functionality. The network moves data around. It does not look into the data. At the same time, the network must act as a system integrator. As users, we should look at more than one

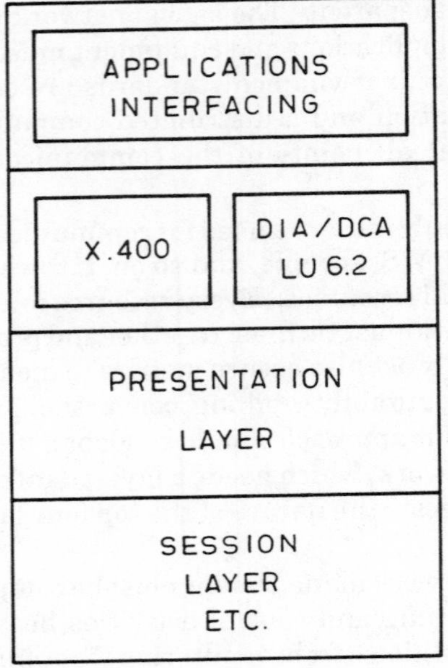

Figure 5.4. In this application DIA/DCA will have priority over X.400 implementation. At the networking level, both SNA and X.25 will be supported.

vendor's products. To assure vendor independence, new architectural designs provide the eighth, higher-up "applications interfacing" layer, also called "midware" or "mapping services." The name is not important but the functionality is vital to any forward-looking system design.

5.5 Technical Characteristics of Network Solutions

Valid solutions require choices which lead to the definition of a communications architecture. This includes the overall architectural concept, backbone specifications (software and hardware), and feeder lines to the backbone, which is typically LAN. While users can profitably employ CAD/CAM for prototyping, it is also good to follow the research and development activities of vendor(s) that are connected to offers they make, including conceptual studies by the vendor firm. Questions to ask are: How many people work in this product range? Where? What's the total R&D expenditure? The budget by subject? The research effort in associated fields? While a vendor's product description will cover current product characteristics, coming strengths and weaknesses can only be seen in the laboratory, hence the wisdom of examining what is in development.

Significant attention should also be paid to value added to the network. This includes the ability to add on services beyond the initial offer, the integration of expert system features to nonintelligent communications characteristics, the attachment of specialized applications servers (file, print, gateway), and the availability of applications facilities such as electronic mail, voice mail, calendaring, phonebook, and online directory capabilities. If electronic mail and voice mail have been implemented, the next step may be to video and framefreeze and live video sessions. The vendor should be asked to document the constraints on teleconferencing relating to the offered software and hardware, but the user should examine organizational constraints and possible international problems that may be caused by different PTT standards.

Prior to fulfilling value-added goals, it is necessary to cover fundamental operations such as PC-to-mainframe links, and alternatives, such as a PBX solution and a LAN solution to provide both PC-to-mainframe and PC-to-PC connectivity in a peer-to-peer manner, must be studied. Constraints posed by nonhomogeneous OS and DBMS must be examined and solutions found. Migration paths, including interfaces to currently existing networks in the organization, should be defined. The ability to match and integrate future developments in public digital or other networks should be guaranteed. The same is true of interfaces to stationary or other satellite linkage.

Component functionality must be examined in detail both in an organizational and in a technical sense. Choices relative to switches are important; they include:

- Digital PBX versus data switch
- Action switches (for international, leastcost routing)
- Line switching versus packet switching
- Time division multiplexing (TDM) versus frequency division multiplexing (FDM)

Distributed control capabilities must also be studied, up-time assurance given, and fail-soft features implemented to improve up time.

Significant attention must be paid to cabling choices; they are classical twisted pair, flexible coaxial, protected coaxial, or optical fibers. Will infrared links and microwaves be of service? Should there be multiplexing on cable? What about software support to be provided through network choice—wide area or local?

Implementation characteristics must be thoroughly studied. They include the maximum covered distance by a single network, the maximum covered distance with bridges, the ability to weed out the lower end of the band in a noisy environment, grounding, physical and logical characteristics of cable closets, signal converting, and supporting services. Power and cooling requirements are an example of the latter.

Responsibility for installation and implementation is another area management should study. The questions here are: Should it be done by the vendor or under the vendor's responsibility? Or should the organization tool up to undertake it? What is the required timetable? How many people are necessary? What are the characteristics of the project team? What testing procedures should be adopted? What object quality level should be reached? Are metrics for reliability and up time required? Other critical factors include:

- Testing procedures by user
- Criteria for acceptance tests
- Pilot installation
- Early verification project

Additional technical characteristics necessary for efficient network solutions focus on operating functionality. Critical factors include central versus local-level configuration, support for the corporate network control center, the number of persons needed for operations, the skillls per class of specialists, training support (what type, where, how much), and expert systems to assist in operations and in maintenance.

A crucial subject is the quality of software. A network operates within a distributed software environment and features remote diagnostics (at a high level of detail) and recovery from single, major, and castastrophic failures. Software is also necessary for each of these functions to help the specialists restart following a failure.

Another important area is security. Passwords must be both system wide and local. A dual system of passwords set by the center and by the user may be advisable. The NCC computer should register all transactions (journaling). Reporting logs must be examined, preferably through expert systems. Alarms must be established and integration made with internal and external security monitoring devices. In short, software for overall security control is necessary.

The observance of reliability characteristics requires the steady measurements of mean time between failures (MTBF), mean time to repair (MTTR), and mean time of system interrupt (MTOSI); there should be contractual guarantees for reliability of the component subsystem, the area system, and the total system. Examples of mandatory measurable criteria are:

1. The mean time to failure for any 1 month period must be greater than *n* hours.
2. The mean time to repair should be less than a specified time frame as an average and a well-defined maximum value as an exception (less than 1 percent of all cases).
3. Up to a five-digit number of terminals must be online without system degradation.
4. 95 percent of all trivial command response times must be less than 1 second.
5. No response time, for whatever reason, should exceed the three second.
6. The system should be fully delivered and operational no later than some specific date for turnkey applications.
7. The system must be able to grow modularly in terms of CPU cycle, central memory, and disk capacity to about *n* times the proposed configuration.

We must integrate the different aspects of a network system study. These aspects range from network development and implementation to network administration and maintenance. They also include expert system support.

The definition of maintenance includes the type and number of people necessary, their qualifications, resident maintenance support versus on call 24 hours per day, recovery and restart with specific contractual references, remote maintenance capabilites, and most importantly, expert systems support for maintenance. As far as maintenance is concerned, vendor specifications should not only answer current requirements but also should focus in the future on a long-term planning basis. One of the key criteria in selecting vendors should be their ability to provide high-capacity communications infrastructures into the twenty-first century—and to maintain these infrastructures at the peak of what technology permits.

5.6 Quality Improvements and Cost Effectiveness

One of the major forces driving industry, business, and financial institutions toward investments in computers and communications is to make better use of existing staff, rather than to decrease staff size. Technology permits us to curtail (but not cancel) paperwork. Technology also changes the way a company markets its products and services.

Management of leading-edge organizations look at technology as a means to improve business. They use the projected benefits in customer service and internal decision making to justify the cost of setting up an electronics environment. Still, justifying the costs is hard. Many of the reasons we bring technology on board are fairly nebulous; how do you cost or justify a telephone? The answer is that in the 1990s we will not only be going after efficiency. Technology will be a key strategic tool for achieving corporate goals, with innovation and quality being at the top of the list.

Furthermore, leading-edge organizations realize that they have to be low-cost producers and distributors of products and services. This view was not prevalent 10 years ago. As a major financial institution has shown, high technology is beneficial both to the clients and to the bank:

- The clients get a faster, well-rounded, more accurate service.
- The bank profits from greater precision and from significant improvements in productivity.

The new way to think of banking is as *information in motion*; the shift from paper money to electronics is as important as the change 2,500 years ago from barter to money. The problem is that our thinking, attitudes, skill, and, consequently, our decisions have not yet caught up with the new reality.

Criteria for return on investment can vary with the organization. At Toshiba its office automation group's philosophy is embodied in the phrase "efficiency of investment." There, an analysis of an efficient investment begins with a method of measuring worker productivity. Unless we can measure productivity, it is hard to demonstrate how we will improve it. An auto manufacturer has found that its world-wide online network has provided positive results from message exchange and decision support, which provides management with an analytical capability. Online systems and decision tools are no substitute for human judgment; but properly used, they enrich the information available to executiv es and professionals, produce needed documentation, permit what-if experimentation, and help clarify mangement's ideas prior to important decisions. Such benefits do however, require preparation and lifelong, hands-on training to provide a direct understanding on how to work with the system. Simple case studies show ways to approach business problems through the new tools that technology makes possible.

Results from expert system implementation, for instance, indicate that they can add a powerful layer of assistance over what has been provided so far by decision support systems. Expert systems make feasible two types of decision support tools:

1. The most important is the "human window." It permits a more effective exchange between the manager and the information in the machine.
2. The other is the formalization of decision rules within the expert system's knowledge bank.

The network enhances communications and by so doing it makes more sophisticated decision support solutions feasible.

Distributed online access to databases brings great benefits. A thesaurus of references permits the contents of a referenced section to be effectively accessed and applied. A "web of links," for instance, allows for the following direct connections:

1. Engineering workstations among themselves (every designer having one).
2. Engineering WSs and the global database.

3. Engineering WSs, supplier WSs, and mainframes.
4. Engineering WSs and manufacturing WSs.
5. Both engineering and manufacturing WSs to sales WSs.
6. Both manufacturing WSs and sales WSs to filed WSs for maintenance feedback.
7. Engineering WSs to quality control WSs, the quality database, reliability statistics, and field maintenance findings.

For such wide ranging linkage to be effective, a numbering plan must be provided for all workstations that includes addressing facilities for frequent number calling and steady addressing for all services through a unique number. Distributed directory services must be supported.

Once a reference database has been established, it is possible to automatically incorporate complete personnel data into the system. For example, employee badges contain embedded magnetic stripes that make them machine readable. Employees use these cards to clock in and out of work. At lunchtime they can purchase food in the cafeteria with the same card. It also lets employees withdraw cash from automated teller machines. In personnel, automated control over networked time clocks means that the company can easily put employees on variable time schedules and still track overtime. Some of the services are obvious; others are more subtle. Still others can be easily added as time and budgets permit.

Benefits of a network can be derived over a wide range of implementation from engineering design to manufacturing. However, the scope of implementation makes it wise to apply the Ford principle. This means, assembly line approach, small models which are easy to handle, interchangeable parts, and emphasis on integration. A modular solution also makes it feasible for a user to see and approve the prototype of an application. Prototyping is a user-driven approach. Visual thinking oriented, it constitutes an experimental way of programming. It also emphasizes the proper procedure. The prototype provides a fully functional working model which is easy to change and adjust. Programming work is done at high speed but after approval of the software model it must be optimized for processing reasons.

The concept of a user-rather than technology-driven design should be the cornerstone of our approach; prototype is not a theoretical system. It is a working model which can be implemented on the machine in the environment for which it has been conceived. The prototype may include traditional DP, WP, document handling, electronic mail, or the network since the return on investment will be the highest if we obtain end-user satisfaction. It follows logically that we must organize ourselves to meet that goal.

5.7 End-user Orientation and Contributions of Artificial Intelligence Research

From the intelligent network to the end-user's workstation, the integration capability and range of information facilities provided should permit text, data, image, and voice to be transmitted, switched, stored, and presented anywhere within the organization. This must be done in a manner that enhances mental productivity, promotes client service, and assures a high-quality product. The overall view of an efficient investment in computers and communications should definitely be end-user oriented.

Eventually, all services of an information society should be accessed remotely. End-user-oriented approaches enriched through artificial intelligence (AI) provide new vistas in communications and computing. From a software developer's viewpoint, the most important new concept coming out of AI research is not a different type of program—it is the *new approach to programming.*

Novel and highly effective apporaches to programming create a friendly world for end-users. They also upgrade the skills of professionals and make their function more interesting. Artificial intelligence enables us to write programs that can cope with unpredictable situations. Instead of telling the computer precisely what to do in every case—as in classical programming—we now tell the machine what to know. This greatly relieves program maintenance which is mostly needed to satisfy steadily evolving user demands and the resulting changes in specifications. With AI, the computer uses the contents of its knowledge bank to reason about what to do as new situations arise. Key to this solution is the way of representing knowledge in a manner the computer understands. This is done through IF ... THEN ... ELSE rules in a way that is similar to the way people reason.

At the same time, networks have become a focal point of interest on the micro and macro levels. The automobile market, for instance, is open for semiconductor penetration. Currently, only such mundane tasks as control of engine timing and ignition or luxury tasks such as digital dashboards and stereo components use semiconductor technology. However, the next generation of increased functionality is upon us. Among current and future automobile functions which could increase semiconductor content are multiplexed car wiring, ignition timing control, fuel usage, and economy control. Multiplexed car wiring is really a local area network confined at the car level. As Figure 5.5 suggests, it permits a wide range of digital attached devices to operate: from speech recognition to real-time navigation and from fuel injection to door locks and electronics-controlled transmission.

Microprocessors have revolutionized the design of computers and communications equipment, automobiles, home appliances, and practically everything else. Because of microprocessors, computer architectures reflect more utility per dollar than any previously made product or larger aggregate. Microprocessors have such an impact because their low cost makes them attractive as work horses which can be distributed to the place where the processing power is required. But we still require a connecting link. That is the role of the networks.

With investments running in billions of dollars, a foward-looking system architecture is a fundamental design requirement. At the same time, competitive pressures see to it that value-added features are part of further refinements in implementation. Value-added design is necessary to assure competitiveness within a sophisticated information society. We must prepare now for the time when economic activity shifts from adding low value on materials to adding high value on services. This is why, when it comes to software and hardware, we should not be primarily interested in technology. We should be interested to gain added value.

Architectural solutions for system projects will become increasingly vital to the successful harnessing of computers, communications, and artificial intelligence constructs. Digital signaling processing:

1. Brings up the need for even higher densities of memory and logic chips to process and store fast-growing bit streams...
2. Pushes toward higher channel capacities...
3. Obliges us to look at transmission, storage, and presentation as an aggregate...
4. Underline the growing importance of a global, accessible, and secure text and database...

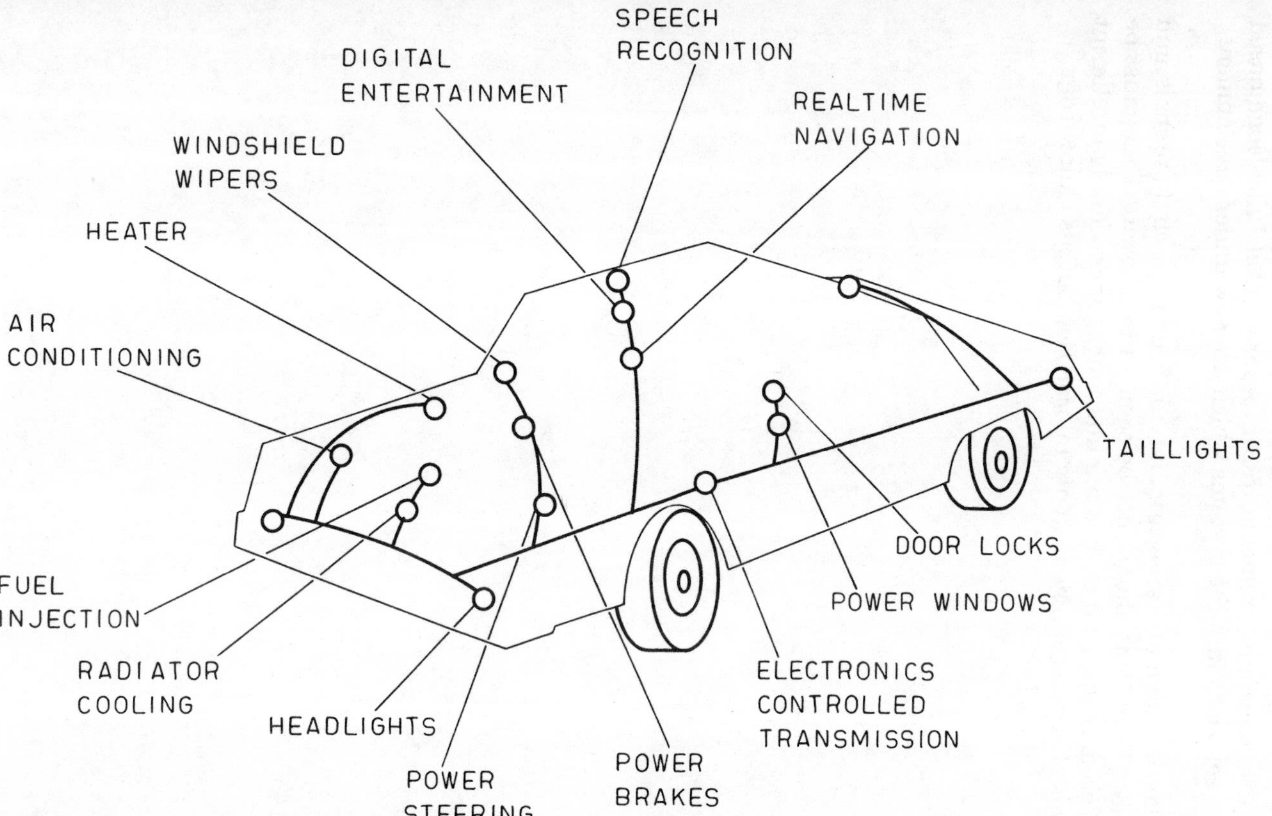

Figure 5.5 Interconnecting through LAN at the level of a motor vehicle.

5. Increasingly promotes the incorporation of knowledge-based solutions into the systems which are now under development.

Classical computer science found it difficult to reach these goals, and networked solutions should not be seen on their own. They must be considered as the vital connecting link among increasingly intelligent systems able to exchange not only information but also knowledge.

PART 2

Characteristics of Local Area Networks

Chapter

6

What Is a Local Area Network?

6.1 Introduction

The real challenge of the coming decade is not computation, but communication. For this reason, LANs are likely to be one of the major growth fields in computer systems. They are destined to cover a wide range of implementation. The use of LANs in the office lags behind their use in the factory because the need has taken longer to develop, but this need is now widely felt. A LAN distinguishes itself from other types of information networks in that communication is usually confined to a moderate-size geographic area such as a single office building, a warehouse, a factory, or a campus. The network can generally depend on a consistently low error rate. Typically this network is generally owned and used by a single organization. This is in contrast to long distance networks which interconnect facilities in different parts of the country or are used as a public utility.

The local network is also different from networks which interconnect components within a single piece of equipment, but together they create a system which brings computer power and communications-intense features to every desk. The main reason for this development is economic; it allows a variety of workstations to share common resources in such a way that the potential of each engine may be realized at the level the end user really needs.

LANs made a new approach to systems design feasible. Its rationale rests on the effective use of technological innovation. Experience from the last 50 years has shown that the implementation of advanced technology often occurs in two stages:

1. The innovation is exploited to better perform tasks that were already being done by other means.
2. New applications are discovered which could not reasonably materialize or even be foreseen prior to the innovation.

Local area networks and personal computers are now on the threshold of this second stage: the real challenge lies in identifying new fields of applications they can make possible. If trends in hardware costs encourage abandonment of large computers in favor of a number of smaller machines, the trends in human productivity are even more overwhelming in this same direction.

6.2 The Vital Communications Link

Literature is full of definitions of a LAN. One of them looks at local area networks as an information transport system that provides a medium-to-high-speed connection between users within a single building or building complex. This is achieved through the implementation of a common wiring subsystem with communication adapters and access protocols. A simple LAN interconnecting workstations was shown in Figure 4.5. A slightly more complex LAN is presented in Figure 6.1. It interconnects minicomputers, some of which act as file servers supporting shadow images and providing for fault tolerance. A number of WSs are attached to the LAN, multithreaded through other minicomputers.

Another LAN definition is end-user oriented. It looks at the local area network as a group of computers connected together through adapters and cables—just as our telephone is connected to other telephones through the phone lines. The LAN makes our workstation more

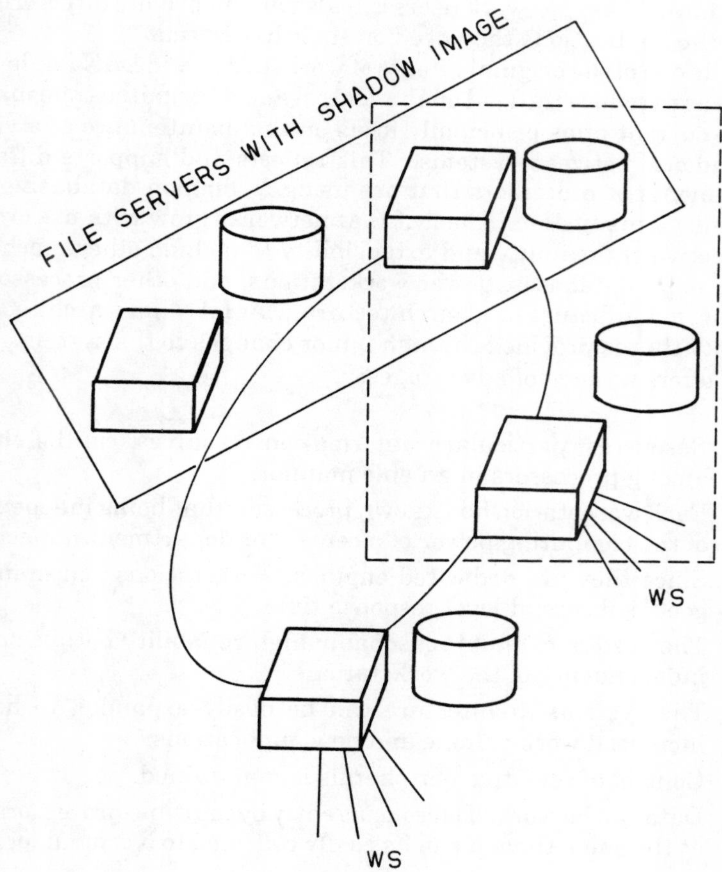

Figure 6.1 Implementing fault tolerance through LAN implementation.

powerful because it makes hardware and software at common servers available to everyone on the network. Applications, such as spreadsheets, graphics, and word processing, are made available to everyone through downloading. We can install many applications in a directory on the LAN server. Users share the directory, select from it, and ask for an application to be transferred to their own microfiles which are stored in their hard disks. Network users can also install private directories as well as the applications they need on their hard disks.

While one of the original intents of workstation and LAN implementation was to reduce the load on the central and distributed timesharing facility, current aims principally focus on the maintenance of a viable independence between systems. This reflects and supports different environments of processors that are using a common databasing and communications system. The fact that networks grow with use creates the objective of flexibility and extensibility to include other machines, such as more databases, newer workstations, and other processors of different manufacture and architecture. A LAN has architectural flexibility that is provided through minor changes to the system structure; it offers a range of advantages:

1. Resources, particularly information resources, can be shared among processors in an able manner.
2. Each workstation has its own processor, thus being independent of the computing power of a central or departmental machine.
3. Since they are dedicated engines, workstations can maintain good, subsecond-level response time.
4. The system exhibits reasonably high reliability because of the independence of the workstations.
5. The systems architecture can be easily expanded to handle increased work volume and new applications.
6. Control of sensitive peripherals is maintained.
7. Data can be worked on concurrently by multiple processors and, at the same time, it can be easily collected to a central location.

This adds up to cost effectiveness and better service: as technology has driven hardware costs down, the trend to replace large shared computers with personal microcomputers accelerates.

The local area network should not only allow processing and databasing equipment to be hooked together, but it should also enhance their capabilities through its interconnection features. The benefits of a common database and the efficient allocation of resources such as printers and gateways must be realized in a way that presents a well-rounded distributed information system. This should be done in a manner which is both application-independent and equipment-independent. Software and hardware must be transparent to the end user. An overriding need for local area networks is their ability to hook up any manufacturer's equipment or programming package. Three other important design criteria are:

1. *Low cost.* This is necessary to justify the personal computer approach. Low-cost connectivity primarily focuses on the bus interface unit (BIU), which on an attached device basis should be below 10 percent the cost of that device.
2. *Modular.* It must include clearly defined hardware and software building blocks, creating the prerequisite for an easy growth path toward different configurations.
3. *Performance.* Low-cost and modularity should not lead to sacrificing performance. Not only should the initial solution be satisfactory in response time, turn-around time, and up time, but it should also be possible to improve upon these times.

Because of technological advances, central processing unit (CPU) cycles are no longer a scarce resource. Therefore large, centralized computers have given way to local, more agile, and more accessible alternatives.

6.3 Profile of a Local Area Network—Baseband and Broadband

We said that a local area network is a medium- to high-speed network operating within a limited geographical area. It is also typically cable based, owned by or dedicated to the user of a single organization and supports any device to any other device connectivity through a commonly agreed upon access method, addressing scheme, and packet format. A LAN provides services beyond replacing the physical link with a logical link capability.

What are the objectives of a LAN? The first and foremost is *able assistance to the user with the problem*, enlarging the communications window through computer-supported databases and electronic message systems. Local area networks provide improved access, including greater connectivity and multivendor interconnection; mobility of equipment, supported through standard cabling with placement flexibility; and efficiency in terms of resource sharing and load leveling.

A LAN is composed of four basis hardware elements:

1. A transmission medium, often twisted pair, coaxial cable, or fiber optics.
2. A mechanism for control of transmission over the medium.
3. An interface to the network for the host computers, workstations, and servers, the nodes of the network.
4. Protocols to govern the relations between processes operating on a given layer.

A twisted-pair network has a limited capacity and cannot handle high-speed transmissions. It will suffice for 16-bit workstations that transmit only intermittently. But video, audio, and facsimile require a higher throughput and will overload such system. In fact, twisted pair is just another term for phone lines leading to baseband implementation. There is no satisfying definition of the terms "baseband" and "broadband" as they relate to local area networks. In general communications usage:

- *Baseband* refers to a signal before it modulates a carrier.
- *Broadband* refers to the signal after the carrier has been modulated.

Some local network transmission scheme classified as baseband might be viewed as the modulation of a carrier by the transmitted data. Because they do not require a modulator and demodulator, baseband systems are generally less expensive than broadband. At the same time they do not allow frequency multiplexing. Since signal attenuation for coaxial cable varies as the square root of frequency, baseband cables of the same length have less attenuation and a smaller dynamic signal range than broadband and may allow collision detection on single-channel systems. At high bandwidth, baseband cables are more affected by phase dispersion, a phenomenon resulting from differing propagation velocities at differing frequencies.

Baseband is typically digital and may run on twisted pair or flexible coaxial. Its distance is limited, but it features a relatively simple design and installation. It is also less expensive and offered by many vendors, but its potential capacity is limited. Because of supported protocols (which we will discuss in the following section), a baseband approach allows transmission by only one attached device at a time. The entire capacity of the system's cable is occupied by each transmission, which can be a limitation if an operation must handle large amounts of information. Response time will decay badly if pictures are transmitted (real-time video) on a baseband system.

Baseband uses the cable spectrum from direct current (dc) to several times the bit rate. Broadband employs the spectrum immediately around some higher-frequency carrier. If frequency division multiplexing is used, it is a broadband system. Broadband usually works on the basis of frequency division multiplexing, is advisable for noisy environments, effectively runs over larger distances, and is implemented through protected coaxial or optical fibers. It also requires sophisticated design and installation, is more expensive and offered by fewer vendors than baseband. Key advantages are higher reliability and significantly larger capacity.

Frequency division multiplexing (FDM) is a primary reason for using broadband transmission. We can operate a large number of separate networks on a single cable through FDM. The goal of some broadband solutions is to use a single cable to carry several networks.

Broadband systems break the capacity of a cable into frequencies, or channels, much like cable television (CATV) does. Any messages transmitted on a particular bandwidth are assigned to their own channels. Broadband enables users to make many transmissions at the same time with different devices.

Until recently, cost was the major deterrent to multiprocessor LAN-based systems because the collection of devices needed to equal the capability of a mainframe was more expensive than the latter. However, technology evolved to the point at which low-cost computer power presents a more attractive alternative to mainframes for many communications tasks. Computers and communications resources on a LAN not only increase accessibility with the addition of each information station but also increase speed and storage capacity. Mainframe-based approaches do the opposite; more terminals mean less power to each user, slower speed, and lesser dependability as the system gets overloaded. However, at the current state of the art, one local network technology cannot meet all requirements. We still need multiple protocols and access methods to handle multimedia requirements: text and data, video, documents, high-speed graphics, and voice (including PBX integration). Currently a wide range of facilities can only be served through multivendor participation.

Thus the able use of local area networks implies prerequisites. The most important is enforced coherence among the methodologies available to users in order to assure their ability to share the resources of powerful computers. At the same time, the communications link can help stimulate a real sense of community among users; their common machine environment enhances a level of compatibility and provides a sense of common language. To make this approach economically viable, the LAN must be designed to exploit— and evolve with—mass- produced VLSI technology. It must also be projected to support wideband communications as multimedia requirements are on the increase. In fact, the supported channel is one of the basic characteristics of a LAN.

6.4 A Bird's Eye View of LAN Protocols

As computers have become smaller and more numerous, the reasons for interconnecting them have grown. Local area networks were developed to promote resource sharing: particularly software and databases. The LAN assures the characteristics of a packet communication network that is limited in geographic scope and meeting a growing demand for high data rate and low-cost communication among computers.

A "protocol" is a rule of conduct all devices attached to a network can understand. The observance of protocols makes information exchange feasible. Which protocols are typically supported on LAN? In Chapter 3 we spoke of the IEEE 802 reference model and mentioned two standard protocols at the LAN level that are medium access mechanisms:

- Carrier sensing multiple access/collision detection (CSMA/CD)
- Token passing

CSMA/CD is like a party-line telephone. It checks to see if a line is busy (if no one else is transmitting) and sends our transmission along when the line is free. If it detects a collision, it waits for a random period before transmitting again. Using multiple access with collision detection, workstations transmit when the carrier is unoccupied. They do so for one frame only, for less than a specified maximum number of milliseconds. While transmitting, the station listens for evidence of competing transmissions. Upon collision, brief reinforcement occurs, transmission ceases, a semirandom wait follows, then the entire process repeats.

With CSMA/CD, access is statistical, not deterministic. There are no guarantees for transmission deadlines. Hence this protocol is difficult to use for real-time applications; it is, however, moderately efficient, though this decreases with decreasing frame size and with increasing wire length:

- Minimum frame size increases linearly with increasing wire length.
- Standard deviation of waiting times increases faster than the load.

A basic advantage of CSMA/CD is its implementation simplicity. Another is the fact that many vendors have adopted it; therefore there is choice in sourcing.

Token-passing is another way to assure that transmissions do not collide. Usually employed in a ring network, this protocol employs electronic tokens to keep devices in an orderly transmission sequence:

- An attached device is allowed to transmit only when the token is passed through it.
- The network has a built-in intelligence that gives each device a chance to pass the token along or communicate in sequence.

Given the way token access works, active stations on the LAN form an ordered logical ring. This may operate as a physical ring, bus, or tree-like topology. Control passes in order from device to device. When a station has control:

- It may transmit and accept immediate responses for less than a maximum number of milliseconds.
- Then it passes control to the next station in the sequence.

Established procedures handle initialization: the first station up must create the sequence. Other procedures focus on demand assignment (adding stations to sequence) and housekeeping for station failure and dropout (deletions from sequence).

Tokens are deterministic, thus usable for real-time applications,

Table 6.1 Network Comparison Based on Technical Characteristics.

Network characteristic	*CSMA/CD*	*Token*
Access type	Probabilistic	Deterministic
Topology	Bus	Star or ring
Structure	Multipoint	Loop
Control	Central node, explicit poll	distributed, no addressing
Priority reservation	None	Anytime
Fault isolation	None	Alternate ring possibility
Traffic collision and performance impact	Yes on heavy traffic	practically unaffected
Network span	Limited width	Wider with signal regeneration
Synchronous traffic	None	3270 datastream, digitized voice
Wiring media	Must be homogeneous	Could be mixed fiber and copper
Target node type	Micro powered	Any network addressable unit

from process control to packetized voice. They are also very efficient. The useful capacity of the LAN approaches the theoretical capacity. Efficiency is less sensitive to the number of stations and wire length than it is with CSMA/CD. However, token passing requires an awareness of other stations on the LAN and knowledge of two other devices: the next and prior in sequence. Table 6.1 compares CSMA and token passing.

As compared to baseband protocols (CSMA/CD, token passing) in a broadband system, a channel controller regulates a different sort of traffic flow. If we want to transmit, we choose a channel and tell the controller which device we want to call. The controller checks to see if the station is busy. If it is free, the controller picks up a clear channel for the transmission. After that, it is all automatic.

Confirmed protocol solutions are essentially standards fostering multivendor device intercommunications. Hence, their function and impact are increasing with time and with LAN implementation. Compared to past telecommunications methods, the latter assures greater flexibility, higher speeds, and improving costs—but such benefits are in direct proportion to the sound protocol choices we make. Eventually, new protocols will be necessary because of the production and implementation of hybrid LANs, the integration of private branch exchanges (PBX) to such hybrids and the necessary wide area connectivity with ISO/OSI or other transport standards. Other forces pushing toward the development of more sophisticated LAN protocols are multimedia gateway and server implementations. The possibility to incorporate artificial intelligence constructs points to the direction new protocols may take.

6.5 Classes of LAN Service

Originally, local area networks supported three main classes of service: local access capability, server sharing, and the ability to develop an integrated system. With a local access approach, computing resources reside in relatively few locations. The requirement is to provide users at terminals with an access mode. This calls for server sharing, which should support high-speed high-volume applications. Stations interconnected through a LAN require large file transfers, feature distributed processing, and demand load share between closely located communicating devices. Since we talk of shared resources, an error control protocol should be provided by the network.

The push toward integrated systems is not limited to the text and data level; it includes other forms of information, such as voice and vector graphics. Also, an increasing number of applications require simultaneous real-time capabilities. The integrated system must assure:

1. *Completeness.* A finite state machine should exist.
2. *Termination.* For any possible sequence, attached devices should conclude in an expected state.
3. *Bounding.* It should be possible to process every message sequence. No infinite queue of tasks should ever be built.
4. *Freedom from deadlocks.* No message sequence should interlock the attached devices. Hence, asynchronous processes should be handled.
5. *Freedom from livelocks.* No message sequence should cause

attached devices to retransmit messages forever. A lifelock occurs when a sender station repeatedly sends the same message while the receiver always returns an acknowledgment.

6. *Single system view*. This is relative to three principal viewers: developer, administrator, and end user.

Single system view is a view of a network of workstations and servers in which one need not be aware of the topology or even that there is a network. More specifically, it refers to a capability provided by system and application software that allows you to see only as much of the network as you wish to see. Such a definition is dynamic. Users typically require an increasingly more detailed view of the system. Thus the system and applications should attempt to both hide the configuration from 'typical users' while at the same time permitting knowledgeable ones to override the defaults and directly control the system.

Given this increasing sophistication in requirements, LANs have evolved over the past several years from being mere resource sharers to powerful multiuser, multitasking systems. They are capable of successfully competing with the traditional mainframes while still harnessing the individual processing power of PC-based workstations to create comprehensive corporate information resources out of hitherto scattered and often repeated information elements. However, products may disappoint unless three critical user concerns are addressed. The first is ease of use. The device a user has must be a true workstation, not a scaled-down complex mainframe. The second is accounting for managerial applications which are heavy users of resources. The third is full networking. The system must not only provide sophisticated server capabilities but must also support any-to-any connectivity.

The advent of valid, reliable solutions through local area networks and the availability of a supporting architecture makes functionality at an affordable cost feasible. That is why LANs are driving the introduction of PC into operating environments. PC based workstations and LAN solutions cut into the market which was characterized by timesharing. They offer a greater reliability; a more user-friendly environment; ample software support at a low cost; and better communications. Among the benefits is compatibility of attached devices in terms of:

- Protocols
- Operating systems

- Data formats
- Data rates
- Transmission media

This makes it possible to handle multiple vendors. Another benefit is that full physical interconnection is provided through a one-time wiring cost. A LAN also simplifies WS interconnection after installation and after subsequent moves.

One of the major benefits from LAN implementation is financial. Cost effectiveness is treated in detail in Chapters 25 and 26, and in the Appendix. Nevertheless, it pays to take a quick look at costs and benefits in a simple case shown in Figure 6.2, which evaluates a PC and LAN against the alternative of installing a small business system with non-intelligent terminals. Leaving aside a most significant difference in applications software and in response time—both to the benefit of PC and LAN—the cost evaluation demonstrates that intelligent workstations cost only 43 percent of dumb terminals while offering much more functionality and reliability.

The future direction of development efforts consists of two major thrusts. One is toward new products with still higher levels of performance and continued expansion of multivendor functionality. The second focuses on global networking consistent with the evolving needs of leading-edge customers. Global networks will feature LANs as feeder lines but will be able to span long distances and connect all types of equipment into one cohesive network that treats all elements as fully functional machines.

6.6 LAN versus Centralized Resources

Bigger-is-better arguments conveniently forget that there is a fundamental limit to the amount of computing power compressible into one box. This limitation is magnified by the existence of a nonlinear relationship between a problem's size and the computing power required to solve it. Hence, new technical solutions have to be found for computing machinery. Over the last 15 years, key design issues have focused on:

- Cache management and cache consistency issues
- Tightly coupled systems

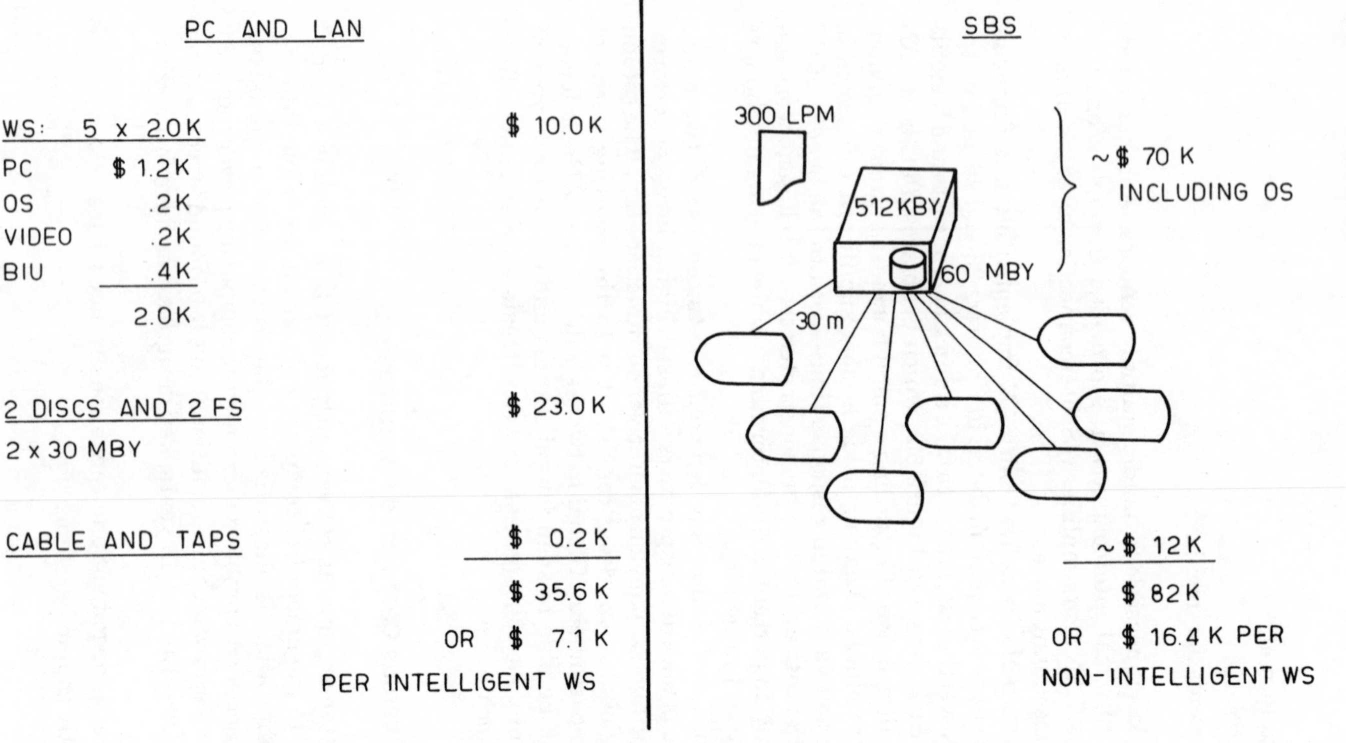

Figure 6.2 Cost comparison: PC and LAN vs. a multithreaded small business system (SBS).

- Attainment of load balancing and the issue of symmetry
- Features of optimizing, vectorizing, and parallelizing compilers
- Fault-tolerant systems

The advantages and disadvantages of tight versus loose coupling (global versus local memory) have been often argued, this being a distinguishing characteristic in multiprocessing and parallel systems. Multiprocessor aggregates can be either loosely or tightly coupled. A loose coupling features a minimum of two semiindependent processors interconnected by a high-speed bus. Each processor runs its own operating system, having its own memory and I/O controllers. It also shares multiported peripheral controllers with at least one other processor. Tightly coupled architectures were the original multiprocessing approaches; in the 1980s they got new life because of significant improvements in myriaprocessor technology. But they also had to compete against local area networks which made it possible to attach independent file servers and gateways on a very high speed bus, minimizing the instructions required to effect a pass through from one system to another, reducing overhead, and improving mirroring capabilities.

Over the same timeframe, fault-tolerant systems were one of the more successful and significant applications of multiprocessing technology. They typically offer the ability to recover from processor failures; maintain database consistency and integrity despite system or disk failures; and sustain repairs online. To assure fault detection capability, the hardware in each attached processor should check for certain types of errors such as parity, then close itself down if a fault is discovered. Integrity is the degree to which a system tolerates faults and the resulting errors which, when processed by the normal software on the system, will produce failures. Solutions involve:

1. Confinement, detection, and diagnosis.
2. Fault tolerance through the isolation of errors.
3. Prevention of further damage.
4. Repair of faulty component.
5. Recovery restoring a stable, consistent system state.

However, performance measurement in multiprocessor and parallel systems has not followed hardware advances. It has been particularly handicapped through the lack of accepted standards which causes great confusion and unrealistic claims. It has also been conditioned by the OS and DBMS running on the machine. But what interests the user most is the end result, not the technical details.

Performance in real-time systems is measured more in terms of response time than throughput—a violation of an application time constraint often constitutes a system failure. Furthermore, real-time events tend to occur in bursts, requiring a large and immediate increase in processing over that needed under steady-state conditions. On an isocost basis, this favors a PC/LAN approach over the mainframe of departmental computing approach.

There is also an organizational perspective to consider. When we have end users sharing the main production machine(s), we are eventually going to have degradation in response time. Implementing multifunctional workstations on a local area network is like moving from a wholesale to a retail business. It's a world in which the customer (the end user) is always right.

At the same time, we need languages which make parallelism implicit, while their compilers will take over the burden of partitioning programs. Some commendable efforts in this direction are:

- Guarded Horn Clauses (GHC), by ICOT, Japan
- Flat Concurrent Prolog, by Weitzman Institute of Science, Israel
- Parallel Prolog, by Imperial College, England

A further challenge is the provision of very high-level user interfaces capable of interacting with managers, scientists, or engineers at a level of abstraction fully understood by each profession. In short, languages must be adaptable to the user's profession. This has proved easier to develop for workstations than for centralized computers, thus presenting another reason why to favor the former to the latter.

With fifth-generation non-von Neumann computers, when we talk of languages, we talk of artificial intelligence. This is consistent with the aims of parallel computing. Fifth-generation computers (5GC) are made for AI purposes and vice versa. With AI and personal workstations, users may see two windows with different solutions. The classical DP window reports that the desired application will take 3 years and cost $3 million. The WS/LAN window shows that it can be ready in 3 days for $3,000.

Another significant advantage of LAN solutions over the mainframe alternative is the able implementation of an NCC in which a maintenance system operating supervisor tests every complement and immediately initiates online diagnostic routines whenever failure is detected. An NCC-based system can be dynamically reconfigured with no interruption.

6.7 Resource Sharing

Local area networks are the blueprint for resource sharing among workstations and other attached devices. Using a service-request model, resource sharing approaches allow any PC on the LAN to offer and use services, which can be professionally developed, user-written or off-the-shelf applications. End users can start several activities that proceed concurrently and that call on services offered by different machines. They can interact with applications running as services at other WSs. Program interfaces are provided for the development of distributed applications. In contrast to older software for LAN WSs, where emphasis is on file sharing, resource sharing emphasizes the services. Remote execution is supported within the service-request framework.

A resource sharing machine project at IBM has taken this approach. A "service" is an application offered on the network. Each service is executed by one or more server processes at the machine which provides such service. Multiple server processes run concurrently at each machine, and more than one server can execute the same service. In this project, a service is invoked by a request for that service. The request may come directly from the user or from a program. The process that issues the request is the "client" (of the request). Client and server may be at the same machine or at different machines without affecting the way the request is made or handled.

An "action" is a request made directly by the user. It may involve multiple services and span several machines. Different actions may be used concurrently. The end user may query a database, compile a program, and format a document—each at a different service machine. Components include:

- A kernel supporting all other devices by providing local operating system features
- Networking for communication between machines
- A service component maintaining all objects related to services, such as service definitions and lists of active services

- An action component permitting the user to start actions and communicate with them
- A request component managing calls for services and communication between applications programs

On this and similar projects that focus on resource sharing and resource management, readily available access to information elements is fundamental. The same is true of sharing peripherals, connecting to central computing and distributed databases, and employing electronic message services. The key is transparent access to *my* information, wherever it may be.

Basically, resource sharing is an interconnect problem requiring software-supported services well beyond the data link level. Both facilitation and protection involve proprietary protocols at the WS level, the workgroup, and departmental and mainframe machines. Able solutions should consider the beginning interconnect requirements as well as the implementation of a distributed file system. This can be done through:

1. *Dedicated* approaches run by a network file system, where the host is dedicated to shared files.
2. *Segregated* approaches where file sharing is compartmentized (DECnet DOS acts this way).
3. An *integrated* solution, which is the most generic of the three.

All three alternatives provide a distributed functionality and at the bottom line they are rather similar in capabilities—even if it doesn't look that way superficially. The contribution of these solutions is that they permit connecting the entire system as a resource aggregate.

A basic requirement for added-value solutions is that of network bandwidth permitting real-time transmission of multimedia not only under normal conditions but also under peak conditions handling the worst case. By contrast, data communications policies looked after the average case, and data had two orders of magnitude fewer requirements than multimedia. There is also need for database bandwidth that is able to handle the large volume of bit streams necessary for future storage. For some time, terabytes will become a unit of measurement. Then this, too, will be too narrow. The other key reference is processing bandwidth. The clocked nature of real-time voice, image, text, and data connections requires that the application be able to schedule itself, hence dispose

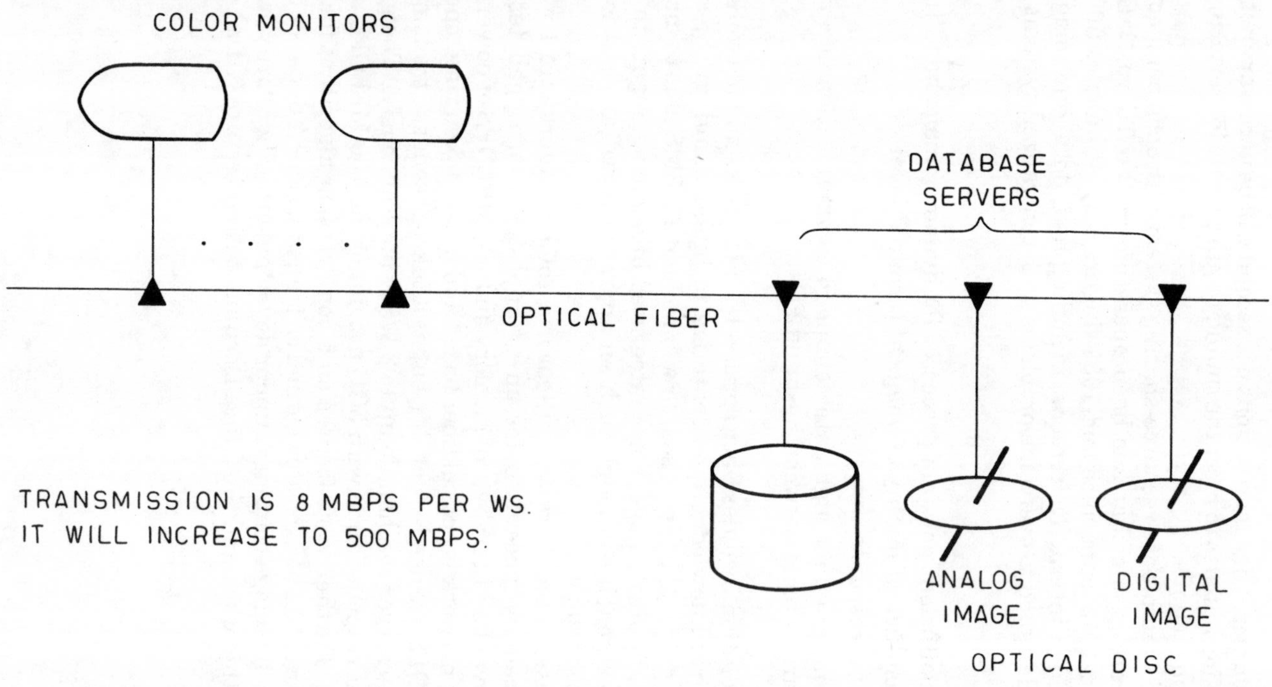

Figure 6.3 Optical fiber LAN at Tokyo National Ethnological Museum.

ample resources. Giga instructions per second will be necessary not only for processing but also to meet the timing requirements for servicing the ongoing connections.

A good example of a resource-sharing system with open perspectives to the future is one that has been operating at the Tokyo National Ethnological Museum since mid-1987 (Figure 6.3). It handles 500,000 cards through interactive screens, including text, data, and image. It has been designed to overcome problems with centralized systems such as:

1. Insufficient power of processor for dynamic image handling.
2. Insufficient quality of image at terminal level.
3. Slow response time.
4. Limitation for high data volume in communication because of narrow band between host and PC.

The solution includes fiber optics—both for disks and networks. It also requires knowledge representation techniques and an object-oriented language. Further research will include a DBMS able to manage text, data, figures, image, voice integrated into one aggregate to overcome heterogeneity—though such an approach is still beyond today's level of technology.

The associated workstation features color monitors (1024 x 1024 pixel), a memory space of 8 bytes, an external storage of 5 gigabytes. The image server has 1 terabyte of memory and 100 MFLOPS of power. The local area network is optical fiber based and it uses token ring topology. 100 MFLOPS are needed per WS, but as it takes seconds to transmit the image, the server can handle up to 3 WSs simultaneously. The goal is subsecond response time with 5GC providing the 100 MFLOPS at the WS level. Further work focuses on a compression algorithm for color image to save bits both on storage and on transmission. A dynamic query capability by image content is under development. There are parallels between this work and the Office Document Architecture (ODA).

Chapter

7

The Nodes and the Topology

7.1 Introduction

In the local area network, a node is a computer resource connected by a link to one or more neighboring nodes. Messages are assumed to be generated locally in source nodes. Nodes for which particular messages are destined are sink nodes. Information is typically transmitted between neighboring nodes in packets through links, nodes, and switches. A topology-connected set of nodes is a network. It provides a communication infrastructure implemented through a set of interconnected processors often featuring store and forward capability. The discipline may be packet switching, circuit switching, a ring, or a bus structure. A topology is usually selected on the basis of maximizing performance and minimizing cost without violating speed, distance, or error rate constraints.

The network of interconnected nodes creates a transmission mechanism. The discipline can be as simple as waiting for the beginning of an empty slot and filling it with a packet, but system services should include the ability to:

- Divide messages into packets
- Handle routing and sorting problems
- Support error detection features
- Face flow control problems
- Maintain internode collaboration

Each node consists of a bus interface unit (BIU) and its corresponding computer resource. The BIU controls the network in a distributed fashion performing three basic functions: interfacing to the carrier, link management, and node management. We will talk of the BIU and its functions in Chapter 9. However, since the notion of a BIU—and most particularly its functionality—is important in the definition of a node, Figure 7.1 gives in a snapshot the essence of interconnecting. Notice that two items— (A) line handling software and (B) network handling software—are fundamental in creating a node. Item A is necessary even in nodes belonging to hierarchical networks, where network handling would be done by the commanding host or its agent (front end, communications engine). However, in distributed control (horizontal) networks management software should reside at the nodes. By contrast, end-to-end software is optional. It does not need to reside at the node. As workstations are computer based, it may be at the WS level. Nevertheless, the able distribution of resources to each end of the network presupposes intelligent attached devices. In their absence, the node must handle this function.

7.2 Nodes at the Network

A node is a basic information-handling unit that is directly connected to the network. This term can, however, have different interpretations depending on the network's architecture and type of transmission. With broadband the single addressable device is the bus interface unit to which may be connected one or more workstations or servers (usually 2, 3, 4, or 8). For this reason the term "node" is often used to refer to the BIU, though it can also mean the workstation or server. With baseband, where the BIU is reduced to a small printed circuit board inserted in a slot of the ultimate attached device, the single addressable unit, and therefore the node, is synonymous with the workstation or server. This

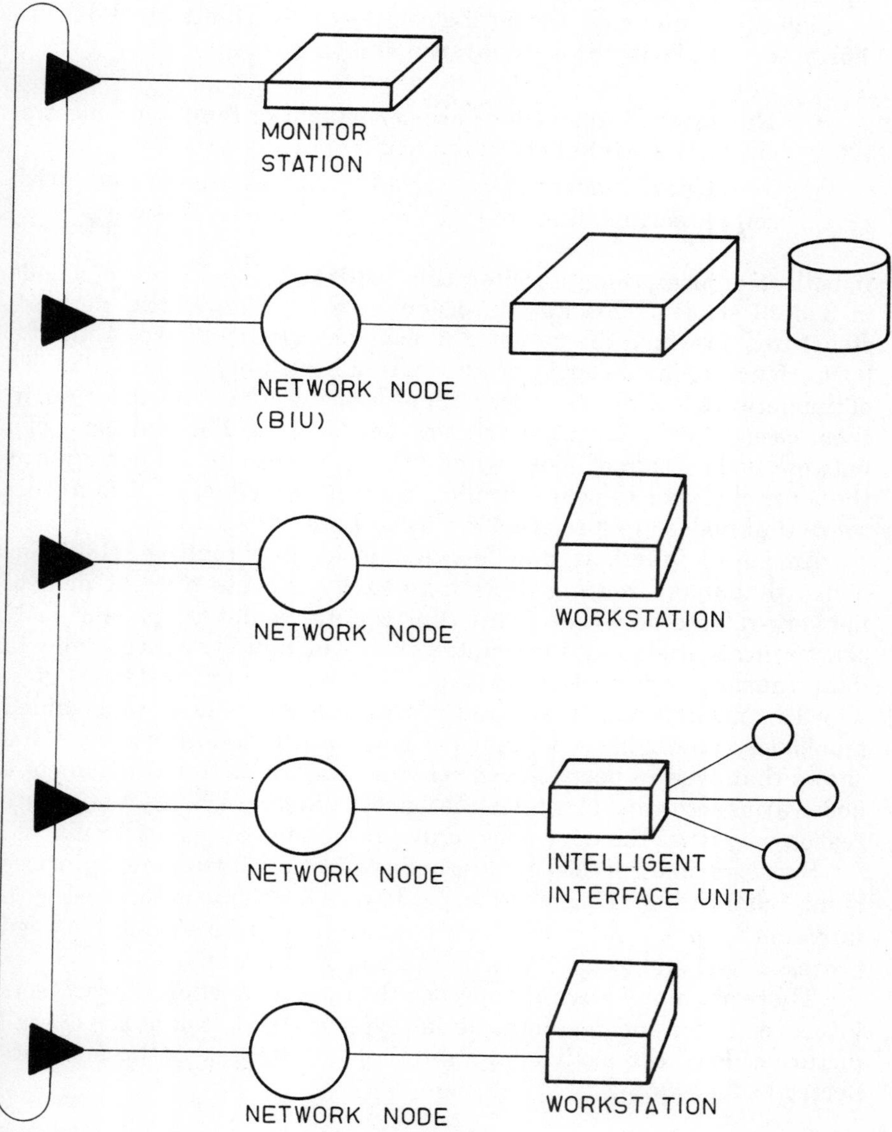

Figure 7.1 **A logical network ring with nodes and links.**

distinction is important, first because it is valuable in identifying functionality; second, it indicates that some definitions are situational.

Nodes communicate among themselves and with attached devices (hosts, servers, WSs) through physical and logical connections:

- The physical connections are permanent or temporary electromechanical circuits between nodes.
- The logical connections require that nodes are endowed with software capabilities to make communications feasible.

In both references, computer literature tends to use the notion of a node in a dual sense. This has its origin in older hierarchical network structures, in which the notion of a node was synonymous to that of a host. Hence, today it is not uncommon that hosts are often called nodes of the network—which they are not necessarily. To avoid confusion, in these cases, it is better to use the term "node-host." The real sense of a network node is that of node-switch. This is the function it performs at the level of a peer-to-peer (parallel, horizontal) network. It is in this sense that nodes are discussed in this section.

Among its functions, a node-switch looks after routing. However, nodes that make routing decisions usually execute a great deal of network-related activities. This runs counter to design goals of LAN communications. It adds unwanted overhead, and introduces delay to data transfer. Routing decisions typically use unconstrained topologies, which are not necessarily required in local area networks; unconstrained topologies answer basic demands of long-haul communications. This shows that even in peer-to-peer network constructs the functions of a node varies according to the destination of the network. This is one more reason why what the node does cannot be defined once and for all.

Speaking in terms of a generic node definition, its foremost purpose is interconnecting. Hardware and software problems associated with interconnections arise every time resources must be shared between processes and end users. We should focus on this issue.

There are many ways to approach the interconnection of processors into a computer and communications system. If we look at the overall picture of local connectivity, we see that a system could be interconnected as follows:

- Through serial I/O links to form a computer network
- In a tight synchronous fashion to build an array processor

- By being organized to share primary memory

Leading to a multiprocessor organization, this last approach has often been chosen because it offers a closer degree of coupling between the processors than do other multicomputer solutions. Known as a tightly coupled system, the sharing of central memory was a favored approach in the past. It is not necessarily so at present nor will it be in the future.

In a tightly coupled system every attached processor is a node, specifically a node-host. Such processors have typically been mainframes. They might also be maxicomputers. There is no point of thinking of WSs in such an arrangement. In this system, the shared central memory could be regarded as a server of sorts. Its resources are shared among different processors in an attempt to overcome one of the limitations of the von Neumann-type computer architecture.

As with practically every solution, tight coupling solves some problems while it creates others. One of the most serious is restart and recovery when one of the nodes goes down—leading to a dichotomy between a *hot* and *cold switch* as well as to a serious issue of software support. Hence, modern non-von Neumann architectures have abandoned this approach, opting instead for dedicated memories in each processor. In Chapter 2, Section 2.3, we discussed a specific example of this, the hypercube architecture.

Bus, ring, and ether—and to a certain extent star-type architectures* —aim at creating local networking capabilities of a loosely coupled type. They don't share central memory, but they do share other servers (file server, print server, gateway) as we will see in the appropriate chapter. This type of connectivity is the kernel of a local area network solution.

7.3 Developing Multiprocessor Capabilities

The essential feature which distinguishes a tightly coupled multiprocessor from other structures is that in it shared memory is not separated from the processing elements but rather a unit of memory and a processor are closely connected in each module. This was thought to

* In this case the switching node is passive. Active star-type connections have hierarchical characteristics.

allow modular expansion of the number of processors and memory modules without a rapid increase in interconnection costs, but it has led to major inconveniences: contention and the reliability of the aggregate are more important. As a result, alternative solutions have been sought ranging from a return to uniprocessors to system linkage through a transport medium such as a bus. The search for solutions is based on efficiency, reliability, and the premise that the interconnection is motivated by economics and the needs of users. Such needs are exemplified by the process of sharing a common database, and the resulting solutions typically have logical and physical characteristics. They are:

1. At the logical end, software routines and protocols are necessary for connecting together workstations and servers into a single computer system. It is difficult to imagine a computer continuing to perform any sort of useful action in the absence of its logical, software-based functionality. Logical characteristics ensure that the network effectively connects a number of autonomous nodes together, each capable of operating by itself if the network is not active.

The network's active status answers the communications needs of the user. A mail system is an example of interconnection based on users' needs. Messages are sent to and received from users of the several host-nodes (practically workstations) of a local area network. Messages can be exchanged via both local and long-haul facilities. Another example is access to specialized computing resources, occasionally required by the workstations of a local area network but too expensive to assign permanently to each one of them (e.g., number crunching or a dedicated graphics processor). Thus we see that both communications and resource sharing dominate the background purpose of a LAN.

2. At the physical side are the devices that provide support for visualization, databasing, computation, and the communications facilities. In a networking sense, they basically consist of the transport media: the cable (carrier) and the bus interface unit. The logical resources drive the physical. Addressing is a precise example of a logical solution made to solve physical problems. The addressing structure is one of the most important aspects of any computer architecture; it is even more significant when cooperation between multiple workstations is to be achieved

by sharing an address space.

In a LAN implementation, addressing is very important. Its impact goes well beyond message exchange. A proper addressing scheme lays the ground for:

- Program modularity
- Variable-size data structures
- Data and program sharing

Agile addressing solutions permit independent programs to access the same physical memory addresses with different program names. All resources within the network may be identified by a user-specified symbolic name rather than by a fixed address. Such resources may be any device or service the user wishes to identify to the network: workstations, printers, disks, application programs, compilers, or gateways. When the network resources are accessed by name, rather than by physical address, application programs and data can be moved freely from one host computer to another or even from one location to another. The address cover can be extended through gateways and the software addressing conventions they implement. A communications device extends the traffic and signal coverage. Addresses can be expanded in two directions:

- Down into the station by adding fields to identify destination ports or processes within a station
- Up into the internetworking level by adding fields to identify destination stations on remote networks

Theoretically, there is no limit to the number of gateways connecting two segments. A gateway only repeats packets addressed to itself as an intermediary. Practical limits are often indicated by experience. A critical question is: "What would be the result of a failure of a single repeater connection in segmented partitions of the network?" This points to two important considerations. First, while peer-to-peer solutions provide significant improvements over both tightly coupled systems and hierarchical solutions, they are by no means free of problems. Addressing is just one of these problems. As the subsequent sections will demonstrate, there are many others. Second, the reason for LAN solutions is universality in terms of connectivity, which means the need for any-to-any capability as far as the attached communicating devices are concerned. Even if it looks as though any-to-any is not needed at present, it will be necessary at some time.

Since the future implementations are multimedia oriented, universality must support multimedia. Restrictions implied on media even in some limited parts of the network will be a great handicap and also very costly. Hence, prior to assuming that we have available an efficient communications mechanism, we must clearly establish what this entails.

7.4 Functions of Network Control

Even if addressing were the only reason for network control on a network-wide scale, it would be important. But there are other reasons. Message exchange must be controlled, scheduling done, connectivity assured, monitoring provided, degradation detected, error correction provided, and store and forward implemented. Both operational and diagnostic reasons imply control center capability. In simple networks, the functionality relevant to control activities can be distributed at the nodes. It may be part of the BIU's mission to look after an end-to-end assurance. This is not necessarily the best solution when we deal with complex networks.

One of the nodes particularly tooled to look after internode collaboration is the network control center. It contains the necessary performance monitoring and diagnostic software to analyze the data transport activity. It can monitor how many packets are being transferred per second on the network or who is receiving the messages. It can also trace a network malfunction. The use of statistics available to the network control center help users establish functionality and possible bottlenecks—thus enhancing the ability to modify the network configuration. With the statistics, the user can study each type of device attached to the LAN, what type of data each unit may handle, and what sort of action is necessary in the short-, medium-, or long-term in network management.

These issues are common to all networks. Networks typically span distances ranging from meters to thousands of kilometers and they have significant similarities to the internal computer structure. Bus structures used in computer systems range from those of microprocessors, which can be as short as 1 to 10 cm, to large scale multiprocessor systems interconnected through broadband, which can be as much as 100 km in length. Thus network control functionality cannot be defined once and for all. It is a function of the solution we provide and should be examined as such. With LANS, for instance, the range of NCC functionality is often governed by the distance over which inexpensive techniques can be used. The distance over which a single LAN extends its activity is typically from about 300 meters to a few kilometers. Solutions to network control are:

- Even if this LAN is connected through bridges or gateways to other LANs, we may wish to exercise network control at the single LAN level.
- Alternatively, some commodity offers consider it better to assure a broader coverage such as controlling all the LANs in the same building.
- Still others take the approach that it is better to exercise network control on a floor-by-floor level—no matter how many LAN buses or rings are at that floor.

Choices are not made at random. They fit a precise strategy which takes into account topology, intended user, prevailing protocols, supported resources, software availability, and bandwidth.

A basic feature connecting the nodes of a LAN is the sharing of bandwidth, which is a continuous sequence of broadcasting frequencies within certain limits. Bandwidth is expensive in wide area networks, but not in a local area network. Hence, there should be greater motivation to exercise appropriate control— and a lesser need to search for features designed to reduce, for instance, the size of the header or overhead bits sent with each message. In other words, we need different design solutions for LAN from those developed for long-haul networks. The fact that LAN bandwidth is relatively inexpensive should carry throughout our design work.

Two principal objectives have to be considered when configuring a network:

1. The total length of cable should be minimized to achieve a low-cost system and to limit overall transmission distances.
2. Concentration points should be provided to facilitate configuration and maintenance of the network.

Topological considerations and structural matters are expressed in a system of hubs and nodes. All LANs are composed of nodes; some nodes are hubs. The hub is the central node of any system or subsystem online to the information network.

The network controller itself is a system hub. The logical connection between subsystems must be done system hub to system hub. It is precisely this hub structure that gives end users on a node system the impression that their reference data is available locally. Control should be able to sustain and enhance this user-oriented functionality. Thus it goes beyond transport proper. It handles requested data that is not available locally; the data is transported automatically from the hub through:

- Application-to-application communication
- Distributed transaction processing
- Electronic messaging
- Database-to-database transfer
- Automatic file and document distribution

A value-added function would assure that critical updates in the node database would be done automatically—and that no errors interfere with this process. Similarly, network control should assure an effective and dependable process-to-process communication. Different approaches are used to this end. For instance, a main purpose of using process names in procedure invocation is to allow the procedure code to be used re-entrantly. But re-entrantly is not always appropriate. Also, accesses that change a resource, such as writing to a file, must be synchronized.

To face the necessary tasks efficiently, network control must support the concept of a resource manager restricting the use of certain resources and facilitating the use of others. When a resource manager is used, a number of synchronous and independent processes may attempt to use a non-sharable resource in parallel. It is the task of network control to assure that only one process at a time uses its critical region. This can be achieved by using a semaphore, supplying a token which may only be possessed by a single process. There are two ways to do this:

- A shared action
- A token which non-deterministically matches with only one of a

possible group of tokens from processes wishing to use the resource

The use of a semaphore concept seems to be a natural way to implement resource managers in a system in which the matching of tokens is the normal instruction activation mechanism. Through it, each process wishing to invoke the critical region uses a request token, containing the process name, to the resource manager. This leads to a number of tokens with identical destination names. As a control mechanism, semaphore tokens match with one of these request tokens, allowing that request token to enter the critical region. When the request has been processed through the critical region, a result token is sent back to the requesting process and the semaphore token is released. This is not the only way to do this, but it is a good example.

I have placed emphasis on network control requirements because I consider them far more important for modern solutions than the lower-level question of start versus bus versus ring topologies. The choice of these topologies was considered important when we lacked the concept of higher-up layers in a network. But experience has demonstrated the wisdom of refocusing our center of attention.

7.5 Star versus Bus versus Ring

Star, bus, and ring are the classic ways of connecting workstations, servers, and hosts into a communications systems. Each has variations, Star connections may be active or passive. We may have a one- or two-channel broadcast bus; transmission may be baseband or broadband.

The topological connectivity we use for LAN configuration, as well as the devices we employ, have advantages and disadvantages. Devices can be connected in a ring LAN configuration. The danger is that the ring will break if one transmitting device fails. Therefore, rings usually are braided or woven to provide backups in case of equipment failures. Buses are the most common LAN configuration. The bus reference typically implies a cable strung like a highway with entrance ramps. Any device that must be connected is simply attached to a ramp. Star is much like a phone network or the old data-terminal solutions. It has a central controller, with branches connected to each device. Other topological characteristics include loops (type of rings), trees (sort of multidrop lines), ether (interconnected buses), spider structures, and meshes. The latter can be regular, irregular, or partly or fully connected.

Figure 7.2 shows eight different topologies; they are:

1. Centralized or star.
2. Bus or unrouted tree, the ether type.
3. Spider (passive star).
4. Hierarchical.
5. Ring.
6. Irregular mesh.
7. Fully connected.
8. PBX based.

All configurations require access methods and protocols to allow the sharing of a single-transmission facility. Each alternative configuration at least features the two lowest layers of the OSI reference model, data link control (DLC) and the physical transmission layer. Generally, functions that exist in the higher architectural layers are assumed to be largely independent of the communication network topology. Therefore, high-layer network protocols can be employed for data communications in local area networks that have different basic topologies.

Star structures have a central point or node that interconnects the attached devices. This affords good control over the network's operation, but it is also vulnerable because a single point of failure closes down the whole network and its interconnected devices. In an active node star-type arrangement, each user station or server is connected to a central facility that is responsible for managing all communications. Both the advantages and disadvantages of this arrangement stem from this centralization. Although communications and resource management can be efficiently handled, the limitations and reliability of the central unit determine all network performance characteristics. In addition:

- Connecting the central host to each individual user is often costly without exhibiting a corresponding reliability.
- The central node itself can become a bottleneck in transmission.
- The connecting distance is limited (usually at 30 meters) while, if repeaters are used, their number must be multiplied by the number of lines.

Star-type networks were the direct outgrowth of terminal attachments in which remote devices having no data processing capability

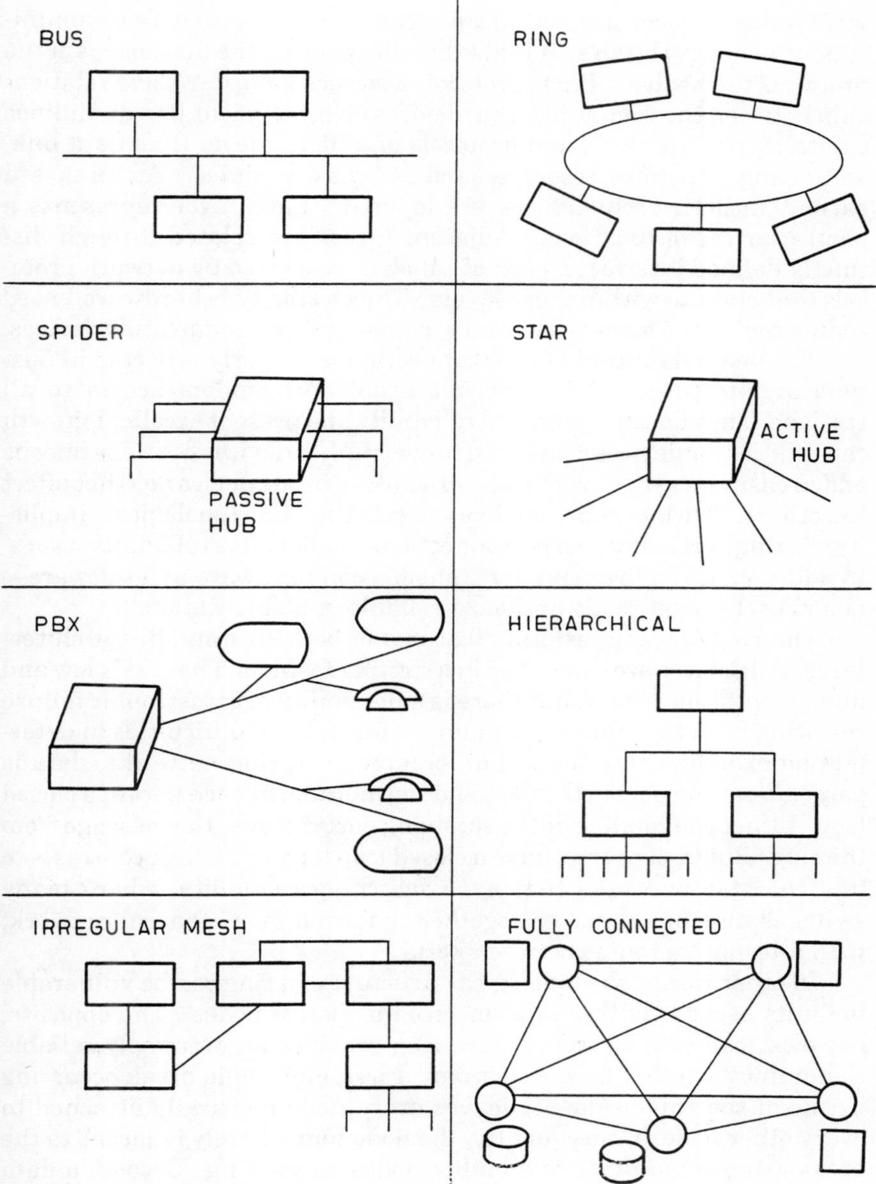

Figure 7.2 Eight different solutions of LAN offerings and their background implementation concept.

were linked to a central mainframe. Such a solution to data communications is limited by size. It is also handicapped by the limitations of the protocols themselves. Early protocols assumed a master-slave relationship between the communicating devices. New efficient line disciplines capitalize on interfaces and protocols of a higher level than data link, embracing hardware resources and software modules. As discussed earlier, modern architectures are layered. Each layer represents a particular set of functions. Adjacent layers are related through distinctly defined interfaces, each of which is supported by network protocols that operate within those layers. Thus a star-type hardware-based connectivity is no longer essential in supporting communicating devices.

The layered concept of interconnection is properly reflected in bus-type architectures. Buses permit equal and random access to all stations. They feature improved reliability and present excellent growth capabilities for devices connected to every other device. Stations may be added easily on a bus structure, and a failure in one device does not affect the others. The bus approach has roughly the same topological simplicity of a ring, but using passive connections, it alleviates reliability issues. In addition, it requires simpler transmission hardware and software—allowing the least costly and most reliable implementation.

The ring (or loop) exhibits features of both star and bus architectures. All devices are connected in a circular fashion. The cost is low and implementation is easy, but there is a possibility of catastrophic failure resulting from the transmission line being cut and difficulties in determining exactly where the failure occurred. In ring networks, data is passed from one port to the next and regenerated at each port in a closed loop. Either the sending or the receiving port removes the message from the ring. Rings, of course, have a closed loop topology which contrasts to bus and star networks that have switching capability, where many switches may be connected together to form a more general network, with alternative routes between ports.

In other words, the topological structure of a ring can be vulnerable to faults because of the serial interconnection of nodes. The opposite, however, can also be true since a ring provides an extremely reliable communication link for two reasons. First, any single break occurring in one of the ring segments leaves every node physically attached to every other node. Consequently, the node immediately adjacent to the break can communicate to all other nodes on the ring. Second, a data packet transmitted on the ring passes sequentially from one data processing node to another until it is removed from the ring. Removal can be performed by either the transmitting node, the receiving node, or a combination of both. This allows different types of control information to be propagated around the ring, thereby providing network management functions. A distinction between ring and loop networks can easily be made based on control:

- Ring networks exhibit a distributed control structure.
- Loop networks have centralized control.

The topology of networks can be discussed from three points of view: the physical wiring, the logical flow of data, and the mechanisms for controlling access. With ring networks, the use of a token access mechanism is often emphasized since it offers more functional capability than other ring access mechanisms. Finally, it must be emphasized that though the topology being selected determines many network issues, it is basically independent of the choice of the transmission media. Local networks may use optical fibers, coaxial cable, flat wire, and twisted wire pairs—and also radio and infrared transmission. Coaxial cable and twisted wire are the favored solutions at the present time.

7.6 A PBX Alternative?

Just as the mainframers try to invent ways which could conceivably extend the life cycle of their systems, private branch exchange (PBX) companies try to promote their wares as an alternative to LAN (Figure 7.3). Experience teaches a bitter-sweet lesson in this regard, provided we talk of interconnecting workstations, not mainframes where a PBX approach has nothing really to offer:

- The advantage of using a PBX to link WSs among themselves and with remote resources lies in the fact that we can utilize the twisted pair already embedded in most buildings.
- The disadvantage comes from the consideration that even the newest PBXs have not been designed for multimedia communications. Besides, beyond a certain level of traffic, all PBXs are blocking in spite of claims to the contrary by their vendors.*

---

* See also D. N. Chorafas, *System Architecture, System Integration and the Role of Artificial Intelligence*, McGraw-Hill, 1988.

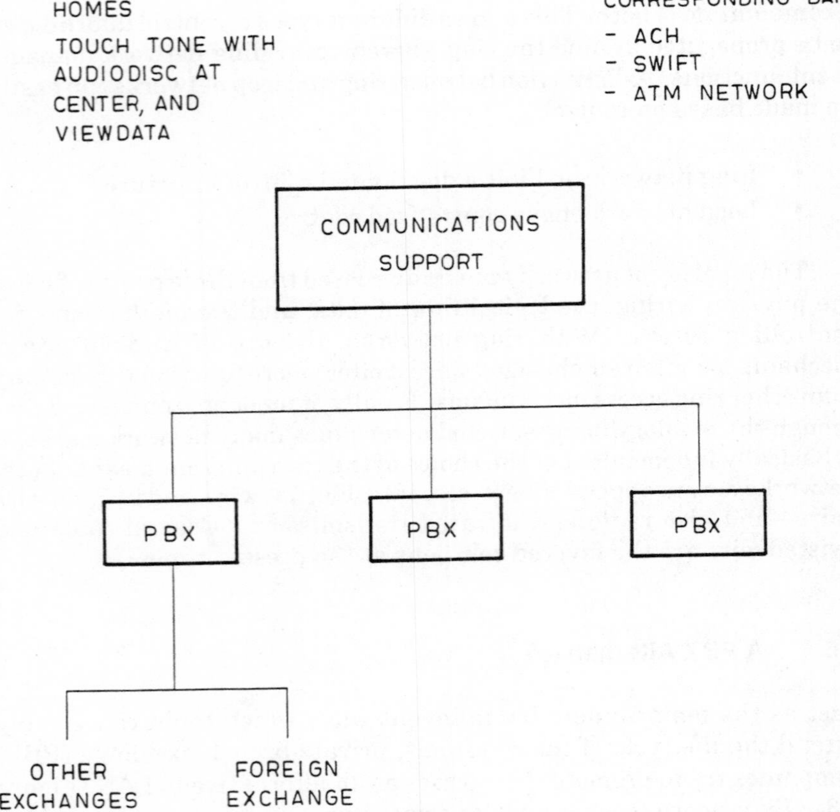

Figure 7.3 Communications support interfacing through Private Branch Exchange (PBX).

In this section we will only discuss whether or not the private branch exchange is an alternative to the LAN; we will not enter into details of its role. The PBX plays a significant role in the medium to large firm for voice reasons. It is the gateway toward the public telephone network. As WSs become multimedia, the PBX must convert into handling data, text, and image. But this conversion has not yet been made.

Let's look at the technical facts. First, the only type of equipment one should consider for LAN supplement rather than as an alternative are digital PBX systems. This is no great constraint since practically all PBXs announced since 1980 are digital and most of them are able to switch interactive voice and data. Second, supporters of the PBX-for-data argue that though they are slower than LANs, they offer valid service in certain applications where data and voice are constantly switched between terminals and telephone. That is so, but PBXs are not really equipped with the appropriate software for such support—though the newest among them feature a large software endowment.

Things may change in the future particularly given the sharp reduction of the average PBX lifetime. In the past, private branch exchanges have had long life cycles, with an average life expectancy of 15 to 20 years. This has changed because of technology, cost reduction, and the competitiveness in the market which, by introducing new features and new services, make the PBX obsolete much sooner. A number of factors make the new PBX machine more sophisticated than the old one; they include incorporating processing power, allowing protocol conversion, and performing multiform information switching. Yet, the PBX is an information switch which is still voice oriented and represents just one of the key nodes of the system.

Digital local handling of voice communication is not new in a nonpacket mode. TDM (time division multiplexing) connections for digitized voice have long been in use by the telephone companies. The new research is focused on the application of local packet switching networks for voice communication. But, the major issue is compatibility with long-haul packet voice communication, not the technology required for achieving the performance needed to support locally a large number of interactive data and voice connections. Of course, local packet voice has its place. It may be used either for support of local communication (intraoffice) or as an access and distribution mechanism for a long-haul (interoffice) system. There are also other applications for real-time packet voice such as voice messages. Under this perspective, long-haul compatibility is the prime design objective for using local switches for interactive voice communication—whether or not other media are integrated into the system.

A third technical fact is that because a remarkable spread of LANs is expected in the coming decade, together with an upgrading of public telephone networks, it may seem natural to think of an integration process: that of the LAN with the public networks and that of text, data, and image with voice. This, however, does not have to happen by substituting the distributed LAN capabilities with a central switch. The PBX can act as a backup switch with a broadband being the carrier of data and voice. It does not need to be the primary gateway. In other words, every solution has its place. The integration toward which we are moving may be much broader than the foregoing suggests, as Figure 7.4 indicates. A global approach will involve:

- Broadband CATV (cable television) technology
- Baseband LAN for PC-based workstations
- An evolution in PBX implementation

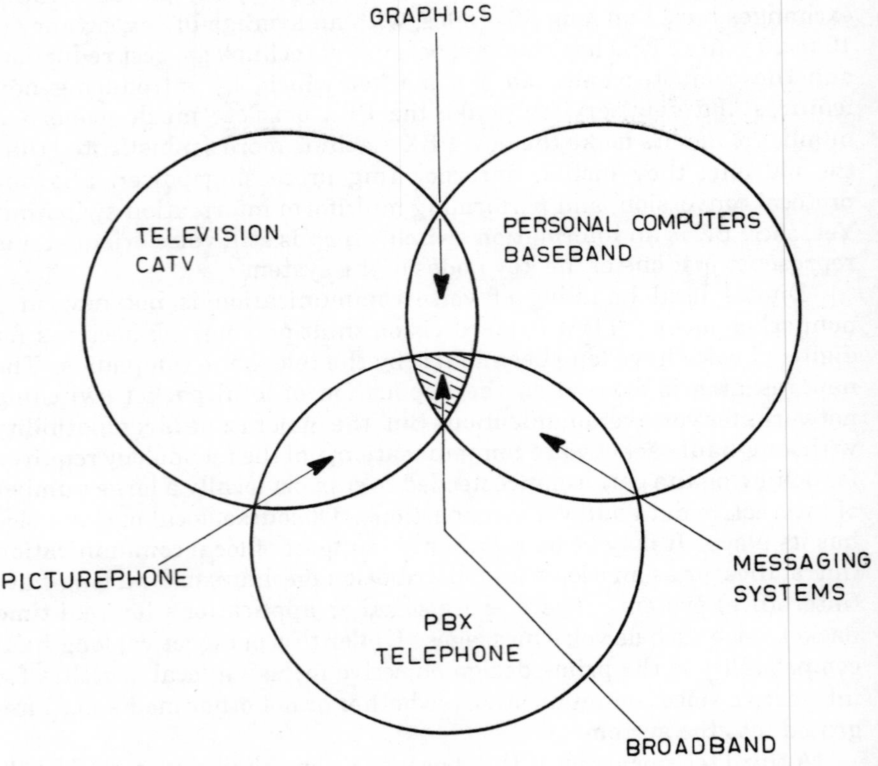

Figure 7.4 Three different technologies may exist for a number of years and we have to capitalize on them.

The PBX itself will benefit from the effect of a mass market as communications requirements keep on expanding.

In terms of engineering, neither will the LAN cable be likely to replace the PBX, nor will the PBX push the LAN out of existence. The former is a carrier; the latter is a switch. Just the same, the phone station will not disappear. Telephone sets will always be at peoples' desks—their shape may be changing, but here again we need the switching capability. What will most likely happen is an integration of PBX and broadband whereby the broadband is the carrier and PBX does the switching. However, there is not yet enough basic research on this integration. It will still require another 2 or 3 years—maybe more—for some successful applications to take shape.

The PBX is no substitute for a LAN, though its functions are very important. One day in the not too distant future, local area networks will carry voice along with data, text, and image. Typically there will be separate wavelengths for services which have different characteristics and pose demands on the carrier which may result in knocking out the other service. While such capabilities will be evolving through time and the market will be offering increasingly sophisticated equipment, the solution to the user's problems will not be found off the shelf. Able solutions need time, patience, money, and above all brainpower. Projects must be undertaken only if the goal is worth the effort—and if it is, projects should be done well.

7.7 Network Throughput

Let's now look at statistics behind the need for integration. PBX, computers, and television merge into a broad polyvalent system. In 1988 there were an estimated 800 million telephones in the world and about an equal number of television sets. This gives an idea of the enormous potential which is offered to a system accessible to the public in general and offering text and data broadcasting. For the general public, microprocessor-based television sets are going to become multifunctional terminals. For business, the trend will involve personal computers and LANs. This is supported by the fact that the use of local area network technology for online interactive voice communication has recently attracted considerable interest.

This brings up a number of issues that largely go beyond using the PBX as a substitute for the LAN. What are we really after in local communications? The answer is network throughput. We know from engineering studies and from successful implementations that throughput depends on:

1. Bandwidth of the carrier.
2. Efficiency of the switch.
3. The nature of the attached devices.
4. The processes running on them.
5. Their communications requirements.
6. Message size.
7. Retransmission timeout.
8. Buffers at every node.
9. Roundtrip delay.

Several of these factors are interrelated. The LAN architecture imposes its own prerequisites. The solution which we must give is global. The real question is not LAN or PBX. It is how we can use both LAN and PBX to best advantage.

The bandwidth of the carrier and the communications requirements of the processes running on the system underscore the traffic problems. For instance, the increase in the number of packets also causes increased delays from collisions and queues. For most networks, local or long haul, delays grow with the number of packets. Therefore, short packet periods are not necessarily the proper strategy for reducing the total end-to-end delay. For any network, load, and data rate, there is an optimal packet size which may sometimes be derived analytically or may be found by trial and error. When several networks are used in tandem, the best strategy is for all of them to use the same packetization period even though this leads to suboptimization.

Furthermore, given the relatively low cost of the local network and the fact that it operates under controlled conditions, when local and long-haul networks are combined, the packetization period should be mainly aimed at the improvement of the long-haul network performance. Aggregation, multiplexing, and concentration techniques can be used to reduce the number of packets without increasing the packetization period—but this leads into technical discussions which are not the subject of the present text.

Chapter

8

Technical Choices for the Cabling Plant

8.1 Introduction

We have considered some of the physical issues connected to a local area network, particularly those relative to the switching system. There are also other physical choices to be made, while still other logical and physical subjects will have a great impact on system performance. In layered networking approaches the lowest level is cabling, and the physical layer is divided into two sublayers, the media access unit (MAU) and the cable, which is the information transport medium. This is the first technical choice which will subsequently affect the services to be obtained from a LAN.

Reliability considerations also contribute to the selection of the bus and its architecture. Besides mean time between failure (MTBF) and mean time to repair (MTTR), noise avoidance and electrical characteristics play a role. The communications system should remain usable regardless of the number of hose interfaces attached to it.

Cable, MAU, and BIU will define whether the application will be baseband (BAB) or broadband (BRB). The communications market of the future will most likely be served at four different levels or reference:

1. Interstate by satellites and optical fibers without necessarily value-added characteristics.
2. Intercity by VAN (value-added networks) largely through optical fibers and radio links.
3. Intracity through CATV-type broadband.
4. Interbuilding by means of broadband and baseband.

Each will feature its type of approach in terms of information transfer. For interstate, "photonics" will dominate the scene, since light waves provide the most efficient approaches so far devised; we can look forward to generalization of their usage.

CATV means coaxial, though here too optical fibers can make inroads. At the end of the solution spectrum we have twisted pair of copper wire, but, necessary bandwidth is not enough. We need solutions rather than components, no matter how valuable the latter may be. In a sense, a LAN without the capacity to integrate voice and image will have a limited future. Yet in another sense, given the prevailing costs and current lack of know-how on LAN implementation, baseband is a good starting point, particularly for LANs which can demonstrate and maintain low costs. To repeat, the issue of cabling is indivisible from the overall solution. The physical layer affects the data link layer and vice versa. Let's recall that the data link layer, too, is split into two sublayers: logical link control (LLC) and media access control (MAC). To answer the requirements of MAC, the AIEEE Project 802 developed three standards, each supported by known computer, communications, and office automation firms; we examined them in the chapter about media access.

8.2 Choosing the Bus

Loosely coupled information systems are the natural result of the evolution of the computers and communications technology and of their merger. The changes in data processing, databasing, and datacom (DP/DB/DC) brought on by a LAN can be far reaching. This is true not only in a technical sense but also in other domains.

1. Organizational.
2. Operational.
3. Distribution of competences and responsibility.

In fact, technical choices have to consider the other three domains, accounting for the fact that WSs and LANs make up a well-defined product that affects managerial and professional productivity.

Ideally, the supported technical characteristics should see to it that the chosen LAN is open to equipment from multiple suppliers so that the user organization avoids the lock-in experienced in earlier times with long-haul network architectures. Another important criterion is multifunctional capability. This should include not only different types of classical DP applications but also the newer polyvalent services such as messenger (electronic mail), calendar, text handling, etc., processed on the same LAN.

What are the options at our disposition? When it comes to the question of choosing the bus, many organizations think about what the vendor has to offer:

- *Building wiring*. IBM's cabling system, AT&T's premises distribution system, the ability of combining voice and date
- *Work area networks*. Ethernets, IBM's PC network or token ring, the server concept

Then they jump on an evaluation of cost and performance. This is the wrong way of going about the problem. The right way is more generic and starts with requirements. Normal and peak conditions must be studied; minimums, average, and maximums established; and foreseeable growth in demand projected. Both qualitative and quantitative estimates should be followed through.

Practically all carriers have been used for voice. Figure 8.1 compares twisted pair, microwaves, coaxial cable, and optical fibers in terms of thousands of voice circuits being supported. To a fair extent such media overlaps with one another, with one exception (microwaves) each covers and area addressed by no alternative. Thus, at the physical level of decision, one of the major questions is which material to use. This puzzles the LAN designer rather than the user, as by the time a local area architecture is chosen, this question has been answered. Under current technology, this bus can be of six types:

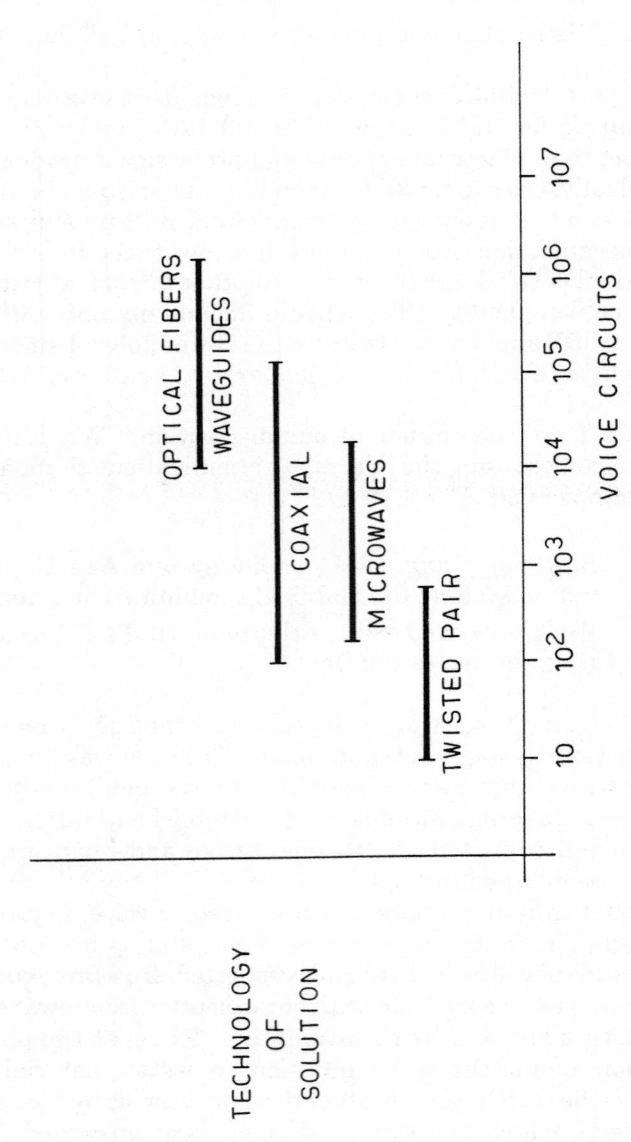

Figure 8.2 Cables of lower quality and long distance cables distort the signal.

1. Twisted pair, the common telephone wire is a widely used medium. The main advantages of twisted pair are that it is inexpensive, widely available, and installed in many buildings. But it is subject to noise. At low speed, it covers short distances with no modem—at moderate speed and distance, with modems. One of the basic reasons why twisted pair cable was selected for baseband LAN is its low cost. Another positive reference is that anyone can install a network: lay the cable and connect the transporters to it, using only pliers and a screwdriver. Furthermore, shielded twisted pair cable is not as susceptible to radio frequency interference as other types are. But twisted pair is only a cable. A whole architecture must be built around it. The performance of the LAN must be enhanced by an efficient low-level acknowledgment scheme. Omninet, for instance, uses a positive acknowledgment protocol in which every message, if received correctly, is acknowledged by the receiving station, and if a message is not positively acknowledged within 15 to 20 microseconds, the sending station will retransmit it after waiting a random time interval. A message is retransmitted until it is acknowledged or until it has been retransmitted a maximum number of times specified by the user.

   In the Omninet LAN, the transporter receiving a message sends the acknowledgment as soon as the message has been validated. The receiving station does not wait or check the line for activity before sending the acknowledgment, but all other stations wanting to transmit are waiting because they will have detected that the line is busy. Therefore, acknowledgments are sent immediately by the transporters.

   The LAN developed by IBM uses twisted pair working up to a stated 4 MBPS. (This is the highest known rate on a twisted pair application.) By contrast, Omninet, by Corvus Systems, works at 1 MBPS. Both are baseband.

2. Flat wire, which is commonly used in connecting peripherals to a central unit. An applications example of this type of bus is Nestar's Cluster/One. It works at 240 KBPS. To a very large measure, the speed of transmission depends on: the quality of the wire, the distance, and the data load to handle. As Figure 8.2 indicates, the cable distorts the signal. It thus becomes a matter how much distortion the application can accept. The lower the quality or the greater the length of the cable, the more the distortion.

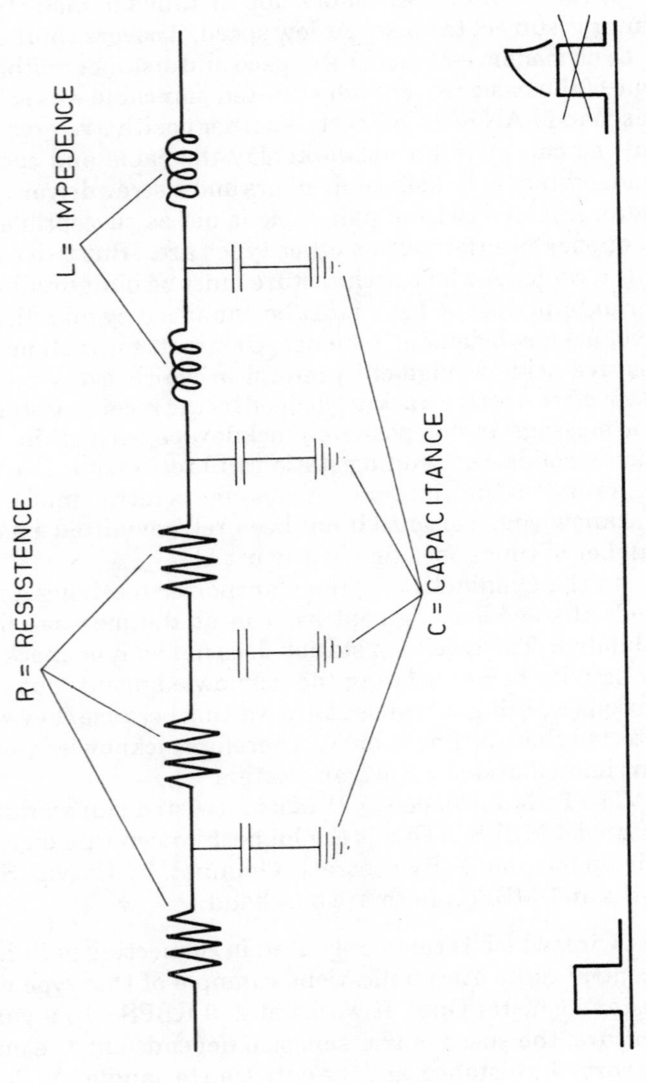

Figure 8.2 **Cables of lower quality and long distance cables distort the signal.**

Solutions can, of course, be found, but they make the interfaces much more expensive. For instance, to overcome this problem, IBM distorts the signals at the beginning, then reconstructs them. This removes worry about the speed. Something similar can be said of the flat wire. Nestar's 240 KBPS band is partially determined by the workstation interconnection (micro to micro), the database access, and so on—and also by the quality of the wire and by the timing device. These physical characteristics make an aggregate. The same is true of the following two media.

3. Coaxial cable, which comes in two forms: flexible (unprotected) and protected cable. Coaxial cable, too, is inexpensive and of known technology. It can support multimegabit transmission, be used for broadcast of point-to-point, and may exist in buildings wired for CATV. Protected coaxial cable is relatively immune to noise.

   There is a range of options in coaxial cable choices. They can be generally defined as follows:

   - Grounded coaxial can pass high information rates but is subjected to ground loops and to magnetic and radiated noise.
   - Underground coaxial can substantially lower the ground loop interference. One version known as triax also removes the radiated noise but does not reduce magnetic interference.
   - Twinax cable possesses only medium information rates but hinders magnetic interference because of a twist in the signal pair. It is typically operated with balanced inputs and outputs.
   - Quadrax cable operates like twinax, but it also gives double radiated noise protection and allows the inner braid to be used for control voltages in some applications.

A key subject is the choice of materials to be used in these cables. National Electrical Code, Underwriters Lab, and local ordinance requirements must be complied with. Flame retardant materials should be used in public buildings. Some cables use copperweld for the center conductor. This is a high-resistance steel wire with a copper cladding on the outside. It was originally intended to give strength to CATV cables when they were suspended from poles or pulled through ducts. Typically, unprotected cable is used for a baseband implementation, Ethernet being an example. Also, typically, protected cable is used for broadband, the more so within a hostile environment in terms of noise, such as in a factory. 3M's broadband LAN has this type of implementation.

There is no reason, however, why flexible coaxial cable cannot or should not be used for broadband. At Brown University, one of the earliest successful campus-type broadband applications, protected coaxial cable was used for the backbones. It was installed in ducts, while flexible coaxial was employed in hallways and classrooms. The latter is easier to install.

The basic argument for protected coaxial cable is immunity to noise. This is a function of the outer screen (Figure 8.3a), which may be mesh (such as copper), foil, solid aluminum tube, or both mesh and foil. The screen makes it difficult for electrical noise to get into the cable. If we apply 2 megavolts on the protecting cover, we may get 1 volt at the copper wire level.

Electrical characteristics are very important in terms of performance. If the LAN should work at 75 ohms, we must assure 75 ohms at the end. Otherwise the signal is reflected back. To do so, at each of the cables we put a 75-ohm resistor (Figure 8.3b). Furthermore, this 75-ohm resistor must be applied at the end of every branch. There are, however, some margins of tolerance. If we forget some of the resistors, say up to 20 percent, we may not even observe a negative outcome. But past a given threshold, the noise can get high.

In spite of the fact that the coaxial cable is an established medium, allows multitapping, and a good experience exists with CATV, some specialists consider it as outmoded.

4. Radio. This is primarily of interest in mobile communications in a metropolitan area network (MAN) sense. Radio is a broadcast medium; it exhibits easy reconfiguration capabilities and has low incremental cost. Some local area applications have used infrared waves. Use, however, has been limited both in terms of scope and of obtained results. While infrared remains a possibility, it is a medium in search of an application which might create a niche in the market.

5. Optical fibers, are typically a broadband solution and the way of

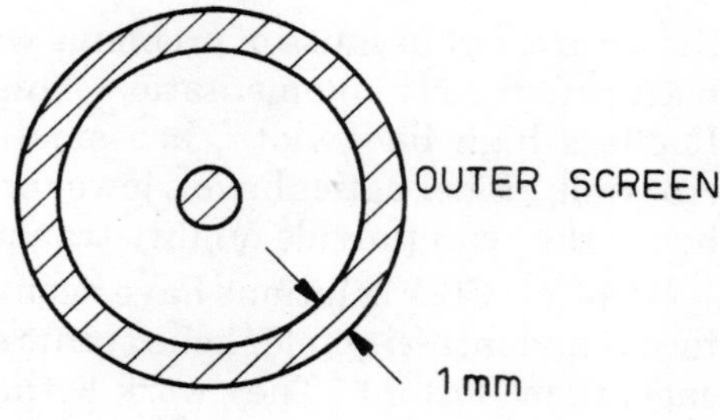

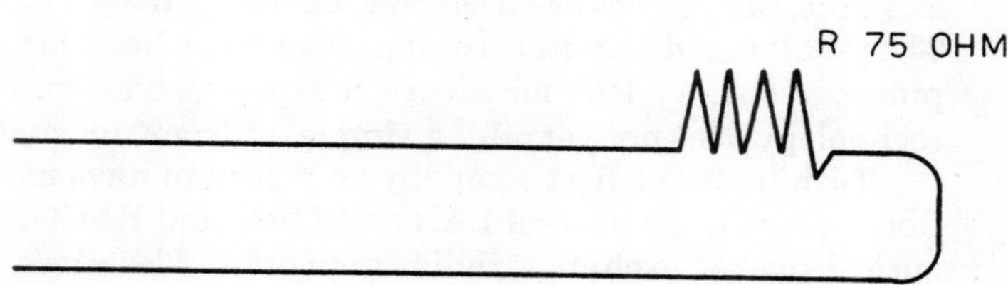

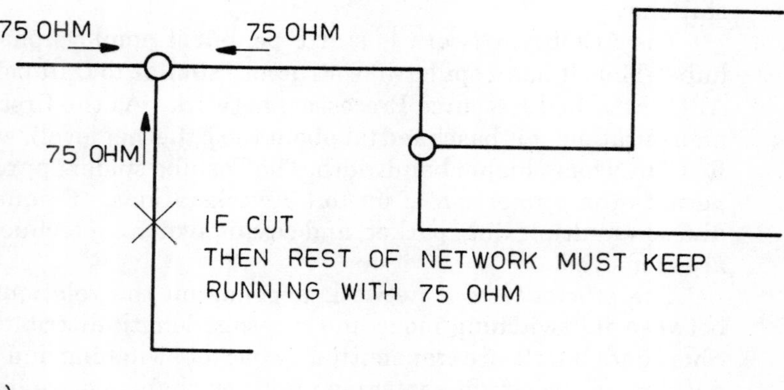

Figure 8.3 Protected coaxial cable. The gain is relative immunity to noise

the future, but because of problems with multitapit, it is not yet mature for LAN implementation. This is the newest technology. It offers high bandwidth, has small weight, and there is no crosstalk. Fiber optics have a lower error rate than other media, hence they can provide quality transmission.

Optical fiber solutions have been successfully implemented in city and intercity telephone traffic since early 1977 (first Chicago, then Boston). They work without repeaters up to 12 km (though for practical reasons telcos keep the distance at 7 km), but they do not allow multitap and the connectors are expensive. However, special applications may justify the use of fibers. For example, fiber optics are used now where security is paramount. The problem is different in communications where, for multitapping reasons, we look for a very cheap, passive tap. The fiber technology does not yet offer a simple, inexpensive installation.

Toshiba is the first company on record to have used optical fibers point to point on a LAN. ACORN and RACORN are its optical packet exchange radial networks. Toshiba's optoelectronics have led to optical passive star networks with good reliability and a reasonably large number of WSs. Both networks follow a time slot assignment controlled by an administrator selected on a contention basis from among the attached stations.

The ACORN network is star type, but it employs passive hubs. Thus it has a spider-like structure similar to Datapoint's ARC (Attached Resource Processor) network. As the first implementation, it is baseband (at about the Ethernet level), while RACORN has a higher bandwidth. The Toshiba spider approach permits the connection of up to 50 workstations. Frequency division multiplexing, packet, and circuit switching technology are employed.

The efficiency of a network depends on the relationship between its switching mode and message length distribution. Short data bursts are transmitted by packet switching and long data groups by circuit switching. Both mechanisms are implemented by FDM on a single fiber cable. Line switching is controlled by the packet switching network.

6. Satellite technology and gigabit-per-second streams. Like optical fibers, satellite solutions assure high bandwidth. Unlike optical fibers, they feature a rather high delay (2 x 0.24 seconds

earth to satellite and back). One of the satellite advantages is distance independence, another is very reasonable cost. Satellites are not LAN media but through earth stations they can nicely help interconnect a LAN on a wide area basis or even in a metropolitan area. That is why satellite transmission should be considered as a supplement rather than alternative to bus choices—though terrestrial microwaves and infrared may be both a complement and a substitute to the media we examined in this section.

8.3 Evaluating Channel Capacity

The choice of transport media is a function of the implementation requirements which we have and of solutions available in the market. Supported protocols and associated software should be bought as a commodity and should respond to our requirements regarding channel capacity, which is the metrics of the network channel which itself is the collection of links connecting the nodes of the network. As stated in Section 8.3, the channel and links are made up of some form of physical media. Capacity is a measure of the range of analog or digital signals that can be carried by such media, and it also indicates the amount of message traffic that a given medium is able to accommodate at one time.

"Bandwidth" is the term commonly used to describe capacity. Each variety of transmission media has a different amount of capacity or bandwidth. Bandwidth is also used to describe the difference between the highest and lowest frequencies of a signal. When dealing with purely digital communications, bandwidth tells about the amount of data that can be transmitted on the channel over time in bits per second. So, in the general case, channel capacity measures the range of signals that can be carried by the physical medium—and therefore the possible amount of message traffic. This definition is, however, only partly correct because in an intelligent network a major role is played by software and topology—neither of which are reflected at the physical level.

At the physical level of estimating the capacity of a network, we tend to divide what is available in a way that allows the most effective use of bandwidth. For instance, through multiplexing, a single channel is divided into many channels that transmit a number of independent signals. This is frequency division multiplexing (FDM). The frame of reference changes when we consider logical functions above the physical characteristics of channel capacity. Top to bottom, these typically involve:

- User application environment
- End-to-end reliability
- Formatting functions to support the chosen applications
- Code conversion functionality
- Data compression requirements
- Session establishment chores
- Flow control priorities
- Path control and optimal routing
- Link control

Of these, all of which are above the layer of physical transmission, only one is addressed by the IEEE 802 recommendation. All nine logical levels have to do with end-user service and overall system functionality.

The average communications requirements of each user in each system may be relatively low. Yet, in a shared data link environment, the aggregate peak communications needs of the multiple WSs can be very high. Certain system functions may demand bounded response times even when many ports are waiting for link access. A mechanism for distinguishing between ports with high and low response time bounds is a necessary part of any priority-type implementation. A generic study traces the guidelines of the implementation as a whole and then backtracks to the fundamental elements that make up the system. Each one should be studied individually and in depth—starting with the switches and the transmission media.

Well-studied and properly-defined applications characteristics imply technical choices: from the forementioned broadband and baseband to distributed control and monitoring. Good performance requirements bring up the need for a physical separation of the distributed elements of a LAN while they remain logically connected: WS(s) or database(s), printer(s), and datacomm links must be supported concurrently. An online connection is established through the cooperation of an entire process on one system and a passive, or listening, process on another. The processes establishing and terminating connections are usually applications programs. Their operation, however, presupposes the existence of a physical medium. Finally, studying channel capacity at the local level might be an idle exercise unless we consider ways and means for interconnecting to common carrier circuits:

- What is readily available?
- What can or should be leased and what should be maintained by the carrier?
- How can we maintain easy reconfiguration?
- Do we want to invest in a variety of speeds?
- Which speeds should be our target?

Effective channel capacity is not necessarily the sort of metric written in theoretical books or given by the vendor. In an intelligent network, it is not enough to say the cable is a carrier. We need much more than a system for supporting channels of information on nude wire. While one part of the process is converting to a form suitable for the transmission media being used, there are many other parts of the transmission process to consider.

It is also not enough to suggest that a link connecting the nodes in a network may have one or more channels operating at the same or different capacities. Bandwidth describes three issues at the same time:

1. The difference between the highest and lowest frequencies of a signal measured in megahertz (millions of cycles per second).
2. The amount of data that can be transmitted over time, expressed in bits per second.
3. The effective use of the network, more precisely, of the signals that can be transmitted over available channels.

The latter is theoretical capacity minus what is needed for housekeeping, security, information dependability, and other purposes plus improvements which we can make because of data compression, store and forward, alternator routing, strategically located information enrichment, and so on. We should keep this in mind when, in the following sections of this chapter, we speak of megahertz and megabits per second.

8.4 Implementing Megastreams

There are several ways for transmitting a communications signal. Normally, transmission takes place with sharp edges, which calls for wide bandwidth. An Ethernet signal, for instance, would need a 100-MHz carrier but transmit only 10 MBPS. A way around this spoilage of available capacity per second is a predistortion technique which employs bandwidth much better but increases the cost of the interface electronics.

Two lessons can be derived from the foregoing:

1. With baseband solutions, there is no direct linear relation between cycles per second and bits per second. The capacity of the coaxial cable used in baseband local area networks primarily transmits a single baseband signal at data rates in the area of 10 to 12 MBPS. In broadband local area networks channel capacity is used to create a large number of frequency subchannels from the one physical channel. Coaxial cable commonly used for CATV (and broadband local area networks) has bandwidths available in the range of 300 - 400 MHz. This translates into enough capacity to carry more than 50 standard color TV channels—at 5 or 6 MHz each—or thousands of voice-grade low-speed data signals, e.g., 9.6, 19.2, 56, or 64 KBPS.

   Broadband uses channel capacity in a more effective way than baseband. This is important since transmission speeds increase in direct proportion to technological developments. Currently available optical fibers have usable bandwidths of up to 4 billion Hz (10^9 gigahertz) compared with the upper limit of 500 MHz for coaxial cable. Data rates of over 1 GBPS (10^9 bits per second) have been supported.

2. No approach offers a free lunch. If we wish to get more bits per second out of the cable we must pay more for the interface. If our goal is to keep the interface simple and low cost, we must accept less throughput from the cable. This makes questionable the idea of increasing the cost of the interface hardware since the carrier cost per linear meter is minimal, well below $1 whether we talk of twisted pair or flexible coaxial. In this sense, it is wiser to keep the interface cost low, as our goal should be that of putting a personal computer on every desk at an affordable cost.

If we opt for higher cost, we could obtain other advantages from the use of new technologies. Error rates are very low with fibers (1 bit error per 109 bits) with the result that most error detection and retransmission overhead can be eliminated. The quality of service can also be significantly improved.

Fiber optics transmissions are not affected by electrical or electromagnetic interference, nor do they emit noise. This sees to it that they are inherently secure. Lesser volume and weight are also attractive propositions. Optical transmission media are very thin and light, allowing space and weight savings. Furthermore, broadband solutions are supported through a more impressive body of knowledge than what we know about baseband. The nonexistence of a linear relation in baseband between cycles per second and bits per second is not necessarily the case with broadband. CATV experience dominates the scene and radio frequency transmission is implemented through Amplitude modulation (AM) and Frequency modulation (FM).

Each technical solution has its own laws regarding how much bandwidth can be used, but the basic law by Shanon is the fundamental reference. It expresses algorithmically the theoretical limits and relates: power, signal to noise, and bandwidth. For a specific bandwidth we must have a certain power and accept a signal-to-noise ratio. If we reduce the power, we need more bandwidth for the same ratio. With broadband, the signal-to-noise ratio is very favorable in terms of end usage. However, because significant changes require order of magnitude swings, the effect of variation is not so pronounced within a given environment. We will return to this issue in Section 8.5.

Cable is by no means the only carrier medium. A good deal of information we receive daily is largely broadcast over the airwaves, an unbounded medium. Signals broadcast via unbounded media are microwaves, millimeter waves, and infrared. While there are currently few commercially available local area networks based on these technologies, they might become more prevalent over time.

8.5 Forms of Modulation

We said that signaling can be digital or analog. The former features a sequence of voltage pulses, the latter a continuously varying electromagnetic wave. Digital signaling is cheaper than analog and less susceptible to noise interference. But it suffers more than analog from attenuation. Analog or digital signaling can be used to propagate analog and digital data. Both approaches are cost effective in the context of LAN.

In Chapter 6 we said that baseband refers to a signal before it modulates the carrier and broadband refers to the signal after the carrier has been modulated. Other major differences between baseband and broadband technologies are maximum station separation, cable bandwidth, and per station connection cost. At this time, the least expensive and most readily available bus interface units use baseband modulation. However, given the limitations inherent in baseband, companies are working to develop low-cost parts for use in broadband networks.

Baseband permits transmission of an analog or digital signal in its original form (no modulation). The entire frequency spectrum is used. There is no frequency division multiplexing (FDM) for LAN; there is a somewhat restricted use regarding baseband. It is practically synonymous to digital signalling.

With broadband, transmission of modulated analog signals dominates. A higher than voice-grade quality channel is available. FDM is often but not exclusively employed with broadband. In LAN implementation we can have FDM broadband or single-channel broadband. FDM broadband will typically employ CATV cables and terminators, feature less than 400 MHz capacity, and run over less than 20 km (about 13 miles). Head end and modems will be needed.

Let's now look more carefully into the algorithmic expression of different forms of modulation on a cable. Any of three types may be used:

- DSB, double-side band
- SSB, single-side band
- VSB, vestigial-side band (which is the more unusual case)

The basic difference is in the way they split the bandwidth. Figure 8.4 shows all three approaches. As seen in Figure 8.4, with DSB, the bandwidth is twice the data rate, each band being symmetrically around the center point of the RF carrier. This double-side characteristic can be used to increase the security of the transmission. With DSB, the signal-to-noise ratio is good, the penalty being that the bandwidth is twice the data rate.

SSB is primarily used in military communications. It is more expensive to build transmitters and receivers for single-side band, but some applications can afford it—and in a noisy environment this is a technically preferable solution. If we have a transmitter with a finite power, we can transmit over DSB or SSB. As Shanon's law specifies,

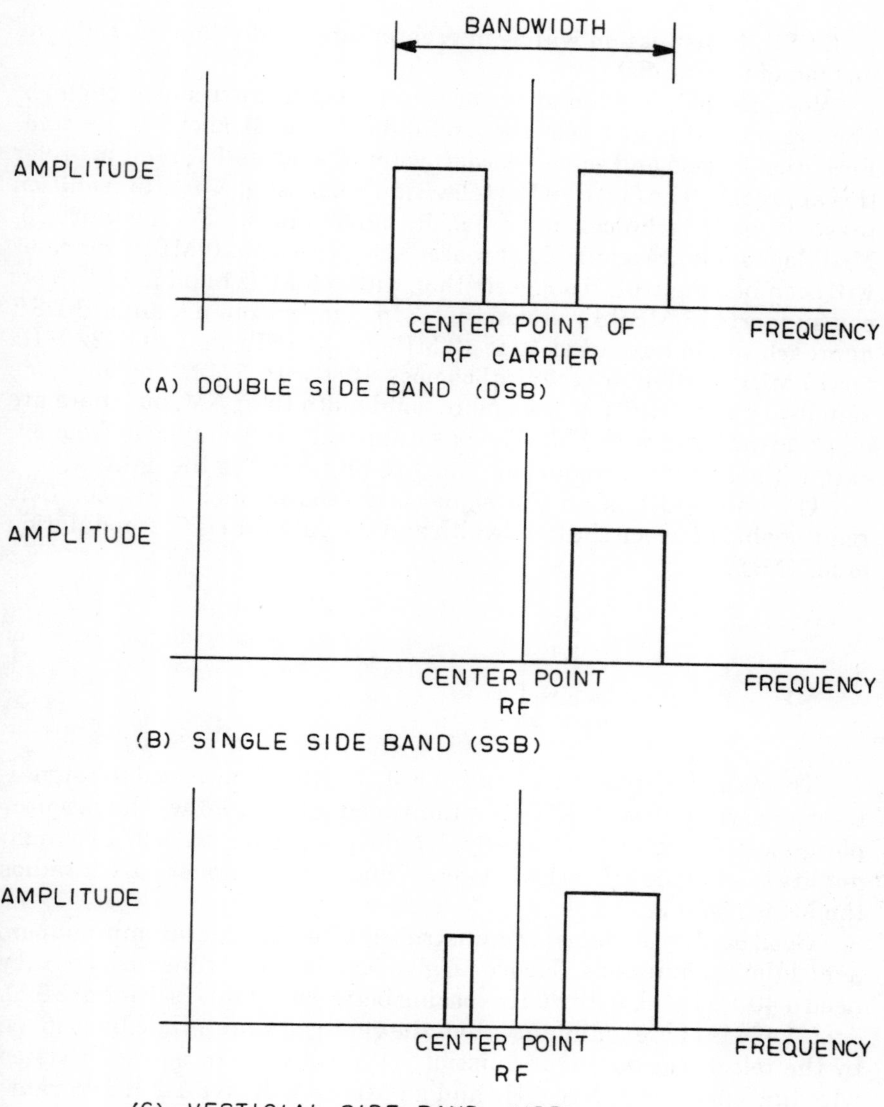

Figure 8.4 (A) Double side band (DSB), (B) single side band (SSB) and (C) vestigial side band (VSB).

with SSB, transmission will be in greater amplitude than in DSB (one instead of two bands).

Vestigial-side band solutions are used to make the receivers cheaper. The extra band is just over the useful data rate, at about 10 percent. Reception is good and some telecom systems, such as TV, tend to prefer this approach. The fact that the television business goes for this solution presents both technical and financial advantages. For instance, 5-MBPS modems are available at reasonable prices, as 10-MBPS modems will soon be. Figure 8.5 suggests that with a 6-MHz band and VSB we can support a 5-MBPS transmission. In comparison, a standard DSB approach would have used 10 to 12 MHz for 5 MBPS and 20 to 22 MHz for 10 MBPS. Similar technical choices exist with FM.* For the same signal-to-noise ratio, FM uses more bandwidth than AM, but there are other advantages with FM. The basic approach is a change in frequencies, with the rate of frequency change being equal to the data rate.

The bandwidth of an FM signal is presented in Figure 8.6. The relationship between the bandwidth and the data rate is the modulation index (MI):

$$\text{Data rate} = \frac{DF}{DT}$$

$$MI = \frac{\text{bandwidth}}{\text{data rate}}$$

This is an important quantity in FM. It defines how good the signal-to-noise ratio will be. If MI is less than or equal to 2, we will have a poor power-to-noise ratio. Technically, MI must be greater than 2. In a high-quality system the MI varies between 6 and 7. For commercial car radios the MI is about 3.

Good quality modems for industrial and business datacomm support a modulation index of 4. Hence, to give 9.6 MBPS of transmission, they need a 40-Hz band, with 80 Hz spacing between signals (see Figure 8.6). An MI of 4 is of higher quality than the classical voice-grade lines given by the telcom for data transmission. Typically a voice-grade twisted wire line operates at 3 to 4 Hz and an MI = 3 will give 1.2-KBPS rate.

Other solutions are feasible and are being developed with LAN. Omninet, for example, puts digital data directly on the twisted wire; no modulation is used. That is why we need repeaters every 300 meters.

---

*PSK and FSK are alternative approaches in frequency modulation.

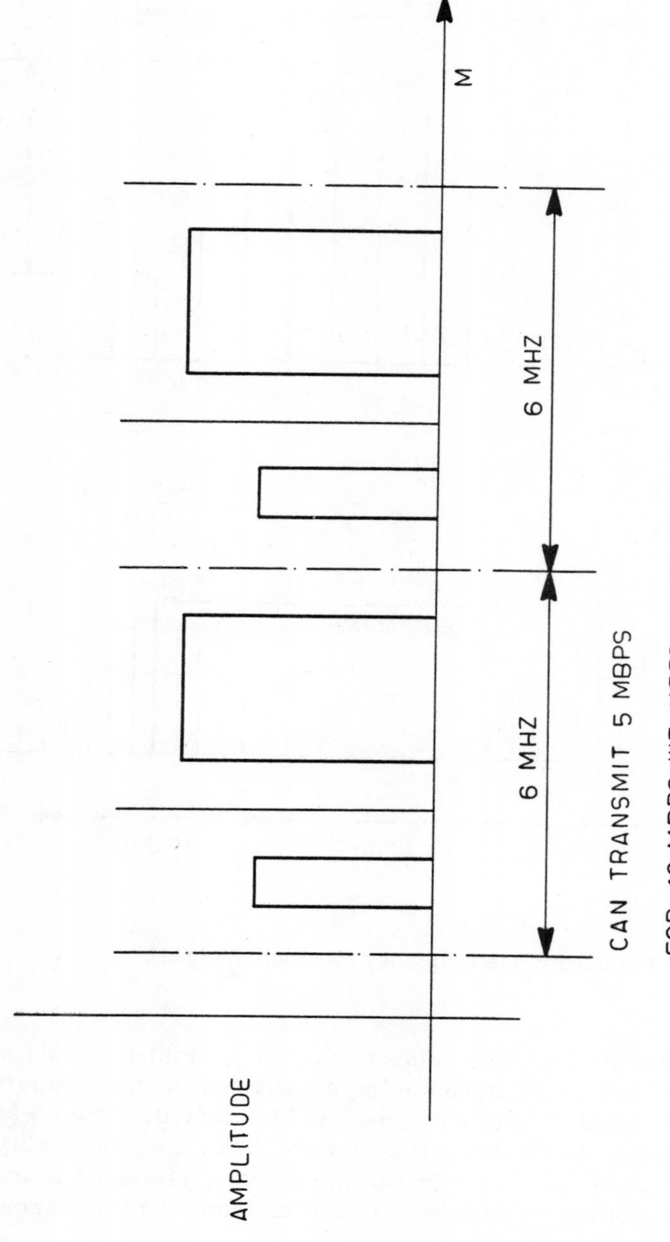

Figure 8.5 Support of 6 MHz transmission by vestiagal side band.

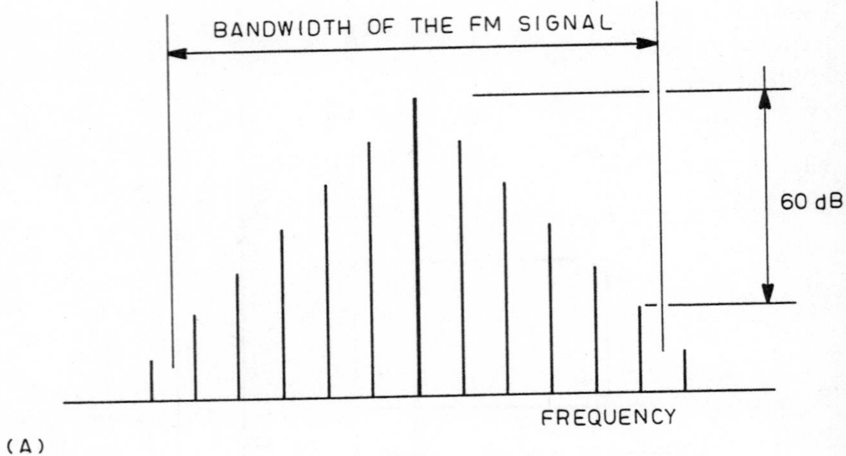

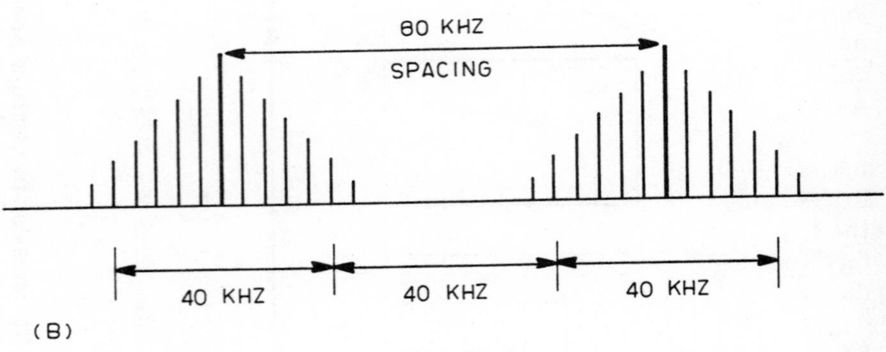

Figure 8.6 Bandwidth of a frequency modulation signal.

Still other technical LAN solutions work through analog signals on the carrier. The ability of datacomm implementation to use standard RF modems is the technical characteristic to be retained: 2- and 5-MBPS cards are off-the-shelf items in the industry. They are good quality and low price; above all they can become de facto standard interfaces assuring compatibility. While the line acts as a concentrator, the modem uses AM and FM together. They handle an AM signal, then alter the frequency. But the more we ask from modulation and demodulation, the greater the cost of the device.

Greater cost and less performance can also result as we try to get around Shanon's law. Mass production sees to it that the classical telephone and TV modems are the best alternatives. In the voice-grade approach:

- The 300- to 1.200-BPS modems transmit tones and work FSK.
- 2.4 KBPS are usually AM modems.
- 4.8 KBPS are also AM.
- 9.6 KBS alter phase and amplitude.
- 19.2 KBPS are expensive modems and therefore little used.
- 64-KBPS transmission is the ISDN recommended standard to be slowly phased into implementation.

Another reference to cycles per second and bits per second concerns voice digitization. Nyquist established the rate of sampling at twice the audio frequency. Through an 8-bit number we can obtain 256 different codes. Standard good quality audio is 64 KBPS; 56 KBPS works just as well.

There are two ways of transmitting voice on a broadband local area network—digital and straight analog—and there are different solutions to band allocation, such as data under voice or data over voice. However, the broadband technology is still under development and many manufacturers advise against an immediate implementation of voice and data.

8.6 Midsplit and Subsplit, Dual Cable, and Bridges

There is more than one way to implement a broadband solution. Midsplit means the use of the available frequency range on the carrier for a full-duplex solution on the same cable. For instance, in the broadband solution by 3M/IS, the division is made as shown in Figure 8.7. Modem identification for this is:

- Forward: 160 to 300 MHz
- Reverse: 5 to 112 MHz

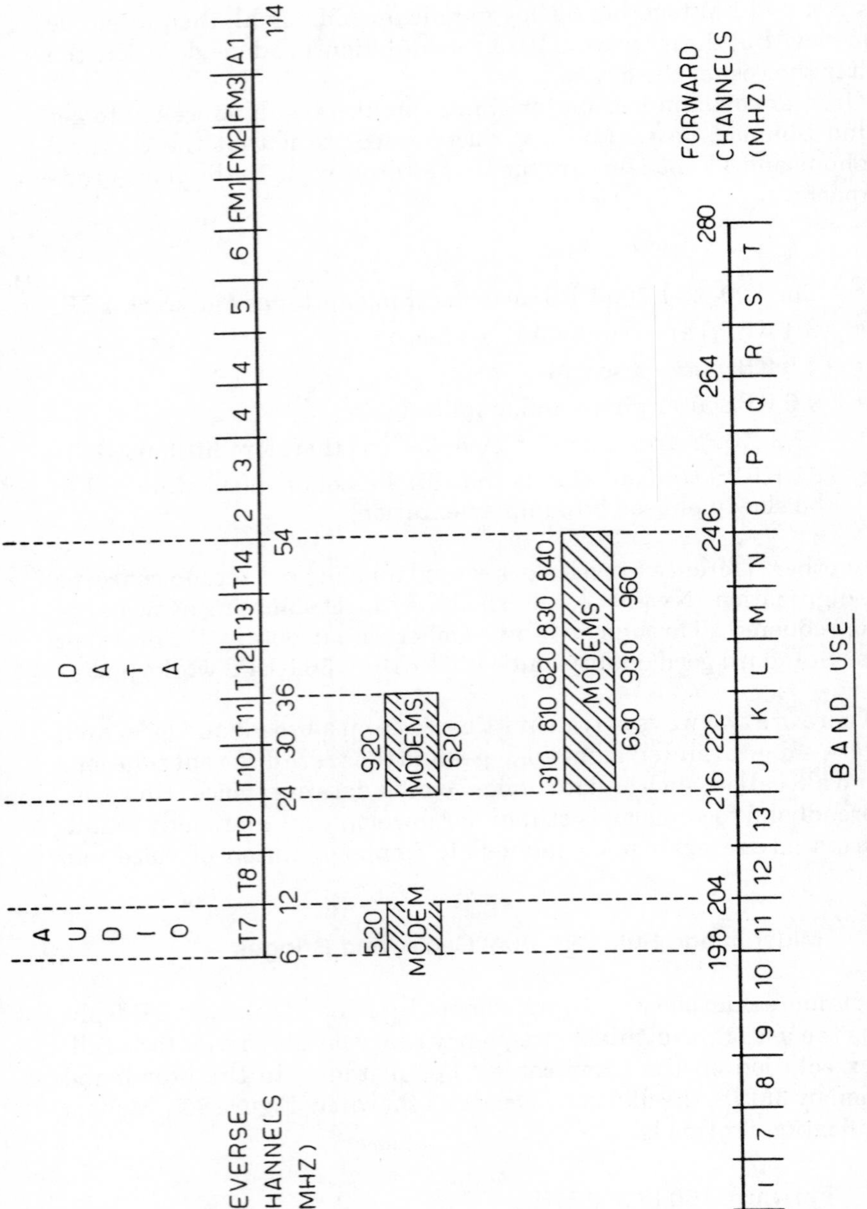

Figure 8.7 Band use with the 3M/IS coaxial cable solution.

The Electronics Industry Association (EIA) proposed a frequency allocation (TR40.1) for broadband networks which has been incorporated into the IEEE 802, and some are using their own frequency allocations and implementation. The IEEE 802 local area network recommended standard specifies a single cable system using a midsplit configuration. Midsplit, single cable requires that a head end remodulator be provided to translate the inbound frequency F^1 to the outbound frequency F^2. Midsplit refers to the frequency spectrum from 5 to 300 MHz being split down the middle so that 5 to 108 MHz are reserved for the inbound frequencies and 162 to 300 MHz are reserved for the outbound frequencies. The frequencies from 108 to 162 MHz are reserved as a guard band to prevent interference between the two major frequency bands. The frequencies from 180 to 216 MHz are reserved for TV channels. A frequency offset of 192.25 MHz has been defined between the inbound and outbound frequencies which are in 6-MHz pairs.

The name midsplit is not appropriate since the two bands are not equal. For capacity we need the same in both directions, but the CATV industry, which leans mainly on forward transmission, has influenced the uneven distribution. This brings up subsplit and lowsplit which usually mean the same thing. The original idea of CATV distribution is to send a lot of signals to a large number of receivers—all going in the same direction. But with pay TV and billing computers, subsplit was invented with a small number of reverse channels. For instance, the CCITT/ European solution is 40 to 300 MHz forward and 5 to 20 MHz reverse. For security systems and most of the CATV-type implementations, subsplit is good enough. We do not need duplex.

As an alternative structure, dual cable systems imply one cable in one direction and one cable in another direction. Starting from the head end, there would be two cables in, say, the 5- to 300-MHz range, one transmitting toward the head end, the other away from it. Dual cable can use cheaper modems—but there is an disadvantage in using two cables rather than one. Generally, products are projected for midsplit work on the dual cable system: the sockets for dual cable are a reasonably simple modification.

The role of the head end is defined through the modem installed there. With the classical CATV installation:

- The transmission frequency (TF) at the head end is high.
- The receive frequency (RF) is low (Figure 8.8a).

Correspondingly, for the modem at the receiving station the TF is

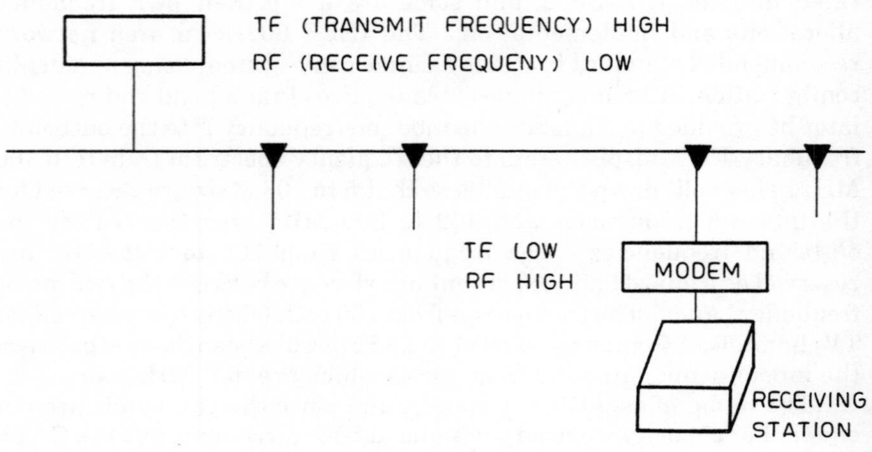

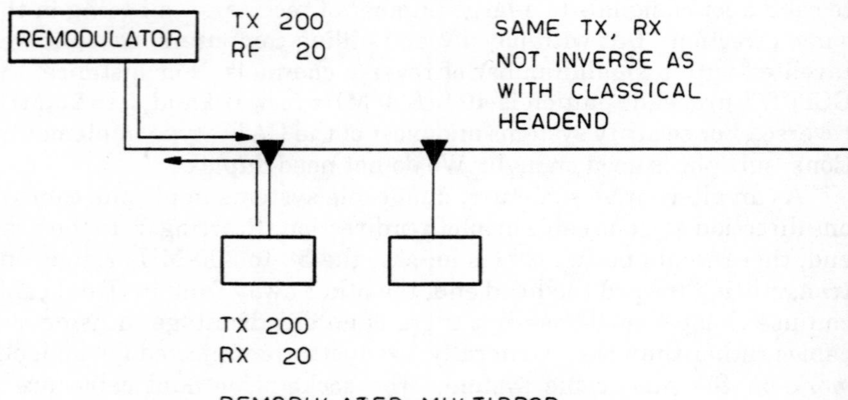

Figure 8.8 (A) Classical CATV and (B) local area network solutions.

low and RF high. With local area networks, at least with one solution (3M/IS), the remodulator at the head end and the station modems work with the same Tx, Rx (Figure 8.8b).

The remodulated multidrop approach is necessary to compensate for the fact that off-the-shelf CATV taps talk back to the system. Standard remodulator units can be employed. With Omninet and other LAN as a head end, 3M/IS uses the "450" remodulator, which generally works on many frequencies and costs about $1500. Figure 8.9 presents the 3M/IS broadband network with the "450" device as the head end. Attached to the "925" off-the-shelf modem is the file transfer gateway of the Nestar LAN. A 3270/SDLC protocol can be added to the interface to enable communication with mainframes attached to the broadband. Either implementation calls for some custom-made software. Baseband LAN manufacturers cooperate in developing the interconnection of their wares to the coaxial broadband network.

Most importantly, the technical solution makes feasible the interconnection of different baseband LANs and self-standing workstations through the RS-442 standard. The latter is assured through a bridge. The sockets necessary for implementing this approach are generalized. All modem aggregates come after the socket; they help make transparent which channel on the cable we use.

The interconnect approach through broadband cable which we are describing gives a welcome distance and topology independence, thus enhancing LAN capabilities:

- The real local area dedicated network will typically work baseband and serve distances up to 300 m.
- A broadband connection will act as a reasonable-cost, powerful gateway between different semicompatible LANs, assuring coverage of up to 10 km or even more.

Not only does piggybacking baseband on a broadband give distance and topology independence, but also the broadband itself can be seen as several basebands on the same physical support. This approach capitalizes on the cable TV technology which gives a valid transmission media without particular errors—making feasible the easy attachment of extra hardware, such as:

- TV cameras
- An alarm and monitoring system
- Modulators (with sound channel)
- Frequency translator at head end
- Normal TV sets for videotex

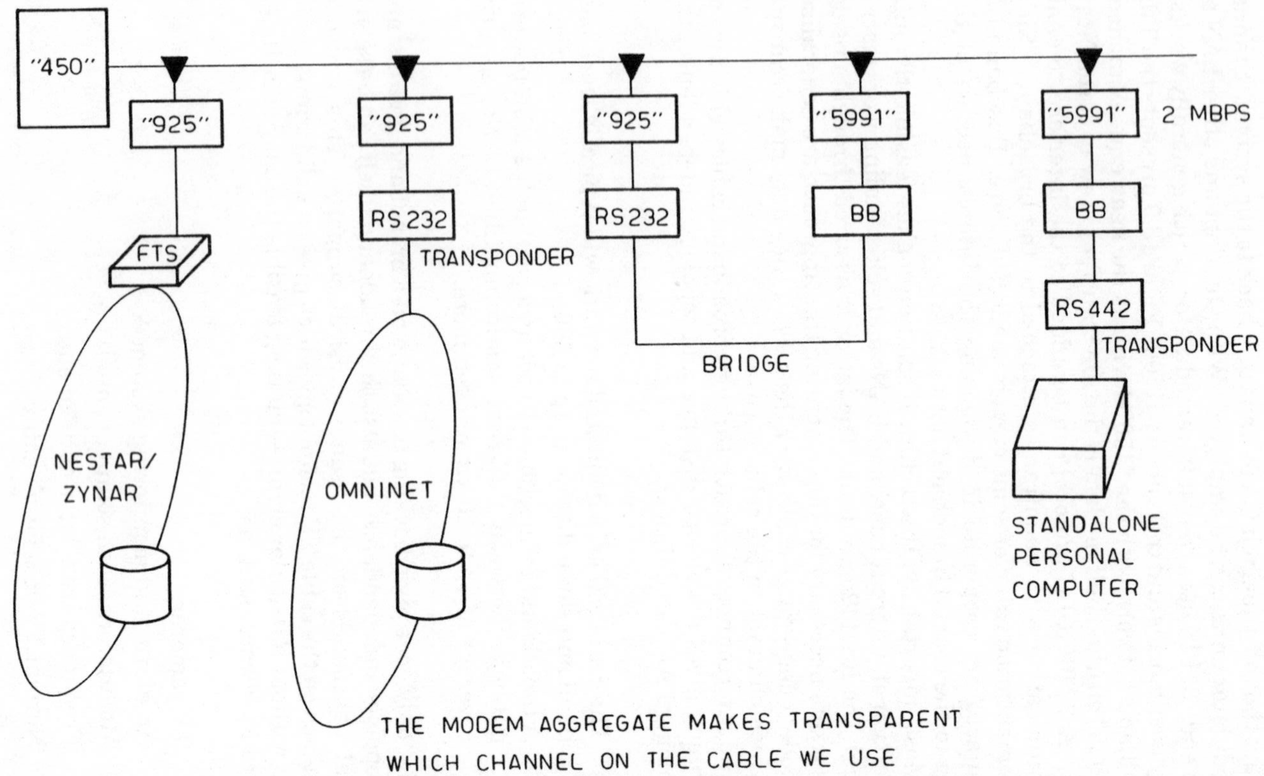

Figure 8.9 This 3M/IS implementation makes transparent which channel on the cable we use.

This range of services permits the integration of multimedia presentation solutions including the appropriate TV equipment at the broadband level—while the add-on baseband channels permit the interconnection of different baseband networks. Cable solutions which do not feature packets or network protocol other than RF transmission help in the latter case: if the baseband is Omninet, the broadbands will transmit Omninet packets; if it is SDLC, then SDLC packets; if X.25, the X.25 protocol. The broadband network is transparent to these requirements. It does not change the form or the data. It neither corrects nor introduces errors. Machine-level errors on broadband are said to stand at the 10^{-9} to 10^{-10} level or better.

Chapter

9

Bus Interface Unit and Control of the LAN

9.1 Introduction

A bus interface unit (BIU) is a local area network node to which other devices (WSs, servers) are attached via a standard communications interface. Typically, at the BIU level end-to-end transmission speeds are limited to those of the communications interface. A valid way of looking at the bus interface unit is as a package of software and hardware which is flexible and sometimes economical. Adaptation to specific user problems requires minimal effort and fits within the concept of modularity, expandability, and reliability.

Network control functions implemented in BIU hardware, software, and firmware are usually those of the physical and data link layers. The BIU translates signals for the node interface into form and format necessary for transmission over the carrier. It also drives the message over the medium, assures error detection, and provides power and ground isolation.

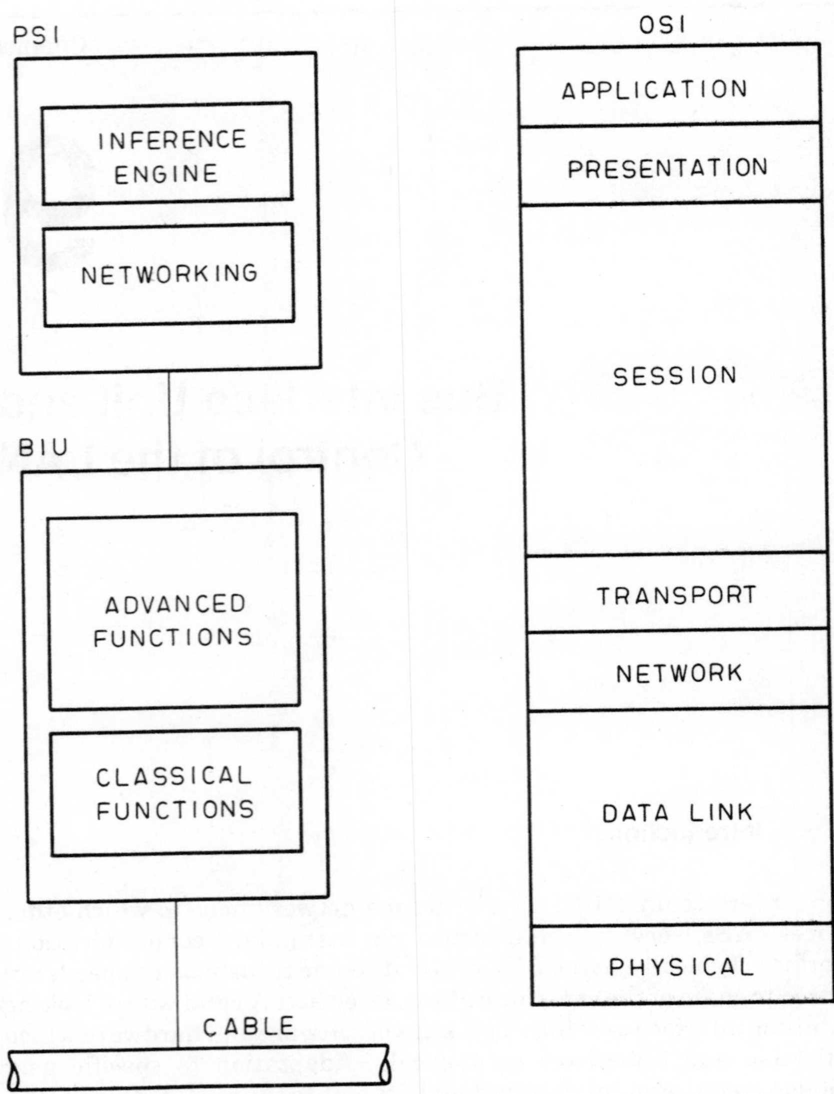

Figure 9.1 Positioning BIU functionality in the layered structure of ISO/OSI.

The BIU functions themselves are evolving. While originally they addressed themselves to level 2 of ISO/OSI, they tend to extend toward the higher-up layers. A good example of this is the interconnection through LAN of Japan's fifth generation computer known as a personal sequential inference (PSI) engine. The LAN connection aims to make the PSI a parallel machine. As Figure 9.1 demonstrates, the BIU is given functions well into session control (layer 5) of ISO/OSI.

The BIU receives information from the LAN and sends it to the attached WS. The latter also sends the BIU information which is channeled to the LAN. Once the data from the BIU is on the LAN cable, it moves at higher speeds, permitting more traffic during a given time than conventional point-to-point communications. Usually the BIU allows connections of any vendor's equipment that supports the standard interface. As such, it is a passive controller. The BIU will permit connection of all terminals and processors which support a standard communications interface to the LAN at any location convenient to the user. This reference concerns personal computers, minicomputers, front ends, and so on. Connectivity is assured through standard communications ports: RS-232C, RS-449, etc.

As the Japanese PSI shows, the functional capability of a BIU can vary from a simple transparent connection to an elaborate implementation of presentation control and terminal management. Ideally, the design of 802-controller hardware and software should enable implementation of a BIU by substitution of standard communication interfaces for the hardware and software support to the bus line.

9.2 Functions of the BIU

Whether we chose to apply baseband or broadband, we need an interface between the carrier and the attached devices. This interface may be:

- External, and in this case we speak of a bus interface unit (BIU)
- Internal to the attached device (PC, mini, front end), in which case reference is made to an integrated LAN controller

Generally, the BIU can be seen as the gateway between the socket domain and the user domain (Figure 9.2). The user domain features PCs or multimedia terminals. The socket domain includes communications and servers of all types.

Though the detailed functions of a BIU may vary from one LAN

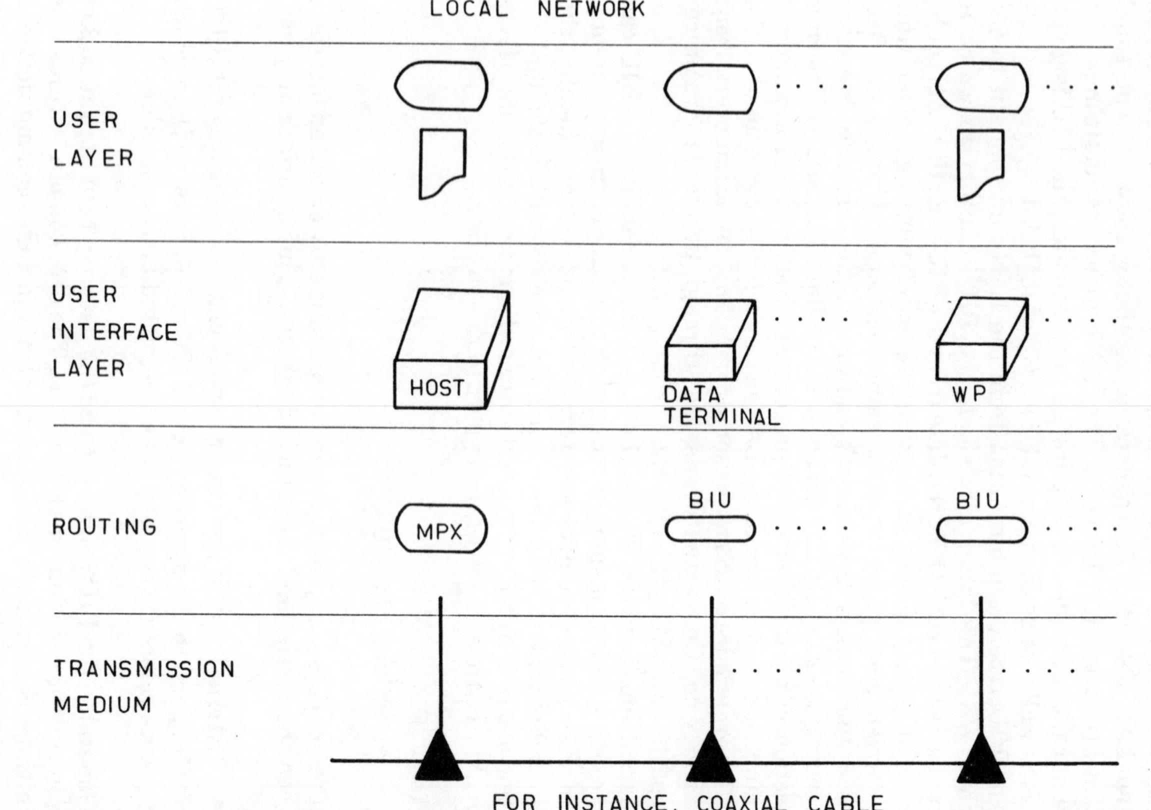

Figure 9.2 The bus interface unit is the routing engine of the LAN.

architecture to another, the control software of the LAN performs four basic functions:

1. Logical link control (LLC) services as described in the IEEE 802 standard.
2. Bus interface with LLC and access control to move data commands.
3. LAN adapter interface. LLC and access control to move data control information between the LAN controller and the LAN cable.
4. Administration and control functions pertinent to the LAN.

These functions should be implemented in a modular manner, with clean interfaces between communicating software to facilitate enhancement (or replacement) of supported facilities.

Architectural considerations should start from the fact that LAN architecture is a distributed operating system residing in the BIU. The logical functions of a BIU derive from this reference. In terms of protocol characteristics (See also Chapter 10):

- The MAC would be specialized by type of access protocol: token or CSMA.
- LLC is a standard service interface for level 2 and level 3 of ISO/OSI.

The goal of the LLC facility is to build a frame. It looks at this frame in deciding where to send it. This is independent of the access protocol, whether token of CSMA.

Not only the design of BIU but also the name of the device varies from one vendor to another: network interface unit (NIU), cable interface unit (CIU), communication interface unit (CIU), and so on. Nevertheless, its function is basically the same. The BIU integrate:

1. An RF modem for media access.
2. A microprocessor-based network control device, usually with random access memory (RAM).
3. A timer chip.
4. A status display.
5. A RAM buffer that functions in the supported workstations per BIU.

6. A microprocessor-based control of the user interface with its EPROM or live memory.
7. Serial I/O interface units (synchronous or asynchronous), for instance one per two ports.
8. The ports attached to this unit feature a physical standard such as RS-232, RS-449, parallel.

This is shown in Figure 9.3, which presents the bus interface unit for the 3M/IS local area network. The interface unit comes in three sizes with 2, 4, and 8 ports. The latter also offers RS-442 and RS-449 connections, plus a parallel port. Device no. 1 in this BIU is the RF modem. Device no. 2 is a vital subset of the unit. It performs the cyclic redundancy check (CRC), recognizes its own address, does serial-parallel conversion, and generally assures network interfacing.

Given this range of functions, in terms of data communications, a BIU assumes the role of a front end. Console commands permit operational activities, such as configuring local and remote ports, calling remote ports, disconnecting, returning to data mode, sending ASCII messages for a testing procedure, displaying statistics (held in the BIU's RAM), clearing statistics, and changing passwords. For a secure system, the BIU should be protected by password, particularly so in the case of remote configuration capability.

Depending on the system solution being given, an important device within a larger BIU configuration is the transceiver attached to the carrier. The transceiver can be internal or external to the BIU and it is responsible for:

- Putting out electrical signals
- Recognizing the traffic on cable

In essence, that is the basic function of the media access unit (MAU). In the broadband version of the modem, the MAU is essentially a transceiver. Baseband uses no modem because it is a digital connection—but it may need a transceiver for reasons explained in the following paragraph.

Transceiver cable interfaces which permit placing nodes at some distance from the coaxial cable are usually desirable. To make this possible, the transceiver taps directly into the cable, and a transceiver cable of up to 50 meters is run from this unit to the controller of the network node. Many LAN specifications describe the transceiver cable

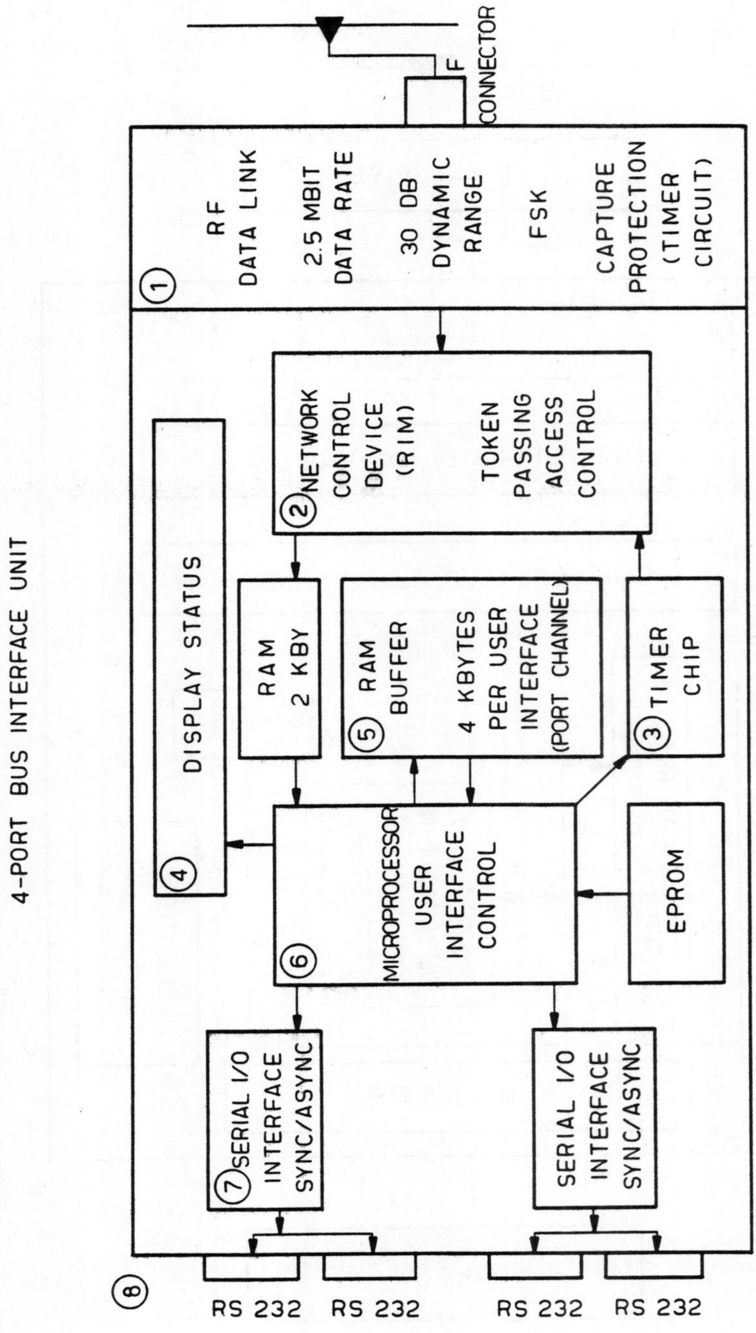

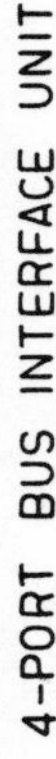

Figure 9.3 Component parts of the 3M/IS bus interface unit (BIU)

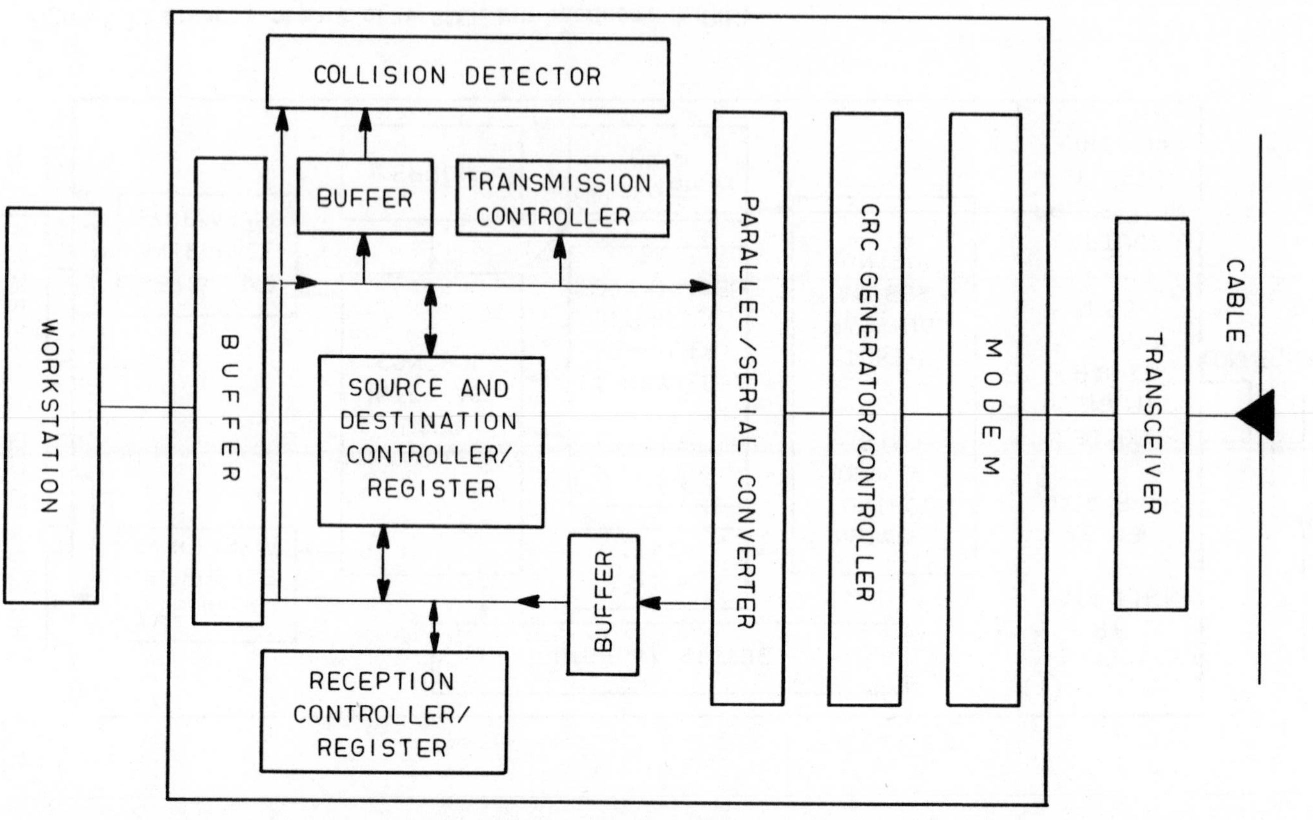

Figure 9.4 Interfacing the transceiver between the workstation and the LAN.

and its interface to assure compatibility when they are used. Ethernet is an example. However, a node can interface to the Ethernet cable without using a transceiver. Here, the transceiver cable is made up of four twisted pair wires, each of which carries one of four signals: transmit, receive, collision presence, and power. All this can be — and has been— put on a chip.

Figure 9.4 positions the transceiver between cable and BIU. It also gives another example of a BIU structure. Comparing Figures 9.3 and 9.4, we see that there are differences in their components and organization.

9.3 A Specific Example of a Bus Interface Structure

We will use ContelNet to examine the structure and functionality of a BIU. As a local area network, it offers four models: two baseband and two broadband, each operating at two different speeds. The four ContelNet networks use the same cable, a semirigid coax, 75 ohms. The models are for baseband: 702, at 2 MBPS, and 710, at 10 MBPS. Baseband has one single channel. By contrast, the broadband offerings each have four data channels, Model 802, at 2 MBPS; 810, at 10 MBPS. Both broadband models are CATV based. A BIU of 2 MBPS can be field upgraded to 10 MBPS. The access protocol is CSMA/CD. The vendor claims up to 5 miles of connecting links. One of the first installations was made at the American Stock Exchange.

Each ContelNet BIU controls four serial RS-232-C ports and a parallel port (8 or 16 bit) for mainframe communication. The BIU components are (Figure 9.5):

1. A Z80 microprocessor with RAM and ROM.
2. An RF modem or baseband cable driver.
3. A power supply.
4. A transceiver (for the 10-MBPS unit only).

The RAM associated with the microprocessor handles the network OS, the table entries, device port parameters, or the control block in the bus interface unit. The BIU software resident in EPROM consists of three components:

- Operating system (TICOS)
- Cable bus software

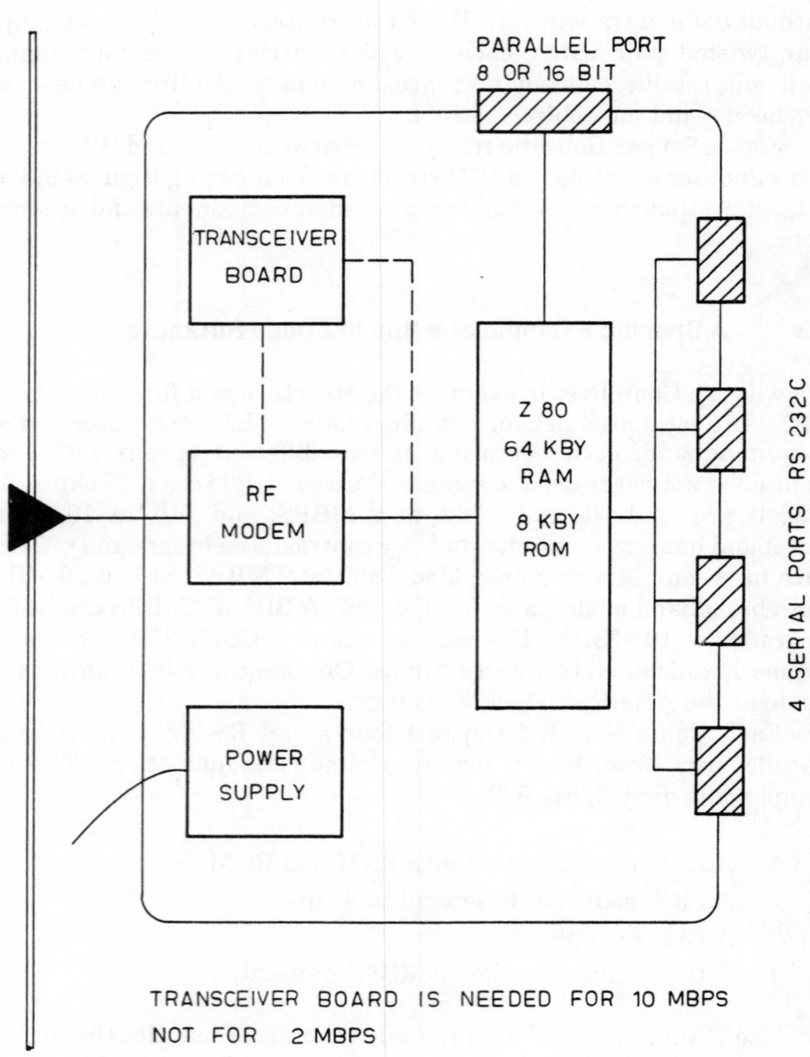

Figure 9.5 ContelNet BIU. Transceiver board is needed for 10 MBPS, not for 2MBPS.

- Support modules

TICOS is a real-time multitasking executive using a queue-driven architecture. The operating system is that of the network and must be designed to act as a resident in the bus interface unit. Ideally, it should be modular in structure (like the BIU hardware) and layered—therefore permitting system expansion through additional features without upsetting the aggregate. TICOS support modules provide for initialization, down-line loading, up-line dumping, online diagnosis for BIU, status reporting, error reporting and alarms, and network statistics. Software initializes the BIU hardware, the random access memory (RAM), and the OS.

Initialization also prepares the intelligent cable interface to accept a down-line load. The initialization software automatically executes following a power-on or BIU reset. The down-line loading software in each BIU enables any portion of RAM to be loaded from a network control center. The entire RAM resident program can be down-line loaded. Hardware enhancements to the BIU need to be supplemented by OS modules to support new features and product options. This is, for instance, the case with the file server, the different gateways, and the printer server. Features can be incorporated by adding printed circuit boards or by substitution of one board type for another. Network attached products such as a file server, print server, or protocol converter are based on the standard BIU with additional printed circuit boards.

The operating system is a real-time multitasking executive providing:

- Task schedule
- Buffer
- Queue
- Timer
- I/O management

Tasks are controlled through the use of task control blocks, which are manipulated using TICOS buffer and queue management. The "ready" queue and the various waiting queues are treated first in-first out with priority scheduling provided for bus and port I/O.

Queue management handles two forms of queues: buffer and task. Buffer queues are single-threaded lists of buffers. A buffer can be obtained from the head of a queue and returned to the end of a queue.

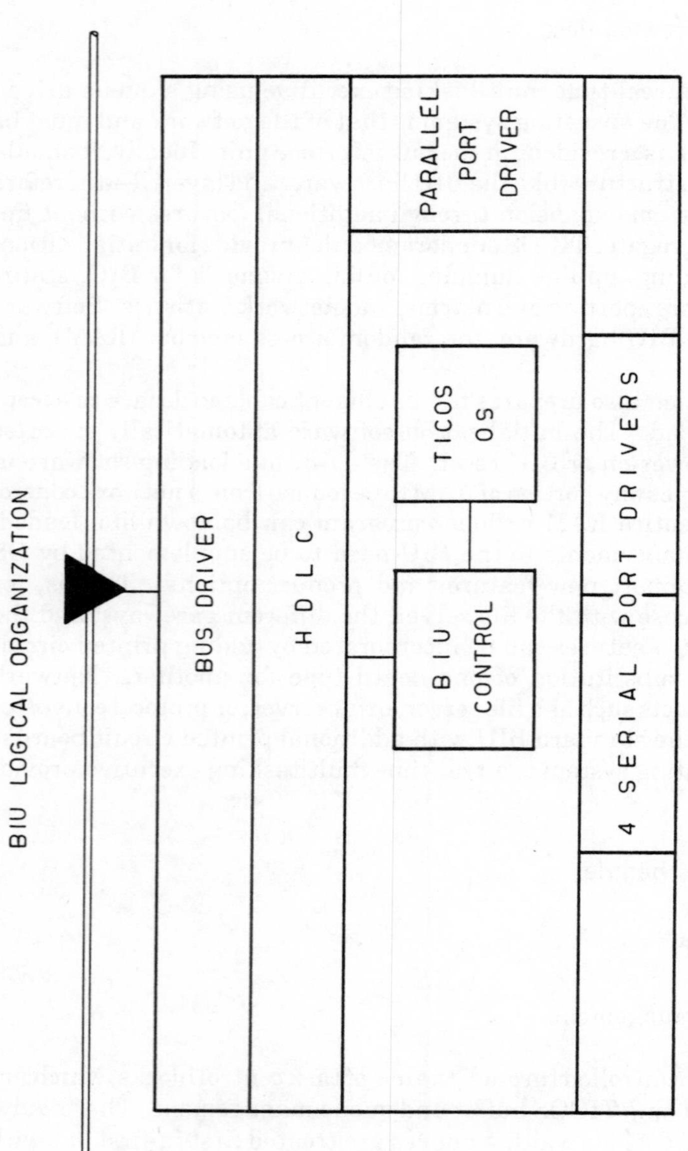

Figure 9.6 Drivers support: X.25 level 3 (Telenet), X.25 gateway, X.25 pad, SDLC/HDLC, VIP.

Task queues may also be of the buffer queue type or represent a queue of tasks waiting for the buffers. An enqueue and dequeue function is provided:

- Enqueue places an item in the resource buffer and awakens the top-most task enqueued in the task queue for that resource.
- Dequeue attempts to remove an item from a resource queue; if no item exists, the calling task is queued to the bottom of the associated task queue.

Hence, task queues act as queues of items, such as buffers, but also as semaphores. Queue management permits the contents of a buffer to be an information communication vehicle. Communication may occur between two tasks or between an interrupt process and an associated task.

The logical structure of the BIU is shown in Figure 9.6. The block diagram indentifies bus driver, data link protocol (HDLC), OS, and BIU control, as well as basic characteristics of the ports featured by the bus interface unit. The bus software uses a modified HDLC frame as the unit of transmission (bus frame). This differs from the HDLC frame in that both source and destination addresses are used. The frame format has been derived from the format developed by the AIEEE Project 802.

The system employs a CSMA/CD access protocol to enable the sharing of each cable channel by the bus interface units. In addition, it uses a link layer protocol similar to HDLC and based on the link protocol developed by the IEEE Local Network Standards Committee. Through a modified TICOS software, ContelNet can follow token protocol as an alternative to CSMA. We will further elaborate on the exchange of access protocols when we talk of the integrated network controller.

With ContelNet a BIU can be converted from baseband to broadband configuration by substituting the modem; it is converted from single channel to one capable of frequency division multiplexing. The baseband/broadband substitution can be done through a plug-in modem in the cable driver. The channel can also be changed from 2 to 10 MBPS through modem substitution and the addition of a transceiver (Figure 9.7). A transceiver board to be included in the BIU operates in conjunction with an RF modem supplied for broadband implementation. Modem substitution affects the speed of the device and not its frequency multiplexing characteristics (both higher- and lower-speed modems can be obtained off-the-shelf from CATV/RF applications).

A down-line loading facility permits the modification, addition, or

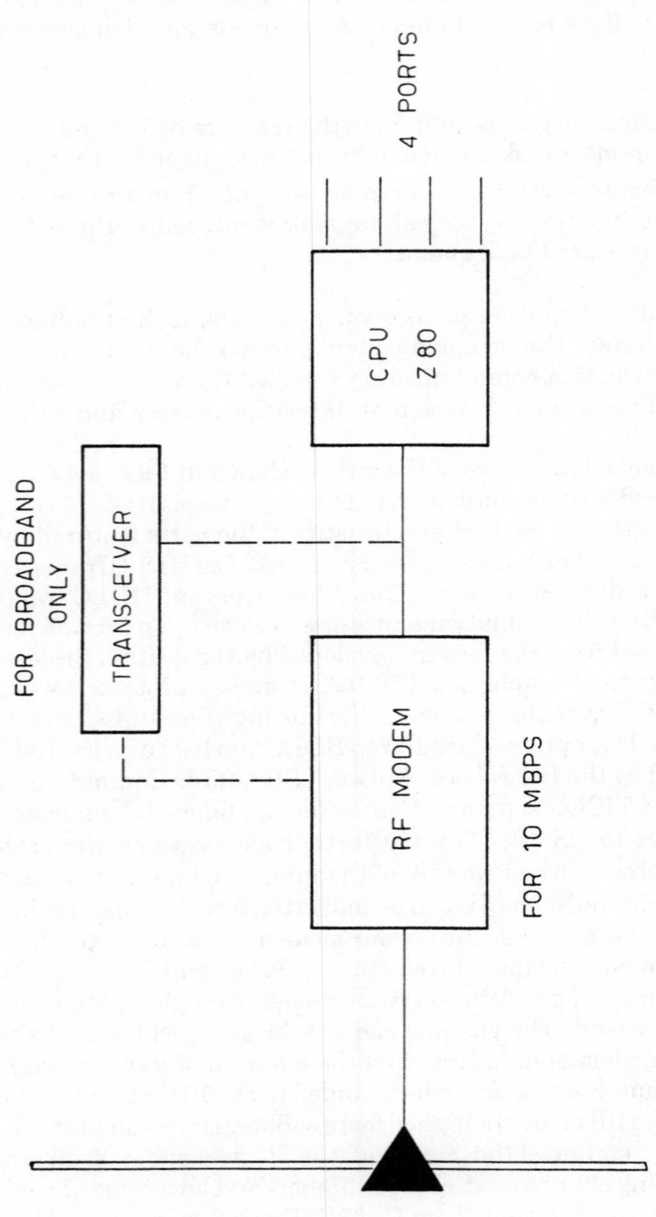

Figure 9.7 Converting from baseband to broadband through component modification.

deletion of data from instructions to table entries (an example can be found in the description of BIU port parameters), which can be done using table identification and entry number rather than an absolute memory address.

The bus interface units in the LAN can be down-line loaded as an aggregate by the network control center. This takes place simultaneously; therefore, at system initialization, the aggregate is rapidly brought online. In many architectures down-line loading frames for BIUs are sent unnumbered and therefore are not acknowledged by the receiving bus interface unit. If an error occurs during a down-line loading, the BIU detecting the error requests an individual load procedure. The up-line dump software in each BIU accepts commands from the NCC. These commands contain a list of BIU memory locations to be reported to the NCC. Such a report can be a one-time event, or periodic table entry numbers can be used to specify the data to be dumped. Errors include:

- Device port failures
- Device line or modem failures
- Device failures
- Device protocol problems
- Bus protocol anomalies

Status-reporting software periodically reports BIU status and statistics. It responds to status poll messages from the BIU. The system error reporting routines guarantee error reporting to the NCC.

A timer device provides two services:

1. Measurement of elapsed time.
2. Event timing.

The event timing routines are designed for ease and efficiency in cancelling or modifying event timers. The communications events normally timed, such as acknowledgment responses, usually occur within the prescribed time frame.

9.4 An Integrated LAN Controller

A LAN controller should be built from standard commercially available components. An important criterion for component selection should be

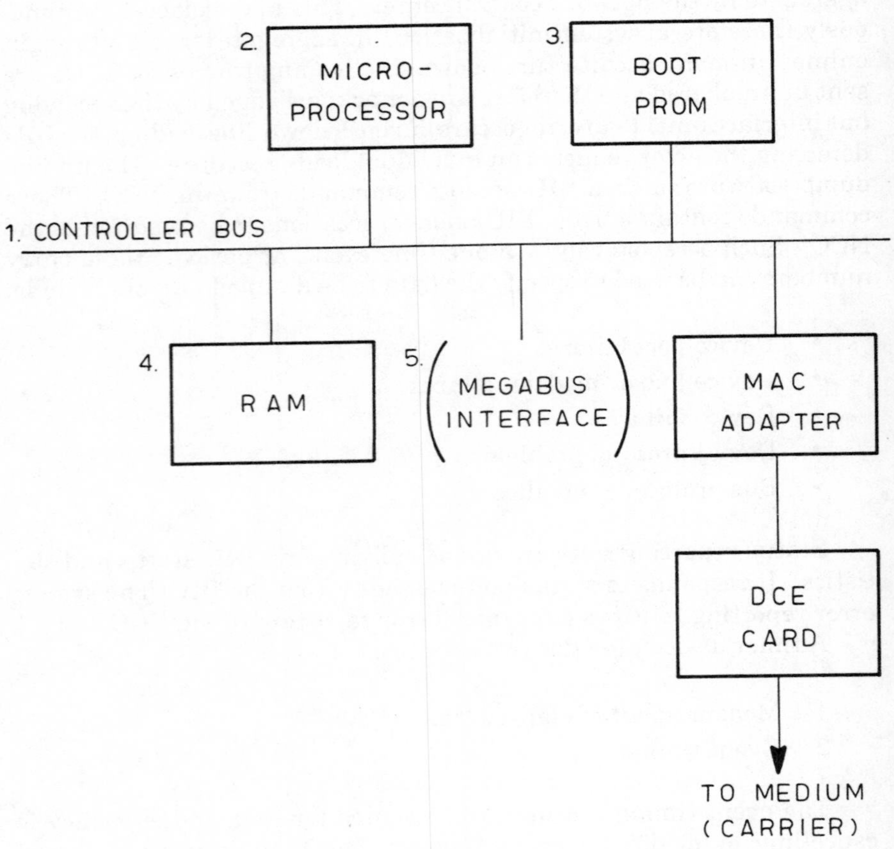

Figure 9.8 Functional representation of an AIEEE 802 LAN controller

future comparability with VLSI chips which implement the 802 standard media access protocols. Figure 9.8 shows a functional representation of the LAN controller; the following paragraphs describe hardware requirements for BIU components.

Let's start with the controller bus. All components at the BIU except the modem (DCE), which implements level 1 (physical control), are interconnected by a standard commercially available component bus compatible with the selected microprocessor. The MAC adapter and the megabus interface will appear as intelligent I/O controllers on the bus.

Software running on the unit's microprocessor will support the:

- 802 logical link control
- Megabus interface
- Software loading (in cooperation with the boot PROM)
- Other functions, such as statistics maintenance

The microprocessor to be selected must be able to execute the real-time OS and handle anticipated enhancements. There are advantages in choosing one of the widely used commercially available microprocessors, but not everybody agrees with this thesis.

The boot PROM is a permanent read-only memory provided as part of the microprocessor memory to support down-line loading of software to the RAM and dumping of random access memory. The boot PROM basically makes tests and talks to the host. Random access memory must be provided to accommodate:

- The microprocessor operating system
- The software processes required for operation of the controller
- Sufficient buffer space for maximum-size (4 kilobytes) data frames for input and output flow control

Some studies indicate that between 128 and 256 kilobytes of RAM are needed.

The megabus interface is, for all practical reasons, a special requirement. It is promoted by those manufacturers who want to anticipate nonmegabus applications, such as a bus interface unit or a front-end processor connected directly to a standard mainframe. The BIU connection calls for substituting a standard communications interface, such as an RS-232C for the megabus interface. Even if the functionality changes somewhat, a similar design is usable for the BIU by replacing the megabus interface with N RS-232Cs. However, too many RS-232Cs may cause the unit to run out of horsepower. (Some designers say that 10 to 12 outlets may be a reasonable number. This is, however, a software rather than a hardware problem.)

The MAC adapter implements an IEEE 802 media access control

protocol. Design requirements specify the bus protocol to be implemented in the MAC adapter. A versatile MAC adapter can be designed so that either a token bus or token ring protocol can be supported with the same hardware—the differences being handled by different firmware to drive the adapter. Just as important are the software requirements. The LAN controller includes a microprocessor; its principal purpose is to execute logical link control software as specified in the IEEE 802 standards. Such software, together with firmware in the LAN adapter (media access control), perform the OSI level 2 functions of link control.

Reference should also be made to the microprocessor operating system. If feasible, a standard commercially available multiprogramming real-time OS should be used to assure operating system services for the LAN control software. The principal criteria for selecting an OS are:

- Fast interrupt handling
- Context switching
- Availability of comprehensive software
- Facilities
- Steady software development

Facilities at the development site will include a macroassembler, a high-level language compiler, a text or program editor, a file system for program storage, a linker/loader, and a debugger for execution control. They should be executable through an interactive command processor.

The LAN control software should be implemented in a high-level language. Development should be facilitated through the use of structured programming disciplines. A measure of portability must be assured. The only exceptions to the requirement to use a high-level language are routines to access microprocessor functions not accessible through the HLL and to reimplement critical high-use routines to improve performance. The LAN controller and its software drivers should provide enough message frame buffer capacity to accommodate reasonable flow control requests either from its own software system or from another receiving station connected to the local area network. A LAN simulation facility should include three functional components:

- LAN controller
- Hardware and software system
- Cable system

This facility can be used for "what-if" analysis and for making LAN performance predictions.

The controller simulator should provide parameterized analysis of all major components of the controller to permit step-by-step evaluation of the controller design. Among the functions to be examined are:

1. Interconnection bandwidth (for instance, sufficient to fill the screen in less than 1 second.
2. Addressing capability to access the database, gateway, and any application or workstation.
3. Facility to bulk transfer data structures (document distribution and archiving, file transfer, and so on).
4. Ability to provide a single communications backbone that constitutes a flexible means to link resource stations—and to support a very wide range of transmission speeds with both asynchronous (up to 19.2 KBPS) and synchronous transmission.
5. Capacity to support varying requirements for a wide range of applications including standard data processing, word processing, decision support systems, and so on.
6. Systems reliability and maintainability.

Finally, the outlined requirements suggest certain packaging for the controller components. A design analysis made by one manufacturer has indicated that the packaging in Figure 9.9 is feasible. The controller consists of three field-replaceable components:

- A motherboard containing the microprocessor and its bus, the RAM, the boot PROM, and the megabus interface
- A daughterboard containing the MAC adapter
- A daughterboard or external unit with the modem card

In a front-end type of implementation, the motherboard performs HDLC-type functions so that the host does not need to do so.

9.5 Solution Selling and the BIU

Part of the Xerox 8000 Network system, the 873 BIU (called a commu-

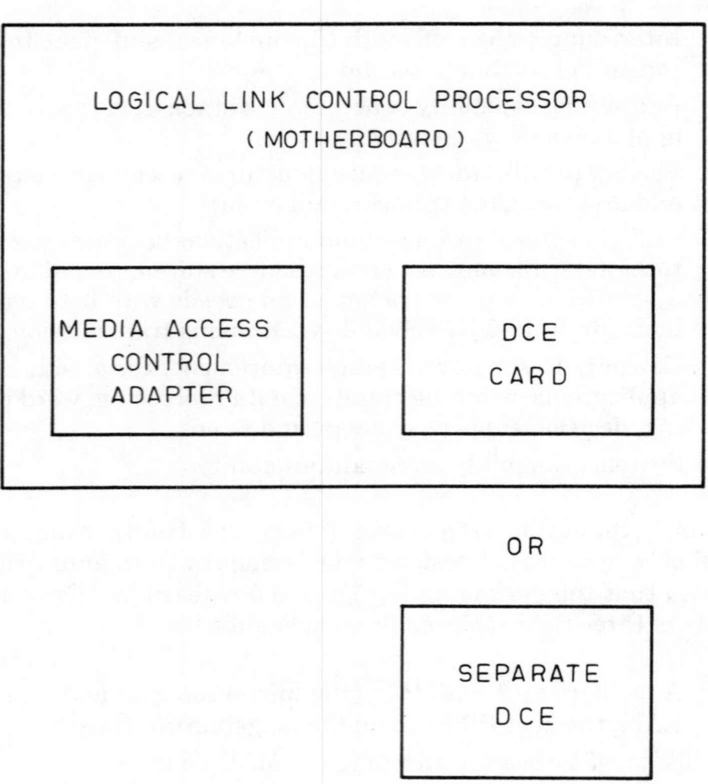

Figure 9.9 AIEEE 802 controller packaging.

nication interface unit) attaches to an Ethernet local area network and provides, as standard, four external RS-232-C communication ports. As an option, an additional four ports may be added. The operation of this BIU is controlled by software in either an 8030 series file server or an 8071 communication server. Such software communicates with the BIU through the Ethernet, thus leaving the port on the server itself free for other uses. Ports on the BIU may be used in:

1. Bit synchronous mode for internetwork routing which joins Ethernets over standard communication lines.
2. Asynchronous mode of TTY communications, permitting Ethernet users access to remote computer systems.
3. Interactive terminal service, permitting remote terminals or personal computers to attach to the Ethernet.

The appropriate packages must be configured in the controlling server in order to support these functions. Supported line speeds are up to 9600 bits per second, full duplex. Throughput of the BIU is 19.2 KBPS for each four-port board. Synchronous lines may be configured at speeds between 1.2 to 9.6 KBPS full duplex; asynchronous speeds range from 75 BPS to 9.6 KPBS. When more than one asynchronous port is configured on a board, all asynchronous line speeds for that board must fall into one of the seven established BPS ranges. The systems administrator has some further options available when configuring asynchronous ports.

Devices are connected to the network cable by transceivers and local drop cables. The latter are multicore twisted pairs, supplied in three lengths: 4.6, 9.2, and 18.4 meters. These lengths may be joined together, up to a maximum of 50 meters. Signals from a device pass along this cable and are placed on the network by the transceiver. Contention between devices attempting to transmit simultaneously is resolved by CSMA/CD, which we will examine in the chapter on protocols.

Thus, BIU solutions are specific to the LAN which we have chosen. Changes in LAN type made subsequent to BIU investments lead to a cancellation of such investments. Though this sounds evident if a baseband to broadband change is made, it is also true for a given baseband solution. Even within a given vendor's wares there are choices. Furthermore, the proper implementation of BIU functions is dependent on network configuration and design. In a network with centralized control, the BIU could be a simple modem that amplifies and modulates signals to their appropriate frequencies, creating a point-to-point connection between the node device and a central controller or switch.

When simple low-speed devices such as terminals and printers are connected to modems, the BIU can conform to industry standards (such as RS-232-C or CCITT V.24) in terms of physical connection and electrical interface. In such cases, the BIU might be a programmed interrupt-driven I/O interface. BIUs for more complex node devices, such as processors or mass storage peripherals, interact with vendor-specific network control software to implement the higher-level network functions. Such BIU hardware is designed specifically for the devices of a particular vendor and can be quite sophisticated. While BIU hardware and software will remain vendor-specific (even as standards develop for higher-level network functions), the network architects of the user organization should configure the nodes as single, addressable entities—thus assuring a local area network solution.

Economics should be an evident factor in making a LAN choice—and therefore a cable and BIU choice. This is valid not only in deciding between broadband and baseband but also between one of the two alternatives. On a per-attached-device basis, the baseband alternative is cheaper than broadband. Other things equal, a BIU on a chip and a BIU embedded into the WS or server are cheaper than alternative approaches. Embedded BIU typically come with baseband. There is also the cost of the tap to consider although, with the exception of optical fibers, this is minor. A tap is a device for physically connecting to the cable while disturbing its transmission characteristics as little as possible.

Figure 9.10 presents a comparison of BIU costs as a function of the supported communications band. However, because of technological advancements and VLSI, cost keeps changing; furthermore, cost comparisons are meaningful only for equal service rendered by the units under comparison.

Caution must also be taken in regard to reliability characteristics. A proper study will assure that likely failures in the BIU unit itself, the server, or the workstation do not result in pollution of the bus. Different mechanisms are provided for reducing the probability and cost of losing a packet; they include carrier detection, interference detection, packet error detection, truncated packet filtering, and collision consensus enforcement. In evaluating functional characteristics, it should be remembered that the BIU acts as a network controller for getting packets onto and out of the bus. For instance, when a source-detected collision occurs, it is the source controller's responsibility to generate a new random retransmission interval based on the updated collision count.

To review, the missions assigned to the bus interface unit, particularly those which it is generally able to perform are:

- Transmission (cable driving)
- Collision detection
- Reception and expediting of packets

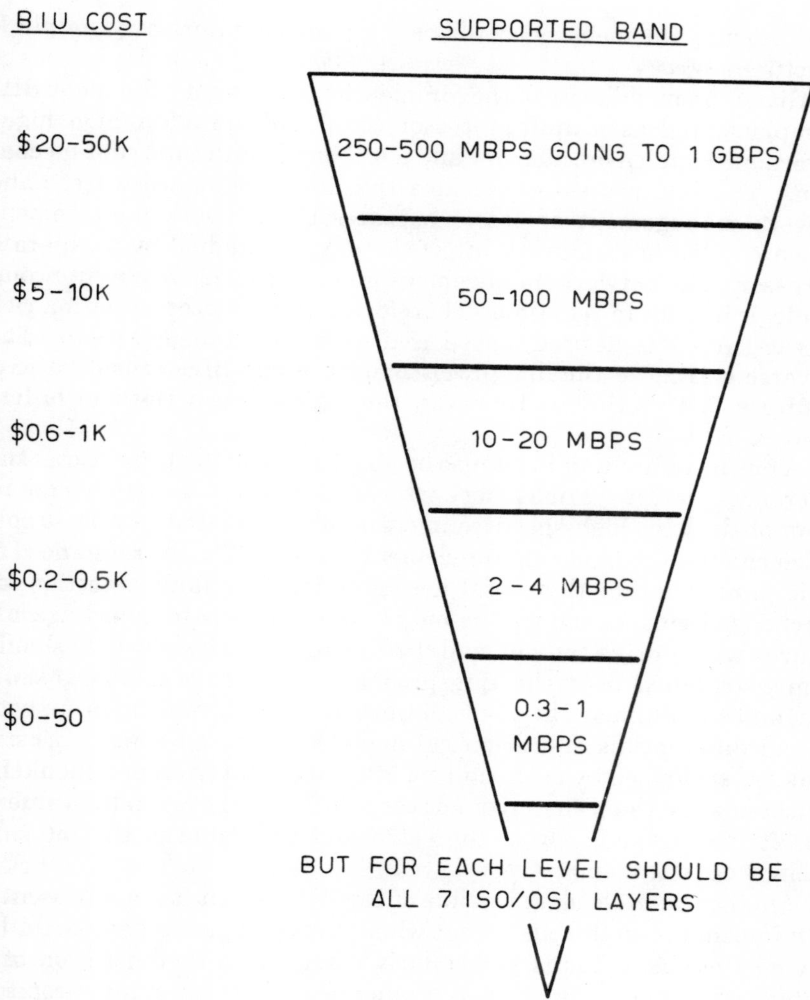

Figure 9.10 **Comparison of BIU costs as a function of supported communications band (just notice the difference).**

- Transceiver fault detection
- Power and ground isolation

Also, a key to the performance of the BIU is in the multiport memory. With multiple lines, a single port memory would soon become a bottleneck. Ideally, the memory should be multiported, interleaved, or block structured.

Given the modularity of the forementioned tasks, a polyvalent BIU is implemented as a multiprocessor connected via a common high-performance multiport memory and a low bandwidth interrupt mechanism. The line processor executes the line handler software. The network management processor executes the network management software. The host-network interface may be handled by a separate processor. The network management processor needs to execute complex logic but not in real time. Therefore, a microprocessor with a rich instruction set is desired; speed is a secondary consideration. The converse is true for the line processor. Here real-time considerations require a fast machine. However, the logic to be performed is less complex.

A bus interface unit must also be able to cope with ground potential differences at the various network attachments. Isolation can be accomplished by high-speed couplers and an isolated power supply which enables the major circuit elements of the BIU to be referenced to cable ground rather than local host ground. The fault detection, or watchdog circuit, examines the output of the driver to guard against failures which drive the bus and disrupt the network. A BIU should endure sustained direct shorting, proper termination of cable transmission, and simultaneous drive by all workstations. It must tolerate both ground differentials and electrical noise encountered when workstations are separated by as much as a kilometer. Interference should be indicated when the transceiver notices a difference between the value of the bit it is receiving from the cable and the value of the bit it is attempting to transmit.

Another basic design principle of the BIU is that it must present a high impedance to the bus except when it is transmitting and actually driving the bus. This is particularly essential to the operation of a contention bus network. The unit must be able to detect and properly receive signals from the most distant point on the bus. It must also be able to detect a colliding signal while its companion transmitter is itself driving the bus. This affects the choice of an encoding scheme for data transmitted on the bus. A number of data encoding schemes can be used, all of which require that the transmitter be able to place the transmission medium in two distinct states. If the BIU drives the cable to some voltage to represent one signaling state and represents the other signaling state by not driving the cable, the problem of overloaded drivers can be eliminated, and the task of collision detection simplified.

Collision detection is accomplished by looking at the bus during the transmitter's quiescent state. Any signal present during that time must come from another BIU and constitutes a collision.

9.6 Forward Error Protection

Developments in microelectronics make new technical solutions feasible. The new V.32 recommended standard by CCITT incorporates forward error correction (FEC) into what is likely to become the next generation of modems. FEC modules are getting cheaper, while their capabilities are being enhanced. They are able to improve the bit error rate performance of a transmission channel by three orders of magnitude without changes to the actual circuit.

Through forward error correction, the receiver reconstructs a data block where error bursts may have altered a hundred consecutive bits without retransmission from the sender. FEC works by processing a bit stream through a series of algorithms at the sender level prior to transmission. The bit sequence is rearranged, sometimes the binary values are changed, and extra bits are added to the original data block. This overhead is balanced by lack of retransmission. At the receiver end of the circuit, the corresponding FEC processor uses decoding algorithms after receiving the message. Control bits inserted at the transmitting end determine if the user block was received correctly. If not, the same bits serve to correct the errors.

Compared to the CRC used in ARQ (the code word for requesting retransmission) schemes, the FEC overhead as a percentage of its total bills is often much higher, but the improvement of the transmission lines saves the need for retransmission. That is why the force working against FEC is not in communications overhead but in the cost of modules to perform forward error correction. But this is changing. The cost of such equipment over the last 10 years has dropped by a factor of 10. As a result, applications that could have used FEC to improve channel performance, but which did not warrant the added cost, are now finding it affordable. For instance, FEC has been included as an integral part of specifications for CCITT's new dial-up modem. The forward error correction CCITT has adopted (Trellis coding) is improving channel quality so that a full-duplex 9.6-KBPS data rate can be accommodated. The recommended standard in the CCITT V.32 modem specification uses a code rate of 4/5: 1 redundant error checking bit is sent with every 4 user data bits. The bandwidth expansion (overhead) is 25 percent.

While forward error protection procedures are in the modem, other methods can be used for network-wide error. Data analyzers are applied in either active, semiactive, or passive. In the passive mode, they simply capture and store all online data. Keeping their buffers continuously full, they retain the most recent data and discard what came earlier. A semiactive data analyzer can be programmed to search for a specified character or bit stream. If the search is successful, it traps the specified sequences and alerts the operator, while also capturing the subsequent data. In the active mode, the data analyzer records and evaluates data but also transmits selected commands and responses into the network. With this capability it can emulate intelligent data terminal equipment or data circuit terminating equipment. The data analyzer can be used for both troubleshooting and development purposes. The operator or another machine exercises the analyzer's various options. Some data analyzers can display a fully decoded protocol. The latter provides ready identification of the frame architecture.

9.7 Very High-Frequency Switch

While the BIU is the interface between the carrier and the attached devices, other technological developments are in the process of changing the nature of the bus itself. The most interesting is the very high-frequency switch, the first of a range of features which will characterize smart carriers. Though the experimentation with very high-frequency switches is particularly focused on optical fibers, nothing excludes use of this technology with the coaxial cable LAN we have available today.

In any local or metropolitan area network, the addressable hub is the first element in the creation of automatic switching. The object is to allow a large number of channels at reasonable prices—well beyond the physical channels the media can support. Logical channels can be created through an addressable hub. In the case of CATV, such community-located receivers can be placed in a smart building installation to serve all offices or apartments or in a central building to supply a neighborhood area. In either case, the hub presents a radically different approach to cable-based services. Instead of constantly feeding all subscribers all channels, it sends only those channels the subscriber needs or calls for.

The implementation of very high-frequency switches rests on the continuing improvements in two-way communications, addressability, and picture scrambling. In itself, it is a manifestation in the evolution in cable technology which has grown from fixed channel video pipelines hooked directly to the VHF antenna terminals (of TV sets) to sophisticated systems requiring set-top converters to tune the signals. Applications requirements have pushed in this direction.

The addressable hub is a switching facility through which a practically unlimited number of channels can be made available without increasing the number of cables entering the subscriber's location. While, with the present day fixed channel solutions, doubling the channel capacity requires twice as many cables, the addressable hub sees to it that channel capacity increases only on the major trunk lines that lead to the hub. In metropolitan area solutions, the trunk can be an optical fiber and the distribution cable, a coax. This single cable from the hub into the office could deliver the one channel requested at a given time. The addressable hub can also create a two-way point-to-point video network: the wideband equivalent of the telephone system.

Within the network itself, the addressable entity can be identified by a unique digital code:

- At the local office level, the appropriate device continuously searches for its code within the unused scan lines.
- By transmitting individualized messages to each black box, a central computer can turn the switch on and off, as well as activate scramblers and descramblers.

What is more, within a smart system, the identity code(s) can be removed from the computer's list of authorized boxes on a programmed basis and, in addition to channel selection, the network can assure two-way services: from instant polling and videotext selection to full-blown voice and live image capabilities.

For instance, in the Times Fiber's system, fiber optic cable links the subscriber's wall unit to the basement hub. Such cable contains one fiber to send signals up to the apartment and another to carry them down, with the hub divided into three sections:

- A digital controller checks authorizations and provides control logic.
- A coaxial distribution network receives the cable signals from the 400-MHz trunks, then equalizes, amplifies, and divides the signals.
- Converter modules take these processed signals, demodulate

the cable channels according to subscriber requests, and convert the electrical signals into light waves for fiber optics transmission.

In this as in other implementations, the outputs are actually two-way lines that can receive messages from the subscribers as well as send programs. The subscribers input a channel request on a keypad. The hub checks the authorization for that channel and feeds it up. The cable into the subscriber's apartment carries only one channel at a time, at the same VHF.

Switched office networks would work in a similar manner. By offering subscribers every signal available on a common carrier basis, telcos and value-added networks can take advantage of this technology. A switched network would allow a wide choice in interactive services and would open up new implementation perspectives.

Chapter

10

Protocols and Multiple Access Methods

10.1 Introduction

A protocol is a rule of conduct which is necessary for shared, switched data communications services. Conceptually, the services are like the dial telephone network, except that the interconnected subscriber equipment consists of computers and computer terminals instead of telephone handsets. Switching centers and communications circuits are shared in the sense that all users have access to the same facilities on demand. The resources of a local area network are switched as calls can be routed to user points. Key to such allocation of resources is the line discipline established by the protocol and supported through its observance. Therefore the protocol must be a well-established procedure that is clearly understood by all parties.

Essentially, the protocol consists of a logical connection to the physical line of the carrier. Its observance enables the orderly exchange of information elements: data, text, image, voice, and commands. The procedure constitutes a predetermined dialogue be scrupulously maintained by both ends of a communications link. Line procedures provide for:

1. Contact including identification and synchronization (e.g., the creation of a virtual channel).
2. Transfer, which comprises not only transmission functions but also error detection and correction and the assurance of delivery of a message the protocol has received.

The access method is itself a protocol. It directly affects response time, reliability, cost, and other issues. A basic premise of LANs is the ability to effectively share allocated resources. Such sharing does not only happen at the data link level. It takes place at all layers of ISO/OSI.

The observance of protocol standards also means other benefits. It helps organizations acquire flexibility to choose the best equipment, organize their business in the way that best suits their own special needs, and harness new hardware and software developments without major upheavals.

10.2 Global Observance of Standard Protocols

In local area networks any-to-any connectivity is very attractive. The problem, however, is that it can also be topologically limited to a network's own domain. It can also be expensive. Yet interconnection flexibility is essential if networks are to deliver the business benefits management increasingly expects, which is why standard protocols are important. An integration picture of ISO/OSI and IEEE 802 standards are given in Figure 10.1.

Below flow control, everything is basically communications oriented; above it everything is OS dependent. For instance, session control marries the OS to the network and vice versa. It integrates computer to computer and includes address finding on the LAN. Presentation control performs data translation. Its protocols are the (now) standard graphic sets (North American Presentation Level Protocol, NA/PLP)—but there are also mail and file access protocols. Some are specialized to the particular application.

Network management actually occurs at all layers. This is the most difficult problem of all. It is really a systems problem which must be solved to improve performance. Network control monitors each layer and reports statistics. The business of network diagnosis is tricky. The

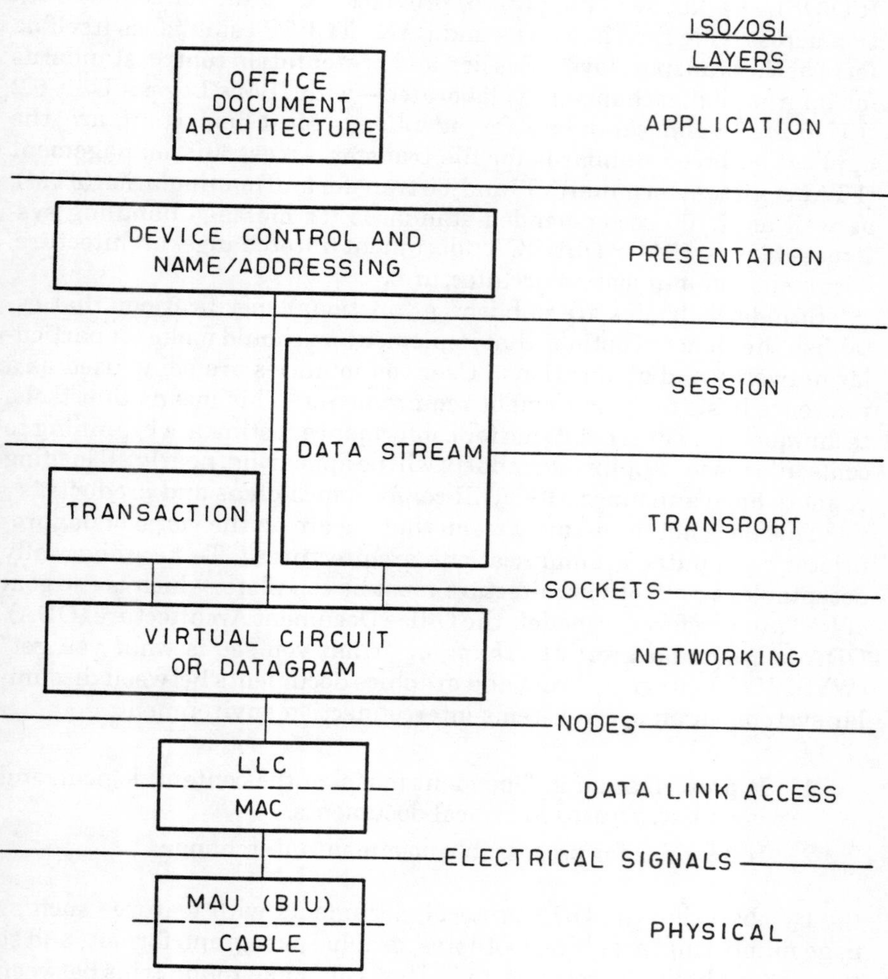

Figure 10.1 Layered protocol architecture for an open system with escape mechanism at every logical layer.

system must support loop backs to run tests. Still, without sophisticated mechanisms we cannot control the network.

While network control standards have not yet been established, a body of protocol standards starts emerging for the higher-up layers of ISO/OSI. Packet switching (X.25) provides standards for communication across wide area networks and LAN. TCP/IP establishes itself de facto at the transport layer. Session and presentation control standards for information exchange are elaborated—with IBM's Logical Unit 6.2 (LU 6.2) a valid candidate for adoption. Most important are the application layer standards for file transfer, access and management (FTAM), virtual terminal (VT) and job transfer and manipulation (JTM), as well as X.400 recommended standards for message handling systems—versus IBM's DIA/DCA (document interchange architecture, document communication architecture).

Standards bodies are publishing functional specifications that establish the choice of options that implementors should make for particular networks and applications. User communities are being used as a reference basis for procurement requirements. This means that tools, techniques, and organizations for conformance testing are beginning to come into place. Approved products will be appearing; nearly all leading vendors have announced ISO/OSI conformance plans and products.

This does not necessarily mean that we are on the verge of nonproprietary computer communications architectures. To be universally acceptable, a network architecture must be complete, which is the goal of ISO's new reference model: the Office Document Architecture (ODA). ODA is a standard for interchanging "what you see is what you get" (WYSIWYG) integrated text and graphics documents between dissimilar systems in an open systems interconnection environment:

1. It prescribes an independent model of the content, logical, and layout structures in typical documents.
2. It provides for processable document interchange.

By observing the ODA protocol, documents with features such as page numbering, graphics, footnotes, graphs, paragraph format, and so on, can be edited and reformatted. They can make round trips between systems without losing information the users did not intentionally delete.

ODA includes document processing, structural, and descriptive models. It features document classes, layout and logical structure, overview attributes, and styles. The content architecture addresses itself to character sets, raster graphics, and geometric graphics. There is a document profile and interchange format as well as interchange mechanisms and document specification language(s).

The ODA's aim is to provide a high-level protocol basis for text and graphics documents to be sent using MHS and FTAM. Increasing availability of X.400 MHS implementations and rapidly growing interest in FTAM illustrates the significance of these services, particularly when attribute qualifiers and defaulting mechanisms are specified; functional requirements, technical specifications, and attribute applicability are included.

While this chapter emphasizes the recommended standards for LAN at the data link level, knowledge of ongoing work at the higher ISO/OSI layers is always valuable. Increasingly we will need internetworking capabilities which have to be supported through the appropriate protocol solutions. This also applies to the availability of sophisticated information exchange services.

10.3 Protocols at the Data Link Level

At the data link (DL) level of ISO/OSI, we need a range of protocols to answer all our requirements. However, these protocols should be transparent to the higher-up layers. Furthermore, whichever protocol is used, the data link layer should assure information integrity. There is no absolute answer to the question: "Which may be the best data link protocol?" The choice should be made on the basis of the physical transmission media to be used and the acceptable level of BIU costs. A valid choice depends on channel capacity, bit error rates, and type of media.

It would be silly to use the data link protocol we need with satellites at the twisted pair level. But it would be just as irrational to stop at the DL level. A minimal requirement above the data link is adaptive routing. This permits the network to automatically configure itself in terms of channel availability, traffic saturation, and up-time characteristics. An end-to-end approach would assure sequencing and the handling or requests for retransmission and acknowledgments. A number of approaches (adaptive routing, adaptive path routing) came about because different architects have different ideas about how the network should be designed to run. Anybody can design a new protocol; the hard part is bringing the system together and making it work as one entity. This has been the goal of the IEEE 802 project. In it, the media access unit (MAU) corresponds to the physical level of ISO/OSI, and the media access control (MAC) is logical level and covers the lower half of the ISO/OSI data link layer.

The responsibility of the MAU is to facilitate the choice between broadband and baseband. To give them meaning, we must associate them with basic applications characteristics and systems functionality. In this sense a reference to bandwidth, as the key to high transmission speeds, becomes meaningful. When, for instance, we talk of integrating voice, image, text, and data on the same network, bandwidth becomes important.

But preoccupation with bandwidth alone is misplaced energy. It is the whole system we should be after—starting with data link control. Specific functions allocated to it include the sequencing of frames between two nodes attached to the network, along with appropriate recovery from transmission errors. Such functionality, as well as that of higher layers, is a controlling supplement to the transmission facilities of the LAN. Link connection functions include the specific encoding of digital information into electrical signals and also the generation and detection of delimiter fields. Such delimiters contain a sequence of signal elements that is unique compared to the sequence of signal elements occurring within the body of the frame. IBM's SDLC, for instance, employs the concept of 0-bit insertion within data to mask any possible false flag delimiters. The attachment of data processing nodes to a link also tends to include some type of circuit switching elements which can be taken as link connection capability.

- Link access functions regulate the transfer of data to the transmission facility.
- For some access mechanisms, information must be within the physical control field of the frame.
- A frame check sequence for error control is also appended to the data packet prior to transmission.

Upon receipt of a frame, the link access protocols perform appropriate validity checks. Dependent on protocols and topology, they may set flags in the modifier field. Furthermore, multiple appearances of data link control may exist within each data processing node. Each DL control appearance is logically associated with one other DL control appearance in another node. Each link is identified by the pair of addresses of the nodes at the ends of the logical link.

The amount of time a node can have the communications channel once access is gained is an allocation issue determined by the size of the message that is allowed or the size of the interval allotted to the node by the control node. Centrally controlled polling can be implemented in any topology, as well as in multipoint configurations. If there is a master station in the network, this master decides which node is to access the network at any one time. Once a node gains access to the channel, there are two possibilities for the course of a message from source to destination nodes:

1. Nodes could be required to send all messages to the master node, which routes them to their destination.
2. Nodes could forward messages directly to their destination.

The trend with LAN is distributed polling. Controlled access to the network is accomplished through distributed forms. For instance, each node could contain an internal timing mechanism synchronized with all other nodes. Each node would own an exclusive slot of time during which it could transmit. In this way, access conflicts could be avoided and control of access would be located in each node.

10.4 Token Passing and Carrier Sensing

The two most frequently discussed methods of distributed polling used in local area networks are token passing and slotted rings. Token passing is most often associated with ring topologies, although it has recently been applied to bus networks as well. In its distributed form, token passing is a mechanism whereby each device, in turn and in a predetermined order, receives and passes the right to use the channel. If there is master control (real or simulated), priority handling can be established through token passing. Tokens are special bit patterns or packets, usually several bits in length. They circulate around the ring (or bus) from node to node when there is no message traffic. Possession of the token gives a node exclusive access to the network for transmitting its message, thus avoiding conflict with other nodes that wish to transmit.

Slotted rings are another form of distributed polling. They employ a variation of token passing access control in ring networks. Usually a number of slots, or frames, of fixed size circulate around the ring. Each frame generally contains bits specified for source and destination addresses, control and parity information, and data. The frame check sequence is not necessarily a function of data link control. This type of checking is strongly dependent upon the transmission medium and its environment. It is a function of the DL control protocols for sequencing frames which have been selected.

An alternative to token passing is carrier sense multiple access. Carrier sense is the ability of each node to detect any traffic on the channel, called "listen before talking." Nodes defer transmitting when they sense that there is traffic on the channel. However, because of the time it takes for a signal to travel across the network (the propagation delay), two nodes could detect that the channel is free at the same time. In such a situation, a collision between the two messages will occur.

Multiple access is the sense of contention which theoretically permits better usage of available resources. However, when collisions happen, node transmissions overlap and interfere with one another. A node can experience a collision during its collision window—the time interval before the signal has had the chance to travel completely around the network. This round-trip propagation delay plus some internal delay is called the "slot time." Once the collision window has passed, the node is said to have acquired the channel, since all properly functioning nodes would have detected the carrier signal by that time and would have deferred transmitting.

Collisions are detected by nodes while they are transmitting by monitoring the energy level (i.e., the electrical signal level) of the channel (known as "listen while talking"). Message collisions change the energy level on the channel. Collision detection (CD) is the ability of the transmitting node to sense a change in the energy level of the channel and interpret it as a collision. The nodes also emit a short burst of noise, called a "jam," to assure that all other nodes involved have detected the collision.

To see to it that all nodes, including the one that is transmitting, are able to hear a collision on the channel, packets must be of a certain minimum length. That size has much to do with slot time. Since there is no predetermined order of access by nodes in CSMA/CD, there is no guarantee of a maximum wait time before getting access to the channel. However, given that each node randomly bids for the channel, a statistical guarantee can be calculated. In many local area network CSMA/CD implementations, the fair distribution of access to the network is combined with a high-speed high-bandwidth channel so that there is sufficient capacity available to allow access by any node at virtually any time.

An alternative protocol to CSMA/CD is CSMA/CA, in which CA

stands for collision avoidance. Its vendors claim that it is more reliable than CSMA/CD because each network node listens twice to the network before transmitting a packet, whereas with CD it listens only once. With CSMA/CA, after the node listens the first time and finds the line clear, it transmits a burst to notify other nodes of its intention to transmit a message. The node then listens again and if the line is still clear, it transmits. Should a collision still occur, back-off routines determine the time interval before a retransmission is attempted.

10.5 Multiple Access Methods

A choice among the alternative protocols should be made with specific goals in mind: work to be done, available work stations, real-time control requirements, and LAN solutions fitting our environment. Objectives are not independent and must be balanced to reach a valid technical and managerial solution. To keep cable lengths to a minimum, a pure serial interconnection of nodes would be appropriate. However, the costs associated with installing, maintaining, and reconfiguring such networks could be high. On the other hand, a pure star-type cabling scheme, where all nodes are cabled to a single concentration point, provides a reliable configuration.

A systems approach would take a network-wide view for the attachment of nodes to a common physical link, keeping in mind that the connectivity of such shared-access links has two aspects:

1. The physical connections achieved through propagation of electrical signals.
2. The logical connections established by the link protocols.

Both the logical and the physical topology should be any-to-any connectivity, the major benefit of which is the capability of a single node to broadcast information to all nodes, or a subset of all nodes, that are physically and logically attached to the link. The link access protocols to be employed should make extensive use of this capability.

Different access protocols can be employed for data link purposes, some being more popular than others. Among the better known are:

1. *Aloha*. With no carrier sensing but explicit ACK.
2. *CSMA*. With carrier sensing, multiple access capability.

3. *CSMA/CD*. With carrier sensing, collision detection, and abort if collision is detected.
4. *CSMA/CA*. Also carrier sensing but with a timing algorithm to provide collision avoidance.
5. *Token passing*. Explicit polling approach under central or peer-to-peer control.
6. *Demand assignment*. Through explicit reservation of time slots
7. *TDMA*. Through either explicit or implicit polling procedures based on time division.
8. *Spatial connectivity*. Exemplified through mesh or, even better, hypercube architecture.

Aloha provides one of the simpler strategies. Each port simply transmits as soon as it has a message to send. Two ports may transmit simultaneously, causing a collision. An error-detecting code is used by the receiver to detect collisions, and a back-off algorithm may then be used to retransmit unacknowledged messages. Aloha works well when traffic is light, but channel throughput falls to zero with even modest loads. For this reason, it is more suitable for exceptional transmission cases. A variation, slotted Aloha, is useful for long-distance broadcast networks, since none of the CSMAs works well when propagation delays exceed typical packet transmission times. Slotted Aloha has TDMA characteristics and the whole process is based on time division.

Carrier sense multiple access is a listen-before-talk protocol in which a port with a message to send checks to see if the channel is idle. If so, the message is transmitted: if it is active, the port defers to the current transmission. When the channel becomes idle, some back-off procedure may be employed to reduce the probability that two ports will transmit simultaneously. This procedure cannot really guarantee that collisions will not occur, but it may reduce the probability of one. The bus interface unit uses a collision-free CSMA arbitration protocol with resynchronizing messages to maintain clock synchronization after long idle periods. In other words, with carrier sense multiple access, prior to initiating transmission, a node senses whether or not a carrier signal is present. If so, another node is transmitting and the new transmission is delayed until the carrier signal is removed.

Once the transmission has started, the node continues to monitor the transmission for a collision—that is, destruction of the transmitted electrical signals, indicating the presence of another transmitting node.

If so, transmission is halted and the node waits either a random period of time before attempting to transmit again or waits for a predetermined (node specific) time interval.

One random access method for a ring topology is called "register insertion," in which a node on a ring can initiate a transmission whenever an idle state exists on the ring. A data packet received while the node is transmitting is held in a register by the node, awaiting transmission following the end of the current data packet.

By contrast, a controlled access mechanism can be employed on a bus (or on a ring). A specific digital signal grants permission to transmit to one data processing node at a time. As a result, the data packets from two different data processing nodes cannot interfere with each other. Responsibility for this special control signal can be centralized within one of the data processing nodes on the link, or it may be distributed to all nodes on the network.

In terms of competitive advantages, star configurations effectively handle broadcasting, as does a token bus. Broadcast media may be arbitrated by token passing. The port which receives the token may transmit one or more messages and then pass the token to the next port in a physical or logical ring. With it, steady-state operation is quite simple. Token arbitration is efficient for modest numbers of ports in the arbitration ring. However, lost token and duplicate token recovery are complex. Token bus systems frequently include some provisions for ports to dynamically enter or leave the logical arbitration ring. The resulting complexity of protocols and the delay time required for token processing are reasons for not using token passing in a large bandwidth network.

Spatial connectivity is a cost-effective method of connecting thousands of dual-port single-chip microprocessors into an information processing system. This is practically a network computer in that each network node is a chip containing memory and a pair of processors for tasks and input-output. Nodes are linked by shared communication buses, each conceptually spanning an N-dimensional M-wide hypercube. Each node shares two buses; each bus is shared by up to M nodes. The number of bus connections per node is fixed to satisfy chip pin limitations. Dual-bus hypercubes can be extended to large numbers of computers. As network size increases, connection costs increase only linearly with the number of nodes in the network. Average path lengths and total delays for nonclonal messages increase only as the logarithm of the existing nodes. This is by far a less costly approach than other interconnection schemes, but its implementation is just starting.

In all these cases, multiple access methods need control procedures. If there is a master station, it should look after ring clocking, token losses and duplicates, ring purging procedures, and station bypasses. The latter is typically centrally controlled (control by the master), but a network operating system could also support it in a distributed sense. Bus monitoring is important to detect token losses, establish if there are duplicates, and provide for virtual ring management. In a peer-to-peer system this is done by software in the nodes (BIU) which also administers the response window, senses the bus, detects collisions, and resolves contention problems.

To recapitulate, a class of access service can be CSMA/CD or token passing. CSMA is applicable with baseband. Token passing is used both with bus and ring topologies. The bus topology can be broadband (multichannel) or single channel. Ring topologies are mainly associated with single-channel implementation (baseband), but the physical medium can be either twisted pair or flexible coaxial cable.

10.6 Protocols Defined by IEEE 802

The data link is composed of two sublayers: the upper logical link control and the lower media access control. MAC calls for a protocol choice, which is somewhat linked to the decision made in the physical layer to use a bus or ring structure. Although, as we have seen, a large variety of protocols are available, everyone wants to see some order in this domain. This is the task the IEEE/Computer Group, Project 802, has thrust upon itself. The two main standard-type protocols that have been elaborated for the MAC sublayer are:

1. CSMA/CD. This standard is supported by Xerox, Intel, Digital Equipment (DIX). Typically used within a bus structure, CSMA sees to it that the stations listen to see if there is any traffic and, if not, they transmit. There is collision probability because two stations may find no traffic and transmit simultaneously. In this case, a collision detection mechanism indicates at the receiver level that a collision has happened.

Figure 10.2 shows the functionality of CSMA layers both at the data link level and in terms of infrastructure to be provided through MAU. In principle, this protocol is good for a large number of low-speed terminals; it is based on the principle that the WSs on the bus fit the protocol's capability. However, the use of high-speed units—such as printers—often leads to collisions.

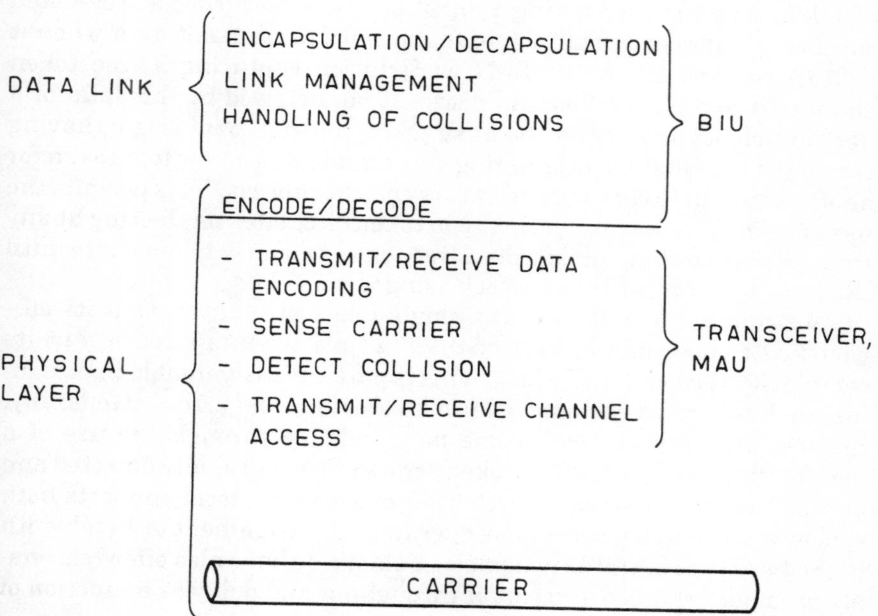

Figure 10.2 Functionality of CSMA layers at data link level; also of the physical structure.

Trying to speed up a LAN is not a valid approach. As the transmission speed increases, the overhead time required to resolve contention becomes relatively more important than the mean message transmission time if a carrier sense collision detection is used. For this and other reasons, it is not advisable to mix applications with different flow requirements. In a baseband environment, the application with the greater communications needs will take control of the cable, shutting off the other WSs.

2. Token passing. Token passing can work with a master-slave or a peer-to-peer solution. In a master-slave relationship, central network control handles the token. The master decides which attached workstation should speak next and then assigns this function to the corresponding party.

In the peer-to-peer case, the WS, which has the right to communicate, passes this right (token) on to another WS when The IBM version of token passing uses a ring control strategy featuring a free-token capture technique. A station gains the right to transmit data when it captures a free token. A LAN workstation capturing a free token changes it to a busy token and passes it on, followed by the data for a destination station. After the busy token returns to its origin, having traversed the ring, the originating station releases a new free token for another station to capture and to carry on the process. This permits the use of a single-token protocol, as one token circulates on the ring at any time. A station that transforms a free token to a busy token waits until the busy token returns before releasing a free token.

A primary advantage of the single-token strategy is that its efficiency is comparable to that of the multiple token approach, but its complexity is considerably less. This is particularly valuable in designing a robust priority scheme and in recovering from errors. Generally, the token operation can become more reliable through the use of a monitor function, with which token errors are more rapidly detected and automatically recovered. Furthermore, a ring protocol supports both synchronous and asynchronous operations. Assignment or bandwidth to the two types of traffic is flexible. Token solutions also offer reasonably good performance in terms of throughput and delay as a function of speed and distance.

There need be no relationship between which station next gains control and the physical location of a station. Therefore, this protocol is valid for real-time and process control-type operations. The architecture can assure that groups of stations are examined to see if there are any messages to transmit. Polling assumes that most of the time every station has a message. Once a WS begins to transmit successfully, it will empty its buffer of messages. These are broken up into packets up to a maximum size.

There could be other solutions than those defined by IEEE 802. One of the most prominent is the tree structure. It provides a distributed approach that runs through truth tables. Each workstation follows the communication going on in the line through two counters: top to bottom and left to right. By updating them whenever the next communication takes place, it is possible to reach the right conclusion on when to speak.

Another interconnecting approach which has been tried without exceptional success is the use of 3270 emulators for access to mainframes. In an IBM or compatible environment, for example, a user gets personal desktop computing power plus access to the host computer at the application level through a 3270 PC attachment.

10.7 Comparative Evaluation

As no solution is fool-proof, it is necessary to always provide for a control and recovery mechanism. At the same time, although it is nonsense to make a priori judgments about which protocol is best, it is possible to establish evaluation criteria:

1. Capability of handling various kinds of information.
2. High efficiency in response.
3. Short response time.
4. Wide service area and adaptation flexibility.
5. Ability to connect a large number of workstations—directly or through bridges.
6. Network expandability.
7. Low-cost interconnect requirements.
8. Packet length.
9. Frame header length.
10. Guard time length.
11. Turnaround time.
12. High noise immunity.
13. Immunity from domino effect (fail soft).
14. Failure isolation and online recovery.
15. Distributed bus access mechanism.
16. Distributed power source.

The software must support local event counting—collisions, message counts, messages sizes—in order to observe and control the communications traffic. Event counting has low overhead but information about the WS is not always coherent. An alternative is to attach a monitor as a passive node. This helps assure a coherent image through direct measurement of the elapsed time.

In many applications, a vital technical requirement is timeliness—guaranteed access delay and assured throughput. Another is robustness—both in terms of availability and of reliability. A third is flexibility, ranging from topology to technology and functionality. Still another is affordable costs—from installation to maintenance and upgrading. Such requirements are written from the knowledgeable user's viewpoint. It is not just the protocol but the network architecture which

Table 10.1 Comparison of Token Passing and CSMA

	Token Passing	*CSMA*
Centralized or semidistributed	X	
Distributed		X
Priority handling		X
No priority basis		X

Table 10.2 Evaluation in Terms of Geographical Dispersion

Protocol	*LAN solution*
CSMA/CSMA-CD	Passive baseband star
Token passing	Passive baseband or broadband bus
Demand assignment	Active ring or active star

should support them. Yet, the IEEE 802 level protocol has a key role to play:

1. As it covers the functionality of the data link level, it influences the type of network solution. Table 10.1 contrasts token passing to CSMA with respect to centralized versus distributed structure and the ability to handle priorities.
2. Each solution provides different perspectives in terms of active versus passive networking approaches. Table 10.2 elaborates on this argument, extending beyond CSMA and token passing.
3. Cost considerations should be seen as an integral part of the evaluation picture.

Chapter

11

Solutions in Baseband and Broadband Environments—Internetworking

11.1 Introduction

The cost-effectiveness of baseband (BAB) and broadband (BRB) solutions must be examined to establish guidelines for implementation. The bottom line is to avoid redundant effort. When we talk of high technology, where experience is still thin, anything short of a generic approach borders on superficiality. But a generic approach has many theoretical elements. Can we take a practical approach? However, without really knowing your problem, we can only made general recommendations:

- In a factory environment use broadband.
- In a limited office topology use baseband with a broadband

running through the building to interconnect the baseband networks.

This will resemble the model in Figure 11.1 with BRB as a backbone and BAB at the feeder LAN. Remember, though, that the key point in

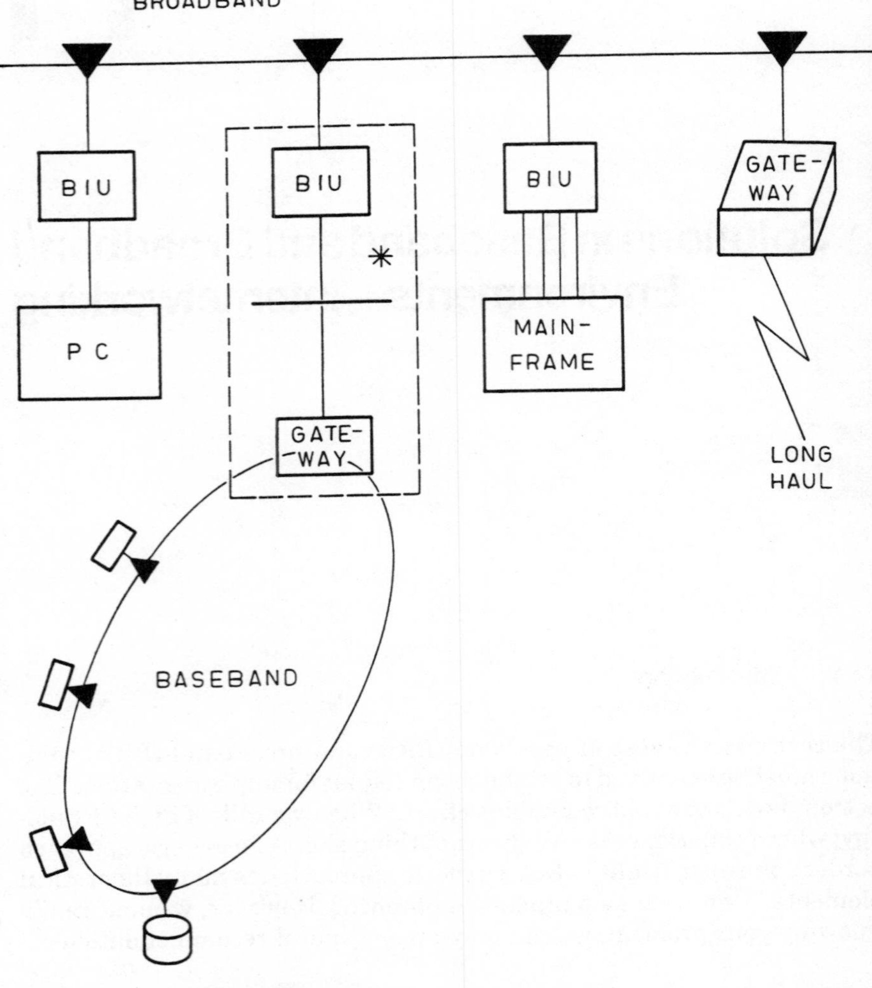

Figure 11.1 Using a broadband LAN as backbone and baseband LAN as feeder.

the decision on whether to use a BRB or BAB network is the definition of the tasks to be performed.

Highly related to this requirement is a changed way of thinking by the people who will do the choice, design, and final implementation. This is particularly true when the organization is moving from a mainframe-based concentration to a fully distributed environment. A wise decision strategy for any user will be:

1. Set objectives.
2. Study.
3. When you have the facts, think, evaluate.
4. Only then make commitments.

A fundamental approach will go beyond computer hardware and software. It will consider human resources and focus on the knowledge of applications as well as technical expertise.

The outcome of a careful study may be the definition of the system scope, functionality, and major entities and a conceptual model representing user requirements. Prototype modeling addresses this issue in an elegant fashion. Through prototyping, the application development team retains possession of the system until final user acceptance. It also experiments and provides improvements. Thus, the key issue is not BAB versus BRB but how our solution will be architectured.

11.2 Cost, Benefit, and the BAB and BRB Technologies

The technical solution of using the broadband to interconnect baseband systems serving local assignments presents a plethora of applications opportunities, causes an upward and downward integration of systems, and extends end-user communications capabilities. But while in LAN literature BAB and BRB have clear meanings, many variations must be evaluated. Some have acquired their own standing. An example is the use of the private branch exchange (PBX) as a complement or alternative to the LAN. Another, more recent, example is the emerging fiber distributed data interface (FDDI) recommended standard. It is promoted by optical fiber use on local area networks. Considerations should also be given to related design issues such as local network servers, network control, reliability, security, and expected benefits and pitfalls. This also applies to back-end and backbone applications which typically affect the planning of a local network in general and more precisely, network management.

The solutions we are after require a long, hard look at all factors in the LAN equation. Figure 11.2 suggests the important components: physical, logical, and supported facilities. Each needs a great deal of detail. In principle, an interconnect solution which is independent of specific protocols employed by the different LAN and which employes off-the-shelf modems as interface devices can assure:

1. Program and product transparency.
2. Greater network functionality.
3. Good price and performance ratios.

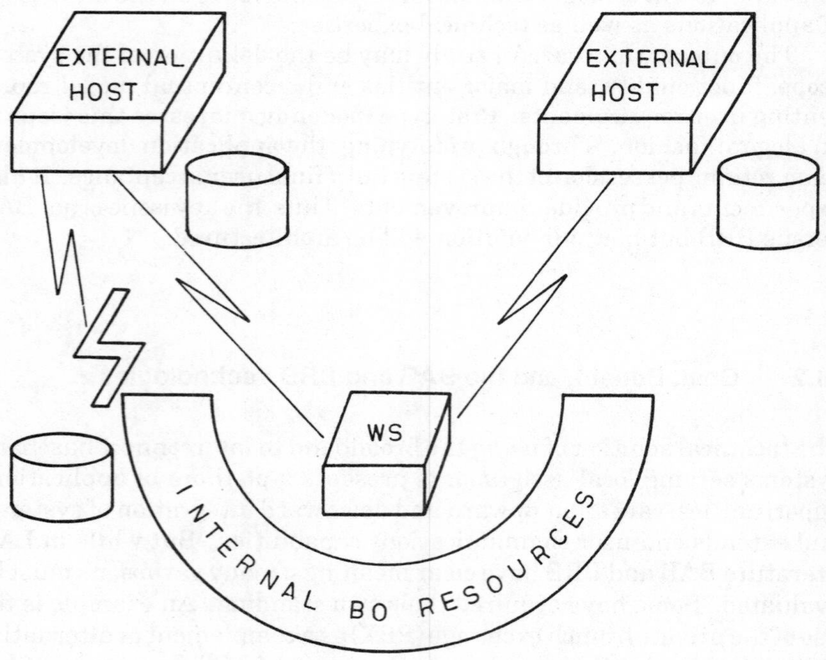

Figure 11.2 Physical, logical, and support facilities in an interconnected branch office (BO) system.

4. More innovations to user.
5. Modularity of upgradeable software products.

Only careful study can tell if this principle is applicable to our case. Once the best technical solution has been located, a legitimate question then becomes: What is the cost of this solution? And since with current market offerings baseband implementation costs stand at a lower level per workstation than BRB, the question practically boils down to the functionality and service of baseband connections in relation to our requirements. Correspondingly, the cost of the BRB implementation is related to the number of channels we will build in as a response to our communications requirements since this will determine if we can find what we need off the shelf. Currently, product line broadband manufacturers are very much oriented toward the larger computer center, office building, and bigger factory, which call for hardware different from that which will suffice for interconnecting a few WSs on a LAN.

Response time is another factor to examine. Delays may seem small in a universal sense but they get multiplied depending on the communications solution the LAN architecture has adopted. In a baseband LAN in which one workstation communicates with another through the file server, the message is unidirectional, but electrically the message goes to both directions (Figure 11.3a). Consider two workstations spaced 300 meters apart. Although logically the message goes only to the file server, the electrical delay in the cable makes both WSs think the cable is free and they transmit at the same time. The result is more collisions. This makes it necessary either to modify the protocol, and therefore alter it, or to provide emulator interfacing as in Figure 11.3b. This could, in principle, be provided through piggybacking a BAB or a BRB, which helps relieve the problem of increased collisions by extending the cable length beyond prescribed limits. However, it is only theoretical until proper implementation devices are provided and the approach is proven valid in our topology.

The point is that we cannot talk of costs until we have a solution that gives valid results. This means that we start with an overall technical projection and end up with a cost estimate. Then, as we work out the details, we have to revise that estimate—and sometimes change it completely. What we are really after is a cost and benefit analysis rather than just a cost figure. The benefit comes from the application. More frequently than not, it will reflect gains in management productivity. Organization-wide communications and subsecond response times can produce productivity improvements, and both are affected by the choice between BAB and BRB.

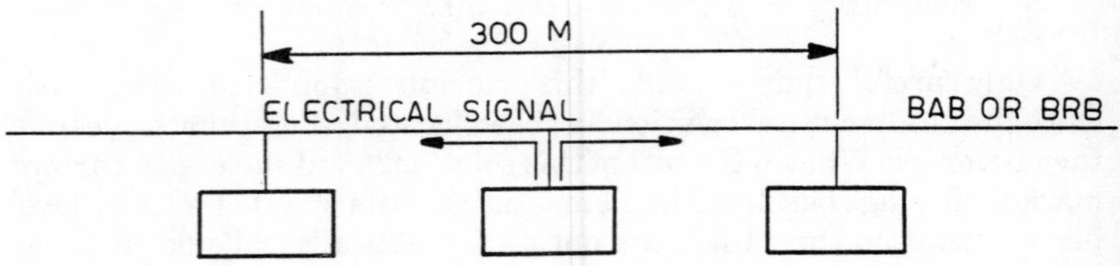

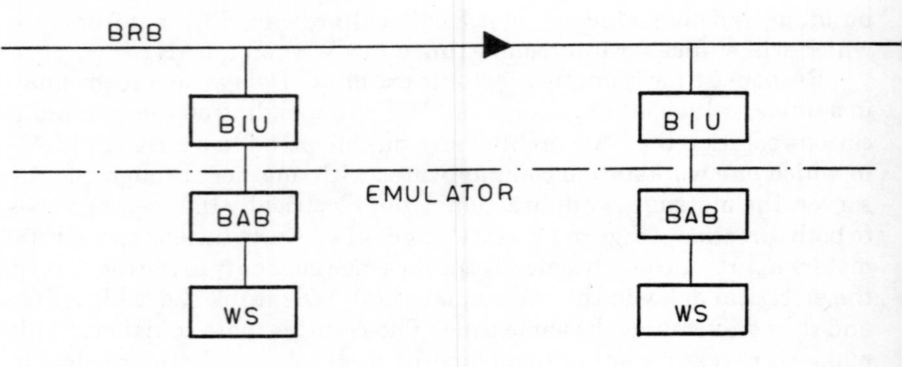

Figure 11.3 **(A) Provision of emulator interfacing. (B) Solution with local area interconnecting.**

11.3 Critical Aspects of LAN Communications

Provision of the proper interconnection capabilities can open vistas toward using remote diagnostic features, online program upgrading, fault tolerances, uninterrupted functioning through built-in system redundancies, and improved software and service support. However, beyond the technical setting, organizational, procedural, and system issues also have to be satisfied.

To enhance the wider use of interconnected personal computers aimed at management productivity and product quality improvement, financial institutions and industrial companies are setting up information centers in which the end user can:

- Try out equipment and / or software
- Become convinced of the usefulness of new technologies
- Receive training
- Obtain support
- Get internal maintenance service

Users who see beyond the limited aspects of their day-to-day functions are given more extensive training which includes:

- The principles of operatorless networks
- Electronic message services
- Ways and means for downloading software (through standard programs)
- The ability to perform access to remote databases (private or public)
- Procedures for database backup and recovery
- Automatic restart and recovery
- Fourth-generation language fundamentals
- Understanding of descriptions and instructions in packaged software
- Some training on assisting other users

With end users devoting their attention to the implementation problems regarding their level of operations, the computer specialists have more time to plan, design, develop, and install local area and remote networks. Among the system problems are workstation access to any connected resource, file access and subsequent transfer, global message exchange, and the observance of security and protection prerequisites. The benefit a user organization can derive from networked solutions can be found within this broader perspective. Time and again the policy of looking at the organization as a whole has proved itself against the alternative approach of considering departments individually without an overall plan for internetworking. An overall plan

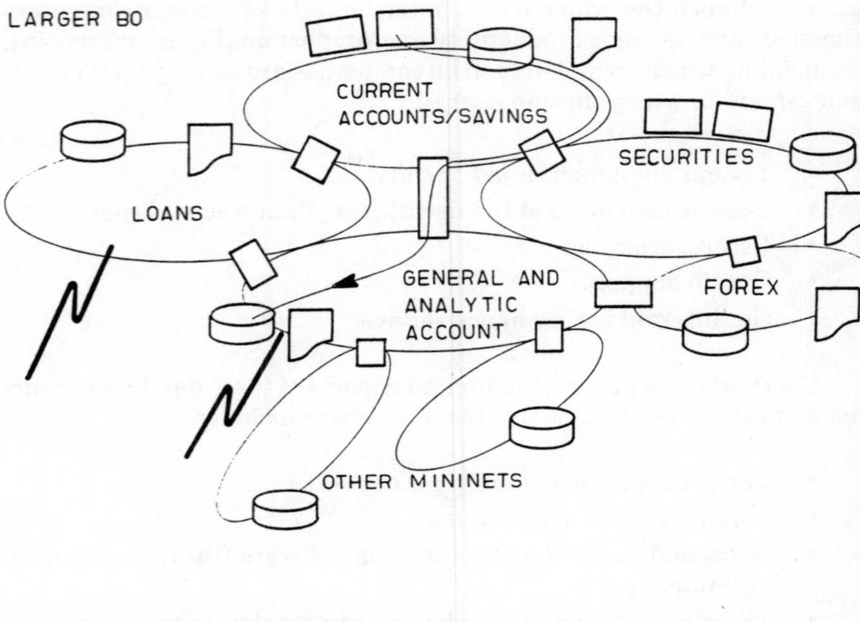

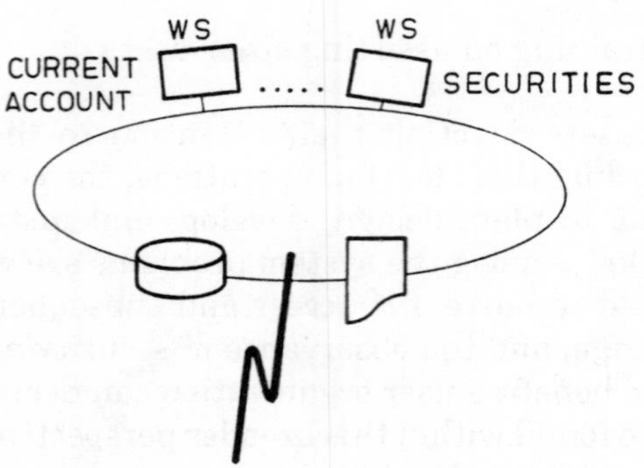

Figure 11.4 Branch office implementation with one or more local area networks.

gravitates toward broadband and high bandwidth, which is where organization-wide communications benefits are found. This does not exclude local feeder baseband LAN (Figure 11.4). The differences is that by first establishing the big picture, we offer ourselves a plan for evolution and integration. Ten key points highlight results which can be expected. They are:

1. The ability to build a flexible network for current and oncoming machines, interconnecting workstations, servers, and mainframes.

2. No cabling costs for the next years. The hardware for datacomm is embedded and has a large carrier capacity. Broadband channels are allocated through frequency division multiplexing (FDM). Bridges can be provided to link the FDM channels together, as Figure 11.5 suggests. This will still leave a high bandwidth available for expansion.

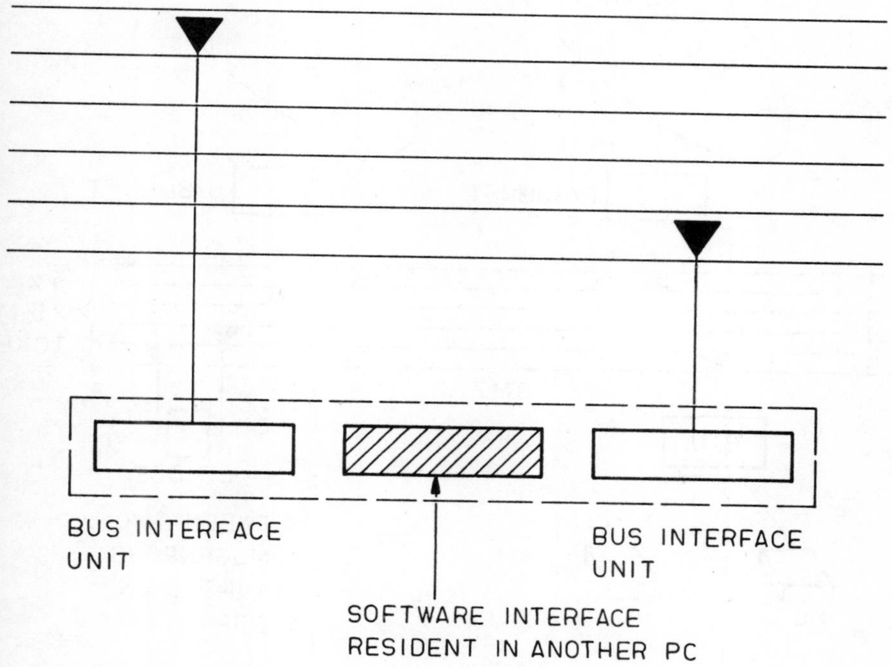

Figure 11.5 **Use of bridges to interconnect distinct bands of an FM cable.**

3. The BRB network is very reliable. It is almost exclusively passive (just one amplifier). Many installed BRB systems have demonstrated an MTBF of 200,000 hours.
4. When new software is developed for a specific application, it can be put on its own frequency. There is no multiplexing with the existing applications. This allows us to separate some of the things we do. It is also one of the advantages of peer-to-peer networking.

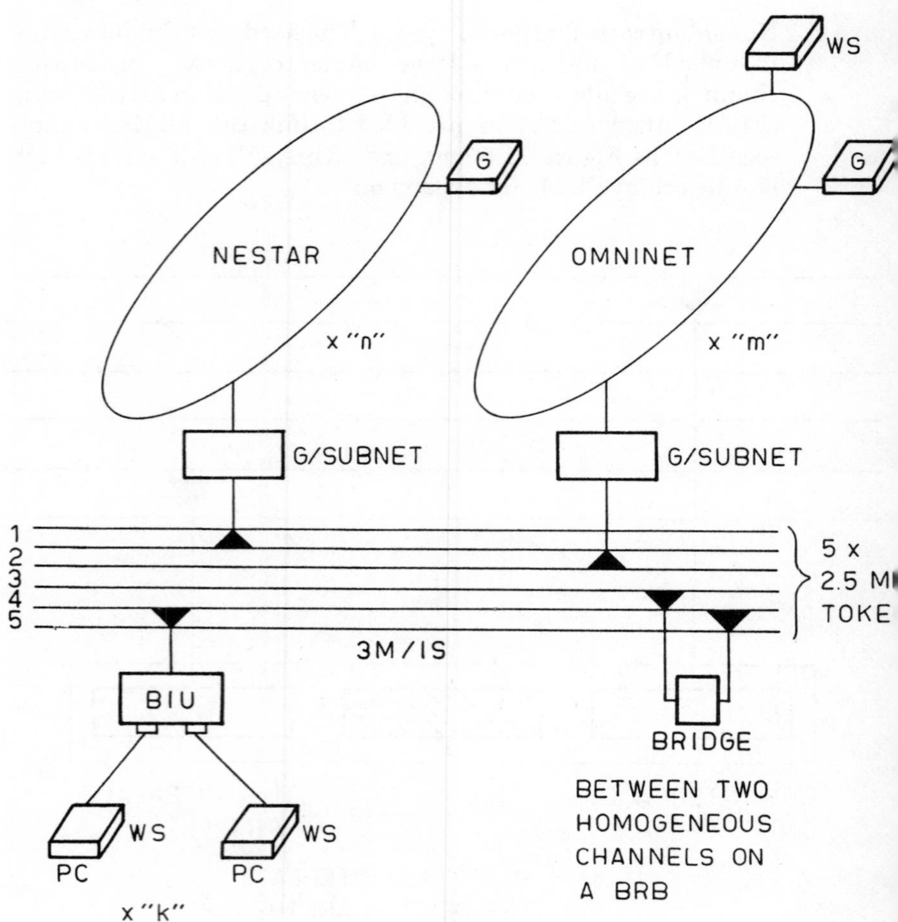

Figure 11.6 **Interconnecting baseband LANs through an FM broadband network.**

5. Security control can be integrated while running on a different type of computer. The overall security issue can also include a number of important applications such as cryptography. Other subjects can be incorporated, such as energy management—dedicating a personal computer by application to do the job.

6. It is always possible to use the broadband network for integrating diverse baseband LANs which might not have communicated with one another in a direct manner. Figure 11.6 demonstrates a solution in which both Nestar and Omninet baseband LANs were already installed and operating at different departments. Among other things the, broadband LAN served as integrator.

7. The system is extensible to further accommodate data communications and databasing—with access to other networks and to text and data warehouses supported by mainframes.

8. There is flexibility in design, depending on job requirements. If some of the clerical WSs are dedicated to data entry, it is useless to have a modem for each WS. We can use a baseband LAN or multithread. Generally, in a restricted area such as a small office with BAB, we can reach 300 meters; with multithread, 10 to 30 meters. The former is a preferable solution and we have seen how it can be attached to the broadband. In addition, a system solution would pay particular attention to choices regarding the interface unit. While for BRB this will be an external attachment, it is preferable for BAB to have the bus interface unit built in the PC rather than added on through a slot, which costs money. Options are shown in Figure 11.7.

9. The ability to add on different baseband architectures and provide gateways is retained. This helps solve the problem of orderly progression toward more complex information systems.

10. With proper planning, we gain speed of action. The BRB network is reasonable fast to build, getting off-the-shelf most of the needed equipment to start working. This includes coaxial cable, taps, and fixtures. Some modems have a 90-day delivery—bus standard units (like MUX) take a shorter time.

These implementation highlights are based on a variety of experiences. Still, while an applications environment looks straightforward, there may be problems in it that require particular attention.

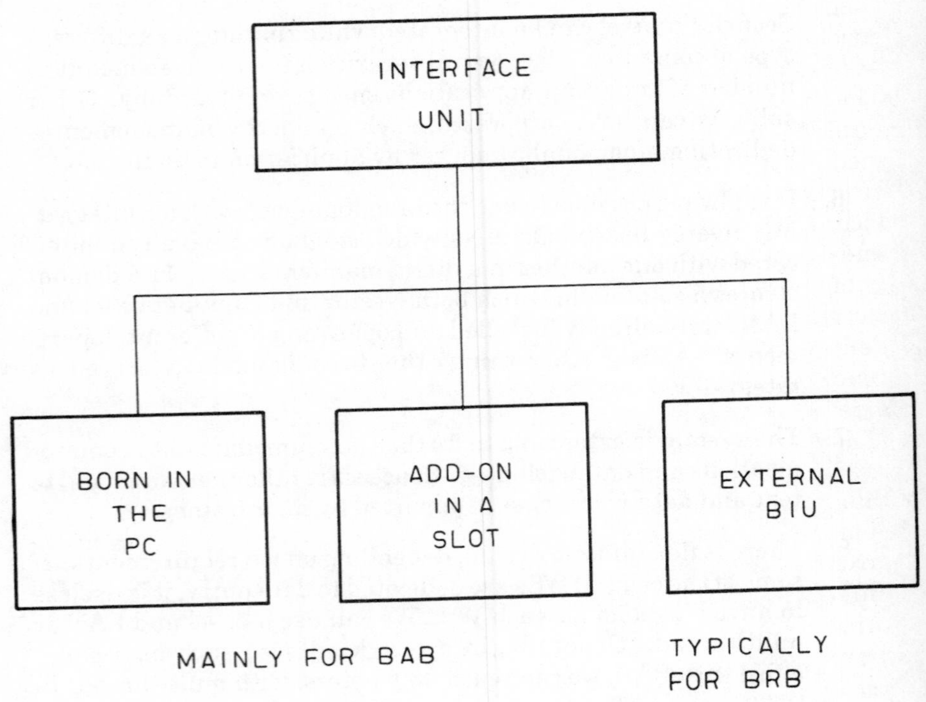

Figure 11.7 An internal BIU has one port. An external BIU may have two, three, four, or eight ports.

11.4 Prototyping and Experimentation for LAN Design

With prototypes we can experiment with technical solutions, evaluate results to be expected, make educated guesses on costs and benefits, check the validity of a global solution, convert some original coarse grain specifications into internal representations. decompose, optimize, and verify the developing design, and lead to the derivation of needed details, The prototype is a representation of the real world. Within limits, it permits us to activate the communication network link together intermediate results, resolve data incompatibilities, and evaluate the wisdom of predecisions critical to LAN performance. The prototype may also focus on specific, rather than global, aspects, such as user applications and query handling functions, distributed concurrency control, or distributed communications interfaces. But it may also be a global optimization verifier or a means of assuring conformity to original LAN definition. Or a prototype could be constructed to help evaluate concurrency control on the LAN or to examine a distributed deadlock problem. A recovery system could be embedded in the model to preserve integrity of data after restart from, say, data access conflict.

In all these examples, prototyping provides the designer with more than an observation of executable specifications. For this reason, it is being increasingly used in development. It offers the benefits of early error detection for less investment and retraining—but there are many different approaches to prototyping. One of the best methodologies is a three-level approach (Figure 11.8) based on:

- Idealization
- Concretization
- Prototyping proper

In the idealization step, the designer identifies the objects of interest in the LAN and the operations necessary to support the tasks identified for the system. At this stage the main concern is to identify in an idealized (abstract) form the objects and operations required. These give the designer a vocabulary with which to plan development. Subsequently, in the concretization step, the informal idealized model is formally specified. Objects are constructed from mathematical types or in physical terms. Operations are defined explicitly in underlying mathematical notation, with linking for sequences. By insisting on a formal, mathematical presentation, this level reveals the ambiguities and inconsistencies present in the conceptual model. The resulting specification forms the prototype itself, allowing the designer to validate the structure through testing and experimentation. A significant class of errors revealed by this process is that of omissions—facilities necessary or desirable but overlooked in the original concept. Validation can

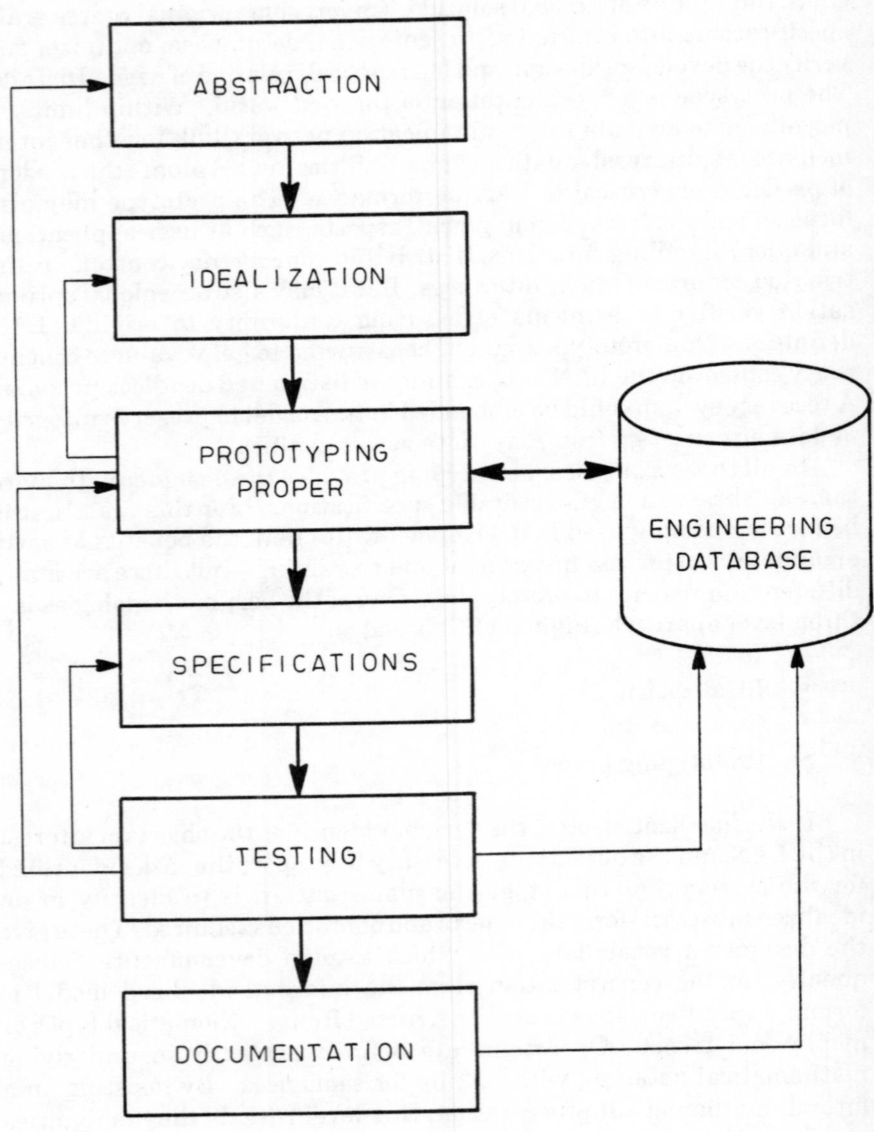

Figure 11.8 Idealization, concretization, and prototyping in an experimental system.

be a source of new ideas as well as a means of correcting the design. The prototype itself is a working model. As such, it provides ways for exploring areas of uncertainty in LAN design.

Common to most prototypes is the requirement that they should be constructed quickly to give timely feedback. Such help is a reflection of the fact that, as a working system, the prototype is capable of providing its user with a tentative system for experimental purposes which can evolve into a production system. Prototypes can also be used for gradual evolution into a production version. System prototypes can be helped by fourth- and fifth-generation languages that integrate system modeling tools and automated application code generators for procedural specifications. This means that current prototyping tools are expected to merge with artificial intelligence (AI). This would allow the design of a system on the conceptual level, relegating the steps of logical and physical design to an expert system.

Enriched with computer aided design (CAD) tools and making use of an engineering database, such an approach will revolutionize the complete cycle of technical development. Hybrid systems will combine conventional and AI-generated modules into a working model of much greater power than those currently available. CAD workstations provide a graphics and documentation facility for representation of logical models. At the level of the engineering database, the integrated data dictionary defines and controls the integrity of objects and relationships characterizing the development environment, hardware, software, and human resources.

Through CAD and AI constructs, the designer validates and balances plans and benefits from graphical images, the test of system specifications, project management capabilities, and technical and training documentation. The designer can also verify consistent implementation of standards and procedures, balancing design solutions to reach goals. From prototyping to final design and subsequent maintenance, CAD makes feasible an integrated framework able to increase development productivity and achieve a reliable, quality system. Computer-based methodologies and technologies serve equally well as a learning aid, assist the thinking process, help in a representation, and make it possible to clarify the abstract nature of many systems. In short, they are invaluable aids in LAN development.

Successful prototyping can also offer other advantages. For example, it increases user's satisfaction since the system can be preoperated, attacking problems of complexity with a higher degree of certainty. Particularly in the context of software development for LAN and workstations, prototyping provides the basis for an inexpensive portfolio of reusable modules while increasing user participation. Prototyping reduces the communication gap between analysts and users. It can also become a decision support facility for analysis of ad hoc requests and what-if scenarios.

Technical experimentation helps to improve planning and hedges against common system development risks, which find justification in the enforcement of methodological procedures and standards in an automated environment. This facilitates planning, controlling, and developing a design project.

11.5 Protocols for System Interconnection — Considerations on X.25

Protocols that control communication on a LAN can be designed with the explicit intention that messages are exchanges between the LAN and the long haul. This approach is usually missing from the addressing and control structure of a computer bus. Networks usually transmit variable-size messages; buses often transfer single, fixed-size words. Depending on the LAN architecture, a bus often has a specialized interface, oriented toward the computer's own addressing and control scheme. Furthermore, a computer bus is often designed for specific, predetermined devices. Historical reasons have tended to limit a LAN's polyvalence, but times are changing. Today we appreciate the necessity of designing protocols with sufficient generality to cope with disparities between the capabilities of devices engaged in a communications process. Among disparities attributable to attached devices, we can single out:

- Characteristic machine design and functionality
- Computer delay between the time a packet is received and the time it is successfully processed and acknowledged
- Windows (buffer space) available at the sender and the receiver
- Possible discrepancies between the rate at which devices can generate and absorb data
- Differences in packet handling caused by software constraints

The latter reference particularly underlines limitations in global addressing. A packet can have as destination all WSs in the network—if it is a broadcast packet. Packet broadcasting networks can achieve the same efficiencies as packet switched networks, but in addition, they have special advantages for local distribution. The point is that we need both broadcasting and switching features in our network.

Different control solutions have been devised to cope with such discrepancies. For instance, with centralized control, the link is assigned on a demand basis, and therefore, the message channels have to be identified every time the assignment is changed. Such identification can also take place through distributed control by using a token, or slotted rings.

The identification of the input-output port for each message is part of the routing information. Typically, this is stored in small translation tables at each port. Interconnection should be studied in a system-wide sense, since network nodes are often built of small machines capable of packet switching, but with limited resources regarding the number of virtual calls and the end-to-end service offered in an X.25 packet switching setup. If such a node has to serve a large number of attached devices, these devices may have to share a smaller amount of virtual calls. Consequently, a transport layer has to be served, using X.25 as an access method of the network. We will look into this subject in the following section. If, on the other hand, only a well-defined number of devices have to be served by the node, each terminal session may be provided with a virtual call of its own. In this case the transport layer is part of the network being accessed by X.25. In case the transport layer has to be served through proper software, a scheduling algorithm for connection multiplexing must be implemented as a part of that layer. The network itself may perform connection multiplexing as well as connection splitting on the lower laying layers, depending on the actual physical architecture.

In any case, X.25 itself has to be flexible. Every time connection multiplexing and connection splitting are brought into use, flow control must be introduced. It may include a simple start-stop, as well as more sophisticated principles for scheduling. CCITT's X.25 recommendation has flow control for each virtual call (ISO/OSI level 3) as well as for the data link (ISO/OSI level 2). The controls are based on similar principles. A receiver may be ready or not ready. If ready, it is able to receive data depending on yet another condition. The receiver has a window, and only packets inside the window are allowed to be transmitted.

Acknowledgment and credit are intermixed, because acknowledgment of a packet will automatically raise the lower edge of the window and thereby move the whole window, allowing for further packets to be transmitted. But an IFIP proposal for a protocol separates these functions, allowing for acknowledgment to be given without raising the credit. Also, credit may be raised even though no packets have to be acknowledged, thus permitting a more dynamic scheduling algorithm. Among other fundamental characteristics, protocols must assure a uniformity. Such uniformity represents homogeneity necessary to handle interhost and intrahost communications. Uniformity must characterize the same layer resident in different devices. This way, a pair of communicating tasks should be able to use the same protocol, like a pair of tasks resident in the same computer.

Knowledge of these functions and how they logically operate has a direct bearing on LAN design. For example, a particular service category may require exceptional care in protocol handling during design so as not to sacrifice its performance during full operational use of the network. Other service categories may be less prone to problems and may therefore represent avenues for design compromise.

Prototyping can be instrumental in assuring that the more critical services may be optimized at the slight degradation of the others. Experimentation can see to it that at the bottom line the total network performs better because of specific, well-conceived design decisions made at the drafting board. Protocol decisions should not be made lightly or taken on the basis that because a given protocol is a recommended standard it will perform well:

- A leading German aerospace manufacturer found that X.25 injected 3-second delays in interactive communications.
- A major French bank found a similar 3-second delay in its X.25 implementation, thus leading to a degradation of client service as compared to point-to-point based lines.

While both examples come from wide area networks, it is not the topology but the protocol which has mainly been the cause. If subsecond response time is at a premium, datagram rather than virtual circuit may be the solution.

11.6 Internet Protocol and Design Control

In the ISO/OSI model, the internet protocol (IP) constitutes the upper half of the networking layer. As such it interfaces with the transport layer. Its function is internetwork routing and delivery. This approach was originally developed for Arpanet. With IP, gateways and workstations share a common protocol for internet traffic—but they operate otherwise undisturbed. IP provides a datagram service, handling each packet of data independently. Multiple packets may arrive out of sequence. To effectively operate in the communications system, each connected host must have the IP sublayer, plus some higher layers. Gateways need only protocol software up to the IP level. Since it works by way of encapsulation, the internet protocol does not need to make assumptions about the other, underlying network protocols. A collection of interconnected networks using IP is often referred to as a "Catanet." An interesting characteristic of Catanet is that its implementation domain includes radio, satellites, and land lines. It is a polyvalent approach as far as transmission systems are concerned.

In the ISO/OSI reference mode, beyond IP and the transport layer is session control. The requirements of a session layer protocol are relatively simple compared with most other protocols, and this simplicity is reflected in the network design. This is particularly important because it reduces the risk of errors in the design phase and in the specifications of the implementation. In one specific LAN implementation, the chosen design makes certain tradeoffs to aid performance. The principal concern is to minimize the quantity of interactions between two session entities because this directly affects cost and throughput. Related provisions are:

- The connection establishment protocol involves only a two-way handshake, both elements of which can transfer session user data.
- Data transfer protocol combines data, delimiters, and marks in one message type.
- Connection termination protocol uses a two-way handshake, the first element of which can transfer user data.

Normal connection termination protocol can be broken out of if the other session user still has data to send, saving the need for an extra interaction to check whether the other user has more to transmit. Such uncertainty is typical of most kinds of dialogue, so the saving can be significant, particularly for short interactions. This demonstrates that specific organizational solutions may be necessary to answer interconnect requirements. This will be discussed in Chapters 12 to 16.

More to the point, a wise LAN policy will coordinate network design with *our* organization's 5-year growth plan, if there is one. A 5-year growth plan should be instrumental in identifying planned applications in areas such as data processing, databasing, data communications, end-user functions, voice, and video. It will help us make our own judgment about how the network will enhance our organization's ability to implement planned goals. In LAN-oriented practical terms, this will probably mean installing more cable, components, and taps, plus providing higher signal levels now than will be used initially. It also means being more versatile in protocol choice. Then, as our organization grows, the network will be more likely to provide adequate access and power to assist, rather than impede, that growth.

In other words, planning the logical and physical structure of a LAN goes well beyond laying the cable and choosing some protocols. We must understand the functional and technical basis of the network we are about to install. On the surface, this means we must know where the network transmission medium goes (geography) and the ups, downs, and twists in between demanded by the technology's configuration (topology). But in reality this is only the beginning. At the moment there are no real standards in local area networking we can depend upon to help us plan ahead. In spite of efforts by users, vendors, and national and international standards organizations to reduce the proliferation of interfaces, formats, and protocols, it is unlikely that significant standardization will be effective prior to 1995.

Furthermore, in any LAN design there will always be unknowns, such as the unstructured information flows with variable characteristics that can best be determined over time. Therefore, LAN designers will need to map both current and potential information flows to roughly determine traffic patterns and data rates. This also helps a company zero in on those system options that make the best use of existing equipment. Finally, after going through this process and finding what we need, it is vital to have the right support from the supplier. Several choices would need prototyping—as there will be a growing need for protocol converters and other communications programming packages that accept disparate formats and protocols, and either change them to the vendor network standard or envelop them so data can be moved not only within the LAN but also the organization-wide, larger network.

11.7 Perspectives in Internetworking

Most of the protocols which we have been discussing are at the data link level. Coming right after the physical layer, this is the lowest of the logical layers of the ISO/OSI reference mode. Right above it stands the networking layer, itself divided into two parts: routing and virtual circuit or in the alternative case, datagram. The networking layer is important because it goes beyond the LAN level of reference into internetworking.

While very large databases—whether distributed or centralized—will continue to be run by big machines, personal computing power will be increasingly distributed among thousands of workstations scattered throughout the corporate office(s). The online WSs will access local data bases and also remote text and data warehouses, and they will communicate with other WSs online to local area and wide area networks. The local area networks themselves will be of two types:

- Small LANs for intraoffice text and data (plus telephone local loops)
- Big LANs for intraoffice traffic covering buildings or campuses and benefiting from PBX services

Most applications services will be designed for both wide area and LAN, a main issue being the difference in the communications facilities being supported. But whether or not common elements exist, the need will be present to define the internet functionality.

Furthermore, the use of a value-added network for the long haul—hence an on-off approach to online—will answer the need for coexistence of both the connection and the connectionless capability. It will also place a requirement for protocols, allowing the applications domain to choose among alternative communications services, without being conditioned by them. Though current technology does not yet successfully solve such wide-scale problems in a fully homogeneous, globally unified manner, the requirements are foreseeable. A particular issue is the scale problem, which is the ability to effectively account for differences in the size and functionality of interconnected information warehouses.

Different international proposals have been made on how to handle the associated internetworking problems. One of them is to introduce a new level between the networking and transport layers of ISO/OSI, an internetwork level (Figure 11.9). The goal is to be able to map a global address into a local address.

This or similar solutions are important since, when we talk of long haul:

- CCITT's X.25 answers up to the virtual circuit level in terms of

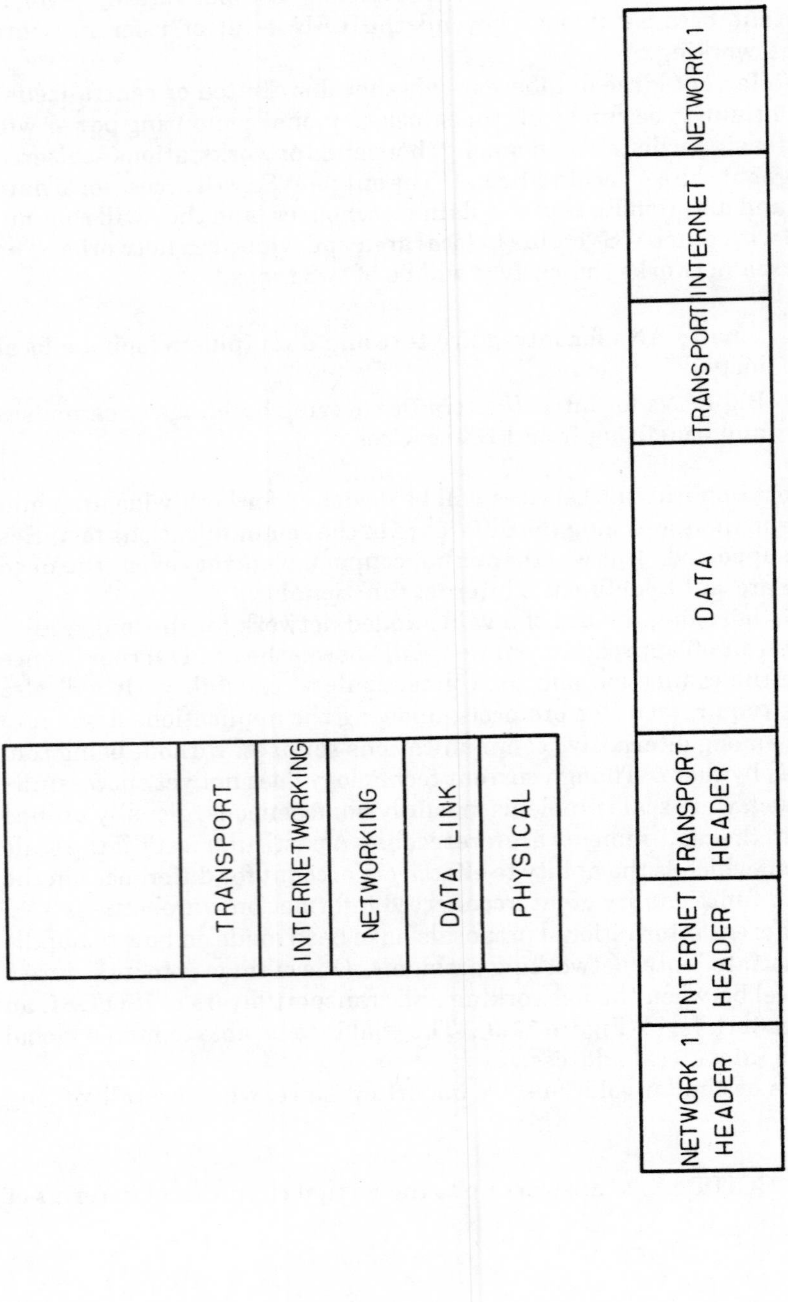

TRANSPORT
INTERNETWORKING
NETWORKING
DATA LINK
PHYSICAL

NETWORK 1 HEADER	INTERNET HEADER	TRANSPORT HEADER	DATA	TRANSPORT	INTERNET	NETWORK 1
				C	R	C

Figure 11.9 Accommodating the internetworking level within the protocol structure.

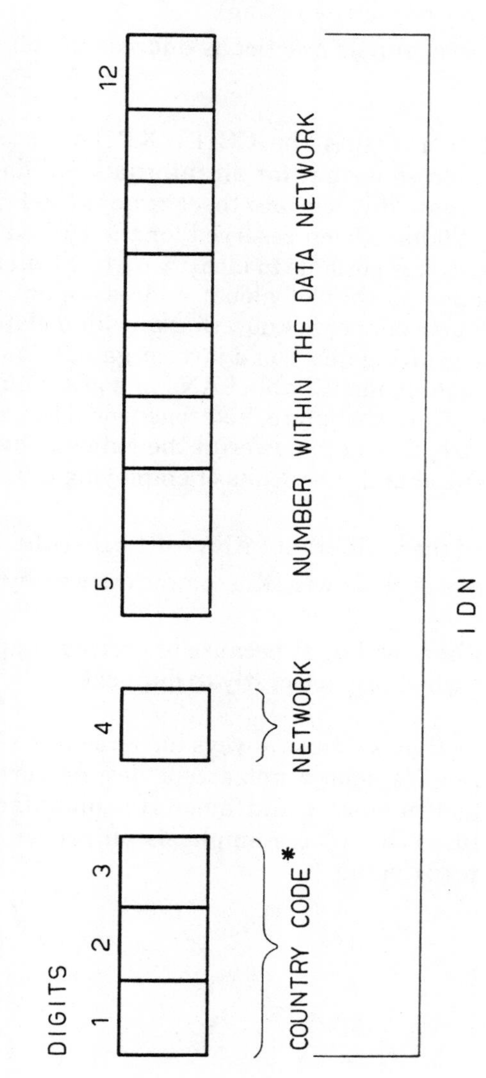

* 20 RESERVED FOR THE U.S.

Figure 11.10 The CCITT X.21 protocol for an international digital numbering system.

standards.

- Leased lines limit themselves to the data link level (HDLC/SDLC for packet switching).
- Satellite channels practically address the physical level, hence X.21.

Figure 11.10 presents the CCITT X.21 protocol. Its goal is to establish an address format for an international data number. IDN consists of 12 digits divided into three groups: 3-1-8. Out of the 999 country codes, 20 have been reserved for the United States. With the network ID digit, it is possible to identify up to 200 networks. The basis of interconnection is that of global address space. Using a proper internal ID scheme (since we know that any kind of network may be too small to fit the growing needs of a large organization), we can support a variety of uniquely identifiable LANs in a given environment.

It appears that the more heterogeneous the different network architectures are, the more powerful the gateway has to be. This also applies to the need and the means of employing different technologies:

- Some of these different LANs will be there because we buy them.
- Others will come with the computers we buy and cannot rip off them.
- Still others will exist because of precious applications environments which are too costly to duplicate.

This means that we must always have room to allow new technologies to appear. We should not accept getting cornered in a certain solution—no matter how big and famous the manufacturer promoting it may be. In turn, this places emphasis on proper planning—and by extension on prototyping.

PART 3

Local Area Networks Offered by Vendors

Chapter

12

Network Systems Corporation's Hyperchannel

12.1 Introduction

Hyperchannel serves large, centralized computer centers, typically containing supercomputers and large mainframes, with high-volume data rates. It supports 50 megabits per second (MBPS), or up to 200 MBPS by using four Hyperchannel cables. Hyperbus products feature a transfer capacity of 10 MBPS. Hyperchannel products work CSMA/CD. They consist of several types of communications processing units (or adapters) and standard multidrop cable. The maximum covered distance is 1000 feet (about 300 meters) locally and 100 miles or more with link adapters. Each adapter consists of a buffered storage area along with a microprogrammed processor designed to interface to an attached device, accept data from the device, and transmit data to another adapter.

Hyperchannel is designed to provide high-speed mainframe-to-mainframe communications in a nonhomogeneous setting. Depending on the adapter, connection is via I/O or DMA channels. Adapters are available for IBM, Unisys (Univac and Burroughs), DEC, Honeywell, CDC, Cray, Siemens, Fujitsu, Harris, SEL, Data General, Prime, Apollo Tandem, Hewlett-Packard, and Perkin-Elmer processors. An adapter can attach to as many as four independent network trunks. It acts as a buffered communications controller to move messages onto and receive them from the network. A computer hooked to the adapter communicates with it at the computer's own speed. The adapter uses a proprietary transmission format and protocol to send the information onto the network cable. The process works in reverse at the receiving end.

Two PC dataport multifunction coprocessor boards complement Hyperchannel. Either permits an IBM PC or compatible to function concurrently as a 3270 terminal, a ASCII terminal, or a computer able to communicate directly with mainframes. A dataport board differs from standard terminal-emulation products in that it allows the PC to trade files with a mainframe through full access at once instead of on a page-by-page basis. PC dataport boards are also microprocessor based with random access memory. The software handles session level protocol.

The 10 MBPS Hyperbus connects computer terminals in multivendor environments and serves applications requiring complex interconnections between different equipment and functions. Installations include settings with mixed RS-232 and IBM 3270 terminals. This equipment is joined to a Hyperbus network through a bus interface unit which acts as both port selector and multiplexer.

12.2 The Network Executive

The Hyperchannel network executive (Netex) represents a family of products which can be grouped into two types: Level 1 and Level 2. These share a common user interface but are internally different:

- Level 1 resides as a subroutine library called by the applications program. This version is implemented on smaller systems and comes as a compact package.
- Level 2 resides as a subsystem within a host computer. It is generally used on larger machines and features an operator interface.

With both Level 1 and Level 2 Netex, applications on the same processor can use the Hyperchannel-Hyperbus facilities without particular concern for other applications which are also using them.

There is a distinction between Netex Level 1 which does not feature cross-memory service—that is the driver addressing the data link level is an external attachment—and Netex Level 2 which does. Here the driver is integrated. The internal structure of Level 1 consists of components performing specialized functions. While characteristics of the different versions of Netex for various operating systems are tailored to the needs of the specific operating system, general functions of the components are similar. For example:

- *User interface* signals the initialization of Netex whenever a first call to the Executive is performed. This module takes optional user arguments passed with a Fortran or assembler call and creates a user identification field to distinguish external user-type requests from internal requests.
- *User request director* resides within Netex and accepts requests from the user interface. Such requests are queued and executed as resources become available. The user request director performs validity checking and calls user-provided exits. It also signals the user when the request is complete.
- *Session service* takes user session-level requests which come through the user request director and processes them into transport-level requests.

We will look closely into the functionality of Netex transport and session control level software in the second half of this section. Other services of Level 1 are as follows:

- *Timer management* takes requests from Netex components and informs that routine when a specified amount of real time has expired.
- *Trace facility* records Netex messages onto a buffer for user reference.
- *Queue management* runs the queues used by the other components of the executive.
- *Memory management* allocates storage at initialization and provides both working storage and buffers for data transfer. Its controls help to minimize demands on the host operating system.

The internal structure of Level 2 consists of several routines also tailored to the needs of the specific operating system. The functionality of Level 2 is integrated. Other subsystems include:

- *Cross-memory services* taking user request packets and data from the user interface and exchanging them with Netex packets and data. These services implement a mechanism whereby both Netex and the user can dispatch to each other if the other party is waiting. Depending on the implementation, this component may reside in a separate address space or require adaptations to the host operating system.
- *Initialization* supplies Netex with user-defined parameters at each initialization specifying the order that processes are to be readied.
- *Operator interface* interacts with Netex only when communications take place with the local machine operator.
- *Transport service* handles user transport-level requests, either directly or through the session software, to establish a matching transport protocol through the use of driver requests. Transport software allocates the transport connection and releases it when the connection ends abnormally or normally. Once the connection is established, data is sent in a continuous series, with responses returned to provide transport error correction and flow control.
- *Network service* addresses itself to network level requests, either directly or from transport software. It formats messages to route data through the network.
- *Driver service's* objective is to handle driver-level requests either directly or from network software, sending and receiving network messages using the network.
- *Task management* queues components or resources in a way that allows one component to activate other. It interacts with the other components in the Netex address space. It also provides an interrupt handler to respond to external events.

Network executive protocols exist for different operating systems and supporting utilities. Netex packages user requests and sends them over the network to another version of Netex on the receiving computer. Since each version of the executive contains an ISO/OSI session-level interface, the receiving software transparently passes the requests to the appropriate application and sends responses back to the computer that issued the initial request. In this sense, Netex may be used in a configuration with computers manufactured by different companies, provided each machine:

- Uses the appropriate Hyperchannel adapter
- Is running the proper version of Netex designed to operate with its specific operating system

NSC has standardized the versions of Netex that exist for different operating systems. There is also a standard language interface that allows language program, for instance, in Fortran or Pascal to be moved from one host to another without changing the logic used to call and function with the executive.

Netex software on each host handles remote links, flow control, and error recovery. Paralellism within the executive maximizes data throughput by allowing simultaneous input-output operations with the hardware adapter, the user file, and buffer management. Netex also contains protocols for long-distance communications over classical telephone, satellite, microwave, and fiber optic links. The Netex user interface is the same for all operating systems, giving programmers a consistent format. Once the network executive accepts data from the caller, it assumes responsibility for delivery to destination. The system provides delay compensation when data is sent through communications satellites.

A comparison between basic Hyperchannel firmware and hardware, the NSC driver, and Netex versus the seven layers of the ISO/OSI reference model is shown in Figure 12.1. Firmware provides the date link level services. NSC's driver sublayer converts I/O for a particular network path into a form understandable by the attached devices. It also supports retry and error recovery.

Netex software covers the upper half of the networking level as well as the functionality of ISO/OSI transport and session control. The transport layer routines provide the actual data movement services. They are responsible for transmitting and receiving user data, along with internal protocol information. They also look after data delivery and integrity. Transport software manages the network path chosen by the session software. It sets up hardware and software tables, provides buffering, and establishes linkages to manage the flow of information. It also assures full-duplex communications between subsystems. Asynchronous reads and writes are permitted.

As the highest layer within Netex, session software looks after the

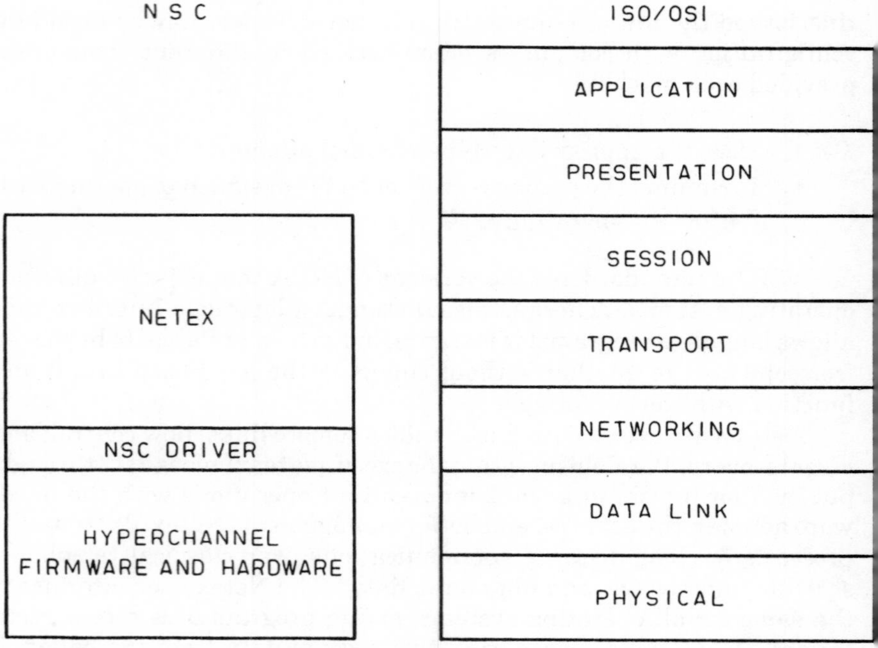

NSC	ISO/OSI
	APPLICATION
	PRESENTATION
NETEX	SESSION
	TRANSPORT
NSC DRIVER	NETWORKING
HYPERCHANNEL FIRMWARE AND HARDWARE	DATA LINK
	PHYSICAL

Figure 12.1 Netex software includes most, but not all, of the session control functionality of ISO/OSI.

general interface to the user's applications and utility programs. It serves the executive to assure program-to-program connection using the best available network path, reading and writing data, disconnection, and gathering of statistics. The user requests these services using session layer Netex requests. Circumstances under which data delivery may fail basically revolve around a catastrophic failure of the physical or logical connection between application programs, such as a disconnect or abrupt program termination performed by the remote application, lack of response from the remote Netex program, or a failure of the Hyperchannel hardware. In all these cases, error recovery consists of terminating the application since its partner application is no longer available or, alternatively, of issuing a connect to an equivalent applications and resuming the task at hand. Such equivalent application may be on a different CPU.

Since OSI is a recommended standard which has been described by

ISO — but not defined — each vendor takes the freedom to define the functionality of each layer. Therefore, while the Netex software of the transport and session control layers is functional, it does not mean that it is compatible with that of another vendor for the same OSI layers.

12.3 A Product Line

The market for Hyperchannel-type equipment consists primarily of the world's 5000 largest computer centers, which typically require the connection of large numbers of mainframes and minis to perform the daily data processing operations. A benefit from a high-capacity channel solution and appropriate software is that the DP center needs only concern itself with explicit access to the data. Database applications can be run in dedicated machines by sending requests to to the database computer (DBC) via the high-speed channel. This type of application has led to a software architecture able to serve DBC connectivity. The specialized database computer is of great interest to large computing centers—and will constitute one of the main phases of fifth-generation computers (5GC) applications.

Large multimainframe data processing centers often have a bottleneck in the corporate database. But it is not rational to use 50 or 100 MBPS to interconnect workstations—at least not until the new breed of intelligent WS is capable of moving images, voice, and text as compound processing systems. In accordance with a layered global networking structure, NSC offers four networks:

1. Top of the line Datapipe, with 175 to 275 MBPS*—which is the highest capacity present technology allows for fully software-supported networking.
2. The current Hyperchannel product, at 50 MBPS.
3. The Hyperbus Hyperchannel "B" series, at 10 MBPS.
4. Datatap, a likely new product at 2 MPBS, to work up to 30 meters.

All four offerings have Netex in common, thus providing for continuity in terms of implementation.

*The design goal for Datapipe, as stated by NSC, is up to 500 MBPS with distance tolerant transmission of 30 km.

However, I feel four layers are not enough; two more layers are necessary:

- A very high-capacity pipe at the 500 MBPS and beyond to be served principally through optical fibers
- A very low-capacity pipe (for LAN reference) at the 200 to 300 KBPS level—but practically at no BIU cost

We can think of a vendor's product line as falling into one or more of the six layers shown in Figure 12.2.* At least the four central layers should share the same operating system and interconnect and utility routines through a process of upward compatibility, thus providing solid bases for the future without handicapping or inhibiting current operations in a way that is not only solid, system-wise, but also permits an escape route in case of vendor catastrophe.

When making LAN choices, system architecture and system integration should be decided first, then the investment can be made with reasonable benefit expectation. In addition, a well-thought-out product line will pay great attention to upward compatibility in layers 2 to 5. This refers not only to network OS routines but also to different operating systems of attached mainframes, maxis, and minis. Such capability is not necessarily part of the ISO services, but it is crucial in enhancing session level functions and beyond.

We must always think in terms of network usage. In real life implementation, the applications programs running on diverse and incompatible mainframes will request connections, exchange data, and generally use and terminate the connection. These functions include:

- Session establishment coordination
- Data transfer
- Lower-level capability like pacing and segmentation
- Path selection and reselection
- Data conversion
- Notification of failed application
- Disconnection services

---

*This figure complements without contradicting a similar one I have included in my book *System Architecture, System Integration and the Role of Artificial Intelligence*, McGraw-Hill, New York, 1988. The difference is one of viewpoint: integration versus product line.

	LAN CAPACITY	PRIMARY GOAL
6	MORE THAN 500 MBPS UP TO, SAY, 2.5 GBPS	HIGH COST VERY HIGH PERFORMANCE
5	MORE THAN 100 MBPS UP TO 500 MBPS	HIGH PERFORMANCE CENTRAL OPERATIONS
4	MORE THAN 20 MBPS UP TO 100 MBPS	CENTRAL OPERATIONS AND DEPARTMENTAL AREA
3	MORE THAN 4 MBPS UP TO 20 MBPS	MEDIUM COST DEPARTMENTAL AREA
2	MORE THAN 1 MBPS UP TO 4 MBPS	LOW COST OFFICE AREA
1	1 MBPS OR LESS	EXTREMELY LOW COST

Figure 12.2 LAN can be classified into six ranges, each with a primary implementation goal.

This is what, in technical terms, Netex is implementing up to the level of basic session control service. It is a protocol embedded in software routines. Though NSC goes to great lengths to explain that Netex is not a characteristic network OS—the functions Netex supports are a significant part of a LAN's operating system.

12.4 Design Philosophy of Datapipe

NSC's Datapipe is currently the highest-capacity LAN in the market. It is a high-speed, fiber optic backbone network capable of interconnecting NSC and other vendors' products over extended distances. Metropolitan area, large mainframe center interconnections, and campus-type environments are its market goals.

Datapipe design goals focus on transmission capacity of up to 500 MBPS and a 30-km distance tolerant transmission with repeaters. The design isolates the so-called front-end personality, the nucleus services of the LAN, and the transmission media. Design rules observe:

1. Function boundaries for modularity.
2. The separation of data and control.
3. The isolation of areas subject to change.

One of the design aims is to anticipate new technology. Media access is time division multiplexing (TDM).

The Datapipe architecture features a star coupler as the focal point with Datapipe adapters at the end. The up to 30-km distance is between the star coupler and the adapter. The link is optical fiber, with a fiber transmitter-receiver integrated into the adapter. The Datapipe has four ports of 50 MPBS each. A Hyperchannel input-output processor (IOP) connects to each at a distance which varies depending on the cable media: coaxial up to 1.6 km (1 mile) and optical fiber up to 2 km. The following can be attached at the IOP station:

- 50-MBPS Hyperchannel A
- 10-MBPS Hyperbus
- 10-MBPS Hyperchannel B

Datapipe I/O processors in full duplex can also be interconnected at the Datapipe's 50-MBPS ports. They operate at 32 bits plus control and make feasible the direct connection of mainframes and/or optical disk memories (database computers). As an alternative, the Datapipe IOP offers 64 bits plus control and parallel interfaces.

The Datapipe architecture features synchronous IOP and will support a standard interface allowing voice, video, or any low-level real-time connection. It also makes feasible peer-to-peer dialing with fast path switching for failure recovery. Another facility is the Datapipe link IOP.

Link IOP has an operating capacity of up to 200 MBPS and works full duplex. Datapipe software supports traffic and operating statistics, profile configuration, loop-back testing, and internal tests. It also features network management interfaces for:

- System identification
- Network mapping
- Transmission bandwidth allocation

As of late 1987, Phase 2 and Phase 3 of Datapipe development status were in beta testing. Phase 2 focuses on the 50-MBPS Hyperchannel A interconnection. Phase 3 addresses itself to the 10-MBPS Hyperbus linkage. NSC has also designed BFX to cover the software requirements of presentation control layer of ISO/OSI—that is, beyond the Netex level.

12.5 Exploring Interconnect Requirements

The PC Dataport plugs into the PC and provides multiple concurrent functions—including serial interface, ASCII emulation, and 3278/9 emulation—for computer-to-computer communications. This is the bottom level LAN offer by NSC and corresponds to Layer 2 in Figure 12.2. The NSC entry into Layer 3 of Figure 12.2 is the Hyperchannel B series. It is compatible with other NSC product lines. Figure 12.3 shows the connection developed to serve Apollo supermicro engines.

The bus interface unit for the B series can connect up to four WSs. However, the available bulk file transfer (BFX) software does not support process-to-process connectivity and, therefore, it is not an interactive utility. The BIU sends a stream of data which the remote host interprets as batch jobs., hence, the bulk transfer arrangements. NSC suggests this unit can also be used to handle smaller files if it is equipped with software tuned well enough to the application. There is no evidence at this point that this is so, and there are also security considerations, since software design avoids complex security problems at this level. One of the reasons NSC gave for the four-port B400-BC 403 BIU is that it can be used to construct a managerial WS with an executive, a secretary, and a couple of staff assistants coupled on it. I don't think there is a market for such a limited cluster.

The NSC bus interface unit for mainframes is coded BC 110/BC222. It was stated that this is good for a medium-level mainframe, given the

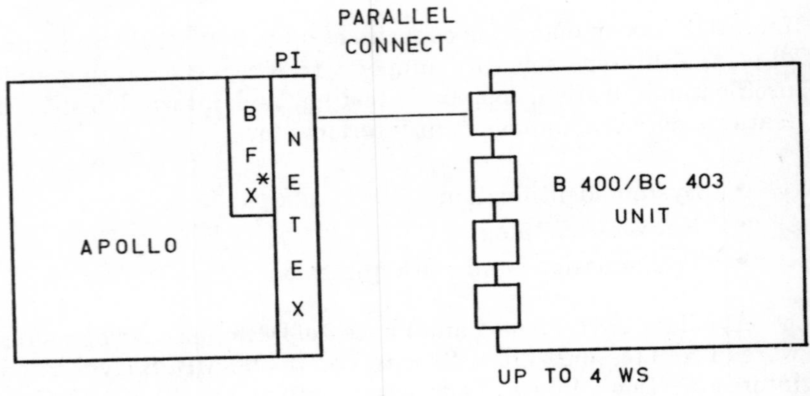

Figure 12.3 Product line modification to serve a specific computer and its OS.

10-MPBS limit. However, the emphasis is misplaced. A channel capacity of 10 MBPS *might* be enough to serve IBM's 4341 and PDP-11 engines—but not mainframes. Any bigger machine than a small mini will find that 10 MBPS is not enough for information exchange. Furthermore, even if the capacity constraint was not present, implementation presupposes a FIPS (Federal Information Processing Standard) channel. To my knowledge, few DP users today have FIPS on their data processing equipment.

Hyperchannel B has other weak points. For instance, there is no technique to map ASCII into IBM, though the design goal is to make EBCDIC transparent to PC software. There is, of course, the possibility of using the IBM Host Database View which runs under VM Bond (VM/CMS environment only). The Host Database View supports ASCII code—but it is a very special case. However, only mainstream solutions should merit serious LAN study; parochial approaches end with the organization being in a dead end. Unless they represent a significant breakthrough in technology, there is no reason to look at them in the first place. Along this line of reasoning, a recent LAN project examined the wisdom of employing IBM's Personal Decision Series (PDS) as interface software with Hyperchannel B. PDS is simpler to implement than Host

Database View and runs under MVS, which was the mainframe OS in this project. However, this study concluded that:

- The B series software is neither an alternative nor a complement to IBM's PDS.
- It is a totally different system, whose purpose is that of covering the bottom five layers of ISO/OSI into a level of LAN at 10 MBPS feeding into a 50-MBPS Hyperchannel.

But the software does not necessarily answer all PC-connect requirements. More precisely, Hyperchannel B aims to make the PC look as if it were a nonintelligent 3270 terminal. This eliminates the reason for buying PC 3270.

Similar implementation perspectives, regarding the B series, are outlined by the vendor for PC-to-mini connectivity, as well as PC-to-mainframe with the stated FIPS constraint. My advice is to clear away from nonintelligent terminal emulations and from solutions which lock a user organization into this line for years to come.

Hyperbus seems to be compatible with both the AT&T Premise Distribution System and the IBM wiring system. ASCII devices that comply with RS-232-C, RS-422 and MIL-188C interfaces can use the twisted pair available from each user area to the communications closet. In IBM, 3278/79/8X terminal devices can employ existing RG62 coaxial cable or through BALUNs use the twisted pair wiring that terminates in the communications closet. The announced NSC BB44x adapters interface with various Dataport boards in the PC via an RG62 coaxial cable, making this connection a candidate to use the same wiring.

12.6 High-Level Logical Supports

While in the early years of implementing computers and communications, major emphasis was placed on physical media, it is the logical solutions which today constitute the competitive element. Both facilitations and constraints are the result of how well the logical infrastructure fits the intended implementation objectives.

Data link protocols are a well-established communications solution. They are offered, in alternative approaches, by all reputable communications vendors. Therefore, attention no longer needs to be focused at this lower logical level. Instead, five issues should attract the serious LAN user's interest:

1. High-level protocols.
2. Network control center software.
3. Distributed data dictionary facilities.
4. Delays and response time as seen by the end user.
5. Network administration.

When it comes to protocols addressed to the higher levels of the ISO/OSI reference mode, there are many organizations attempting to set standards. The following have (or will have) significant importance in the implementation of computers and communications:

- Manufacturing Automation Protocol (MAP), by General Motors
- Technical Office Protocol (TOP), by Boeing
- Logical Unit 6.2 (LU 6.2), by IBM
- NBIOS, by IBM
- Transport Control Protocol/Internet Protocol (TCP/IP), sponsored by the Department of Defense
- XNS, by Xerox

As far as support for these protocols is concerned, the graph in Figure 12.4 tells the story. A network port to which different devices are attached is served by:

1. A network engine handling higher-level protocols.
2. A network driver for the physical and lower-level protocols.

The network driver addresses itself to RS-232 and, say, 3270 and the network engine to a range of protocols, from XNS and TCP/IP to LU 6.2 and MAP.

The importance of these evolving de facto standards is to guarantee the proper operation of virtual terminals. A network may have either homogeneous or heterogeneous composition. Homogeneous is a rare case. Heterogeneous is the rule. How can we manage the system? The rational approach involves the definition of virtual terminals— and this in a layered scheme. As such, it guarantees basic and other functions to serve the end user in an able manner. We then design the network software to serve the basic functions—common to everybody.

For this reason we should examine the efforts currently under way both by vendors and by large user organizations, such as Boeing, General

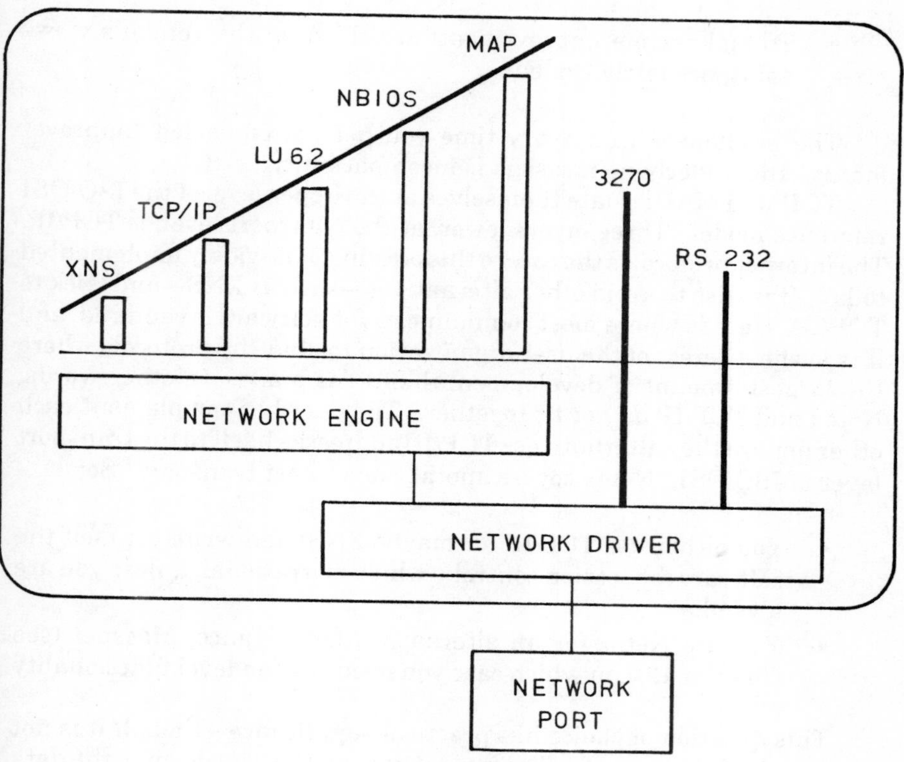

Figure 12.4 A network engine and network driver can support different protocols whose functionality is felt at the port level.

Motors, and the U.S. Department of Defense. The Technical Office Protocol has been developed by Boeing and is particularly important in engineering (CAD/CAM) implementations—but it can be expected to spread throughout business and industry. TOP can be seen, at the level of the technical office, as the alter ego of the Manufacturing Automation Protocol (MAP) developed by General Motors. Both TOP and MAP have been adopted by vendors, and the list of compatible offerings is growing. The problem is similar to that of ISO/OSI. Every vendor's interpretation is different:

- To better fit MAP/TOP to the vendor's hardware and software

- To make some improvements which, from the vendor's viewpoint, are fairly evident

The problem is that every time you hear of one-sided "improvements," the underlying message is incompatibility.

TOP and MAP situate themselves at the upper level of the ISO/OSI reference model. Three layers lower, at the transport level, is TCP/IP. The internet protocol is the core to this offering; it is widely implemented today. It is wise to avoid other alternatives—such as XNS—and stick to TCP/IP. Here is where most communications software is centered, and it is in the interest of the user organization to abide by protocols where the largest amount of developmental effort is made. In other words, Netex and TCP/IP *do not* fit together. They neither complement each other nor are they alternatives. TCP/IP addresses itself to the transport layer of ISO/OSI. Netex covers another layer past transport. So:

- You either use TCP/IP (or maybe XNS) and write yourself the software for session control—which is irrational, unless you are a vendor
- You use Netex (or an alternative, for instance, Massnet (see Chapter 13)), in which case you need session level functionality

This question of choice has practical significance—though it is not often appreciated as such. The impact goes all the way down to the data link layer and beyond. For each unique protocol implementation we should have a specific I/O driver in the operating system and appropriate interface routines. In a multivendor environment, each operating system would have multiple I/O drivers and, depending on resources required, driver interfaces. That is where solutions like Netex are good. They allow multiple applications with different lower communications protocols to use a single network and—just as important—a single hardware connection to the network. Still, answering the top- and middle-layer requirements in terms of ISO/OSI reference is not enough. We must also adopt solutions for session and presentation control.

Netex is not the answer at the ISO/OSI layer of presentation control. The leading candidate is IBM's LU 6.2. Trouble is that TOP, MAP, and LU 6.2 overlap to a certain extent. And so does Netex. Table 12.1 demonstrates this point by taking three network functions as an example.

Table 12.1 MAP/TOP, LU 6.2, and Netex Functionality

Function	*MAP/TOP*	*LU 6.2*	*Netex*
Establish a connection	SConnect	Allocate confirm	SOffer SConnect SConfirm SDisconnect
Exchange data	SData	SendData ReceiveData	SRead SWrite
End a session	SRelease SuAbort SpAbort	Deallocate	SClose SDisconnect

12.7 Primitives for Networking Requirements

MAP/TOP have ISO session compatibility; a shell on Netex that will support ISO applications like FTAM might help provide MAP/TOP applications support—though this is still to be seen. A similar statement can be made about IBM compatibility, but NSC thinks that the support for IBM LU 6.2 will be a more complex implementation because the protocol is owned by the vendor. It is also subject to change without notice.

Shell-type solutions basically focus on the primitives. When the native commands are different—and they usually are—an LU 6.2 application will not interface to, say, a TCP/IP application. In fact, interfacing might be difficult (or even impossible) even with similar native commands, but close similitude applications can use the same communications system to exchange data and code with peer applications. In a way, close similitude in the primitives helps in providing a gateway to implementations, allowing the application in a network to interface to an application on another noncompatible network. This can be done without very expensive emulation which eats machine cycles and slows down the system.

For a user organization, the benefits of this strategy are speed, flexibility, and cost savings as well as fewer changes in the operating environment. A system or application can be chosen for its features and benefits, with the user organization implementing protocols and applications without costly hardware and software overhauls. Savings will result from close similitude in primitives because a single aggregate can provide multiple system functions. A good solution stresses on degrees of homogeneity rather than an absolute approach, which we know does not exist.

There are other requirements to which the user organization should pay attention. Whether it rests on one of more vendors, the network environment must be supported through a network control center (NCC). Another key logical resource is the distributed data dictionary. At the present time Netex does not address the data dictionary issue nor does alternative software from other vendors. But when session capability is added, NSC intends to provide a logical resource name, though the WS will be unaware of it, the mechanics rest in session control and the session interface (Netex session level). The attached WS can define logical names for the mainframes, directing the transaction.

Basically, in terms of design criteria, the distributed data dictionary should be transparent from the user's viewpoint; this may require a front-end machine. With front-end capabilities, the data dictionary function might be more easily supported through minor upgrading of currently available software. Configuration also plays a role in selecting the kind of data dictionary which is necessary. If a data center has only two machines, a crude solution will suffice. If there are many mainframes, a sophisticated approach will be needed.

From the viewpoint of the user organization, a good NSC product is the Netex Administrator. It allows the centralization of housekeeping and some logical issues that affect end-user performance, such as delays. They depend both on hardware and software resources: the type of equipment, its basic software, and the local or long haul configuration. If we are talking of transactions per second, and not of seconds per transaction, the key question is dimensioning. The principal delay may be in getting the request out of the machine—but this changes with communication. These examples point to another group of primitives that networking software should exhibit: the administrative and control part of the picture.

The way NSC handles the latter problem is through dedicated lines so that it is possible to use its own protocols. Links employ a low-level service but could take advantage of line capabilities. No doubt, interfaces introduce delays. There is, for instance, a delay of 2 to 3 milliseconds per box for forwarding. Still another shows up if the line is loaded with traffic. Hence, it is wise to employ 50 MBPS or more for mainframe-oriented networks.

Again from the user organization's perspective, a properly designed and implemented network management structure will constitute the next fundamental step in the direction of valid solutions to multivendor problems. This should include:

- Nonstop networking, able to detect faults, reroute traffic, inform system control, and so on
- Network administration, regarding state and status, NCC database, operations control
- Added user services, including self-testing, fail soft, user reports
- A wide range of security considerations—from encryption to access control, ID, and authentication

The time has come to take a systems view of these problems. We no longer talk of independent instances. Our goal is corporate-wide practices supported by valid technical LAN solutions. That is where our interest should be.

Since no LAN software is currently responding to the requirements of process-to-process and field-to-field implementation of diverse and incompatible mainframes, an alternative solution has to be found. One has been to contract with the main vendor or a third-party for an ad hoc solution covering the presentation control and application of layers of ISO/OSI. There is no question about the wisdom of finding a solution. That's how the protocol shell approach was developed.

Let's first start with the objectives: apart from ISO/OSI application layer service, what else do we wish to accomplish? A whole list of items suggests itself:

- Simplify both the professional's and end user's training.
- See to it that the system specialists have only one interface to understand.
- Speed developments related to the communications interface(s).
- Make sure enhancements are consistent across all implementations.
- Encourage third-party software vendors to produce applications.

Further goals should be included in the specifications, such as tying the LAN into PBX. However, while conversion capability is there, the implementation for this is not yet ready.

For PBX, NSC looks at digital systems, providing data services but not voice integration. This rests on their premise that there will be separate data and voice channels for the next 5 years. Though some vendors developed a WS with full integration of text, data, image, and voice, NSC has not come up with a generalized solution yet. But, for an organization which foresees that a high-capacity LAN should tie into the PBX (and vice versa), the development of protocol shells should be an opportunity for providing such facility from the beginning.

The opposite argument could also be valid. Not all functionality that will be necessary in the future should be implemented right away. However, the design established now should not only account for such developments, but it should also provide the necessary exits and assure that its inner mechanism can handle the logical flow when it develops.

The concept of a protocol shell is simple enough. Whether at network architecture level or with reference to mainframe/mini OS, it presupposes a free flow of processes and fields—including the support of routines and functional prerequisites addressing themselves to the presentation control and application levels of ISO/OSI. Just the same, whether we talk of network or mainframe, a basic decision must be made in terms of the standard to be used for the shell. My suggestion is that the first, second, and third choice should be LU 6.2. It is a de facto standard.

Another key point about protocol shells to be taken up at the drafting board is global database connectivity—more specifically, DBMS interfacing. All major relational DBMS, DB2, Ingres, Oracle, and so on, should be supported. While in the past networking and databasing were the two antipodes (respectively front ending and back ending), today they have merged. The need for database interfacing goes well beyond the now-classical LAN file server (see Part 4). The database perspective must also account for the distributed data dictionary.

Most importantly, the global database interface is necessary for field-level access through DBMS services. This is a key element in making the use of the nonhomogeneous mainframe environment transparent.

As far as NSC is concerned, the implementation of Netex on many diverse operating systems provides a base on which it can develop the shell that users require to efficiently do multivendor business in the future. This may not be so for OS and DBMS. The next few years will be challenging as standards change and user requirements evolve.

A protocol shells solution may be the way out of the standards confusion and an alternative to blindly following IBM. A question most often asked today at leading data centers is "How can we integrate?" Protocol shells try to answer this question. The method is explained in Figure 12.5. Say, we want Honeywell mainframes to participate in an SNA network. To enhance the interprocessor communications facility we can add at the Honeywell side (beyond the teleprocessing calls) an LU 6.2 library. The same solution can be followed if Cray, Unisys, or other mainframes are added to the SNA network. An alternative approach is *run-time* resident routines:

- LU 6.2 library at, say, the Honeywell side
- LU 6.2 gateway in the IBM mainframes

However, this alternative means bracketing and debracketing the different applications programs through add-on layers of header and trailer, hence delays, costs, and possible errors.

Seeing the application as a bit stream (like in an X.25 packet switching protocol) increases the overhead, but it has other advantages. It can provide multivendor attachment capability on the LAN with IBM mainframe(s) or other OSs. Any processor can be active in the system, be used for transit only, or even not be present in the network at any given implementation instance. Flexibility in configuration can be achieved provided all mainframe vendors have an LU 6.2 library capability—or the bracketing and debracketing solution.

The approach shown in Figure 12.6 is consistent with the overall concept of networking. It is the principle of having one big datapipe and avoiding run-time converting. It has other advantages. Resource usage is not fixed but is allocated and dynamic, permitting bit streams to travel freely between machines.

The hinge is providing efficient interconnect features spanning all layers of the ISO/OSI reference model—though not all layers will be needed in all applications. Here is precisely where the protocol shells implementation has its rationale. How long will a shells solution take and what's the estimated cost? The budget is not forbidding. According to one projection, if only IBM mainframes are involved—with different OSs, say MVS and VM/CMS—roughly nine calendar months will be necessary for a team of two to three top-level system programmers. Hence, +2 programmer years of investment.

It is also estimated that for every additional mainframe OS to be

PROTOCOL SHELLS

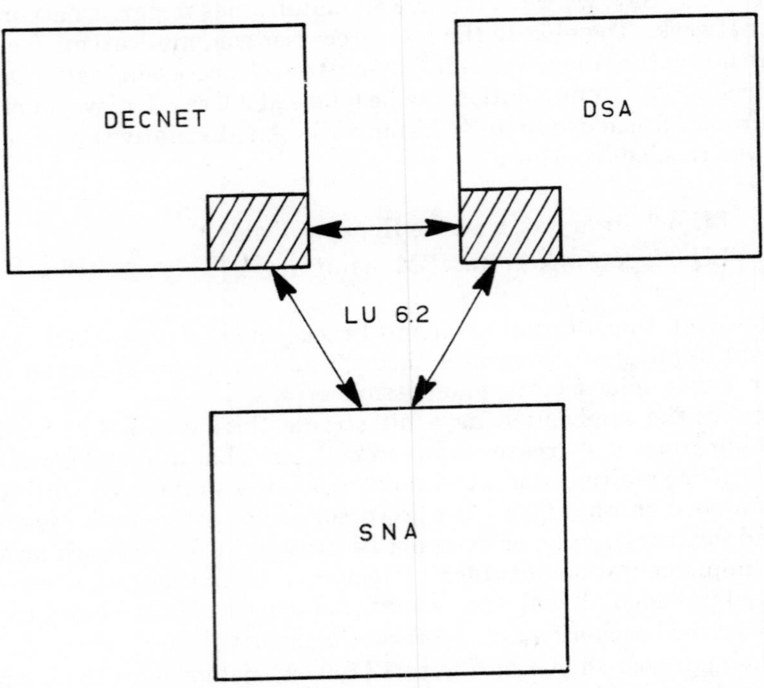

IBM INDEPENDENT
PROCESS TO PROCESS AND FIELD TO FIELD

Figure 12.5 An IBM-independent implementation; process to process and field to field through protocol shells.

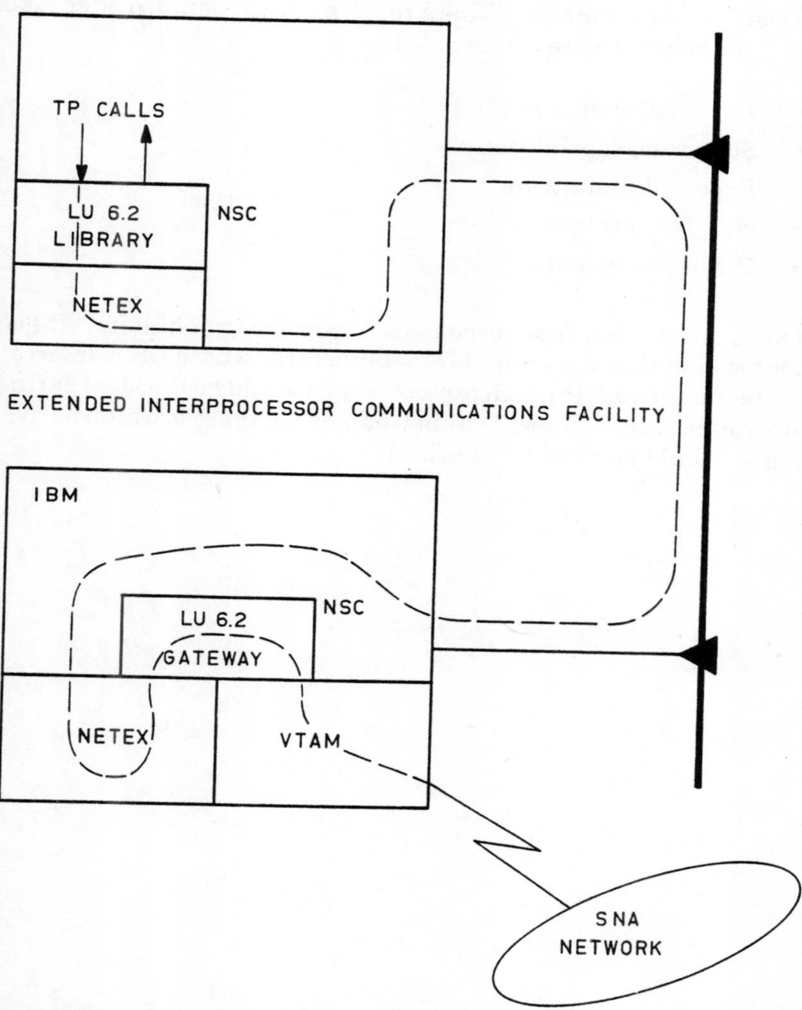

Figure 12.6 Extended interprocessor communications facility by means of interfacing.

supported, an additional $100,000 will be needed, with about 3 months more work for *the same team*. This a rough guess. A detailed offer takes about 6 weeks to prepare. It includes:

- Technical characteristics
- Supported capabilities
- Expected limitations
- Nearly exact cost
- Precise timetable

Obviously, such a first response will be a design *objective*. It goes without saying that the computer manufacturer whose OS is interconnected to the network through protocol shells would be the ideal partner in the project. But as we will see in Chapter 13, there are alternatives. And they should be considered prior to decision.

Chapter

13

Massnet Plus, by Masstor Systems Corporation

13.1 Introduction

This chapter builds on Chapter 12. The infrastructure of the local area network solution we will be discussing is the Hyperchannel by NSC. But the network software from ISO/OSI layer 3 (networking) and above is different. It is known as Masstor Network: Massnet. (Masstor stands for mass storage.) This networking-to-session control communications software was written to interconnect mainframes with large-capacity mass storage devices through a LAN architecture. Its implementation is based on the following:

1. A state-of-the-art high-bandwidth, reliable LAN. Hence, the Hyperchannel choice.

2. An agile software able to interconnect database machines to mainframes through a well-supported high-capacity pipe.
3. An ad hoc solution since at this point there is no standard for the type of problem just described.

The designer, implementor, and vendor of Massnet is Masstor Systems Corporation (MSC). This is not a communications company; it is a mass storage manufacturer. Masstor's main product, the M860, is a cartridge-based, online, high-capacity storage system consisting of proprietary hardware and data management software. It is the linkage of this data management software to different operating systems which created the need for a high-level LAN-type implementation.

13.2 The Database Machine

Prior to looking into the mechanics of software support of Masstor's networking approach, we will consider the need for database machines and what they represent in terms of current and future perspectives. They are the modern version of file servers, which have been the pillars of local area networks—if not their original reason of being. The development of complex and complete software for local area networks originated in the need to serve database engines. Masstor Systems correctly appreciated that this support was necessary if its M860 database computer was to provide an attractive mass storage for IBM and IBM-compatible MVS- and MVS/XA-based systems. Originally written for these OSs, the networking-to-session control communications software has been extended to cover Sperry and Honeywell OSs through the Massnet interface.

Even if the M860 is not a subject of immediate interest to a user organization, the Massnet LAN software may very well be so. Experience teaches the wisdom of learning well all aspects of a system even if only part of it is to be used. Outside the IBM world there is, for instance, a Massnet application with Unisys (Sperry mainframes). It concerns the Auto Secure product offering and online data backup. In anther example of Massnet's LAN-type usage, Unisys 1100 mainframes are linked to an IBM back-end processor to which the M860 is attached. Masstor Systems Shared VSS Software provides for control and sharing of data across the Unisys host systems interfacing to the back end. Figure 13.1 shows this connection. The back-end processor is an IBM machine. There are more examples—particularly at the communications end. We will come to them.

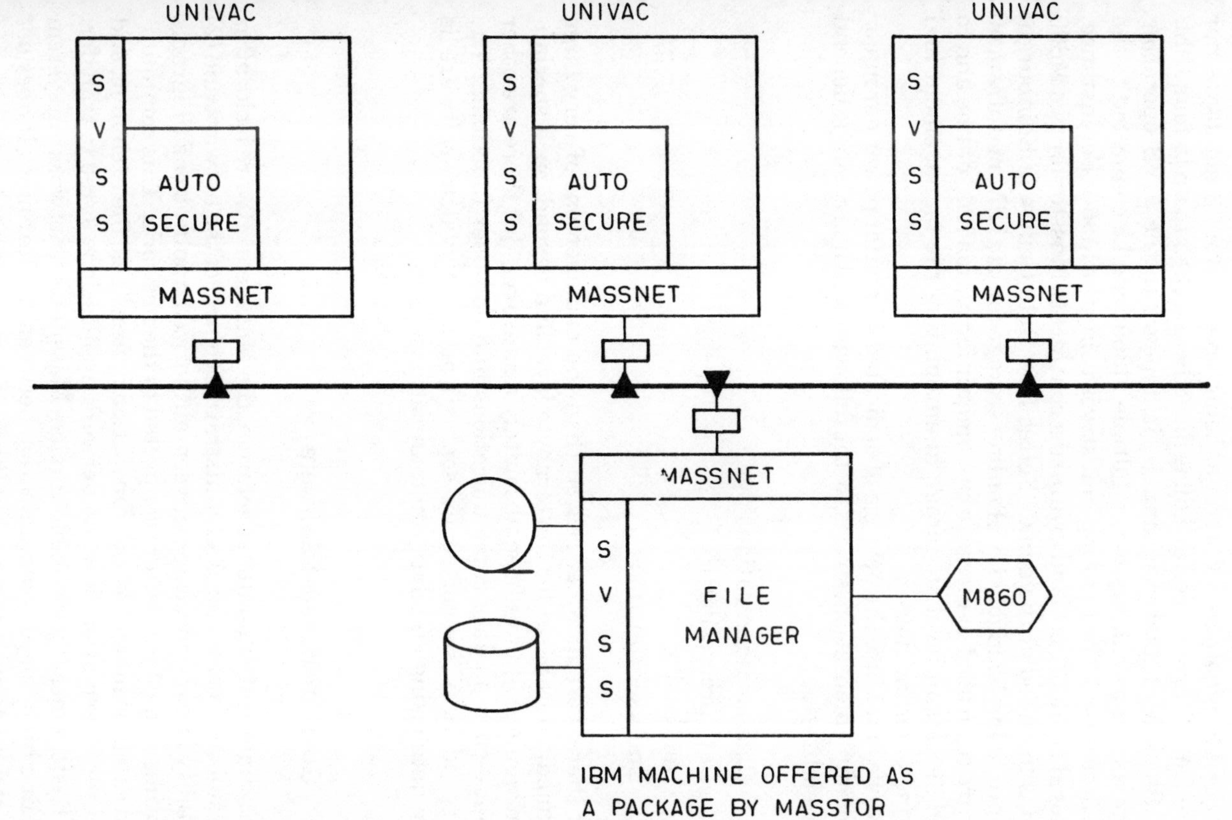

Figure 13.1 Interconnected Univacs to master storage through LAN interface (Massnet).

The M860 provides a modular growth from 55 billion bytes (gigabytes) to 440 gigabytes of storage, being able to store 3 gigabytes per square foot of floor space. (M860 is directly attached to up to four IBM/PCM Block Multiplexer Channels; it appears to the MVS operating system as a tape sub-system. Multiple M860s can be connected to the same processor.) The banking industry is using the M860. For instance, the Royal Bank of Scotland awarded a contract to Masstor for two M860 systems installed at the bank's Fettes Row Data Centre in Edinburgh, each providing 55 gigabytes of online storage for the IBM mainframes. They are to be used to increase customer information held online and to provide a second level of storage in automating the management and securing of online data.

As we move into the new era of dedicated computer power per major area of implementation, success of the following will increasingly depend on specialization:

- Data communications
- Data processing
- Databasing
- End-user functions

If there were no other reason than the management of very large multimedia databases for the terabyte level and beyond, such specialization would still have been absolutely necessary. But there are other reasons—such as data communications and end-user functions. The high-speed LAN supported by sophisticated, polyvalent software is where databasing and data communications meet.

13.3 Goals of Massnet Software

As a communications-intense solution, the Massnet software looks after two issues: (1) centralized administrative control of the network and (2) the ability to communicate between authorized applications programs executing on host computers connected to the network. This communication can take many forms: transactions, messages, file exchange, and any other information flow the network applications agree to transfer. In its basic, generally available version, Massnet is a networking system providing high-speed communication between mainframes. It *does not* support applications as such, but it provides management and control of network functions. Its features include:

- Inter-host communications at computer I/O channel speeds
- The ability of host-resident applications to communicate and exchange data
- A centralized audit and accounting function
- Error detection and recovery
- Integrity and configuration control

These are functions which in the ISO/OSI model occupy the lower four layers and part of the fifth: physical, data link, networking, transport, and the lower level of session control. The functionality of the physical, data link, and part of the network layer is covered through solutions provided by the Network Systems Corp. The rest of the network layer, the transport layer, and part of session control is addressed by the Massnet software, which consists of software modules resident in the attached mainframes. Still not covered are the upper ISO/OSI layers. This is why higher-up proprietary software is so important—as the General Electric case demonstrated (see Chapter 4). There, the Massnet Plus programs (developed jointly with Masstor using General Electric specifications) cover the balance of ISO/OSI session control, presentation control, and most of the application layer functionality. They address field-level detail—as compared to file-level detail of the basic Massnet software (up to session control). Even at the latter, file transfer facilities are provided between nonhomogeneous computers. Processors attached to the network can be treated as a single, logical processing resource. Multiple computers attached to the intelligent LAN share information storage and peripherals (such as printers). Network communications between applications programs take place in parallel.

In a typical operation, a program in one computer sends a message. The recipient of this message in another machine must issue a corresponding receive. Multiple logical connections can take place concurrently over the same adapter hardware with available software support. Figures 13.2 and 13.3 show the General Electric and Northwestern Bell applications. They:

- Reflect nonhomogeneous environments: IBM and Honeywell (HIS) mainframes
- Feature front-end communications engines: GE through VAX; Northwestern Bell through IBM, SNA compatible

Both installations have characteristics of interest to the larger organization. The opportunity to learn from them should not be missed.

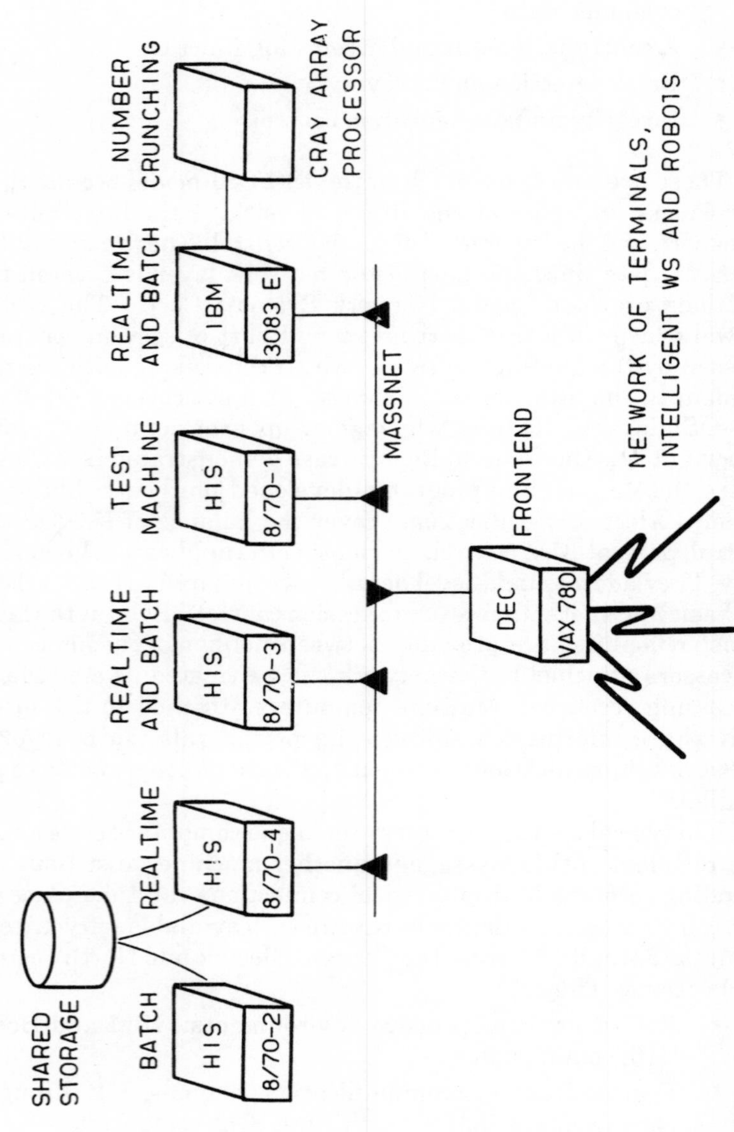

Figure 13.2 Massnet interconnecting mainframes at General Electric aircraft engines division, Lynn, MA.

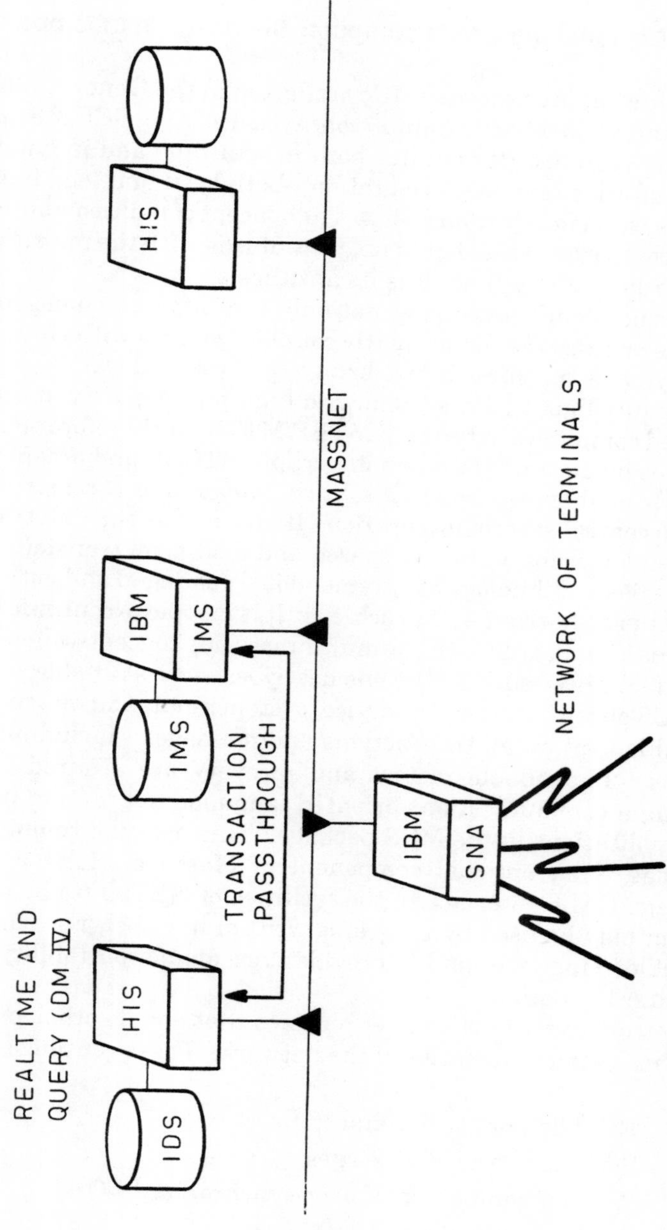

Figure 13.3 Massnet networking solution at North Western Bell, Omaha, NE.

13.4 Establishing a Multicomputer Service with Incompatible OS

The multicomputer service (MCS) reflected in the General Electric implementation involves the interconnection of the GCOS 8 and MVS operating systems. It operates both in real time and in batch, and it offers real-time terminal orientation—both local and long haul with a unique system integration vision. The concept of multicomputer service with incompatible OSs should not be confused with the multiprocessing of yesterday. If anything, it is its antithesis.

Classical multiprocessing not only presupposes homogeneous operations but also results in tightly coupled systems with shared central memory. Any machine failure brings the system down.

The intelligent LAN system with high-pipe capacity uncouples the attached computers in terms of MTBF/MTTR. It therefore significantly improves mean time of system interrupt (MTOSI) and accepts computers with nonhomogeneous OSs, thus overcoming a major stumbling block to central system integration. It also makes the link transparent to the end user for database search and field-level transfer.

The basic technology has tremendously changed and with it the implementation horizon we can achieve. It is myopic to continue operating with traditional, failure-prone multiprocessing concepts when new high-power facilities—such as the one described—are available.

MCS offers file transfer service, system input, and message mail. A journal is kept on all transactions and messages—including access to reasons. Dependable restart and recovery are assured. GE used Netcom, a communications-oriented language to program its proprietary applications in the MCS package. This network communications language is an optional component of Massnet. It is a high-level language CALL interface to the facilities of NETIO (to be discussed). Netcom may be used by programs written in Cobol, Fortran, PL/1, or assembler language, and it provides reasonable portability from one computer to another.

Netcom consists of a set of routines that enable other programs to interface with the facilities of the network. These routines:

- Establish network connection
- Send and receive messages
- Wait for completion of user-synchronized I/O
- Return error information
- Terminate a network connection

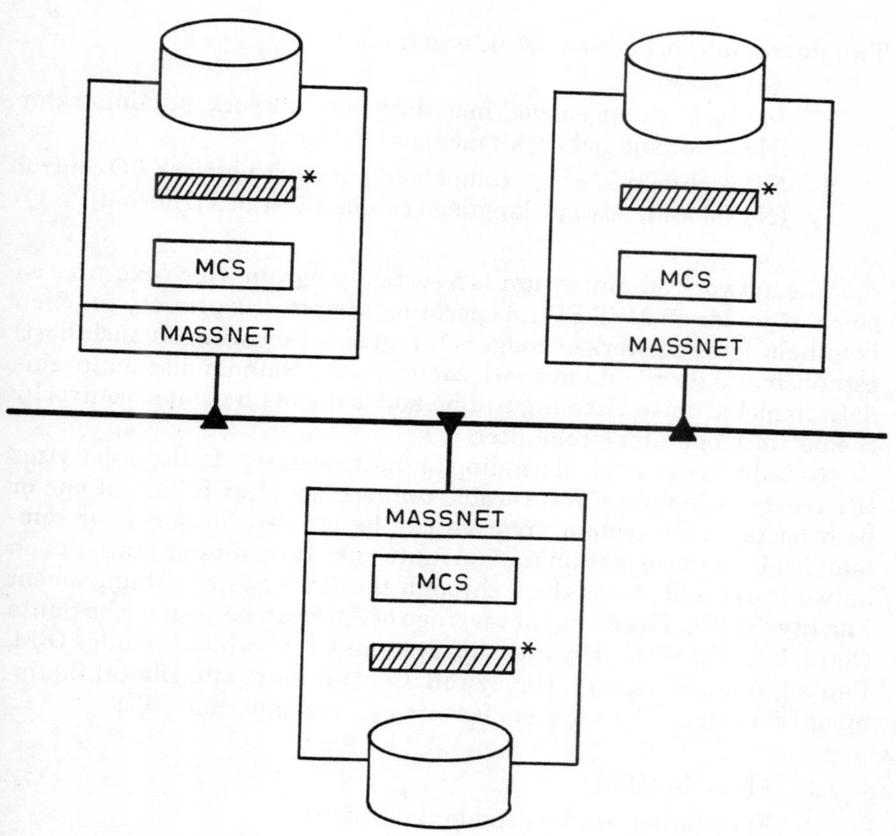

* SOFTWARE TO BE ADDED BY USER ORGANIZATION OVER THE MCS LAYER.

Figure 13.4 Positioning the MSC software for interconnection purposes. A system perspective.

The positioning of the MCS software within a system perspective is shown in Figure 13.4. Transfer activities can be launched by the user through simple commands. Information transfer works both ways among dissimilar mainframes—and this is important. Over the MCS layer is software by the user organization. Message Mailbox routines (MMS), proprietary to GE, are an example.

Let's now look into a more technical description of the Massnet layer.

Two important packages must be understood:

1. *Network management*, including the network administrator (Netadm) and network manager (Netmgr).
2. *Network access*, whose component parts are network I/O control (Netio) and network language communications (Netcom).

The network administrator is a system program which executes on one host under an MVS SP 1.3 operating system. Its primary function is to help local network managers (programs executing on each host) establish and terminate network connections. Netadm also maintains data on global network configuration and is the main point of control by the network operator's computer.

Netadm keeps track of pending connect requests. It also supervises the reestablishment of recoverable connections after failure of one or both hosts. This system program can be queried for status or commanded to perform certain control functions. It maintains statistics on network use and stores them through the MVS System Management Facility (SMF). The extent of coverage of SMF can be seen in the Santa Clara, CA, installation by Masstor Systems Corp. which includes IBM, Fujitsu, Amdahl, Sperry, Honeywell, Control Data, and Digital Equipment computers. This system features six incompatible OSs:

1. MVS/XA (IBM).
2. MVS (other vendors Amdahl, Fujitsu).
3. OS 1100 (Unisys).
4. GCOS 8 (Honeywell).
5. NOS (CDC).
6. VMS (DEC).

Network I/O control is the access method of Massnet. It interfaces all user programs to the network, whether or not a high-level interface is used or Netio is called directly. Netio has responsibility for overall control of the networking hardware, including interrupt handling, exception processing, and request queuing. Hence, the Netio caller does not need to be concerned with network adapter capacities or trunk and node configurations. Netio dynamically allocates and initializes a network logical unit. It establishes a connection with a program on a host computer. It also specifies that the remote applications program should be automatically started on a given host.

It is part of Netio's job to transmit a message across a given connection. With a few exceptions, a send request operation includes an automatic receive response. Finally, Netio terminates a connection and releases a logical unit. Masstor defined Netio as the driver embedded in the transport layer. Massnet also has an optional software feature used to extend the scope of networking beyond the local site. This is Masslink. Through the use of link adapter software, Masslink permits hosts using Massnet to communicate with each other over land line and microwave systems (leased and private). The method supported by Masslink is half duplex over a full-duplex line connection.

Also supported is a Netio protocol acting as the delivery mechanism for network transmissions:

- Incoming messages are delivered to central memory buffers for the receiving process—typically an applications program.
- Outgoing data is delivered to the network from user program buffers.

The inter-Netio protocol is based on exception reporting: successfully delivered messages are not specifically acknowledged to a remote Netio by a local Netio. Acknowledgment is the responsibility of the applications programs. The latter can defer a response until the message has been successfully processed.

Protocol exceptions reflected to a remote Netio include network error reported on the channel interface, receipt of unsolicited transmissions for which there is no user, receive active or no connection, incorrect transmission sequence number and/or incorrect length of associated data, and response timeout. Masstor stated that user application, programmers are free to design their own interapplication protocols within the rules and constraints of the lower-level Massnet layers. Among such rules, a proper connection must be established between applications programs via the connect protocol provided by the network manager and the network administrator. Except for multiblock chaining:

- Only one request can be sent on a connection before waiting for a response.
- Every request received must be acknowledged by a response to the sender within the agreed timeout limit.

Applications programs can individually specify request and response timeout values via Netio. Consistent user program names and connection protocol must be used in identifying applications to the network managers and the network administrator. There must also be a steady agreement regarding the content, format, size, and meaning of network user messages and associated information.

To see how the technical fundamentals have been applied for networking purposes, we must follow a real-life case study. For this we will use the General Electric implementation.

13.5 Technical Solutions for Open Vendor Policy

The concept of an open vendor policy simultaneously looks at the past, the present, and the future. The past is very important because of the large investments computer-user organizations have made in programming. The practice of throwing away software when changing equipment is over. There is neither time nor people nor money now to rewrite an application because of changed computers. Dai-Ichi Kangyo, a major bank, has 20 million Cobol statements invested in applications programs. Another leading bank has 16 million statements in applications inventory. These represent nearly 4500 programmer years of investments. We simply cannot throw away such wealth.

The overriding demand at the present is for continuity. Every self-respecting data system center cares for its users and their work. We simply cannot disconnect operations. They have to continue and to steadily improve. That's the target we can hit with intelligent LAN solutions. The future should be open to new developments. It should not be blocked because of past decisions. This, too, is an issue to which intelligent, high-capacity LAN can provide a valid response, making feasible in the process an open vendor policy.

Let's take a closer look at the GE case study, as it is not only instructive but also a good example of what other organizations will be facing in the not too distant future. In 1982, General Electric went through a process of mainframe interconnection. It involved the introduction of IBM mainframes into a part dominated by another vendor, Honeywell. It was decided that if the interconnection proved successful, the approach would be applied GE-wide. The time had come for open vendor policy.

IBM was chosen for mainframes and DEC for departmental machines. There were also CDC and Cray for engineering applications. The internal study on technical objectives done by GE personnel was given to major vendors, but none offered a satisfactory solution. Then GE turned to a smaller company with experience in the field. That's how Masstor Systems Corp. came into the picture. Their system specialists studied GCOS 8 (the OS) and made a proposal with a fixed price and a timetable for implementing multicomputer services (MCS). Figure 13.5 shows an overview of the logical components of this system. MCS is delimited by two address spaces (AS). The different operating systems (MVS, GCOS 8, VMS) are found beyond the upper address space.

The goal of MSC in this implementation is to provide a set of integrated application services for network users in a multimainframe, multi-OS, multivendor environment. Such a goal is reached through high-level access to a variety of applications programs. It is executed in a uniform, centrally managed way. The multivendor services software resides in the attached mainframes. Each host must also ba a Massnet network host:

- The computers are called MCS nodes.
- The group of hosts connected with Massnet and MCS is an MCS complex.

Quite importantly, an MCS complex may include geographically separated host computers, connected via the Massnet MLink capability. MCS software helps to make network and related services a uniform frame of reference.

Regarding the ISO/OSI model, MCS provides the application and presentation layer protocol. The underlying Massnet software handles the session and transport layer protocols. A vital systems reference is the way of adjusting form and syntax of requests for MCS services to fit the applications environment:

1. There is a Masstor-supplied standard end-user syntax.
2. Subroutine calls for programmers are typical of library routine calls for assembler and high-level languages.
3. Operations-related applications are easily embedded in normal operating procedures.
4. Subroutine interface allows the construction of a variety of general- and special-purpose MCS distributed network applications.
5. Functions such as integrated network data management are provided.

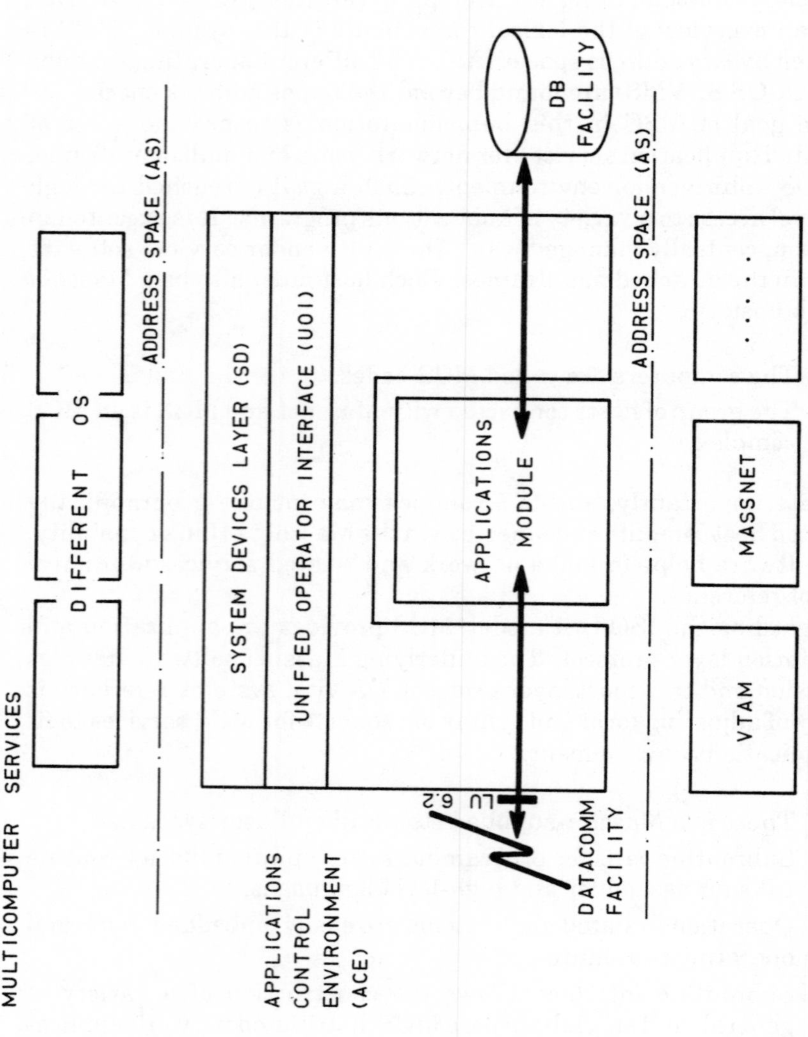

Figure 13.5 Logical structure of the multicomputer services solution implemented by MSC.

In this sense, MCS facilitates the integration of multiple sourcing computers into a single unified system.

In the process of moving files, routing input and output, and handling network-based data management, MCS addresses itself to resource allocation, data format conversion, job scheduling, access security, network protocol, and catalog management. To make effective use of MCS services, applications entities need information about the network configuration. MCS provides a logical name facility permitting changes in the network configuration to be made transparent to end users.

The MCS network configuration is defined and managed through operator commands. This definition is accomplished by adding appropriate application records to the Massnet Network Administrator's (Netadm) database. The definition of MCS to Massnet is performed only once for each Massnet network, regardless of how many MCS nodes are present. Typically, the amount of configuration information needed for one MCS node to communicate with other MCS nodes in the network is quite small. The MCS node must know the name by which it will refer to each of the other nodes and it must know its own name.

13.6 The Applications Control Environment

Key to MCS functionality is the Applications Control Environment (ACE) and the Applications Module. ACE is a run-time facility. Like a real-time OS with program development capability, it includes consistent macro, utility service, real-time (RT) system service calls, support requirements for memory, and so on. Interfacing through an addressing space and system service layer is important in order to:

1. Keep immunity from OS releases by different vendors.
2. Provide consistency, e.g., fence off combinations of errors.
3. Assure the capability to recover from failures on a subsystem basis.

The system service layer executes the conversion of system calls by different OS into one reference base.

ACE is a proprietary program that facilitates the decision and implementation of a range of real-time event-driven applications. It creates a programming domain that is host independent; its structure and functions are common across various host architectures and operating systems. ACE is the key to multicommunication system functioning. It provides a wide range of commonly used facilities for the real-time applications programmer, including operator handling, interjob communications, multitasking, access to database (through keys), network interfacing, restart and recovery, tracing, hardcopy, and logging to debugging.

Routines which must be present in any real-time program are provided within ACE. MCS makes use of ACE throughout its structure. Since ACE is the basis for many Masstor program products, the recovery characteristics, operator interfaces, installation procedures, and overall architecture for these products is common to all. Furthermore, the ACE environment permits an application to be divided into a number of largely autonomous tasks, each of which performs a specific function. Such tasks work together to deliver the full integrated function of an ACE application.

Both databasing and communications facilities reach the applications module through the ACE interface. The communications link can be Massnet/Hyperchannel, SNA, or other. Each application running in the so-defined domain has one master task (MS) specific to the OS from which it depends, such as MVS. The master task is responsible for process handling in the environment in which it runs. Its functionality is similar to that of a demon in Unix 4.3 BSD. (Demons are network-wide supervisory processes.)

As seen in Figure 13.6, the master task can have several subtasks (STs). An MS can provide changing operator parameters. Different programmers may develop new processes at the task or subtask level.

Each MCS service is a defined network application. It provides a facility needed in a networking sense. Individually defined application services are integrated into a single system. The positive aspect is that such MCS services feature a broad range of facilities for user processes. Services can be called by applications programs which also may combine the functions of multiple MCS services, treating them as building blocks.

A session control concept is used for communications purposes. Each user process must establish a logical session with MCS before issuing MCS information or service requests. An MCS session may consist of only one command or may involve many varied MCS operations to be grouped within a single session. During a session, all of the services are available to the user. Information destined for that user from MCS is routed to the session. Termination of a session will not necessarily terminate the requests that the user has issued, but it will end the reporting ability of MCS for those requests.

Two different approaches to user access are supported through MCS.

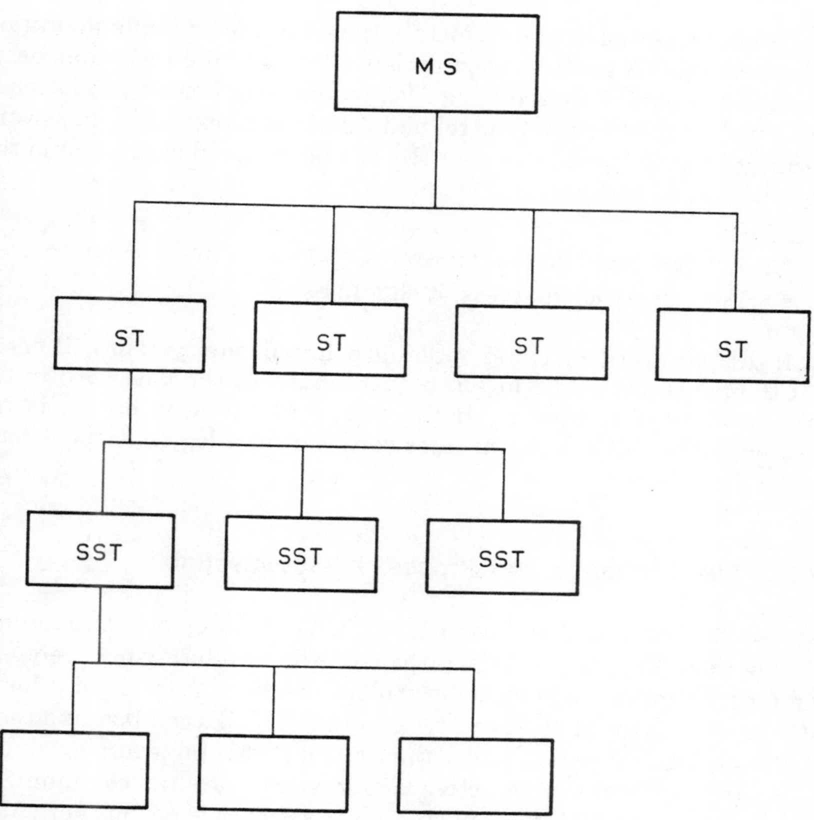

Figure 13.6 **Dividing the master task into subtasks in a hierarchial tree.**

The user access may be treated as a restricted access operation or as an open access. In the restricted access approach, users must properly identify themselves by supplying an MCS user ID and password, in a similar fashion to accessing a timesharing system. Only users supplying a correct user ID and password pair will be allowed access to MCS. Each user ID may have specific limitations on the MCS functions being invoked. In the open access approach, any user of the host system may use MCS freely. Defaulting is provided so that users need not specify their user IDs or passwords and need not be aware of the distinction between MCS user IDs and system user IDs.

The MCS Site Administrator must determine which access approach is to be implemented in a given installation. Each MCS implementation makes available a configuration option which specified whether password validation is to occur during a log-on request. Log-on validation is performed by the Service Control and Administration task. Password checking for privileged MCS user IDs can be enforced regardless of the check password option:

- For restricted access, password checking should be on.
- For unrestricted access, it should be off.

If the password checking option is selected, the system will verify that the password in the log-on request matches the password in the corresponding user profile. If the password checking option is not selected, MCS will accept any password during a log-on request for a nonprivileged user.

13.7 File Exchange and Process Interconnection

Service Control and Administration (SCA) provides overall management of the MCS system. It is responsible for validating user requests and for maintaining a Massnet control connection. A focal point for all MCS services is the MCS Executive program (MCSExec). It runs on each host in an MCS/Massnet, under the control of this program.

A large number of interactive and/or batch users can communicate concurrently with MCSExec to obtain the services of one or more MCS applications. Through its SCA component, MCSExec validates and schedules each user request and then passes the request onto the appropriate application for execution. Validation of user requests is accomplished by accessing an MCS-use database each time a user attempts to log on to MCS or issues an MCS service command. The novelty is a user-oriented database containing a list of valid MCS users, their passwords, and the facilities or services each is permitted to access. Entries in the user database are created, modified, and deleted by the MCS site administrator through the use of privileged commands.

Control links are used to exchange scheduling and status information about the overall MCS system as well as individual user requests. SCA also provides a system console interface allowing operators to obtain MCS system status information and manage the system. Through this approach SCA manages a modular set of application services conforming to a common architecture and design, therefore providing a consistent image to user entities.

The division into task and subtask facilitates run-time execution. A subtask may be assigned to dispatching, recovery, queuing and dequeuing, and so on. Other important system functions are shown in Figure 13.7; SIFS stands for standard interface subroutine (reentrant code) and SUIF is the standard user interface. SIFS provides the cross-address-space communication required to formulate and handle requests for

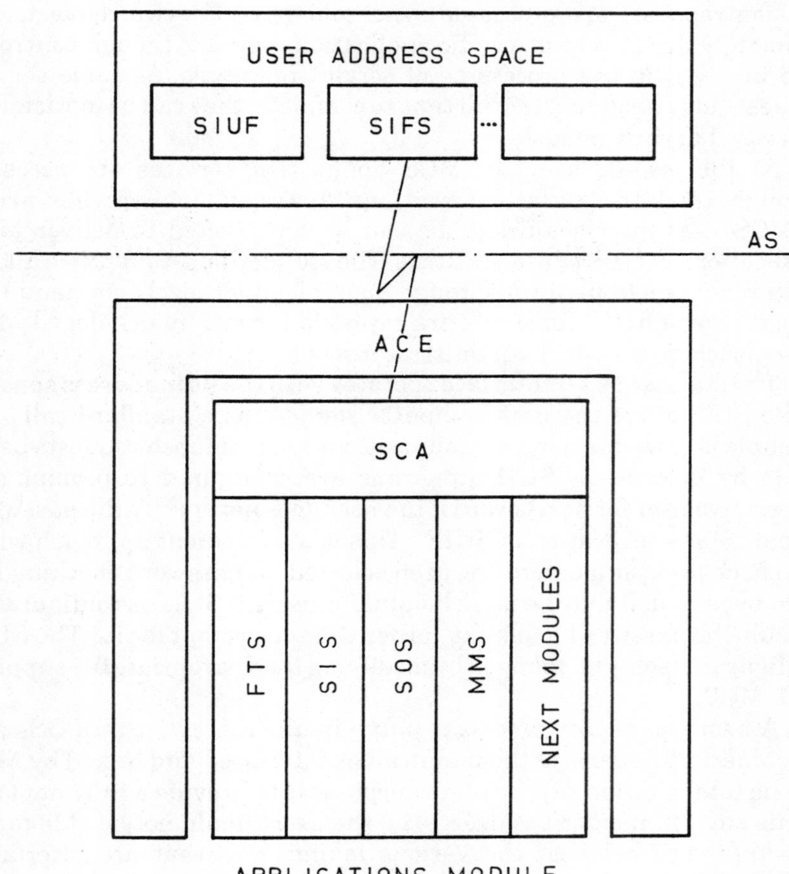

Figure 13.7 User address space and applications modules included in the ACE/SCA software.

MCS services and to also return the results. Additional functions provided by SIFS include:

- Management of an MCS user session
- Editing and validating user input before initiating cross-address-space communication

SIFS calls are divided into two categories: session requests and service requests. The former are only passed on to system control. Session requests are processed synchronously. Service requests are ultimately directed to a specific applications service, though control is also involved in the processing of service requests. As some service requests may need substantial time to complete, they can be (optionally) processed asynchronously.

At the lowest level, all MCS application services are accessed through standard interface subroutines. At a higher level, a wide variety of MCS user interface programs can be constructed to deliver MCS application services to user entities. The standard user interface allows MCS functions to perform through a simple, high-level command language. Some SUIF functions are reserved for use by privileged MCS users, such as the MCS administrator.

The standard user interface operates with the user address space—while SIFS offers the multicomputer services as a standard call. An example is cross-memory communications to accomplish requests being made by processes. SUIF programs are configured to prompt and interactive user for a password if the user does not specify the password as part of the invocation of SUIF. This is a convenient approach when the check password option has been selected. If password checking has been bypassed, it may be more helpful for users if SUIF is configured to default the password to blanks rather than to prompt for it. The SUIF configuration may be changed by modifying the appropriate file supplied with MCS.

A user can be *any process* running in *any context*. Since OSs and machine architecture of the mainframes interfaced and linked by MCS can be totally different, one of its purposes is to provide a fully homogeneous environment to the user, e..g., the user should not be able to tell the difference between the various mainframes that are interfaced through MCS or that are being addressed by a workstation.

Figure 13.7 also details the components of the applications module under the system control and administration (SCA) layer. They are

- File transfer (FTS)
- System input service (SIS)
- System output service (SOS)
- Mail and memogram service (MMS)

Other modules are being implemented by users of MCS, as well as planned by Masstor Systems.

The FTS service may be employed directly by end users to facilitate exchange of information between nodes: a user may copy a document from one node to another, edit it, and return it to the original location. Hence, editing features supported by one manufacturer may be combined with document preparation capabilities of another vendor. The object of the system input service is that of transmitting a JCL file to or from a remote node, submitting that JCL file for execution on the target hose. The message mailbox service transmits and receives messages via mailboxes (electronic mail).

File transfer can be affected in a number of ways:

1. Files between similar nodes may be transferred as physical records, such as disk tracks or blocks. MCS terms these physical transfer modes, or native modes. Each MCS implementation supports one or more native transfer modes since they yield high performance and guarantee identical file copies.
2. Files between unlike vendor types may be treated in one of two ways. If the file is a sequential text file, it can be transferred as blocked logical records consisting of characters. Character set and file format translation is handled by MCS. However, complex files, such as MVS partitioned data sets cannot be transferred in this way, though facilities to treat both fixed- and variable-length records are provided as MOVE options.
3. If there is no need to create a readable copy of the file on the destination node, the file may be sent using a native transfer mode. A physical record is recorded at the destination as a logical record in a sequential, or literal, file. A literal file can store a foreign file's contents in a way that the original file can be recreated by reversing the MOVE operation.

Files transferred between like nodes will generally move as physical tracks or blocks across the network. Files transferred between unlike nodes will be moved as translated logical records unless the MCS-supplied defaults are explicitly changed. Important is the fact that MCS has the ability to make intelligent default choices for the user.

13.8 System Control and Administration

SCA can be used as a facility interlinking attached machines and it can also look at and receive status information. SCA acts as virtual circuit, assuring programmatic and run-time interfaces.* It communicates with users through SIFS using cross-memory communication services (provided by ACE) to handle control information.

Multiple user programs may be in communication with MCS concurrently, with SCA being responsible for managing and routing user requests received through SIFS. When a request is posted to SCA, it will be routed to the appropriate service task or to another SCA node across its network connection. Such service is a subtask to SCA, which has the ability to respond to interrupts or initiate a message. Status information is exchanged between services and SCA in response to SCA-, operator, or user-initiated inquiry.

Requests for a service are handled asynchronously; therefore, SCA may go on to other work while awaiting a response. A message is always held by the sender until an acknowledgment is received from its destination. In this way, recovery is possible from a variety of conditions. SCA also maintains a dynamic database that records the current status of a number of operational parameters. This permits dynamic configuration of an MCS aggregate, as well as recovery across system interruptions. Dynamic status information maintained by MCS includes:

1. User definition.
2. Network connections to other nodes.
3. Service status.

The operational status of each applications service is thus maintained. Such information includes whether a given service is active or inactive, as well as resource limits and user requests.

The division between ACE and SCA allows a layered vision of im-

---

*ACE and SCA represent 2 to 3 million lines of code, plus 3 to 4 programmer-years of implementation effort.

plementation. The alternative would have been a monolithic interfacing solution. The network interface for SCA is provided by ACE. When started, each SCA attempts to complete a network connection with every other SCA in MCS:

- There is a virtual circuit connection established between each pair of nodes.
- Over this connection, which is essentially a control link, SCA is able to exchange control information with other nodes with good performance.

Operator interface is assured by the facilities of ACE, and it plays an important role in MCS control, although close operator surveillance and control of MCS is not often necessary. The system operator must have the ability to start and stop MCS, but the interface also supplies control capabilities.

When necessary, the operator may investigate the configuration and status of nodes, users, and services; modify a site configuration; monitor and modify MCS job scheduling; and also bring individual services online or offline, although the typical operation will be that of an unattended environment.

SCA manages a modular set of application services which actually perform the end-user services of MCS. Each service, though distinct in function, conforms to a common architecture and design, therefore providing a consistent image to end users. To repeat:

- ACE supports system services, addresses itself to devices, and includes unified operator routines and interfaces to SCA.
- SCA interfaces to ACE and acts as supervisor of the towers in the applications module (FTS, SIS, etc.).

Such a layered solution simplifies operations as it contains specific functions per layer. Concurrency-limited services are constrained by local, remote, and total limits. Concurrency limits can be used to control the consumption of system resources by MCS. Also MCS traffic statistics are valuable in evaluating service management.

Concurrency limits and history queue processing apply to such services as the file transfer service and the system input service. Transaction-oriented services like message mailbox service (MMS) are not managed through concurrency limits. The process of sending a message through MMS takes place in two steps:

1. The user generates a message. When message entry is complete, it is transferred from the sending user to the mail system, where the message is queued for delivery—posting.
2. The mail system attempts to insert the message into the destination mailbox(es)—delivery. MMS will try to deliver all new messages immediately. If unable to do so, it may hold the message and try to deliver it at a later time.

MMS only communicates with the sender if there are problems in delivering the mail. For instance, if it encounters a difficulty in delivering the message, MMS informs the sender of the problem by posting internally generated mail back to the originator and describing the delivery problem. A fatal error occurs if MMS determines that a message is permanently undeliverable, for instance, if it has been sent to a mailbox on a nonexistent node. But other errors, too, may prevent the successful immediate delivery of a message, e.g., if the destination mailbox for a message is located on a host computer that is temporarily down. In this case, MMS holds the message in transit.

Multiple concurrent user address spaces can simultaneously obtain services from MCS. Each user job uses the standard interface subroutines which communicate cross memory with the MCSExec program. Through such programmatic interface, a variety of links can be constructed. Each subroutine entry point executes one primitive MCS function. Other interfaces to MCS, such as the standard user interface, call the SIFS subroutines to access MCS.

Masstor Systems is in the process of implementing MCS for VM, but it already assures VTAM/SNA as a communications access method. MCA uses a LU 6.2 macro-to-macro approach. With SNA becoming a virtual standard in data communications, LU 6.2 will be the common ground. As contrasted to MCS, the Data File Interchange Utility (MDX), which is included in the current Massnet software as the upper layer, provides the capability to interchange files between any Massnet interconnected computers. It also supports RJE from any network-connected computer to any other.

Another important software module by Masstor Systems is MTAM (Massnet Terminal Access Method). This is a network applications product interfacing ACF/VTAM and Massnet. It links 3270 or compatible terminals attached to one IBM host to VTAM applications programs on another IBM host. MTAM allows terminals in one domain to access applications in another domain using Massnet instead of SNA Multisystem Networking Facility. Given the Hyperchannel interconnect, it permits resources to be relocated in different hosts without affecting the user.

Masstor Systems maintains that MTAM leads to reduced 37xx hardware requirements as well as interhost communication at 50-MBPS speed, either for local area hosts or for remote hosts connected via MLink. It relieves the need to maintain VTAM cross-domain resource tables for remote terminals, thus enhancing terminal flexibility for cross-host 3270 access.

Finally, administrative functions must be assured. Four categories are important:

1. Network configuration.
2. Service configuration.
3. User access.
4. Capability management.

User access and capability management call for defining MCS user profiles in the MCS user database on each host in an MCS site. Static network configuration management consists of supplying data to describe the network configuration to each MCS node.

Dynamic network configuration management determines which parts of the network will be active at a given time and includes responding to temporary outages and changes in the network configuration. The MCS site administrator acts as the central authority of MCS resource control for the user community. That administrator should, therefore, have a thorough understanding of the MCS system concept, functions, features, and capabilities.

Chapter

14

IBM's Local Area Networks

14.1 Introduction

In the last 5 years an IBM local area network product has created a de facto standard, and other vendors have announced products that make their LANs compatible with or adaptable to the IBM system. Therefore, a thorough understanding of token ring technology and IBM's LAN products is essential.

As of early 1988, IBM statistics indicated that there were over 12,000 token ring LANs installed interconnecting an estimated 200,000 attached devices at an average of 16.67 attachments per LAN. A 20 to 25 percent increase in token ring nodes was foreseen for 1988. Such statistics are meaningful in comparison to another network architecture such as Ethernet. As of late 1987, Ethernet was installed at 8,000 customer locations with an estimated 115,000 attached devices, or 14.37 connected devices per LAN. However, many of these connected devices were larger machines, including an estimated 20,000 Vax and PDP 11.

Intensifying its market effort, IBM is in the process of expanding token ring installation in smaller firms. For example Covia, United Airlines' information services subsidiary, is installin thousands of PS/2 Model 50s and 60s and hundreds of token rings in travel agencies and reservation offices nationwide. Each PS/2 will allow travel agents to view multiple databases relating to airlines, rental cars and hotel availability. IBM has also adopted much of Microsoft's LAN technology, primarily for workstations rather than for the server. But Microsoft has entered into a third-party agreement with 3Com, a rapidly growing LAN hardware vendor, to market Microsoft's OS/2 LAN Manager software with 3 Com's hardware—which is thin Ethernet.

A recent study by Paine Webber viewed LAN software as an extension of the operating system. Microsoft's OS/2 LAN Manager takes this approach by having the same operating system running on the workstations and servers, thus being in a position to offer transparent, distributed processing. Given the wide variety of LAN products and the impact of IBM's strategy, what sense can be made of the technology and direction of this market? The answer to this question can be found only by carefully reviewing trends and products. A comprehensive response requires the examination of IBM's strategies and assessment of future directions for IBM LANs as well as of IBM's personal computer and departmental computer lines.

IBM local area network and personal computer strategies are indivisible from software policies and interconnection architectures. OS/2 is an initial participant in IBM's strategic solution aimed to overcome OS diversity in its systems application architecture (SAA) product line. SAA guides the development of software to run across IBM PC, System/36, System/38, System/370, and through the LAN. Most importantly, SAA is destined to play an important role in the data processing industry, as IBM seems to have decided to make the technical specifications of SAA interfaces available to its customers and to third-party hardware and software developers. SAA has four major elements:

1. Common user access.
2. Common programming interfaces.
3. Common communications support.
4. Common applications support.

A new interface management group has been formed at IBM that will oversee development of various SAA components for all IBM products, including the LAN. OS/2 offers a common user access, programming interface, and communications support. This way IBM hopes to lock in large corporate accounts through the microcomputer. To preserve the huge investment in existing software and provide a migration path to new applications, OS/2 contains a compatibility mode that emulates the DOS 3.3 environment.

IBM's solution for a microcomputer-to-mainframe link revolves around its advanced program-to-program (APPC) LU 6.2 protocol. Its promotion rests on the premise that the most effective computing environment of the 1990s will consist of PCs integrated into large corporate DP systems.

14.2 New Life for SNA

If we carefully look at available network architectures, we will see that IBM quietly introduced a nonhierarchical extension to SNA. Advanced peer-to-peer networking (APPN) is the first product to support this structure. It is also the first component of SNA's low entry networking (LEN) extension. Understanding the transformation of SNA and APPN is fundamental in following IBM's local area network strategy.

APPN is the first in a growing array of IBM peer-oriented building blocks. It rests on APPC and LU 6.2. One of the merits of APPC is that it permits interprogram exchanges. The Physical Unit 2.1 (PU 2.1, now referred to by IBM as Type 2.1) comprises the lower-level basis of LU 6.2 in the SNA/LEN architecture. LU 6.2 is not just a workstation-to-workstation communications protocol between intelligent systems. It is a major departure from IBM policies—as well as those that have been followed by other mainframe vendors. Unlike the older SNA session protocols, LU 6.2 drops the master-slave orientation. APPC does not have primary and secondary session partners. Instead, two systems communicate as peers.

Establishing a SNA session usually requires the involvement of a system services control point (SSCP). The latter is located in the mainframe's VTAM software that interfaces the terminal and application that requires interconnection. It also:

- Provides network directory and address conversion
- Maintains status information on all active network sessions
- Permits centralized control of a wide area SNA network

Such an arrangement does not make much sense for local area network communications. This master-slave orientation is utterly unnecessary for workstations communicating in an office environment. Eliminating this restriction requires support for an intermediate routing capability, which is provided. With wide area and in-house networking solutions becoming prominent (Figure 14.1), both SNA- and LEN-type features will be necessary. The workstation-to-workstation communication may directly involve a WS coupler, baseband or broadband LAN, LAN plus PBX-to-PBX communication, and so on. For every approach the user organization wishes to take, the appropriate architectural and software should be supported by the vendor.

IBM's LEN Version 1 is a point-to-point interface between Type 2.1 nodes, which currently include the IBM PC, System/36, and Series/1. Like LU 6.2 and PU 2.1, LEN Version 1 is just a point-to-point link, but it supports APPN, thus adding dynamic routing and directory protocols. There is a structural difference between a LEN and an SNA. As they presently stand, SNA networks have three levels:

1. Hosts, always mainframes, are on top.
2. Communications controllers (front-end processors) form the middle tier.
3. Everything else (smaller processors and cluster controllers—peripheral nodes, or PN) are underneath.

By contrast, a network running under LEN has only two levels:

1. Network nodes (NNs).
2. Peripheral nodes (PNs).

To participate in the network, NNs contain directories of the PN attached to them. They also feature an internal representation of the topology of the NN network. An important reference is that the NNs function as peers, sending each other messages on behalf of the PN that they serve. This differs markedly from SNA, where each subarea node must contain information about all the peripheral nodes in its own subarea. LEN is also a departure from SNA in its operational services: connection, disconnection, directories, routing, session initiation, and termination.

The SNA-LEN architectural solution largely rests on logical unit

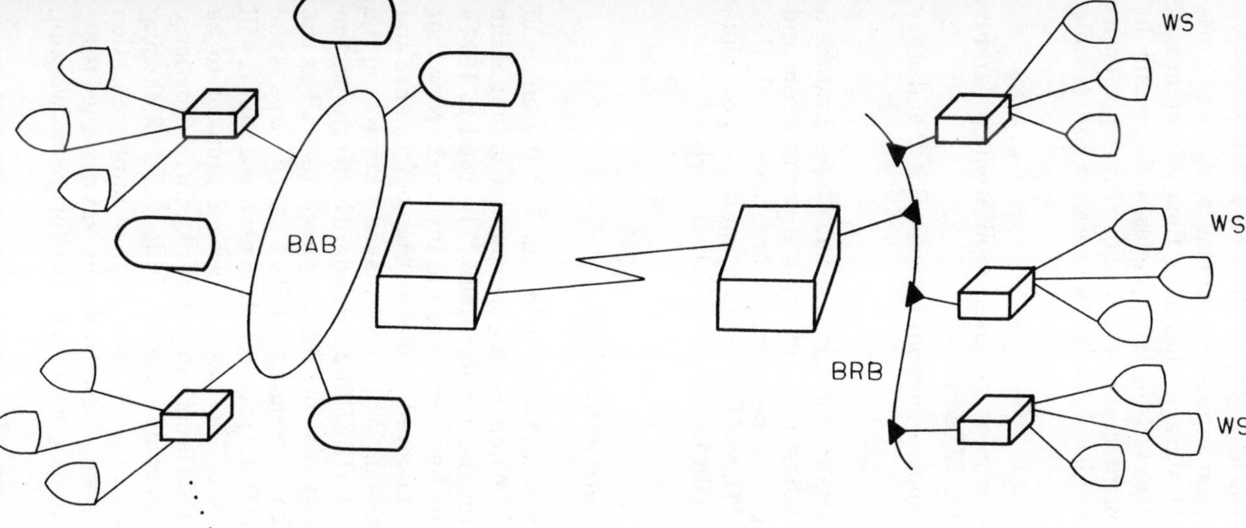

Figure 14.1 Integrating broadband (BRB) and baseband (BAB) LAN into an inhouse network.

(LU) functionality. They are the logical ports through which end users gain access to network resources: input-output devices, machine processor cycles, real and virtual storage, database files, direct access storage devices (DASD), as well as WS displays, queues, and sessions. In any communications environment, sessions are temporary, logical connections. In SNA, sessions take place between two network addressable units (NAUs):

- Sessions that directly connect end-user applications programs or devices are called LU-LU sessions.
- All other sessions are control sessions between SSCP and other SSCP, PU, or LU.

All of the non-LU 6.2 program-to-program session types assume a hierarchical session between a host-resident applications program and a dumb I/O device. LEN's peer-to-peer feature does away with this assumption. Still, APPN, APPC, and LEN are a framework of concepts and possible products. The applications will tell their worth.

14.3 Personal Computer Networks by IBM

IBM's entry into the local area network field has had the effect of legitimizing the technology. The impact has been similar to that of the original IBM PC in the personal computer field. The road to IBM's commercial token ring offering has been long and involved. Now that products are being formally announced, issues such as conformance and patent rights are being addressed. While IBM played a key role in the IEEE 802.5 recommendation, the IEEE 802.5 standard had its impact on the token-passing media access control (MAC) protocol as well as the physical signaling aspects. The interface that IBM uses for this is the IEEE 802.2 data link control (DLC) protocol. It is expected that it will continue to use it regardless of the medium access protocol to be employed. At the same time, IBM is defining new link control functions, such as source routing, that may or may not be included in 802.2, causing concern among third-party vendors. Another area of implementation interest is the IBM cabling system, which IBM says was designed to accommodate not only current equipment but also future networking products.

Some of the standards elaborated by IBM for the cabling system are incompatible with previous ones such as AT&T's twisted pair. However,

IBM's cabling system is intended to eliminate the multitude of cabling methods that exist for current IBM equipment. Based primarily on data-quality twisted pair, some of the components of the wiring system have been used in comparable forms in other data communications approaches for decades. To counter questions of cost, IBM added to this family of wiring components by specifying a Type 3 telephone-grade twisted pair. This has put severe restrictions on the network, particularly in terms of sizing and the number of supportable devices. Subsequently, IBM announced a Type 9 (lower cost) go-between twisted pair designed to accommodate the token ring.

IBM also introduced repeaters into its token ring family. They allow extended distances and offer the capability to bring fiber optics into the system (Type 5 fiber optics cable). From strategic and marketing viewpoints, IBM is at an important point in its communications product plan. By announcing its token ring LAN product and cabling system, it indicated how it intends to tie its mainframes, PCs, PBXs, and other office automation products together. But current announcements fall short of mainframe connectivity as well as of the ability to integrate text, data, voice, and image into a multimedia system. For this reason we will limit the discussion to what IBM's local area network can do.

The token ring related products IBM has announced will have a great effect on the future of networks as well as on IBM and compatible computers. Many IBM watchers expect all computer products—from the IBM PC AT to the Sierra 3090—to cooperate in a token ring environment, though I personally greatly doubt mainframes can even intermittently be served by anything that has been announced so far.

IBM's PBX is beginning to enter the token ring implementation perspective as new connectivity products are announced. The Rolm bridge 5250 Link Protocol Converter allows a System/36 and System/38 to support PBX-connected asynchronous terminals. With the addition of the System/36 LAN attachment feature, these terminals can access other resources attached to the token ring. There are, however, serious doubts whether current PBX can hold both voice and data traffic. At the same time, several technologists think that IBM's 3725 and 3174 controllers will be crucial in achieving system integration. The 3725 acts as a front end to large IBM SNA-based host computers. The trunk coupling unit allows the 3725 to participate in the token ring. The 3174 is a new class of low-cost cluster controller that makes IBM competitive with third-party vendors. Key to the 3174 products is the optional token ring interface that allows 3278 and ASCII terminals to use the token ring as transport. It also directly supports attached IBM PCs running in 3278 emulation mode.

Following IBM's announcements, there are products from third-party vendors that add compatibility or value-added services between their local networks and IBM or offer an alternative to the token ring which might be taken as nearly compatible. Third-party offerings are highly varied; they include compatible wiring products to use their existing LANs on the IBM cabling system; gateways between systems; software that sits on top of the token ring; and fairly compatible hardware and software that plugs into the PC. Many claims are being made as to compatibility with the token ring, but products typically rely on an interface, such as Netbios, to operate properly. There is also RM, a LAN resource-sharing machine system that allows personal computers to act as application servers within a service-request framework. A user can engage in concurrent activities supported by different network service machines. A prototype implemented on an IBM PC, using the IBM PC DOS and the IBM PC Network LAN, has been used to support project development work.

The term "action" refers to a user's unit of work that is carried out by a LAN service. There are possible variations to the action concept as well as an action management facility, with emphasis on use of the service-request framework. Software for managing the user interface and for supporting user interaction with remote servers is under development.

Understandably, IBM announcements place significant importance on software. Unlike the underlying LAN hardware, the software that operates in the upper layers offers many choices:

- It is widely expected that OS/2 will evolve toward networking and multiuser systems.
- IBM introduced the new APPC interface to run on PCs in the token ring or with stand-alone SDLC adapters.
- Netbios and the IBM PC Network Program have been carried over from the IBM PC Network broadband LAN.

The APPC interface allows access to SNA protocols, making possible communications with PC and other hosts attached to the token ring. Netbios gives access to the widely adopted interface for PC LAN.

Currently there are over 15,000 SNA installations worldwide. With a series of steady enhancements during recent years, IBM has significantly expanded SNA capabilities, counting on its programming products to be the network standards for a long time. Yet, there are still major areas that have not been fully addressed by SNA. In addition, critical incompatibilities between some IBM products will still remain.

At the core of software developments are possible extensions of SNA which are intended to allow peer, dynamic, and easy-to-use networking functions for a variety of node sizes down to new generations of personal computers. There are special requirements posed by small systems, and the need for including them as peer partners in networks can only be met by following a sequence of steps beginning when a logical resource requests a session with a remote logical resource of an unknown location. After connectivity with the preexisting network is established, directory services locate the remote object, route selection services determine the preferred path, a session is activated, and deadlock-free flow control assures a useful flow of data. IBM expects that APPC will have a major role in integrating the various computers together, using SNA for the intermediate protocols and token ring as the basic transport mechanism.

14.4 The Cabling System

In its initial 1984 announcement, IBM's token passing LAN was composed of the cabling system and logical components scheduled to be marketed over a number of years. The focus on the cabling system extended over a range of traditional types of connections to be made between devices with a common cable consisting of twisted pairs. In an office, the aim was to connect wall outlets to wiring closets. 'Such information outlets are installed in the walls for computer devices and, optionally, for telephones. Each office wall outlet interconnects to a distribution panel. The panel can accept up to 64 cables from different devices.

As announced, the cabling system covers only the bottom two ISO/OSI layers: physical and data link. Cabling is grounded and shielded double twisted pair. Four types of cable were announced:

- Type 1 cable supports data only.
- Type 2 has two more twisted pairs for voice. Hence, from the start the IBM solution featured separate wires for voice. There is no problem carrying voice at 64 KBPS (the ISDN recommended standard) and no contention with text and data transport.
- Type 5 is optical fibers (2 fibers) advisable for high bandwidth (eventually) and immediate needs regarding security and noise.
- Type 6 is patch cable, used to rewire in a distribution panel only (not as data carrying wire).

According to its specifications, this shielded twisted wire LAN can run up to a maximum distance of 16 km (10 miles).

The current offering supports baseband, single channel, and any-to-any capability. IBM selected baseband for a number of reasons:

- TDM (time division multiplexing) implementation
- Use of digital signals
- Any-device addressability
- One wire to support all requirements
- Lower cost per attachment

IBM's twisted wire baseband works at 4 MBPS, though it has been driven under laboratory conditions up to 8 and 10 MBPS. Higher speeds will be supported by fiber optics. The 4-MBPS level refers to twisted pair, which is where IBM will stay because of background electronics. At the present time, the optical fiber option is preferred when electrical noise, the weight of copper, and security reasons pose problems. The challenge with fiber optics is that a suitable connector has not yet been found that can be installed routinely in buildings.

Regarding the protocol, token passing was chosen because of its deterministic performance and the handling of priorities necessary in certain environments, and because token solutions are to a certain extent distance independent.

In terms of topology, the adopted solution is a logical ring but a physical spider (star structure with passive nodes). The reason for the choice was:

- Reasonable noise immunity
- Good application approach for fibers
- Simple design for problem determinations and isolation (star wiring)
- No need for network customization to balance signal strengths
- Delay performance not so sensitive to network distance
- No penalty for total building rewiring (star wiring)

Equally important design factors are the ability to fit a PBX and its similarity to current wiring systems for telephone.

Figure 14.2 shows a wiring concentrator per floor that brings wires

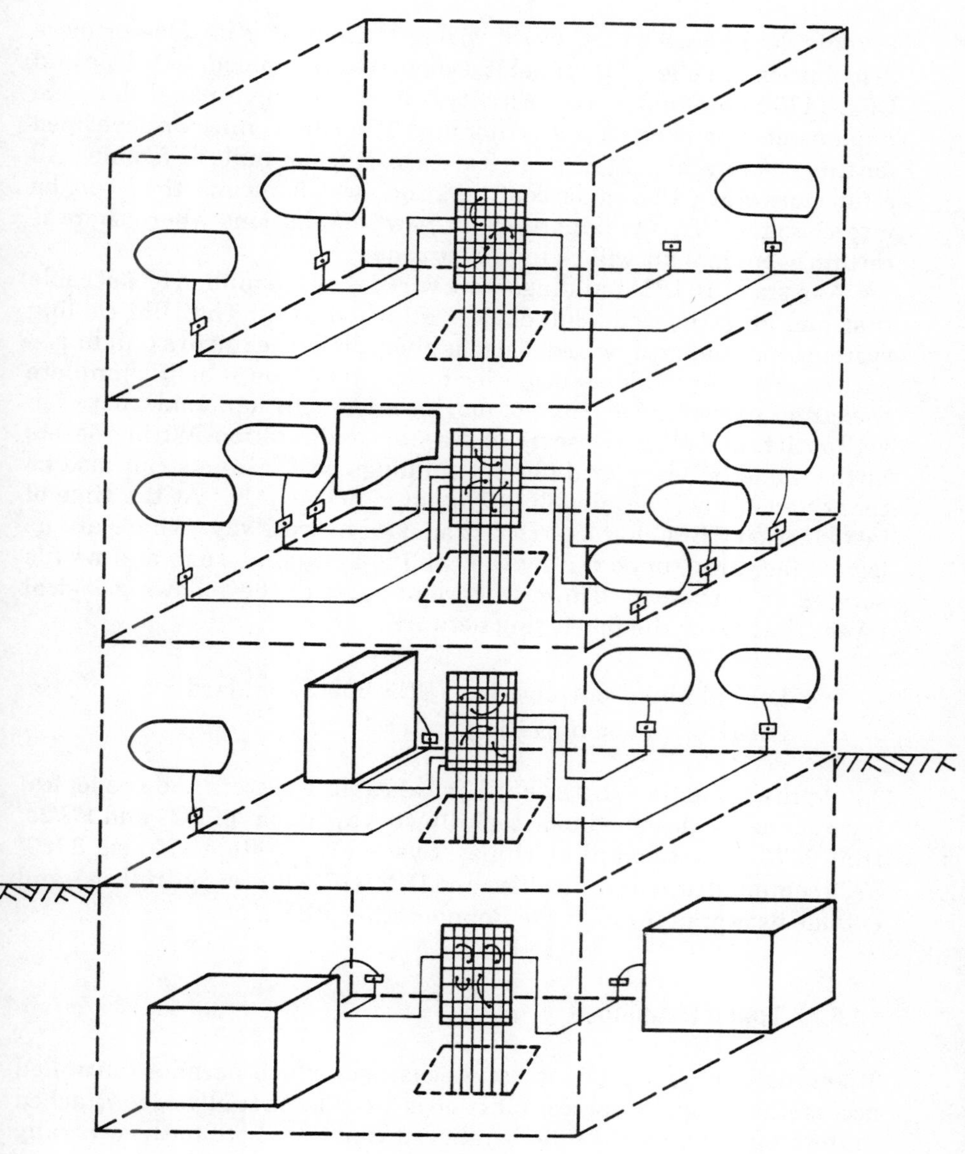

Figure 14.2 Baseband and wiring concentrator per floor in an IBM LAN solution.

to individual phase shifts. Each wiring concentrator has one or more distribution panel(s). The panel is designed to accommodate B-loop and DCA (4700 equipment) connectivity. It is a passive panel, but one implementation is electronic switching. The IBM connector developed for this network has interesting features. It is not male or female. All connectors have the same configuration, which means they can be interchanged. This is important for new installations where there is certainty equipment will change over time.

As a start, 10 IBM buildings were wired with 3.5 million feet of cable that had an estimated 2800 devices attached to it. The IBM cabling system is permanently wired—just as phone lines are run in a building—with connections made to outlets in office walls. Thus, it helps eliminate the larger part of the expense of moving a workstation. Links between wall outlets and wiring closets run in a star configuration. Wiring closets in the same building or different buildings on a campus can also be connected. However, a cabling system is not a LAN. At the time of introduction, IBM characterized it as data expressway. There are no logical facilities supported by the cabling system as such and no file servers or gateways. These require support of the following logical layers that make the token ring network:

- Logical Link Control (LLC) IEEE 802.2 standard
- IEEE 802.5 token-passing protocol

At the same time, both the physical cabling system and the logical layers must be designed to accept direct attachment of PCs and PS/2s, IBM 9370 departmental machines, System/36, System/370 (via 3720/3725 communications controllers and IBM 3174 cluster controllers), and outside networks through the Rolm or other PBX.

14.5 Token Passing

Token passing is a cable access mechanism which permits controlled access to the ring. The access function is distributed to all nodes attached to the ring. In terms of functionality, it contrasts both to the centrally controlled loop access and to carrier sensing multiple access.

An implicit token consists of a unique delimiter followed by a physical control field that contains an indication of whether the token is free or busy:

- Each attached node must observe a free token in order to transmit a frame upon the ring.
- The token indicator is then changed to mean a busy token and the data packet is appended to the token.

Following transmission of the complete frame, a new free token is transmitted to give the next node on the ring an opportunity to transmit information. Housekeeping is important. The node transmitting a frame is responsible for purging the frame from the ring. Therefore, the node keeps the flow of information on the ring interrupted until the frame circulates completely around the ring. However, the transmitting nodes do not perform any address recognition to remove frames from a token ring.

The IBM 2790 was one of the earliest rings. It is also the only segmented ring in existence which introduced the notion of the segment bypass feature. Subsequently, the Series I ring used twin axial cables for data transmission at speeds of 2 MBPS. The maximum internode distance was about 5000 feet for twin axial cables and 2000 feet for coaxial cables. This ring operated with either kind of cables and accommodates up to 16 nodes. Series I ring is a typical token controlled ring. An elementary token model is shown in Figure 14.3. It can be seen that progress in token passing ring structures is evolutionary. The current IBM LAN is a synchronous token ring, with synchronization provided by means of phase lock loops. The LAN uses a packet switching protocol. A frame is delimited by a start and an end and consists of:

- A transport control field
- To and from link address
- A transport information field
- A frame check sequence field

Transport control servers supervise cable access, multiplexing of traffic, ring functioning, and recovery. The frame is the basic transmission unit and has the format shown in Figure 14.4. The starting delimiter (DEL) for a frame consists of 1 byte. This is followed by the starting physical control (PCF) field of 2 bytes. It handles information necessary for managing access to the ring:

- 3 bits are allocated to priority information

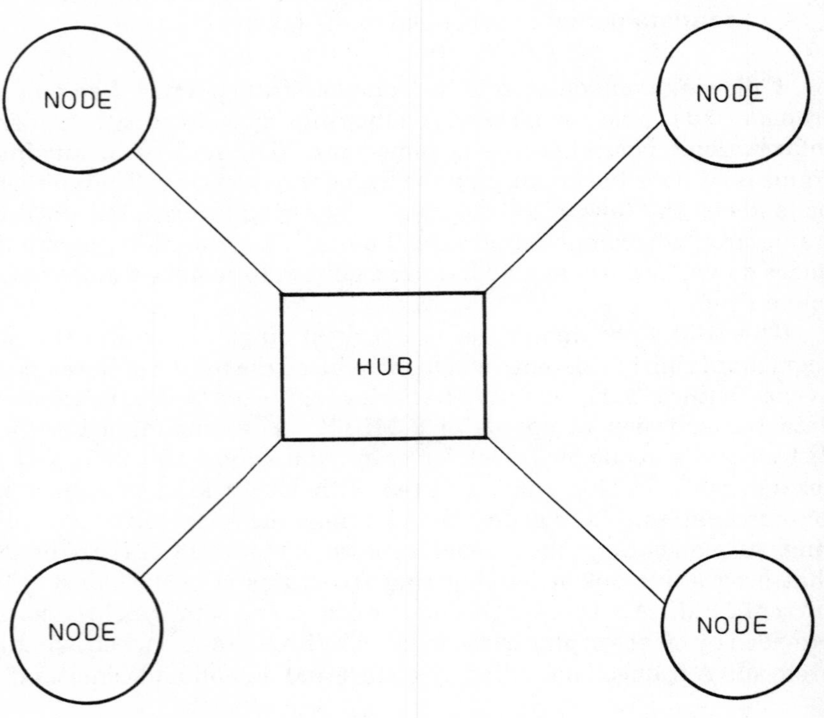

Figure 14.3 A token model. Hub retransmits to all WS (nodes).

- 1 bit, token
- 1 bit, monitor count
- 3 bits, priority reservation

This makes up the first PCF byte which is unchecked. The second PCF byte is checked and contains the following fields:

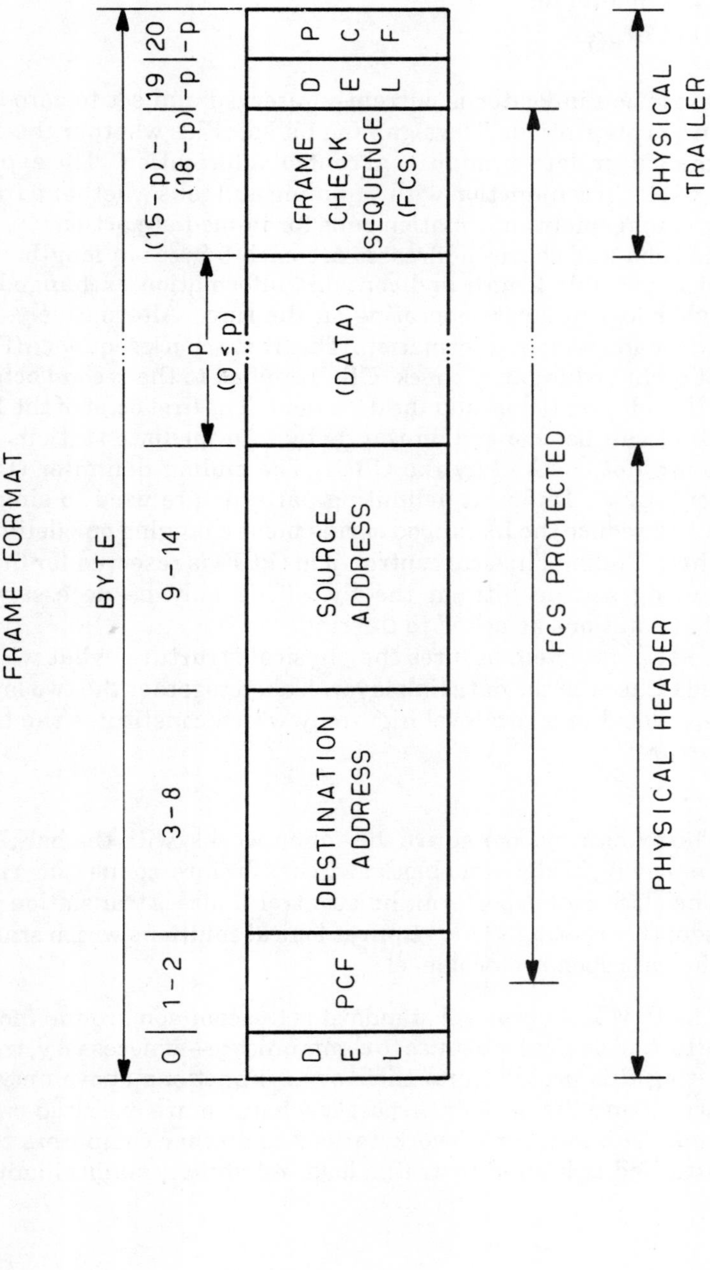

FRAME FORMAT

BYTE							
0	1 – 2	3 – 8	9 – 14	p (0 ≤ p)	(15 – p) – (18 – p)	19 – p	20 – p
DEL	PCF	DESTINATION ADDRESS	SOURCE ADDRESS	(DATA)	FRAME CHECK SEQUENCE (FCS)	DEL	PCF

FCS PROTECTED (PCF through FRAME CHECK SEQUENCE)

PHYSICAL HEADER (bytes 0 – 14)

PHYSICAL TRAILER (bytes (15 – p) – (20 – p))

Figure 14.4 **Frame format, including header and trailer by the physical resource.**

- 5 bits are reserved
- 1 bit, extension
- 1 bit, signalling
- 1 bit, express

The extension indicator is currently reserved and set to zero by a transmitting ring station. The signaling bit specifies whether the data field contains user data or additional control information. The express indicator works in conjunction with signaling and tells whether a frame with ring management information calls for immediate action.

Destination and source addresses are each 6 bytes in length. The data field is variable length and contains information exchanged between higher logical layers operating on the ring. Alternatively, this may be ring management information. The frame check sequence (FCS) is a 32-bit cyclic redundancy check (CRC) applied to the second octet of the PCF, the address fields, and the data field. The first octet of the PCF has bits that can be changed on the fly by intermediate stations and therefore are not checked by the CRC. The ending delimiter (DEL) consists of 1 byte. Different delimiting patterns are used to simplify detection and reduce the likelihood of ring noise changing one delimiter into another. Ending physical control field (PCF) is reserved for future uses requiring setting bits on the fly. This may be necessary at intermediate stations attached to the ring.

If the cabling system assures the physical structure, what we just considered focuses on the data link layer. Taken together the two layers can be remodeled in a two-level hierarchy which constitutes the basic LAN structure:

1. The token rings per se are the subnetworks, with the backbone employing bridges and block switches for interconnecting rings. The block switch performs link control, address translation, and adaptive routing. This requires logical solutions which start at the described protocol level.

2. The IBM LAN protocol standard is the common ground facility attached devices must use to communicate—if necessary, translating this protocol into their own. Functions above network access and the basic transport mechanism are executed end to end. The number of workstations and other computers to be attached is limited by traffic load, reliability, maintainability,

network management needs, and by their type of communications discipline. The latter is overcome through interfaces.

IBM industrial computers can become a link on the chain via a new version of the basic board-level link, Token Ring Adapter II. The ingredients necessary for System/370 support include hardware and software for the 3725 front end processor. For the hardware basics, network connections are based on 3725 Line and Token Ring Attachment Base and a Token Ring Interface Coupler. The Attachment Base supports up to 16 communications lines, but a maximum of 8 Token Ring Nets can link to the host through the 3725. PCs on the LAN get access to the mainframe via the:

- PC 3270 Emulation Program Version 3 Personal Services/PC 1.2
- Advanced Program-to-Program Communications (APPC) for the PC

But System/36 attachment stipulates a dedicated PC AT to be the go-between. This PC AT must be outfitted with a System/36 5360 LAN Attachment Feature or a 5362 Attachment Feature depending on model of System/36. Also needed is a Token Ring PC Adapter II.

The software includes the System/36 5360 or 5362 LAN Communications License Programs. That software supports communications with the System/36 via the LAN and allows most of the System/36 SDLC protocols to circulate around the network. PCs on a token ring with a System/36 can use the latter to store files and share data, emulate System/36 workstations to run System/36 applications, or emulate IBM 3270 terminals to get to the 3725 to, in turn, get to the 370.

All this sounds rather complex and it is so. Therefore, it can become counterproductive. Some machines have not been designed to operate on a LAN, particularly on a token ring structure. While the token ring mechanism is sound, forcing them together brings in complexity, significant costs, and unreliability.

14.6 APPC and SNA

The original SNA implementation was hierarchical, limited to single-host networks with attached programmable cluster controllers. Improvements resulted in its use in both large and small networks for terminal access to hosts and communication between hosts. SNA became nearly peer-to-peer, but it remained a host-based architecture. The computers and communications requirements of user organizations demanded more than that. The goal became an architecture that allows the interconnection of widely differing sizes of machines into networks of arbitrary topology. These networks should be easy to install and flexible to grow, allowing:

- Autonomous control of each processor on its own behalf (peer rather than centralized)
- Dynamic definition of network resources

The networking kernel developed to satisfy these basic concepts exploits LU 6.2 and builds upon PU 2.1:

- The logical units (LUs) in SNA are the means for end users to access the network.
- The physical units (PUs) are typically communications controllers, host processors, and interfaces. These are subarea nodes. LUs are insensitive to the details of session routing.

But not everything is in hardware. The PUs also are software-based resource managers within SNA nodes. PUs provide a location for configuration services, request software downloads into nodes, and generate node diagnostic information, including storage dumps and activity trace information. They are classified into PU types 5, 4, 2.1, 2.0, and 1, depending on the SNA node function which is provided. Figure 14.5 suggests the SNA/LEN relationship and target area. The term "LEN" should be seen as being closely associated with APPN and its APPC 6.2 protocol.

In IBM jargon, "entry levels," or entry points, are logical locations within SNA components that forward data concerning their own operations (and that of components under their control) to focal-point applications. Commands or control protocols for the manipulation of these components and resources flow between focal point and entry point. Examples of components that house entry points include 3705, 3725 or 3720, and 3174 or 3274, as well as System/36 or 38, distributed processors, and any other physical unit in an SNA network.

Entry points contrast to SNA service points. Service points are components in the SNA network that can serve as gateways to focal-point applications for network management data; the latter may be coming from non-SNA products, such as PBXs, LANs, and other vendor

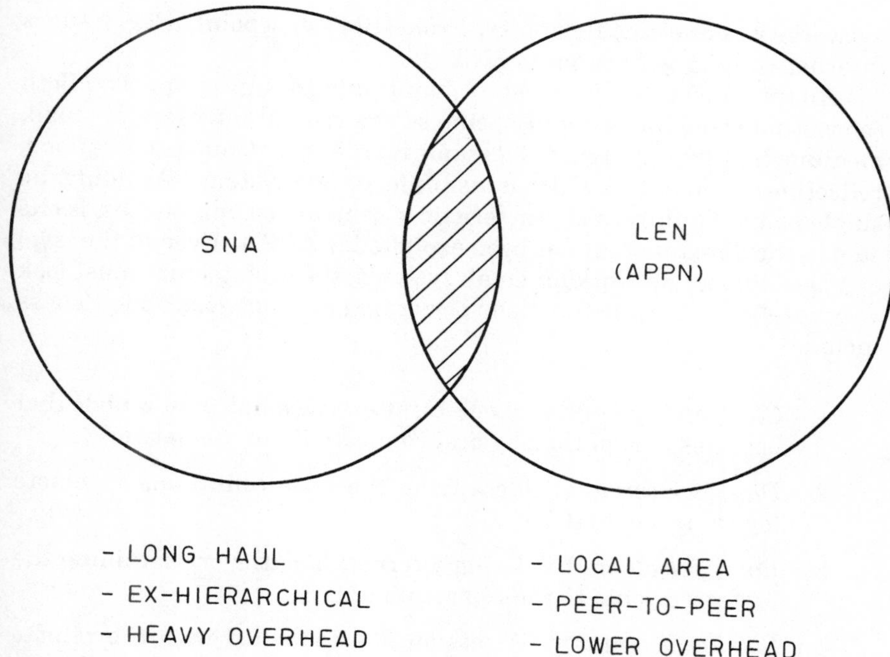

Figure 14.5 SNA and LEN partly overlap and partly complement each other.

networks. The service point, however, does not transfer end-user data.

In the case of APPC, a peer-to-peer dynamic style of networking control was perceived to be important to many users who felt that they would like to maintain control over when their machine joined and left the network. This peer emphasis reflects the fact that small machines are mostly found at the departmental and individual level. While APPN is peer and decentralized, we must distinguish between control, communications network management operations and maintenance functions. The latter are a focal point mechanism for centralized operations that allow the network owner to work in a manner that is in accord with the organization's established lines of responsibility.

Functionality is at a premium at the local peer level (e.g., the ability to configure any technology easily, rather than being restricted to a star, a bus, or a hierarchy). This is particularly important when we are dealing with an arbitrary topology. Another requirement for peer networks is connection flexibility. From IBM's viewpoint, a key issue is internetworking with subarea SNA.

All this must be achieved while maintaining design simplicity. Both conceptual streamlining and openness are critical for users of small, medium, and large systems. The same is true of continuous operations, reflecting the emphasis which is visible for online systems. Avoiding the single point of failure, a characteristic of centralized approaches, is one step in the direction that has been exploited in APPN. Even at the level of a peer-to-peer network for small systems, the architecture must look very carefully after the functions performed by a network node. These include:

1. *Connectivity services*. Looking after a new link or new node that becomes part of the physical connectivity of the network.
2. *Directory services*. Identifying the node containing a remote logical resource (LU).
3. *Route selection*. Exploring alternative paths or sustaining the preferred route to the remote node.
4. *Session activation*. A session is established with the remote logical unit using the preferred route.
5. *Data transport*. Establishing and supervising traffic flows on the session between local and remote LU.

Connectivity services may be provided on switched or nonswitched lines. They may involve connections across packet carrier or LAN facilities. Once connectivity is established, identification information is exchanged between attached nodes. A session is activated between control points in the two adjacent nodes. This control point session is used to exchange network topology information. With APPN, the result is a table in each network node constituting the topology database. It captures the current network connectivity by identifying each network node and its links to adjacent network nodes. This approach to network configuration was first introduced by Arpanet.

In terms of directory services, IBM's APPX approach is based on the concept that the most efficient way to share applications is by doing one task from the menus. To do this, all of the applications must be in one subdirectory. When the subdirectory that contains the applications is shared, all of the applications are available to the network at once. Some applications have program files that need to be in a subdirectory with read, write, and create access. For example, a text editor application can create profiles, so the application needs to be able to write a profile in a subdirectory. Since only one remote computer can write to a file at a time, each remote computer needs to have a copy of the files.

Remote computer users may want to store files on other user disks in a private subdirectory so that only they have access to the files. To do this, the server computer needs to have separate subdirectories for each remote computer user. If the remote user wants applications that have profiles or other program files requiring read, write, and create access, the files are stored in the PROFILES directory. This directory is created with the assistance of the installation aid and an APPEND command entered when the remote user starts the network. The APPEND command causes the PROFILES directory to be searched first for any applicable applications program files.

In terms of route selection service, each network node maintains in its control point complete knowledge of the current topology of the network portion it works on. It uses this topology database to calculate the preferred route from itself to every other subnetwork node for various classes of service—batch or interactive. Routes are maintained and updated in a database of rooted trees. Such combination of dynamically maintained topology databases and automatic path computation eliminates the need for manual definition of the physical configuration. It also provides automatic adaptation to configuration change.

Session activation provides an effective handshake. A session is activated by transmitting a special set-up message over the path that the session is to follow. It contains the names of the session origin, the session destination, and the route description. It is transmitted one hop at a time, with each node using the route description to determine the next hop. As it passes through each of the nodes along the path, it leaves behind table entries (session connectors) that cause subsequent packets to always follow the same path. Typically the packets belong to the particular session in reference.

The management of data transport is important. Assuring a smooth flow of packets is an exacting matter. Typical problems that arise in the attempt to control the flow of bursts of data traffic can be magnified if the proper conditions have not been maintained, such as, if there are nodes with very low buffer capacity or we lack experienced network operators who understand network congestion. Three functions are provided by the software to take care of such situations:

1. Long messages generated at one node may be repacketized later into shorter units to fit the buffer sizes of nodes encountered along the route.

2. Different flows can be given different priorities. For instance, control flows are favored so that they travel ahead of all user data.
3. A flow control algorithm is used to keep traffic moving in an efficient fashion, practically eliminating the possibility of deadlock and preventing nodes along the route from being overrun to the point that messages are lost.

In mid-1986 IBM further enhanced the pure networking functions through announcements addressed to the WS domain that are still close enough to the concept of network functionality. Topping the list of new software were versions of TopView, the PC Network Program, and PC 3270 Emulation Program. The main point was to get the three programs to work together on the token ring, as well as to get them to communicate with some of the other new software IBM brought out, including a new release of Personal Services/370.

The PC LAN Program can function on the same PC as TopView as long as the PC is functioning as a plain network workstation instead of a workstation that doubles as a file and print server. Applications that normally run with TopView 1.10 can have their requests for system resourced redirected onto the network as necessary, and messages can be sent and received between the TopView user and any other node on the network.

14.7 Other Types of IBM-Sponsored Approaches

Local area networks announced by IBM, but purchased from other vendors, are typically CSMA offerings originally brought to the market to fill a gap subsequently, maintained for competitive reasons, but in reality downplayed. There is no rush by user organizations to install these LANs. The principal characteristics of IBM's CSMA offering, a converted LocalNet 20 by Sytek, are 2 MBPS throughput, CATV-type coaxial cable at 75 ohm, but only a 300-meter (1000 feet) distance. Such distance can be extended through converters.

In terms of topology, the PC network looks like a spider with passive hubs as the expansion base (tree structure). Each expansion base can handle both simple WSs and WSs defined as file servers (Figure 14.6). The manufacturer suggests that up to 72 stations can be supported in the basic configuration. The number of attached stations depends not only on the LAN technical characteristics but also on system design in terms of implementation—including the type of work they are doing and,

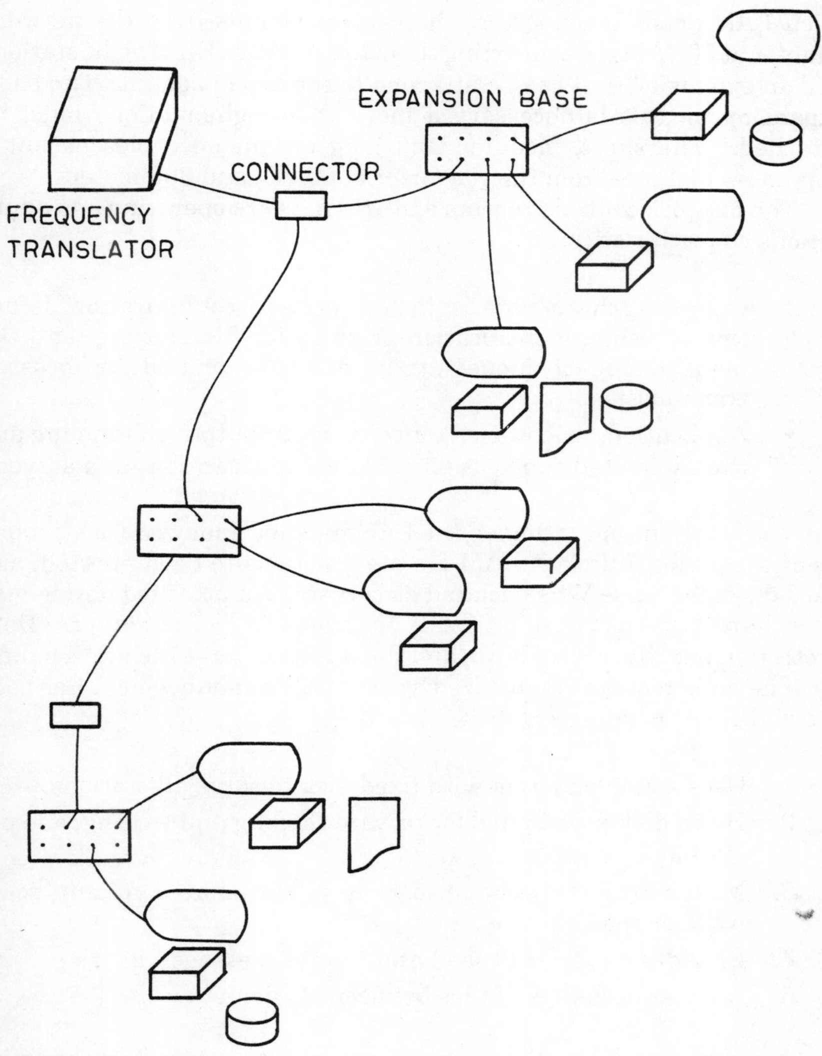

Figure 14.6 Implementing a spider-type LAN with attached workstations.

therefore, the traffic. Hence, a quarter of the stated (theoretical) amount of workstations will be plenty for a first use.

The BIU employs an Intel 80186 microprocessor and uses Netbios functions embedded in ROM—hence, it has firmware and is protected.

Each LAN needs a converter. It receives signals from the network adapter at 50.75 MHz, converting them to 219 MHz. Up to eight stations and an expansion unit can be attached to the expansion kit. The basic expansion module is necessary if more than eight stations must be attached. The short, medium, and long expansion cables permit a maximum distance from the converter of 60, 80, and 300 meters.

The network control program features network operating and applications characteristics:

- Operating characteristics include network configuration, definition of users, identification or rules for file sharing, and the management of queues at the print server and for message transmission.
- Applications orientation concerns input-output channeling and the associated supports for attached workstations and servers.

Workstations operating on the LAN must be endowed with attachment adapters, sufficient RAM for the functions to be supported, and hard disks for those WSs declared as servers. An attached device may have hard copy whether or not it functions as a file server. Data protection is at the record level, and there is a message file interchange.

The main feature emphasized by this LAN announcement has been the ability to share a hard disk. It:

1. Uses a single system with fixed disk to serve all stations.
2. Has a disk partitioned for private reading and writing, one per station.
3. Makes available storage space as public, shared volume, read-write or read only.
4. Provides a carrier to send and receive messages.
5. Assures exchange of files between stations.

As with any LAN, the network operating system can recognize addresses, identify and localize workstations, and handle switching.

Stations send and receive messages and transfer files. As such, this LAN can be useful in small business and educational environment and for filing assistance. The disk server station can contain two general information libraries: a public volume is read only and the private read-write volume for each station is protected. Figure 14.7 presents the distribution of storage at the file server level. An information transfer

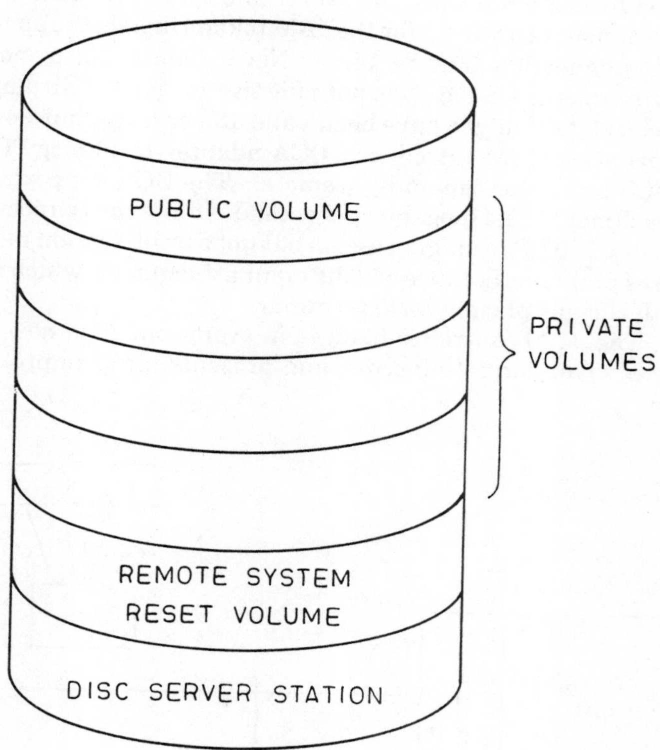

Figure 14.7 IBM cluster file server.

program permits transfer from private volumes to the public database on the server.

While they cannot be considered LANs, IBM has other locally connected systems. Two are:

- The 3600 banking loop and its successor; they use token passing but are slow, in the 600 baud to 4.8 KBPS range
- The 8100 loop, which is also token passing

The 3600 banking loop has been followed by the 4700, whose controller is reoriented toward file server and communications mode aspects. The announced wiring for the IBM token ring also supports B-loop and DCA connection (Figure 14.8). Nevertheless, in a modern banking environment, 4.8 KBPS is not effective for formal display and printer. Such solution might have been valid 15 years ago but not today. As an alternative, IBM introduced DCA adapter technology (in house) and SDLC connector capability (remote). The DCA supports a star coaxial attachment of 2.4 megabits per second. One of the connected devices can be the 3270 PC in single-session but not a multisession mode. The latter poses problems because of a different attachment, which is also the case with the gas plasma 3290 terminal.

The 4700 controller itself is in evolution. The new product introduces error correcting codes and presents other improvements, mini-

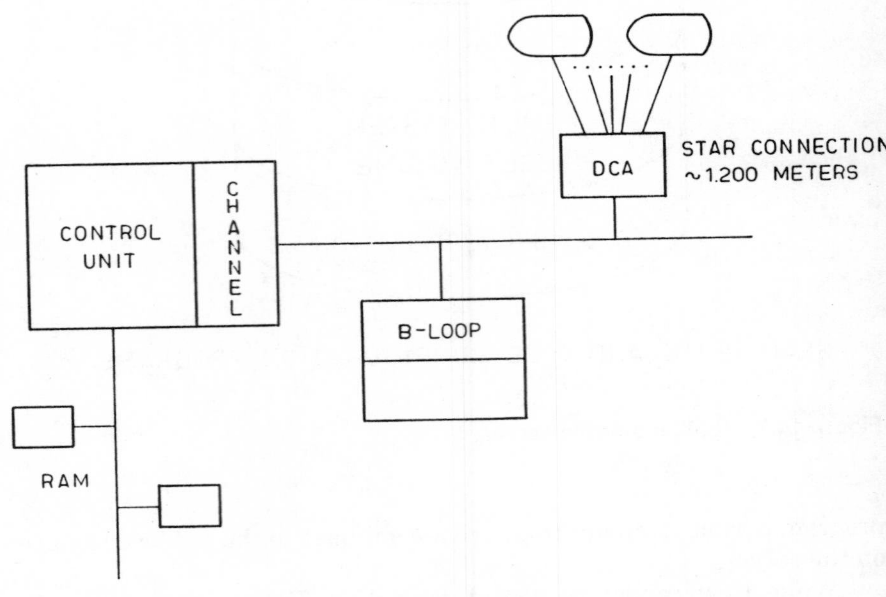

Figure 14.8 B-loop and DCA connection in IBM's token ring.

aturization being one of them. For the token passing LAN, IBM has developed a supercompact 4700 controller. This unit looks like IBM's plan for a LAN panel at floor level. This 4700 controller unit not only gets miniaturized but, in terms of supported facilities, it develops into a family of products. A metric advanced by IBM is the maximum aggregate band rate (MABR), which represent the sum of all communications adapters: B-loop, start-stop, and bisynchronous. MABR is the maximum transfer rate supported by the controller.

14.8 Netview—A Means for Network Control

Though it is possible to operate a computer network without the facilities of a network control center (NCC), it is highly unwise to do so. NCC functionality is an essential part of a network solution and should be treated as such. Netview's goal is to provide a single presentation structure at a host-based terminal. This permits the network manager to run the operation of the physical network from the same place that the operation of the logical network is managed.

Through NCC activity, component failures are flagged and diagnosed from the same location as are failures in end-to-end logical sessions. The network manager can be alerted to degradation and failure to meet service criteria. We can investigate the cause of that failure and remedy the problem by treating its source or activating backup machines, nodes, and links. Netview is a standard VTAM application, but it requires only commonly available VTAM facilities. The command list (CList) facility permits precoding of relatively simple command sequences that can automate many standard network operational tasks. IBM's Netview/PC permits data to be monitored from non-SNA sources.

Like other vendors of network architectures, IBM recognizes that as the size of a network grows, it becomes increasingly difficult for a single operator to monitor and manage it. Since the volume of operational alert messages coming into VTAM is so large, the messages often roll off the screen and into the log before they are monitored. It is just as vital to maintain the ability to implement operator commands from a central facility. IBM provides more that 150 command lists with Netview. However, a user who wishes to implement automated tasks in a sophisticated manner must add a lot of custom software. IBM should offer much more in this area.

However, the command facility is good. Through its usage, the network operator need only cope with a single presentation structure for all component parts. It is not necessary to switch among multiple products when tracking down a problem. Also, any Netview command can be entered at any Netview screen. From such screen the operator can:

- Activate or deactivate network resources
- Recognize problems as they occur
- Isolate a failing component
- Invoke line and resource tests
- Take corrective action

Data is presented in a reasonably consistent manner. CLists may also be built to handle more involved tasks of network diagnostics and recovery functions.

A separate facility at the network control center handles alerts coming from common carriers, T1 vendors, private branch exchanges, and generalized sources of non-IBM equipment. It is a problem addressed through Netview/PC. In this sense, Netview/PC is a problem management and alert tool, a bridge by which the central monitoring facility in the host is able to access operational information from sources beyond the SNA environment. References include non-SNA-addressable networks, voice networks, and networks supplied by other vendors.

Netview/PC forwards data to the host in two ways:

1. Standard VTAM-to-PC system service control point. During an SNA session, Netview/PC sends the data to the focal-point application through the same VTAM interfaces from which it regularly receives data.
2. Establishment of LU 6.2 advanced program-to-program communications (APPC) session between Netview/PC and a host application. CICS is currently the only 370 host application that supports LU 6.2 communication. Properly used, information such as alert records from PC-managed LANs is valuable to LAN management. Device-specific applications reside in the PC housing Netview/PC. The PC application accepts the alerts coming from the specific source and converts them to a common format, such as IBM's Communications Network Management format, acceptable to the focal-point application.

IBM is offering applications for the Rolm PBX to interface with both the alert monitor and the call detail records collector. An application for the IBM token ring network is expected to follow soon. No doubt, the need for network control center activities at the LAN level will be increasingly felt in the future. In fact, a background reason for 4700 integration at the passive node level of the token ring is its ability to act as an NCC node. What is missing is the necessary software. That will be coming in the near future.

Chapter

15

Ethernet by DEC, Intel, Xerox, and Others

15.1 Introduction

Ethernet is today one of the more popular privately owned data communications systems. Its geographical area is usually limited to a section of a building or the entire building. Because of the CSMA/CD protocol, Ethernet is not advisable for campus-type or metropolitan area applications. Although Ethernet is a baseband LAN, it can be implemented in BAB flexible coaxial cable or broadband CATV cable. In the latter case, it occupies one of the channels. Standard coaxial cable is recommended for communications between floors and buildings. Another alternative, thin wire cable, is recommended for interconnecting workstations or other personal computers, generally in low-end systems in local work areas on a floor.

Ethernet on CATV offers the ability to use other channels for video, voice, and other communications with the same network wiring. It can be used to distribute multiple information services but not necessarily in the sense of integrated multimedia implementation. Other CATV channels and additional capability can be employed without disturbing the operation of the installed network facilities.

Because of different solutions supported by the Ethernet sponsors, being able to connect devices to an Ethernet cable and having them exchange meaningful information are two different things. This seems likely to remain the case for the foreseeable future, since the Ethernet-board business is being handled through a variety of suppliers.

15.2 A Multivendor Environment

Like Corvus did with Omninet, Xerox sold many Ethernet licenses, and the licensees are fairly free to work out the solution to their environments. The first multivendor standard was announced in 1980 by DEC, Intel, and Xerox. This, however, is not the technical solution accepted by the more than 60 manufacturers with Ethernet licenses. AT&T, for instance, made Ethernet adaptors reportedly using its standard Bellmac microprocessor. Other computer makers went into the Ethernet-board supply business. Honeywell's gear was supplied by Bridge Communications, NCR contracted with Excelan, and both TI and HP have sought out 3Com for their micros. Other deals are outstanding.

There is also the IEEE 802.3 recommended standard to account for. Digital Equipment stated that all DEC second-generation Ethernet products support the IEEE 802.3 LAN standard. The IEEE 802.3 itself is technically very similar to the original Ethernet which Digital's first-generation products supported, but it is not necessarily fully compatible.

There is a way to set up a small Ethernet local network without connecting transceivers to coaxial cable. It can be done with the Intellink cluster module from Intel and plain old twisted-pair wiring. The Intellink module allows users to connect up to nine Ethernet workstations without using coaxial cable or transceivers.

The resulting cluster can be optionally connected to a main Ethernet cable through a single transceiver. Nevertheless, provided they follow the IEEE 802.3 specification, the lower layers of Ethernet (levels 1 and 2) are today aligned closely enough so that compatibility at these level is reportedly no longer a problem between different boards. Still, because of the radically different board designs, factors such as relative user throughput can vary in a significant way.

Some vendors maintain that this difference is caused by the type and configuration of the hardware employed on the boards. Others say it is caused by software-based issues such as memory management and firmware efficiency. The fact remains that there are differences, and it is wise to account for them. Furthermore, user organizations may buy add-on products from several vendors. That is good in terms of freedom of sourcing but bad for interconnectivity. It can lead to major compatibility headaches—especially if the user intends to employ boards from different vendors in different computers on the same Ethernet LAN. This is because each board product is built and programmed differently. In addition, the user is responsible for the often-complex task of assuring that the host software is properly tuned for the Ethernet board.

Some computer vendors are performing this integration themselves to make sure that users can employ the coaxial cable for something more than a mooring device for their computers. This makes the task for user organizations a lot easier—provided that their Ethernet handles only 3Bs from AT&T or DPS from Honeywell or DEC VAX. Still, users with the inevitable dichotomy of computers from different vendors are left with incompatibility problems. Prevailing differences among alternative offers are not just at the level of the physical solution—from microprocessor to BIU board—though such differences can be significant:

- The BIU buffer ranges from 2K to 128K.
- Correspondingly, the estimated throughput from host to Ethernet LAN varies from 100 KBPS to 1–2MBPS.
- The microprocessors themselves are a diverse source of supply.

Supported host OSs vary from MS-DOS to Unix, VMS, RSX, and others. One of the compatibility risks is the possibility of mixing the source of supply in a Unix environment. The latter can be explained by examining the protocol support at the transport layer of ISO/OSI.

- For Excelan it is TCP/IP, the recommended standards of the Department of Defense.
- Interlan and Bridge Communications support Xerox Network Systems (XNS).
- CMS tends to address both XNS and TCP/IP.

In other words, Ethernet boards typically employ one of two protocols: either XNS or the TCP/IP protocol combination, a carryover from Arpanet. Both protocols perform essentially the same functions, but an XNS-based board will generally not work with a TCP-based board.

There is no agreement over the relative merits and demerits of these two different protocols. The XNS proponents maintain that TCP's use is limited to the Unix operating system, while TCP advocates say that XNS may work well in business environments but is poorly adapted for scientific and laboratory applications, including CAD/CAM. Both suggest that the other requires more overhead and CPU cycles. The only agreement seems to be that both do more or less the same job, though they are of different conception.

This diversity in terms of Ethernet solutions, up to a certain level, makes sense. To enter the market early, the Ethernet-board suppliers had to make certain design decisions, which resulted in incompatibility; they cannot change now without creating undue hardship to current clients.

Despite their diversity, Ethernet LANs share certain advantages and disadvantages. Among the advantages we notice reliability, because there is only a small number of shared active components. Also it is easy to install and expand, with no preplanning of expansion particularly necessary. Disadvantages can be divided into two classes: fundamental and engineering. One of the fundamentals is that the Ethernet approach cannot make effective use of high-speed transmission media and, at the same time, maintain effective usage of such media. As speed increases, a lesser fraction of channel capacity is used. Another fundamental disadvantage is that no traditional link-level encryption is possible with Ethernet. Thus, security threats, including traffic analysis, are difficult to prevent.

There are also some engineering negatives to take into account in terms of implementation:

- Ethernet technology uses a large number of analog components.
- By contrast, token ring uses mostly digital components.

Furthermore, the coaxial cable is an unbalanced transmission medium. Electromagnetic compatibility between the network and adjacent equipment is more difficult to achieve than with balanced media such as shielded twisted pairs. At the same time, coaxial cable has other engineering advantages over shielded twisted pair, bandwidth and dependability being two of them.

15.3 Technical Fundamentals of the Ethernet Solution

The shared communications facility with all versions of Ethernet is the branching ether, which is a passive coaxial cable. A station's interface connects bit-serially to a transceiver, which taps into the passive cable. Figure 15.1 identifies the coaxial cable, connector, terminator, and BIU functionality. The latter includes the transceiver, transmit-receive logic, and user interface. The component parts of the transceiver are the line driver, line receiver, and collision detector.

Transmit and receive logic make up the next layer. The user interface can be conceived in three sections: input buffer, output buffer, and interface logic. However, workstations can be connected to Ethernet without transceivers using the Intellink cluster module, which is compatible with the specifications contained in the 1980 Version 1.0 of the DEC-Intel-Xerox Ethernet. Any Ethernet-compatible device may be connected to the module and communicate with other connected Ethernet devices. Intellink connector signals are identical to those outlined in the Ethernet specification. The Intellink module performs the same functions as a standard Ethernet transceiver. It

- Buffers receive and transmit data
- Detects attempts by two or more stations to gain access to the line simultaneously
- Signals the presence of a collision to the transmitting stations
- Transmits the jam signal

To establish an Ethernet connection the ordinary way, without Intellink, the user must first consider the workstation, which, in the case of Intel products is a Multibus workstation. The bus scheme is a predetermined wiring pattern that a particular manufacturer adheres to in tying together the printed circuit boards in its word processor or other terminal device. Multibus is the name of a unique parallel bus used in Intel products; Unibus and Q-bus are similar parallel bus schemes used in Digital Equipment products. Manufacturers standardized on parallel buses long before local networks and Ethernet were developed. Now, however, there are many serial buses, and they are easier to tie directly into local networks.

Within the chosen bus configuration and subject to acceptable limits in terms of distance, the user organization can extend the topology of its

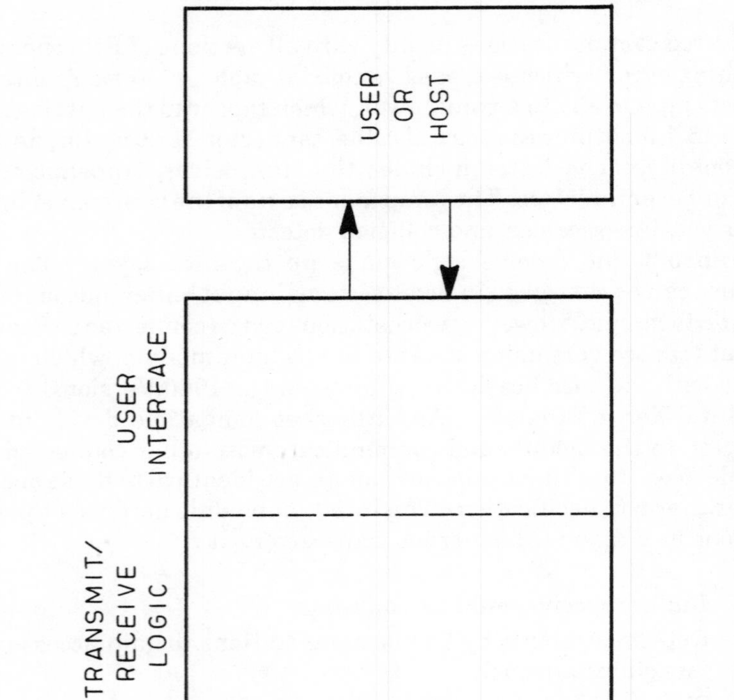

Figure 15.1 Coaxial cable connector, terminator, and BIU functionality with Ethernet.

Table 15.1 Minimums and maximums in supported services by different Ethernet version.

Design Criterion	*Minimum Supported Service*	*Maximum Supported Service*
1. Data rate	2.94 MBPS	10 MBPS
2. Maximum length end to end	1 km	2.5 km
3. Maximum segment	304 m	500 m
4. Impedance	75	50
5. Preamble	1 bit	64 bits
6. Cyclic redundance check (CRC)	16 bits	32 bits
7. Address	8 bits	48 bits

Ethernet LAN through repeater stations. This is one of the basic advantages of the ether approach. Acceptable limits are determined by the two most remote workstations, usually at the 0.5- to 2.5-km distance. The DEC-Intel-Xerox solution typically supports a length of 500 meters per Ethernet segment. The segment can handle up to a maximum of 100 transceivers. Four to five segments can be linked together through repeaters, but users with experience advise using only three interconnected segments. Table 15.1 compares supported distance by different Ethernet versions.

Next to installing the cable, a user who wants to link two workstations on a LAN must put an Ethernet controller board in each workstation. The controller board, for instance, converts the parallel Multibus to a serial bus; it translates from multiple connections inside the workstations to a single serial connection. The DEC-Intel-Xerox approach supports 2^{47} physical addresses and 2^{47}-1 multicast group addresses. The latter is important for broadcast possibilities.

For the Ethernet LAN actually to do anything, software is necessary. Depending on the Ethernet solution adopted, this software resides in random access memory (RAM) in the bus interface unit or in the workstations as is the case with 3Com and Interlink. If the Interlink solution is adopted, the next requirement is to connect the nine transceivers to the cable. Two bolts in a U-shaped bracket are used to tighten the cable into the bracket's anchor hole. Next, the cable is reamed out down to the center tap. A small needle protruding from the transceiver connection makes contact when the transceiver is plugged into the receptacle. With coaxial cable-based Ethernet implementation, each vendor presents its distinct solution particularly adapted to its wares. An example is the Etherseries by Texas Instruments.

15.4 The Ethernet Packet Structure and Carrier Sensing Mechanism

The Ethernet packet structure is divided into preamble, destination, source, type, data, and trailer for cyclic redundance check (CRC). The goal of the preamble is synchronization through a known waveform. The Ethernet packet format is shown in Figure 15.2. Packet length can vary from a minimum of 72 bytes to a maximum of 1526 bytes. The message of the multicast bit is: "I can receive a message." A packet is:

1. Broadcast into the Ether.
2. Heard by all attached devices,
3. Copied from the ether by the destination(s) which select(s) it,

Packet selection is made according to its leading address bits. Ethernet can be extended using a packet; there are repeaters for signal regeneration, filters for traffic localization, and gateways for internetwork address extension. The protocol provides for 48 bits allocated for a unique network-wide station address. It has a 32-bit checksum on each packet. In a network-wide sense, the 48 bit destination address field specifies the station(s) to which the packet is being transmitted.

Each attached device examines this field to determine whether it should accept the packet. The first bit transmitted indicates the type of address. If it is a 0, the field contains the unique address of the one destination station. If it is a 1, the field specifies a logical group of recipients; a special case is the broadcast (all stations) address, which is

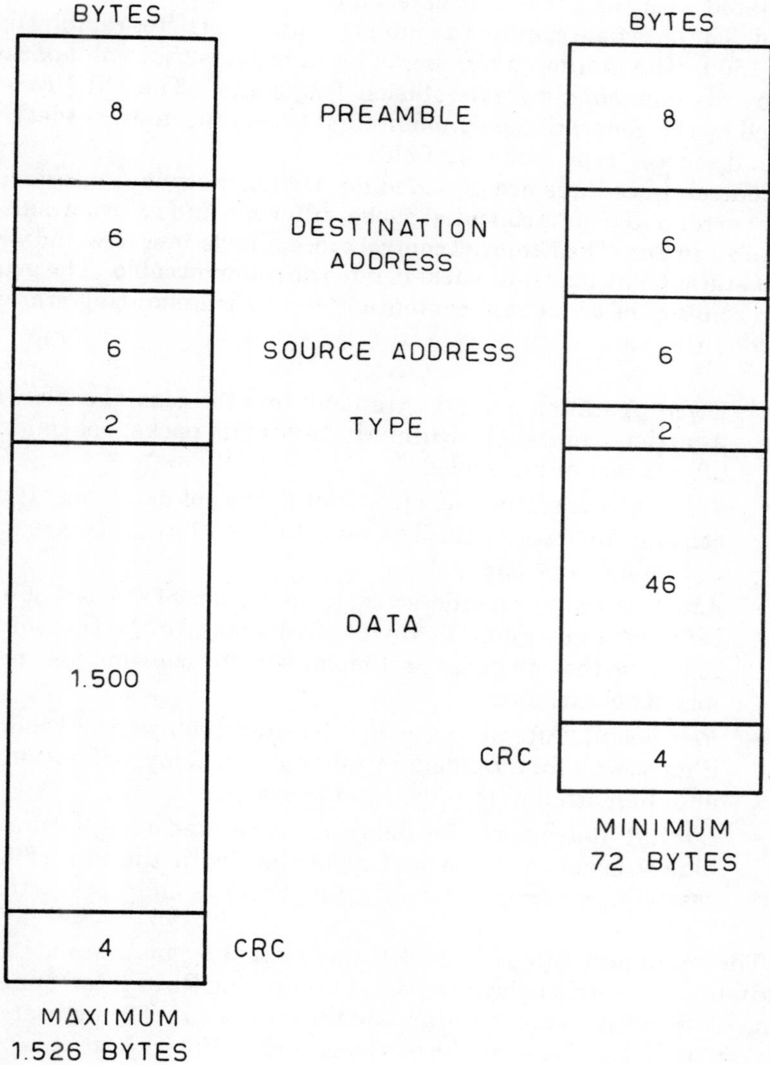

Figure 15.2 Maximum and minimum Ethernet packet formats.

all 1s. The 48-bit source address field contains the unique address of the station that is transmitting the packet.

The 16-bit type field is used to identify the higher-level protocol type associated with the packet. It determines how the data field is interpreted. The data field contains an integral number of bytes ranging from 46 to 1500. The minimum number of bytes assures that valid packets will be distinguishable from collision fragments. The CRC code is defined by the generating polynominal. It covers the address (destination and source), type, and data fields.

Control procedures are provided for carrier detection, interfacing, packet error detection, truncated packet filtering, and collision consensus enforcement. The Ethernet control procedure defines how and when a host station may transmit packets into the common cable. The goal is fair resolution of occasional contention among transmitting stations. The conditions are:

- *Defer*. A station must not transmit into the coaxial cable when a carrier is present or within the minimum packet spacing time after a carrier has ended.
- *Transmit*. A station may transmit if it is not deferring. It may continue to transmit until either the end of the packet is reached or a collision is detected.
- *Abort*. If a collision is detected, transmission of the packet must terminate, and a jam (4 - 6 bytes of arbitrary data) is transmitted to assure that all other participants in the collision also recognize its occurrence.
- *Retransmit*. After a station has detected a collision and aborted, it must wait for a random retransmission delay, defer as usual, and then attempt to retransmit the packet.
- *Backoff*. Retransmission delays are computed using a truncated binary exponential backoff algorithm, with the aim of fairly resolving contention among attached hosts and workstations.

The minimum Ethernet packet pacing is 9.6 microseconds. The maximum round-trip delay of a packet (supposing three interconnected segments of 500 meters each) stands at the level of 50 to 52 microseconds.

As a packet is placed on the bus by a workstation or host, it is phase encoded like bits on a magnetic tape. This guarantees there is at least one transition on the carrier during each bit time. The passing of a packet on the cable can therefore be detected by listening for its transitions. An attached device listens before talking and defers if the cable is busy. It also listens while talking. Since it can sense a passing packet on the carrier, it can delay sending one of its own until the detected packet passes safely. Without carrier detection, efficient use of the transport media would decrease with increasing packet length and/or packet frequency. With collision detection, network efficiency increases with increasing packet length—but decreases with packet frequency.

A collision resolution algorithm can be with nonadaptive retransmission delay, with random delay time chosen from a fixed uniform distribution, or it can feature adaptive retransmission delay (binary exponential backoff, geometric backoff, global approach). As with all CSMA/CD algorithms, carrier detection makes it possible to implement deference. Once a packet transmission has been in progress, during the end-to-end propagation time, all stations are hearing carrier and are deferring. Still other controls are necessary.

As a packet is placed on the bus, a checksum is computed and appended. As the packet is read from the bus, the checksum is recomputed. Packets which do not carry a consistent checksum are discarded. Hence, transmission errors, impulse noise errors, and errors caused by undetected interferences are caught at a packet's destination. Interference detection and deference cause most collisions to result in truncated packets. Colliding stations detect interference and abort transmission within the data transfer round-trip time.

With Ethernet there are automatic retries for packets truncated because of collisions. There remains, however, a possibility that apparently successfully sent packets may not be accepted at their destination. For this reason, the lowest-level protocol requires positive acknowledgment of all numbered packets. If this acknowledgment is not received after a suitable time, the transmission is repeated. Both the number of retries and the intervals to wait are taken from tables. This provides the flexibility to allow a few short interval retries followed by longer waits and a smaller number of retries during requests for connection than when contact already exists. If there is still no acknowledgment after the maximum number of retries, it is assumed that the corresponding station is no longer operating or the cable has broken, and the virtual connection is closed. During a connection, a watchdog message is sent every few minutes to verify the connection.

To reduce the processing load that the rejection of damaged packets would place on listening workstation software, truncated packets are filtered out in hardware. When a device (WS, host, or other server) determines that its transmission is experiencing interference, it momentarily jams the bus to assure that all other participants in the collision detect interference and, because of deference, are forced to abort. This collision consensus enforcement mechanism is very important. Without it the transmitting workstation, which would otherwise be the last to detect a collision, might not abort since the other interfering transmissions successively abort and stop interfering.

Emphasis on carrier sensing and collision detection is appropriate, since the Ethernet design started with the basic idea of packet collision and retransmission developed in the Aloha Network. Like the Aloha Network, Ethernets carry bursty traffic so that conventional synchronous time-division multiplexing is inefficient. Ethernet designers saw promise in the Aloha approach to distributed control of radio channel multiplexing.

15.5 An Example with TI Etherseries and Thin Ethernet Software

Thin Ethernet is a cabling method using flexible coaxial and designed specifically for the entry level of interconnection, addressing itself to PC equipment. Thin Ethernet cables and connectors maintain the standard Ethernet specifications at the lower end. Thin Ethernet can be routed easily for installation, with each segment up to 304 meters (1000 ft) long.

Because there are no agreed-upon standards in the higher levels, local, not interconnected, approaches can be expected to proliferate for some time. There is little use in connecting one workstation to another that does not use the same Ethernet software. Eventually, some standards might evolve. Then users will begin to communicate with each other at the higher protocol layers. But until users standardize on all higher protocol levels, this is not going to develop. The only way to see this happen now is to buy from the same vendor, which will put the same software on all its equipment.

Cost is evidently one of the basic criteria. While the price per connection is decreasing at an estimated 30 percent per year, there is always a difference between the cost of BIU designed for larger hosts and one addressing itself at the PC level. There is also a need to keep a certain ratio between what is paid for an attachment and what the attached device is worth. One rule to use as a guideline is 10 percent to 15 percent.

Etherseries is a family of Ethernet-oriented hardware and software networking products for increasing the productivity of personal computer users. The Etherseries products include Etherlink, Ethershare, Etherprint, and Ethermail. There are also variations in implementation. A thin Ethernet cable is most often used with TI personal computer networks. Each personal computer or server node in the LAN requires an Etherlink package. The package includes a user installable plug-in board and the client software to connect a personal computer to Ethernet. Etherlink combines controller and transceiver functions onto one board to handle data link functions.

To a considerable extent, the Etherseries example is based on thin Ethernet software by 3Com. With an Etherlink board installed (Figure 15.3), a personal computer can tie into a network that shares disks and printers. The Etherlink printed circuit board (PCB) plugs into an expansion slot. It has 2 kilobytes of buffer memory. The Etherlink PCB can be connected to standard Ethernet cable (4/10 inch) or thin Ethernet cable (2/10 inch).

Networking functionality is managed by dedicated PCs. A single network server typically manages up to eight users, but multiple servers can be employed to manage the load for larger networks. A network server runs the fixed disk space, the printers, and mail delivery. Servers may be dedicated to each function or may manage all three of them. Users may access the servers' common files, obtain hardcopy, and exchange mail.

Ethershare software allows users in a network to share a network server's fixed disk space. It reduces duplication of programs and data and permits efficient use of storage. Ethershare divides the fixed disk into volumes, allocated to users dynamically as they make requests. A volume can be as small as 64 kilobytes and is limited only by the available disk space. A user can access up to four volumes at a time as if they resided locally with the unit. Operation of the disk and communications across the net are totally transparent to MS-DOS and the applications program. The user designates whether a volume is:

- *Private*, used by only one client at a time
- *Public*, read-only files which a number of clients can access concurrently
- *Shared*, read-write access to multiple WSs

To prevent two users from trying to change the same record at the

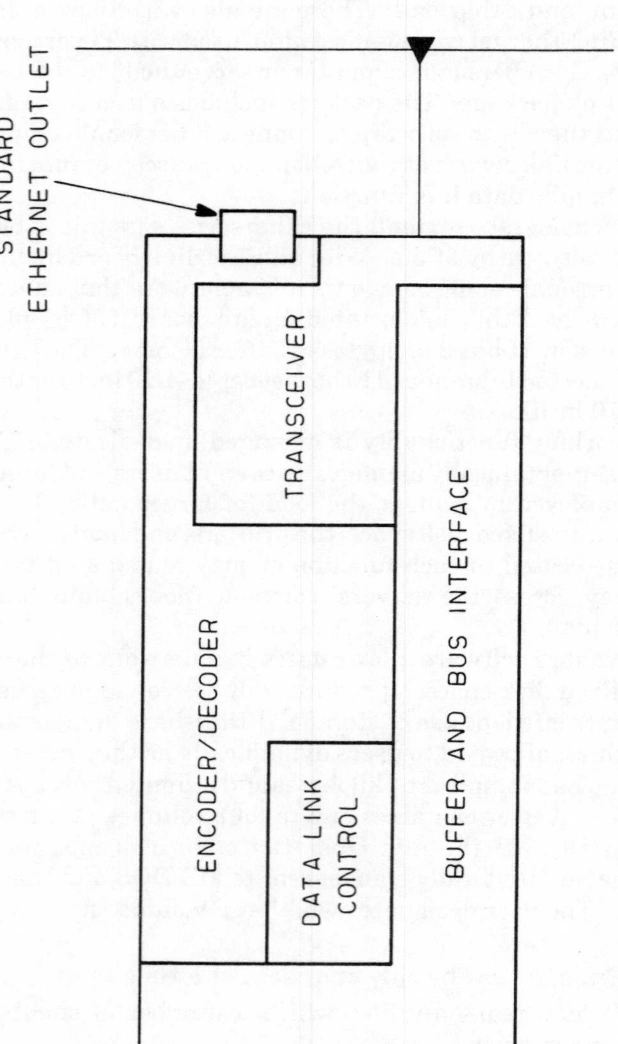

Figure 15.3 Etherlink PCB configuration.

same time under the shared access, semaphores signal that the data is being updated. Security and protection are provided with Ethershare by requiring one password for log in and a separate password for use of a particular volume. Passwords can be assigned to control access and prevent unauthorized use of information elements.

Etherprint permits users in a network to share printer resources. This eliminates the need to have a dedicated printer for each personal computer. Sharing printer resources makes print operations more efficient through print spooling. Data is transmitted over the network and is transparent to normal program operations. Etherprint software is installed on the personal computer designated as a print server. This machine has one or more printers attached for shared use. Normally a print server is also a network server, which is a personal computer dedicated to managing networking function such as Ethershare and Ethermail. Network users can use any printer attached to any server. Online help provides a description of available printers.

An Etherprint command sets up a link into a shared printer. Data is transparently sent across the network to the server. Once the printing operation is accepted, the server spools the output to the disk. The user may then proceed to the next task, while the print server queues printing jobs from different workstations and manages the printing tasks.

Ethermail provides the capability for message composition. It includes function keys and prompting to facilitate message creation, as well as message addressing to a person or distribution list. Mail is routed to all users in a network. Responses to messages are facilitated by built-in routines. Ethermail helps in interoffice communications, making it easy to send messages through the network electronically. It governs the reception and distribution of messages. The editor contains features such as word-wrap, block move, and copy. It can also be used in a stand-alone mode to compose documents outside of Ethermail when a full-featured word processor is not required.

Ethermail is composed of two modules:

- One resides in the network server and acts as a post office.
- The other runs on user personal computers and does message creation and distribution, as well as retrieval and display.

Ethermail on a PC requires 192K, the Etherlink board, and the MS-DOS. The user software for Ethermail is loaded across the network from the network server. Each network server needs a copy of the appropriate resident Ethermail software.

15.6 LAN Interconnecting by Digital Equipment Corporation

As with any other implementation of local area networks, in its environment DEC aims to off-load communications functions from host systems, provide resource sharing, and improve network reliability. Design aims are to enable modular growth, enhance topological flexibility, and provide adaptable approaches to changing communications needs.

Figure 15.4 introduces the concept of a terminal server. It provides logical terminal connectivity to hosts on or off an Ethernet, and in the DEC environment it supports asynchronous terminals. Attached VAX and PDP 11 computers can also act as terminal servers. Use of a terminal server is suggested for multiple logical terminal connectivity to multiple processors, and when higher-performance connectivity is required in an environment where nonintelligent data terminating equipment are in the majority.

By definition, a server is any network node where shared resources are located. There are terminal, compute, disk, application, gateway, and print servers. A computer in a LAN that offers these types of services may be viewed as providing server functions. An attached host providing server functions can be time-shared or allocated to dedicated functions such as applications processing. A computer node providing CAD services, using software provided by the user, might be viewed as an applications server.

Among terminal server benefits are lower interface cost per attached terminal, reduction in cabling expense, and host-independent terminal connectivity. Ethernet communications servers are dedicated special-purpose subsystems that promote resource sharing across many host systems within the local area network. Currently, there are four types of communications servers for use on a DEC-supported Ethernet:

- Terminal servers
- DECnet router servers
- DECnet router/X.25 gateways
- DECnet/SNA gateways

Gateways provide communications with foreign architectures via protocol translation. Routers assure communications between DECnet nodes on two or more Ethernets and remote DECnet nodes. Terminal servers address themselves to terminal connectivity with multiple hosts on and off an Ethernet.

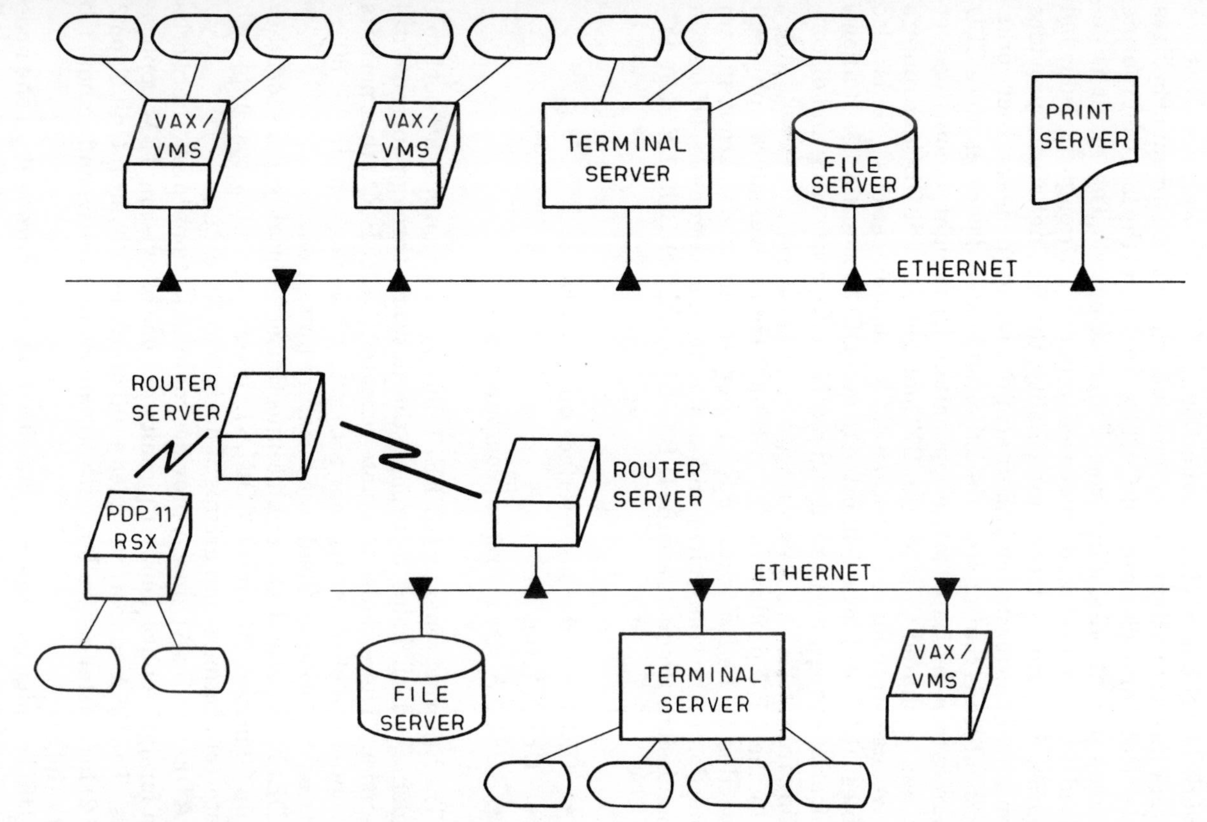

Figure 15.4 Applying the concept of a terminal server.

DECnet router servers find their application in large DECnet networks, LAN-to-LAN interconnection, and LAN-to-wide area DECnet network interconnection. Benefits include the establishment of bridges between local and wide area DECnet networks and the fact that routine functions permit off-loading from Ethernet hosts. The result is decreased load on host and increased reliability through a dedicated resource. In terms of basic functionality, the DECnet router provides communications to another Ethernet and to remote nodes and networks. It both off-loads routing from the Ethernet host and permits more CPU resources to be dedicated to the application. Up to eight remote lines per unit can be shared through the DECnet router. All DECnet routers feature user-transparent DECnet/X.25 communications. This also enables DEC hosts to be connected to non-DEC hosts of X.25. It allows applications programs to send and receive data, connecting and disconnecting from X.25.

In the DEC product line, the H4000 transceiver allows physical connection to the Ethernet cable. Ethernet controllers permit system connection to the transceiver and also perform a diagnostic self-test on transmission. Products are the Q-Bus-DEQNA, UNIBUS-DEUNA, PC-DECNA:

- DEQNA is the bus interface unit for PDP 11
- DEUNA, for VAX
- DECNA, for a personal computer

The Ethernet repeater (DEREP) allows connection of Ethernet cable segments, which helps to expand the network through incremental expansion. There is also a remote repeater (DEREP-RA) that permits the connection of segments that are up to 1000 meters apart. It offers electrical isolation and features moisture protection.

DELNI is a stand-alone unit connecting eight local systems together within 50 meters (150 feet) of DELNI. It serves as a low-cost approach to interconnecting small groups of devices to Ethernet.

A DECnet-SNA gateway provides communications to SNA networks with foreign applications. It permits the use of existing IBM applications. The SNA support includes 8100 protocols, Physical Unit Type 2 (PU 2) for cluster controller, data stream compatibility, and remote job entry (RJE).

DEC emphasizes the fact that Ethernet can be brought up one node at a time. A newly installed node can communicate immediately with all other active nodes on the network. Quite importantly, additional devices and cable segments can be connected without shutting down the network. Also the absence of master-slave node relationships and the need for routing nodes eliminate most single points of failure, while online diagnostics minimize the time needed to locate and to repair a failure. Implementation statistics add to the confidence level. There have been some 20,000 VAX PDP 11 installed worldwide on Ethernet as of mid-1987, of which about 2000 were installed the last quarter prior to this estimate.

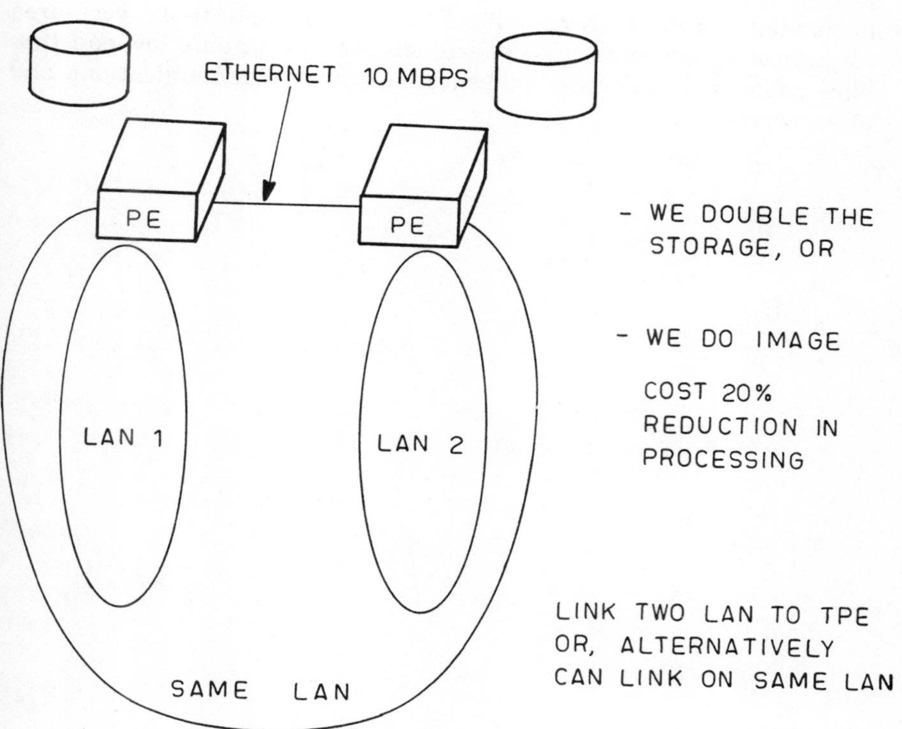

Figure 15.5 A duel file server configuration for greater reliability.

Some of the better-known Fortune 500 customers distribute services such as security monitoring, energy management, and building access control using Ethernet channels. But more frequently, the Ethernet channel is used for transmitting reports and electronic mail. By piggybacking Ethernet on CATV channels, a single medium can transmit teleconferencing, data communications, and security. It provides access to a variety of databases, while sharing the cable with other applications.

A DEC competitor uses Ethernet to interconnect two professional engines (PEs) which function as database servers to a twin system. Each PE runs its own LAN. In this manner the vendor offers its clients the alternative to double the available storage per supported dedicated LAN or to maintain shadow image to improve system dependability in case one of the two file servers fails. This approach is shown in Figure 15.5. TPE stands for twin professional engine. This is but one example of the flexibility which can be obtained when system designers understand the basic facilities the LAN can offer. In another application, work-area configuration optimizes cost effectiveness by combining low-end thin wire cable with standard Ethernet supporting communications and other servers.

Chapter

16

A LAN Operating System

16.1 Introduction

For mainframes, steadily expanding OS routines mean overhead; for LAN, it is another matter altogether. A local area network needs an operating system, though it may be called by a different name, and the functions which it performs are not necessarily the same as those on a mainframe. Such functions are highly distributed. Netex and Massnet, the evolving token passing architecture and Etherlink, Ethershare, and Etherprint of Ethernet are examples of OS fuctionality in a LAN. So is the role of the network control center (NCC) and, in general, of system control and administration. Both the importance and the plurality of OS functions call for very careful planning. Lower overhead can come from specialization:

1. Data processing functionality is assured by the personal computer OS.
2. Databasing is managed by the OS of the specialized file server.

3. Printing capabilities are handled through the print server.
4. Graphics and voice input-output are run through dedicated microprocessors.
5. Gateway to other networks are assured by dedicated servers.
6. The global data communications capability has to be run through the networks OS residing at the BIU.

This type of distributed structure is consistent with the notion that an OS is a control program for allocating resources among competing tasks. Layered OS functionality helps distribute competence among software modules supporting different devices. Specialization makes it more evident that an operating system is a software extension of hardware primitives implementing a virtual machine that serves within a programming environment. The focal point is, and should always be, quality of service (Figure 16.1). More than data consistency is at stake. With communications the central point of reference , LAN-wide operability and availability should be given a lot of attention.

With mainframes and minis, one of the greatest problems for OS designers has been maintaining the consistency of data about the current state of resource allocation and the state of each piece of hardware in the system. Yet we know from experience that consistency is difficult to maintain when multiple processors and I/O controllers have access to a common database.

16.2 Meeting Design Objective with Network OS

With LAN architectures, distributed OSs work on a virtual machine base. They make extensive use of equipment independence. Changes in the hardware affect only a small portion of the logical set-up. Distributed operating systems:

1. Look after procedures that enable users to share resources.
2. Manage the common resources on the network.
3. Provide control action for programs and data.
4. Look after communications-intense activities.
5. Protect against unauthorized usage.
6. Supervise the ongoing functionality of the system.
7. Follow-up administrative and accounting prerequisites.

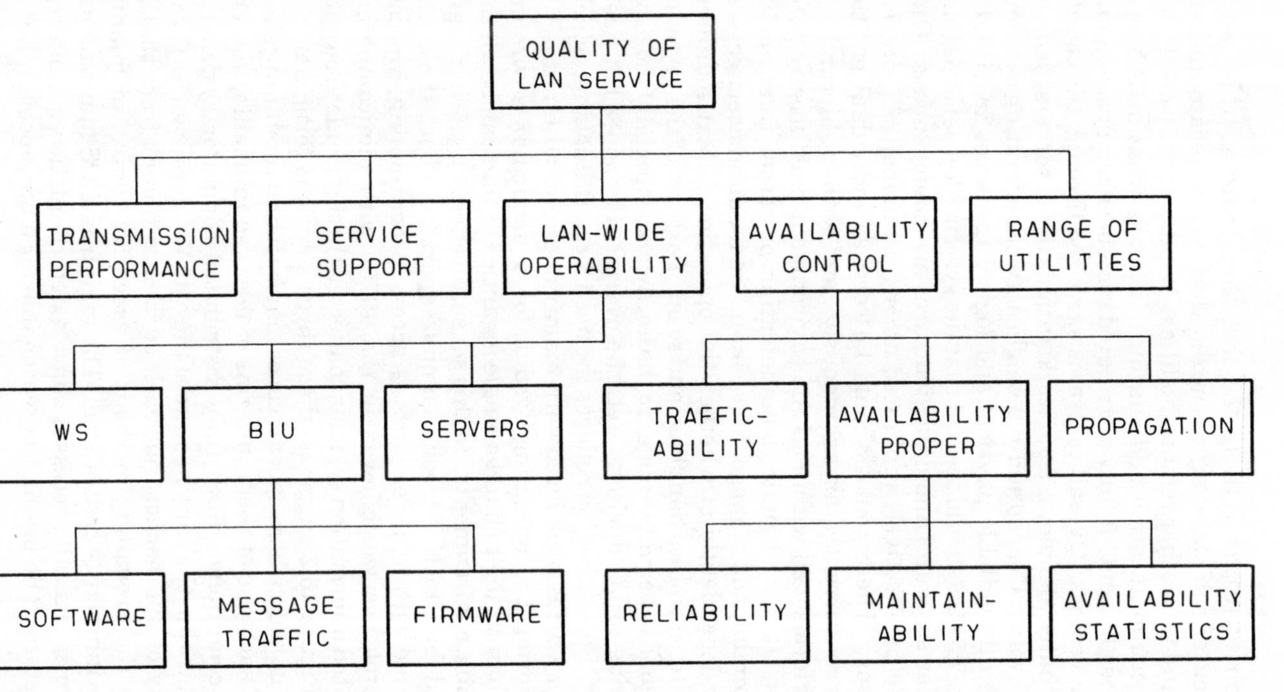

Figure 16.1 Functions needed to ensure quality of LAN service.

Their structure reflects the fact that with a LAN, we have a collection of self-standing resources that communicate among themselves and with other remote facilities. What we really need is supervision in communication and sharing. That is what a LAN operating system is all about. A fully distributed system encompasses a multiplicity of processors. Overall control is exercised through the coordination of distributed elements: from workstations to file servers, print servers, and gateways. Conceptually, a single network operating system should manage all available physical and logical resources in an integrated fashion. The OS should see to it that the system's kernel logic (hardware as well as software) and data structures are homogeneous. Only then can they be effectively replicated among a number of processors and databases. These copies should be seen as individual entities that execute concurrently, asynchronously, and without hierarchy. An OS that performs well within a LAN environment must assure polyvalent services. It must handle communicating processes from applications programming and manage their contention for database access. It must do so independently of whether the operation is text handling, data processing, graphics handling, and so on. Portions of the system should be designed to permit changes to the hardware, especially those portions interfacing to I/O devices. Yet, the overall effort does not need to be complex. Specialization relieves the need for multitasking, which is the way this job has been faced with mainframes and with minis.

Tailoring the operating system for a particular environment is better than trying to build a single gigantic OS that can be all things in all possible environments. In this sense, an operating system aggregate designed for a LAN is a solution quite apart from both the centralized mainframe with its three parts — access, programming, processing — the approaches we followed in the 1970s with minicomputer-based distributed information systems connected through wide area networks.

As Figure 16.2 suggests, these three solutions form, among themselves a domain where specific cases may be found combining characteristics of each one of them in terms of user requirements, and environmental conditions. Such fully distributed computer systems are, in general, within the current state of the art. Vendors bring to the market a variety of approaches, but each of them different from that known through the prevailing methods of executive control of mainframes, which is inherently centralized. The mainframe OS approach rests on the premise that all processes share a deterministic view of the entire system state. The premise is reasonable for a uniprocessor but not for

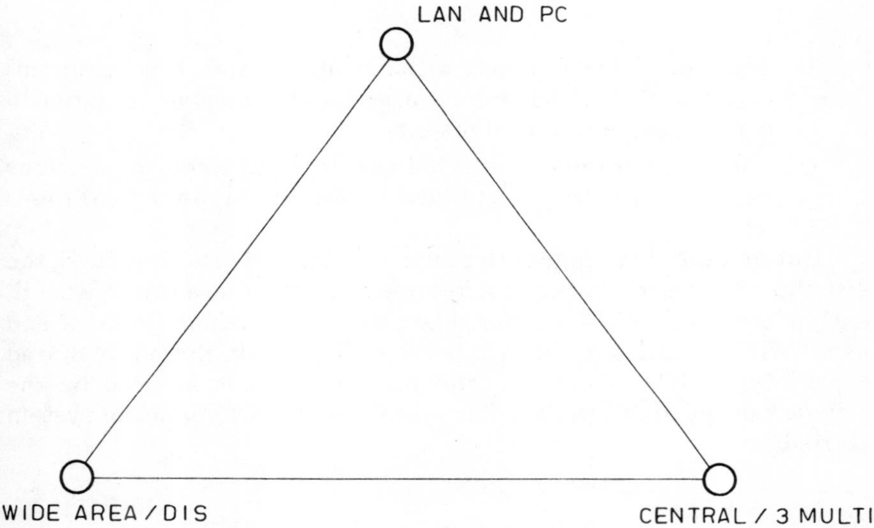

Figure 16.2 Solutions are defined by three concepts dominating information systems depth.

a distributed system. Truly distributed resources call for a different perspective in terms of their management. In a local area network, connections are made only when they are needed. Data traffic is controlled by software between two or more devices on the network, serving either:

1. Lengthy transfers of data between various devices, particularly communicating databases.
2. Fast, transaction-type operations between workstations and the local databases, and among the workstations themselves.

With LAN architectures, no operating system is used in the mainframe sense, although most of the functional design is extracted from the operational uniprocessor for comparison purposes. All attached devices to the LAN are task driven, using a simple system of ranked input and output queues to schedule and coordinate activity. The fact is that since our concepts regarding the management of new systems evolves from what we already know, two disciplines have influenced LAN design:

- The centralized approach with multiprocessors, this being converted to a sort of distributed large mainframe-style operation in a star-type hierarchical manner
- The long haul interconnected real-time time-sharing systems particularly with packet switching Arpanet-type capabilities

But concepts do change with practice and experience. In a LAN, the distributed resource rests on microcomputers and these run independently of one another in a manner able to provide functionality to the end user. While each micro is dedicated to a single task, there is a shared capability, such as databases and printers, that is assured by the software of the architecture. The mission of a LAN operating system starts here.

16.3 Goals in Operating System Design for LAN

Experience from long haul distributed information systems has influenced LAN designers toward the implementation of a set of protocols able to assure that although the attached machines are autonomous, they are also coordinated in their function. The essence of such approach has been cooperative autonomy. Four broad areas have interested us during the last dozen years of OS design:

1. *Device independence*. The distributed operating system of the LAN should implement standard interfaces between user programs and devices. This calls for coordinated software and hardware solutions. Within the LAN environment, a user program can obtain input and output from any attached device by reading the file corresponding to that device. This insulates programs from changes in the hardware properties of devices and permits new units to be added without changing the I/O conventions of the system.

   Communications services relative to basic LAN functionality should be supported by error control and a dynamic activation of processes. This leads to the need for concurrency control on the transport medium and in the global database. Identical ordering provides unique time-sharing, hence mutual exclusion. To study a real-life implementation we must look at arrival statistics for transaction, and the scheduling policy when multiple transactions are present for the serial resource.

2. *Process handling.* The operating system must maintain process coordination from messages passing to the scheduling of the processors attached to the LAN. Control software for process handling must be completely distributed and include four basic components:

   - A kernel code supervising communications and processing starting in each machine
   - Peripherals control through the different servers
   - Routines needed for command and log-in processes
   - Software able to support a methodology for interchange of data and processes (semaphores, pipes)

   Utility routines are also necessary. They work in coordination with the OS of the attached workstation which typically features a range of services; some of OSs to be found in such a network are shown in Figure 16.3.

   Coordination between LAN routines and the OS of attached resources (WSS, servers, hosts) is of critical importance. In a mainframe situation, this approach typically involves low-level details such as memory locks, interrupts, and context switching with the high-level concepts of sockets, message queues, and semaphores. Distributed resource management maintains a good deal of the aspect, but the mechanics largely depend on the protocol to be chosen: carrier sensing with collision detection, token passing, or other tree-like structures.

3. *File manager.* This is the server dedicated to the handling of the LAN database. To a fair extent it can be seen as a component part of the overall operating system. Although this software may or may not feature database management system (DBMS) capabilities, it must be able to handle the local storage in the longer term by maintaining directories and managing objects. It must perform operations on them copy, rename, open, close, read, and write and also exhibit qualities which are useful for organizing and sharing numerous files.

   LAN implemented file servers must be designed to help

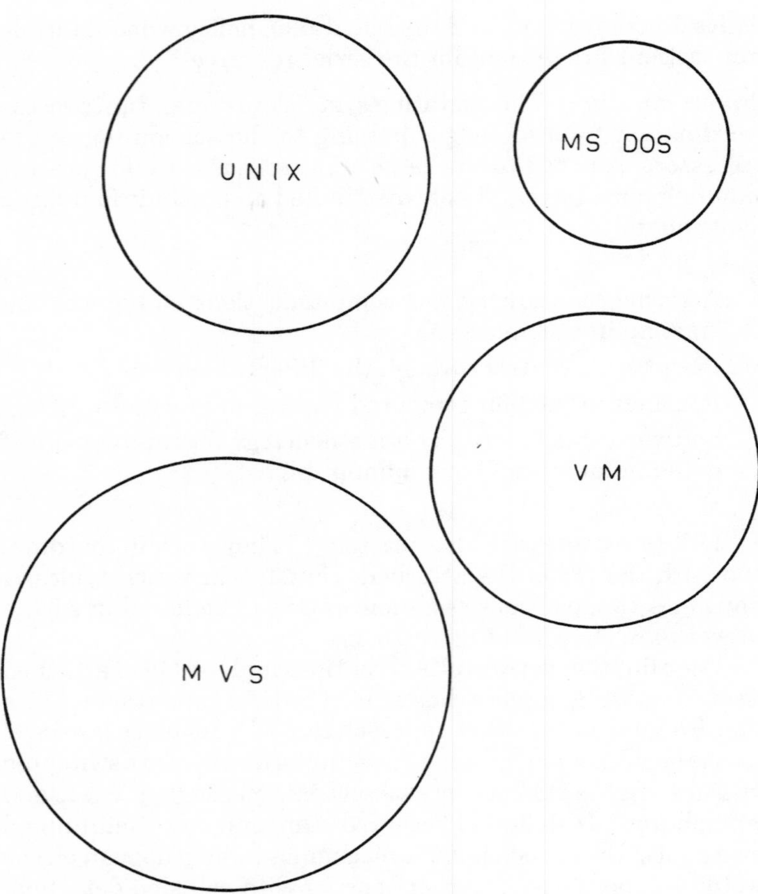

Figure 16.3 Too many OS do bad service to system depth goals.

users keep track of increasing amounts of permanent data. Shared file stores greatly ease saving text or data and handling projects in which several online users cooperate on a single file or document. While this stresses the file server, a LAN requires other server functions as well. The existence of a printer server can be fundamental. Hard copy should be avoided at the WS level, keeping instead a soft-copy (video) orientation. Another vital server is the gateway, for data communications purposes.

4. *End-user functions.* This, too, is a component part of the overall OS, not necessarily supported by all currently available LAN architectures. End-user functions run on the workstation and each WS has its own OS. But end-user function coordination should be done through the network. Examples of user-level software running on the attached devices (workstations) include assemblers, compilers, link editors, a document preparation system, text editors, a distributed debugger, and different utilities. The network itself will coordinate services connected to a distributed file management system, gateways, and measurement tools.

Within the overall system architecture of the distributed resources, programs construct a virtual architecture from processes and interprocess communication paths. This virtual architecture is mapped through layers of software and multiplexed onto a substantially different real architecture. As a result, a variety of implicit relationships may arise. The effects of virtual-to-real mappings are fundamental in an effective LAN, OS design. Other activities, too, must be accounted for, such as what in a mainframe environment is referred to as job control. It concerns the software that interacts directly with the users, allowing them to specify commands (command interpreter). Schematically this is the outermost layer of the logical machine implemented by the operating system. Since several of these concepts come from mainframe OS implementation and mainframes are batch-type engines, the more classical command languages are also batch oriented. Much better solutions have been followed both in terms of efficiency and in the human interface in interactive systems such as time-shared minicomputers and interactive online personal computers. In fact, personal computer and word processor system designers are paying considerable attention to the user interface; they have learned that a well-engineered approach greatly improves the user's ability to communicate. This is one of the fundamental design prerequisites as systems move into a LAN environment.

A further critical issue with end- user-oriented resources is identification. In a distributed environment, resources (whether devices or services) may have aliases, and multiple resources may have the same name. In principle:

- A resource rests on logical (SW) and physical (HW) devices.
- A device is necessary to support a resource.

- The goal of this support is to offer a service.
- The devices and the services they support must be callable from any other device or service.
- Models help characterize how distributed software structures use the network. Services such as file access and message exchange that take place between processes establish LAN functionality and define the utility it can present to the user.

16.4 Supervisory Activities from Source to Destination

As far as the cooperative processes, the file accesses and the communications capabilities are concerned, the common ground is the message passing through an interprocess mechanism that is assured by the aggregate OSs which comes into play in a LAN. Such mechanism is logical in its nature. It should, however, also be clear that it will be subject to physical-, logical-, and applications-oriented limitations. (begin propagation, routing, queuing, duplication because of lost acknowledgments, misrouting, reordering because of rerouting, and undetected damage).

In a layered architecture like ISO/OSI, each layer is dedicated to a function and has a protocol. These protocols form a hierarchy. In general, we can distinguish the following three layers:

1. The virtual machine.
2. The communications support.
3. The physical management.

From the virtual machine layer through communications support and logical and physical management, demons are instrumental in assuring supervision and control. They watch registers, indexes, values, or blackboards for indications that they are needed, at which time they are activated. If more than one demon is activated at one time, priority is decided by the system's rules.

There is a correspondence between the ISO/OSI model which has seven layers and the above three-level structure. The virtual machine layer involves the ISO/OSI applications level, presentation control, and session control. Communications support corresponds to transport, networking, and data link of ISO/OSI. In a LAN environment, the data link and the physical layers are further exploded into two sublayers each. In IEEE 802 the logical link control (LLC) and media access control (MAC) correspond to the ISO/OSI data link layer. LCC occupies itself with data transfer; MAC interfaces with the upper sublayer of the physical layer which is divided into the media access unit (MAU) and the cable. In a local network, the functions of MAU are signaling, encoding, and medium handling.

A network may broadcast, narrow cast (multicast), or transmit messages point to point. In a broadcast application, a message can be transmitted to all the attached workstations. Narrow casting uses a selected distribution list. Point-to- point routes messages only from one station to the other. These communications capabilities are necessary for stations on the same local area network to communicate among themselves, with the file server, the printer server, and the gateway. This underlines the nature of a distributed system and the supervisory activities which are needed from source to destination, taking into account:

1. The multiplicity of general-purpose resources.
2. The fact that they are both logically and physically distributed.
3. The need to have them coordinated through high-level operating system routines.
4. The ability to assure system transparency.
5. The possibility of having resources addressed by name, not by location.
6. The coordination necessary for assuring a cooperative autonomy, not a competitive structure.

Figure 16.4 suggests a decision matrix for LAN supervisory activities. Most of the entries are valid from source to destination. Usage classes and functional subsets are properly identified. They should be examined with an open mind toward effective implementation.

When we look more carefully into the system characteristics, two approaches come to mind. One is to build upon existing network operating systems like this. The other is to start from scratch and avoid the pitfalls of the past. The second approach is the more elegant and the most efficient. It also helps make the local OS subordinate to the network OS — not vice versa as with the long-haul solutions (and resulting network architectures) of the last 20 years. But a newly

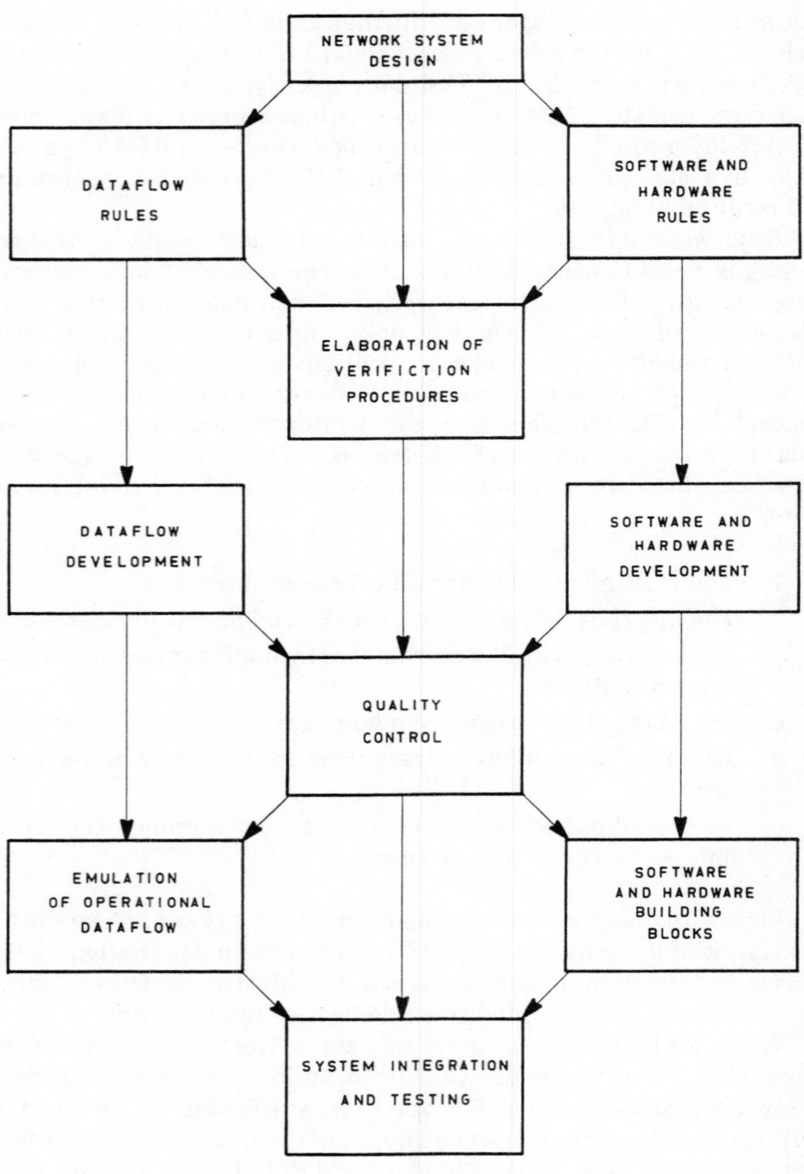

Figure 16.4 Decision matrix for LAN supervisory activities.

designed LAN OS must also assure:

- Robustness
- Reliability
- Transparency
- Extensibility
- Configurability
- HW supports
- SW supports
- Cooperative autonomy

Design guidelines advise the wisdom of exploiting existing software investments, minimizing modifications at a later date, avoiding interruption of the current system of operations, and adopting advanced concepts which can be valid for many years. For these reasons, virtual machine solutions seem to be the right answer for LANs. Extending virtual technology from mainframes to multiple microcomputers introduces new considerations, especially if the virtual machines are cooperating rather than executing in isolation. For instance, a decision procedure is needed to take into account:

1. The resources available at each workstation and server.
2. The resources required by the virtual device.
3. Communications bandwidths between the different processors.
4. Logical and physical file exchange requirements.
5. Communication load generated by the attached engines.

There is also the virtual nature of tasks to be used primarily to help structure the separation between logical and physical entities and to provide a well-defined mechanism for communication between processes running on different computers. Some of its specific obligations include the assignment, switching, and multiplexing of local physical resources among virtual machines; the control over the execution of sensitive instructions; and error recovery procedures. The LAN's distributed operating system should handle resource allocation and global monitoring functions.

The network software should provide hardware support mechanisms for system control and interprocess communication. There is also a need for standardization in methodologies and protocols.

16.5 A LAN Operating System and the Network Architecture

A network architecture should be designed in a layered manner, each layer performing a specific set of functions. The inverse is also true. The interconnecting of layers sees to it that the network architecture looks after the whole range of implementation: from data link to end user. A LAN architecture does not concern itself only with text and data transport. Once the transmission of information is achieved, the most important portion of LAN functions starts: interacting with the operating systems of the attached devices (WSs, servers, hosts) and the programs running on them.

The architecture's higher layers define the way in which network intelligence is implemented and the rules for information exchange between nodes of similar or different design. They:

- Manage end-to-end information to be delivered
- Provide users with needed interfaces to the servers
- Channel text and data within and between networks
- Make feasible network management and control

Through local area networks, the user may obtain a reasonable freedom to use equipment of different vendors if the architecture permits it. We can interconnect different networks through gateways, assure performance improvements by the addition of new hardware and/or functionality (such as graphics), and experiment with the way in which change can be accommodated. The standard software interface, with the addition, deletion, or substitution of support packages, relinks user programs to allow them to exploit performance advantages of the optional features.

For communication-type applications, text, data, graphics, images, and eventually voice must be carried between attached devices while, at the same time, particular attention must be paid to shared resources. The OS must be able to locate required entities, devices, programs, and information elements; manage the resources residing on attached devices; create needed process (es); service the device (s); and resource (s); and connect the process together.

The bus interface unit connecting the attached devices (WSs, disk drives, printers, gateways, etc.) has an OS which can be in firmware. This makes the overall system tree-like. It has:

1. User processes.

2. OS processes.
3. Kernel of the LAN architecture.

Taken together these layers constitute a functional aggregate which is essentially what we mean by the basic software, OS functionality, and application-oriented tasks. Such software drives the hardware. It runs the system, accesses the shared resources and makes feasible the implementation of advanced workstations and of communicating databases.

Since workstation resources are dedicated to the user, LAN performance is most frequently defined in terms of throughput rather than response time. But response time is critical at the WS level. Distributed resources overcomes inherent ceilings imposed by mainframe implementation where, at any particular time, performance beyond a certain level can be achieved only through greater system complexity, which degrades both throughput and response time. Centralized solutions present poor service to the end user because of the switching overhead and the contention for available resources. The distributed architecture of the LAN avoids performance degradation caused by the exponential rise in software overhead as the maximum performance of the processor is approached. LAN architectures can overcome the performance bounds when executive control is itself distributed when the LAN OS is appropriately designed.

The selection of an interconnection mechanism is oriented toward a broad range of custom-made solutions. This can be easily achieved through message exchange, which becomes a linking mechanism from source to destination. On several occasions, the determining factor in system throughput is the speed of the disk system and the processor attending it. Workstation response time is determined by the applications program it is running and by the amount of I/O it must do. Under no condition, should the maximum wait for a file server transaction exceed 20 seconds, and the average delay at the WS should be below 1 second.

The correct choice of protocols is instrumental in a successful operation. For instance, in a given implementation four protocols are required:

- *Name inquiry* for lookups
- *Rendezvous* to open and close the connection to effectively examine connection

- *Data transport* to carry the requested information elements

The kernel of the LAN operating system provides the interprocess communications facility through the exchange of short messages. The interface of the kernel consists of only one primitive: "end of the current processing step" and it has a parameter set of messages. For the sake of homogeneity, communication with the kernel is also seen as an exchange of messages: some give parameters for the selection for the next processing step, others for the switch of the next processing step, and still others for the timeouts to be enabled or to be sent on ports of processes. A distinction is necessary between a message intended for the kernel and a message for a process, which is made in the name of the destination port. The process may not even be aware of that distinction. Thus when a process is started, it receives the message which triggers the processing step. During the whole execution of the processing step, it may access only this message and its local data. When the processing step ends, the process returns to the kernel transmitting all its messages. This, too, is an architectural solution.

16.6 OS Functionality for Message Handling

Looking at the local area network as a system, we automatically consider a collection of entities: active and passive process, active and passive object, and demons and other functions which act as guardians. Each one of these entities has a name and is of a certain type. Kernel, forks, pipes, semaphores, and demons are process-oriented entities. Records, files, stacks, messages, etc., are user-defined entities. Both process- and user-defined entities are examples of the different types.

Connection establishment implies complete binding of the parties entering in a communication. Within this context, control action (guardians) is a special process. Typically, it is cyclic in nature or carries specifications for the entities which it guards. This may be the state of information, synchronization constraints, scheduling algorithms, or local resource management capabilities.

Message systems running on a local area network provide particularly clean mechanisms for communication between processes and attached devices. In the past, a drawback to message systems has been the substantial operating system overhead in transferring a message from one process to another in a fully protected way. Today, LAN architectures offer an opportunity to build a fully protected message system which can be used with low overhead. Typically, a message port, or mailbox, will be assigned. Messages will be passed by the LAN's transferring capabilities. Two representative operations are:

1. *Send (message).* This transfers message functionality and a reply mail address from the caller's list to the mailbox. If the mailbox is full, the caller is suspended.
2. *Receive (mailbox).* If the mailbox contains a message, the capability associated with the message and a reply command will be transferred into the caller's list. Otherwise the caller is suspended.

A message-based communications system (such as Ethermail, described in Chapter 15) permits a clean separation between the transport mechanism for the messages and the interpretation of the actual message content by the receiver. The main role of the communications routines becomes that of routing and switching messages and establishing and controlling communication channels between processors. Higher-level tasks, such as destination process identification, message numbering and acknowledgment, and CRC generation and checking, are left to the protocols observed by the LAN's communication system. This provides the most flexibility at the expense of some overhead for the workstations wishing to communicate. It also assures a high degree of computational concurrency leading to a large number of messages traveling through the network at any one time. Many of these messages may be routed over the same link, and an obvious design goal is that a single, very long message must not monopolize a link, and no stalled message should render a link completely unusable.

The LAN operating system should account for the fact that messages move in bursts, and that switching from one message to another is associated with overhead. As far as the communications subsystem is concerned, the standard routine task involves:

1. Looking at the header.
2. Decoding the target node address.
3. Determining the proper link over which message must be sent.
4. Finding an available channel slot on that link.
5. Updating the translation table.
6. Giving a go-ahead signal to the input port.

These tasks can be handled by hardware or software, the decision being based on the frequency with which the task has to be performed and on the influence that its execution speed has on the overall communication bandwidth.

While the routing of individual bytes through each node, after the message channel has been established, should be performed entirely in hardware, less critical events, such as reporting the status of all links to the operating system, can be handled by software. For instance, transaction-oriented data may be exchanged between a workstation and the local database by using a single packet of information: the datagram. Datagrams are like telegrams. An addressed unit of information is sent to the destination in a single, one-way transmission. If required, a response may be sent with another transmission.

Datagrams involve little overhead. Therefore, they are ideally suited to LAN environments since they feature short information-exchange transactions rather than a long-term circuit session. (In contrast to a datagram, a virtual circuit can be thought of as a telephone connection, where the destination is dialed, a two-way information exchange session takes place, this two-way information exchange terminates, and both parties hang up.) Datagrams also allow maximum use of the multiaccess, broadcast technology featured by LAN to be made. Flexible packet-addressing modes provide the capabilities necessary for a fully distributed resource sharing system. This is fundamental since many LAN characteristics are determined by network structure, including the number and means of the buffers used for intermediate storage of packets passing through nodes:

- A system using a small number of buffers is more likely to become deadlocked than one with more buffers.
- But a large number of buffers implies increased memory and greater complexity in organizational software.

In both cases, the network OS must continually ascertain which ports have live neighbors connected to them, tell the neighbor connected to any particular port when the buffer associated with that port is free to accept a packet, and on reception of a packet, decide whether to discard it, pass it on to one destination, or transmit it to all other live neighbors excluding the one from which it was received. This type of activity goes well beyond the requirements imposed by conventional multiple-processor architectures whose hardware and software for interconnection typically imposes high-cost configurations and a low limit on the maximum number of processors. By disassociating the data processing component from data communications, the LAN operating system is more versatile than that of a mainframe; it is also less costly since the system which it supports is more modular.

Versatility, modularity, and consistency in a LAN environment can be further enhanced by following the proper message management policy. Figure 16.5 suggests an approach with consecutive layers of message encapsulation. LAN software and hardware uses control bytes to allocate and deallocate a channel slot to a message channel. A routing controller looks at the message header to decode the destination and choose the appropriate output port. As with any other communication system, this approach is not concerned with the content of the message.

16.7 Intratask and Intertask Communications File Exchange

In a local area network environment, logical parts of a single program reside in and are executed by different computers within the system. Each process and each object is under the control of the organizational entity responsible for the node in which it resides. Work is focused on language primitives to support modularity and communications between the parts. By distributing the program, contention for any one section of it is reduced. Access speed is increased because the entity most likely to use a part of the program will be located close to it. Each attached resource has a greater control over its part of the program. These are definite LAN advantages.

Decisions relating to program simplification should be based on the fact that in any computer application the cost of software predominates. In networked applications involving multiple computers, the effort of providing specialized software for each type of machine can be limited. Since this effort benefits from potential economic advantages of a critical mass, the cost per WS is reduced. By any standard, simplicity is the best policy.

Attached devices typically exchange end-to-end session messages at the transport level of ISO/OSI. Into this is reflected the packet structure of the networking layer, the frames format of data link and the bit streams characterizing the physical level of interconnection. Functionality at session control and higher levels is characteristic of the attached devices but not of the networking node. We can have a task classification which may be a type defined by function (manager, system, file) or service (virtual user, virtual resource). Another example is an OS task

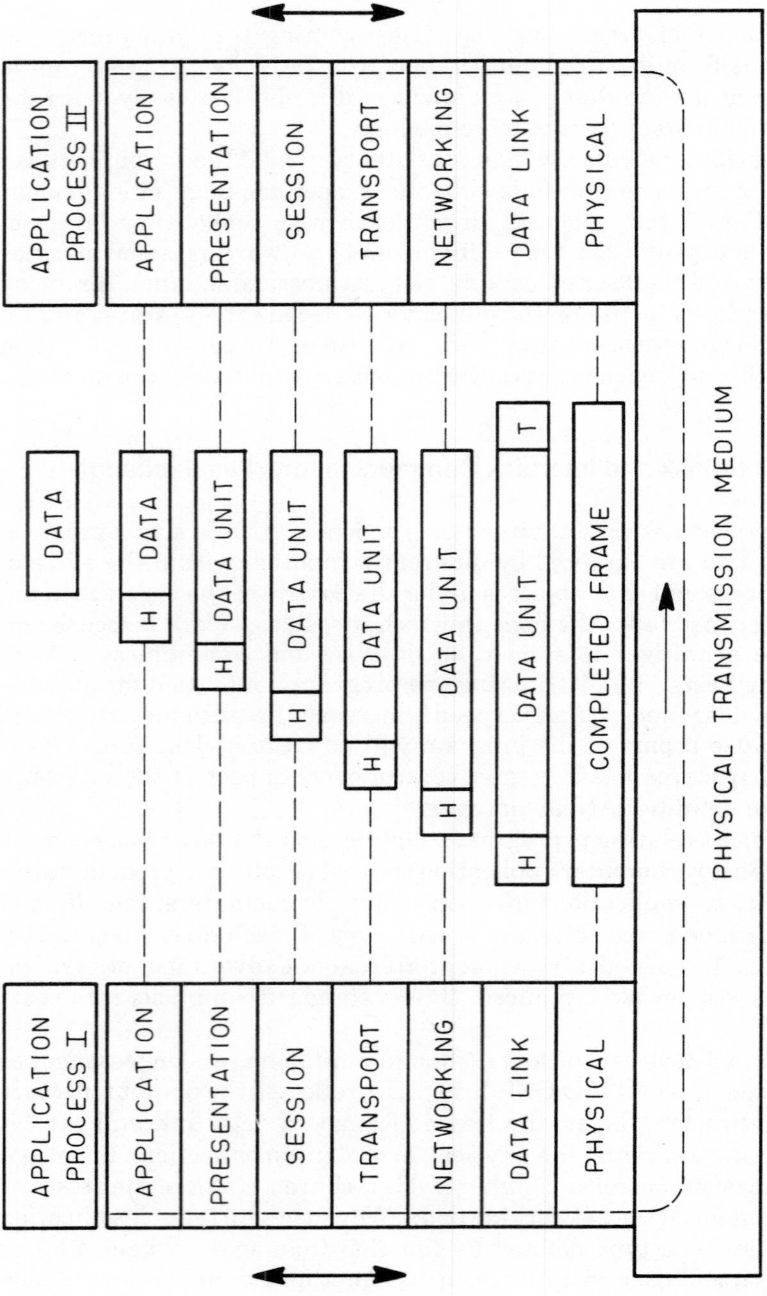

APPLICATION PROCESS I

APPLICATION
PRESENTATION
SESSION
TRANSPORT
NETWORKING
DATA LINK
PHYSICAL

DATA
H DATA
H DATA UNIT
H DATA UNIT
H DATA UNIT
H DATA UNIT
H DATA UNIT T
COMPLETED FRAME

APPLICATION PROCESS II

APPLICATION
PRESENTATION
SESSION
TRANSPORT
NETWORKING
DATA LINK
PHYSICAL

PHYSICAL TRANSMISSION MEDIUM

Figure 16.5 A layered protocol structure implies consecutive levels of message encapsulating.

relating to the local operating system (at the resource level) online at the LAN. With all these considerations in mind, design characteristics must assure that:

- System transparency is observed
- Generic services are logically equivalent
- An autonomous operation, at the device level, is guaranteed.

The network OS must be accessible throughout the LAN, with device interconnection upheld at all times. A valid model will operate at two levels:

1. *Intratask communication*, which can be either synchronous (for procedural innovation) or asynchronous (for message passing).
2. *Intertask communication*, which is mainly message handling.

A task consisting of OS primitives and objects should be resident in one location in the network. These simple considerations describe the general overview of an architecture involving a set of interconnected sites (personal computers, servers, hosts) within a local area, able to handle a range of processes considered to be local objects.

At each site, a kernel must be assured. This will see to it that, among other things, ports can be attached successively to processes. The OS will create (open) and close ports. Processes will use these ports to send messages. When a process does not need the port anymore — say to access the file server — it closes it. Another process can then access it.

Given that the typical office environment for managerial and professional activities does not require synchronous-type operations, it is a good policy that the process sends messages only at the end of a processing step, not during processing. This is important for system reliability. It also helps to achieve simplicity. In this sense, system services will be performed through the:

- Scheduling of processes
- Selection of next message to handle
- Switch on an entry point
- Local transport of messages
- Management of timeouts
- Assurance of security and protection

The necessary software must be provided so that errors can be detected by the processes, the local OS and the kernel, and in general, by the system itself. Such errors must be reported as messages.

This further underlines the need for a LAN architecture to guarantee extensive use of messages, uniformity in the communications domain, clarity in the processing of messages, and good overall performance characteristics. Performance characteristics will, to a large measure, be a function of the efficient handling of common resources. File administration requires file access, file management, and file transfer. For flexible polyvalent file transfer purposes, the user should be able to move an entire file and its attributes across networks even with dissimilar file systems. Such capability can be effectively supported when the LAN operating system, its communications routines, file management utilities, and supported end-user functions have the necessary software for driving the local resources and activating the right protocols according to the user requests. Typically a mapping process will interface with the local file system and will perform the mapping between the local file structures, standardized file format, and vice versa. Routines must also be activated to simultaneously process user requests, although the maximum number in instances is dynamically limited by the OS.

16.8 Silicon Nodes for a LAN

The idea of casting parts of the local area network OS into silicon rests on two pillars. First, major advances in computers and communications depend on achievement in hardware technology. Second, and just as important, the acceptance of LAN solutions will greatly increase by shrinking the implementation cost. A decrease in the implementation cost is directly related to the number of functions that can be put on silicon. To keep designs simple and costs low, components must be specialized to a function. Hence, functions with the broadest applications perspective should be chosen first and studied in terms of a conversion to hardware. Cost reduction will be accomplished by placing as much of the network interface as possible in silicon using very large-scale integration (VLSI).

At least one semiconductor manufacturer has taken the approach that a LAN can be divided into two distinct groups in terms of networking characteristics:

1. The front end part of the network represented by devices that

have bit transmission rates ranging from a few thousand bits per second to a few hundred thousand bits per second (kilostreams).

2. A generic group of devices contained in the rear end network, supporting data rates of megabits (megastreams) and gigabits per second (gigastreams). The latter appeal to database functions.

This underlines the need for different chips: kilostream, megastream, and eventually gigastream levels. Not only the data rate but also the functionality is different in each class. Front end devices usually support low-speed units such as query terminals, data collection gear, and so on. Since many of them are inexpensive, it is important that the first consideration be that the connection costs are a small fraction of device cost.

The consequence is that designers must restrict themselves to a range of applications that have similar requirements. Thus a VLSI solution will be projected in an application specific manner to assure the product will deliver maximum intended performance at minimum cost. By casting it in silicon, the physical medium supplies data to and receives data from an integrated transceiver via a cable tap; the transceiver chip and its support components fit inside the cable tap. In line with this approach, a LAN node connects to the transceiver and is composed of five basic blocks: a serial interface adapter, the local area network protocol chip, a memory chip, a microprocessor, and peripheral controllers. The purpose of the first block is to provide node data and clock encoding and decoding functions.

The LAN protocol chip handles the link layer and also interfaces this layer to the network via a 16-bit microprocessor bus. Depending on the design, the node microprocessor can be used to implement layers 4 through 7 of the ISO/OSI reference model. Link level address permits physical and logical addressing functions. The physical address match is the filter, and it is unique to the node. Frame check sequence generation and control is done automatically in the LAN protocol chip. On transmission, the frame check sequence is automatically checked for errors. The LAN protocol chip also contains the logic to perform binary backoff.

Also cast in silicon and associated with the processor, a memory interface is divided into sections: initialization block, transmit descriptor, receive descriptor, transmit data buffers, and receive data buffers. The host is responsible for writing the initialization block, the transmit descriptor ring entries, and so on. The LAN protocol chip updates the received entries. Error indication is handled through:

- Cyclic redundancy check (CRC)
- Collision detection
- Bubbling error on transmit timeout
- Framing error definition
- Missed rear end error
- Memory error possibility

While these references correspond to front end requirements for workstations, solutions for rear end networks should focus on interconnecting CPUs and high-speed devices such as disks. This requires a different design approach from the described VLSI for the front end. In heavy-duty rear end approaches, hardware-intensive features are dictated by:

- Network architecture
- Bit rate
- Encoding
- Access protocol
- Link protocol

The range of transfer capabilities for the rear end can vary widely from 50 MBPS to 1 GBPS or more. The current ANSI specification of a bit rate of 50 MBPS can be achieved with a bipolar implementation of a high-speed node. Higher bit rates mean larger packet buffers and higher interconnect cost. Good reasons also exist for casting interface devices in a variable bit rate design. Both in the front end and in the rear end sense of implementation, the specifications for integrated circuits to be worked out with criteria such as flexibility in transport and ease of programming.

Current experience indicates that from 50 MHz down, the physical layer is easily programmable. Also relatively easy to handle are link level protocols for bit stuffing, address field (length, position) management, and CRC (16 or 32 bits). The casting into silicon of higher-up layers presupposes the establishment of data flow characteristics, the definition of flow control type, the study of response time constraints, and the proper analysis of other time-sensitive issues which may imply limitations on the implementation of the LAN operating system.

PART 4

LAN Servers, Gateways, and Distributed Databases

Chapter

17

Concepts and Practices with LAN Servers

17.1 Introduction

Servers are network devices that perform both resource interfacing and intelligent sharing for workstations and hosts connected to the local network. A file server, for instance, controls mass storage sharing under LAN software. It allows single-user operating systems to share database resources. Other servers do the same for other peripherals. Security is also supported, access being restricted through user identification names and passwords. Each user has access to a set of volumes on the shared database. Computers running similar operating systems may share files by logically mounting the same volume on their own systems. Incompatible operating systems might communicate through the disk via byte-serial first-in, first-out (FIFO) pipes.

The printer server provides printer spooling and despooling. It also handles shared access to a printer for LAN connected workstations. A printer spooler and despooler can use pipes to buffer files destined for the printer server. Communications servers interconnect similar or dissimilar LANs. Modem servers help interconnect remote sites through telephone lines for transfer of data via pipes. Gateways bridge one network. Specialization is a key feature with communications servers. The use of bridges is instrumental not only in linking network segments but also in promoting partitioning concepts in the design of local area networks. However, partitioning into subnetworks might introduce protocol issues between subnetworks with different characteristics, which emphasizes the need for compatible protocols.

A LAN's servers maintain the network's shared resources. There may be several servers connected on the LAN with different sets of files on each, pairs may be run in tandem to provide security copies of all transactions. A local area network is unconceivable without servers, as is servers without a network.

17.2 User Stations and Servers

Solutions to end user problems are based on personal computers, servers, and local area networks. This system provides a distributed environment, a high degree of cohesiveness, transparency, and autonomy provided it has been implemented in a fault-tolerant way, using interfaces, communications protocols, distributed operating systems, distributed databases, and distributed applications programs. Attached LAN processors can be generally divided into user stations (workstations) and server stations. The workstation can be polyvalent, employing an impressive array of applications software. The choice of servers is more restricted and (in a number of cases) closely connected to LAN choice.

Servers should feature standard hardware interconnects and software protocols, they should be optimized for data integrity, and they should be able to accelerate throughput. A server system should be designed for expendability and easy maintenance — ideally assuring generic, device-independent operating system drivers. Device-independent solutions are most important since all requests are passed along the bus to a server. Device independence is also necessary since not only WS, but also (depending on the installation) shop floor collection devices, time and attendance recorders, digitally controlled machines, process control subsystems, and so on, may use common network resources managed by servers.

There are three important types of server stations (Figure 17.1), one

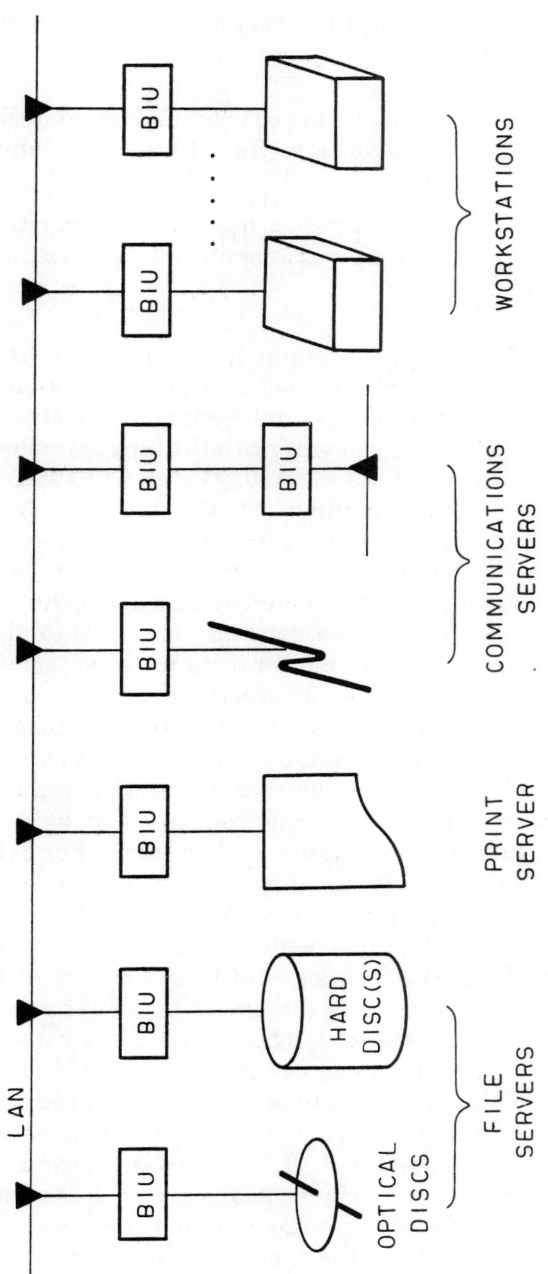

Figure 17.1 Server stations are many types, the file server being one of the most vital.

of the most vital being the file server. We need to share database resources because:

- The size of accessible shared volumes has changed by more than two orders of magnitude: from 10 to 20 megabytes to 1 and 2 gigabytes and beyond.
- New technologies introduce much larger capacities and features which have to be shared among WSs (e.g., document images on optical disks).

Today the file servers can be augmented through DBMS capabilities. Tomorrow the network-wide availability for interogation by any WS will be enhanced through artificial intelligence (AI) constructs.

File server functions can vary with the type of implementation and nature of supporting software. It may be an addressable virtual disk, read-only shared disk, or read-write not shared disk. The file itself may not have virtual characteristics, feature file and record locking, and operate as a shared relational database. Whether we talk of file-, printer- or communications-oriented functionality, the servers, as such, are not generally visible to the operator. The operator does not have to take any specific action because, for instance, a system is being used as a database server. The definition of servers, the functions they perform, and who will use them is part of the software configuration and installation process. From that point on, all interaction can be automatic.

There are, however, situations where the LAN administrator may be asked to respond to specific requirements and will need access to network control commands to accomplish them. For example, the site may decide to give priority to an application or group of users. A LAN operator may be told to implement that priority by directing servers to give preferential treatment to requests from a specific system. When one WS in the local area network is executing test software, the administrator may specify that servers reject some or all requests from that system. The result is that a new set of operator-administrator commands for dynamic control of network access must be provided. For example, the printer server allows key-ins to direct which printer servers a system may access and which requestor systems a printer server should currently accept requests from. LAN software permits the operator-administrator to redirect print from one server to another for availability, security, or load leveling reasons. Other servers implement similar key-ins as appropriate to the functions they perform. However, the communications, database, and file servers do not require extensive key-in support since they are extremely transparent to the administrator-operator, as well as to the end user.

However, administrative transparency is a matter requiring solutions which are highly situational. MIT's Project Athena built an authentication server primarily because each private workstation is owned by a student, and each public workstation is captured by individual students as superusers. Given this situation, there must be a way to protect the services, such as mail, printers, and file systems, from inadvertent errors. A prevention approach requires pair wise agreement between each two communicating entities. Implemented in an individual LAN, this approach can be cumbersome. It would require a global authentication service with a distributed implementation.

Problems, such as making sure to avoid using untrustworthy authentication services, become far more serious in a heterogeneous environment. Other problems arise because different environments often have different views of the level of protection that is necessary or desirable. Also, different authentication and authorization boundaries may exist within a single system as a function of user entities (persons, terminals, applications programs). In several implementation cases, files can be shared between applications running on the LAN, but the application has to take care of the sharing capability. Furthermore, file sharing needs networking links to allow the application to make network calls. Semaphores are available in most systems today, but they are not enough for LAN-wide handling of security and protection.

Another important file server contribution has been the journaling of all transactions and messages passing through the networks. However, the journaling and statistics mission must be enriched with more sophisticated software, such as the forementioned authentication and authorization mechanisms which are intimately related to the local operating system. Since authentication and authorization mechanisms are relying on being built-in to both prevent and detect tampering, the question arises: "Is it possible to accommodate such low-level OS dependencies in a distributed, heterogeneous environment?" This is a critical question when we talk of user stations and servers.

One of the more successful system solutions to the authentication problem is:

- Building appropriate-size barriers to discourage casual breaches
- Logging activities at each node
- Performing cross checks at intervals to ensure consistency
- Instituting a network police force as well as educating the users

Still, providing a solution to the authentication problem is only half the battle. The authentication information must also be interpreted in a consistent manner across the local area network and other interconnected resources. Performing this interpretation is a problem at least as hard as the original authentication.

Other duties relative to managing shared LAN resources have to do with optimization tasks. Network administration must take advantage of the fact that currently available software permits the time that the server uses to perform foreground and background tasks to be adjusted by defining time-slice intervals with which the server will perform foreground tasks for end users at "this" LAN and will perform background tasks for remote users. Some of the foreground tasks in a given LAN environment are: the user at the server entering DOS commands, the user at the server entering network commands, the user at the server running applications, and printing files from the print queue. Among background tasks are receiving and logging messages from remote users, handling remote users accessing a shared file server or directory, and accommodating remote users who are sending files to a shared printer.

Specifying a large time interval for background tasks means that remote users receive a good response for their tasks. However, response time to the LAN's immediate server users may be slower. Some operations by ongoing programs could also inhibit the time-slicing mechanism. Therefore, the administrator should experiment with new applications on the server in a controlled environment before using them when the network is fully active.

17.3 Managing Databases in a Network Environment

The core of the discussion about the agile handling of LAN servers is databases. The subject of managing multimedia databases is so fundamental that it requires the proper focus from the beginning. This section introduces the concept of a database and discusses what file servers can do by way of end-user support. We will go into details in Chapters 18 and 19.

A multimedia database is the sum of all information elements (IEs), data, text, graphics, voice, image available to the organization and handled by computers. It contains all documents in the organization stored and managed through information technology, as well as voice messages and other computer-assisted processes. In this sense, the database is a computer and communications-based system:

1. *Composed* of information elements.
2. *Organized* to serve the data, text, and other needs of the organization (voice, image, graphics).
3. *Accessible* by authorized entities (people, machines, programs, other databases).
4. *Distributed* in a physical sense but structured as one logical entity.

The information element is the building block of the database. It is an addressable entity; it can be bit, byte, field, record, file, or subdatabase, but it is usually structured as an object, page, or multiple. Such IEs are: stored, downloaded, received, and retrieved between machines. Data structures (i.e., text structures) must be normalized throughout the system. Modern retrieval mechanisms follow heuristic approaches which have richer results than deterministic ones. The emphasis of heuristic approaches is now being increasingly placed on an office document architecture which will characterize the file servers of the future.

The developing office document retrieval theory specifies the properties for query language in office documents:

1. *Incomplete specification of assertions.* The user needs a report or text but may be vague and/or uncertain about its specifications.
2. *Flexible specification assertions.* The end user may define a range of queries; may take a look-alike approach to document handling; or may express ideas about what is needed and let the machine make the proper identification.
3. *Relation assertions about different views of documents.* This calls for a manipulation language associated with text and data models. In all cases the inference capability of the computer system must assure an able interface for the specification of query predicates and associated uncertainty on behalf of the user.

In the future, uncertainty will be a very big part of retrieval. It will also be a basic ingredient in managerial and professional productivity:*

---

* This has been both the evidence and the conclusions reached in April 1987 at the NBS Symposium on Office Automation (Gaithersburg, MD).

- The basic concept is that of database search under certainty.
- The hypothesis is that a database search which is vague and stochastic gives much better results than a crisp and precise search.

This is a totally new concept that is alien to classical DP. With certainty, only very limited goals can be satisfied. Partial match gives far richer results.

But a partial match also implies significant design requirements incorporating artificial intelligence tools. Figure 17.2 gives a view of an approach which includes constructs to enhance the manipulation of a multimedia database. Design-wise, the fundamental characteristics of a database are:

- Storage in physical media is made in a device-independent manner.
- The handling of multimedia is based on relational and virtual memory (VM) principles.
- Location-independent access to the IE with idea database characteristics goes beyond key words or menu access.
- Depending on the application, access is implemented with encryption possibilities.
- Link to the applications programs are made applications-independent.
- Unique data definition and identification are on a system-wide basis.
- There is a *communications-oriented* structure. A message is a file in the DB and every file must be designed as a message.

Databases run through LAN servers are distributed in nature and a distributed database requires:

1. Directory services.
2. Online control capabilities .
3. IE definition and identification in a system-wide manner.
4. Synchronization in update and image consistency.
5. Assured privacy of data subsets (private versus public).
6. Dependable backup.
7. Online recovery capabilities.

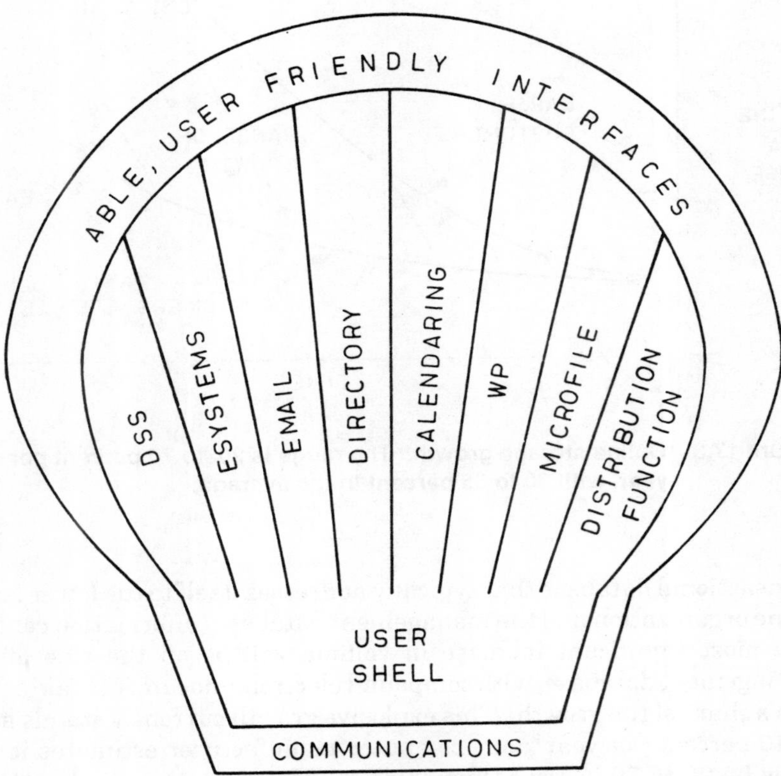

Figure 17.2 **Personal assistance functions to enhance multimedia database manipulation.**

8. Data dictionary services — with distributed data definitions.
9. Steady administration.
10. Consistency in usage.

In terms of volume, there is a significant difference between the

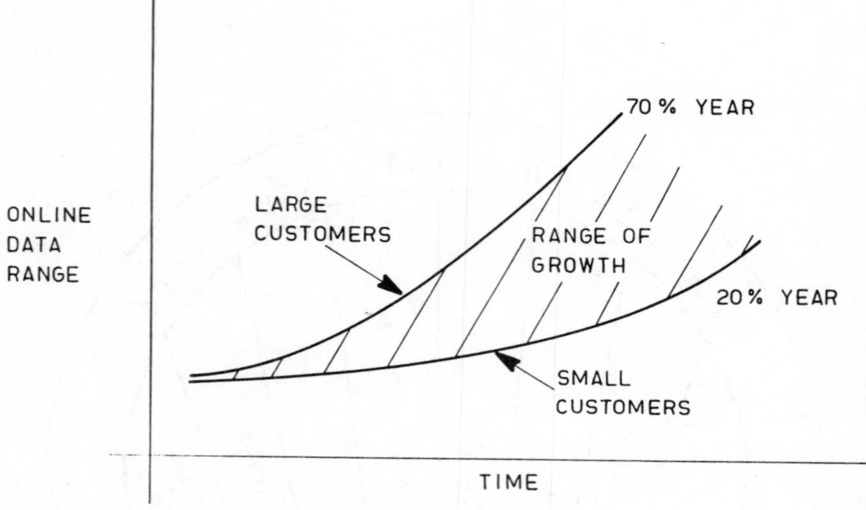

Figure 17.3 Online storage growth. The range is 20 to 70 percent per year, with 30 to 35 percent in the average.

transactional database that typically addresses itself to the lower levels of the organization and the management database (information center). The most significant increase in volume will be on the side of the management database, with compound electronic documents taking the lion's share of the growth. This explosive growth currently stands at 25 to 40 percent per year*; one computer manufacturer estimates it will grow by 20 to 70 percent (Figure 17.3). However, this vendor placed emphasis on company size, which is misleading. Therefore, we need an orderly progression. The implementation of microfiles and corporate files requires rules:

- No personal files should be kept at the WS level on an exclusive, uncontrollable basis.
- Files should be properly organized and stored in the local database, thus highlighting the role of the file server.
- Files should be both shares among users and protected and managed through the same discipline.

- A central text and data warehouse must provide for consistency, backup, and effective control of information elements.
- Pollution of corporate records should be avoided at all times.
- Recovery possibilities must be assured in an able manner.

Both long and short-range database planning are important. Proper pruning of the distributed database is a must. Although controlled replication may be — and often is — necessary, a database should never contain superfluous, obsolete, or unwanted copies of information. A database's contents should be regularly subjected to an extruder function, and all information elements should carry sunset clauses. Morgan Stanley manages an impressive online database. In 1987, this database stood at 100 gigabytes, growing at a rate of 25 gigabytes per year. The growth would have been much greater if sunset clauses were not in effect, cutting down unnecessary references and weeding out obsolete IE.

17.4 File Servers on a LAN

A LAN file server (FS) allows a group of workstations to plug into the interactive multiuser network. Each workstation maintains its full computer power using local processing, and storage yet has the ability to share a convenient mass-storage device. Among other benefits, such configuration provides a bonus for users, who may purchase and maintain one copy of applications software for their system, downloading when necessary. With stand alone approaches, they have to purchase a separate license for each floppy used on their WSs, a messy process, subject to errors and slow response time. Software vendors require an additional license for each micro on the LAN, considering the configuration as a time sharing arrangement, but even so, there are financial and operational benefits to the user organization from the management of one program copy rather than many.

The file server on the LAN allows users to display, create, delete, and copy files stored in the local database. They are provided with the means to protect the files, accessing the FS services to:

1. Back up file(s), copying onto departmental computer supports, central resources, or local media to be stored for safekeeping.
2. Copy files, moving information elements to a different support medium or operational node on the same or other LAN.

3. Change protection level; giving the user a means to guard against inadvertent file deletion while keeping the freedom to add or delete files as the job stream demands.
4. Display file(s), either the entire contents or part of a file on the screen.
5. Rename files, change file type(s), affect a range of administrative processes needed for proper operations.
6. Restore files in the event of accidental file deletion or system failure, recover, restart.

In addition, data dictionary and directory services may be available, including the ability to view the current directory or change directories. Intelligent file servers make available to individual workstations the services of complex software and hardware supports. Once in place, file server services may be shared by all of the workstations and possibly by other servers.

Large print files might be spooled to a database server and requested by the print server when it is ready for the job. Gateway(s) attached to the LAN feature store and forward capabilities, thus enhancing both message and file exchange. The capabilities and requirements of file servers differentiate them from other classes of storage control products — whether or not DBMS functionality is supported. In the typical DBMS environment, a single software package running on a single computer comprises the complete facility, with the end user or programmer interfacing at the top and the storage interfacing at the bottom. In a LAN, output formatting and language processing are the domain of the WS and may differ significantly from one application to another.

Thus file servers provide a common denominator in information element storag,e permitting workstations to specialize regarding the job they have been assigned and still share resources and have available backup. Figure 17.4 presents a real-life LAN application in a small company with five workstations and a file server. Each WS has its own microfiles on business partners (clients, suppliers). The local database (LDB) supports the common elements such as article files, stock balance, and order detail. In many large organizations, functional departments resemble this setup. Most user-oriented databases have locality whether they have been handled in a centralized or a distributed manner. There is no question that the locality issue exists. The problem is synchronization. This brings into perspective:

- *Access control* (which is reasonably well understood, hence rather cheap)

- *Integrity control* (which can be very expensive)
- *Design semantics* (the ability to differentiate and to imply controls)

In a distributed environment there should be no accidental deletes and no propagation effects. Propagation effects confuse the design issue

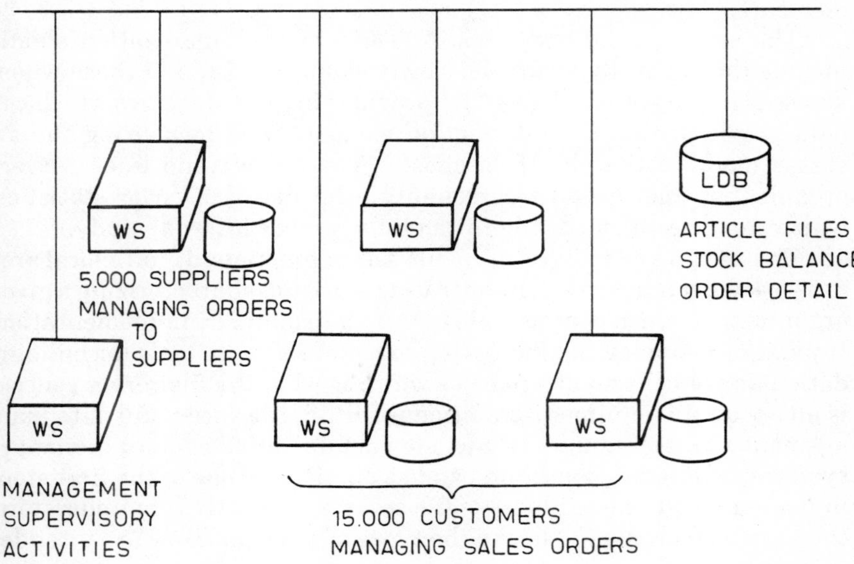

Figure 17.4 Database distribution among workstations and file servers.

and affect the integrity of the distributed database. That is where the challenge lies with file servers not in the act of installing a file server on a LAN.

File server organization is no different from database organization. Information elements must be properly defined and streamlined. Supported IEs must be distributed, with proper integration capability. Access to the IE must be secure, only by authorized entities. Database growth must be planned. The overall concept must cover three levels of references:

1. Microfiles (personal files) driven by microcomputers.
2. Local and regional files driven by minis, midis, and maxis.
3. Text and data warehouses managed by mainframes or, better, through dedicated rear end fift-generation computers.

Statistics help in deciding how a system architect should look at IE distribution. Generally, 90 percent of a firm's transactions involve only the 10 to 15 percent of the IEs in the global database. An estimated 80 percent of queries and management-type information handling usually makes reference to 3 or 5 percent of the computer-based information elements.

The text and data warehouse (T&D) of the organization should include the generally available, slowly changing IEs, and those whose access is an exception. Table 17.1 provides further statistics which can help in positioning the information elements and measuring the accesses made to the global database. These are trend lines. Every organization has its own personality (and distribution of statistics) which can be confirmed only through the proper internal study.

The design and integration of file server functionality on a local area network must account for the operating statistics characterizing a given organization which contemplates (or updates) a LAN implementation. It must also employ the increasing array of software tools for building data management applications — which is what the file server concept is all about. In addition to traditional DBMS, the successful data management strategy must now include such facilities as data dictionary systems, relational generators, and so on. Hence, one of the first steps in maximizing the usefulness of file servers on a LAN is to understand the various tools available and the types of problems they are intended to solve.

Data resource development is still a rapidly evolving technology, but proven concepts and techniques are now available for database admini-

Table 17.1 Positioning the Information Elements and Accessing the Database.

	Local Dynamic Storage(%)	*Corporate T&D Warehouse*
Volume of text and data	20-25	75-80
Database access	96-98	2-4
Data dictionary access	98	2

stration. Database technology is at the core of all future activities. Successful pursuit also requires a greatly expanded understanding of what constitutes the organization's data resources and of the techniques needed to manage data. File servers are one of the professional developments in this area.

17.5 Goals and Functionality of Printer Servers

Another shared resource on a local area network is the printer server. Depending on LAN software, it can support one or more printer devices, and the local area network itself can have one or more printer servers. The technology may be laser or matrix printers, plotters, or facsimile machines. Printer servers can provide a variety of functions, work steadily or on an exception basis, spool and despool in connection to mass storage media, and (if required) keep a log for maintenance functions.

Depending on supported software and printer buffer availability, the server can determine how much of a print file it can keep in memory before it has to go back to the file server to get more of the print file. The larger the value for a printer buffer, the better the overall network performance at the server computer.

With some LANs, it is possible to choose and preset printing priorities: low, standard, high, or overnight. Workstations can ask for printout or graphic presentation from data they currently handle, as well as information elements being retrieved from mass storage or from other LANs, whether nearby or remote.

Print priority features characterize the more sophisticated printer server devices. Priority parameters are employed to determine how much of the foreground task interval is used to print files while we may employ LAN communications capability for other tasks. Because printing and data transfer are foreground tasks, we must determine which has the most priority. It makes a difference when we have user activity going on at the same time that a file is printing and therefore downloading from the file server.

Some LAN architectures provide file and print server functionality, allowing the users to access a range of services. In one LAN offer, Xerox 8000 Network System, this range consists of the:

- File server proper, for bulk document storage
- Print service, for electronic printing
- Mail service, for communication with users at other workstations

The activity identification page is typically displayed on the screen. Selecting one of the options outlined causes the available services to be accessed. To reduce typing overhead, information on these services may be held permanently on the profile page. During operation, the activity page displays relevant information about file drawers and folders, mailing documents, and print options.

Typically, all print utilities allow files to print concurrently with other applications. The user may submit one or more files for printing. If the printer is busy, the user is notified that the print request either has not been accepted or is queued in a stack. Similarly, a message notifies the user of the termination of a print job. The user is then free to print out a new document. With another LAN architecture, the user may print out material in one of two ways:

- Pressing the Print Screen function key, causing a screenful of text or graphics to be printed
- Having the contents of an entire text file printed with the printer utilities

The printer utilities menu includes functions such as abandon printing (this function stops the printer), continue printing (resumes printing at the point where the printer left off operation), pause printing (temporarily suspends a print job to allow the user to add paper or adjust the printer), print file(s) (submits one or more files for printing), restart printing (starts the printing process from the beginning), set printer characteristics (allows the user to specify printer type and certain printout characteristics such as page length), and view status (presents a printer status message at the bottom of the screen: printer busy, disconnected, and so on).

There are also system utilities: queue documents at the server, decompose and reformat them, reproduce a full range of text and graphics, and print and out documents, in either landscape or portrait mode. System utilities permit the LAN administrator to select, under software control, the paper trays that are to be used for normal printer output and for separator pages. The latter may be inserted between complete print jobs or between documents within jobs. The systems administrator can also control the order in which a job is printed: first page first or last page first and so on. There are a wide range of status commands available to monitor the activity at the server.

Different print and language fonts are available and may be installed and removed dynamically. The Xerox 8000 Network Systems printer server features a basic classic fonts package consisting of a digitized representation of a classic font in 8, 10, 12, 14, 18, and 24 point presentations and: normal, bold, and italic styles. There is also a math package. Quality output is achieved by digitization and high-resolution capabilities on the printer itself (with a character image of 90,000 pixel per square inch). Communications-intense activities are taken care of by a range of external communication facilities. They include: connection of remote workstations, of teletype compatible terminals, and of remote computing resources to permit workstations to access these resource.

File servers can be polyvalent and their sophistication increases as offerings steadily show up in this highly competitive field. Electronic publishing capabilities can be expected to further enhance the quality and variety of offers.

17.6 Communications Servers, Gateways, and Organizational Prerequisites

Communications servers come in many types. They can support synchronous or asynchronous transmission and PC-to-mainframe connectivity, minis on a central or distributed basis, bridges to other LAN, stand alone remote users, remote databases, and dedicated print mechanisms for DP, WP, or DP/WP:

- We talk of *bridges* when the linkage applies to identical networks to be interconnected because of topological range restrictions.
- *Simple gateways* are used when networks of compatible architecture are to be interconnected, requiring added value on a bridge. Encapsulation and decapsulation techniques are normally adequate in this case. The exact nature of added value depends on the implementation environment.
- A *routing server* is more than a bridge. It interconnects nodes and networks of like or dissimilar architecture supported by the same vendor.
- A *complex gateway server* is a system that connects the nodes and networks of different architectures by performing protocol translation.

Besides joining networks of different architecture, complex gateways attach mainframes, minis, or long-haul carriers, typically in a heavy-duty fashion. High-speed LANs endowed with software addressing itself to all seven ISO/OSI layers make interprocess communications independent of mainframes and of minis. They can connect dissimilar LANs and other resources that understand different high-level protocols, they can link LANs and wide area networks of different architectures, and they help mainframes of dissimilar OS effectively communicate with one another.

Among the high-visibility functions of communications servers are the off loading of communications chores from hosts, the overall improvement in systems reliability, and the provisions of resource-sharing capability, modular growth, and remaining adaptable to changing needs. It is easy to recognize that most of these benefits are a direct result of LAN implementation and of the host-independent connectivity which it makes feasible. As new communications server products are introduced, their range of functionality increases. Software-based communications features today include:

- Selection of appropriate services for applications handling
- Code conversion and data formatting
- End-to-end coordination between applications processes
- End-to-end data integrity and quality of service
- Switching and routing of information
- Transfer of information units to the other end of the physical link

- Handling of bit streams at the transmission medium level

Top to bottom, these are functions of the application, presentation, session, transport, networking, data link, and physical layers of ISO/OSI. The function of a communication server designed to satisfy the requirement of the seven layers is shown in Figure 17.5. A complete frame is transmitted by the physical medium.

This includes the data link header and trailer — and between them a DL-level data unit.

Each ISO/OSI level implies a header reference. The communications server must assume responsibility for its handling. In addition, the movement of data on a packet basis poses problems. The solutions that involve partial transmission of a page have their own overhead: we must identify and correctly locate the changed information. But the communications server is a shared resource, and therefore problems and opportunities with other attached devices must also be considered. One of the biggest limitations at the user end is DOS and its constraints that prevent background operation, easy entrance and exit to the operating system from a transfer in progress, and sharing resources without major investments in additional software. The next serious bottleneck is the network itself, especially as far as speed and application-to-application communications are concerned. Standards and products have not yet been developed that will permit us to take advantage of conceptual capabilities a shared network server can offer.

Ideally, and at reasonable cost levels, network users should be able to access devices and services anywhere on the LAN by means of clearing house directories run by the server. One of the problems that come up is compatibility. Does the communications software product run on all our hardware?

- Some products will work with different engines, others will not.
- There are tradeoffs in the functions they perform or in their efficiency and speed.
- Can we use the product under all the operating systems, application, programs, and DBMS we use?
- If not, what are its communications capabilities?
- Does it support our current data access methods directly or indirectly?
- Must data extraction routines be written before we can do file transfers?

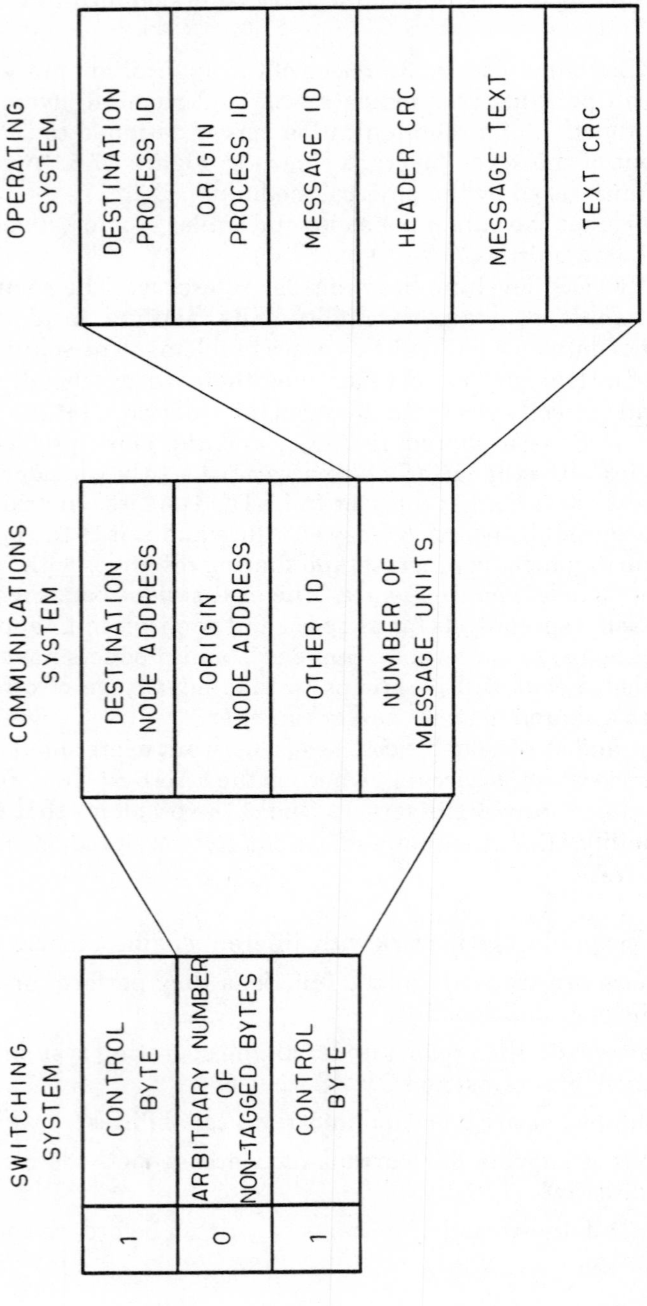

Figure 17.5 Several functions of the communication server are reflected into the protocol structure.

Understanding our present and future needs is critical. So is ease of use. In some cases, communications products provide very friendly interfaces. Some use menus or permit users to create stored procedures which can be recalled with a few keystrokes. But others require a great deal of knowledge about the import-export software itself as well as the frame application.

Significantly, in many organizations, the absence of standards for software packages on workstations complicates the selection of a micro-to-mainframe link. Few companies step back and consider their true needs. Yet caution is appropriate in dealing with high technology. A prudent approach is to assure ourselves that the communications products we select will do what we need for the next few years, because by then things are likely to be very different.

The functions of the communications server do not end with data transfer. Communications is the key through which we enter databases. Access to databases must be defined and controlled. Security needs vary widely. Some questions to ask are:

- Will the communications server integrate with our existing security policies?
- If so, how easily does it enhance them?
- Does it instead, or in addition, provide its own security methods, and do they meet our standards?
- How easy are they to implement?
- Must data be uploaded as well as downloaded, and what security procedures must be in place or established?

As these questions help document, the business of the communications server is much broader than one would have suspected by reading the typical text on how to make machines talk to one another. Not only technical solutions but also management policies must be examined. For security reasons, an estimated 80 to 90 percent of organizations today do not permit any upline loading by users. The communications server can do the job, but organizational and security prerequisites command otherwise.

17.7 The Administrator's View of LAN Servers

Like any well-functioning system, local area networks, particularly the larger ones, require a well-tuned administrative function. The administrator is responsible for defining the hardware and software configuration and giving system users the necessary information to permit an efficient implementation. The design, installation, usage, and maintenance of local area networks will increasingly require a great deal of intelligence and knowledge of intended use patterns and performance requirements. The administrator must consider performance, resiliency, and security, among other things, in setting up the configuration. For example, file servers may permit any user to access all the files in the network. However, this will not necessarily provide the response time needed to access the files of dedicated drives and may endanger security.

The administrator will be responsible for setting up user groups. It is also the administrator's function to study the implications of LAN use. In years to come, there will be great potential for better applications design, but also huge amounts of training and many lines of changed code will be needed to take advantage of new features. Communications servers in LU 6.2-style applications are a practical example. The roadblock to be faced is that millions of programmer-years have been expended on the development of current applications. Changing them will require tools we just do not have today. We can expect those tools to emerge, but we must also learn to use them.

Chapter

18

Implementing Efficient File Servers

18.1 Introduction

The LAN file server has evolved toward an intelligent database machine. Supported functionality includes efficient message exchange, transaction management assuring data integrity, and protection features eliminating unauthorized access. A nonprocedural query capability is developing, making it easy to access and update information, with artificial intelligence constructs increasingly incorporated into the system. New solutions feature automatic concurrency control, data administration facilities, and commands that ease the restructuring and expanding of database contents. Crash and recovery features, including checkpointing and transaction journaling, become standard features while shadow image capabilities significantly improve dependability.

Idea database features and associated capabilities increase the server's utility and functionality and also its sophistication. The same can be stated of multimedia approaches. A file server which can manipulate text becomes a far more effective building block for integrated office systems. While some of the information in the office can be presented as structured records, much more can only be expressed as bits streams of: text, digitized images, graphics, and voice encodings. Databases supported by a network of mainframes, departmental computers, the local database at the LAN, and microfiles on hard disks at the WS level form a unified logical aggregate. Able solutions can be approached in a valid manner only if we account for complexity in our initial design, paying particular attention to divisional assignments between the WS, the files included in local databases, semaphores and other protection mechanisms attached to the files, 24-hour-a-day backup, and the close connection between the LAN file servers and the information elements residing in the global database.

Accumulated experience suggests that at least three features beyond what is available today will have to be provided in the next few years:

1. The availability of a workstation on a LAN to transparently access the global database.
2. The ability of a file server to request subsets of central files for local retrieval purposes and analytical queries.
3. The need to implement dynamic file allocation among communicating LANs, central text and data warehouses, and public databases that make information available for a fee.

This is no the environment of the simple, rather static file servers of the last few years. The change has been continuous. First the concept of multiple file servers took hold. Then, better LAN-to-mainframe communications were established. Subsequently interest focused on security in file server messages and transactions. Let's look more carefully at some of these developments.

18.2 Security Procedures Connected to File Server Operations : A Controlware Architecture

The reasonably high bandwidth and low delay attributes of local area networks not only make possible distributed systems with information sharing through file servers but also requires attention to the implementation and maintenance of secure operations. Rights controls are made feasible through:

1. Passwords, with authentication procedures.

2. Assigned privileges and authorization chores.
3. The management of dynamic usage rights including their real time update.
4. Encryption algorithms including not only information elements in transit but also those stored for retrieval.

The file server handles semaphores, regulates the traffic of access requests to its database, manages the pipes set up on request by the workstations, and, depending on the sophistication of its software, does the journaling, handles transaction logs, maintains backup files, performs recovery and restart, and keeps file management statistics. All this is part of a controlware architecture which typically consists of several building blocks, each providing a specific function. Some of these functional modules are:

- Multimedia manager
- Multitask dispatcher
- File security manager
- Memory and buffer manager
- Encryption/decryption module
- Sign-on and sign-off supervisor
- Communication device driver
- Interprocessor driver

Such modules must be configured by the developers into standard control programs performing activities of I/O and communications processors together with the more classical memory management functions such as system reset, open file, close file, search for file, add and delete file, read and write (sequential or random), name and rename file, set attributes, lock and unlock record, log in, log off, set compatibility attributes, and return server configuration.

Controlware interface attributes help define the shareability access mode for a specific file and its access. Four possibilities are:

1. *Exclusive access.* Once a file has been opened no other user may access that file until the opening user closes the file and gives access permission.
2. *Shared access.* Any number of users may have a share file opened simultaneously and all users may read and write to the file

under controlled conditions. A Record lock and unlock function can be used to manage the access of specific records.

3. *Read-only access.* Any number of users may have read-only file opened simultaneously, but only reading is permitted.
4. *Permissive access.* Any number of users may have a permissive file opened simultaneously for reading, but only if any user writes to the file, that user becomes the only one permitted to write other records to the file until it is closed.

Passwords have been and can be used to protect a disk file, but while necessary, passwords are not enough. Disk encryption software is necessary. Through passwords, the file server will not allow a station to mount the file unless the proper password is presented; neither will it permit unauthorized read access. But if an intruder manages to gain access, the files are open. By contrast, the proper encryption of the microfile contents prevents the intruder from reading files. Proper encryption can be enacted through software and sign on and sign off by the user. Logical shredding of microfile contents is also a necessary measure.

At the level of the more classical password protection, the right to create information elements (IE), read and/or write an IE, insert one or more IEs, and delete what is already in the database is controlled by the privilege control mechanism run by the file server. Some workstations (and their users) can be limited to read-only access rights, others may have both read and write access, and still others may insert and delete files. In every case, the file server must provide controls and assurances. Not only is the protection mechanism important as such but so is the way it fits into the applications environment. Depending on the sophistication of the available software, controls and assurances may be provided to:

1. Identify damaged IEs (for instance, through the application of a cycle redundancy check in data storage).
2. Assure the proper sequence number of stored IE and other characteristics which might reveal unauthorized manipulation.
3. Provide ACK/NAK responses in WS communications beyond the mechanism assured through pipes.

Security typically involves the proper identification of IE origination, responsibility associated with IE usage, documentation of access procedures and supervisory activities, correct (and updated) definition of access rights, and the ability of supporting a distributed environment without losing control over its functions.

A global view in the management of data resources should involve the administration of all information (including manual and automated data), as well as all methods used in communicating, manipulating, or presenting information. A well-timed responsibility function involves both storage issues and flows. Receipt, storage, and delivery of text and data and the supervision of all automated systems used in the production, reproduction, and delivery of information should be covered. One of the security parameters in an operating environment is the number of file servers to be protected, This question is linked to the answer which should be given to the query: *How many file servers*? One per LAN, one per *n* LANs, one LAN per group of WEs dedicated to a given function hence *n* file servers per LAN? Similar questions could be raised foe gateways.

Better-defined security approaches should be assured in the case of multiple file servers on a given LAN. If the number of file servers increases, it becomes more efficient to put the look-up activity on a master file server supported through a data dictionary. This, however, increases the number of accesses per query and therefore the response time. In other words, the latter solution affects system design. It leads to the institution of a master file server, adding disk access time for look up purposes to every local database search. The location of dictionary and security directory has to be decided by a careful study of the application with the dual goal to track down the database traffic, and make it secure, as well as fast.

To a large extent, decisions on how to distribute the data dictionary and associated authentication and authorization measures depend on security and privacy to be built into the system. Hence, such decisions are applications dependent. The same is true of control functions embedded in the system. Control functions not only accept or reject the transactions being executed but also enhance security and privacy featured by the system.

18.3 Evaluating Approaches to File Allocation: Absolute and Relative Naming

File management statistics are needed to dimension the file server, switch files between physical disks (if more than one are attached to the

LAN), and perform the extruder function for text and data. Additional file server faculty supports may include remove application (allowing the user to remove an application from the hard disk), show current directory (displaying the directory which is online or a list of names of all directories on the disk), lock or unlock a file, and shred a file or fraction thereof. If an application performs file operations incorrectly, the file server can lock the file in an attempt to protect its contents — with further operations on the file blocked until the user unlocks the file with a command.

System design must take a network-wide view since the file server accomplishes its task by permitting WSs to share resources. File accesses happen repeatedly, often in a burst mode. Files may be stored by both their names and version numbers. When a new version of an existing file is created, the old version is not necessarily deleted, reducing the possibility of accidental file deletion. (A sound approach is that files must be deleted explicitly by the user; no autopurge except through sunset clauses). The naming of information elements is one of the critical issues in planning file allocation. This is particularly true in heterogeneous systems and in situations requiring accommodation of evolutionary growth. Name resolution, transparency, and name acquisition are impossible methodologies. We know how to provide many styles of services, but which are the right ones? Can multiple right approaches be combined without discontinuities or interruption?

One of the often-discussed puzzles is whether names should be relative or absolute. An absolute name refers to the same object regardless of context. That is, the site, the user, and possibly the application should be transparent. Absolute names facilitate sharing since they provide a common vocabulary with which to refer to objects. A relative name is context dependent. For instance, each user creates a set of easily remembered mnemonics to be used in place of more cumbersome, network-dependent message or file names. Another example of relative names is file names in a shared file system. A standard mechanism for providing these names imports a portion of a foreign name space and attaches it to a local root. Particularly in a heterogeneous environment, this flexibility is an asset. Different contexts may have fundamentally different requirements of the naming scheme.

A subset closely linked to that of absolute and relative names is whether there is a single global name space or many local name spaces. Design decisions are very important in the context of WS access to global databases. But although a global name space appears to be desirable, the cooperation and extent of changes required to implement it are considerable, with no really elegant solutions available. This creates a dilemma. If there is no global name space, it is impossible to name all the objects in all name spaces because some naming environments will have no way to translate some names. But because file sharing is so important, we have to provide name services. Some distributed heterogeneous environments approach this subject by providing for some type of relative and absolute names. This is an attempt to solve issues related to heterogeneous systems where name syntax and operations may differ significantly from one site to another. Yet, it also presents its own problems.

The possibility of using different name strategies is generally a function of facilities available in the command language rather than the operating system primitives. Even then, ad hoc name strategies can suffer from drawbacks such as path compression. Finding alternate paths may be difficult with ad hoc solutions. Both current and the most likely future system problems must be examined prior to deciding a naming strategy. The same is true of the dynamic aspect of naming. The autonomy characteristic of heterogeneous systems requires that there be provision for recovery from system failures and online changes to the name space. The establishment of a name-management system is indivisible from the decision on name space and vice versa.

The type of a name strategy to be adopted influences the range of shared file activities, which vary from one server environment to another. While all possible solutions share one central feature—they make available system resources which cannot be dedicated to a single WS—the answers to be given are not necessarily the same from one organization to another. Sometimes a variation exists from one site to another. The increasing interest in the implementation of multimedia will further complicate naming procedures as will strategies regarding multimedia file allocation. Among the presently conceived critical parameters for file allocation in a distributed environment are:

1. The level of data sharing, which indicates whether the information elements are partitioned or replicated and to what extent.
2. The nature of the access patterns, which may range from a simple query to an analytical query or a total database update and can even vary significantly from one time to another.
3. The nature of the access pattern, whether it is deterministic or probabilistic.
4. The database search procedures, algorithmic or heuristic.

5. The available database management system (DBMS) to run the database locally (relational, networking, hierarchical).
6. The artificial intelligence-based access and eventually management

The dynamic nature of file allocation must always be kept in perspective. While a valid estimate will be helpful at the start, still more important is the monitoring of file use and reallocation of files because of requirements posed by interactive work. Further, the integration of WS microfiles into the global database environment sees to it that another problem to be carefully studied is workstation identification and replacement. When we replace something having to do with file access and management, there should be an update of all interconnected workplaces, not only the one affected — and the global dictionary. This, too, is part of design semantics to be considered.

A LAN file server is an integral part of a global distributed database. The fact that it is widely accessible poses prerequisites quite different from those of centralized processes. We must change our image of system design and adapt it to the new requirements. Some of these requirements will be situational. Others will only exhibit a limited perspective weighted along the lines the current system operates — but these lines can change faster than we think.

18.4 Software, Organization, and Access in File Server Environments

The specialization of labor is fundamental to the utility of a file server. Functions such as data entry, text processing, and output formatting are workstation domains. A word processing terminal has different requirements from a data entry terminal but they both need access to files. For each, the file server receives requests and must provide access functions without including special format characteristics or limiting interface design. However, requirements are somewhat different when it comes to managerial and professional workstations. Here, communications capability is the primary criterion, along with analytical queries such as file downloading for spreadsheet analysis or expert system usage. At the file server level, this is a much more demanding operation than data entry. It also imposes bandwidth and network OS requirements.

A management-decision-oriented LAN installation requires state-of-the-art file server software designed to provide analysis-oriented operations in the network environment. Such software should be designed for high performance, data integrity, and security and also for large file capacity and simplicity of operation and access. A long list of supported features will determine the quality of the software. This list includes functional interfaces, the ability to accommodate and access multiple processors (number crunching, graphics, and so on), independence of file format, rational file organization, and multiuser facilities. Password security, standardized interfaces, and mailboxes should also be on this list, as must online diagnostics and quality databases.

Workstations and servers interconnected through the LAN typically use functional interfaces in which explicit functional requests are sent to other servers. This is practically a communication method permitting file- and record-oriented functional requests to be made by one system and performed on another. The LAN may contain multiple processors dedicated to specific functions and aimed to improve performance over what a WS can deliver.

The notion of independence of file format can be seen from different viewpoints. The more common are machine- and applications-independence. But independence for a file format can also be interpreted as a process of storing and retrieving files on disk in a manner facilitating efficient space utilization and file access. A WS or another server makes functional requests for the data within the file server files without concern for file location or format. This permits future updates of file formats without affecting user applications. In principle, each record in a file may be accessed either sequentially or randomly. More than one device attached to the LAN may access particular files for which available software should provide file- and record-level interlocks to permit simultaneous multiuser access. Implicit file-level interlocks must be automatic, require no user program participation, and support multiple inquiry tasks which might run concurrently with an update task. For performance optimization, buffering can provide a reduction in the number of physical disk accesses in both sequential and random operations.

Critical to longer-term dependable performance is the assurance of a diagnostic facility, which provides several forms of fundamental capabilities. For instance, at boot time, diagnostics should include memory test, memory mapping, sensing of devices and major components, and checkout of disks and network functions. Automatic error logging is necessary so that whenever a software or hardware failure occurs, the information regarding the error or malfunction is immediately posted to a log file. Not only may this file be read at any time to assist in problem correction, but also an instrumental quality history analyzer should be provided to enhance the network control functions.

A sophisticated file server is a sort of DBMS in a box, with security and diagnostics added to top it. Its functionality is like that of other types of database machines that have received a lot of attention in the past few years. Known as database computers (DBC), these engines are very different from the large, architecturally obsolete mainframe-based DBMS. They are coarse-grain fift- generation machines. The normal evolution of a local area network's file server is toward DBC. In this, as in any other case, the able management of a database on a LAN relies on distributed intelligence. But while the design of the large database machine is motivated almost entirely by considerations of price and performance relative to mainframe software, for a LAN engine:

- Cost is definitely a constraining factor.
- Performance requirements focus on distributed resources.
- Communications are a vital part of the picture.
- Hardware efficiency is not a burning issue, but software sophistication is.

One of the points of emphasis in design is on achieving low cost for functions rather than steadily accelerating transaction rates. The file server is a somewhat autonomous node in a nonhomogeneous network rather than a peripheral attached to a host's input-output channel. This suggests that the interface to the user processes requires a complex, efficient communications protocol instead of a specialized channel or bus discipline. The goal should be to:

- Accommodate more flexible node-to-node relationships
- Assure reliable delivery of packets
- Allocate a single serial channel among multiple conversations

The associated overhead affects performance and is affected by available software and the bandwidth of the network. Able solutions require a careful look at the traffic to be supported — with applications programs being a good candidate to move into the workstations' microfiles rather than steadily moving on the LAN. This is consistent with the requirements of properly documented design and of a continuous watch on the traffic evolution. A network is a dynamic entity and feedback is necessary to finely tune any dynamic structure.

18.5 File Servers as Systems Components Combining Databasing and Communications

For internetworking reasons, it is advisable that system architecture follows the ISO/OSI approach and its open system characteristics including the definition of activity boundaries or WSs, servers, and hosts. This involves support of:

- Port(s), which are hardware bound
- Sockets (end points; entities with both software and hardware definition)
- Logical communications paths which connect socket to socket

Sockets are similar to a telephone number. They are a software convention, conditioned by hardware characteristics. The software-hardware boundaries assure that the data transfer will follow formatting rules. The goal of a virtual terminal service regarding workstations and servers is to define how terminal management looks to the inside of the system. Toward the higher-up layers, terminal management action can be schemabased. In facing the lower-level layers (communications proper) functionality includes the drivers, which should reflect exact specifications of each entity.

A number of routines are necessary to support the online communications characteristics of the file server system, such as the common exchange interface able to handle the information exchange between the flow control layer and session control. Typically, session control will define authentication and privacy for all exchanges. Next to it, presentation control will take care of the finer programmatic interfaces, among which is encryption. A standard device protocol interface will look after the formatted form of data transfer supporting the way presentation control talks to the applications layer.

File and record selection can be affected through filters. Each record consists of a number of fields; each of these has a name, value, and some properties. Through a WS the user can establish a number of logical views. The records that are displayed when any one view is open depend on the filter associated with the view. The latter consists of a set of field patterns. Only information elements whose fields match stated patterns are selected for display. At the workstation level, the precise format of the resulting display depends on the data form in use. Fields in a given form whose names match those of fields in the records file would be filled in with values from the selected records. A sort order can be used to define the order in which the selected records are presented.

When the LAN file servers have been architectured to work in such a structured manner, implied by a layered solution, a dedicated software routine exists for every function. The dialogue between stations, programs, and users is not casual. It is also structured, providing a well-organized support for interactivity. The concept of structured interactivity between WSs and file servers is far reaching. Basic commands needed to support an interactive system, such as submission, display, cancellation, priority handling, reentry programs, and conditioned operations, should operate network-wide. Procedural requirements call for the support of data independence, data structures at multiple indexes, automatic back-out, and the ability to restructure text and data.

Projecting, designing, and implementing database and networking capabilities are much more successful if some key requirements are observed. These include a common data dictionary as well as an online development facility and applications modeling (test, documentation, maintenance). The computer based data dictionary should be able to handle processes, tables, data, text, and graphics and also data definitions, links, and cross-references. Within a distributed information systems environment, the data dictionary is instrumental in terms of the feasibility of supporting central control, local autonomy, and the end usage. This is very important since the implementation of any distributed information system must be made between these three points of reference.

The system development language to be chosen should facilitate the creation of information elements and should be supported by a number of utilities. Applications modeling should follow a valid methodology in projecting network-wide file server services, interfaces, and processing routines. The designer should consider the elements which can be found in the company's storehouse of system knowledge. This activity should consider all LAN components. The common ground of a good design is efficient file sharing augmented by networking capability, which is itself enhanced through reliable LAN communications. File and file access activities must be organized in a comprehensive group of logical and physical resources required to serve the end users attached to the network.

Design experimentation can play a key role in the development of a successful file server system. Typically, such a process must account for six concrete phases: conceptual modeling, information element definition, IE integration, program development, program and system test, and steady maintenance. There is an interplay among them and what exists in file server capabilities. The rising cost of systems development not only necessitates the adoption of a good methodology from the start but also, if not primarily, requires a policy of avoiding redundant effort. For this reason, combining databasing and data communications should be considered.

18.6 Contributions by the Data Dictionary

The aid a data dictionary (DD) can provide in designing, implementing, using, and maintaining a local database has many aspects. One of the important contributions is to reduce file server maintenance costs over the total life of a system — while at the same time it increases the level of control made available. Another key benefit of a dictionary is that it standardizes terminology. It is next to impossible to properly maintain complex business records if users in each department in each LAN use unique methods and terminology. Yet that is the way many companies maintain computerized data, whether centralized or handled on a distributed basis.

Precisely because in many instances there is little or no standardization, a DD is a valuable tool. The data dictionary is to information management what the general ledger is to financial management. At the DD level the user documents all the components of the information management system — beginning in the planning stages, when a business model is developed. However, major benefits can be attained only when we follow DD-based procedures with consistency:

- The data dictionary must be used for all the file servers on the LAN.
- It should be applicable to all the files.
- It must be possible to distribute parts of it down to the WS level, if this is necessary.
- All information elements (including records, fields, images, etc.) must be defined in the dictionary.
- Every element in the database must be contained in the dictionary.
- Detail must be supported down to the name of the IE.

Typically, the role of a data dictionary will include: data resource management, information element definition, links to processes, the promotion of functional distribution, a better ability for system development and documentation, database control functions, and user ID for protection against unauthorized access. An able approach to system conversion and maintenance should also be among the DD features.

Just as built-in redundancy takes care of local database failures, the approach to be followed in the implementation of a data dictionary for file servers should assure that the facilities to be supported are available even if there is a partial system failure. System planning must account for this need. The data dictionary will help manage the information flow; document ownership, usage, and relationships help identify redundancy and ambiguity; protect current system investment; assist in reducing the cost of future development; and contribute to the modeling of the corporate environment and its operating perspectives. Correspondingly, the role of the DBMS is to manage the data storage, provide data description and data manipulation language, assure a reliable and secure data access, guarantee data value integrity, stage the ground for data independence, provide common program interfaces, and help model the applications environment. Table 18.1 identifies existing relationships and characteristics proper to DDs and DBMS.

In the specific case of multiple file servers on a LAN, the DD is to be used as a dictionary to tell which node contains needed data. In this case, a lot of work must be done to determine where to put the dictionary. To a large extent, decisions on how to distribute the DD depend on security, privacy, and efficiency to be built into the system. They are, therefore, applications dependent.

How to distribute data definitions in a cost-effective manner is an issue involving the language and the DBMS to be used. One of the requirements is the existence of the DD where the IE reside within the systems aggregate. There is a tendency toward including in the data dictionary information on powerful tools for the preparation, maintenance, and storage of a wide variety of documents. One reference includes the following major areas of functionality:

- Text input and editing
- Text layout and page formatting
- Inclusion of graphics in documents
- Multiple character sets and fonts
- The control and storage of documents
- Protocols for handling compound electronic documents

Table 18.1 Relationship Between Data Dictionary and DBMS

Data Dictionary	*DBMS*
1. Directory	1. Logical definition
2. Data description	2. Support of data view
3. Data flow and usage	3. Physical design
4. Data and program links	4. Text and data validity
5. Identification of responsibility (security)	5. Database access
6. Control and consistency	6. Privacy assurance
7. Documentation	7. Recovery

A global view of the management of data resources should involve the administration of all information (including manual and automated data) and all methods used in communicating, manipulating, and presenting information. Such a function involves the responsibility over communication flows, but it primarily focuses on storage, retrieval, and file server administration. There must be control information able to assist in the receipt, storage, and delivery of text and data and the supervision of all systems used in the production, reproduction, distribution, and delivery of information.

The analysis of information flows involves compiling information sources, establishing an information library, standardizing forms and reports, and classifying information usage. A database administrator will typically require DD services to analyze user requirements, coordinate user reviews, and record and describe information element usage. The administrator will also develop standards, establish priorities, elaborate on security and privacy, and look after all issues regarding usage support. Parallel to these activities, other specialists should look after distributed databases and supporting data communications facilities:

- Type and number of file servers
- LAN bandwidth to guarantee unimpeded file exchange
- Conventions for a uniform file server environment
- Networking solutions to be adopted
- Standards which should be followed

- Reliability and uptime
- Response time considerations
- Cooperating transactions (synchronous and asynchronous processes)
- User-machine interfaces

Reliability in communications is to a certain extent a matter of cost: How much money we wish to invest in a solution. The easiest and least-effective way to increase reliability is to throw more hardware in the system. Not only is this very, very expensive and often unwarranted, but it rarely if ever gives the expected results. System solutions should be sought after. They require precise definitions, imaginative approaches, and experimentation. That is an area where the contributions of an online data dictionary can be significant. Both databasing and data communications are bound to profit.

18.7 Making Better Use of Query Facilities

Since the office world of the future will be centered on the workstation and the file server, one of the basic features to be supported is intelligent, polyvalent query. To be user-friendly, this should be done through nonprocedural, English-like statements designed for use by a nonspecialist. Fourth-generation languages (4GL) fit this requirement. Typically, a nonprocedural query statement can generate a fairly complex report that would otherwise require a special program. Queries can be used to:

1. Automatically generate a file sorted according to user-defined criteria.
2. Support selective retrieval from file server(s).
3. Match features by facilitating comparisons.
4. Assist in nonprocedural text editing and manipulation.
5. Help select options on page and text layouts and formats.
6. Incorporate graphics and pictorial representations in documents.
7. Help select multiple fonts and character sets.
8. Assist in document filing and management.

Through powerful 4GLs, users can obtain pictorial representations (icons) of items in a manner familiar to them. There are icons for objects such as documents and folders and also for other devices on the LAN, such as file servers and printers.

In the course of a query process, the contents of a user's desktop changes continually to reflect the work being done. Between sessions, the desktop may be left on microfile, or it may be sent to a file server on the LAN. This latter option enables it to be retrieved and used at some other WS on the network, thus freeing the user from a particular place of work.

Document creation is an important aspect of query facilities. Once a query is opened, text may be put into a document. This is done by simply selecting on the WS the place in the document the text is to be positioned. A document may be created from scratch or inserted from system files.

The data dictionary can be queried. A query statement can be executed by submitting a single word. For increased retrieval efficiency, expert system constructs can optionally construct and maintain an index for particular views as well as handle transitory filters which may be used for increased selectivity. A special error folder can be associated with each record file through query statements. Such a folder can hold information on records that a user attempted to move into the record file and which were rejected because they contained data that failed to match the constraints laid down for the information element in reference. Query output can be displayed on screen, routed to a printer, or saved on a file for subsequent use. File extraction is subject to security conditions. Reports may be customized. The user can specify control breaks, define output formats (such as column headings, report title, value labels), set page width, depth, spacing, and so on.

Each information element can have a property sheet associated with it to define its characteristics. These characteristics may include:

- Type (any character, text only, numeric or data, icon)
- Required or optional inclusion
- Format and length of contents
- Permitted range of contents

The contents of a field may also be defined by fill-in rules. They allow the contents of another, named, field or fields in the document. A variety of operations may be used to manipulate and process IEs in those other fields. Arithmetic and logic operations (mean, total, standard deviation) are examples of processing activities that might be specified through queries.

The user may select the order in which fields in a document are to be filled in. This is not necessarily the order in which they appear in the document or are stored in the file server(s). Graphical objects can also be stretched, magnified, and moved about the screen. Composite objects constructed by the user many be defined as clusters and stretched, magnified, and moved in turn. Frequently used shapes may be stored in a document for later use. Varients can be provided at the user's choice. These are examples of the power of AI-enriched query languages.

Intelligent user interfaces take care of the mode of interaction, handle lockout mechanisms, follow-up on record type and record occurrence levels, and search for error messages. General consistency checks are performed by the query system. Various types of command status messages can be available and these are not exceptional features. Most database systems today provide an interactive query language for selective retrieval and display of text and data and also for modifications to the IE. In the past, query languages tended to be difficult to learn and remember and required a significant amount of keying-in. New systems are simple, low keystroke, and screen oriented. What you see is what you get.

The goal is to make this tool suitable for updates, insertions, editing, browsing, and retrieval. Able query tools reduce the need for detailed, step-by-step coding to convert ideas from human language into instructions the computer can act upon. That is why they are valuable. Many produce (or generate) programs, but they differ in: ease of use, complexity of tasks that can be performed, and the efficiency with which they use resources. Query products also differ in technical characteristics, as well as in the types of machines, operating systems, and communications protocols with which they are compatible. User-friendly 4GLs allow users with only slight training to search or manipulate records in complex ways, employing language very close to English. But 4GLs can also be used to update data and express logical operations.

Tools are now developed for WS-oriented systems and file servers. Many of them use system commands from the DBMS on the file server. Among the criteria for a valid query language are:

1. The use of simple English to retrieve information from multiple sets simultaneously.
2. The ability to design attractive screens: blinking, bells, color,

and so on including customized screen layouts with automatic editing and integrity checking.

3. The facility to protect data with IE and field-level access controls.
4. The use of structures approaches able to support applications development including conditionals.

Powerful generators are typically part of a database management system. While this is particularly helpful for information element manipulation and presentation facilities, in some cases users can also have the generator perform arithmetic or logical operations on data prior to displaying them. At this level query tools can also be helpful to software developers.

Using very high-level languages and applications generators, the analyst or programmer expresses instructions in general terms that automatically evoke the detailed code required by the computer. The principle behind generators is that many computer-based operations are routine. Therefore, the code for them can be stored and used repeatedly, rather than being rewritten each time it is needed. This not only saves time and effort, it also helps standardize programs and the use of computer devices as well.

Chapter

19

Choosing File Server Protocols

19.1 Introduction

A protocol is a rule of conduct that is observed by all attached devices on a LAN. In choosing the proper one, a long, hard look with global reliability in mind is necessary, since reliability is a basic requirement with computer-based file systems. In a LAN environment, file transfer is a pivot point for reliable operations. The ability to move information elements from one source to another presupposes protocols for file transfer and exchange (not just for data transfer). It also calls for systems and applications software, network-wide look-up capabilities, and protection measures.

Sharing is a demanding activity. Supervision is necessary to look around the network and find things which require corrective action. File transfer is one of the fields where supervision is steadily needed. Error detection and correction is a type of basic supervision. A simple, error controlling file transfer protocol (FTP) is relatively easy to understand and implement. It can also provide valuable services. Ethernet's FTP, for example, uses five packet types: data, ACK, abort, end, and end and reply.

The hardware checksum is present only on the bus and is not counted as part of the protocol. (The checksum is a 1's compliment and cycle over the entire packet, including header and content data.) Within the overall datacomm procedure followed by Ethernet, each data packet is retransmitted periodically by the sender until an ACK with a matching sequence number is returned from the receiver. The destination computer ignores all damaged packets, packets from a station other than the sender, and packets whose sequence number does not match either the expected one or the one preceding. A packet with a sequence number less than the expected by one is acknowledged and discarded. Packets with the appropriate sequence numbers are acknowledged and maintained. Basic functionality rather than a high-level reference frame is provided with this approach. However, all ISO/OSI layers from data link to application should be supported, with a focal point being the transport layer.

19.2 Common Characteristics of File Transfer Protocols

Work done on Arpanet has been the origin of file transfer protocols that are made available to the user as an explicit command to move a file from one device to another. For protection purposes, users may be required to identify themselves at the other machine or take similar measures. This, however, should not obscure the need for other supported services. A protective approach has two advantages. First, it helps control the overhead associated with moving a file. Much of the delay in moving the file has nothing to do with the time required to send the data through the network. Rather it is time spent establishing the connection and identifying the user at the other site. Second, it permits a certain integration of network routines into the file system. It also makes feasible an authentication mechanism so that interchange of information between the various machines can be transparent to the end user.

Protocols do not only provide the groundware for data linkage or limit themselves to the format of information elements. Protocols address themselves to the security domain of sessions and files. They compare the security level of the file to the security level of a session and decide accordingly. Still, the management of bit streams is in itself very important.

Several LAN file servers can transfer ASCII 7- and 8-bit character sets. Various parameters can be specified through the file transfer setup menu to control file transfers: allowing or disallowing file copy, selecting specific files to be copied, specifying a password which must be provided before a transfer takes place, and establishing whether files coming into the workstation can supersede existing ones. To transfer files, users need to connect their WSs to the FS and invoke the file transfer utility. Subsequently, the utility program may display a form that the user fills out to effect the file transfer. Other services supported by the FS occur when the server is programmed to do something more than simple storage and retrieval for files. Consider a feature whereby a file can be described to the server as containing a document in some standard representation. Say that the server is endowed with the ability to search document files in response to commands such as "find all paragraphs in document A that contain the phrase 'Decision Support'."

Associative capabilities increase the server's utility and functionality and also its sophistication. An FS which can manipulate compound electronic documents becomes a far more effective building block for integrated office systems. The same can be considered for software at the file server and WS levels to support office document architecture (ODA).

Although characteristics just outlined may seem to be a departure from strict database management, they are appropriate since information in the office is becoming much richer and less structured. In the evolving applications environment we do not only deal with formatted records, we also deal in streams. If under the current release the file server software does not support bit and byte streams, the new release should provide such facilities. It should also be able to handle backup procedures and communicating databases. Similarly, from the user's viewpoint, the file management level protocol should support a file image capability either on the same LAN or on backup (Figure 19.1). For years this has been a value-added consideration. Today it is one of the basic requirements to be satisfied through LAN software — or by attachment of a database computer (DBC).

Short of implementing a true database computer, added capacity might be accomplished by putting two FSs logically together, sharing or switching the disks (see also in Chapter 15). Our concepts of how to design and integrate interconnected or independent database servers on the same LAN are continually evolving.

Other component parts of the file server protocol structure address themselves to configuration information involved in a network exchange (OS, file system), to FS attributes (i.e., details relative to the representation of the information elements being addressed), and to access proper. The latter helps specify:

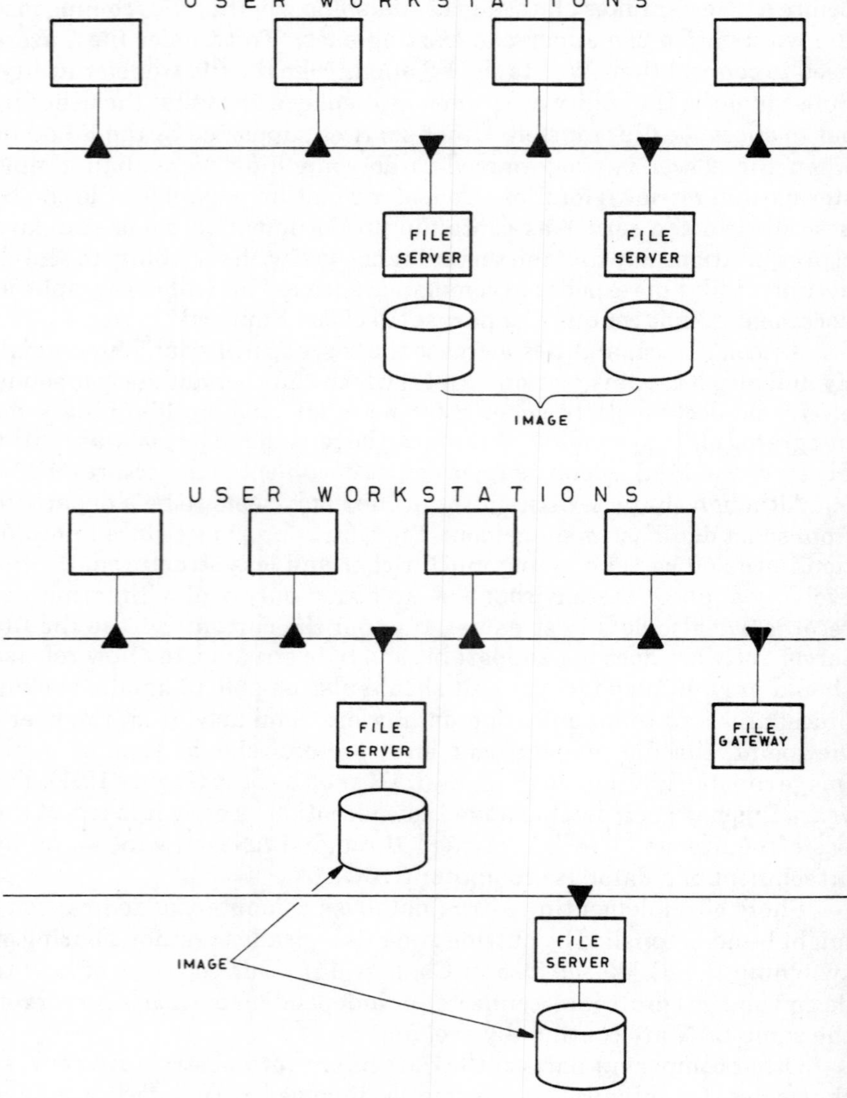

Figure 19.1 Alternative solutions to file image help to increase system dependability.

1. Type of access, for example, type of operation to be performed such as open new file.
2. File name and file specification, in the format required by the remote node.

One of the first problems of file management is to establish a consensus structure for data. This is followed up by the problem of figuring out what to name the elements of that structure. Data integration's primary problem is to provide the ability to add to the consensus data structure without violating or arbitrarily changing any of the existing protocol agreements:

1. Access mode (sequential, random, keyed, and so on).
2. User-oriented access operation — as requested (get, put, etc.).
3. Optional file and record processing features, such as user exits.

Control activities are necessary both at the device and the file level. Control commands also allow the access mode to be changed from previous settings.

Another part of the file server protocol structure is continued transfer. The object is to permit alternative recovery strategies to be activated (try again, skip, abort). This is also true for acknowledgment and access completed. The latter involves information on termination of access to the remote system and recovery procedures for record transfer.

19.3 A File Transfer Architecture

Two basic components constitute the file transfer architecture: (1) a server both storing the files and providing access to these files which are managed by a DBMS and (2) a control activity supervising and synchronizing the operations of the server. The three key players in the general file transfer process are a control activity and two servers. One of the servers is at the host, where the source file resides. This is the *producer*. The other, on the destination WS or another host to which the file has to be transferred, is the *consumer*. Transfer can also take place WS to WS. Then one workstation is the producer and the other is the consumer. The control activity on a host (file server) represents the interface to the user. It supervises the other servers (Figure 19.2).

Data flows are supplemented by command flows for the synchroni-

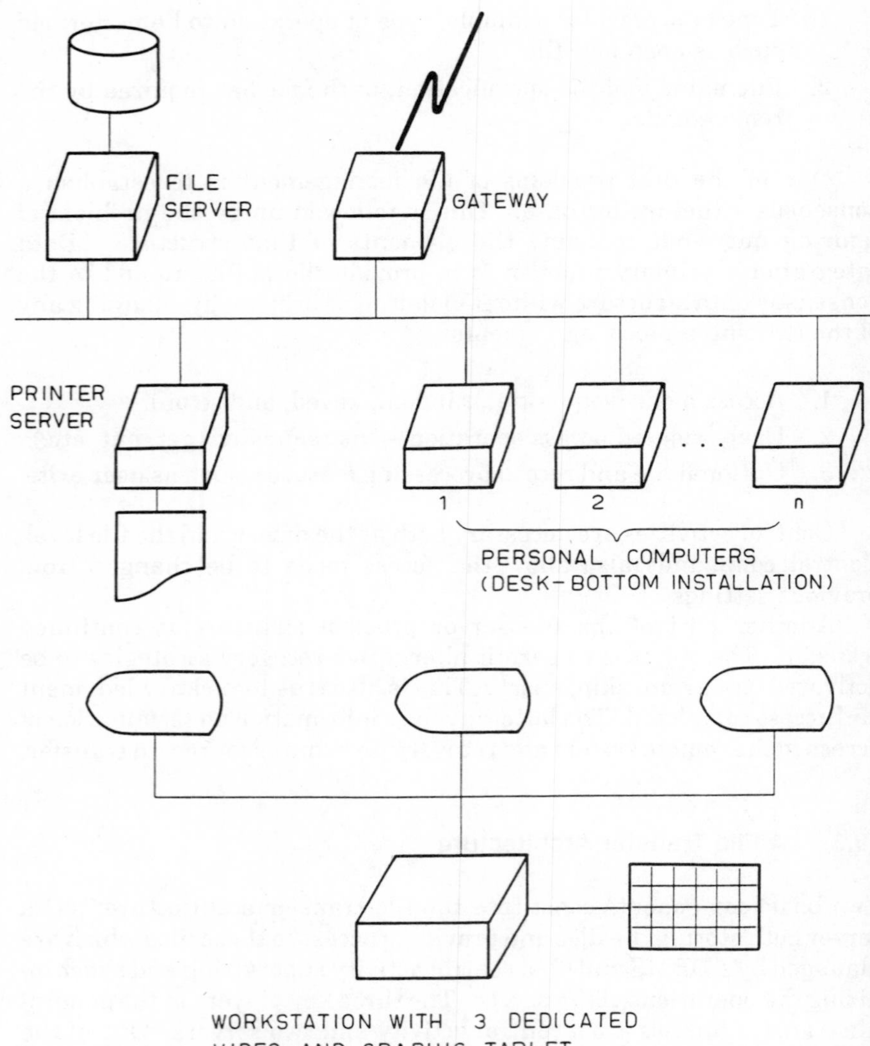

Figure 19.2 Workstations with three dedicated videos and graphic tablets waiting for the 2 megapixel screen.

zation and controlling of the server(s). Hence, the network must provide a transport system with communication facilities such as flow control, error detection, and recovery. Synchronization leads to the need for file transfer protocol establishment. Most files have a structure that is ignored by a conventional file transfer protocol but could be exploited by identifying elements that are invariant under the mappings likely to be encountered. A data structure compromise can be attained by synthesizing different information requirements, each with its own particular data structure, into one standard data structure.

Since, there is no international standard, ad hoc solutions will be followed. But they should be organization-wide. They will be valid only if each of the source data structures can be recreated from the form to be adopted as a standard. Furthermore, the best consensus structures are those that have the lowest probability of change, given new, valid information requirements. In this manner, an organization-wide data structure protocol would become a model of the organization's information elements. It must be extensible, accessible, consistent, and transformable into the physical structures necessary for building files and databases on computers. It must also be transformable into an arbitrary number of user-oriented data structures to service particular information requirements.

Using the data structure protocol as a frame of reference, classes of files could be identified according to their content. For each class, the file transfer protocol should be a specific rather than a general approach, which risks being not so efficient. A simplified file transfer model can be derived from the general organization-wide model by combining one server process with the associated control activity, and user interface with the contents of other file servers and the commanding process(es). The latter can be either the source or the destination of the transferred file. Emphasis thus needs to be placed on the primitives to be supported by the file transfer protocol. In a nutshell, these are:

- Set up and termination of a connection
- Identification of source and destination file
- Interprocess communications
- Agreements about file structure
- Data conversion accords
- Additional file manipulation requirements
- Data transfer protocols
- Error recovery capabilities

The choice of user-oriented data structures should observe data life cycle requirements. From a system viewpoint, a data life-cycle parallels the life cycle of its environment. In a way, data is born when the system is born and dies when the system ends. However, experience shows that data does not die when the host system dies. It simply assumes a new form in the new system. The concept of data growth and change can be traced directly to the business life cycle. The best of personal data becomes common data, and common data is treated as a business asset. An organization establishes its own sense of data ownership. Managing this evolution is most important in assuring corporate survival.

There is merit in looking at file transfer from this global aspect. The movement of data from private to share form must be accompanied by technologies and organizational responsibilities appropriate to the organization's needs. Technology levels must be defined consistent with data usage. The migration path must be clearly understood. The actual migration is managed by using methodologies and tools to create databases and assure their system-wide interconnection. For intra-LAN distributed databases, it is desirable to support efficient protocols for data transport. If bridges are used as inter-LAN gateways, WSs on one LAN can communicate with other WSs external to the LAN. A gateway may also provide the link to one or more mainframes, manage wide area links, and translate messages between the LAN protocol and the protocols native to the remote hosts. In these cases, more than one protocol will be necessary.

A network of mainframe- or mini-supported databases, the file servers on the LAN, and microfiles at the WS level form an aggregate which can only be properly approached if we account for all database resources in our initial design. This calls for paying particular attention to the:

- Division assignments between the WS
- Local databases and files included in them
- Semaphores attached to files
- Use of memo posting procedures (for 24-hour reservations which may not be fulfilled)
- Connection between the LAN database and the information elements residing in the mainframe
- Protocols to be used in this connection

It is important to choose an appropriate information modeling tool for defining the conceptual schema. The tool must have a semantic form, include precise rules and procedures, and be based on sound theory, such as the relational model. One of the primary roles for the conceptual schema is to provide a set of conventions for managing the data life cycle.

The associated protocol makes feasible a data-driven software implementation for maintaining alignment between private views and models and organization-wide data management technology.

I emphasize these issues because accumulating experience from LAN implementation suggests that at least four issues will have to be looked after in the next few years:

1. The ability of a LAN workstation to access network-wide files.
2. The facility providing a file server with download capabilities from any files to any files for retrieval, updating, and merging.
3. The feature of dynamically distributing database subsets among communicating LANs in ad hoc fashion.
4. The attention to be paid to data life-cycle issues not only in a system sense but also in regard to the extruder function (sunset clauses).

This is a much broader view than the strict transfer activity would warrant. It is nevertheless a necessary approach. By contrast, the simple transfer of files between databases can be regarded as a service involving six steps: access to a file, typically administered by a DBMS; activation of the selected protocol; transfer of file data by a transport medium; provision of added services, such as code conversion; creation of a file copy in another physical or logical resource; and assurance of security, recovery, and protection. Even at this more limited level of reference, online file transfer has prerequisites: control languages, OS, DBMS, and file management. The operation on the transferred file must be organized under the system control.

The benefits to be derived from a properly conceived transport system are fast, reliable, controlled activity. A protocol-based file transfer service should present only one standard interface to the user. Additional operations on the copied file that might need to be managed during the transfer of the data are:

- Copying of data files from and to file servers
- Conversion of file structure
- Handling of data structures
- Recovery procedures
- Transfer of program modules, tables, etc.
- Remote spool capabilities

These are among the common characteristics of file transfer services. Though no two vendors offer the same solution, protocols, software, and hardware available today provide reasonably good services. If there is something wanting, it is found not in the fundamentals but in the more sophisticated supports whose need is increasingly felt. Both the lower and the higher-up levels of a file transfer architecture are important as are the organizational prerequisites.

19.4 Looking at a Basic Protocol Structure

We will look at Hminet* as an example of a well-studied protocol structure. Its attraction is its simplicity. This file transfer protocol consists of three phases:

1. Association
2. Data transfer
3. Break association

The association phase assures the identification of the access rights to the remote host. It also provides for connection set-up, establishment of file identity and properties, definition of the transfer direction, conversions of file structure and data, and specification of additional operations on the transferred file. The data transfer phase includes the local file operations, the mapping into virtual format, the actual data transfer, and the administrative exchanges required to regulate it. The conversions of the file data and structure are automatically done in this phase by the applications process. The break association phase finishes the local file operations and performs the additional functions on the transfer file (spool, job entry, etc.). It also closes the connection and indicates the final state of the transfer.

The protocol format is simple. A protocol element consists of a fixed-length header part, a data part, and a control part. The parameters in the control part depend on the type of protocol element. The header definition is as follows:

Byte 0	TYPE (protocol/element type)
Byte 1	RCODE (return code)
Byte 2–3	BCOUNT (block count)

* Hahn-Meitner Institute fur Kernforschung, Berlin.

Byte 4– 5 DATA LENGTH
Byte 6–7 RCOUNT (record count in block)

Typical types of protocol elements are: INIT (initialization of a process, with user access rights parameters), FFDB (function and file

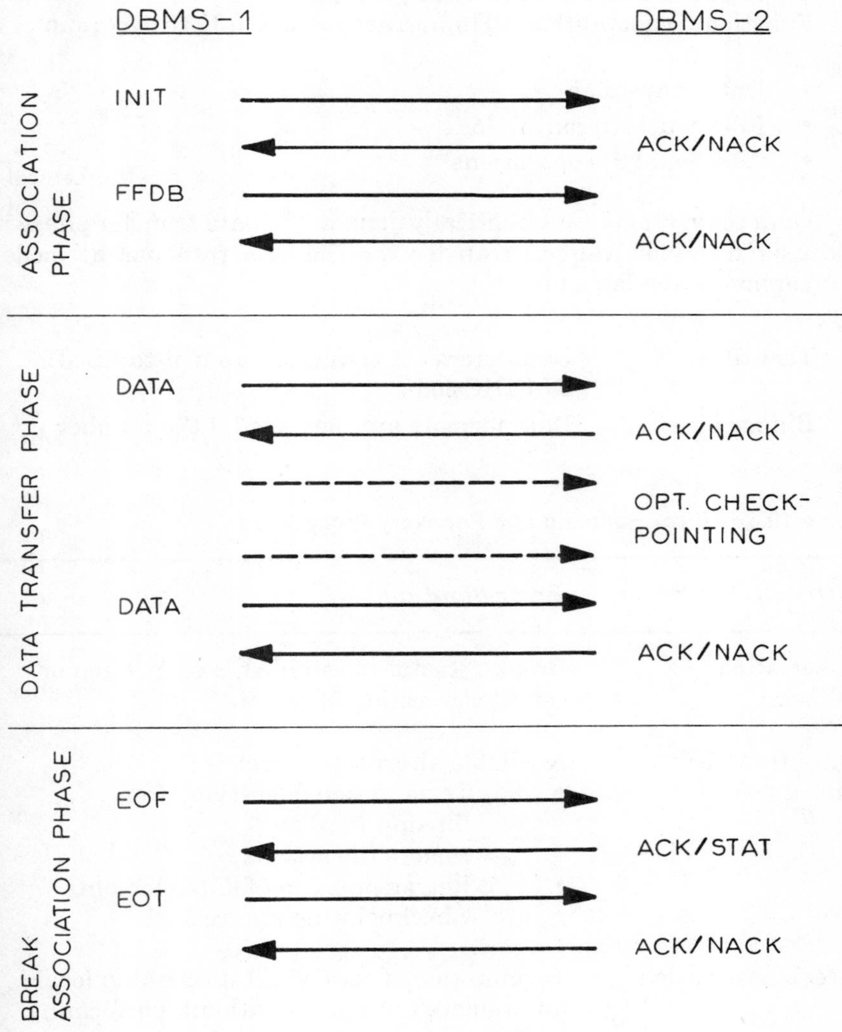

Figure 19.3 **Handshake for a typical file transfer operation.**

descriptor control, for identifying the file by filename, properties, and additional file operations), DATA (file data block according to format), EOF/EOT (end of file or end of transmission), and ACK/NAK (acknowledgment for synchronization, error detection, and recovery). Figure 19.3 shows the handshake for a typical file transfer operation. In each of the three protocol phases an error handling and recovery service must be provided. Table 19.1 presents these procedures.

Functional capabilities of Hminet are divided into three groups:

- Data conversion
- File structure conversion
- Additional file operations

Data conversion is automatically done in the data transfer phase if the user does not want to transfer the file in a transparent mode. Conversion is available for:

Text files	Characters are converted from or to ASCII/ EBCDIC code.
Binary files	Data formats are converted if the number

Table 19.1 Error Handling and Recovery Procedures

Error in	*Error handling*
Association phase	Break attempt to establish a connection or cancel connection at remote host
Data transfer phase	Available alternatives are: • Termination of session after finising local and remote file actions • Retransmission of data elements • Checkpointing and restart
Break association	Termination of session after finishing local and remote file actions without performing additional functions

	representations of the involved hosts calls for it (no mixed data files can be converted).
Graphic files	The standard graphic files of the HMI GRAFIX system can be automatically converted from and to each host representation.

An exception is that if a complete file is to be sent to a remote place for storage and subsequent retrieval for use by the originator, there seems to be no need to transform its structure of stored data. It can be simply accepted as a package by the store and returned, on demand, in the same state. However, if the store is operated as a common service, providing backup and archiving facilities for several computer systems, a uniform protocol is needed to govern the transfer of files to and from memory. Such a protocol can also be used to transfer files directly between different computer systems, again treating them as packages whose contents are absolutely independent of the transfer mechanism.

If the different computer systems concerned with exchanging files are all of the same type or are owned by a single organization, their software may be tailored in such a way that the files transferred between them are meaningful to each of them.

File structure conversion relates to the transferred file and integrates it in the destination file management system (FMS). Because of the possibilities of the destination FMS, the following file structures and organizations can be selected:

- Sequential
- Index sequential
- Block access
- Contiguous organization

Additional operations are performed after the transfer and are available for both the source and the destination file: PR (print the file), DE (delete the file), SP (spool the file [PR and DE]), and RJ (enter the file as a job in the job entry queue — only for destination file).

On each host computer in the Hminet are three different file transfer (FT) processes running:

1. An FT master, which is called into action by the user from a terminal and handles the FT commands, protocol control, and local file operations (Figure 19.4).

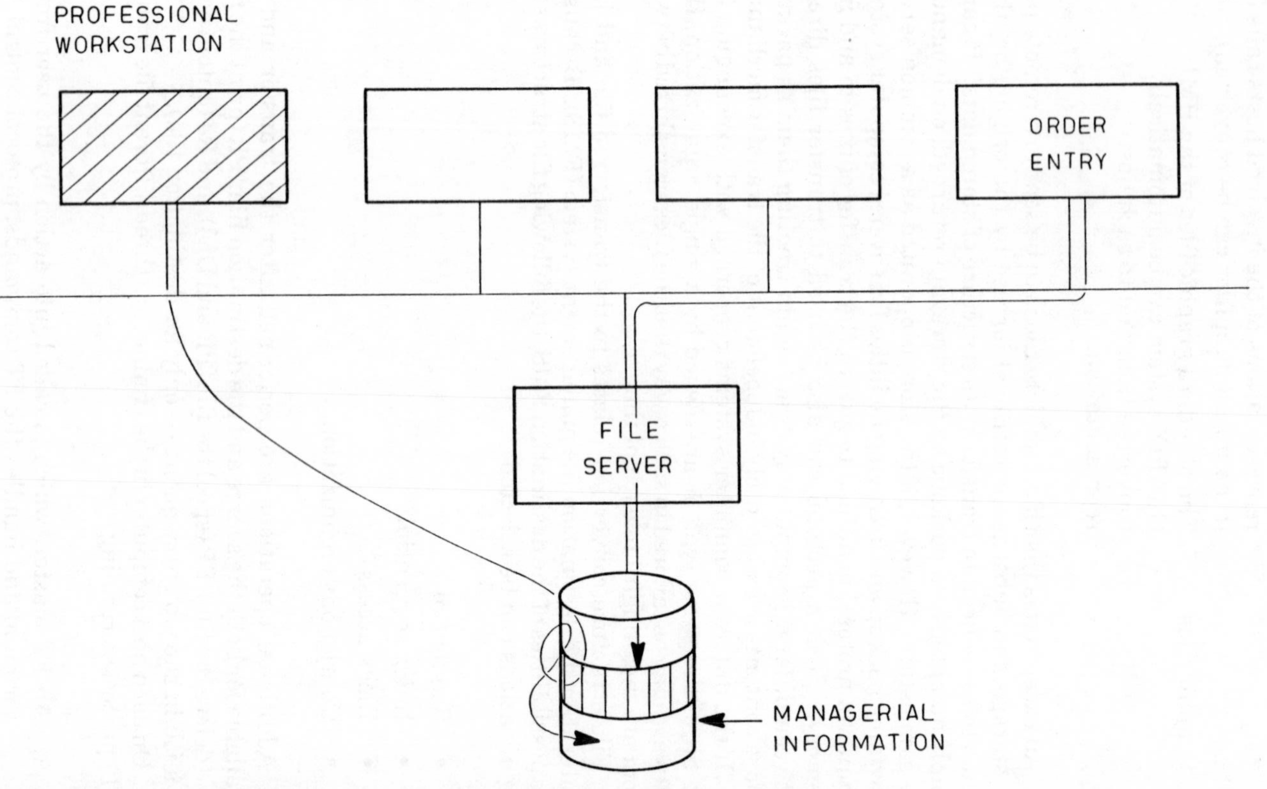

Figure 19.4 Execution of the transfer commands in a workstation environment.

2. An FT dispatcher, which is always running and waiting for incoming FT requests (from any supported point) in the network.
3. An FT slave, which serves the FT protocol and handles the file operation on this host.

To access the files, file name conventions must be known to the user. One solution is the definition of a network-wide standard file name convention. Chapter 18 explained why this can bring difficulties by mapping standard file names into local FMS conventions. The user must be familiar with both the local and the network standard names. In the Hminet FT protocol, the conventions of the accessed host FMS have been adopted in connection with tables reflecting the uniform name space.* An obvious problem with this solution is the handling of file duplicates. With the Hminet approach, on each case of file transfer the copied file is treated as a new file which is independent from the source file. This is not an efficient alternative as far as distributed databases are concerned.

The user interface of the HMI FT is organized in a two-level command language. In the first level the remote host access identification is declared. In the second level the source and destination file identification and additional functions are specified. The processing of a file on reception can, therefore, become a multipass, multilevel operation whose functions can be defined either network-wide or at the local site only—relying thereafter on the network's data transfer mechanism.

The solution EIN (European Informatics Network) proposes is as follows. The originator creates a file, with whatever local conventions about codes, structure, and so on, that apply. If the file is sent to a foreign site through the network, it is treated by a pre-transmission process that replaces all the local non-standard uses of symbols, codes, and commands, expanding them into explanatory strings. Upon receipt of such an expanded file, the strings are replaced by the equivalent symbols that happens to be understood by users and systems at the reception site. The overriding consideration in this approach is ease of understanding and implementation.

19.5 Data Units and Transport Protocol Services

In the ISO/OSI reference model, the transport layer is defined in terms

*However, the distinction made by Arpanet between ports and sockets is a more sound alternative.

of the transparent transfer of data between two end systems. An end system can be a host, a server, or a workstation. The purpose of the transfer protocol is to shield the transport user from concerns about the way in which reliable data transfer is achieved, providing a uniform service to the transport user regardless of the type of underlying network.

The functions of the transport layer invoked by the protocol are dependent upon the quality of service requested by the user and that obtainable from the network service provider. An ISO draft proposal includes five protocol classes intended to provide a constant service to its users on a variety of networks:

- Class 0 is the transport protocol for the international Teletex service over very reliable networks.
- Class 1 extends the functions of Class 0 and performs limited error recovery.
- Class 2 is also intended to be used over reliable networks and includes functions allowing multiplexing and flow control (but provides no error recovery mechanisms).
- Class 3 protocol includes added functions for the recovery from signaled errors.
- Class 4 protocol adds functions for error detection and recovery.

Table 19.2 compares the five classes of ISO transport protocols with regard to basic functionality criteria. Only the Class 4 protocol is intended to be used over networks with error characteristics unacceptable to the transport user. ECMA and NBS are also working on transport protocol classes. NBS has selected two of the ISO transport protocols: Class 2 and Class 4.

The Class 2 transport protocol assumes that the network is reliable. This assumption allows it to provide a minimum of functions in addition to those already performed by the network. Reliability means that the network service provides a low rate of data corruption, in-order delivery, unduplicated data, no loss of data, and notification of errors. It assures mechanisms for flow control on each transport connection independent of the network flow control, expedited data transfer, and unique identification of a transport connection for demultiplexing a single network-provided data stream into several transport connections. This protocol provides no enhancement of the network service in terms of reliability. It delivers data in sequence and without errors only as long as the

Table 19.2 ISO Draft for Five Transport Protocol Classes

Subject	*Class* 0	1	2	3	4
Assignment to network connection	Yes	Yes	Yes	Yes	Yes
TPDU transfer	Yes	Yes	Yes	Yes	Yes
Transfer TPDU length and segmenting	Yes	Yes	Yes	Yes	Yes
Concatenation and separation	No	Yes	Yes	Yes	Yes
Connection establishment	Yes	Yes	Yes	Yes	Yes
Connection refusal	Yes	Yes	Yes	Yes	Yes
Implicit termination	Yes	No	Yes	No	No
Reassignment	No	Yes	No	Yes	No
Reassignment after failure	No	Yes	No	Yes	No
Resynchronization	No	Yes	No	Yes	No
Multiplexing and demultiplexing	No	No	Yes	Yes	Yes
Use of checksum	No	No	No	No	No*
Retransmission and timeout	No	No	No	No	Yes
Resequencing	No	No	No	No	Yes
Interactivity control	No	No	No	No	Yes
Treatment of protocol errors	Yes	Yes	Yes	Yes	Yes
Splitting and recombining	No	No	No	No	Yes

*Mandatory

network service delivers the data correctly to the transport protocol entity. Of major importance is that if an error is detected by the Class 2 transport protocol entity, the transport connection is released.

With Class 4 transport protocol, the user is assured that the data is delivered in sequence and without error regardless of the reliability of the network. The connection established by the transport protocol entity is maintained as long as the user requires the connection or until there is a break in the network connection between the transport protocol entities. The protocol makes no assumptions about the behavior of the network. Therefore, in addition to the functions of Class 2, it looks after functions to resequence data, retransmit lost data, discard duplicated data, and detect and discard corrupted data. The aim is to help maintain the reliability of the transport service regardless of the reliability of the network in use. In this sense, the Class 4 protocol is designed for a network which is not reliable, may change, garble, lose, misorder, or duplicate data. This is why additional mechanisms are required in Class 4. The lower quality of network service makes them necessary.

Transport protocol description begins with the format of transport protocol data units (TPDUs). It includes peer-to-peer exchanges typical of the various protocol mechanisms. Peer transport entities communicate by sending and receiving TPDUs which serve to exchange either protocol control information or transport user data. In some cases, a TPDU may do both.

Data integrity measures the frequency with which transport protocol data units are corrupted while traversing the network. Data sequence and duplication errors measure such events in relation to TPDUs in transit. Data sequence errors measure how often TPDUs arrive at the destination out of order. Error notification is a measure of how often errors are not detected and reported by the network to the transport protocol entity. Network availability measures the amount of time the network is available to the users. A TPDU consists of an integral number of bytes. Its maximum size is negotiated during connection establishment. Typically, bytes are numbered starting from 1 and increase in the order of transmission. All TPDUs are divided into four parts:

1. Header length indication (LI) field .
2. Fixed part of the header.
3. Variable part of the header.
4. Data field.

The variable part of a TPDU header contains optional or infrequently occurring parameters. Thus, it may contain zero or more parameters, each structured as in Figure 19.5. Within each parameter included in the variable part of a TPDU header, the parameter code specifies the particular reference being represented.

Parameter length indicated the length in bytes of the parameter value field encoded as an 8-bit unsigned binary number. The parameter value field contains elements characteristic of each parameter, its coding depending on the parameter code. A data field is present only in those TPDUs which carry user data. Only user data is contained within a data

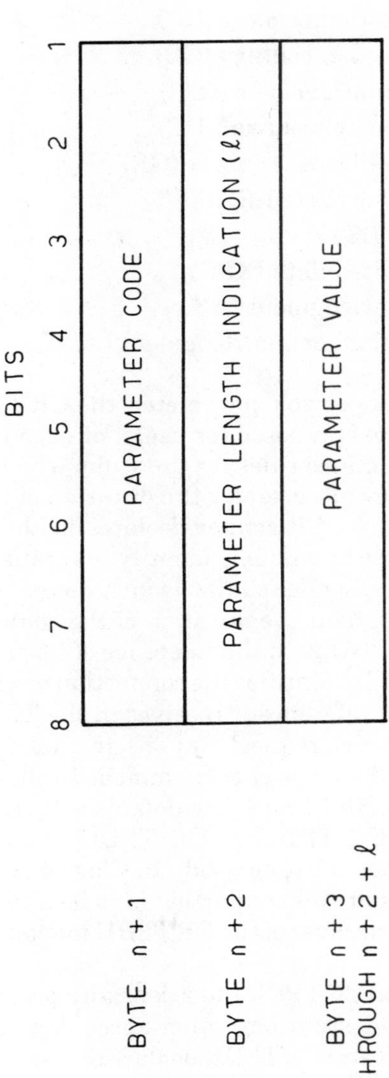

Figure 19.5 Structure of TPDU header with parametric approach.

field. Ten TPDU types are defined for the transport protocol:

- Connection request (CR)
- Connection confirm (CC)
- Disconnect request (DR)
- Disconnect confirm (DC)
- Graceful close request (GR)
- TPDU error (ERR)
- Data (DT)
- Expedited data (XPD)
- Acknowledgment (AK)
- Expedited acknowledgment (XAK)

For each negotiable parameter, the CR TPDU may contain a value (or set of values) proposed for use. For each negotiable parameter, the specification defines rules for the value which may be contained in the CC TPDU, they are used for the duration of the connection.

Typically, the CR sender declares in the CR TPDU the reference which it will use to uniquely identify the transport connection in its own system. The CC sender similarly includes its unique reference in the CC TPDU. Throughout the duration of the connection, a transport entity marks each TPDU with the reference of its peer (destination reference) when sending. It identifies the connection to which each incoming TPDU belongs by the reference it receives in the TPDU (source reference).

The connection request may specify that the TPDU of the connection should or should not be checksummed. In Class 2, use of the checksums is not allowed. In Class 4, the default is to use checksums; in addition, if either the CR TPDU or CC TPDU explicitly specifies the use of checksums, they must be used. In Class 4 , the CR TPDU may declare as an option that this connection is to be a two- or three-way unit data transfer. The receiver of the CR TPDU must agree or reject the unit data transfer.

The CR and CC TPDU must contain a protocol version number. Both sides (source, destination) must agree or reject the establishment attempt. The CR and CC TPDU declare the size of the largest TPDU which the respective transport entity is prepared to receive. The CC sender may choose a smaller value than given in the CR. The specified size must be a power of 2 between 128 and 8192 inclusive. The CR and CC TPDU contain an address, the transport suffix, for each transport user. Also, they may contain each side's declaration for the value of the security parameters. Neither the format of these parameters nor their use is stipulated as part of this specification.

CR and CC TPDU may contain each side's declaration of the quality of service desired for the connection. The quality of service specified in the CC must not be a higher quality of service than that specified in the CR. The attributes which may be specified include:

- Minimum acceptable throughput
- Residual error rate
- Priority
- Maximum acceptable transit delay

The size of the data sequence space and the size of the flow control field are selected during connection establishment. Allowable values in the CR TPDU are 7 bits for the size of the data sequence space and 4 bits for the flow control field or 31 bits for the size of the data sequence space and 16 bits for the flow control field. The values returned in the CC TPDU must be equal to or less than the values in the CR TPDU. The default values are 331 bits for the sequence space and 16 bits for the flow control field.

In conclusion, the assumptions implied by Figure 19.6 are the stated class characteristics. Class 2 transport protocol is used with reliable networks and the Class 4 transport protocol is used with not so reliable networks. In selecting the actual pairing of transport protocol class and network, the user organization's needs must be considered and the appropriate scheme selected. A great deal depends on the network environment. Any user of a transport protocol has a set of requirements concerning the service expected from the transport layer. To select the appropriate class of transport protocol, the characteristics of the network being employed and the enhancements provided by each class of transport protocol must be considered.

Whether with wide area networks or with LAN, during the selection process of protocols, the characteristics of the network must be determined. This can be accomplished by examining published performance literature for the networks or by interference from the network type: token passing, CSMA/CD, or X.25. The criterion for selecting the transport protocol class are the user's reliability requirements: lost TPDU, duplicated TPDU, out-of-sequence TPDU, errors in TPDU, and network availability.

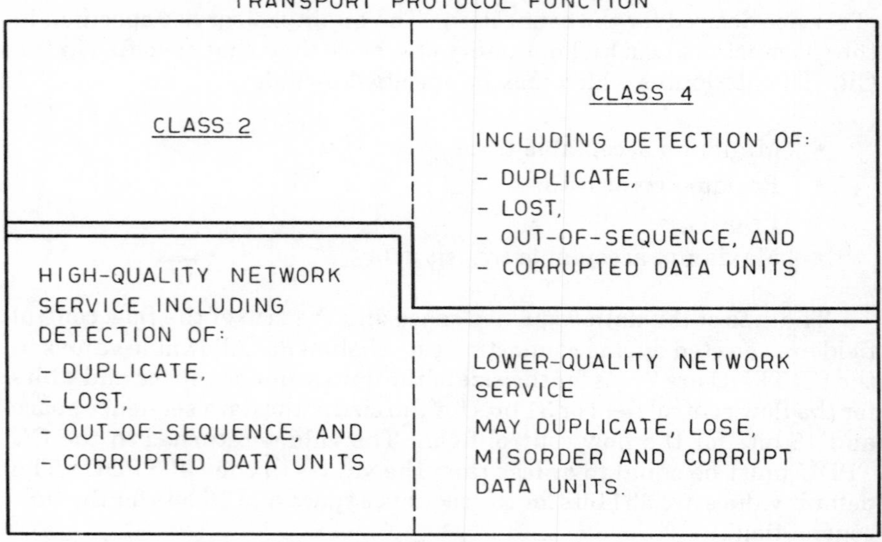

Figure 19.6 Enhancements of underlying network functionality and quality of transport service.

The selection of which class of transport protocol to use is dependent on the user's requirements and on the error detection capabilities of the network under consideration. The users' requirements can be summarized in terms of how often they are willing to accept a transport service that often releases the connection, since this requires substantial user overhead foe reestablishing the connection and resynchronizing the data transfer.

19.6 Session and Presentation Level Message Management

The ability to perform message management in an able manner within an interactive environment calls for an architectural solution. It also involves data description capabilities, data manipulation language(s), and protocols. Data manipulation is done in three layers:

- Internal, concerning data as it stands in the system and in the files
- Conceptual, an interface situation
- External, as seen by the end user and/or the user program

Figure 19.7 gives an example of a commercial application in which two layers are involved:

1. Session layer, acting as start—stop mechanism of the distributed activity.
2. Presentation layer, which will handle the formatted data.

The external and the conceptual schema have correspondences such as name associations, reformatting rules, and rules to localize relations. Protocols allow the computer to perform conceptual data manipulation, calculation of corresponding status, coding into messages, error control, and flow control. An executive controller mechanism is necessary to initiate and terminate a transaction, prevent concurrent conflicts, proceed with commitment studies, provide solutions to deadlock conflicts, and augment reliability.

Needed algorithms must assure concurrency conflict prevention, deadlock detection, distributed query processing, data translation and mapping, and reliability assurance. The user interface is both logical and physical, involving information elements, data models, database access, and database architecture. Solutions must be common to all users and devices, support multiple views of data, assure view-to-view translation, and guarantee schema and subschema flexibility.

Information elements must not only be defined in a precise manner but also in a comprehensive and compatible way, with established relationships among them. Relationships are known correspondence between two IEs. As such, they link one entity to another. For example, bills and clients are related since it is known that every client has an accounts payable file opened by the firm. Similarly, products and sales offices are related since products are sold by the sales office. Relationships between IEs are identified by asking what is the:

- Know correspondence among them
- Meaning of each relationship, expressed either formally or informally

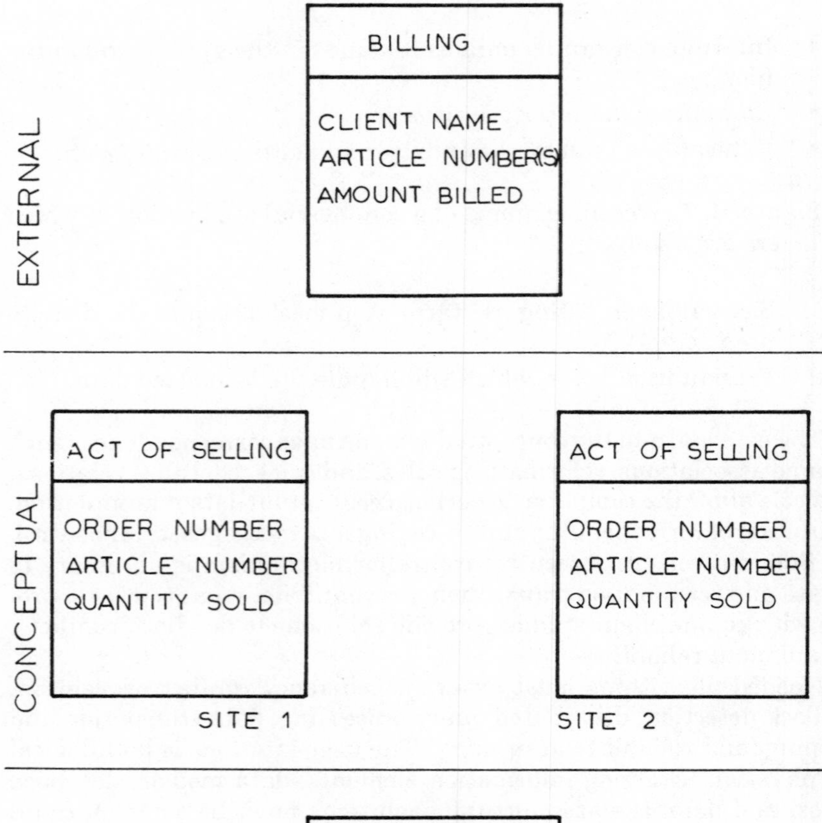

Figure 19.7 Example of a commercial application involving session and presentation layer.

- Appropriate handling for each relationship
- Mapping property for each relationship — one to one, one to many, many to many
- Possible relationships which are not used but are still meaningful
- Probability of occurrence (connectivity) of each relationship
- Probability of occurrence of each IE (both average and maximum number of expected occurrences should be identified)
- Average number of additions and deletions of each IE over a given period of time and of updates
- Average and maximum number of additions and deletions of each relationship for a given period
- Average and maximum size (length) of each IE
- Role(s) of each attribute being used (primary key, security, sort key, linkage)

Data management requirements pose challenges at three different levels:

1. Query level in regard to query decomposition.
2. File level in terms of file placement and migration and also relative to data compression.
3. Task level in regard to task scheduling.

The relevant issues include logical organization, architectural solution, user interface, operational control, and future evolution.

Most of these issues have significant interdependencies among them. Differences exist in types of detail and in order of complexity:

- Single relation query
- Multiple relation query — decomposable
- Multiple relation query — nondecomposable

Query is regarded as an access made by a user in which one or more files are involved. When multiple files are accessed by the same query, these files usually have to reside at a buffer location (stack) before the query can be processed. It is necessary to decompose a multiple relation query to as many single relation subqueries as possible. However, not all queries are decomposable. Even if they are, they may require a significant amount of file transfer.

A message exchange system is more cost efficient if the designer is able to estimate:

- The type and frequency of occurrence of different queries
- The reaction by type and frequency of queries
- Query decomposition and file placement
- Addition and deletion of redundant information
- Cost and access of prerogatives

Heuristic approaches can be used to give valid estimates of the behavior of these factors. A basic objective must be to minimize complexity — both logical and physical.

Data redundancy must be transparent to the user. First, the logical issues must be attacked — such as frequency of processing, types of queries, and the need for nearby IEs. Then, the user interfaces should be studied. Physical supports must also be given careful consideration. Communications overhead may be involved when files are geographically distributed and/or a copy of each file has to be transferred to another location. The search for efficient alternatives has at its origin the goals of minimizing operating cost while increasing the robustness of the system and providing adaptability to user locations.

19.7 Cooperating Transactions and Pipelining Requirements

Cooperating transactions affect the recovery and restart capability and make solutions more complex. But we do not really need synchronous operations—they imply too many commitments and are not characteristic of a managerial and professional environment. The cascading of cooperating transactions creates the risk of a breakdown in the transmission chain and subsequent difficulties in the processing of recovery. It also involves a significant overhead. In terms of network operations, both references are negatives.

Cooperating transactions are made up by at least two parallel processes whose execution agrees on certain rules and common variables in given formats. Modeling for reasons of: verification, performance analysis, or adequate specification of the implementation demands a great deal from a communications method. The variety of methods is restricted to exchange of messages. Shared storage locations can, however, be modeled as a separate process, and communication solely by messages seems to be sufficient.

Process naming requires that processes have access to each other's names, thus an agreement upon the significance of the variables used should be settled. The number of messages sent or received can vary for different processes. A more modular approach is to declare a number of ports for each module. Individual processes would thus define particular variables: the port names, to be accessible externally. Port names present an external mechanism which allows dynamic port linkage.

Another communication method is to define public message variables to be accessed by any number of other processes. Under this discipline it would not be possible to communicate without explicitly naming receiver or sender. Processes can thus communicate without knowing the names of their adjacent communication partner; the name of a receiving process can be part of the message. Naming of processes or ports hide an underlying architecture which is a substantial part of a layered protocol.

A further implication of this approach is that a network topology can be hidden behind a dynamic call structure of executing processes. Such topology can become changeable during execution, with connection between processes established and cancelled during run time. Fundamentals, such as network topology, would be defined by the state of the communicating processes rather than by fixed locations. Given the name matching principle, and communication can be easily limited to a subset of processes. That forces the user to define the communication on the basis of unique names. Nevertheless, hierarchies could be more easily defined if processes call each other by name, although the overall structure is a layered system with communication partners on each side of a layer. Calling a lower-level process on a procedural base and defining the directed graph for the call hierarchy would not, however, be applicable.

Whether the more sophisticated approach which we are outlining or any other one is taken, it is wise to implement a thorough journaling, backup, and restart and recovery procedure. In this domain, a number of critical questions should be answered. For instance, how long to keep a journal? The answer depends on the goal:

1. If it is restart and recovery, we must keep online trace as long as we have such requirements. Operational needs overlap with one

another; a rolling journal can handle them—but we usually change the live journal once a day.

2. If it is security, this poses a long range requirement, but it can be managed offline.
3. If legal prerequisites exist, they have to be met. If not, 5 or 6 years in keeping the journaling trace on optical disk would be a good policy.

A concrete effort should be made to emulate and benchmark the operation of the online, interactive environment under development to avoid unpleasant surprises after it becomes operational.

The last few references point to the fact that means must be provided both for the journaling function and for the restart. The ideal case would be the use of a shadow image of the active database at the LAN level. Beyond the journaling procedure, we must assure a policing mechanism for message exchange and access to files. This can be provided through pipes and semaphores. A pipe is a buffer that collects data from a sender, and makes it available to a receiver. Senders and receivers may be different programs and/or different computers, running at different times. Pipe commands are processed by the file server. Before a pipe can be used, it must be opened for write through an Open Write command issued by the sender. A Close Pipe command closes a pipe for writing.

The size of a pipe can vary with the network architecture. With Omninet, a maximum of 512 bytes could be written with one pipe command — but multiple pipe write commands could be employed. In this sense, pipe handling resembles the datagram approach. Pipes provide a communications mechanism necessary to build LAN applications and serve as a utility. This enables different computers connected to the same file server to communicate with each other, and share common peripheral equipment. A Pipe Status command reads the name and pointer tables from the disk. A Purge Pipe commands allows the user to delete an unwanted pipe. As Figure 19.8 indicates, while message exchange through a pipe mechanism is a solution for baseband, broadband usually adopts a protocol-based handshake:

- Station A questions the BIU of Station B for window availability.
- If the answer is yes, Station A sends the message to Station B.
- The message transits through the BIU buffer.
- When it is received at the destination PC, it is checked for error.
- If correct, the BIU of Station B sends an acknowledgment.

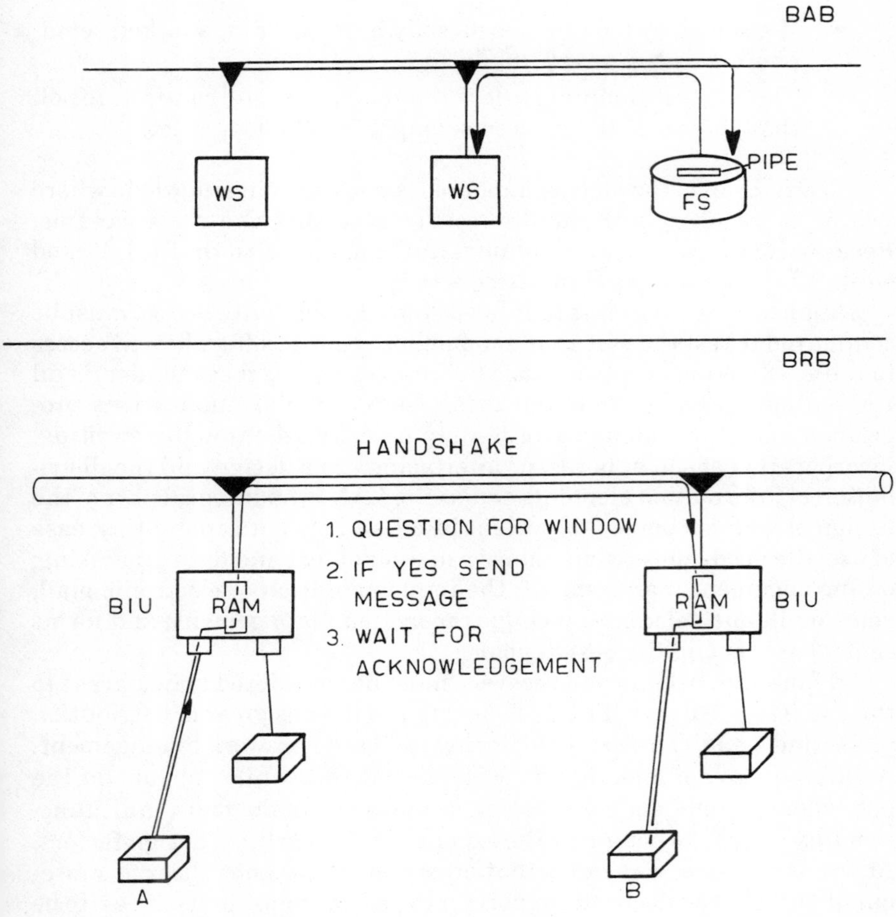

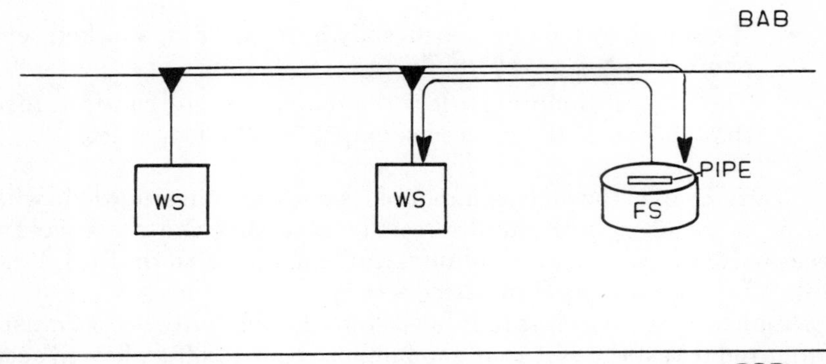

BAB
WS
WS
PIPE
FS
BRB
HANDSHAKE
1. QUESTION FOR WINDOW
2. IF YES SEND MESSAGE
3. WAIT FOR ACKNOWLEDGEMENT
BIU
RAM
RAM
BIU
A
B

Figure 19.8 Handshakes for baseband (BAB) and broadband (BRB) connectivity.

The Lock and Unlock commands applicable to the database are the *semaphores*. Through them, a semaphore is either placed or removed from the semaphore table managed by the file server.

Each program (or computer) on the LAN may, at any time, ask to lock a semaphore. (Their number varies with the architecture. Up to 32 are available with Omninet.) The request is granted if no other entity has already locked that particular semaphore:

- If a semaphore name has already been entered, a locked semaphore message is returned.
- The entity attempting to lock the semaphore will continue to poll the table until the desired semaphore is no longer locked.

Traffic control through semaphores is necessary in situations where two or more users are simultaneously accessing the same volume. Read–write access to shared volumes can be made safe if the file is locked while any program has Write Access to it.

Applications programs that need shared read–write access must be configured to test the status of a semaphore before being allowed access to a file. This is one of the basic differences between stand alone and LAN-oriented applications routines. Conversion of applications programs from stand alone to LAN may be affected through rewriting, incorporation of semaphores, or interfacing. File design and the distribution of information elements across the LAN is an integral part of the design of workstations. Polyvalent input and output capabilities; ease of use; the forgiveness of mistakes; a merger of text and data processing; online document management; the implementation of electronic mail, voice mail, and teleconferencing; transaction management; and forms control are among the design goals.

Reliability, backup and recovery must be considered transparent to the end user. This must be done during the file design and distribution phase and steadily ascertained during local area network management. A different way of making this statement is that while support for the polyvalent, intelligent workstation is one of our main goals, multifunctionality cannot be bought at the expense of other critical design factors. At the same time, if the distribution of the IE does not observe subsequent DP/WP and decision support (or expert systems) procedures (to be executed at the workstation level), the aggregate of PC and LAN will not work properly.

Chapter

20

Communications Challenges and PC-to-Mainframe Links

20.1 Introduction

The explosive growth in personal computers, sparked by attractive price and performance attributes, has moved the workstation to a status of full partnership with the mainframe. This development is further fuelled by advances in communications technologies which have now made PC-to-mainframe links not only technically but also economically viable. Possible solutions are too many rather than too few. Therefore, we need strategies for linking micro and mainframe systems and expert guidance on how to gain the maximum benefits from networking approaches. LANs and their gateways provide effective means for interconnecting WSs and corporate information services, linking micros to minis, and micros to micros, all of which are growing in significance. Among questions to be answered are: How can micros and mainframes be linked? Which applications benefit most from a PC-to-mainframe link?

Other critical issues regard new applications opportunities created by micro-mainframe link technology; the proper balance between micros and mainframes; available and advisable PC-to-mainframe connectivity; ways and means to acquire, implement, and manage these technologies; and technical standards to be followed. Answers cannot be given in an abstract sense. As with all integrated systems, tradeoffs are involved in configuring them. To be considered are:

- Type of applications
- Workload
- Communications geography
- Access to attached devices
- Costs

A simple link provides only a connection and terminal emulation. Its file transfer capabilities are extremely rudimentary, limited to full files and operating at a very slow speed. A simple data link assures *no* mainframe extraction or use of micro-based applications, although many of the hardware products do provide means for the user to perform micro functions and then return to a mainframe session.

There are two methods of providing simple links: asynchronously through software — with a modem dialing up a port on a communications front end, such as a 3705, or a protocol converter — and synchronously through a printed circuit board (PCB) and coaxial hookup to a controller, such as a 3274. Link refers to the physical process of establishing communications between the devices which will be joined. Links should not be confused with modems, although modems are part of the link. They are necessary for communications over telephone lines. Most PC users are more familiar with asynchronous modems, but high-speed synchronous modems are also employed for terminal communications over distances where LAN cabling is not practical.

Enhanced link products extend the functionality of simple links through hardware and software. But some offerings share many of the same constraints. More complex interconnect solutions have additional features at either the mainframe or the mainframe or the micro end and occasionally at both. These include:

- Support for multiple-file types
- Attractive user interfaces
- Script and macro capabilities

Some products support only specific link types; others are independent of the physical link. Many are more or less limited with respect to their mainframe extraction capabilities.

Enhanced links break down into two subcategories: vendor-specific, and application- or process-specific. Vendor-specific products work with the vendor's mainframe. Their approach is to bring some capabilities of the mainframe to the PC user. In some cases, however, not much more than terminal emulation and downloading is provided.

20.2 Links, Files, and Message Tasks

A data link between the PC and the host needs to have certain attributes. It should support a flexible, intelligent communications subsystem, establish connections transparently, and provide a simple easy-to-use file transfer. It should assure easy data extraction from host database, for local analysis and processing, while featuring unattended operation capability. Complementing the basic PC-to-mainframe data link, further support services should offer the following functions: offload creation, editing, reading, filing, printing, and automatic mail delivery and pickup. The entire structure must be consistent with the host system. Menu structures and the means to navigate through them should be as similar as possible, allowing users to move back and forth between applications and even between types of workstations with maximum freedom, minimum learning time, and minimum discomfort.

Figure 20.1 reflects a simple PC-to-mainframe connection. It identifies four problems:

1. The application running on the host.
2. The protocol at the front end processor (FEP).
3. The line choice.
4. Protocol and application at the PC.

Simple PC-to-mainframe solutions typically are unable to handle access against multiple physical storage facilities unless the user aknows how to move from file to file and storage device to storage device on the mainframe, which requires a technically knowledgeable user. In practice, it means significant DP involvement from the start and increased support requirements as time goes on. Simple micro-to-host links often end up consuming a significant amount of programming effort to make the data usable. What is more, the absence of extraction capabilities

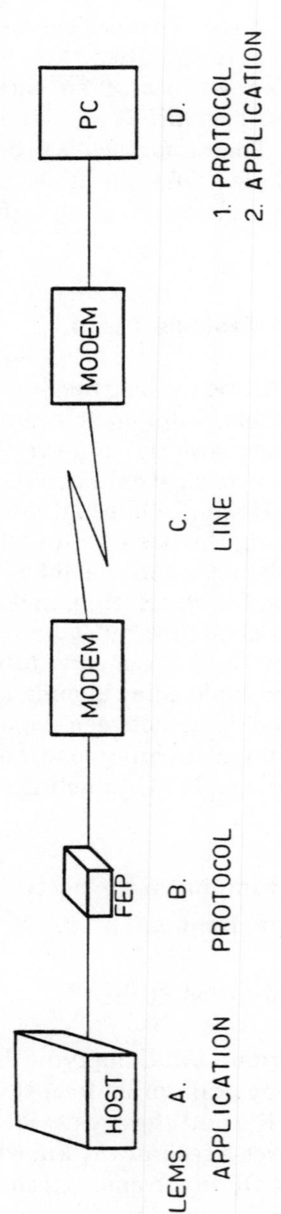

Figure 20.1 Component parts of PC to mainframe connectivity.

against the mainframe files means that unless prior extraction is done, the data must be brought down in very large chunks, possibly outstripping the capabilities of the micro and also taking a great deal more time to perform the transfer.

The proper amount of preparatory work can ease some of these restrictions. A response to this requirement involves:

- Extracting from mainframe files relevant to different applications
- Formatting for eventual end-user retrieval
- Loading the formatted files on to a minicomputer dedicated to infocenter purposes
- Making this minicomputer available online to WS user communicating through simple PC-to-host approaches

A fairly complex procedure is necessary to respond to these requirements. It is wise to use a layered structure, as Figure 20.2 suggests. This not only helps overcome some of this type, but it also provides elegant solutions. One of its key advantages is flexibility. In case one of the design parameters changes, we only need to update the corresponding layer. However, it is also true that layered solutions consume greater computer power.

There are two types of simple links at the end user's end: software-based and hardware-based. Software-based links involve modem-equipped PC-emulating terminals. Several emulators have file transfer capabilities that are more sophisticated than their hardware counterparts. Physical connection is required. The capabilities of hardware-based products have been continually upgraded through software. Since a PC-to-mainframe link is made to serve some purpose, chances are the purpose is file handling or messaging. Chapter 19 spoke of messaging. In this computer we will focus on prerequisite file manipulation which includes:

- Extracting, the purpose of retrieving data from mainframe database. In general, this includes anything from copying a whole file to performing retrievals against one or more file types, handling various vendor-specific file structures, and/or selecting IEs according to parametrically established criteria. Extraction can also be performed with a variety of tools, including fourth-generation languages (4GLs), database management systems (DBMS), and applications programs created ad hoc.

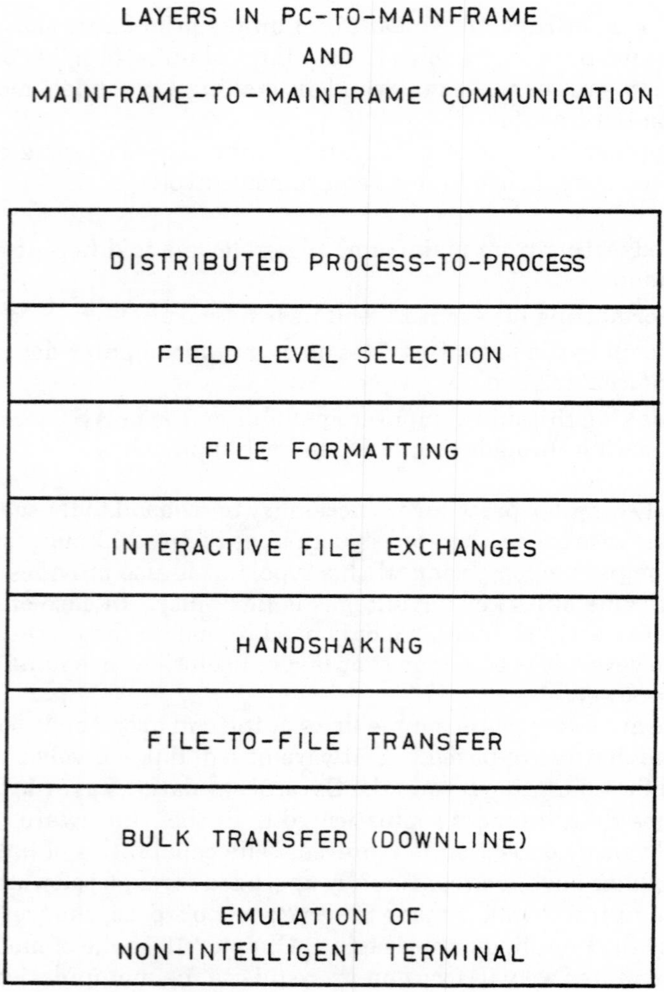

LAYERS IN PC-TO-MAINFRAME
AND
MAINFRAME-TO-MAINFRAME COMMUNICATION

DISTRIBUTED PROCESS-TO-PROCESS
FIELD LEVEL SELECTION
FILE FORMATTING
INTERACTIVE FILE EXCHANGES
HANDSHAKING
FILE-TO-FILE TRANSFER
BULK TRANSFER (DOWNLINE)
EMULATION OF NON-INTELLIGENT TERMINAL

Figure 20.2 Layers in PC-to-mainframe and mainframe-to-mainframe communication.

- Formatting is typically done by programming products which format data before or after downloading has taken place by whatever method is in use. Before is done by mainframe products; after by PC-based programs.

While necessary, formatting and bulk loading are not enough. A micro-to-mainframe product must be able to locate a file in a particular operating environment before transfer can take place. After transfer, the product must be able to store the transferred file properly in the new environment.

20.3 Enhanced Products for Communications Links

File transfer software is necessary if we have different hardware and need to use files from two or more machines. Another basic component of file management is the ability of the software to store and access the downloaded or uploaded data. The following lists some commercial products that are enhanced for communications links:

1. *Goldengate and Infogate from Cullinet Software.* Goldengate serves IBM's System 370 and compatibles. It works under MVS, VM/CMS, and VSE. It supports VTAM and centers on IMS and IDMS database management systems. The format is ASCII and DIF. Another Cullinet entry is Infogate. Both products are designed to work with the vendor's Information Center Management System. Log on scripts are supported, as are VT 100, Kermit, and Xmodem in asynchronous links (only asynchronous communication is supported). Cross-loading through the mainframe is possible, even crossing formats in the process.

2. *Model 204/PC 204 from Computer Corporation of America.* Model 204 is also asynchronous and appeals to the System 370 market. It works under MVS/TSO, VM/CMS, and VSE. The format is ASCII and DIF. Model 204 runs on mainframes. DB Designer is intended to assist in analyzing file requirements, creating a design, translating the design into either Model 204 or (IBM's) DB2 models, and tuning the resulting product.

3. *Focus and PC/Focus from Information Builders.* Focus is a fourth-generation language operating under MVS, VM, VSE, and VMS. PC/Focus is aimed at the functional implementation of the mainframe product. Application development can be performed on the micro using extracted data before moving the code up to the mainframe. The front end is Tabletalk for

reporting and Filetalk for file definition. Nevertheless, the communication capabilities of Focus and PC/Focus are relatively constrained.

4. *Ingres / PC Link from Relational Technologies.* Operating under Unix, VMS, and VM/CMS, Ingres/PC Link aims at the relational DBMS market. It patterns its user interface after the Lotus 1-2-3 model. On the mainframe side, it reads only Ingres files. At the PC level, it includes a context-sensitive help facility and creates menus from the Ingres Integrated Data Dictionary. DIF and ASCII are the formats. Communications are asynchronous, but Ingres/PC Link runs on Ethernet.

5. *PC Contact from Cincom.* PC Contact, is also aimed at the relational database market. It is specifically for Mantis users who can access file types and download and upload in asynchronous mode. Supported OSs are MVS/TSO and VSE. The formats are ASCII and DIF; it runs on Ethernet.

6. *Ramlink by Martin Marietta Data Systems.* Ramlink connects to Ramis II, supporting mainframe formats. It allows generation of code for mainframe execution, the transfer of files, and the export of DIF files. It operates under MVS/TSO and CICS, VM/CMS, and VSE. Formats are ASCII and DIF. Available features are dictated by the installed capabilities of Ramis II and the user at the WS level. Ramlink is asynchronous, bisynchronous, or packet switching (SDLC) under SNA. Supported DBMS include DB2/SQL, Adabas, Total, IMS, and IDMS.

7. *A range of IBM PC-to-mainframe offers.* IBM has two main entries. Host Data Base View (HDBV) is designed to be used with Query Management Facility (QMF), the Information Facility (TIF), and Info Center/1 (IC1). When HDBV is employed in conjunction with the Mainframe Communication Assistant (MFC) or PC/VM Bond, data extraction can be performed transparently. Downloaded data is sent to the PC as reports and can be browsed for further extraction and reformatting. HDBV operates under MVS/TSO and VM/CMS. Data formats are DIF and ASCII. Another IBM product, the Personal Decision Series (PDS), also supports ASCII on mainframes. It comes in two parts. One is resident under System 370 (MVS, VM) and System 36, the other is PC resident. It supports a full range of integrated

software packages, acts as micro-DBMS, and provides PC-to-mainframe connectivity.*

In terms of sophistication, a newly emerging class is the open architecture products with any-to-any features. Some use IBM's LU 6.2 as a framework, adding intelligence at both ends: extracting data effectively and manipulating information elements at the user end. APPC provides an intelligent handshake, but the new generation of link products go beyond this. They are application driven (not based on terminal emulation) and a good deal more sophisticated than what has been available so far. There are vast differences in this class among products. Some are command driven with a great deal of mainframe functionality. Others are menu driven, insulating users from much of the command syntax of the operating system, access methods, and transaction processing.

An example is Any Databridge from Cipherlink. It is said to provide the capability to transfer information between programs regardless of hardware, software, or operating system. It does not need to know what the data format is because it duplicates the process that would be performed by a data entry clerk in extracting, downloading, reformatting and uploading the data, reading the screen, selecting the records and fields needed, and then rekeying into the new application. Any Databridge operates as an expert system featuring IF...THEN logic and process chaining. At this point, the product treats a micro, mini, or mainframe at the receiving ends in the same way: The data entry procedures duplicate those of an operator, being essentially an application generator. It runs on a machine under Unix or Xenix.

20.4 Plus and Minus in PC-to-Mainframe Connectivity

The problem and the challenge in solving PC-to-mainframe connectivity is that personal computing addresses a broad spectrum of applications. Hence, it demands a wide range of facilities. Their provision requires the correct identification of needs of common applications and calls for a thorough examination of possible functional conflicts. The products listed in Section 20.3 are necessary but not enough. While PC-to-main-

---

*See also D. N. Chorafas, *Fourth- and Fifth-Generation Languages*, Volume 1, McGraw-Hill, New York, 1986.

frame links should have been a matter of course in terms of implementation, experience teaches this is not so. This type of communications has been a marriage of three dissimilar cultures:

1. *Philosophical, at the overall implementation level.* There is a dual objective in emphasizing differences: first, to transmit experience and second, to draw the attention of DP/MIS managers and system specialists, who come from mainframe background, to the fact that the WS has totally different characteristics.
2. *Logical, at the code, protocol, and language levels.* Even the IBM mainframe and PC 3270, designed by the same company, don't match. New departures are necessary — and a good deal of soldering iron.
3. *Physical, with reference to the connectors, modems, and so on.* The need for online PC-to-mainframe is undeniable, but we should properly appreciate that we can only achieve an effective solution if we integrate the workstation, its files, and the communications disciplines. The WS must access and effectively use the data which is already in our organization's own private database and in public databases. This is the key to management productivity.

Island solutions have little effect on management and professionals. In 3 to 4 months the happiest users of a stand alone PC will not be happy anymore. They will require online services. Integrated solutions are needed, but this answer has a price. Integration can come at different levels. Multimedia integration will bring voice, image, text, and data to the user's terminal either through a local approach or by means of a fully integrated network, like the Japanese solution shown in Figure 20.3.

While full integration will still take a number of years—and LANs will become one of its basic ingredients—even at the current level of implementation, solutions leave much to be desired. We need:

1. Consistency in handling current requirements.
2. Ability to apply the higher levels of the ISO/OSI model.
3. Dependability in database access.
4. Versatility in electronic messaging.
5. Costs which are reasonable.

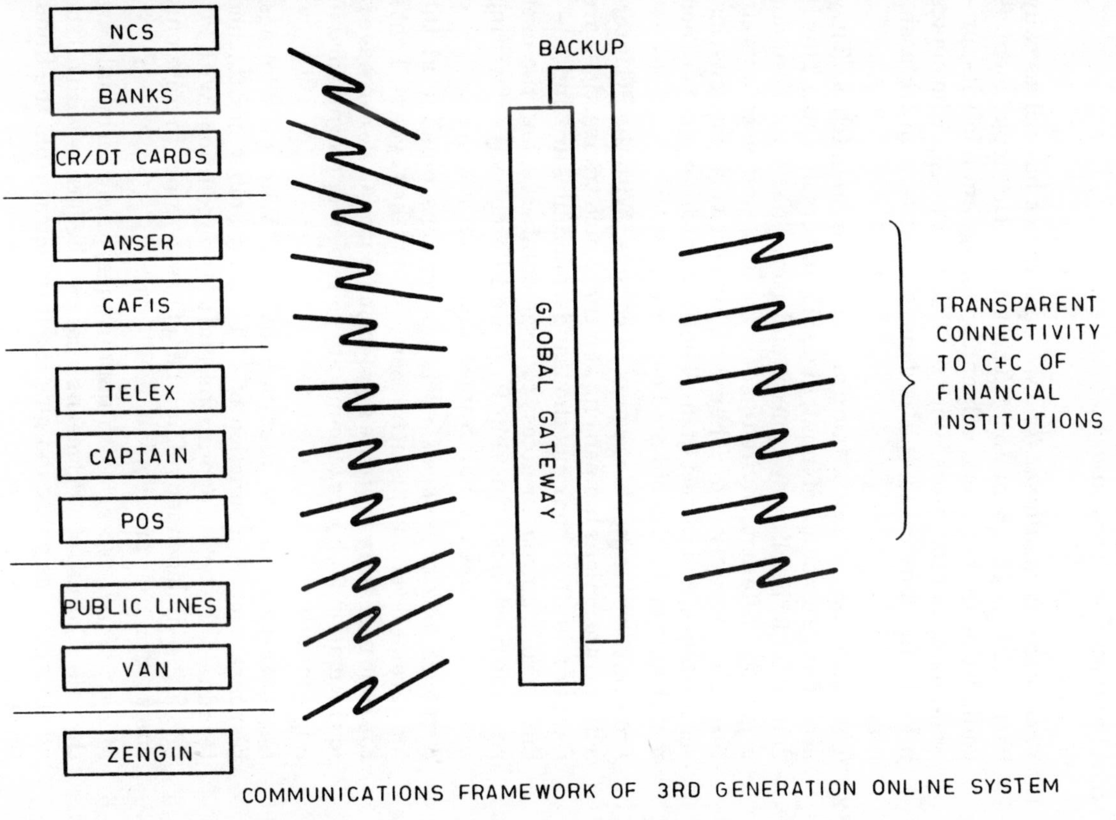

Figure 20.3 Communications framework of third-generation online system.

But optional solutions are handicapped by implementation differences (we call them philosophical). Mainframes and PCs have vastly different backgrounds. They are:

1. *There are organizational issues.* Mainframes have classically been a DP department tool. The typical DP department is equipped with managers, submanagers, system analysts, programmers, and operators. With the PC, it is the user who makes it kick. In many cases, this is done without central DP assistance.
2. *The type of processing.* Mainframes grew up in batches. They accept huge amounts of input, digest it, and crash it out. This is done at high speed, away from the end user. The PC works under a greatly different environment. Creator and user operate through softcopy (video). They work interactively, pose queries, see mistakes, and correct them. The cultural difference between mainframe and PC could not be greater.
3. *Problems in user-machine communications.* With the PC interactive transactions happen one at a time, such transactions are few per minute or hour, not thousands, microfiles are limited — but there is a need for access to large databases, and the user runs the machines. This calls for quite different ways of writing programs from what mainframes have so far required.
4. *Response to user requests.* The applications pipeline at the mainframe level of implementation usually takes 2 years. That's the time necessary to create a program. With PC we can have it in the mail in 24 hours (commodity software) or downloaded in a few minutes.
5. *Response time, as the user perceives it.* With mainframes, response time is a function of CPU, the number of attached terminals, the type of operations, and the line solution. With PC, it is fast — independent of number of users—since there is only one user on the same engine.
6. *Machine intelligence.* With mainframes, dumb terminals are the rule. The use of a PC means local intelligence — with all the advantages this gives and also the differences from the dumb terminal solution.
7. *Interactivity.* Even with line disciplines, mainframes are very remote from the end user. Many users are simultaneously sharing the same CPU, none of them controls its usage, and at

the same time lines are expensive. That's the reason why mainframe hardware (and to a substantial extent software) is designed to make minimum use of phone facilities. The host sends a screenful of information to quickly free the line and talk to the terminals. The PC, the intelligent workstation, uses lines only for file exchange. It reacts immediately to input and gets its operator's attention during the dialogue. Under these conditions, it is much more efficient in enriching information through personal computer support. Workstation implementation should capitalize on this possibility which opens horizons not known before.

While some of these differences may seem self-evident, what is not evident is the readiness of system analysis to capitalize on the new facilities which are available with PC-based workstations. If we don't do so, we will not exploit as we should the powers of the intelligent workstation for which we will be paying good money.

20.5 Logical Differences Handicapping Efficient Solutions

There are six logical differences which characterize PC and mainframes, therefore handicapping efficient interconnection. They range from codes to linguistics:

1. *Character sets.* PCs and mainframes don't speak the same language—except at the binary level, which is too low. The character is the nest higher level in a coding scheme, but (talking of the IBM line which accounts for about 75 percent of installations), with the exception of PDS and HDBV, communicating between PC and mainframes involves translating EBCDIC to ASCII and vice versa. Hence, even when transferring simple data, like numbers, characters, or words, between the two machines, something must be done to translate between ASCII and EBCDIC. If the translation is not done, communication is impossible. Even ASCII is not standard. And there are also the NA PLPS graphic sets.
2. *The instruction set.* This reference basically concerns the logical instructions that the computer is capable of performing, such as add, subtract, and multiply. PCs and mainframes have different instruction sets: not only the number is different (about 132 for

the mainframe versus 96 for the PC) — but the instructions which exist are also noncompatible. Most don't map together 1:1. Therefore, translating a software product from one machine to another requires considerable work—and should not be done in the first place. Incompatibilities exist at the machine language level; however, not all programs use low-level instruction. Higher levels were created to abstract from low-level (basic) instruction sets. Why not use them?

3. *Incompatibilities also exist with higher-level languages.* Mainframes typically use Cobol, Fortran, and PL/1. The PC uses (or at least should use) C, Basic, and Pascal. Thus, at a higher linguistic level (computer), these two classes of machines also do not speak the same language. Even if Cobol runs on PC, or Basic on MF, there are a great deal of problems. MS Basic, a standard, does not exist on mainframe. Cobol on mainframe is not exactly the same as Cobol on PC.
4. *Program size.* Sometimes program conversion is fully unwise. The PC has too small a central memory, disk space not always present, and the program runs too slow.
5. *Protocol translation.* In human communications there are also different disciplines: the lecture protocol (one to many, broadcasting) and the dialogue protocol (interactive). For machine communications purposes we have SDLC, HDLC, BSC, S/S, and their dialects. Both the mainlines and some of the dialects are incompatible among themselves. Furthermore, the PC mainly works asynchronously (start/stop, S/S). The mainframe mostly works in BSC and SDLC. The large majority of currently available PC-to-mainframe products provide for asynchronous communications. This suits the PC world, but it makes mainframe usage suboptimal. It is one thing to provide a feasible solution, it is quite another to assure that this solution is really using available equipment (software and hardware) to the best advantage.
6. *Data handling.* The mainframe works ISAM, VSAM, and other generally complex data structures. The PC has only recently started with ISAM. Usually it works sequentially. Generally, it handles simple data structures. There is incompatibility in the manner data is stored in files. Mainframes have evolved elaborate schemes for storing information elements and then being able to find them again. They are also fast and can store large amounts of data using complex programming to do it. The PC

cannot yet compete on this ground. There is also the problem of providing a way for the PC to ask the mainframe for some data and have the mainframe retrieve it and send it to the WS. Design and programming time must be involved in creating this type of environment unless one of the products in Section 20.3 is chosen — which is the better approach.

In conclusion, speed and microprocessor power conditions the solution we choose. Files can be transferred from PC to mainframe sequentially and then translated in another structure. Still, because this is not a compatible environment, we have delays, possibilities for errors, and costs. While these logical problems have solutions, it is correct to properly identify them. When we describe a certain problem, we have solved it more than half way. We know the limitations. We are able to decide whether or not we can overcome them—and how.

At a leading bank, the renewal of the foreign exchange application introduced personal workstations, a local area network, and file servers. But the ongoing software on a couple of minicomputers had to be kept in the picture — one because of the charting capability it supported, the other because of a unique fees structure. Linking to the dedicated mini, the datacom engine became a fees server.

Able solutions should involve experts both from the PC and the mainframe side of a user organization — precisely the way IBM did with the Personal Decision Series. Such solutions should account for the fact that the operator of the workstation is the creator of the input. If there is a mistake in the input, the computer should call attention to the error immediately. This is the sense of an interactive environment. When the user is running the computer, transactions happen one at a time. Errors can be corrected as they are made. Transactions are only a few per minute or hour. Within such an environment, we can help provide logical solutions by using the powerful ability of microprocessors to emulate other devices such as channel connected units.

The most commonly simulated channel connected device is the 3274 control unit, a cluster control unit, configured to connect to channels. However, the channel itself is not the most desirable connection point. Channels were designed to control local devices, and in the workstation environment, most of the devices are remote from the mainframe. There are really two ways for a PC to connect into a 3274 control unit. The other is to emulate the 3274 control unit. Which method is chosen depends upon whether or not there is an existing 3274 controller at the workstation.

The now-aged 3270 emulation has become a popular method for

connecting a workstation into the network. 3270 is the standard way since every IBM mainframe is already speaking into several, possibly hundreds, of 3270 devices. The software was designed for them. Also, 3270 line speed is not that bad nor is its error checking. A single communications line can connect several devices. The device is easy to emulate, and the hardware required is not too expensive. However, the fact remains that our sights should focus on the future, not on the past.

20.6 Overcoming Physical Differences

In a PC-to-mainframe linkage, physical differences come to the foreground because we need common forms of I/O to exchange information. The five main most important factors follow:

1. *Input devices.* Mainframes typically input batch, but PC input is through keyboards, graphics tablets, badge readers, the mouse, and menu selection capabilities.
2. *Output devices.* The mainframe output for human usage is hardcopy. With a PC, it is mainly softcopy. It is also interactive.
3. *Storage at floppy level.* The mainframe has none or 8 inch, rarely 5 1/4 inch. The micro typically has 5 1/4 inch; newer models have 3 1/2 inch. Furthermore, neither the 5 1/4 nor the 3 1/2 inch are standard in terms of read and write.
4. *Modems.* For communications purposes, the mainframe uses a sophisticated modem. The PC often employs an acoustic coupler. Although PC-level modems are getting more complex, so are mainframe-oriented devices. The difference remains.
5. *Line speeds.* Lines for mainframe connectivity are 9.6, 56, 64 KBPS. For PC we often use 1.2 KBPS or slower.

The modems and lines factors are related. We cannot put slow modems to work with fast modems. On the other hand, slow modems on a mainframe or high-speed modems on a PC are very expensive solutions. And there is the technical fact that in the sense of a fundamental electrical connector, there is no RS-232 C "standard." RS stands for recommended standard by the Electronics Industries Association (EIA). It is not mandatory, and there are many implementations of the signal connection for an RS 232 interface; they include:

- RTS/DCE
- DTE
- Round female DIN plug
- IBM male to male DB-25
- IBM female to 9-pin C-Shell

What was defined by EIA were the electrical signal characteristics, the mechanical elements of the connection, and a functional assignment for the interchange circuits projected to cover the important elements of telecommunications:

1. Transmit and receive channels.
2. Communication rate.
3. Signal quality checks.
4. Back-and-forth handshaking connections.

But the connector itself was not defined in detail. It was only described, hence, the variations which resulted.

These RS-232 compatibility problems concern all applications and not only PC-to-mainframe connections. This makes their solution much more vital. Although it will be good to standardize on a variant of RS-232, technically this is not feasible. Too many variations are already in use. Overcoming the physical differences has another interesting aspect. Able solutions for PC-to-mainframe communications are necessary to support both ad hoc and preestablished real-time operations between workstations and corporate information resources. A fundamental difference between a real-time distributed system and other types is that the highest and lowest layers of protocols interact with the real world and must reflect its constraints:

- The application layer interacts with one or more physical processes whose dynamics are dictated by laws imposing constraints on communication delays and execution times.
- The physical and data link layers must send and receive signals over transmission channels which are again governed by a basic physical law: the speed of light.

This imposes a minimum delay on the transmission of a signal over the required distance, which fixes an overhead on the time required to access the channel at the medium access control layer. Delay and performance restriction impose constraints on the next upper layer, right up to applications. This upward propagation of time overheads should be minimized so that the application's real-time deadlines can be respected.

The tasks to be performed by a real time LAN dictate the approach to be followed. These may be both transactional in nature and message passing tasks. Messages may be obtained from or sent by sensors or communicated processor-to-processor. From the type of application, it is possible to identify different types of timing requirements—probabilistic or deterministic. A communication system is deterministic when it can be demonstrated that there always is a predictable finite number of state transitions between message arrival and message departure for any given message. This translates into the existence of a physical upper bound for access delays for any given implementation. By contrast, probabilistic timing requirements are expressed as probability distribution functions, with no upper bound. Access delays are characterized by an expected value, a variance, and/or a confidence interval. For example, 90 percent of access delays are less than or equal to 50 milliseconds.

While fast response time is better supported at the PC level using local dedicated resources, access delays to physical storage are at the lowest level in mainframe implementation. This provides a basis for optimization but also contrasts the two support systems, providing ground for careful study regarding resource optimization. Applied to local area networks, this leads to the notion that both ongoing coordination and evolutionary characteristics imply flexibility requirements related to the functionality of the services provided, integration of technological advances, and possible network topology and physical dimensions. It must be possible to perform adaptation and modification without disrupting the functioning of a real-time LAN.

Constraints imposed by the environment include resistance to moisture, high temperature, chemical pollution, and so on. Depending on the nature of the environment, the LAN might have to tolerate physical damage. With classical mainframe implementation, such damage can be catastrophic, resulting in multiple common-mode faults visible in all attached terminals. This is controlled much better through the PC and LAN, where the failure of one WS can leave the system nearly intact.

20.7 Internetworking—Short Haul and Wide Area

Local and wide area networks must communicate with one another. Interconnectivity is typically supported through long-haul solutions provided by telephone companies. Since no single global public networks are likely to be constructed, it is necessary to assure the right disciplines for multinational linkage. There are two objectives of network interconnection:

1. To permit resource sharing between nets.
2. To provide for an efficient exchange of transactions and messages.

The first requires network-network, host-host, and terminal-process communication in some form and may also call for higher-level applications-oriented exchanges. The second brings up the need to determine what the physical and logical points of interconnection should be.

There are three basic interconnection possibilities: packet switching, host, and applications levels. Connecting networks at the packet switch level raises the question of whether there is any distinction between intranet and internet packet protocol. If not, there is little point in distinguishing the demarcation between networks. If the demarcation between networks is an issue, we must study the best way to provide the gateway (see Chapters 17 and 21) — that is, the link between different data transmission disciplines. There are two types of gateways:

1. Working through translation, a solution recommended for point-to-point use.
2. Working through developing, or packaging, recommended for route through.

The gateway may actually be composed of two halves, each associated with its own network. Each half would be responsible only for translating between the internal packet form of its own network and some common internetwork format.

The common format and signaling conventions for data exchange among networks could be standardized in much the same way that the host-to-network interface is standardized. International recommendations specifying the means of connection between public packetswitching networks are being developed. CCITT Study Group VII has produced a specification for the international connection of public packet switching networks. Recommendation X.75 makes extensive assumptions about the overall architecture of interconnected X.25 virtual circuit service to be provided at both ends of the connection. Transaction-type operations are not anticipated, and it is assumed that such services (added later) will require associated changes to the X.75 definition.

The CCITT contribution states the assumed architectural model. It shows some of the requirements of the model not covered by current recommendations. The service is to be provided by concatenated virtual calls across each network that is supporting the call and between the network interconnection nodes that are providing the contact points between the networks. For every call made there are corresponding calls set up across each network and across the internet links. End-to-end significance is assigned to call set up, interrupt, and reset functions but not to flow control.

CCITT projects three interdependent and telecommunicating levels:

1. *Handler*. Includes the physical interfaces which are necessary for X.25 DTE (data terminal equipment) and X.75 STE (signal terminating equipment).

2. *Link*. Addresses itself to the packet transfer procedures.

3. *Packet*. Is concerned with the signaling procedures that provide a reliable mechanism for packet transfer.

Routing information may be included in the call setup packet sent between STE. This routing may be formulated by the source computer, a switching node, and STE, or even the subscriber. If no routing information is provided, best efforts are made by each to route on an appropriate international path. But the procedure is left undefined and subject to local implementation. Also, no mechanism is supplied to update routing information that is no longer valid because of the failure of a node, a network, or a change in routing policy. When a failure occurs in an international call, a reset will normally be required. If a component of the route suffers more serious failure, the call will fail and the user will have to place a new call to continue.

International recommendations specify the nature of the interface between the networks without making any statement about functions performed in the connected nodes. It seems likely that the specified circuit will be high speed and full duplex, low-level signaling being in accordance with X.21 with a procedure from HDLC. If local network packet sizes are other than the standard 128 octets for the internet link, the STE must perform fragmentation and reassembly. Shorter packets that are part of a packet sequence must be combined, and longer packets must be broken into sequences of standard length packets.

Both X.25 and X.75 include window mechanisms for limiting the flow of information on a call. In unspecified references the reasons for this depend on buffer availability, acknowledgment of successful transmission to the next node, and other factors. The size of the window and the number of buffers to be reserved at intermediate nodes can have a critical impact on performance.

Records of each subscriber's use of the network must be maintained, with charges determined on usage. Conversion of usage to charges may be complicated by different charging rates for equivalent data loads in different networks. Hence, tariff information has to be exchanged. The gateways of interconnected networks (STE) must perform full virtual circuit functions for all traffic passing through them on a per-call basis. This means maintaining separate status information on windows, sequence numbers, routing, accounting, and so on for each call. This translates to high processing and memory requirements.

The host-level model of network interconnection assumes that there is a logical gateway between nets, which is viewed by the networks as an ordinary host. This does not rule out a variety of physical implementations ranging from the actual use of a host on two networks as a gateway to a collection of gateway halves taken pair-wise to form a logical internet engine.

To accommodate networks which have not yet been designed to support internet service, it is possible to postulate a packet format with an internet header encapsulated in a local network packet. The latter can be used to transport internet packets from the point of entry to the point of exit in a local network. Gateways use the internet header to select the next local network address and the appropriate local network services. This way, source and destination hosts share a common end-to-end protocol. Another alternative consists of maintaining the X.25 links to subscribers on each side of the connection but operating a single virtual circuit segment between the source and destination data communicating equipment. This has been successfully used internally in several networks, notably Datapac in Canada and the Arpanet in the United States.

performed in the [illegible] It seems likely that the situation [illegible] will be [illegible] [illegible] from HDLC. [illegible] [illegible] must perform [illegible] and reassemble smaller packets [illegible] packet [illegible] into [illegible] packets.

[illegible] information on a call [illegible] [illegible] [illegible] number of [illegible] [illegible].

Reassembly [illegible] cannot be [illegible] [illegible] different networks. Hence, [illegible] gateway [illegible] must [illegible] [illegible] [illegible].

The [illegible] interface [illegible] [illegible] [illegible].

To [illegible] [illegible] possible [illegible] packets [illegible] The latter [illegible] point [illegible] network [illegible] [illegible] [illegible] United States.

Chapter

21

Interconnecting and Managing Distributed Databases

21.1 Introduction

The key to the handling of multimedia databases is the able design installation and management of gateways. A gateway is an electronic link between two computers that allows:

1. Users having access to the first computer also have access to the second computer without needing a separate connection. This second, third, or fourth computer can be housed in the same building or can be located thousands of miles away. The connection itself may be made through baseband LAN, broadband LAN, terrestrial microwaves, satellite link, or plain old telephone service.
2. Databases needing to exchange information with other databases do so without requiring special solutions or ad hoc connections. There is a significant difference of requirements between

> implementation Class 1 and Class 2. This difference suggests that the gateway will either connect online interactively or provide remote batch processing. For both, the gateway operator will be responsible for developing and maintaining the service. In a LAN environment, this operator will be the user organization itself.

The user organization also has another major duty to fulfill for interconnecting and managing distributed databases. This is properly planned, able and punctual database administration (DBA). While the need for DBA duties has been known for a dozen years, never before were we faced with trillion-byte (terabyte) volumes and such great diversity from megabyte microfiles to terabyte database computers.

21.2 Bridges and Gateways

"Gateway" is used as a general term, but it is often reserved for the more complex implementation of data communications. "Bridges" is a term often employed for simpler, homogeneous channel connectivity. Figures 21.1 and 21.2 help explain the difference. In Figure 21.1, a broadband network directly interconnects workstations through the appropriate BIU. In this particular installation, channels 4 and 5 are reserved for the type of attachment being shown. These two homogeneous channels of the broadband are interlinked through a bridge. It makes communication feasible between devices attached to channel 4 and those on channel 5.

The broadband local area network can be divided through frequency division multiplexing into channels which are distinct from one another but use identical software protocols, compatible packet sizes, and a single overall homogeneous address space. These channels are interconnected by bridges, which are midway in complexity between the repeaters used in a multisegment contention bus network and the gateways employed in an internetworking environment. Looking at Figure 21.2, we can see that two baseband LANs are connected to channels of the broadband. Although more than one BAB of the same type can be attached per channel, these connections call for a subnetworking discipline. The latter is typically supported through a software interface resident in an intelligent device. This is a relatively simple gateway and the cheapest way to do it is through another PC.

Gateways are often protocol translators and may vary in terms of

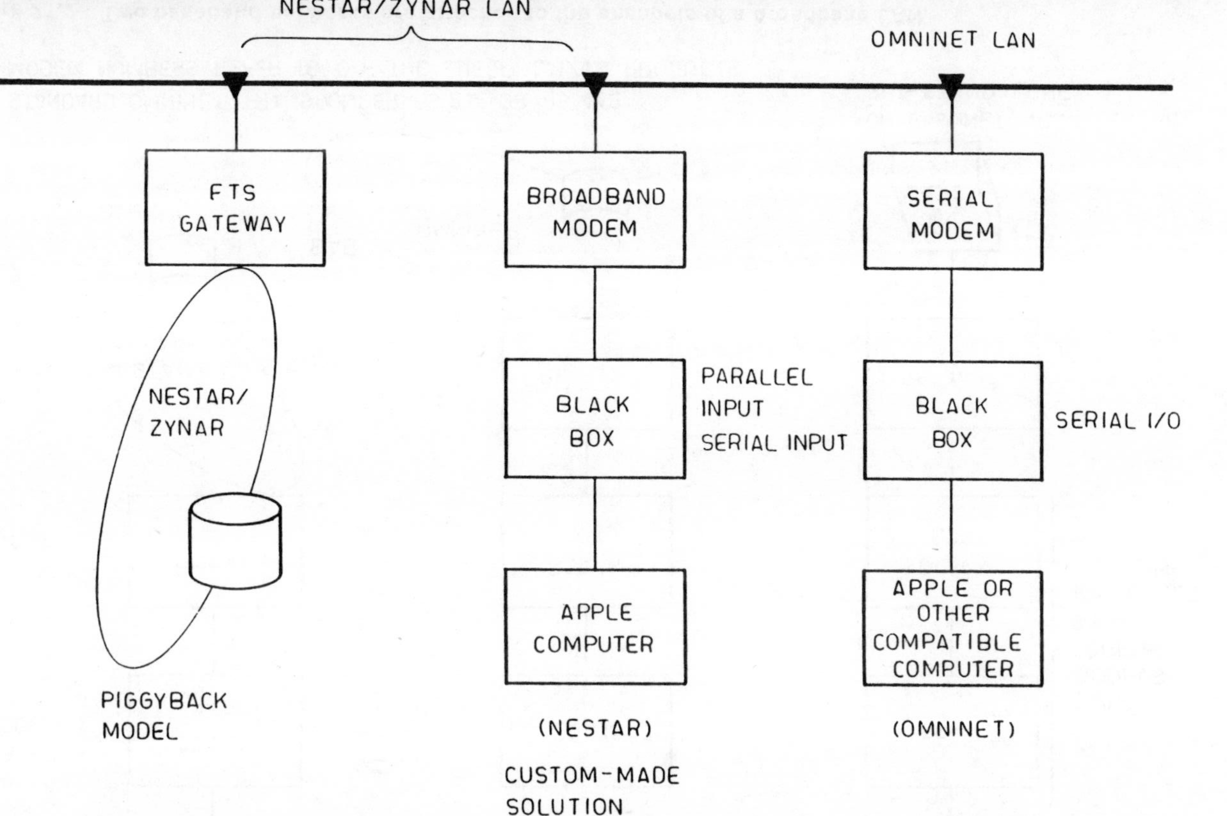

Figure 21.1 A broadband network interconnects WS through appropriate BIU, as well as a baseband LAN.

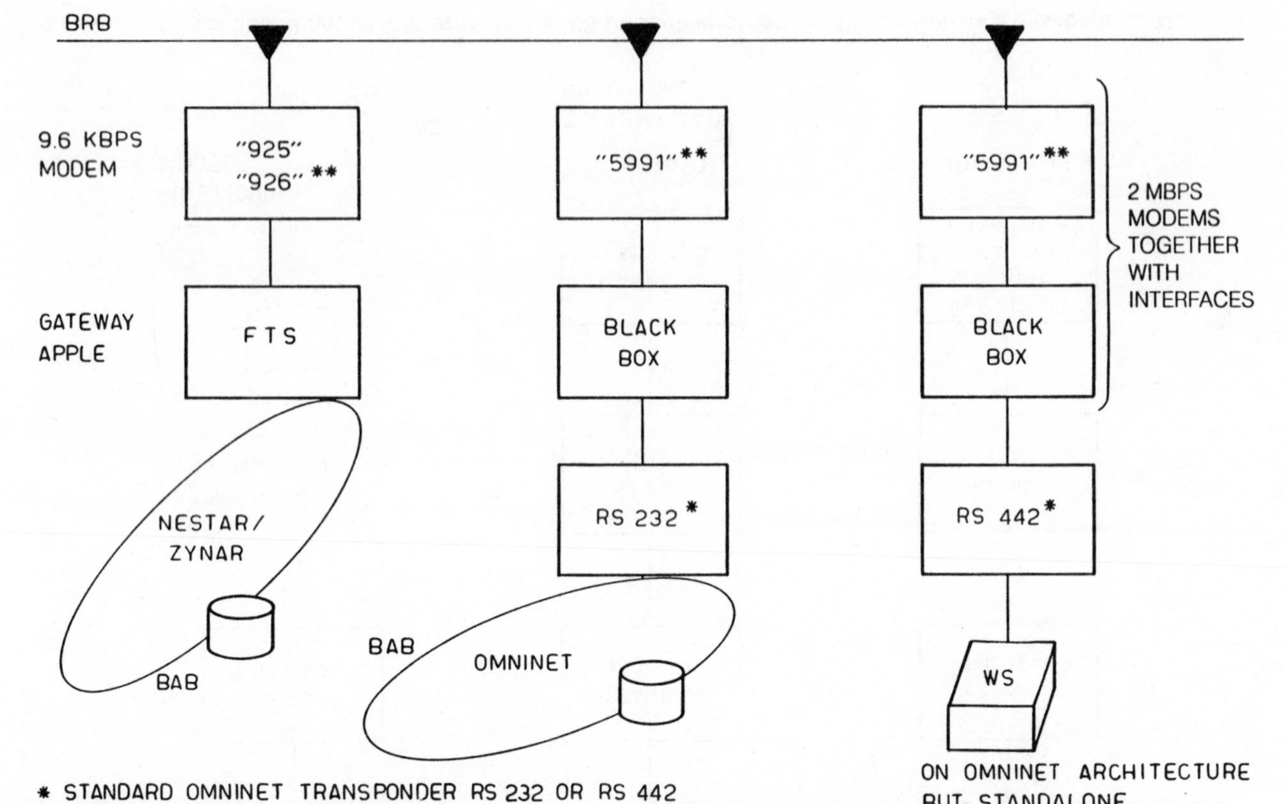

Figure 21.2 Two baseband networks are attached to the channels of a broadband LAN.

supported functionality. A protocol translator unwraps the packet to recover the original message; it analyzes the header to determine whether this, say, datagram contains control information intended for the gateway or data intended for a host farther on. In the latter instance, the gateway must make a routing decision. There are four possibilities. First, the destination host is directly connected to one of the networks to which the gateway is attached. Or, a second possibility, the destination host is on a network that has a gateway directly connecting to the present one. This is known as a neighbor gateway. A third possibility is that to reach the destination host, more than one additional gateway must be traversed. This is known as a multiple-hop situation. Fourth, the gateway does not know the destination address. In this case, it returns an error message to the source of the datagram.

In any case, before actually sending data, the gateway may need to proceed with certain administrative operations (e.g., to fragment the datagram to accommodate a smaller packet size). Each fragment becomes an independent datagram, wrapped in a lower-layer packet, and queued for transmission. The gateway may also limit the length of its queue for each network it attaches to so as to avoid having a slow network penalize a faster one.

In larger networks, this process is repeated through as many gateways as it takes to reach the destination. Eventually, the destination host recovers the datagram from its network wrapping. If fragmentation has occurred, the fragments must be buffered and data reassembled. This activity requires end-to-end error control. Control is made feasible through the cyclic redundancy check of the packet. A checksum is computed at each gateway for error detection and the appropriate corrective action is taken.

Gateways can also act as transmission speed converters. Most local area networks typically operate in the range of 1 to 50 MBPS. By contrast, wide area networks generally work at much lower speeds, usually less than 64 KBPS. Often the long-haul link is 1.2 to 9.6 KBPS. The LAN, moreover, usually uses no intermediate switches to route packets, and it is fast enough to deliver one packet before another is transmitted. In a wide area, there may be a number of packets outstanding, or undelivered, while still more are being transmitted. This type of speed mismatch can result in a local area network flooding a slower long-haul network with packets. Without an effective flow control procedure, the wide area network may simply discard excess packets. Other housekeeping routines are also needed and performed by the gateway. If packets do not arrive at their destination in the order in which they are sent, it may be left to the LAN host to buffer and reorder them. This is a policing task the gateway may be asked to perform.

Some of the gateway functionality is present in the bus interface unit, as shown in Figure 21.3. It suggests different attachments on a

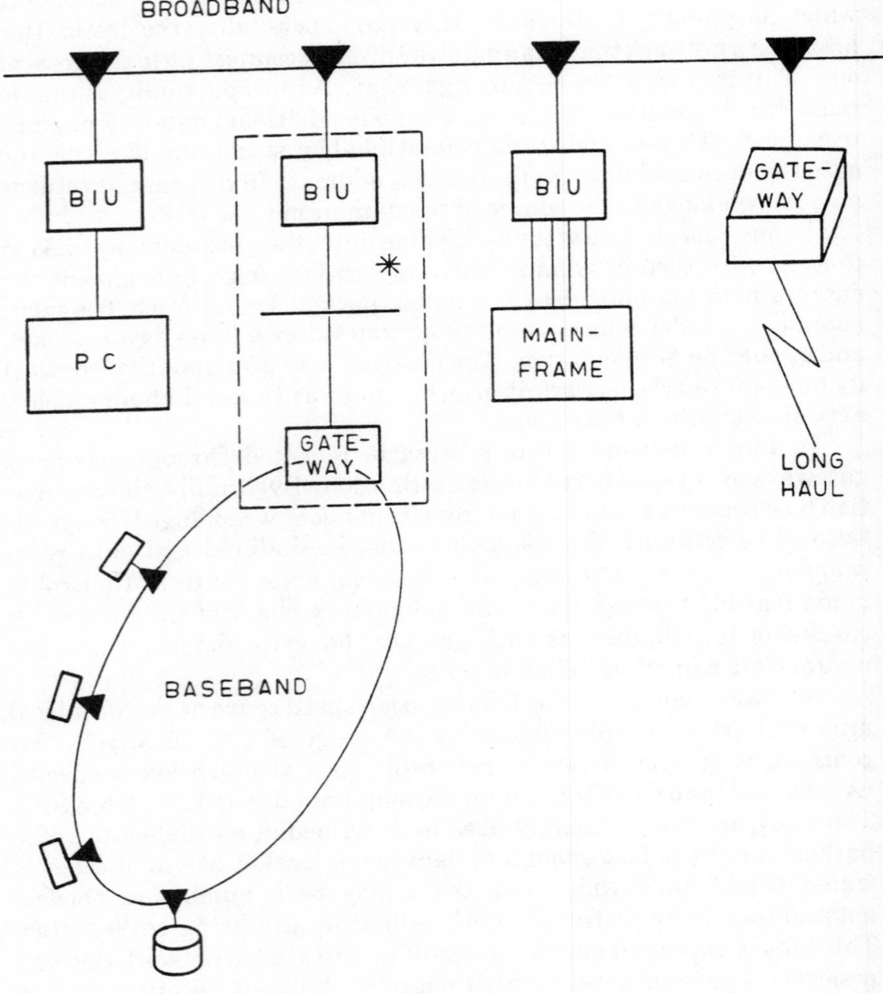

Figure 21.3 Gateway functionality supported through the bus interface unit.

broadband LAN, one of which is a gateway for long-haul communications, another is a BIU for mainframe interconnection. The gateway generally includes:

1. Addressing schemes.
2. The ability to handle different packet sizes (fragmentation)
3. Provision of interfaces to long-haul networks (for instance, X.25, SNA).
4. Intranetwork routing, including flow and congestion control.
5. Access control functionality.
6. Connection-oriented (virtual circuit) and/or connectionless (datagram) services.
7. Connection-oriented transport service (a file transfer, as opposed to electronic mail) able to handle timeouts.
8. Internetwork timing procedures to facilitate successful transmission.
9. Error detection, correction, and recovery.
10. Status reporting on internetwork activity.

Compared to gateways, a bridge is a relatively simple device for linking two local networks that use the same protocols. The functions of the bridge are few and simple:

- It reads all packets transmitted on network I.
- It buffers each accepted packet for retransmission on II using the medium access protocol.
- It does the same for II to I traffic.

The bridge makes no modification to the content or format of the packets it handles. It does not encapsulate them with an additional header. If any modifications, additions, or other operations are necessary, a gateway must be used. Nevertheless, the bridge provides a transparent extension to the local network so that it appears to all stations on the two local networks that there is a single network. This is typical of a connection between two homogeneous LANs. The function is performed by two half bridges, one on each network.

A bridge links two channels or subnetworks, generally at a location at which they are physically adjacent. It selectively repeats packets from each of them to the other according to a filter function. In addition, since it buffers the packets it repeats, it can also perform speed matching functions, if necessary. Typically, a bridge contains:

- Two channel interfaces, one appropriate for each of the two it interconnects
- A limited amount of packet buffer memory
- A control element, able to implement the needed filter function

The goal of the latter is to decide which messages to pull off one channel and buffer until it has an opportunity to retransmit it to the other. This becomes slightly more complex if the two channels are not equal, whether in a physical or logical sense, with each acting as a subnetwork.

21.3 Subnetworking for Electronic Message Services

With subnetworks a variety of technologies, protocols, and data rates can be used in a single logical network. When we have alternatives, we can use each to its best advantage. For instance, a subnetwork can be constructed with a contention protocol, using CATV coaxial cable. The next one may be a ring subnetwork, using twisted pair already installed in an office environment for voice communications purposes. These two subnetworks would typically work at different data rates, the interface between the two handling the speed difference. Subnetworking also provides an orderly means for facing growth in traffic.

The modularity made feasible through subnetworking can be most helpful in optimizing both the servers and the workstations attached to them. Contention-based local area networks perform best, providing high throughput with low delay, when they are not heavily loaded. If a higher-speed technology is not available or change is too costly, as traffic grows with time, it may be desirable to split the network into two or more interconnected subnetworks. Since the gateways interconnecting the subnetworks are selective in their repeating of packets, gaging prevents the saturation of one of the subnetworks. both flow control, and store and forward are necessary to assure that traffic density on each subnetwork will be less than that of a monolithic network structure.

The gateway can buffer packets if a store and forward activity is available. The intelligent gateway will follow strategies, such as waiting for an opportunity to transmit on a given subnetwork, according to the control structure of that subnetworking, which reflects the prevailing line discipline. The latter should be chosen based on the work of the network or subnetwork. Packet buffers also aid a system in handling instantaneous cross-traffic peaks during which the traffic offered by one subnetwork exceeds the available capacity of the other. Design decisions require a great deal of perspective in implementation requirements. Fine tuning cannot be done without sensitivity to type and load of dataflow.

The partitioning of the workstations and servers into subnetworks should be executed along properly defined lines. A subnetwork, for instance, would group together WSs that have high traffic rates among themselves and substantially lower traffic rates to other hosts. Traffic across the gateway can thus be minimized. A greater fraction of all packets will stay within their subnetwork of origin if information exchange has locality. Subnetworking can also be advantageous with a number of solutions to problems involving computers and communications. Figure 21.4 suggests a hierarchical network structure as applied by ICOT, the Japanese New Generation Computer Project. It has been used to interconnect fifth-generation computers the Personal Sequential Inference (PSI) engine. and intelligent databases.

Delta is the forerunner of the file server of the future. It features both international database capabilities with knowledge bank management system (KBMS) and a relational extensional database run under a relational DBMS. This is an excellent example of local area network use to construct loosely coupled systems with flexible configuration and wide connectivity. It brings together different technologies but also helps document how LAN approaches and interconnect capabilities may be a pivot point of future solutions.

In this, as in similar implementations, one of the functions to be assigned to the gateway is routing. Routing techniques which have no impact at all on addressing can also be implemented with bridges, usually at the expense of the greater complexity:

- A simple routing function can be assured using a finite state machine as its control element.
- A more complex one may involve a periodic exchange of information among interfaces on the network to determine correct routing according to dynamic requirements.

When both messaging systems served through WSs and heavy duty database communications are involved, sensitivity to type and load of data flow becomes critical. Electronic message services are a good

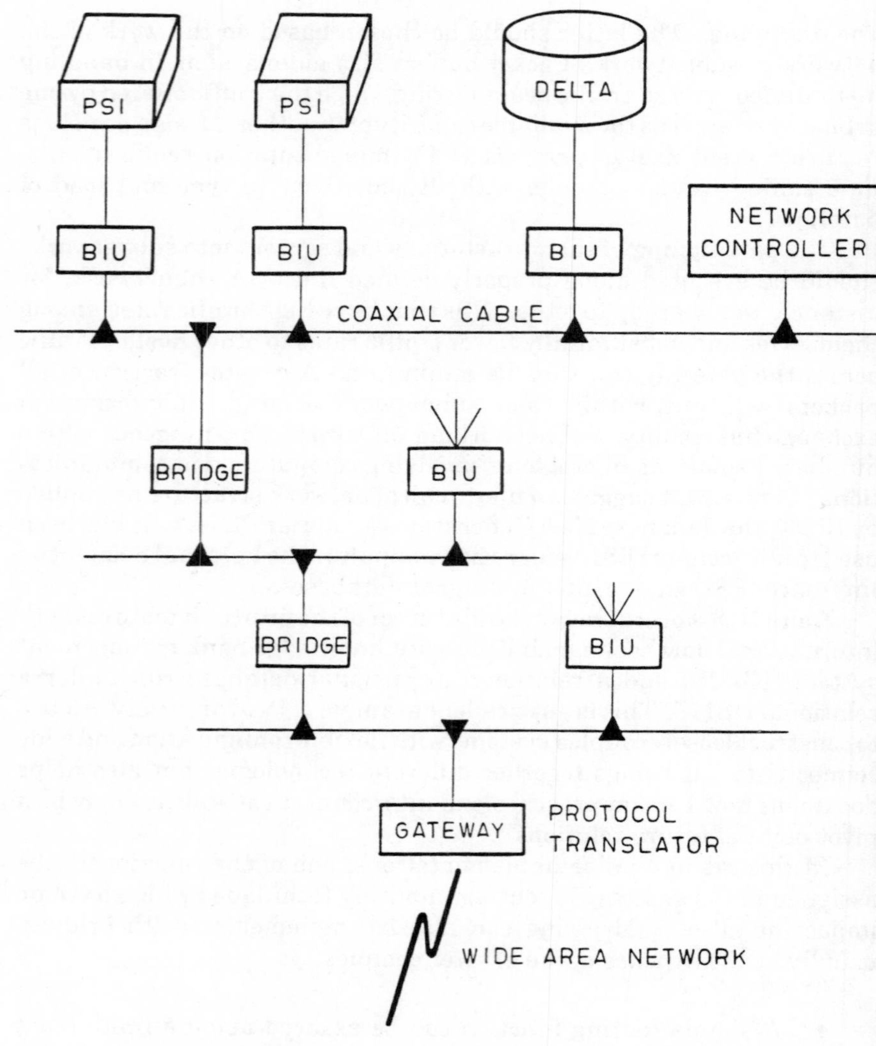

Figure 21.4 A hierarchical network sturcture implemented by ICOT, Tokyo, Japan

example of this. Electronic mail, for instance, requires a mail naming system to assure mail is sent to the right place. Data retrieve is a distributed capability, including text and data collection features. All addresses of attached devices to a network must be unique, but the technology of the two subnetworks being bridged can be different. It is important for the interface to connect the networks together in a transparent fashion.

Electronic mail, data retrieve, decision support, and expert systems are fundamental in an environment servicing professionals and managers. All these activities are highly dependent on communications — hence on networking. Dependence on electronic mail, for example, has become as big as dependence on the telephone. This brings up three basic problems: office-wide connectivity, home connectivity, and business travel connectivity. It also emphasizes the level of sophistication which is presently required from networking. X.25 is generally treated as a communications facility—but what is really needed is a complete communications and computer architecture.

Solutions must not only allow task-to-task operation but must also permit effective handling of a range of applications. End-user-oriented applications need to have no knowledge of the line they use — but they do require a value-added capability. The basic premise is to move communications processing out of the host and into a network switching node. This is not a new idea. It has been used for many years in front ending (FEP). But front ending is good for mainframes. It does not make economic sense to FEP a mini by a mini or a micro by a micro.

Moving the communications disciplines into the node switch opens a wide horizon of gateways, which is absolutely important to managing complex environments. It also permits low-cost devices to be attached directly to the network as opposed to multithreading bigger computers. Thus, subnetworking solutions can give computer independence. If we need to add more computer power, we add another computer. We do not have to rewire the attachments of low-cost devices. In addition, as low-cost devices move from dumb terminals to PCs, windowing becomes a challenge. It can be handled effectively through node switches and bus interface units.

The networks of the future will involve integration of different technologies, making it feasible to have choices depending on needed services and availabilities. The key issue is that of designing an environment which is flexible and adaptable.

21.4 Database Access to Serve Management Purposes

Since we do not know what the technological environment of year 2000 will look like, we have to keep our options open and build a flexible adaptable architecture:

- Technology is largely unpredictable.
- Applications — particularly those of a managerial type — evolve outside known patterns.
- New systems being designed are extremely sensitive to both technology and applications.

The network is a utility upon which we can build more services. It is not a monolithic communications approach. Nowhere is this statement more valid than in a computer and communications environment designed to serve management purposes. Management queries are ad hoc. They are not preestablished in their nature nor do they steadily address the same set of information elements.

Managers and professionals use workstations, local area networks, and gateways to access online collections of interrelated information elements stored at different places to serve different users. Access to distributed databases for retrieval, modification, addition, or deletion of IEs may use the same or different modules of code — but the IEs in the database are structured, and the database has an existence independent of the programs which use the IE. Distributed databases are typically accessed and manipulated concurrently by many different users and applications. They support online transaction processing, interactive query response, and electronic message services. All these are communications-intense activities.

While the communications network and the database network are two distinct entities, they are also interrelated. Databases can be private or public, but they are all accessed online. In London, for example, there are some 10 major sources of financial and stock market information and many minor ones. As far as users are concerned, this is rich information. The users' problem is the lack of one logical system supported through gateways. The end user should not be exposed to heterogeneity, which is the typical case today. Each public financial database requires a quite different terminal and presents a user protocol that is incompatible with the others. Hence, some service companies are developing a set of gateway facilities to allow the connection at several such services into a single protocol system.

Once the homogeneity problem has been solved, other salient problems will arise. The manager and the professional accessing databases would like to be assisted through an online data dictionary that contains:

- Definition of all available information elements
- Identification of all data sources and users of the data
- Cross-reference between information elements and user definitions of logical IE
- Logical and physical interrelationships, organization, and representation of IEs
- Relationships between the various information elements including semantic relations

The data dictionary is a management tool for control over information resources embodied in corporate and public databases (Figure 21.5). It is also a corporate resource which must be highly protected. Only the database administrator (DBA) should be allowed to add, update, or modify the data dictionary.

The DBA defines the global logical description of the database. This is the schema (or view) considered by the ANSI Data Description Committee. The user view (or subschema) is a description of a portion of the database, a specification of which record types from the schema, and which IEs in each of the record the user is entitled to obtain. It also defined interrelationships between the different record types the user is permitted to consider. As networks have intelligent nodes and gateways, databases are supported by DBMS and data dictionaries. They also require security mechanisms, integrity constraints, and audit trails which should be integrated with the security facilities supported by the communications proper system.

Thus, it can be seen that the development, implementation, and maintenance of a modern data communications and database system is not just a matter of adopting a LAN or providing long-haul linkages. It requires an interactive database organization as well as algorithms and heuristics to permit the efficient handling of information. We must also establish techniques for temporary relations as the user defines the functions to be executed. The levels of detail may be general index, analytical index, glossary, abstracts, parts, chapters, pages, paragraphs, or special functions. The types of interactions a user employs may include:

1. Menu selection to define an operation (browse, locate, query).
2. Menu selection to specify the type and level of response to be shown on the screen.

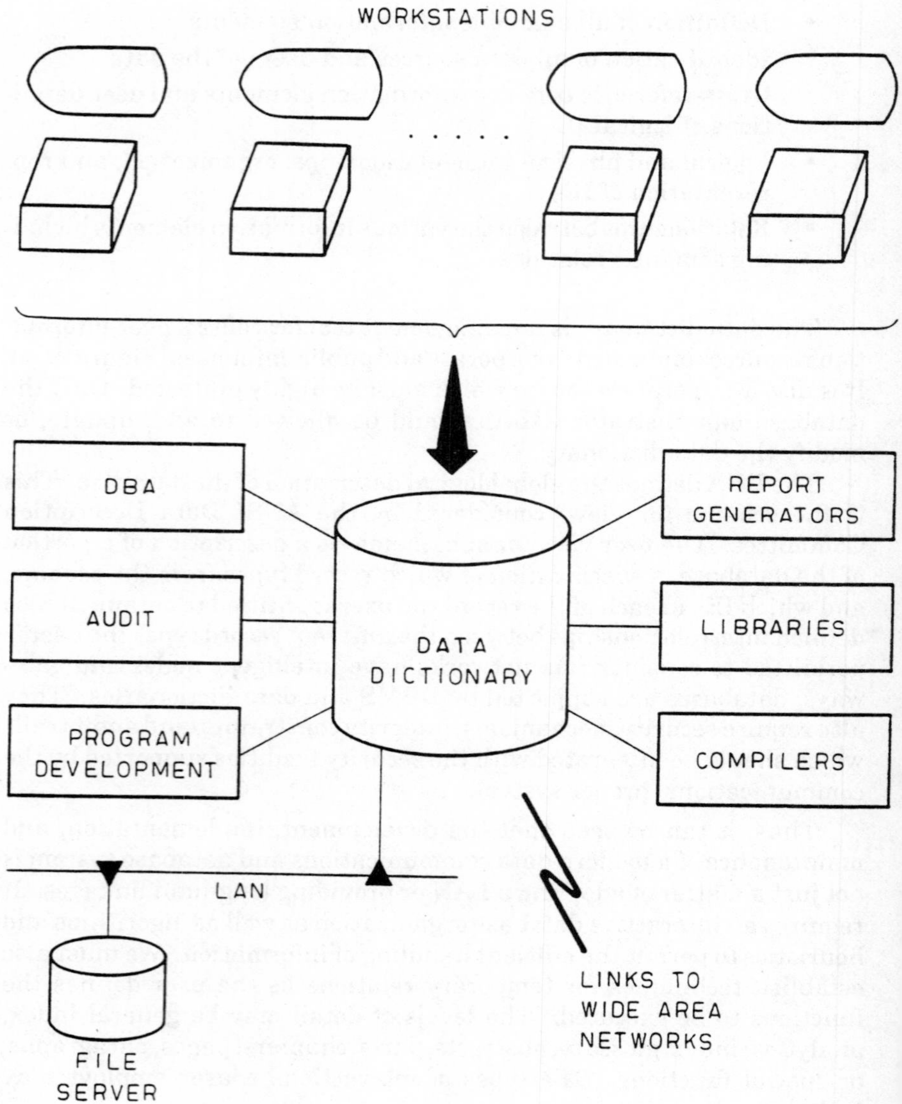

Figure 21.5 Role of a data dictionary in private and public databases.

3. Control to stop browsing action and select an information element.
4. Direct access if the address is recalled.
5. Forward-backward page switching.

At the user's workstation, a split screen may be needed to present different displays. The user may specify that text and data should be presented as graphically as possible. A sophisticated system should be able to interact with the user to define the desired presentation.

21.5 Morgan Stanley and the Database Challenge

One of the best examples of successful approaches to facing the growing database and data communications challenge is offered by Morgan Stanley, which has good database engineers but a database communications and database culture. Morgan Stanley also uses 4GL. When Natural came out, they decided to rewrite backoffice applications and obtained a 500 percent improvement in productivity. They also radically altered their orientation to information systems priorities and direction on the premise that management needs have changed substantially and technology has made huge strides, leaving behind the concepts of the past.

Today, 98 percent of the code running on the Morgan Stanley mainframes is 4GL, while the cost in machine cycles has been contained at 10 percent. The 500 percent productivity gain (through 4GL) permitted management to specialize its information systems on serious problems such as expert systems. One of these is Plumpicker, which is a shallow artificial intelligence construct able to exploit the bank's own database as well as public ones. A client firm asks the bank for advice on the possible acquisition of a company meeting a number of characteristics. Typically some 40 to 60 specifications are given — yearly business, product line, market appeal, center of operations management culture, and so on.

The classical approach to an acquisition problem has been researched by the bank's professionals. This takes time, as most of this work has been manual. Now such information is available in distributed databases — both the bank's own and public databases. But it is also necessary to exploit online database contents and to do so in an expert manner. This is the mission of Plumpicker for acquisition and of White Knight for a defensive policy against a predator. The expert systems, each in its own domain of specialization, are given the client's specifications. They operate online, use communications disciplines as required, execute an intelligent database search, and return a documented list of suggestions. This is a good example of data communications and database implementation with expert systems support. It is also a sound approach to savings in software development. In a business applications environment, routines for most of the 3600 terminals operating online in this financial institution are mainly of the database access type.

The link to Europe is through London, and public facilities are used when valid. Morgan Stanley has written its own software for cooperative processes, mailbox management, and so on. This application permits scripts (calls through smart keys) for mailboxes. Two routines hook IBM mainframe: ADACTC is a channel-to-channel link through adapter; AVTAM is part of the networking concept. The system is efficient. Morgan Stanley is handling 45,000,000 database calls per 24 hours.

Fourth- and fifth-generation language implementation should not be indiscriminate. If all computer-intense programs were written in 4GLs, the data center might double the installed computer power. Selective database-type usage reduces the cycle's overcharge to less than 10 percent. But, in terms of productivity gains, it is wise to obtain a 500 percent improvement for the 98 percent of the works, at 10 percent of total hardware costs. Besides, machine cost is steadily dropping while human costs are on the increase. Economics dictate the 4GL road as the wise course. It is even better to use AI-enriched constructs.

One of the significant gains Morgan Stanley obtained is that there is no more backlog. This has had its impact on the way the infocenter is implemented. They centralized the database and systems development staff and since all development is in 4GL, there is no reason to have dedicated staff for the infocenter or for end-user programming. This is an important effect of a full-scale 4GL policy and it should be given full attention: no backlog, no strong desire from the user community to do their own programming. Only the internal auditors and controllers write their own software. There have been other positive results. Ad hocs are generated with new ventures, such as the opening of the Tokyo Stock Exchange.

Morgan Stanley closely follows technological developments, and it is right in doing so. Innovation cycles with computers and communications differ greatly from what we have known in the past. To protect one's investment, this has to be kept in mind. Morgan Stanley also manages a very impressive database of over 100 gigabytes — growing at the rate of about 25 GB/year. This growth would have been much greater if sunset clauses were not in effect.

21.6 Focusing on Distributed Database Design

Morgan Stanley and others have shown that a great deal of emphasis should be placed on data communication and database design — particularly so when we deal with multimedia environments. The goals must be reasonable, attainable, and technically sound. They could be divided into three classes:

1. *Device independence.* All protocols used for communications and databasing, as well as all routines at the gateways or relating to memory devices, should be transparent to the user. One logical network and one-level memory must be adopted as a policy and served through virtual storage and virtual terminals.
2. *Location independence.* This means that within a distributed environment, database handling should assure that the specific information element location is transparent to the user, the program, or the process. This presupposes that no physical addressing is being employed, relational and associative-type solutions being the favored choice.
3. *Tuning of the update mechanism.* This is one of the most challenging problems with distributed databases. It means that the system must provide for continuing updating in the face of steady change and with the probability that some of the component database sections may be failing or may crash. But simultaneously microsecond-level update is not always necessary. For business environments 24-hour database synchronization goals are realistic. They point to a desire to obtain practical results with good assurance of functionality and at reasonable costs.

Design decisions on the timing of database and data communications actions should account for the fact that the system we develop and support will be integrated into an applications environment that both supports other facilities and imposes operating constraints. Supporting software should be modular. Modules of the transaction software will handle the transaction proper, traffic issues, and system commands. The command interpreter executes commands and operates on one logical but distributed database. The command distributor routes the commands to the place where IEs reside and handles transaction recovery.

While database handlers administer the local database segments on file servers and other hosts, the communications software acts as the transport mechanism. The mechanism should see to it that structure and organization are horizontal. With the exception of data dictionary and control functions, every nodal file server is at the same hierarchical level as all other nodal file servers — whether on LAN or stand-alone. In a peer-to-peer system, each nodal database section is an entity by itself. But all nodes taken together compose one integrated database — at least in a logical sense, if not in physical reference.

Every end user communicates with this integrated database via the communications network and its components (LAN, long haul). A transaction may involve the examination and/or updating of various parts of the integrated database, parts which may reside in different nodes. A transaction may be divided by the communications system into subtransactions; each subtransaction is concerned with information in only one node. A database command distributor can:

1. Establish in which node the relevant information is located.
2. Control the overall handling of a transaction.
3. Assure data is brought in an error-free form from the node where it resides to the location where it is needed.

A command interpreter program receives the database commands and is responsible for their execution with respect to the local database. At each node, the database handler manages the access to the database. The following commands are typically used:

- *Start transaction.* This indicates that a new transaction has started. The database software responds with a (unique) identification for that transaction.
- *Operating command(s).* The start transaction may be followed by any number of commands.

After all commands have been executed, a transaction may be ended in either of two ways:

- *Back-out transaction.* The transaction is revoked. The commanded changes are not executed.
- *End transaction.* This is the counterpart of start transaction and is used when all commands have been executed. The transaction is made final; all commanded changes in the database are incorporated definitely into the information elements.

A data manipulation language provides an interface between database control and the outside world. The commands used by this language consist of the following parts: Operation defines the function to be performed, trans-ID identifies the transaction to which this subtransaction belongs, and key specifies a value to be used in locating the node where the data is stored. Parameters tailor the execution of the operation to current requirements. A transport protocol able to provide an interface between the communication software in different nodes is another necessary component. Its mission is to handle those aspects of the transport which are not covered by the underlying communication network, such as the division of messages into packets:

- It is concerned with getting the information to the other node in a reliable way.
- It may be aware of the format of the information, it is completely unaware of its meaning.

The contents of the information which is passed is known only to the two database handlers involved in the transaction. User packets should be segmented at the level permissible by the network. Segmentation of the message can be actuated from the user terminal (if qualified) or from the proper interface packet assembly and disassembly concentrator. This assures that not only packet segmentation but also terminal characteristics (buffers, code) will be observed. Transport characteristics necessarily interface with database management, sharing common interfaces at the levels of session and presentation control.

21.7 Agile User-Level Interfaces

Data communications and databasing are two of the basic networks on which we should focus attention. Data processing is a third; the fourth is that of end-user functions (EUF). New software solutions are necessary regarding form and screen handling for interactive communications. Both message-driven and transaction-driven real-time monitors are needed to control communications, including protocol and formatting capabilities. Other facilities should be provided as the application demands. In a data entry situation, the software on buffered video displays and/or intelligent terminals performs data entry checks:

- In case of a data error, the cursor is positioned in the corresponding field.
- An error message is displayed in a special field.

An error message is displayed on the screen, for instance, when there is an error in an input message or when a program error is discovered. All error messages are stored in a library on disk, but the most recently used error messages will be found in a dynamic pool in main memory.

Most computer-assisted applications demand the creation of all screen forms in a dialogue manner with the user defining the starting position on the screen and the length, format, and position for each field in the record. A message-control table can be used for each form. Its job is to connect each of the workstation's function keys with an applications program (or a new screen form). Master forms can be used for starting terminal routines.

Since all references to the library are logged together with the form number and user identification, it is possible to get useful applications statistics. The processing of a dialogue step can easily be divided into more program modules by a call statement that transfers a message record to the next applications program. Formatting, correction, and sending and receiving messages can be kept independent of the processing in the applications programs. Programs can be created, tested, changed, compiled, and linked at any of the LAN workstations by users with authority to use appropriate functions.

Save areas can be provided for each WS. They usually dynamically vary in size depending on how they are used. For security and authentication purposes WS users must identify themselves to get access to the system, the identification being followed by a password. Unauthorized attempts to update a file or use a form should interrupt the terminal routine and an error message should be output to the screen. All calls resulting in any kind of file update must be logged on a special recovery file.

Recovery, security (to field content), dynamic manipulation of descriptors, ability to handle screen masks, cross-referencing (programs, tables, screens), and output and input control functionality are among the basic supports to be featured by the online system. Distributed database characteristics should be featured by location. Messages and transactions must be handled with equal ease. The end user should be able to logically handle defined views over distributed areas. These tools must be easy to learn and menu driven. LAN and wide area connectivity must be transparent to the user.

Integrated software, such as spreadsheet, graphics, and calendaring, should be available to every WS. Systems specialists should control, document, and confirm operational criteria. They should study the maximum number of transactions per second, response time, large database access, and formatting capabilities. They should also assure flexibility in the configuration of end user's multiple resources.

PART 5

Applications of Local Area Networks

Chapter

22

Focusing Computer Technology on the End User's Needs

22.1 Introduction

Computer technology in business and industry has become increasingly distributed. Slowly, but surely, it is designed and controlled by functional line managers. By all indications, while this trend will continue, we are on the threshold of another basic change: the integration of a firm's disparate computer systems within an overall architecture which will comprise both local area and long haul networks, center on communicating, distributed databases, and involve tens of thousands of workstations per unified logical network. Such developments will not come overnight, but neither will it take decades to materialize. IBM projects for 1992-94 client networks, with 150,000 or more terminals shared between LANs and wide area connectivity, access terabyte databases located in many sites. (IBM already has on its own worldwide networks an estimated 180,000 terminals.)

To take advantage of evolutionary trends, we must have available an architecture for planned system design, building every module in the architecture to a carefully defined framework. For consistency reasons, such framework should remain steady through generations of online systems. The system architecture should be stable for 20 to 25 years and see five or six different product generations. Such continuity will allow a thorough exploitation of LAN advantages:

- Local-level integrated capability for workstations and servers
- High-speed data channels
- Sharing of database resources
- Logically routed switched circuits
- Common gateway to long haul
- Store and forward through file server and gateway
- Printer spooling

Precisely because of these advantages, local area network suppliers expect sales to grow explosively, since LANs are the most efficient way to link personal computers. One of the most recent driving forces is the belated appreciation that the solution lies in networking and in paying due attention to the complexities of the job.

22.2 Procedure for LAN Implementation

A good way to decide whether or not to employ a local area network solution is to ask the question: “Am I *really* happy with my current system based on minicomputers and mainframes”? If you are, stick to the approach you now have. If not, try WSs and LANs. The preceding 21 chapters help provide the information about what a LAN is and what it can do. But it is also wise to visit installations with LANs and WSs and to use specialist advice. The proper know-how is the key to getting good results. If an organization chooses to use outside resources, (consultants, software makers, hardware suppliers, or LAN manufacturers), it should make a solid contract with clear-cut objectives. It should definitely train and involve its own specialists in the project. Understanding what is being done and learning from it has always been a valid approach. Management should also set up a timetable for the technology transfer. It should not just focus on the current application.

The following list outlines 15 rules for LAN implementation. They start with proper emphasis at the workstation level.

1. Establish current and projected need at the WS level.
2. Do an analysis of current work, then integrate the improvements that high technology makes feasible.
3. Think about and study your findings in interactive terms.
4. Examine selected applications, collect references, establish how other firms did the job—and the results they have obtained.
5. Quantify the text, graphics, and data load: (I/O, storage, DP/WP, communications).
6. Evaluate alternative solutions—within the operating environment of the projected implementation.
7. Make a prototype (DB, DC, DP, EUF). Thereafter, proceed with a critical test.
8. Write a report—to clarify your own ideas and derive lessons.
9. Select a user to involve in the design of the WS solution.
10. Review your prototype and, in the light of this experience, evaluate how, when, and why.
11. Decide OS, language, applications, and specifications.
12. Report to management suggesting a solution (WS, LAN), a budget, and a timetable.
13. Get approval and get going. Take the first LAN and some WSs—but set yourself a *short* time period (4 to 6 months maximum) for the implementation.
14. Train the user, then handhold.
15. Do not saturate the system. Remember that at a fraction of rated capacity, contention will slow down transport.

Solutions currently employed in terms of office automation must be taken into full account in order to avoid incompatibilities or inconsistencies as the work goes on. Commendable results can be achieved if we pay attention to WS design, obtain end-user observation, correctly project database access, assure that applications are hardware independent, and avoid overcrowding the application. Once the first application is complete, we should proceed with the second. We should not lose time. Neither should we worry about perfection. If we are careful, we will approach it the second and third time around.

It is a sound advice never to lose sight of the technological advances affecting PCs, disks, LANs, and practically every systems component. But it is even better advice to look at user requirements in a realistic manner and try to satisfy them. A system is designed for the consumer of the service. Our search for successful solutions will have much to do with the perception of user needs and their satisfaction in a timely, accurate way. *Perception is knowledge*. We should not follow traditional paths. We should look for the unusual, the nonexplored field. That is where the business opportunity will most likely reside.

There is an Automated Analytical Trading Group at Morgan Stanley. The group is involved in the development and execution of algorithms that buy and sell securities—and its work is subject to rigorous experimental validation. The group maintains its own computational facility based on state-of-the-art parallel and vector processing computers and high performance workstations, all connected be Ethernet and running within a uniform Unix BSD environment. Areas of particular focus include neural networks, connectionist models, catastrophe theory, combinatorial optimization, computational physics, econometrics, and forecasting. That this is done by a financial institution is, in itself, impressive. Who would have thought that investment bankers would employ neural networks, computational physics, and connectionist models? Notice that not only are artificial intelligence constructs involved in this application, but they also run on powerful personal workstations interconnected through LANs.

A valid procedure for LAN implementation will largely rest on communications. LAN-mainframe partnerships offer the really distributed data processing and databasing for which users have been striving. The democratization of computing can also be achieved through a microlink; the opportunity for greater individual freedom comes with the danger of microcomputer anarchy. There is a very critical requirement for effective management: the responsibility for assuring that the partnership runs smoothly and productively. A key prerequisite for effective management of the links is the development of an effective plan. Local area networks are part of such plan. If active planning for the microlink is not undertaken now, the result will be a major loss of opportunity in the future.

A systems approach will also account for the fact that mainframe software has been profoundly influenced by the database revolution and, in recent years, by the information center concept. Hence, sound solutions should analyze the management processes required to use new technologies, investigate the importance of strategic planning, and describe a proven methodology. They should reflect on attendant organizational issues, present predictions of trends, and provide guidelines for success gained from practical experience. Such a task is challenging since the choice of technologies is further confused by the vendors, who are competing through differentiation, not standardization. Traditional computer vendors are developing a line of products around their protocols, equipment, and software. LAN vendors are offering their wares as the basic building block, with gateways as links to long distance and outside networks.

IBM is offering several different approaches, and in the future it seems likely that they will be offering wholly new approaches. To sort through this confusing array of choices, users need a thorough understanding of the correct alternatives:

- What are the strong and weak points of LAN and PBX?
- Are LAN and PBX alternatives or complements to each other?
- How should we approach the economics of LAN and PBX?

There are no universal answers to these queries. A properly focused reply is situational and requires the appropriate in-depth study. If you are building an in-house communications facility, examine both systems. If you have heavy data volumes, lean toward LAN. You cannot handle large volumes on a PBX—but the PBX also has its role.

22.3 Three Successful Applications Examples

The Bangor Punta Corporation had an interesting top management experience. The applications to which personal computers and local area networks have been put to work were served for many years by a timesharing service. All 35 companies in the Bangor Punta Group had been working through GEIS to serve their management information needs and to handle the financial results at the holding level. With the change in system design through the implementation of PC and LAN, the 35 companies in the group are now extracting data from their MIS for presentation to the president and the board. Monthly, weekly, daily, they download data to the LAN file server, including different graphical and tabular presentations.

This application includes 5 years of historical financial data, to be used by the chairman of the board, the president, the senior VP of finance, and other authorized executives. The gateways of the LAN also access public financial networks. A decision support system with graphics capability has been developed on the LAN's workstations. It includes historical evaluations, forecasting and other projections, graphical presentation for decision support, and dynamic slides and color capabilities. The system is menu driven and user friendly. Management wants graphs, not numbers. Security and protection are enhanced through an allocated area on hard disk, with passwords and pathnames for individual users. Both top management financial data and the personnel function feature password protected data.

The implementation timetable for this application was reasonably fast. After the decision was reached, the needed time was 4 weeks for the installation and 10 weeks to get the system running. Top management's reaction was most enthusiastic. The chairman of the board and two senior vice presidents started using it consistently after 2 weeks of part-time training. The chairman also uses his workstation and a protected region of the LAN's file server for stock price quotations, portfolio management, and other applications.

Quite important in a management environment, reliability is high and replacement and service are very fast. They expect to have to upgrade the system in about 3 to 5 years, but the savings realized were so high that the system paid for itself in 1 year's time. This is the *typical* experience of companies which have acquired myria-processor experience.

A signature recognition application was set up through WSs and LANs by the Chemical Bank of New York. They approached the problem of PC-based teller terminals with signature recognition capability, linked through the LAN as follows:

1. In January (1982) the LAN to be used was identified (Nestar).
2. In February, the system went under development.
3. In July, the programming phase was completed.
4. In August, demonstration to management took place.
5. In September, the first life test was done: a pilot installation in a branch, followed by user training.
6. Based on the positive results, three more LANs were ordered during the same month.
7. In October, the first LAN installation went in production.
8. In November, the second, third, and fourth installations started operations.

The target was to realize 100 LAN installations in an equal number of branch offices—two per week, with the next step being the implementation of another 150 systems.

The key to Chemical Bank's success has been that management first took the time to set goals, cared to properly understand the system, and installed the pilot in the branch—it did not let it rot in the DP shop. Management also had the courage to make tough decisions. Two more points are important in this project. First, it only takes 2 hours of teller training to become proficient on the WS usage, including the online signature capability. Second, while other signature systems required (at the time) 1500 bytes as a minimum on the disk, this solution demanded 490 bytes as a maximum. The software has been projected to handle up to two signatures per account. Response time has been very fast. Removal of signatures is not allowed. This is a good example of an application which not only substitutes first-generation online systems with the third generation (WSs and LANs), but it also provides a valid solution to the substitution of paper that the earlier online approaches could not realize.

It takes a lot of discipline to make WS and LAN implementation a success. But the results can be very positive. There is no reason for not expanding further beyond PC and LAN to incorporate expert systems support. This is precisely what another major financial institution has done. First, management sorted out all operations into those that were transaction-oriented, mainly appealing to the operations level, and those that were message-intense, primarily addressed to managers and professionals. A second criterion was then used, separating those that were predominantly interactive from one-way-type communications (downloading, upline dumping, asynchronous-type operations). Figure 22.1 presents this dichotomy.

After the proper definition of online activities, management focused on those which should be particularly enriched with expert systems. This bank already had a well-structured decision support systems (DSS) implementation. It was based on multifunctional workstations, largely served through a LAN and aimed to provide management with an analytical capability. Managers and professionals looked at expert systems not as a substitute for human judgment but as a means to enrich the information available to executives, produce requested documentation, permitting what-if experimentation, and helping clarify the ideas of cognizant people prior to important decisions.

The goal of proceeding with a new generation of AI constructs was to provide participants with a direct understanding on how to work with an

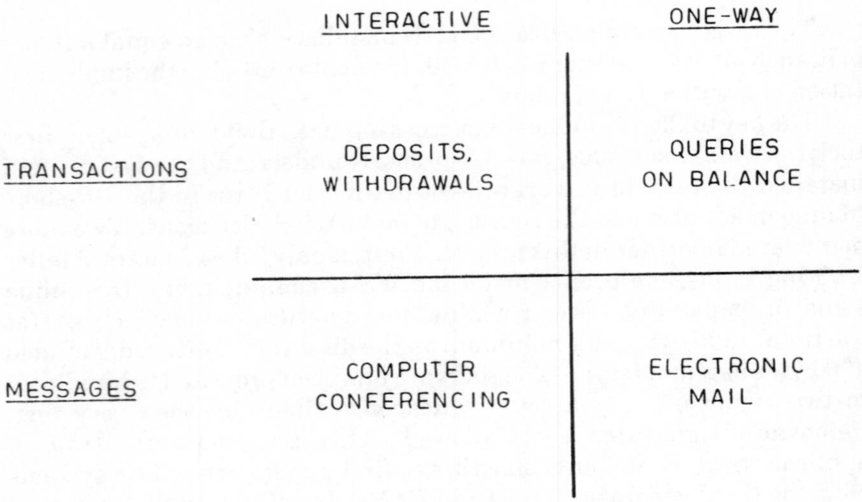

	INTERACTIVE	ONE-WAY
TRANSACTIONS	DEPOSITS, WITHDRAWALS	QUERIES ON BALANCE
MESSAGES	COMPUTER CONFERENCING	ELECTRONIC MAIL

Figure 22.1 Four quarter spaces can be defined using transactions vs. messages, and interactive vs. one way as criteria.

expert system. Through three simple case studies, managers and professionals were shown how to approach business problems through artificial intelligence tools—adding a powerful layer of assistance over what has been provided so far by decision support systems. In this particular implementation (and in a score of others) expert systems made feasible two types of decision support tools:

- The first and most important is the human window. Expert systems permit a more effective exchange between the manager and the information in the machine.
- The second is the formalization of decision rules within the expert system's knowledge bank.

Both subjects demonstrated a significant amount of user acceptance. The implementation was helped by previous experience on the users' behalf with spreadsheets and graphics. Instrumental in the introduction and support of the new system has been the ongoing Information Center operation at the bank.

22.4 Contributions to an Information Center Orientation

The targets of an information center implementation are business and management profitability, which are served through a range of applications from online data access to management-oriented databases. This requires standard formats at the server level, with the needed analytical work done either at the host or executed through appropriate software at the PC. Data management and intelligent host-PC communications are at the core of an infocenter implementation; it also demands a growing family of data analysis tools. Other ingredients are modularity and an open environment.

It is precisely because of managerial and professional usage within an infocenter environment that the micro has evolved form the status of stand alone subordinate to that of a full partner with the mainframe. Personal workstations developed from basic and limited terminal emulation to sophisticated distributed data processing capabilities. Despite these advances, however, there are serious limits to the creation, movement, and presentation of documents, especially those involving noncoded (image) information. Users are hesitating to extend the level of WS technology because of concern that the product will not perform really useful functions. Another concern is compatibility. Because of the latter reason, an open architectural environment can be vital. It can help integrate hardware (device independence) and software. It can also assist in choosing high-productivity tools and applications to be developed by professionals. Here we talk well beyond financial modeling, focusing on means which enhance an office system strategy in the enterprise.

Information center approaches have originally addressed the needs and requirements of the larger organizations—which were instrumental in evaluating the capabilities and limitations of proposed applications as well as basic software and hardware solutions. The key to a successful infocenter is recognizing the implication of the management services to be supported while offering:

- Personal terminals, connected to a high-speed local area network with direct access to central computers
- Support for interactive software development and software productivity
- Able management decision assistance
- Quiet and comfortable work environment

As experience with infocenters accumulated, planned approaches also focused on the smaller organizations that had a broad range of applications: record keeping references, management accounting, inventory and sales handling, marketing data, and auditing tools. Decision support needs exist with these organizations, but they are a subset of other overriding requirements that characterize small business. Business modeling tools are not the most important—but a link to accounting is critical.

In both larger and smaller organizations the high performers—the people making the greatest contribution to final results—should be the focal point of infocenter support. Figure 22.2 presents statistics from three distinct fields: patents, authors, and air-to-air victories during World War II. In every enterprise there are high and low performers. The message is that the high performers should be getting the lion's share of attention. Therefore, leading companies today use the new generation of managerial and professional workstations. The now-developing scenario is one of focus. Attention is particularly paid to activities which lead to high personal productivity and performance when they are supported by computers and communications.

End users work at their workstations, into which are mapped their workspaces. Thus we need a workspace definition which contains a problem description and problem status. Knowledge banks, global databases, and communications provide the user with:

- Domain knowledge
- Concurrency of access
- Distributed operations
- Security and protection
- Systems reliability

A workstation is becoming an inference engine. It has deep knowledge, and eliminates information inconsistency.

This is what we are after with the new generation of workstations and LANs. We have come to appreciate that managerial requirements call for totally different forms of support from those needed at the operational level. These different forms of support can be defined in terms of four variables:

- Types of data
- Nature of applications

- Information volume
- Response time

With the advent of information centers and personnel computing, the complete cycle of information handling for management needs revamping, with decision support and appropriate expert systems tools

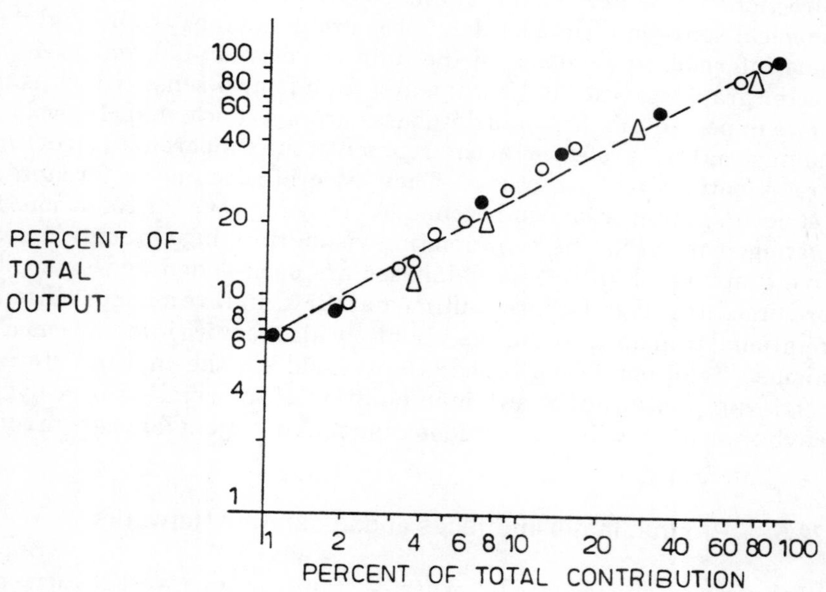

Figure 22.2 Personal contribution to final results, as percent of total population.

positioned at the nodes. Computers and communications are becoming an increasingly vital element of an organization's managerial fabric.

Managerial needs will determine the prime applications of information systems for the next decade and, therefore, will form the major influence on information systems strategy. There is a difference between operational and managerial requirements, just as there exists a full cycle of data handling. Implementing workstations at the executive level is a most challenging task. One of the reasons for management information system failures is the inability to provide an infrastructure for decision support. Another reason is the lack of strategic information systems orientation—as well as the inability to define prime applications for the next decade: therefore, new directions and developments in information technology are needed.

Multimedia databases (MDB) are a new concept and one of the chief directions in the new computer and communications orientation. In a physical sense, multimedia databases are defined as traditional data plus information elements in the form of voice (audio), image, icons, vector graphics, text, and documents. In a logical sense, which is the more important, multimedia databases are object oriented. In evolving managerial and professional environments, the support data structures are essentially text structures. They integrate documents for storage, retrieval, presentation, and exchange. They improve the conditions for management decisions by promoting visual thinking through interactive graphics. Multimedia databases are open-ended and extensible architectures. They feature multimedia DBMS and are managed through relational principles at the base, but they also require inference mechanisms. Solutions to multimedia issues address the capture, storage, retrieval, presentation, and manipulation of information in a hybrid environment. It will be the predominant environment for years to come.

22.5 Programmatic Interfaces and Local Area Networks

We have spoken of powerful, expert system-enriched workstations and of multimedia databases. Both are end user-oriented supports. What is the role the local area network should play within this evolving picture in which management productivity is the dominant factor? It can contribute in management productivity. One of the key answers is response time. For any given WS, network response time is largely a function of:

- Speed of the line that the terminal is on
- How busy the line is that carries the messages of all the users' terminals that are attached to it

Line speed is easy to understand. A message of a given length can be transmitted faster on a high-speed line than on a slow one. Busy line, however, is a more complex topic. It is also more important.

The local area network component of a user's response time can never be better than the time it takes the communication line to carry the input message to the server and then return the response. But it can be much worse. LAN slowdowns are usually caused by overly busy communications lines and queuing delays associated with that increased load. Queuing delays result when one user's message has to wait in the queue because the line is busy transmitting another user's message. Thus, the number of messages per unit of time that the line must carry is a critical factor and so is the message length.

The number of messages per unit of time is largely a function of the number of WSs attached to the LAN and the kind of work the end users are doing. Another critical but often overlooked issue is the organization of the work as it affects message traffic. In PC/LAN applications the blocking factor in network traffic is usually caused by programs, not data. In attached PCs without hard disks, programs' traffic has the largest impact. In one specific implementation simple program accounted for 3 KB, medium-size one for 15 KB, and rather complex program for 45 KB at about 30 bytes per Cobol statement. Therefore, LAN saturation led to the rule that program downloading should be the rare exception in local network traffic. In this particular application, files were the next longest objects transported by the LAN. There were three typical sizes: 300, 1000, 2000 bytes. However, the largest file transported featured fewer kilobytes than the smallest downloaded program. In another LAN application, transactions were the typical frequent traffic. A simple transaction had 30 to 100 characters. A more complex one, 400 to 600 characters. These statistics apply to every WS LAN implementation, but they should be kept in mind.

Because every application has its own characteristics, it is wise to establish the actual statistics on message size from the terminals to the host system and back again. Maximum, average, and minimum message transaction size should be established, together with the corresponding frequencies. This is necessary for optimization. We can always try to improve network response time with faster LANs. This approach carries the benefit that our messages are transmitted faster, and users spend less time waiting. Faster LANs are expensive, however. Not only are the BIU costs higher, but vendors bet on the user needs for faster LANs, adjusting prices accordingly. Short of losing a number of infocenter users, the only way to reduce traffic on a given LAN is to add another LAN and divide the terminals among them. This solution stands a good chance of being less expensive than completely changing the current local area network—but it is limited by the number of bridges the LAN we have adopted can accept.

Evaluating the throughput on its LAN, one financial institution found that in a software development application, four WSs (Datapoint) saturated Arcnet and its file server. In a data collection and encoding, implementation, six WSs saturated Arcnet—but the bottleneck was at the gateway. An industrial company used another way to improve network response time. It reduced message sizes, but this is not always practical, particularly under some protocol solutions. In one specific case, one of the major drawbacks was that no message smaller than an entire screen could be sent to or received by a terminal, resulting in messages that were unnecessarily large. Other protocols have features that address this problem. With the 3270 protocol (which by now is obsolete), for example, an application can format the screen into a number of fields:

- Only fields modified by the terminal user are automatically transmitted back to the host when the user presses Enter.
- All other fields are left behind unless the application has marked them as premodified.
- Premodified fields are those that the program has marked so that they will be returned when the user presses Enter.

Some protocols let users write individual fields or individual characters within a field independent of whatever else might already be on the screen. An application can display a series of screens that are identical except for a relatively small number of characters required to change the current screen into the screen the application wants the user to see next.

Flexibility is the keyword, and this has not only to do with PC and LAN choices but also with protocol selection. The next challenge is to structure the implementation so as to fully exploit the features a given protocol presents. A reason for this is that an application does not necessarily know what is on the screen to which it is writing a message.

For example, the current screen might have been written by another application or altered by the user. When an application cannot be sure what is currently on a screen, there is no opportunity to use, for example, the feature of sending only changes to that screen. Also, in a number of cases the programming effort required to take advantage of basic software and hardware facilities is very complex. To replace a long stream of characters using control sequences, an application must build its own data streams rather than use the higher-level interfaces. Such features make a protocol more functional but also much more difficult to handle.

22.6 Looking into the Implementation of a New Operating System

The need for fine-tuning the programming interfaces goes all the way from applications to special software. Chapter 13 described the Masstor System Corp. (MSC) solution of providing field-to-field communications in an environment which includes diverse mainframes with incompatible operating systems. Say, then, that our company is seriously considering to buy this solution if the OS running at three of our mainframes can be added to those supported through MSC. Let's call this OS Z and its computer vendor C. What we want is for all our users to be able to access OS X by vendor A, OS Y by vendor B, OS Z by vendor C. The X and Y are supported by MSC, but Z is not. Which approach can be followed to extend the coverage of OSs?

The challenge is not simply one of writing the interfaces. The real challenge is determining how to assure that the support to be provided will be effective. This goes beyond the technical requirements. Among the main queries are:

1. Will vendor C collaborate in a three-party team (our organization, MSC, and C) to help with deep knowledge of Z primitives?
2. Should our organization be the only user company entering such an agreement or should we look for other Z users?
3. What is the timetable to be established to assure that the project is not pushed into the background, that there are no slipages, and that the end users will get what they need when they need it?
4. Which are the specific evaluation criteria to be established and observed by all parties at the final tests?

These four issues are interrelated. In this specific case they are further complicated by the fact that vendor C has a limited routine running under Massnet LAN software created ad hoc for a specific installation. This is essentially a storage management software which saves, restores, rolls out, and rolls back. The logical attachment of OS Z is further complicated by the fact that vendor C stated that its existing SNA Gateway should be chosen instead of Massnet interfaces. However, a careful study found that when C tells its clients it offers an SNA gateway, what it means—without saying it—is that it provides a low-performance approach with no process-to-process capability.

The LAN vendor's specialists look at the online interconnection of Z as follows:

1. From a technology viewpoint, implementation is not an issue.
2. The issue is the business side, which has been outlined above.

There are also technical requirements. C owns and controls OS Z. They can make life easy or difficult in providing the information necessary for interconnection—there is a major difference if C cooperates or not in this project. For instance, for OS Y, vendor B did some of the low-code development.

In terms of a time budget for doing the job, Masstor Systems has estimated 3 to 4 programmer-years, assuming that the current OS X/OSY implementation will be ported to the OS Z environment and no changes will be made to it. Regarding a realistic timetable, an objective estimate was put at about 1 year (12 calendar months).

What are our alternatives at the organization's side? In line of preference—but not in terms of probability—they are:

1. Getting vendor C to pay for it.
2. Convincing the LAN vendor of the revenue opportunity.
3. Having the project financed by the user organization itself.

Item 1 is not so likely, but it would be optimal, leaving the user firm in charge of benchmarking the resulting interconnect system. Based on this premise, the better strategy is to put pressure on vendor C and to explain to its management what it means for their firm to have this capability: account control, entry into the competitors' strongholds, and so on.

Furthermore, while necessary, the development of the appropriate

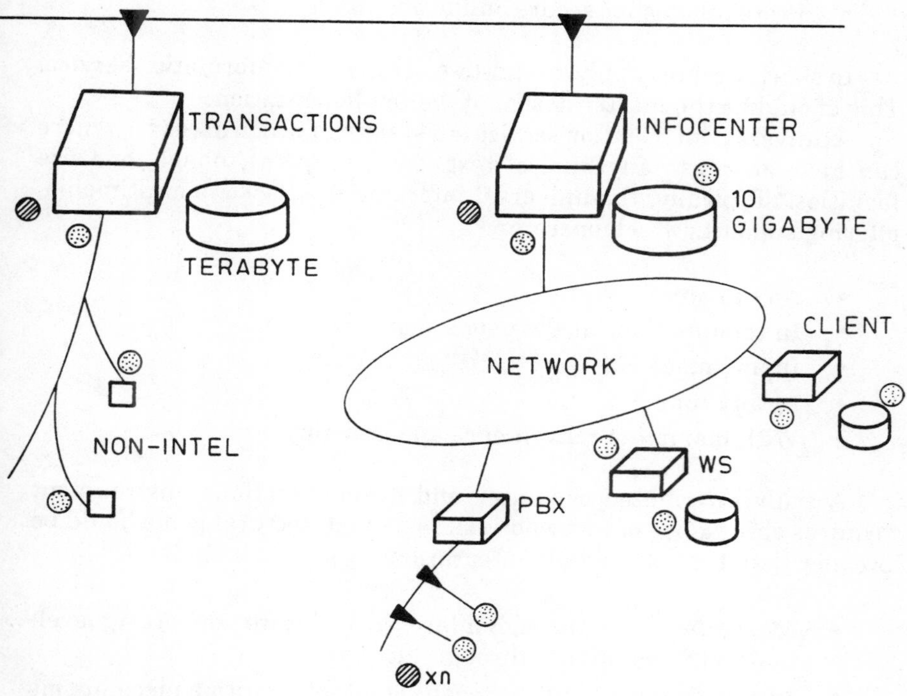

Figure 22.3 Global perspective to be satisfied through integration of transactional and information center networking

programmatic interfaces will not necessarily answer all system questions relating to the interconnection of mainframes through a high-capacity seven-layer ISO/OSI-type LAN. As Figure 22.3 suggests, the global perspective has to be satisfied in a manner which fully integrates:

- Transactional requirements for the operation

- Infocenter services for managers, professionals, and clients
- Network control center needs
- Prerequisites for secure online activities

In short, we must apply an end-to-end universal information service. This should be the master design of the implementation.

A universal information service is a system in which users anywhere can have access to any kind of text, data, graphics, image, or voice facilities. Typically, the universal information service is multimedia, offering supports which operate:

- Any-to-any
- In combinations at the user's choice
- In any place
- At any time
- With maximum convenience and economy

A truly distributed computer and communications environment requires observance of these notions. The architectural goal should be broader than that of a simple integration. It should include:

- *Maintainability*, through a layered structure supporting level-by-level functionality through interfaces
- Increased *reusability*, by means of interconnection mechanisms
- *Portability* among different software constructs and hardware devices

Solutions should support concurrency in operations within this defined distributed information environment. This has been the reason for integrating through the LAN operating system Z with OS X and Y.

22.7 Obtaining and Holding End-User Acceptance

There are many aspects of applying LAN and WS technology to meet end- user needs. A valid procedure for LAN implementation is a must, successful applications examples are very helpful, attention to detail is a basic ingredient of valid solutions, and information center perspectives must be considered. Significant attention must be paid to the finer programmatic interfaces. System tuning must be done not only once, but steadily. Availability and reliability must be high. These are largely technical factors. As such, they are necessary but not enough. It is also important to obtain end-user collaboration. The following case study focuses on this matter.

The organization had 6 years of experience with LANs, but it was not widespread through the operations. The larger-scale implementation was only 1 year old and aimed to interconnect the proliferating WSs purchased and used by professionals in different departments. This was the focus of the auditing study. It became obvious from the meetings held with the end users that they have fully accepted the LAN system. They:

- Judged to be more powerful than multithreading on a mini
- Considered its mode of operating very predictable
- Appreciated the manner in which it worked, making it possible not only to effectively communicate but also to have one's own files in the database being updated in real time

The users now have their own communications machine which gives them what they wanted to have for years. System implementation has been smooth. Because of personal computer usage and a LAN, it has been possible to try new solutions on a small scale and, when they proved that they work, to concatenate.

Their very imaginative approach to developing applications software is impressive: not only did the end users participate actively in the process, but it was possible to develop software as the project went along, showing the user how and why, always being flexible.

The approach was novel and effective. The analysts took one user at a time and spent half a day explaining and adjusting the system to that user's needs, gradually building up the computer and communications support permitted to follow this policy. End-user response was overwhelmingly positive; they were changing the approach to computing. As the project continued, it was discovered that personal computers and LANs permit a layered capture and use of information. This occurs as electronics facilities improve the end user's capability to communicate both with databases and with other workstations. The response time is steady: 1 to 2 seconds. There is no delay because of overloading.

Database access implementation through the file server assures that the personal computer looks at fresh input and products, in real time, a summary page of all pages available for general access—to be displayed at any user's station on request. At the same time, each attached WS gets a summary of requested operations on softcopy, followed by detail when needed. An electronic notice board runs an electronic message system and produces management reports. Users can access this information in 1 second WS to WS without going through the server. The file servers are, nevertheless, an important way of handling the environment. The approach taken to supporting software can be largely divided into two main classes:

1. *Systems software.* This is provided by the supplier and assures file server, printer server, data communications, and electronic mail functionality.
2. *Applications packages.* Here the main task has been to identify software system houses, of which there is a large supply. Although in the past, most routines were written for stand alone WSs, their high quality was useful to the networked application, and several were converted. Examples of types of off-the-shelf packages which have passed a stringent test are ledgers, sales processing, invoicing, stock control, and bill of materials.

Systems specialists converted existing and acquired stand alone packages for multiuser use, with record locking and security. The local network's file server locks records and files, looks after security, and defines groups of users. Every WS has its own local microfiles. An important point concerns *reliability*. There is a temptation to move bits of the personal computer around, but experience demonstrated a better solution: change the whole unit. Reliability is a very important subject which should be approached in a system-wide manner. It should not be tampered with at the workstation level of operations. For a given implementation, failure statistics should be kept in an accurate manner and exploited to provide trends and quality histories. A study done along this line indicated a 4 percent failure rate. On average, one workstation failed once per year. The MTTR was at the level of 10 to 20 minutes. To facilitate maintenance, personal computers were provided with diagnostic disks, which the user could easily learn to load.

Switching a WS on the network requires 1 to 2 minutes, including loading by the file server. Significantly, during a WS switching everybody else carries on—one failure does not affect the other users. Personnel and equipment costs have been kept down and managers have found that their staffs can handle more tasks with greater efficiency and house a broader organizational overview than with traditional communication techniques. Rather than schedule meetings, issue memos, and write formal reports, the general manager, for example, easily obtains the marketing manager's most recent sales projections through the network. One application in which WSs and LANs are particularly useful is in costing. Costs are continually updated on the network so that quantitative decisions can be made quickly and accurately. Decision-making is pushed down to a lower organizational level than is typical in operations where data must be compiled, formatted, and reported to a higher-up manager.

Chapter

23

Requirements and Prerequisites in Implementing the LAN

23.1 Introduction

A system view of the requirements and prerequisites for LANs must be taken. Within an applications environment, in the broadest sense, it is very important to define areas of applications whose basic characteristics are quite similar, or quite different. It is usually convenient to standardize approaches to solutions applicable within a reasonable range of implementation cases. This is valid both in regard to baseband or broadband choices and in reference to the programmatic interfaces discussed in Chapter 22. We must think not only about installing a local area network but also of subsequently maintaining it.

At the same time, similarity does not mean equality. Each application has its own specifications. To establish them, traffic characteristics, holding time, duty cycle, and response time must be studied. Ideally, every workstation and server on the LAN should address all hosts in the network. High-duty-cycle networks should be made to allow for dynamic host and mode reconfiguration, and new device connection with a mini-

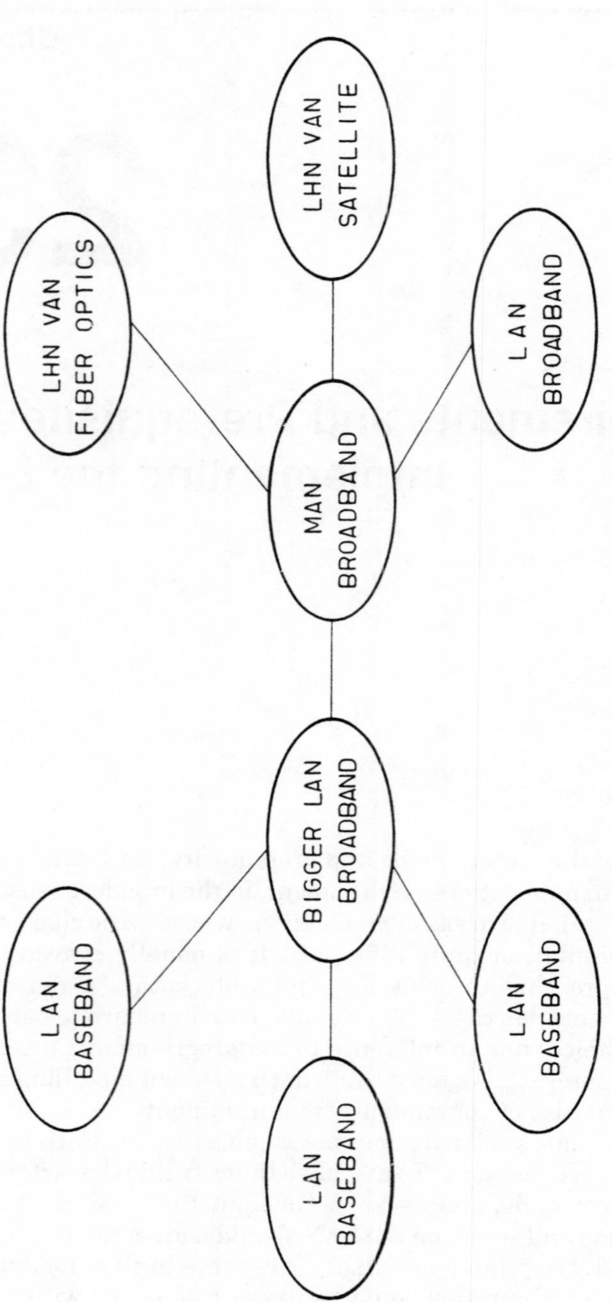

Figure 23.1 Interconnection of LAN, MAN, LHN (Long haul), and VAN into one system.

mum of effort and no disruption at all. Local area networks must be open to future evolution and equipment compatibility. Given the ever-expanding requirements for databasing and data communications, long-haul networks, metropolitan area networks (MANs), LAN broadband, and baseband eventually form an interconnected aggregate (Figure 23.1). The capability must be there for any workstation in any network to communicate with any other. The total systems view goes well beyond the cabling of a building, the servers, the interfaces, gateways, and other attachments.

23.2 An Establishment Information System

An establishment information system (EIS) has broader capabilities than those porting a more restricted number of services and operating over a narrower span. The difference is one of mission and objectives. At the time of its announcement, IBM's establishment LAN supported only the lower ISO/OSI layers. Slowly its functionality has been extended, the goal being to eventually meet the levels of implementation outlined in Figure 23.2. End-user functions call for:

1. A valid global architecture.
2. A wide variety of connectivity options.
3. Facilitated access to shared resources (files, devices, applications).
4. Transparency to the user for creation, deletion, filing, searching of information elements.
5. Expanding inventory of available applications .
6. Fault detection and correction.
7. Open possibility for extension and flexibility in implementation.

One of the coming major areas of application is electronic document distribution. Such service must be independent of the people and processing using the files—which is contrary to the present manually oriented practices in an office environment.

As expected, there is a very significant difference between IBM and DEC as suppliers of LAN services and, on the other side, third-party vendors in the LAN product line. The major computer companies look at the LAN as a means to enhance their wares at the client site. For them, LAN sales are not the goal but the means. By contrast, LAN sales

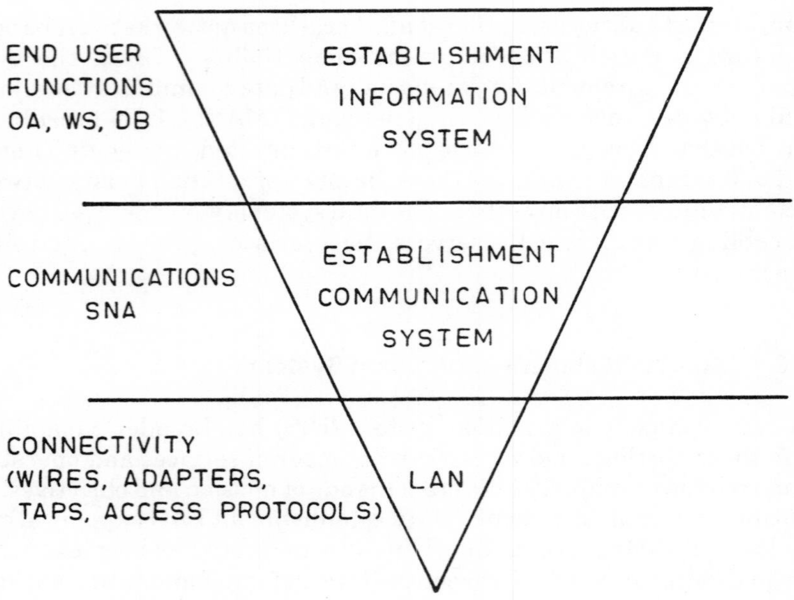

Figure 23.2 Three layers on implementation of corporate information network.

are the goal of the third-party vendors, influencing their implementation perspective. The larger computer manufacturers are well positioned to understand that an establishment information system must be reliable. Otherwise it will not serve its purpose. The LAN should become the infrastructure of the establishment information system and, to do so, availability must stand at 99.99 percent—usually known as "the four 9's." Furthermore, fault detection and correction must be implemented, and it should be totally transparent to the end user.

Emphasis should be placed on applications, and this underlines the need for software support. Software support usually develops after the hardware is available for a few years. This is no longer an accepted practice in a networked environment. The in-house communications system requires an impressive applications dowery as an initial condition. An in-house communications system has more functionality than the EIS at the communications end of the line. It includes telephony, which is most important for the multimedia environment of the 1990s. It also assures the gateways for long haul as an integral part of its definition. By contrast, it does not necessarily incorporate hosts and all of the workstations. Both concepts should be kept in perspective, and both require software support in their foundation.

The classical software objective is to adapt the hardware to user requirements. With PCs and LANs,we have a new freedom and should use it:

1. We can choose hardware *after* the software has been selected.
2. We can dynamically configure both software and hardware to best support the user.
3. We can replace hardware and/or software modules so as to make system development and upkeep much easier.

It is useless—if not destructive—to implement a new technology with the old EDP viewpoints. Not only should applications software and system software be adequate for the goals an implementation proposes to reach, but databasing and data communications are also much more vital to solutions than DP/WP.

The structure of the networks sets some basic choices. Lower nodes perform user and I/O tasks. Upper nodes manage resources and provide for regional control of the nodes underneath. In any type of topology, a higher level of OS support can enhance:

- Multiuser communications (electronic mail, calendaring, etc.)
- Interaction between loosely coupled processes
- Virtual machine concepts
- A variety of gateways
- File protection features
- Database backup
- Transparent recovery and restart
- Network monitoring and diagnostics
- Resource allocation function
- Reconfiguration capabilities, including isolation of faulty devices

Network software should be able to present an increasing amount of support. At the same time, attention must be paid to choices that are able to keep costs down.

In the balance to be struck between flexibility, serviceability, and cost, the LAN must facilitate device movement, simple error recovery, problem determination, agile configuration, installation growth, and maintenance. At the same time, it must protect current hardware, software, and applications investments. It is, as well, necessary for the user organization to fully understand the role of a LAN within the perspective of an establishment information system. A LAN is a means for physical and data link connection and is composed of physical and logical resources. It allows a building block approach and provides a means for attaching devices that are able to communicate among themselves. A LAN is not a substitute for the need for careful planning and implementation, a guarantee that communication takes place end-to-end, or a complete establishment information system. It is only the backbone of it.

As technology develops and user requirements expand, information will move both in coded form (data and text) and in uncoded form (voice and image). A valid system will handle both. Solutions with long life cycles will be device independent and will reflect an open architecture. This, by definition, imposes constraints and the need for standards to assure wider interconnection capabilities. The change of information in an establishment information system can be conversational (interactive) or store and forward (message taking for deferred delivery). Text, data, and voice may be of a transactional or message exchange nature. The LAN must accept facsimile, text, charts, and other services of increasing importance (Figure 23.3).

Data is subject to calculation and can be spaced out at about 2000 characters per page (CPP). Text (letters, memos) is subject to composition spaced out at 6000 CPP. Data, text, and images are structured into documents presented in one or more pages. To these should be added voice and image. If softcopy presentation is to be made, to feed a video at, say, 30 images per second, we need transmission links of 80 MBPS. Hence, the LAN will have to work at the MBPS level—while digital voice can be served with only 64 KBPS. These are issues that the in-house communications and the establishment information system should consider. IBM seems to have built its strategy for the 1990s around such an implementation. For the moment its answer rests on the cabling system. But this is only a beginning.

23.3 Search for Solutions and the Impact of an Architecture

Since user organizations make investments and have to stick to them, management will be well advised to use a well thoughtout and properly policed search methodology, given the large-scale computer and communications systems we are now designing—as well as the

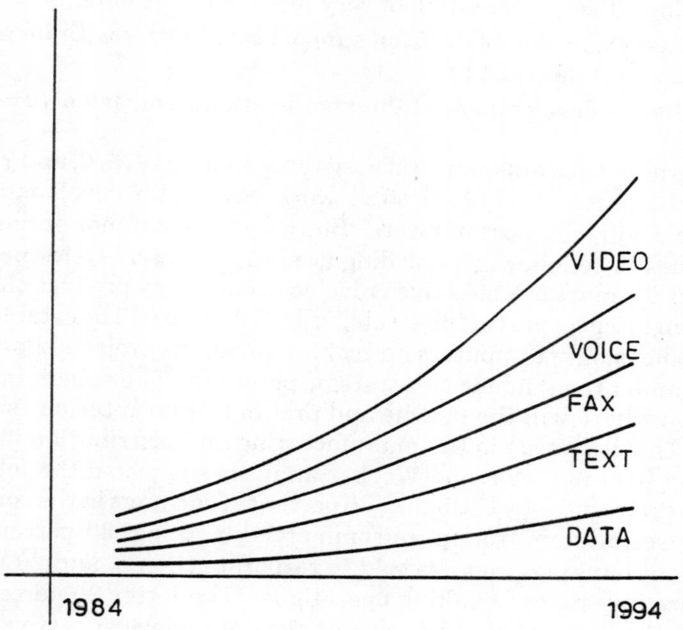

Figure 23.3 Growth of transmission requirements over one decade.

plurality of problems we have to face and the money we spend on them. Top problems faced by dynamic organizations in their search for computers and communications solutions are end-user and product oriented. They include:

1. Able online handling of new types of products (product innovation).
2. Emphasis on automation of delivery, not only of design and production.
3. Service differentiation by client group.

4. Fully automated solutions oriented to simpler products (low-cost production and distribution).
5. Cost effective handling of very large volumes of office work.
6. Fast expansion of decision support capabilities with increasing usage of multimedia.
7. Steady development of the organizational infrastructure.

Local area networks can be of assistance in items 4, 5, 6, and 7. They help in the automation of all office work beyond the levels currently achievable with classic computers. But they have a minor or no role in approaches to be followed regarding items 1, 2, and 3. Here the major questions we must ask ourselves revolve around new product planning and are an integral part of the strategic directive we will be establishing.

The choosing of computers and communications projects should also be done under the guidance of strategic planning. The salient question is: "From where will the income and profits to guarantee our survival come?" This is as true in the manufacturing and distribution industry as it is in banking. A Paine Webber analysis suggested the following highlights on profits by Citibank: 50 percent of earnings in the corporate banking sector stem from pure commercial banking, 30 percent from investment banking products sold to corporate clients, and 20 percent from pure investment banking operations. The latter 20 percent was growing the fastest; the 50 percent was the slowest. Given such projections, where should we be making our high-technology investments? Once this issue has been answered, we should decide on an architectural perspective. Never underestimate the impact of a system architecture.

In all studies concerning computers, communications, databases, and supported end-user functions, the systems study alone, done with the right know how, is at a premium. There are two main reasons underlying this statement:

1. *The compatibility problem.* This concerns the ability to be independent of the manufacturer's wares (hard or soft), using the LAN not only as the carrier but also as the interface between resources to be made available and user's requirements. This is the sense of the emphasis placed in Chapters 12 and 13 on NSC and Masstor—as well as of the discussion in Section 22.6 of Chapter 22.
2. *A complexity problem.* Through a self-managed transmission mechanism and distributed resources which are also self stand-

ing, we try to be less complex than typical mainframe implementation. Results show up when complexity is reduced at least by an order of magnitude.

This calls for modeling the entire local network, if necessary using iterations for solving problems such as queuing and servicing. Traffic studies are just as important. In a local area network, we must think about how to describe the whole process from source to destination within the projected environment and during a foreseeable time frame of operations.

We have often underlined reliability. The measure of robustness used is availability: The fraction of time that the system is usable for its mission. However, while the ratio of *time on* over total time might be satisfactory with mainframes, it is not so with LANs. Mean time of system interrupt (MTOSI) is more significant. Since the main resources attached to a departmental LAN are personal computer-based WSs, file server(s), printer(s), and gateway(s), it is necessary to look at the network both as a whole and by specific class of equipment. The ease of WS roll-in and roll-out leads to a substitution unit bootstrapped to architectural software. In practical applications, this has been achieved with a minimum of upheaval. All that is necessary at the WS level is to save the last operation. Something similar can be said of the printer and gateway—but the situation is quite different with file servers.

The database can easily be the LAN's underbelly, and it should be treated as such. This means the ability to keep a journal (which will also be necessary for security and protection) and to update the file structure to the last transaction should the disk fail. Better still is a shadow (or mirror) image of the database available online that is steadily updated and ready to play the primary function if the master disk fails.

Another critical characteristic is throughput. In networks, flow control schemes are necessary to ease congestion which would otherwise cause a variety of problems:

- Speed mismatching, when different processing rates prevail at the sending and receiving nodes
- Deterioration in efficiency, hence throughput degradation
- Loss of security or reliability because of buffer overflow at some node
- Monopolization, in the sense that certain classes of message or transactions may be allowed to dominate

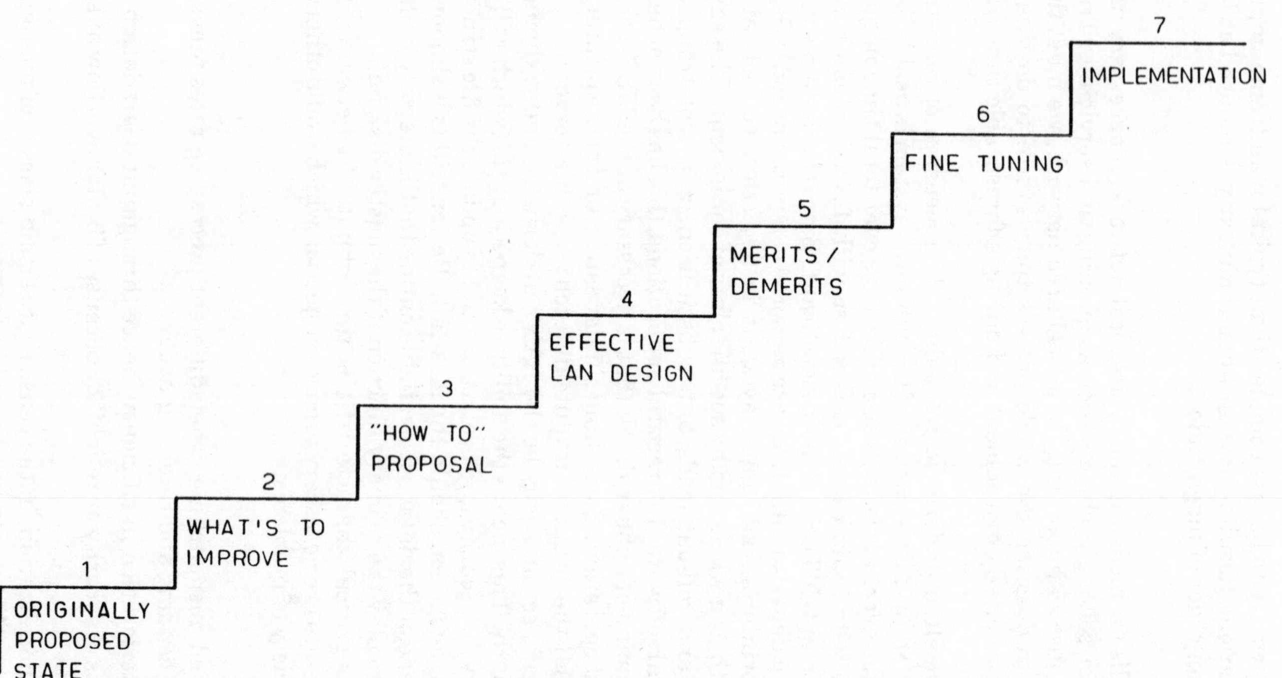

Figure 23.4 Suggested step-by-step networking from original proposal to its improvement and implementation.

A performance prediction of flow-controlled networks is important for the adequate attainment of the original objectives. Flow control studies can be addressed through analytic models by varying window size, buffer limitations through assignment of threshold value, and message acceptance.

Studies of the type which we are describing can lead to a refinement of the network in a step-by-step approach going from the originally proposed state to a definition of what is to be improved, a "how to do it" proposal, and effective LAN design. Next, the network must be studied for merits and demerits, which is followed by fine tuning prior to implementation. Figure 23.4 suggests a methodology. However, since the first step is that of looking at the originally proposed state of a LAN architecture, let's evaluate the criteria which help differentiate local area architectures among themselves:

1. Overall network architecture: services and conformity to international standards.
2. Number of logical layers supported by the LAN's software.
3. Gateways to other LANs and wide area networks.
4. Network structure and topology (ring, ether, star, and so on).
5. Megastreams carried per second as well as broadband versus baseband.
6. Protocol being used (token, collision detection, truth tables, slots. etc.,).
7. Physical medium (twisted wire, flat wire, coaxial, optical fiber).
8. Type and cost of the bus interface unit (or modem) to be used.

Logical and physical issues taken together define the faculties supported by a given LAN architecture. Every unit, every device attached to the LAN will make use of both physical and logical resources. We all know that as a function of time, the hardware costs drop while the software costs are on the increase (Figure 23.5), but are we taking advantage of this opportunity? Design-wise, there is an interaction between the physical, logical, and supported facilities. Quite often the latter imply physical choices and logical provision—either during a planning phase or right after the installation. The former alternative is preferable in terms of functionality. It is also less expensive. Thus, the mechanics of LAN implementation should focus on the selection of a given architecture and, after this is done, on the organization of the workplace. Solutions must be quite imaginative. Efficiency is the single most important factor for installing LANs and workstations.

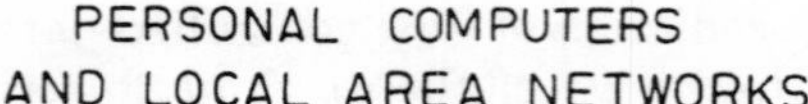

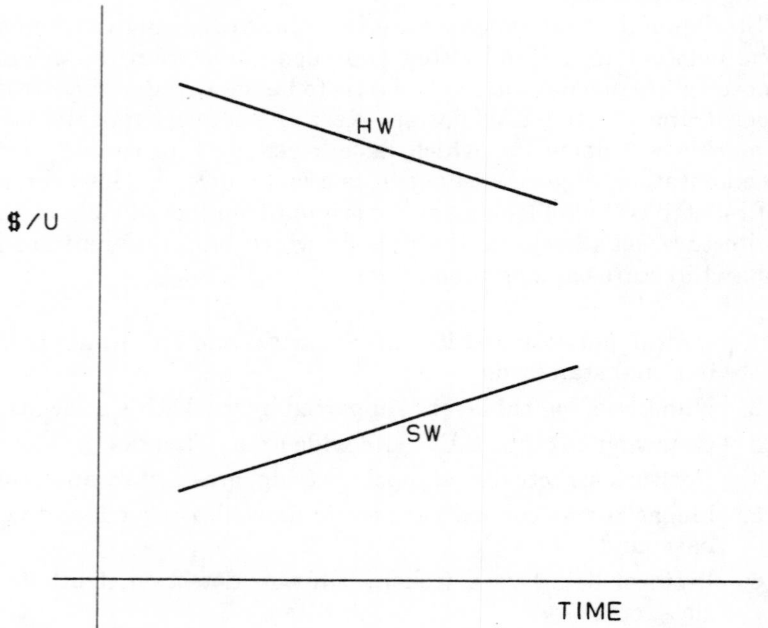

Figure 23.5 Trends in hardware and software costs with personal computers and local area networks.

23.4 LAN Implementation in an Office Environment

When we talk of office system, one thing seems certain: the office automation systems planned for tomorrow will increasingly depend on networks, and a great many manufacturers with varying motives and strategies will try to meet that demand. At the same time, faced with an onslaught of often incomprehensive and typically contradictory proposals, the user organization will be well advised to keep its own counsel for several reasons. Not the least is the going war between computers and office equipment manufacturers who belatedly discovered the advantages of the LANs and are trying to make market headway with a variety of incompatible offers.

It is not enough to know, or even appreciate, that personal computer-based WSs interconnected through local area networks provide a user-information interconnection method but differ in their physical extent, logical supports, transmission delays, and the dependability of their service. We must know precisely what each of these factors means to our organization. We must also conceptualize the mechanics of implementation in our office environment in order to capitalize on the facilities for moving information produced by workstations through online communications. We should also understand why it has become progressively less desirable to move text and data by hand: it requires paper shuffling by people and physical movement of both people and paper.

The answer to cost reduction and greater efficiency is the adoption of electronic forms for information transfer. The LAN (as well as the WS) is only a component of the efficiency equation. The equation itself will be successful only when design is based on the way the end user—and not anybody else—wants to look at it—when it answers the end user's prerequisites in an able manner.

It is quite understandable that all the big computers, communications, and office systems manufacturers are eager to present a "me-too" position in local area networks. But this does not help the user organization. Just as clear should be the fact that each vendor has a long way to go in capturing a big enough piece of the office systems market to assure future growth; in the meantime, the user organization can depend only on itself to do the needed job. One of the cultures largely missing in user organizations is the acceptance of applications packages as the way to proceed. This is particularly important in an office environment where the applications needs are many but packaged software is also particularly rich. Computers are not meant to be programmed in office systems—a concept to be applied in other fields as well.

This affects LAN choice. Not all PCs have the same rich libraries of applications packages. Not all PCs run on a given LAN. So part of LAN choice is the supporting application software. We should rather have that than have to invest in writing new applications programs. This change of emphasis in the users' mind has had and will continue to have a major effect on the structure of the computer industry as IBM compatibility in the PC line shows; leadership is assured by those companies that can provide applications programs support and system expertise while processing equipment and LANs become off-the-shelf commodities.

Having placed emphasis on commodity-type software, a careful office automation study should outline projected benefits to our organization from the implementation of local area networks. In a general sense:

1. They are operationally more resilient. The LAN will continue to operate even with one or more of its constituent machines taken down.
2. Transactions between users and their microfiles tend to have the same response time regardless of how loaded the network is.
3. The workplace can be the subject of an individualized design aimed to solve the end user's problems in the most effective manner—rather than being the image of a monolithic approach projected to serve all users in a standard fashion but none too well.

These are lessons taught through LAN and WS experience in other organizations, but what about our company? How would they apply? Only a thorough study of our requirements can tell. Still, we will always be well advised to learn from the experience of others.

At Nomura Securities, for example, all account executives are attached to the network. Every employee has a workstation. The goal of the new network design has been to:

1. Develop the best solution for account executives, managers, and other professionals.
2. Integrate all information sources into *one* intelligent terminal.
3. Create a global database of in-house information and outside information (financial, market data).

In network design, the goal was to achieve one logical, artificial intelligence-enriched solution. A number of physical structures integrate into it; the top logical layer is universal.

The Mitsubishi Research Institute (MIRI) developed one logical network, projected for:

1. Managers and professionals.

2. The handling of large distributed databases.
3. The incorporation of personal sequential inference engines to support artificial intelligence.

For an any-to-any architectural solution, MIRI is studying MAP (the manufacturing automation protocol by General Motors). This solution aims to integrate diverse networks operating at different levels of ISO/OSI which today are incompatible among themselves.

At the corporate level, the Sumitomo Bank actively supports the client's computer-to-computer link. In parallel to this effort, there is intensive marketing to assure good market size. At the Sumitomo Bank, electronic banking solutions are embedded in their Brain service. The concept is technology integration of:

- Telephony
- Intelligent terminals
- PCs at client site
- Facsimile
- Voice answer back

Any Sumitomo customer is able to access the network through any of the forementioned media. The system is largely interactive. Not only banking transactions but also economic and financial information are supplied through Brain.

These implementation examples focus on the changing landscape of office work. They underline the new look in office chores, which is not just LANs and workstations but also artificial intelligence and global database access. In turn, such requirements imply much more powerful WSs and, consequently, higher-capacity LANs.

23.5 WSs and LANs in Foreign Exchange—An Example of an Application

The mechanics of implementation start with the choice of a local area network architecture, and that choice is much more effective when the applications environment has been brought under correct perspective. A sound approach is to:

1. Dedicate a LAN to one application.

2. Provide gateways between different LANs which must share files.
3. Use one or more file servers per LAN, as needed.
4. Initially keep the number of WSs per LAN to no more than a quarter of that stated by the manufacturer—and less than half the stated number after expansion.
5. Standardize on one type of workstation to make an exchange easy in case of failure.

The foreign exchange applications at a major, money center financial institution supports these rules. Local area networks are dedicated by applications area: forex, commercial and foreign trade, and money markets. There is one for development work and another available as backup. The structure is flexible and, if need be, more can be added to the system and the file server size can also be increased. Not only is the functionality of this setup well proven, but also its size makes it easy to manage. The designer can think both in hardware and in software terms.

The designers have also avoided having to rewrite existing software. This way, an application such as the foreign exchange and Eurocurrency system programmed some years ago on minicomputer stays there. A datacomm engine has been created with this mini as an online server to handle the linkage without having to change anything on the software (Figure 23.6). A new control system procedure avoids the classical double entry made to guarantee a separate control channel. In projecting the LAN and WS system, the analysts projected a new procedure, making use of the new system's capabilities.

One of the problems has been obtaining the controllers' accord. In the adopted solution, the counter confirmation remains in the hands of the controllers—but double entry of the order is no longer necessary because of the logical signature by the dealer and the signed hard copy ticket which is produced by the computer. In fact, the classical double data entry in banking forex environments has been nothing more than a single entry made twice in terms of keying-in. If the deal ticket is replaced through online entry by the dealer, there is no risk of an operator misreading or mistyping it. Neither is there a translation error possibility. These are reasons why the double entry was eliminated: the risk which used to be present is no longer there.

Through LANs and WSs, this solution handles the deal online and puts the information into the forex database. The whole operation becomes the dealer's personal responsibility and eliminates the error

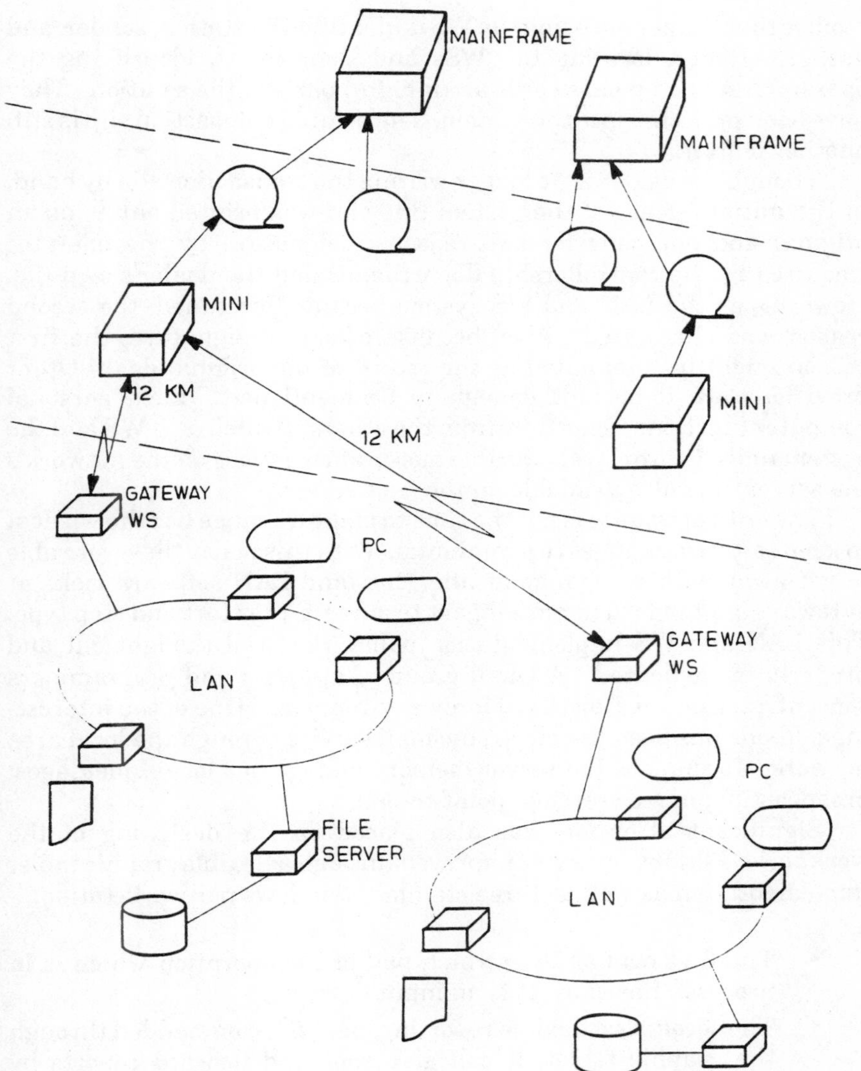

Figure 23.6 Example of an established network using LAN, WS, servers, mimi, and mainframes.

risk down the line—whether intentional or accidental. Let's, however, underline that for control reasons the responsibility of the confirmation remains with a separate department. The important control at the forex room is that the person using the WS is identified by station, sender, and author. Hence, locating the WSs and their input, identifying the operator, and using passwords are integral parts of the solution. They have been projected into the system. The printed transaction slip is still another matter.

Though the dealer is no longer writing the transaction slip by hand, in the initial release of the system this slip was printed online as an original and one copy for two reasons: signature by the operator (required by the controllership department) and the dealer's own file. However, as the LAN and WS system became fine tuned, the second reason was eliminated. Also, because of logical signature, the first reason might be eliminated as the record of the original deal. Other provisions are important enough to be mentioned. Each personal computer functions separately from the others. Switch on a WS and the system finds its own level. Furthermore, when a file is on the network's file server, it is also available on the fee's server.

The critical issue was not the time to make a change but the wisdom to keep software changes to a minimum. With this policy they were able to get away with no change at all. Host and LAN software looks at gateways as standard nonintelligent terminals, the start and stop type. This LAN and WS implementation policy was well thought out and properly implemented. A small group of analysts and programmers concentrated on the functional forex environment. One of the interesting add-ons has been the electronic mail service through the local area network. It employs the server memory and carries lots of messages: broadcasting, narrowcasting, point-to-point.

Significant attention was also placed on the designing of the workplace. Performance was improved through a flexible graphic tablet implementation as well as three standard windows per workstation:

- The first acts as the scratch pad of the operation which is in process. Basically, it is an input device.
- The second is a flexible reporting medium; commanded through the graphic tablet, it can give spot and forward reports by currency as well as other types of information.
- The third has polyvalent software in the background whose functionality is defined by the nature of the workpost: Reuter's prices, closed circuit TV, and so on.

Softcopy design, response time, and personnel training are among the tasks which absorbed part of the project group's time. A general characteristic of all applications has been feeding a common database: feasibility, economic advisability, business opportunity, and employee acceptance are influenced by this reference. This LAN and WS implementation has given very good results in a production sense. It also achieved user satisfaction.

23.6 Local Area Networks in Factory Installations

While some white-collar office systems are similar to those projected for the home market (though not in the sense of systems studies), blue-collar solutions tend to be different. Factory installations are an important market for LAN vendors and have a great future for productivity reasons.

In a typical industrial environment, the attached devices on a LAN must work in real time. Both robotics machinery and planning and control activities are put on the network. Typically, the LAN is broadband, features a modular approach to the incorporation of local computers, and has redundancy designed to meet any availability requirement for a specific application, through the same software and hardware building blocks. Intrinsic redundancy should apply to the component level, with an orderly overlapping, as opposed to a complete system redundancy which is more costly and less reliable. Within these three conditions, a local area network may use packet switching and routing technology, be based on token passing, and handle messages in the order of their priority.

A LAN solution implemented in a factory is a departure from the older control approaches which featured a centralized configuration, mainly star, with a master computer at the center. The master controlled message traffic, the remote stations being dedicated to data collection and actuation functions. Like all centralized systems, this approach presented weak reliability. The complexity of the data communications structure added unavailability and increased the maintenance problems. Another disadvantage was the excessive length of the communications paths. Today practically all industry experts agree that local area networks offer flexibility. They also suggest that LAN solutions will take as many forms as users require. No single approach can hope to dominate the market because of diversity of user needs, but an astute vendor may win a profitable market share.

To achieve this, manufacturers will have to produce low-cost broadband LAN capable of handling high-level languages and equipped with sophisticated operating performance communication facilities. Such a system should have large bandwidth communication to serve workstations and robotics. It should be easy to expand and able to incorporate many different machine types. The failure of one component should not affect the operation of others, and the system should be easily hooked up to wide area networks. Vendors meeting these criteria can serve a broad spectrum of industrial users, particularly users who master LAN technology and understand that distributed control systems by their nature assure a better message traffic. They are peer networks able to guarantee:

- Monitoring and reporting
- Surveillance and disturbance evaluation
- Interactive supervision
- Data collection, storage, retrieval

Analyzing the data, filtering the acquired information, verifying reports, validating, storing, and handling alarms, constitute parts of the application domain as does scrutinizing incoming data from different sources (testing message flow, keeping account of frequency or erroneous or missing messages, disabling failing components, and so on).

Local databases can handle production floor data with much less content than centralized mainframe-based operations. They are more easily accessed by monitors, response time is minimized, reliability improved, and security and protection increased. Faulty units can be replaced without discontinuing the system. This also permits a more complete testing of channels from sensors to the receivers of messages.

If both the production floor and the factory offices are to be served, it is important to incorporate into the LAN study:

1. The layout of the buildings.
2. The location of the individual offices, to assure a data socket per office.
3. The location of the telephone and power cables.
4. The expected data load on the network.
5. The associated interdependencies and priorities.

The protocol standards under development by the IEEE Project 802 and ISO/OSI are particularly oriented to the business environment. As a result, the solutions elaborated through LANs in process control implementation do not necessarily fit the ISO/OSI model. General Motors' MAP approach is projected to cover the huge diversity of equipment at the production floor and associated incompatibilities.

One example of process control applications is power engineering. This is also a case where a LAN approach cannot directly benefit from the developing data communications standards. We will briefly look into MIT's EMCS (Energy Management Control System) project as a case study. Its object is to reduce the cost per needed attachment. To start with, the stated goal is a common one throughout business and industry: assure a low-cost LAN which is reliable and has low overhead. Searching for a valid solution, the MIT researchers rejected the use of power lines for data transfer. Power wiring has communications capabilities, but the bandwidth is very limited and noise can be high. The following premises were made:

1. The bulk of messages in a power system are rather small.
2. The message density is variable.
3. Messages are typically short—hence cannot afford high overhead.
4. A priority structure is needed.
5. Cost is a critical factor.

Within this perspective, the LAN design must assure priority groups by order, multiple independent systems, numerous connected components, low cost per attachment of the single component, and robustness of the architecture and the protocols. Other criteria have been that the solution to be adopted should require no extensive planning, programming must be reasonably easy, the distributed link function assured, and passive links used for greater reliability. The decision was similarly made to work on a solution which requires no central link control, guarantees handshaking between stations, places no restriction on message format, and sees to it that the data rate is acceptable. Power control imperatives demanded that the method to be chosen is suitable for modulated encoding, there is the possibility of arbitration to avoid collision, and variations in distance create no hardship. In an industrial environment distances typically vary between 1 m and 1 km or more.

System specifications outlined that each part will be in one of three states, monitor, master, or slave. A monitor status characterizes a station active system. When a station is activated it is typically slave, an arbitration mechanism makes a port master, and it will then designate other ports to be master. Within the context of this model, to become master a station issues a bus access request. To keep track of its place, a station gets a number function of the stations in the network. From this, it subtracts 1 every time a station releases the bus. When the count is zero, it is its time to talk. The arbitration unit is a piece of link port hardware which connects the station to the carrier. The Manchester encoding scheme was selected to delimit the command words. Crash recovery measures required a collision detection mechanism. If two masters start talking at once, this mechanism comes into action.

Generally, with industrial process control schemes, urgent information can be coded into a short high-priority message and routed to the destination node through a privileged path. The latter was created by means of dedicated memory buffers, formatting procedures, and high-priority transmission. The activation mechanism together with the privileged path guarantees the delivery of urgent messages as required by the application.

For security reasons, the protocol must be able to detect faults or failures occurring in the transmission line or in the nodes connected to it and start recovery procedures. Every message must be acknowledged by the receiving interface: positive acknowledgment means correct message; negative acknowledgment means wrong message; busy acknowledgment means message refusal because of buffer or line saturation; and timeout means message refusal because of failure in the equipment. Monitoring action should reflect on the node liveness and the network status. Events out of control that can be caused by the failure of one or more nodes connected to the network must be detectable by the protocol.

While this example is concerned primarily with a process control environment where data acquisition, signal processing, alarm monitoring, supervisory control, and action set the pace of the system—several of the considerations being made are just as valid in other environments. In general, a distributed information system of this nature can be implemented at four levels:

1. Microprocessors for data acquisition.
2. Monitoring and actuation at the factory floor.
3. Distributed computer control in a plant-wide sense.
4. A broader data communications environment with wide area connectivity.

In any and every application, decisions must be reached in terms of the design characteristics. Should the nodes be passive (no master, no slave) or active (master and slave)? Should the local network be bus or ring? Which kind of intrinsic redundancy should be accepted? Which way to error recovery? And, above all, what is *our* strategy in factory automation?

23.7 Management's Strategic View of Networks

Whether they are in an office or in a factory, local area networks are there to fill a need that fits into a broader strategic perspective established by management. The more advanced a system a company has the better it can control its costs. In a competitive market, this is of the greatest importance. Previously existing structures are, from a certain point of view, practical standards in the network systems evolution. They represent processing availability and focus on commitments which have taken place and therefore on investments. But there is no guarantee that they continue to serve *our* company's current and future requirements.

With LAN, long-haul communications, workstations, and robotics, emphasis must be placed on development planning. New systems have to be balanced to avoid any trouble in the company's communications either for lack or complexity of information. The balance between the need and availability is the result of planning and control activities about costs, resources, and time involved in managing and developing the systems themselves. To satisfy our company's developing requirements we should carefully examine both the present situation and our future goals. Strategic decision making and long-range policy formulation should be prerequisites to WS and LAN implementation, while at the mechanics level we should exercise project control and provide for proper organization. The organization process calls for specific actions in following fundamental parts of the management: systems and strategy, structure and skills, style and staff, and objectives control. It also needs operating guidance via budget, balances, operating analyses, reports, indexes, yields, and relating the different phases of management and technological process into one comprehensive system.

Both logically and physically the system's online structure has to provide:

- Horizontal correlation to exchange information between elementary areas, implementing the logistics cycle
- Vertical correlation to exchange information between different management levels for planning, programming, executing, and controlling

- Time correlation to synchronize operations and divisional business belonging to each area and depending on management action
- Environmental correlation for knowing, filtering, foreseeing, and analyzing the external environment
- Market correlation for promoting, selling, handholding the client, and assuring feedback

Based on these premises, one of the better-known manufacturing firms projected a network configuration, taking into account the following considerations: price and performance ratios, software and hardware investment protection, system reliability and availability, obsolescence of the used technologies, modularity and compatibility in hardware and software, geographical and logistic constraints, and different operational methods in network use. Largely reflecting the same considerations, a well-known financial institution restructured its national and international voice, text, and data network in a manner shown in Figure 23.7. It also installed LANs using the existing PBX cabling.

Other organizations have moved toward value-added applications, capitalizing on an already existing and operating communications infrastructure. For instance, Diesel-Electric Locomotive Troubleshooting Aid (DELTA) is an expert system built by General Electric to assist maintenance personnel in isolating and repairing diesel train engine problems. It is a consultation system incorporating a software architecture which consists of a domain-independent inference engine with a domain-specific knowledge bank. It:

- Uses a hybrid inference mechanism allowing both forward reasoning, from facts to conclusions, and backward reasoning, to confirm or disprove hypotheses
- Features over 500 rules to assist a technician in locating and repairing problems with diesel engines

Diagnostic and repair knowledge is contained in approximately 300 rules. The other rules provide a help function to answer user queries and provide additional information. Quite important in a factory environment, DELTA uses CAD files, such as schematics of the diesel engine system or its parts that are being analyzed, to provide help to the user, thus enhancing General Electric's locomotive repair facilities.

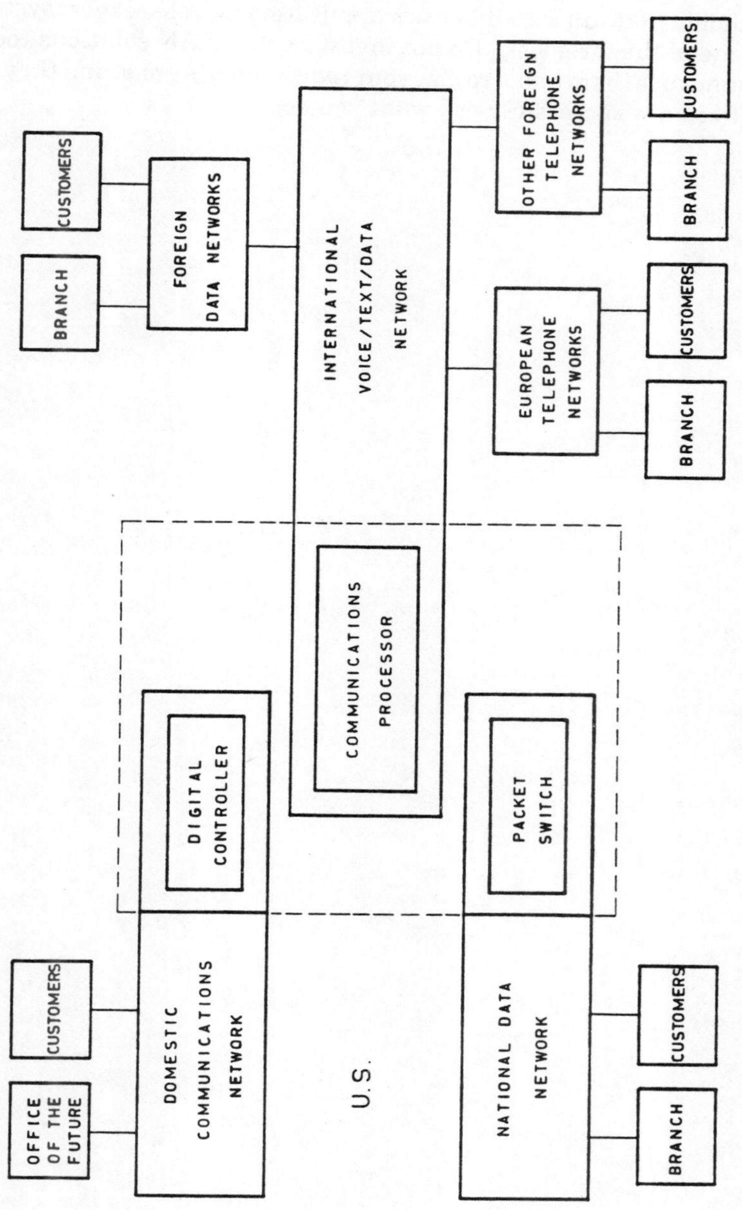

Figure 23.7 Organization chart of a restructured voice and data network in a major financial institution.

Planning and implementing local area networks for the years to come should take full account of new applications areas—expert systems being one of the foremost. Do not invest in slow LAN solutions today. You cannot use them tomorrow as your requirements grow, and they will grow if you are successful with what you do.

Chapter

24

Myriaprocessors—The LAN as System Integrator

24.1 Introduction

"Myria" means 10,000. There is no LAN with 10,000 terminals on it, but some internetworked LANs, plus wide area capabilities today, exceed this mark by an order of magnitude. In this sense, the WSs, servers, and LANs form a myriaprocessing system. They also provide for system integration of the attached devices among themselves and toward the environment in which they operate.

Total system integration has become a key word for new online systems; this involves simultaneously approaching several areas of activity with the concept of integration in mind. This concept itself is in full evolution, changing over time. With distributed databases and distributed communications, the integration concept today emphasis the ability to make diverse equipment (hardware and software) work together over extended geographical areas. The key is the ability to establish and observe a high-level protocol—making this exchange of information possible in a transparent manner. Further, in an integration sense, network design must make sure that we build a system which is flexible and expandable. It is almost certain that as applications experience accumulates, we will need to:

- Increase the number of nodes
- Accommodate new types of servers
- Attach more powerful workstations
- Blur the distinction between the one processor and the other
- Pay particular attention to end-user considerations

Integrated workstations and end-user facilities are a major contribution of the LAN, as the WS and its software are our major concern. Another important integration factor is the operation of a distributed database. There is a general principle, known as the 80/20 rule, which suggests that, of all the data traffic in a network, 80 percent never leaves the immediate area, hence the LAN. Only the remaining 20 percent must be communicated remotely.

24.2 Ways and Means toward an Integrating Capability

If we plan to use the local area network as a system integrator, and there is no reason why we should not do so, we must select a LAN architecture which is flexible, easy to implement, and maintain. We must also choose protocols which provide reasonable assurance of error correction and guarantee message delivery.

Since the typical office worker interacts with diverse workstations, each having its own set of languages, procedures, and databases, a basic challenge is to:

1. Make office workstations an aggregate of functions while remaining flexible and expandable.
2. Provide solutions using the best current technology can offer.
3. Identify the workstations concepts and applications that will be carried over into the next generation of workstations accepted in the implementation area of which we are responsible.

Requirements analysis and software processes involve design problems and bridging methods. Both call for study and research. Our designs should be instructed not to jump to conclusions before they have all the facts. Nowhere is this advice more important than in the development and use of distributed databases—where current experience is thin on a worldwide basis.

When installing a distributed database, every step, from assessing the needs of end users to assigning data administrators, is crucial. A carefully thought-out plan would see to it that before we discuss installation, we should clearly define duties and responsibilities from computer professionals to every single end user. We must convince our computer and communications specialists of the wisdom to paying attention to the total environment capability. We must also train them to do so. As described in Figure 24.1, this turns from network management to system management, including the central computer resources.

Against this background the basic steps in system integration studies should be followed: identifying the problem, planning the activities, establishing the criteria (success and benefit), selecting a pilot group, trying to understand the department we are selecting (early and late adapters), comprehending the specific technology we propose to use, and involving the users in the process. Quite clearly, much of this work will be iterative: replanning, reevaluating, settling milestones; explaining the milestones to users, implementors, and management; showing results; and providing documentation. We should also migrate the experience to cover, in an orderly manner, all departments in our organization.

Our plan should definitely be to make the acquired integration know how operational on a larger scale. Then, to postaudit it—as well as to maintain and update it. Our policy must also account for the fact that obsolescence, always a creeping phenomenon, is visible more rapidly as technological development accelerates. Two forces push computers and communications systems toward obsolescence: economics and functionality. A system is ready for replacement when the costs of keeping it exceed those of changing to another one—or when it cannot meet the ongoing and projected needs. Thus, there are two criteria pushing toward system change.

Figuring a system's operating costs is mainly mathematics. The challenge is to include all costs. Depreciation and maintenance are only the start. There are also expenses for space, cooling, and power. Costs for technical support increase as a system approaches retirement. Ancillary costs make a system uneconomical even if we get it free. A serious systems integration study should project 5 years into the future, with firm plans covering the first 2 years. Design reviews must be

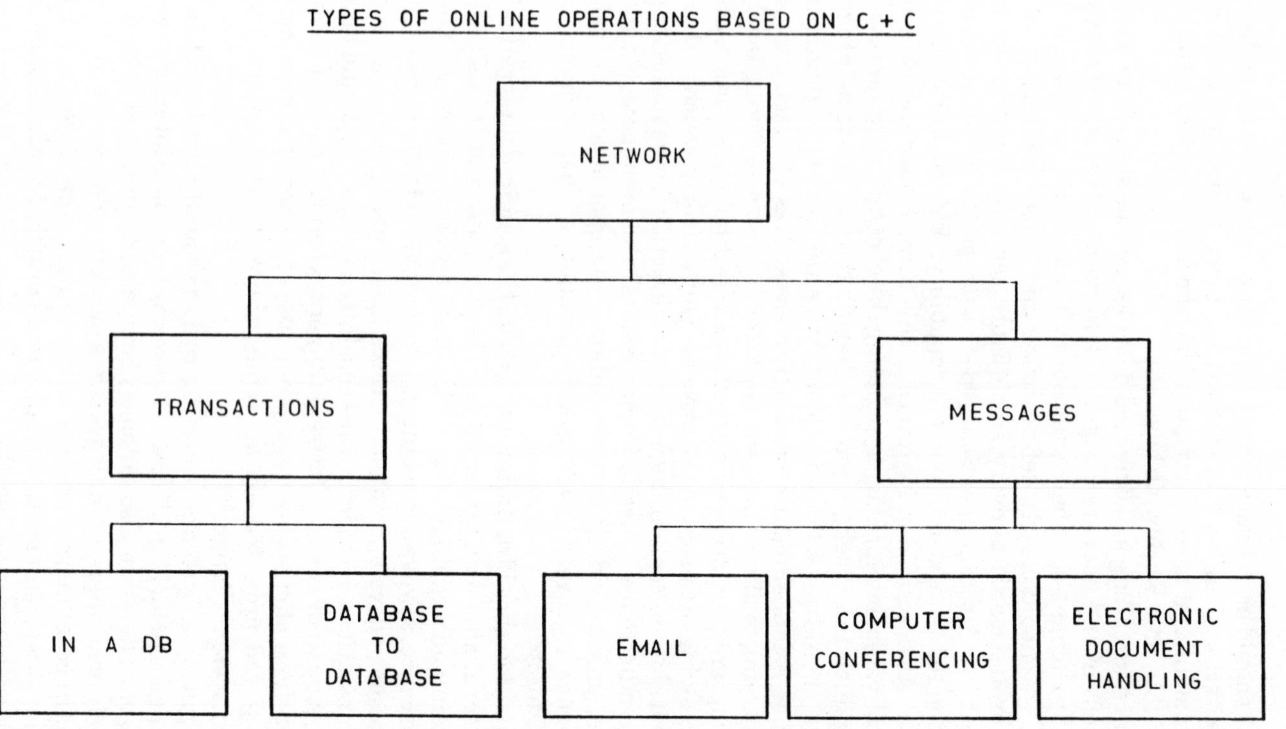

Figure 24.1 Types of online operations based on computers and communications.

established to ensure the continued validity of our myriaprocessor projects.

In order to achieve system integration we need a concept and a plan. Figure 24.2 answers an integration query by presenting a classification into high and low data rate resources—from host to workstation. Different levels of capabilities are distinguished. Notice that the same network supports databasing and datacomm functions which, in the last analysis, help define what a WS can (or cannot) do. Sometimes the latter list can be impressive. The most common trap is not technical. It is a fundamental management issue. Physically connecting WSs together is only part of what is needed to integrate a work group or department, making the system run in a satisfactory manner.

Many companies think they can solve a problem by throwing money at it. Vendors encourage this by positioning LAN hardware to be purchased within the existing budget and approval process. They also promote the ease of hardware connectivity. This approach is popular, since even partial connectivity of the workstations in an office normally improves productivity. The pitfall is:

- Lack of sufficient planning
- A resulting underspecification of the network
- Total lack of integration perspectives

Connecting workstations might create a multiuser environment, but it does not necessarily make an integrated one. There is no substitute to proper planning. If we really want an integrated application, this concept should always be in our minds throughout the planning process, the design, implementation, and maintenance of the LAN.

24.3 Conceptual Transition for Effective Implementation

To start the integration study in the right way, it is important to keep in mind that we have two poles around which our project should revolve: The first is system integration in a corporate sense, with databasing and data communications being the connecting links. The second is end-user activities at each and every workstation we place within our organization. The basic axiom at the WS level should be that rather than spending precious time to reinvent the wheel (software), we must apply brain power to rethink and reorganize the procedure. Part and parcel of

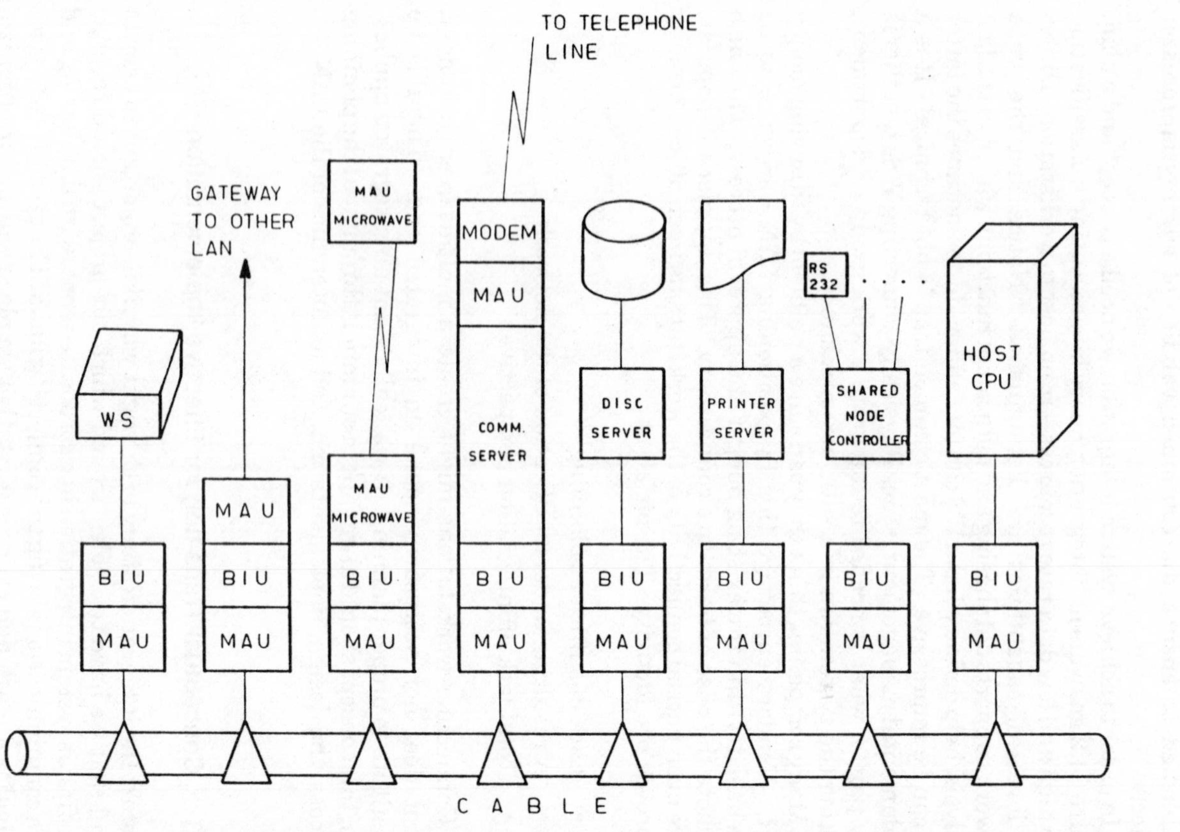

Figure 24.2 Concept and plan for local networking used by a Japanese computer and communication vendor.

this work is classifying and identifying all entities (logical and physical) which come into play in our project.

One of the benefits of an integration study is that it can expose many of the things that ought not to be done at all. The change in the workplace should reflect the gradual conversion from an industrial to an information economy. Such goals need conceptual transition. How well this transition will be met is going to determine the quality level at which our office and factory system will function well into the 1990s. The approach to research and implementation of integrating capabilities should be characterized by fundamental studies which include:

1. Structural aspects (responsibilities, indicators, objectives).
2. An analysis of the information flow (origins, links, nodes and switches, store and forward, destination).
3. Processing proper (to be executed whenever possible through packages).
4. Final presentation (online communication, video as a rule, hardcopy as an exception, color, and graphics).

A comprehensive presentation, short response time, and assistance in timeout should be integral parts of our preoccupation at the system analysis level. They are also key elements in assuring the proper integration capability throughout the LAN.

Myriaprocessor-type studies should be more extensive (and more fundamental) than any similar studies made for computer applications. In a major application the WS study for a second-generation myriaprocessor involved:

- All phases of office work
- Decision support systems
- Managerial and professional productivity
- Document filing, retrieval, and distribution
- Security and protection
- Reliability and availability
- Steady, distributed journaling
- Automatic error recovery
- Human engineering

System definition was well documented. Selected software was standard incorporated open-ended approaches (user exits), easy compatibility (system-wide), and efficient communications approaches.

Some OSs provide the utilities needed for file and record locking, but they are not automatically implemented. The applications must be specifically written for the network or adapted to it. For instance, even in the most recent network version, dBase requires that the source code of database programs be modified for multiuser access. Furthermore, some applications are advertised as multiuser but actually provide only primitive file locking on access. File locking is normally adequate for word processing and spreadsheets but not for a highly interactive business environment.

A major pitfall is to assume that existing PC applications will run properly on the LAN, which will take care of issues automatically. Vendors too often reduce the issue to simple compatibility: whether or not the application runs at all on a single workstation in the network. Because the LAN acts as integrator, WS accesses create increasing demands on the servers which hold common files and applications. Network traffic inevitably exceeds projections as users discover the benefits of electronic mail and time management. These are issues to consider when projecting the LAN—whether it for a first-, second-, or third-generation implementation. This is also true for determining possible handicaps. A survey of large users conducted for Honeywell by Hammer and Company found that the number of PCs attached to minicomputers and mainframes was projected to increase from 26 percent in 1985 to 44 percent by 1988. Yet, over 50 percent of the respondents went on to point out that inadequate facilities for connectivity and information exchange with other systems were significant in inhibiting the implementation of departmental systems within their organizations.

Other aspects, too, should be considered. Some traditional computer vendors place a high value on their mainframes base because "the mainframe is the backbone," the key to account control. This was true in the past, but it is not so today. The network, not the mainframe, will increasingly be viewed as the backbone. Eventually the mainframe will be regulated to the role of a server: the database server, gateway, and number cruncher of a network.

As myriaprocessor applications multiply, compatibility issues will increasingly focus on compatibility with the existing network, not compatibility with the mainframe. This has major ramifications for all systems since it will become considerably easier to install WSs on a LAN than to share the mainframe's or mini's cycles. But easier attachment does not answer all compatibility requirements. Even in a single-vendor environment, there are compatibility problems between different PC configurations. A frequent problem is video: an application configured for a black and white monitor on one workstation will not run on a workstation with a color adapter. Two copies of the application may need to be installed, complicating system administration.

Planning, installing, and supporting a LAN is further complicated when multiple vendors are involved. Typically, no vendor accepts responsibility for a problem. Therefore, unless we have a LAN supplier who can support a mix of different PCs, peripherals, and software at our site, we need to budget additional staff time for support.

Figure 24.3 integrates the foregoing and leads to two pivot points: the development and operation of fault-tolerant systems based on myriaprocessors and the able administration of an information system for management. LANs, PCs, servers, and gateways are the tools. The object is to:

- Bring computer power to every desk
- Make the access to large databases transparent
- Improve managerial and professional productivity through communicating workstations

The systems integration study should see to it that the background factors are properly studied—and the foreground mechanics are supported properly. Both issues are vital to implementing a valid solution.

24.4 Effective Approaches to Personal Computing—A Recycling Policy

As most user organizations have found, the essence of the PC evolution is individual access to computing power at an affordable price. Besides cost efficiencies, a personal computer in the executive, professional, and clerical environments combines the benefits of:

1. Fast response in interaction with a powerful local computer.
2. Distributed processing.
3. Locally accessible databases.
4. Access to public databases.
5. Online to mainframe and minicomputer resources.

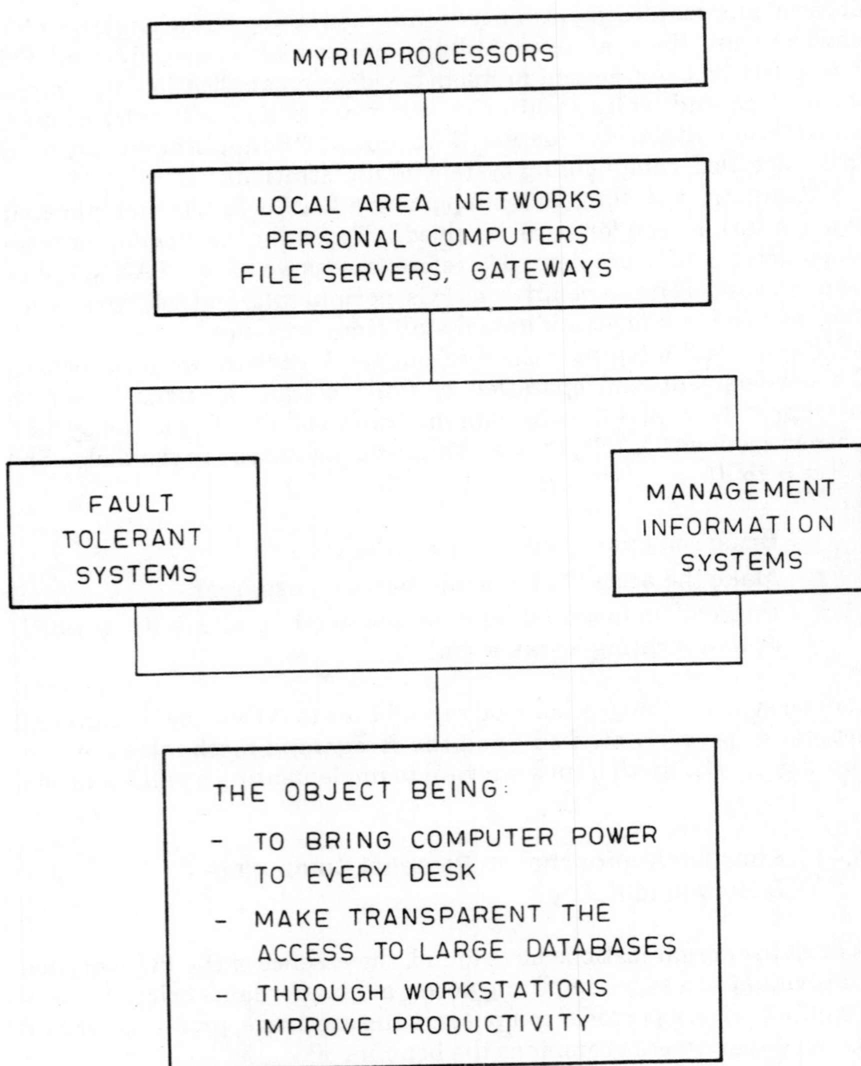

Figure 24.3 Fault tolerant systems and information systems for management have common requirements.

6. Interconnection with the environment (clients, suppliers) through gateways.

The personal workstation should be seen as a monotask, one-user, one-terminal, multi-processor, low-cost, high-capacity device. A valid approach to personal computing equips such WSs with ample applications libraries, use-programmable facilities, and user-friendly interfaces.

Both individually and as an aggregate, workstation solutions should present the user population with a greater reliability than centralized resources with nonintelligent terminals, better supported facilities than those so far available, faster response time, internetworking capabilities, and polyvalent messaging systems. There should be flexibility in applications programming choices, while an open architecture offers significant advantages in WS selection. Figure 24.4 divides WSs into mono- and multiple function machines. The former are nonintelligent terminals and the latter are based on PCs. Among intelligent, multifunctional WSs, the simpler are for word processing. The most complex are the engineering WSs to which the new generation of supermicro (IBM RT, Sun, Apollo, etc.) address itself.

At the mid-range professional level, the workstation should be seen as one substitute for 12 office elements: paper, pencil, memos, reports, charts, calculators, typewriters, copiers, filing cabinets, dumb terminals, telex, and to a certain extent, voice. The implementations environment should coordinate these 12 elements in a planned, integrated manner with one intelligent terminal per desk. There is no room for more. Even at the secretarial level, the use of PC and WP software makes unwise the employment of independent word processors or terminals for electronic mail and a host of other applications:

1. We should capitalize on software to specialize the hardware functions.
2. We should remember that products are convergent.
3. We must look at the PC as an integral part of the mainframe resources.

Trying to do everything on the mainframe has resulted in a situation where the smaller the problem, the larger the overhead. Today, in many mainframe-based installations, more than 90 percent of the effort is for the environmental connections, less than 10 percent for the problem

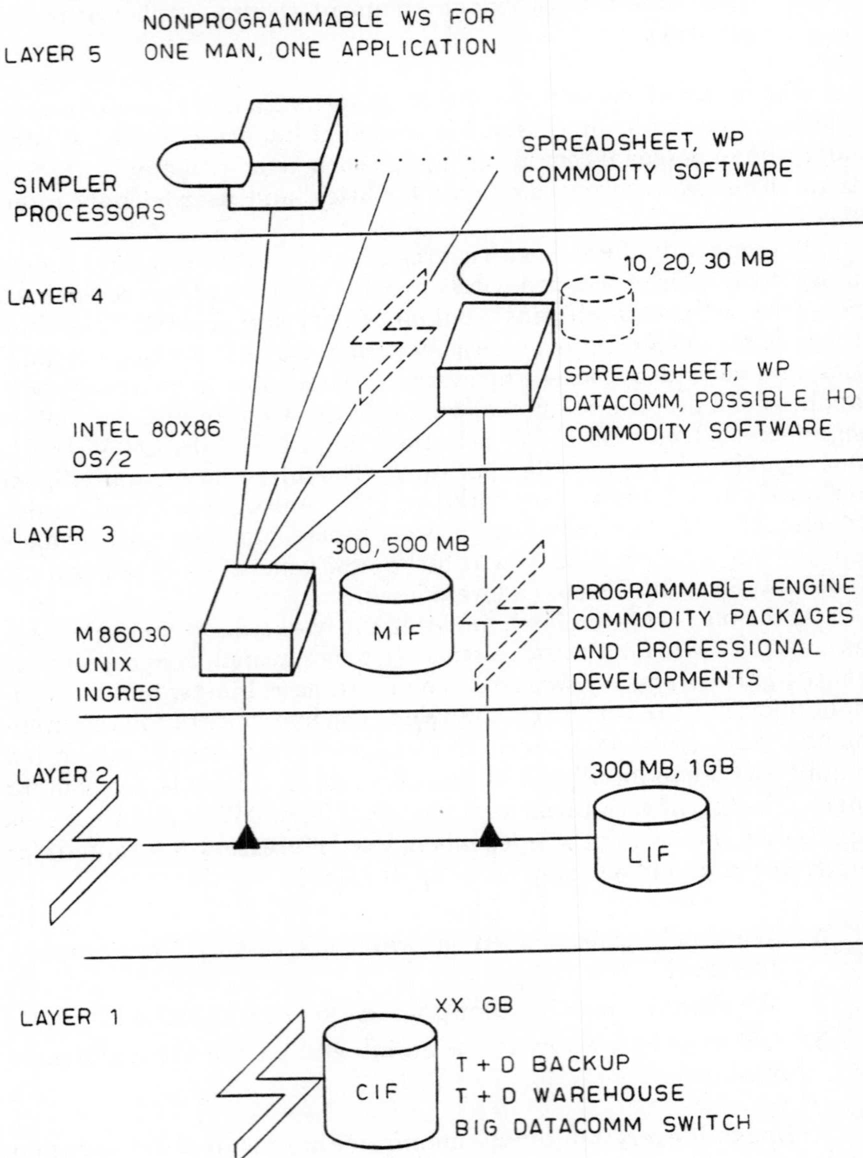

Figure 24.4 A layered approach to the organization of workstations as well as departmental and central text and database (T+D) resources.

itself. A good rule is that only very large projects should be put on mainframes. But should there be very large projects? Isn't it better to break them down into small, manageable parts? There are background factors to be considered:

1. The mainframe approach keeps the functions separate. But with intelligent WSs, we do all functions at the workbench level and this produces faster results.
2. The end user must get personally involved with the application of computers and communications from analysis to 4GL programming.
3. We should assure a steady transition from dumb to intelligent terminals. Most organizations have thousands of them installed. They are still in the majority. Even many PCs work as dumb terminals with 3270.

Intelligent workstations have different degrees of ability to handle dumb connections in emulation of dumb terminals, local storage of downloading with only error control, structure and formatting of downloaded data, and local work on data. The functional capabilities include local formatting prior to sending upline, microfile handling on a file access basis, microfiles with DBMS, the use of DBMS as a programming language at run time, a variety of increasingly sophisticated communications protocols, and simultaneous processing and communications with one or more mainframes.

A study for a leading financial institution aimed at putting some metrics in the PC reference. Figures 24.5, and 24.6 present a snapshot of this study:

- Figure 24.4 outline a layered approach. Five levels have been identified: from central resources to recycled aged PCs used at the teller level.
- Figure 24.5 focuses on managerial WSs. All routines, whether basic software or applications, run in parallel.
- By contrast, Figure 24.6 defines how the monoprocessing line of the applications environment (whether under MS-DOS or another OS). The basic software is present, but the machine is dedicated to one application at a time.

The LAN acts as the integrator. A result of the difference in OSs has

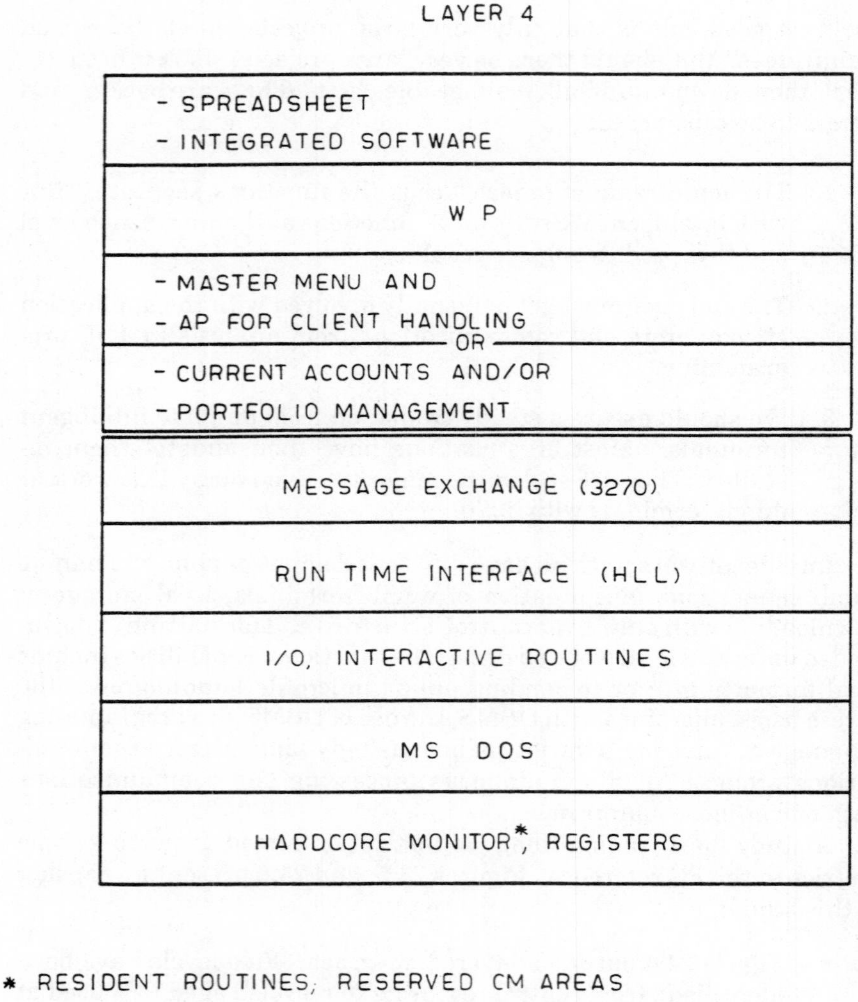

Figure 24.5 The managerial WS is multifunction.

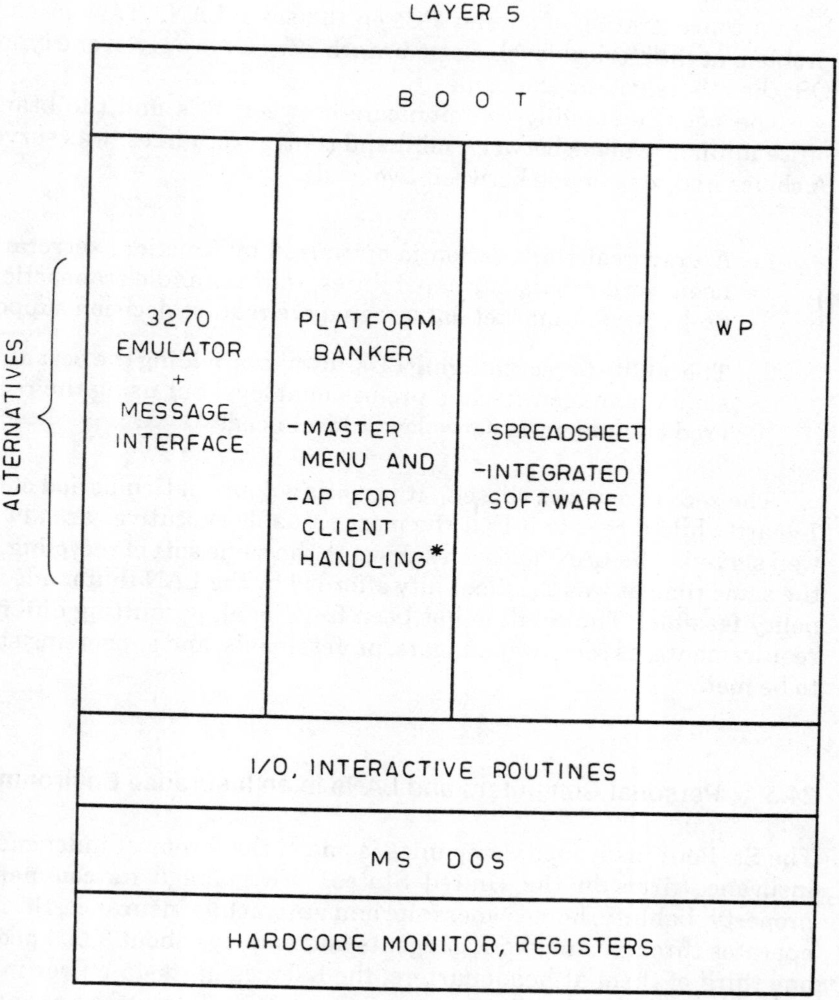

* CUSTOMER PROFITABILITY, CASH CONTROL, INVESTMENT CONSULTING, LOAN ORIGINATOR, OR LOAN LOSS CONTROL SYSTEM

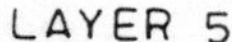

Figure 24.6 Layer 5. A lower cost WS for low level functions, executing them one at a time.

been a concentration of similar PCs on the same LAN. This posed no problem at the clerical level. Some branch offices were given one type of OS; the others got another type.

The need to steadily communicate between PCs and the branch office mini, as well as between mini and central resources, was served. A choice had to be made between two goals:

1. A universal workstation is optimized by function; secretaries need word processing capabilities, tellers handle transactions, brokers want market data, managers require decision support.
2. The ability to recycle aging PCs, always providing the best at the senior management and professional level but using the recovered equipment to serve lower-level needs.

The second one was chosen. It permits a depreciation period of 6 to 7 years while it sees to it that the most valuable executives are always well served. The LAN has been subject to the same sort of recycling. At the same time, it was the flexibility afforded by the LAN that made this policy feasible. The solution has been functional, permitting different requirements, as seen by managers, professionals, and supporting staff, to be met.

24.5 Personal Computers and LANs in an Insurance Environment

The St. Paul Insurance Companies is one of the foremost independent insurance firms in the United States. To manage its commercial property, liability, homeownership, and automobile insurance, St. Paul operates through a network of agents and employs about 9,000 people, one third of them at headquarters, the balance in its 45 offices in the United States and Canada. Responsibilities at the home office are policy making, product development, marketing, accounting, and data processing. Operations at branch offices include underwriting, handling of claims, and management of agent accounts. The major effort in automation—particularly the PC and LAN—is directed at this level. They had 47 Arcnet LAN at various locations around the United States. At each remote location, there are some 5 to 15 terminals, one or two printers, a file server, and a communications processor.

To understand the use of this myriaprocessor solution we should first look on the mechanics of the procedural work. The insurance products are sold by independent agents. Agents quote the premiums, but they also have access to several insurance companies, hence, the competitive importance for the insurance company of having online quotation of risk in the agent's terminal. For the St. Paul Insurance Companies, this rea- time dealer service developed in three steps:

1. From mainframe usage the company moved to distributed data processing with datapoint installations at the regional office. The Datapoints were basically used for data entry, the handling of files, remote printing, and as commercial processors.
2. The Datapoints at the offices were wired together through ARC. The same was done at headquarters, beginning with WP applications. The ARC local area networks started being used in 1980 and expanded within 1 year as the company converted to LANs from stand alones. Significantly, there has been an easy software conversion. The process took about 3 months, and the stand alone machines became part of a LAN operating environment; performance and reliability rapidly increased. Per office it now stands at a better than 99 percent. With stand alones, reliability was at 95 percent, and four points is a major improvement.
3. St. Paul Insurance Companies work actively to place personal computers at the agent's site. The IBM PC was originally chosen for this application, but the implementation plan goes much further than this and includes the whole issue of linking long haul the agents' PCs to the LAN and the LAN to the mainframes.

Such a problem is not unique to any one firm. Every major computer user has it and it has two levels:

1. Tie together the company's own offices rather than using leased lines.
2. Connect the agents to the offices and the headquarters.

The insurance office LAN and the agent's PC started communicating through automatic modems. Every effort was also made to convert the user's mentality to interactive systems since office automation is not going anywhere unless most senior executives and middle managers employ workstations as an everyday tool. The company realized that when executives, middle managers, and professionals—not just clerks and secretaries—start using the microprocessor-based workstations, the new system's potential will break through. Next to organizational-wide training and change in culture comes the streamlining of procedural problems. These, too, relate to people.

Another insurance company used the myriaprocessor to institute a clearing house. It provides user names to network address correspondence, thus insulating the user from the need to understand the topology of the network.

Another service is internetworking routing, encapsulating LAN packets within the transmission protocols of LANs and WSs to be logically tightly connected. It constitutes another issue where local area networks and value-added networks (VAN) come together. In this case, an approximately designed gateway translates the low- and medium-level protocols of foreign networks into the corresponding in-house LAN protocols. This way, dissimilar network types can be interconnected. Furthermore, an interactive terminal service permits remote workstations to access filing, printing, electronic mail, and other services available on the in-house LAN.

24.6 Supporting an SNA Gateway

The salient problem of one project has been the provision of an SNA gateway on a high-speed LAN interconnecting a number of mainframes. It has to do with the Massnet implementation discussed in Chapters 13 and 22—with Hyperchannel as infrastructure. The application would not have been feasible without a tested approach to the SNA gateway. Therefore, a search was made to locate already existing approaches operating in a satisfactory manner. The main one found was the McDonnell Douglas/Masstor Systems implementation involving some 20 IBM mainframes—from 8300 to 43XX—some of which support computer-aided design (Figure 24.7).

VTAM is the consistent interface on all mainframes. Masstor System's MTAM is the gateway. McDonnell Douglas searched for a more fundamental solution than the 3275 because they concluded:

1. There was considerable risk that by the end of the interconnect project more money had to be invested in 3275 than in the attached mainframes.

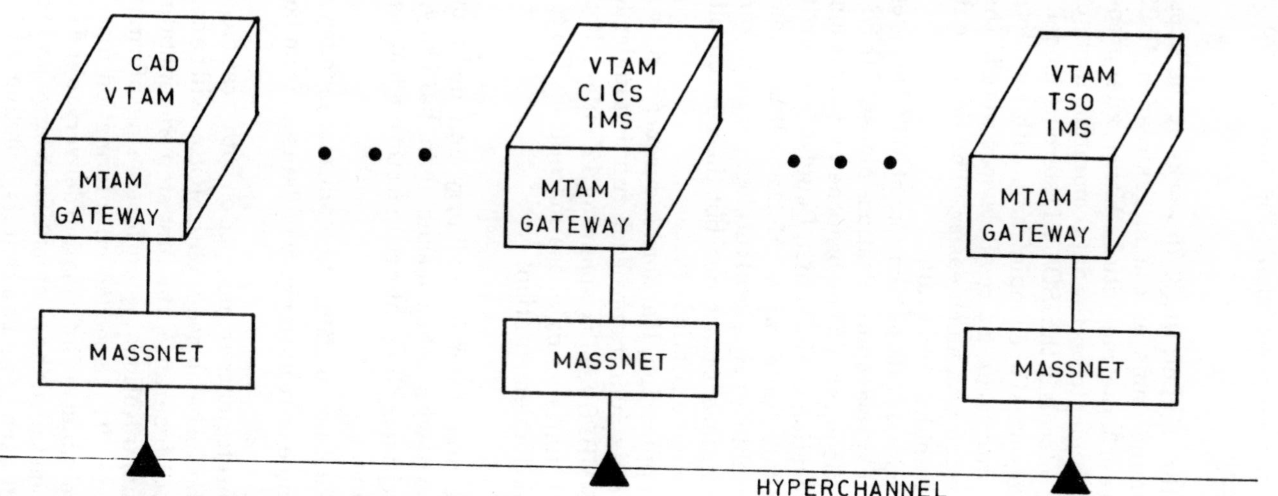

Figure 24.7 Hyperchannel/Massnet implementation involving a two-digit number of mainframes.

2. Even with such investment, the solution provided very slow response time.

In terms of throughput, the 3275 works at the kilostream (KBPS) level. Hyperchannel runs at the megastream (MBPS) level. The difference is three orders of magnitude. Hence, after proper examination Hyperchannel was adopted as the data communications engine enriched with higher-up protocols in the ISO/OSI reference model. This approach supported local terminals per mainframe with complete transparency (through VTAM interface). Since all devices were in the local domain, system configuration was much easier. The implementation involved text, data, and graphics screenfulls.

VTAM applications talk as partners of MTAM servers and requesters. In doing so, they use communications pipes at MBPS capacity. Wide area communications can also be branched into this aggregate. While the current application at McDonnell Douglas is about 10 miles apart, a new one will be 2000 miles wide. McDonnell Douglas runs a catalog management capability using local catalogs per mainframe. The catalog entry points are different machines, but there is consolidation through the multi layer communications system.

In another application, Hartford Insurance has two computer centers with five to six mainframes each running under MVS. They are linked with 1.5-MBPS facility spanning 12 miles. Both employ mass storage (M 860) units as database machines. Three goals seem to characterize this implementation:

1. Provide processing in Sudburry and make output available downtown with other means than hardcopy. The adopted approach is spooling, interconnect through Massnet, then microwave link.
2. Assure data management on Masstor memory.
3. Guarantee critical recovery of datasets from both locations.

Information elements are mapped on both locations. Originally, this was accomplished in batch node. With MCS, it will be done interactively.

For Hartford Insurance, the first step was installing the Massnet high-speed communications system for sharing information between the two data centers. This speeded up information distribution. It also improved the reliability of information delivery to end users. As a second step, Hartford installed the forementioned large-scale storage management system at each of its two centers, together with integrated data management control. This assured automated systems control, while also containing growth of online disk storage. With this solution, information elements are systematically migrated among storage levels to achieve reduced storage costs and improved user service responsiveness and to assure minimal impact on established data processing applications and equipment investment.

A study currently in process at Masstor Systems aims to answer the question of how to use communications techniques to partition query service from query response. This is in reference to a split transaction processing environment. A query interface assures memory residence for a short path designed for simple queries (about 90 percent of all cases). It filters the complex queries, pushing them to a background machine for answering. Such a two-tier system seems to simplify handling and assure better response time for the user.

From Hartford Insurance to McDonnell Douglas, the cases all involve the search for solutions which go beyond what we know already that "can" and "cannot" be done in DP. Many of our current policies and practices are largely conditioned by experiences which grew from relatively small computing centers. They fit neither distributed information systems environments nor very large central computer resources. These examples present a different picture. They are forward-looking and search for effective solutions to present and future problems. They employ technology to satisfy end-user requirements and incorporate high-capacity LANs not only as transmission media but also as integral, active parts of user-oriented solutions.

24.7 Instituting a Network Control Center (NCC)

There are several problems in network management, particularly when we have different equipment installed. In a myriaprocessor environment, some of the problems come from peer-to-peer communications and the lack of a master machine. IBM promotes Netview to assure that network management is expressed in the same way. While this is one of the possible approaches and there are other, more sophisticated NCC offers by third parties available, the problem remains that many users overlook proper facilities for network management. Some even miss the concept, thus failing to understand the need for NCC.

The most common case is that user organizations, even those heavily involved with computers and communications, fail to acquire the necessary tools and put all their trust on the network manager, as a person able to do everything. Fairly rough going for several years proves to them that this cannot and should not be the case. There are no cut and dry figures available to tell when a network control center is needed and when it should be installed. A rule of thumb is that:

- When we get more than 1-digit number of nodes in our network, the of managing our network steeply increase.
- When we get more than a 2-digit number of nodes, these problems become horrendous.

As the experience of the St. Paul Insurance Companies and other organizations in PC, LAN, and wide area networks help document, when we speak of the functionality of a total information system, a number of key components must be considered. The NCC is one of them, but there are more:

1. Within a distributed environment with PCs and minis, the mainframe is a main switch—not the DP handler—and it has to be examined as such.
2. Another main switch is the PBX. In many companies, there may be 5 or 10 different LAN technologies implemented. The PBX can serve as an interconnect. Furthermore, just as the PBX switches lines in a building, the action switch switches trunks. It optimizes FX, Watts, and pay lines (dial up).

The action switch is also necessary to keep costs under control, the more so since, for many companies, data communications expenses have doubled each year for the last 2 or 3 years. This helps reduce the workforce in the field through greater productivity, but carries its own cost and operational factors. For instance, when we enter the PBX into the equation, we should keep in mind the coming integration of text, data and image with voice as well as the wiring of the building necessary to handle the load. The telephone handset is empty now because all electronics fit on the chip. The size remains because it fits our hand, hence the drive to integrate the telephone set and the terminal.

What is happening is an integration of functions into a professional WS, including voice. Some LAN offerings capitalize on the second and third cabling of telephone twisted pair running through the buildings for expansion purposes. But they forget to capitalize on the benefits which come from the implementation of a NCC. The object of NCC is to assure needed services for smooth, uninterruptable operation of the LAN. Its various functions can be invoked manually by a terminal operator, automatically on NCC start-up, or remotely by special request over the network. Tasks involving quality data should be performed automatically without operator intervention. This includes:

- Network status monitoring
- Network activity monitoring
- Quality histories
- Identification of malfunctioning components

If abnormal conditions occur, the operator should be alerted by special messages on the control WS. The NCC should have a menu of commands available for network control, security, remote diagnostics, and generation of different operating reports. These commands must be executed in a foregoing-background mode without interfering with the normal functioning of the LAN.

Remotely initiated tasks will be typically used for access to the local, regional, or central databases. For instance, requests for downline loading of executable files will be handled through software in BIUs, gateways, and workstations. Downline dumping and upline loading may involve text and data files, programs, directory files needed for logical addressing, or other inquiries by network users. They must be managed automatically by the NCC.

BIU status messages are a primary input to the NCC for monitoring purposes. The NCCs messages can be used for supervisory tasks and reconfiguration. Logical and physical network configuration involves communications links, nodes, workstations, BIUs, gateway(s), server(s), hosts, and the NCC itself. The physical processing, transmission media, and also the software support can be affected. Network status information to be maintained includes:

- *Traffic.* Load on channels, BIU, statistics of sessions, messages, peak periods
- *Performance.* Throughput, response time, uptime availability
- *Equipment status.* State of BIU, gateways, servers, and workstations

Network management is an area in which little standards work has been done despite its significance for users. On the one hand there is a lack of NCC standardization and on the other exists an urgent user need for network monitoring systems. By employing them, network managers can count on maintaining performance and avoiding pitfalls in implementation. Among the benefits to be gained when we talk of NCC at large (both long-haul and local), we notice:

1. Automatic remote monitoring, allowing the central operator to obtain all pertinent network status information, eliminating the need for remote site test personnel.
2. Color-graphics monitoring, displaying line, modem, and terminal status in easy-to-read color charts.
3. Management reporting, enabling control site equipment to prepare comprehensive reports on system trends and behavior.
4. Network system restart and recovery from a remote site.

Polyvalent NCCs are software based, capable of monitoring today's most sophisticated online communications systems. Computer-based controllers can easily supervise multipoint and distributed text and data processing networks. Each control module maintains an ongoing check, collecting status data and responding to commands from the main controller.

24.8 Quality Histories to Manage Myriaprocessor Resources

The importance of keeping and exploiting quality histories should be properly underlined. They are vital to an agile and punctual network management—indivisible from its possibilities—just as instrumental to the proper management of a myriaprocessor implementation as they are to the long haul. Good, all-inclusive solutions should bring PBX data as well as LAN data and WS references into the quality history. The whole must create an integrated, comprehensive system. Partial approaches are not long lasting and they can prove detrimental in the longer run.

At the current state of the art, the NCC should maintain a quality database of network resource information. Data can be collected from BIU status reporting messages. One of the basic contributions of a quality database is that it provides an interactive, standardized information reference for control purposes. This makes it feasible to examine failures, test for weak points, evaluate fail-soft paths, and analyze the network traffic load. A more sophisticated quality history approach would stimulate the behavior of attached devices on the basis of warning signals, thus providing a forward control capability. Preventive maintenance is a must. The NCC should periodically check circuits to detect gradual, marginal degradation, which under normal circumstances goes unnoticed.

Isolation of network failures by maintenance personnel must be facilitated. This involves the ability to remotely execute diagnostic tests to isolate workstation, server, or network problems. Intermittent software problems should also be analyzed by dumping the memory contents of the component to the NCC. Maintenance-related data should be integrated into the quality history network database. Related activities consist of fault detection, identification, isolation, repair, and preventive maintenance. The log produced when performing the remote diagnostics function can be a major source of this information.

As the LAN implementation expands to sensitive areas, other necessary activities are security and user-access control. User-access control occurs during log-in and log-out. The minimum level of validation consists of authentication of a user password. Log-in permits the user to initiate a network session; thus an association between the user's workstation and other network nodes can take place.

To perform these functions in an able manner, the NCC requires administrative information:

- A myriaprocessor hardware directory typically contains a list of all registered hardware devices with their descriptions, including names and chassis serial number.
- A myriaprocessor configuration table includes a current configuration description: nodes, WSs, servers, communication link, and channel parameter—and a history of all reconfiguration changes including the description, date, and time.

A configuration status table focuses on the current operational status of hardware and software components. A list of all registered network software names, release versions, source code, and object code, should be found in the network software directory. The traffic log files contain the traffic measurements from the network data collection points, plus traffic statistics computed through a traffic analysis tool. The object of a user directory file is a list of user names, addresses, and authorized functions; that of a function directory file is a list of functions, with names and addresses. The user menu file contains a list of all user menu screens for display at workstations—and the operator command file and a history of all operator commands.

This brief description of an enhanced functionality helps document that while PC and LAN is the way to enter the new era of computing—we have to do considerable preparatory work to make the system successful. Productivity is improved with WSs—but if we don't find the right standards and implement them, this information system can become the bottleneck.

Chapter

25

Cost and Effectiveness

25.1 Introduction

One of the strategems employed by the computer and communications sales engineers is trying to convince the user organization that it is getting the vendor's "best deal." This may be expressed either in terms of a price offering ("a true bargain"), of technical characteristics, or both (the "preferred customer" policy). This strategem is more successful when the supplier can convince the customer that their business relation should follow a standard contract that the vendor provides and from which no deviations are accepted. At times, the vendor may go along with some minor concessions to the user firm "because of their long-standing business relationship." However:

1. The fine point of any standard-type contract from the computer and communications manufacturer is always against the customer's best interest.
2. The "concessions" are often trivial compared to what the user organization can obtain if it knows how to twist the vendor's arm.

Arm twisting needs two key factors to be successful: the one is a strong negotiator who is respected by the vendor's sales personnel. The other, is a thorough know how of the field, including:

- An intimate acquaintance with LANs, WSs, servers, hosts
- The knowledge of how to define goals, establish specifications, and choose among alternatives
- The ability to discard the nonessential in order to focus on the most important issues, both technically and financially

25.2 The Supplier Problem—How to Handle It

Knowing all the variables involved in dealing with manufacturers of computers and communications gives more control over the contractual situation. Critical factors include the type of a contract which safeguards the user organization's interests, the ability to optimize charges—whether "fixed" prices or other, and the thorough screening of the equipment proposed for the job (software, hardware) in an attempt to establish alternatives, evaluate them, and make choices. The mastery of alternatives can play a dual role:

1. In developing a better understanding of what the market has to offer in terms of solutions. This cannot be done by reading the vendor's own literature. It takes field research to establish all relevant factors.
2. By gaining the proper amount of self-confidence. This permits the contract negotiation to be approached through tough working sessions establishing the ground rules and seeing them through. Such a policy helps eliminate a lot of problems for the user organization—but it creates an equal number for the manufacturer.

Just as important is the cost evaluation of the alternatives under study. As a first approximation, order of magnitude will do; precision is not necessary at this stage. It is more important to know what each alternative means in terms of an eventual expenditure and how the one compares to the other.

When we talk of the supplier problems for local area networks, we should always recall that many vendors are still relatively small companies, their wares are not necessarily directly comparable, and there is no real taxonomy of LAN prices, though we can strive to create one to help in the task of making valid comparisons. Table 25.1 represents orders of magnitude. It helps classify commodity LANs in terms of cost, type of cabling, data link protocol, data transfer rate, number of workstations, and prevailing local distance. PBXs have not been added since the service they provide is of a different nature. The lowest pricing range includes BIUs born into the PC and actuated by the vendor at a typical price of $50 per unit; they are often at no cost, as part of the deal. The over $3000 BIUs are for frequency division multiplexing (FDM) solutions and include the price of modems for mini and mainframe attachments. PC-level modems are cheaper.

These prices do not include the cost of file servers, print servers, and gateways. Neither the distance nor the number of attached devices considers interconnected LAN and wide area access. The references are given strictly on a local level and they are approximate. No two vendor offers are precisely the same. There can also be hidden costs in a vendor's offer. Training, for instance, is a fundamental cost of implementing a LAN. So is the software. Some vendors tend to price training and software separate from the hardware of the BIUs, taps, and cabling. Never examine a proposal without a clear view of the alternatives. If you do so, you are preparing yourself for self-deception. And you will regret it.

There are no precise rules on how to look at BIU pricing, but rules of thumb may be helpful. One is that the bus interface unit should not cost more than 10 to 15 percent of the cost of the attached device. The goal is 10 percent or less, but on special occasions 15 percent can be acceptable. In cases of baseband of the ±1 MBPS variety, there is a one-to-one relation between the BIU and the WS. This is not true of other faster baseband solutions or with broadband. In the latter case, the BIU's number of ports should be taken into account for the cost evaluation. The question then arises whether the number of the attached devices (per BIU) or the maximum number of ports should be taken as the reference.

Cost is not the only factor to consider. A thorough evaluation considers the weight of the LAN's technical characteristics and the way in which they fit the projected applications environment. As outlined in a preceding chapter, among the technical factors is the transmission medium to be used, the topology, and the protocols. The population of users is one of the basic criteria for evaluating a vendor's LAN offer. Other things equal, the larger this population is the better the supports

Table 25.1 Taxonomy of LAN prices at the WS interconnect level Cost per BIU

	Under $100	$100–$500	$500–$1,000	Alt. $500–$1,000	Over $1,000	Over $3,000
Cabling	Serial	Baseband twisted pair	Baseband twisted pair	Broadband coaxial	Broadband or baseband	Broadband
Data link Protocol	RS-232	CSMA/CD	Token ring	Token ring, CSMA/CD	Token ring, CSMA/CD	(FDM)
Data transfer rate	Up to 100 KBPS	500 KBPS–3 MBPS	1 MBPS – 5 MBPS	2 MBPS–10 MBPS	10 MBPS–50 MBPS	1–400 MHz
No. of WSs	About 4	2–20	10–50	10–150	50–200 or minis, mainframes	50–500 or minis, mainframes
Local distance (in meters)	30–150	150–500	150–1,000	1,000–3,000	Metropolitan area	Metropolitan area

of the LAN will develop. A similar statement can be made about the featured software able to enhance the higher-up layers of the implementation architecture.

25.3 A Computer Manufacturer's Viewpoint

While this text is written for the user, it is worthwhile to consider the opposite viewpoint: that of the manufacturer. This helps to get insight on the way vendors prepare themselves for their new drives in the market as well as on the way in which they handle the user organization. It also helps explain the problems vendors face in reacting to the market drives, to the advances of the new technology, and in advising their customers in terms of systems solutions. Let's then consider one equipment manufacturer whose products divide into two lines roughly equal in terms of business: office equipment and minis, PC, and other terminals. The personal computer challenge affected this manufacturer throughout its range of products. It was compounded by the LAN, an issue with which they had no previous experience but tried to gain through rights acquisition.

A market study demonstrated that lack of action would result in failure to match the shifting requirements of the client base. But action confronted management with three problems:

1. Technical, boiling down to the development and sale of a cost-effective equipment to hold the line against competition.
2. Marketing strategy: myriaprocessors could kill the minis and terminals product line, particularly the cluster solutions this manufacturer classically marketed.
3. Cultural, calling for a thorough revamp of images from the top all the way down to the line personnel.

Product planning got to work in order to provide solutions to the technical problem. The company produced a new series of machines: Delta-1 is a personal computer but without a LAN solution in its first release. Delta-2 and Delta -3 are cluster-oriented equipment. Should Delta-1 be converted to LAN orientation, provided with baseband solution, and marketed as a myriaprocessor in competition with its two bigger product brothers? Or should it be restricted to the hobbiest market and local friends?

A senior management meeting was held to evaluate the level of development and technical capabilities of the Delta-1 personal computer, the presence or absence of needed technical features, and the need for LAN features and applications software. This was a prelude to strategic decisions, as top management started realizing the importance of IBM-compatible personal computers in the marketplace. The conclusion of the meeting was that the evolution of the Delta-1 PC product would be a function of:

1. Its integration in the current line, with the Delta-2, and Delta-3 models.
2. The adoption of a low-cost LAN providing functionality without directly competing with multithread solutions.
3. What the competition will do along similar lines.

This is not necessarily so. While keeping both a PC/LAN product line and multithread on supermicros and/or minis (with non-intelligent terminals) makes sense for a period of time, this is not a longer-term solution. The short term is a transition period and may be necessary so that the vendor learns myriaprocessor skills, trains its people (both sales and system experts), sorts out all facets of a technical nature, and acquires or manufactures the components. Most importantly, a vendor should use this transition period to judge the impact of PCs and LANs on the client base and try to convert the client's image to the new technology.

A computer and communications manufacturer should always be on the look-out to offer customers the best solution, to make them partners in technological evolution. A fundamental decision was therefore needed as a starting point: "Is the PC and LAN solution more functional and more reliable if supported with adequate products?" The company meeting concluded that the cost to the company and its clients is lower with cluster (multithread) approach, with mini and nonintelligent terminals being taken as a reference. As Table 25.2 shows, this is not true. At the four-terminal level that was used during the management meeting for product line decisions, a LAN solution is lower cost by about 10 percent and much more reliable, functional, and user friendly.

Figure 25.1 dramatizes this. Given that both the micromini and the PC are microprocessor-based, rather than having one microprocessor divided between four people in terms of service as in a cluster solution, the first, second, and third choice should be four microprocessors per WS: the PC, frontending, graphic tablet, and the shared one for DB/DC/printing. Eventually, the real reason why the manufacturer pressed for

Table 25.2 LAN versus Cluster: Costs to the User.

Delta-3 / Cluster, 20 MB 4 nonintelligent terminals	*Delta-1 on a baseband LAN*	
About \$25,000 or slightly over this mark	\$4.5 K unit price	
	minus 1.2 K for the printer	
	minus 1.2 K for the floppy	
	2.1 K unit price	
	For 4 WS, we need 4 machines, plus a dedicated file server and a printer server.	
	6 units x 2.1 K\$/u =	\$12.6 K
	Printer	1.2 K
	Hard disk	5.0 K
	6 interfaces	2.4 K
		\$20.4 K

cluster came out. If they were to sell only Delta-1 on LAN, they would go out of business. With Delta-3 they made a good profit. In production costs, patting the four Delta-1s online cost 30 percent more than the cluster machine. This is a problem—but it is not the user's problem. By putting its best people on the job, they could solve the issue of high costs. This is precisely what it did 2 years later.

25.4 Economic Justification of the Way Users Look at the Problem

One financial institution conducted a costing study of nonintelligent terminals connecting long haul to mainframes versus a LAN solution. Both alternatives were examined for real-time applications. The comparisons which were made established some interesting data. Since the real-time application with nonintelligent terminals was ongoing for 12 years, the study contrasted the classical banking terminal to the PC, without considering (at first) telecommunications, which are heavy. Account was only taken of central computer costs and those incurred at the BO level (terminals, concentrator). When it became evident that a

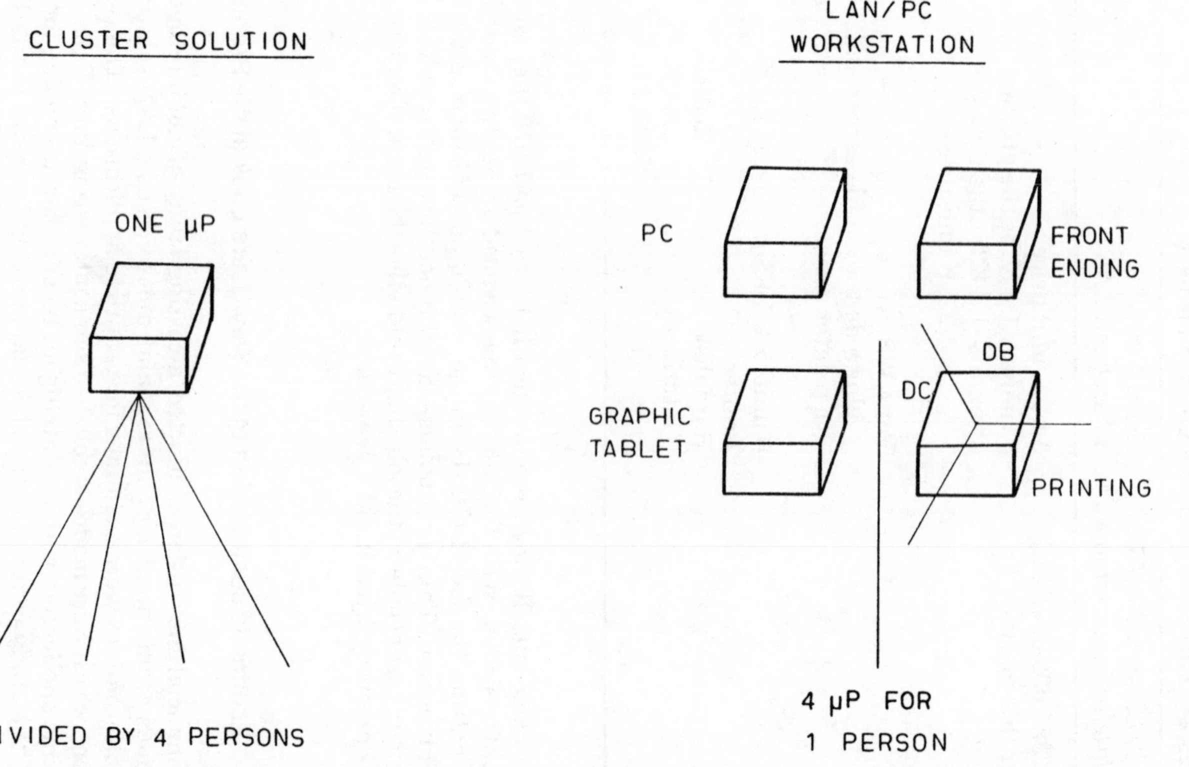

Figure 25.1 In a cluster solution there is a microprocessor for, say, 4 workstations. With PC and LAN, every user can have at his disposal dedicated microprocessors.

PC and solution was tremendously advantageous, the telecommunications costs were added in to get the total picture.

Table 25.3 gives the costing information, including the full telecommunications mainframe and terminal costs. Other costs were the operating and housing expenses for the mainframes. They were not accounted for since the data processing center had to remain no matter what. At the LAN side, telecommunications costs were repeatedly found to be slightly less than one-third the cost of the private lines necessary with a centralized solution using nonintelligent terminals. At the same time, the PC/LAN/file server system was much more robust, as far as the branch office operations were concerned.

A comparison was also made with minicomputer installations, and the result was very positive for LANs. These are not theoretical questions that can apply to any and every organization. The information systems costs always find their way into the budget, often by big strides. Decisions made today load the budget for the next 10 years. We simply cannot afford to forget about efficiency.

There is, however, the cultural aspect to keep in mind. This, too, has associated costs and challenges, particularly since the spread of personal computing, computers, and communications have come to constitute a corporate infrastructure. But personal computing has implications beyond the provision of processing and communications facilities to end

Table 25.3 Comparison of Mainframe and Noninelligent Terminals versus PCs and LANs—Yearly Cost per Workstation*.

Mainframes, long-haul lines, nonintelligent terminals (million $)		*LAN/PC (million $)*	
Terminals	1.92	WS	0.64
Telecommunications	1.60	LAN database and interfacing	0.40
Real time, shared mainframe	.90	Telecommunications	0.50
Real-time operating expenses	0.80	RT mainframe	0.20
		RT	0.10
	5.52		1.84

*Nonintelligent terminals, PCs, and servers are depreciated on a 5-year basis, mainframes on a 7-year basis. The telecommunications and operating costs are taken yearly.

users. It poses the need for new organizational structures which can create forms of organizational renewal. This goes beyond dollars and cents. Organizational renewal can be achieved only through a sound management policy for technology investments and when the senior management of the organization is keen to gain hands-on experience with new tools. Thus, dynamic companies should keep abreast of developments in computers and communications and carefully examine the prime importance of a detailed, documented study of information management requirements.

Another interesting cost evaluation is relative to a PC and LAN implementation which took place in a tough, dust-prone environment—freight forwarding. It employs some five to six WSs—a small LAN. Big crates, lorries, and drivers are registered through the WSs—which also produce the freight manifest. The myriaprocessor installed in this company does all the traditional data processing, some of which was previously done on a service bureau basis. This company moved from pencil to LAN. At the WS level, a printer (front-feed) is used given that, for export purposes, management needs four to five different types of documents—in fact, with the now standardized internal forms, only seven different documents are used at all.

PC and LAN was not the first choice when the manager of this firm decided to move out of the service bureau. This was a small business system (SBS), which would have involved a minicomputer and four nonintelligent terminals. But the manager and owner of this firm knew about reliability. So he examined the minicomputer vendor's offer from an availability standpoint and found it wanting. The PC and LAN solution gave him much more confidence. Costs were the second critical factor. The myriaprocessor solution was not only much more reliable, it was also less costly by an appreciable margin—30 percent.

Two workstations are devoted to the two secretaries, one is used by the manager himself, and another two are made available to the truck drivers. The latter operate directly on the machine, without secretarial interface. To assist the direct user, a prompt asks: "Have you got the right paper on the printer?" Procedural solutions provide further assurance. For backup purposes, a secretary makes a copy of the disk every night on streamer tape.

The experience of a manufacturing company in the Midlands (UK), which makes coin and note counting equipment, has been quite similar. It is attaching this equipment to a local area network and keeps accounts on the file server. The LAN controls the coin equipment and provides information consolidation. This LAN and coin equipment is sold as a system to banks, with the small personal computers integrated into the measurement machines.

Using the foregoing, we can generalize on a LAN-system structure demonstrating how an aggregate of interlinked microcomputers can serve within an interactive sale-oriented environment. The capture of information is simplified with personal computers—whether it is for management or bread-and-butter-type applications. There are four reasons for the increasing success of PCs and LANs:

1. The zero cost of the microprocessor.
2. The steady drop in the cost of central processing units and storage while telecommunications costs remain high.
3. The fact that intelligence dedicated at the personal implementation level adds very little to the budget, but it can give a great deal in efficiency.
4. The results which we can get by using intelligent WSs the right way, including zero defect software—which until recently was a dream.

The cost of central processing units roughly drop by 35 percent per year, and those of high-speed memories by 40 percent. But telecommunications costs drop only slightly, keep steady, or even increase (depending on the country). These facts often tip the balance to the benefit of PC and LAN. They also provide for economic justification of the way user organizations look at the problem. This higher quality of service has many aspects; zero-defect software is one of them. Figure 25.2 shows a steady improvement in a 3-year period reflected in warranty claims per 1 million licenses.

25.5 Budgeting for the Myriaprocessor

Like any other product or service, myriaprocessor solutions must be budgeted. The budget of PCs and LANs will typically depend on four major factors:

1. *The local area network plant.* Cable, taps, bus interface units—but also the hard disk and printer(s) attached to the LAN.
2. *The online workstations.* The personal computers, graphic

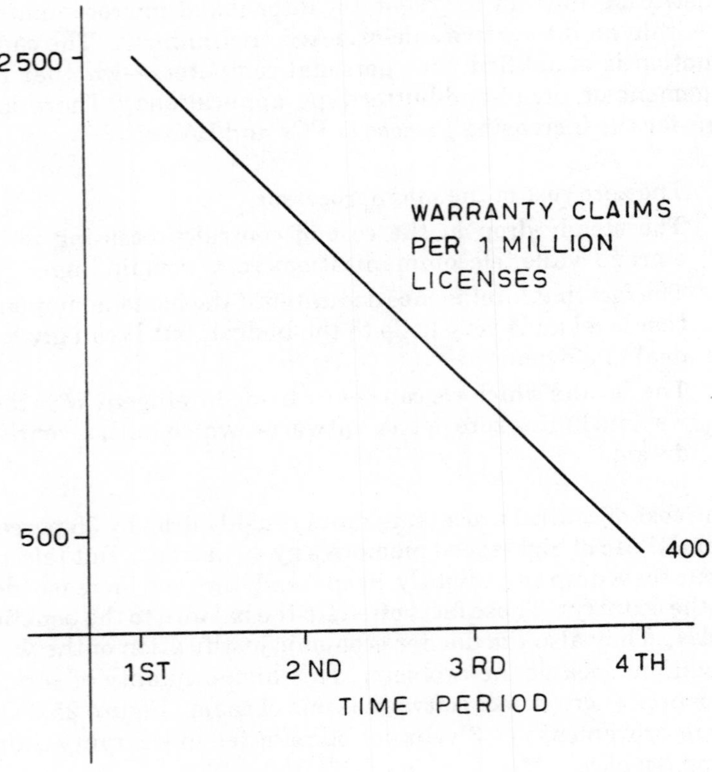

Figure 25.2 Zero-defects software and its aftermaths.

tablet, high-resolution video unit(s), voice recognition, and other I/O media.

3. *The applications programs.* Preferably bought as packages.
4. *The systems effort.* For myriaprocessor implementation, upgrade, expansion, maintenance—as well as the well-rounded end-user and specialist *training* which is necessary.

Looking into similar installations and their cost figures helps a lot in terms of budgeting. Table 25.4 presents summary figures based on 4 years of experience regarding a broadband solution with a university-installed LAN connecting mainframes, minis, micros, terminals, and the student's own personal computers. A sound methodology is always necessary when comparing costs. The first basic principle is to proceed with a well-documented study and to do so on a limited, well-defined area. This will provide necessary internal references and offer a vision of the whole applications domain. The second is to develop internal resources able to attack and master the myriaprocessor subject—not to depend on the manufacturer. With LAN and personal computers, DP/DB/DC has become an issue of human dimensions.

For every myriaprocessor project:

- The working team must be small—preferably two to three people, four people maximum.
- The timetable should be short: 4 to 8 months from decision to implementation—not years
- The projects must be well-defined and precisely stated and of reasonable dimension so that a small team can master and implement it in a few months.

These observations answer the issue raised by many companies regarding project size and ways to get started. When followed, they will

Table 25.4 The budget of a University-Installed LAN

	Cost ($)	*Factor*
1st year (first implementation)	18,000	Overall expenditure
2nd year (operations)	12,600 40,000	Staff Equipment
3rd year (operations)	27,000	Staff
4th year (major expansion)	27,000 80,000	Staff Equipment

help keep the budget low and the work will be focused and will proceed along manageable lines. The small team should occupy itself with mastering the LAN concept—not with writing applications software. The programs should be purchased from those available in the market as microcomputer packages: an estimated 2,000 programs are available today for business applications.

The cost associated with the workstation is variable according to the configuration we choose and the value-added features we wish to obtain. Stripped-down versions for personal computers typically sell for about $1,000; with video units, graphic tablet, and I/O card interface they are something more than $2,000 at the lower end. The high-end today means an 80386 or 68030 microprocessor with a 50- or 60-megabyte hard disk and 0.5 or better megapixel resolution. The price stands at $7,000 to $8,000. A $4,000 to $5,000 price tag can thus be taken as an average price—but a proper budget should be based on details, not on averages.

These are American prices. They are marked up when sold in Europe, and this significantly increases the cost of the workstation but not in a way that upsets the balances. In a budgetary evaluation of this kind, an American bank in London found the cost at the $5,000. If it was not for the manufacturer's mark-up, the cost would have been nearer to $3,000 per WS.

A local area network's physical plant needs a cable. It may be twisted wire, flat wire, or coaxial cable (protected or unprotected). Typically, from the cheapest to the most expensive the cost varies from $0.75 per meter to $1.40 per meter, not even a 1:2 ratio. When we talk of, say, a 300-meter network, we mean a very limited expense. The same is true of the taps. Taps, cable, and other simple jigs and fixtures will together represent a cost of about 1 to 2 percent of the total LAN expenditure. Much more expensive are the bus interface units (transducers, transceivers). The cost for baseband and broadband solutions are in Table 25.1. These are today's prices. Developments in VLSI and high volume will bring the prices down. Different estimates suggest that in a short time prices may drop by a factor of 2.

25.6 An Open Vendor Policy

To get more mileage out of the dollars invested in PCs and LANs, user organizations should follow an open vendor policy (OVP). This means diversity in procurement, always choosing both prime and second sourcing, and:

- Buying hardware based on software availability—not vice versa
- Assuring the manufacturer has development plans for workstations, attached user-friendly devices, and LAN connections
- Giving preference to ready, off-the-shelf packages which can be tested
- Testing data communications protocols, DBMS for file servers, and other horizontal software offerings to guarantee availability and efficiency

Whether the purchase concerns hardware or software, it is wise to make the same type of contract with all vendors in a given class. The client organization should write the contract to protect its own interest, and the contract should include penalties in case the vendor does not meet the promises made.

An OVP implies the need to follow organization-wide standards. Established for a major financial institution, Figure 25.3 offers an example. It talks of prime and second sourcing for PCs, suggesting work-alike solutions to the IBM PC (PS/2 and successors), not just look-alike offerings. The next major factor is LAN compatibility. As a further example, Figure 25.4 presupposes that a token ring LAN choice has been made. Immediately a number of token ring interface levels show up. The higher-level interface is the advanced program-to-program communication (APPC). Based on the logical unit 6.2 (LU 6.2), it provides the top-layer support for LAN-based program-to-program exchanges. Immediately thereafter is the network basic input-output system (NETBIOS) architecture.

The NETBIOS interface on the token ring LAN consists of five basic services:

- General control
- Name support
- Session control
- Datagram
- Debugging support

The general control services allow program-to-request status information—stop operations for a given name or reset the complete NETBIOS

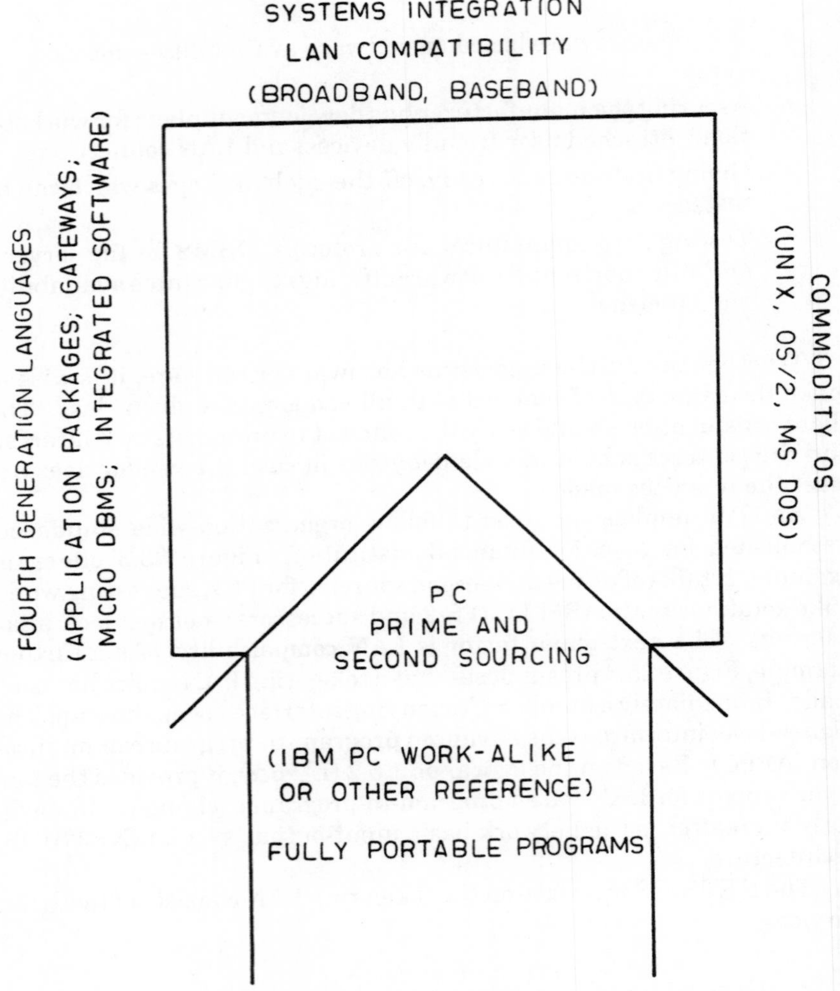

Figure 25.3 Frame of reference of an open vendor policy to guarantee the interests of the users.

interface. Figure 25.4 also identifies the layers belonging to the logical link control (LLC) interface, the media access control level, the adapter support interface, DOS, and the PC token ring adapter. This is the level of detail necessary when we speak of defining LAN compatibility.

An OVP requires detailed technical references to be effective. There are also legal and functional prerequisites to be met. The latter can be expressed in terms of vendor selection criteria, dividing into critical, quality-oriented, and other requirements.

Critical requirements are those that must be met in order to proceed

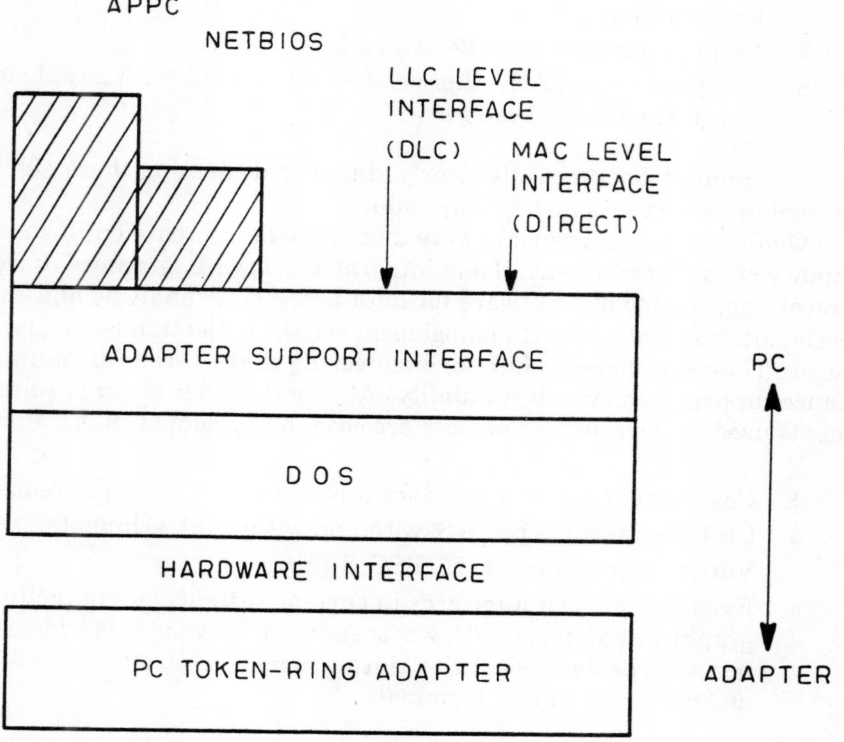

Figure 25.4 Token-ring interface levels, from APPC to MAC.

with implementation. The following list is an example based on a recent study on workstations:

1. The vendor must offer quality products with contractually defined MTBF and MTTR.
2. Communication must be possible between all workstations, databases, and mainframes.
3. Response time must be less than 2 seconds, preferably subsecond.
4. There must be software menu access, with direct access as an alternative.
5. Support of LAN is an integral part of the offer.
6. Data must move between the host and the PC—without excessive overhead.
7. Prototyping tools must be available.
8. In regard to the LAN, other vendors' equipment must be able to be attached to the system.

The request for proposals clearly stated that meeting these eight critical factors was a must for any vendor.

Quality-type requirements were those used for comparison, such as quality of commercially available integrated software, graphics, word processing, commodity software for data processing, analysis and experimentation tools, project management software, electronic mail, and so on. They also included human engineering characteristics, maintenance support, and overall suitability. Among the other major requirements used in the selection process are economics, compatibility, and:

1. Cost comparison to a standard prototype taken as a reference.
2. Cost effectiveness per WS, with and without attachments.
3. Variety of gateways (X.25, BSC, TTY).
4. Existence of good interfaces to current systems and of picture graphics at all terminals, whether or not the vendor is addressing voice processing and, in this particular case, offering teller and other specialized terminals.

Legal requirements were not much different from those used by the organization in contracting other types of computers. The following items were at the top of the list:

1. Our own contract, which should be one type for all vendors, per class of equipment (hardware or software).
2. Have reliability and availability clauses with penalties established at the 99 percent up-time level.
3. List price was only a beginning reference level. Discounts had to be negotiated.

PCs and LANs were bought, but mainframes were rented. The policy was to sign a 5- to 6-years contract with steady prices on rental but not on maintenance. Maintenance had to be indexed to inflation to avoid the excuse of service degradation because costs were not covered. Also the contract implies at least 2 years of spares and skills after the vendor closes down the selected product line. Further, a long-standing policy required that prior to prime sourcing being selected, it was fundamental to verify that the vendor had the software and hardware product promised, when it was promised. Second sourcing was chosen going through the same verification steps.

Designing the personal computer and LAN configuration for headquarters and the periphery was always based on both prime and second sourcing. This required consistent tests to assure compatibility and program portability and to establish contractual clauses to that end. For PCs and LANs the contracts always included maintenance as the contractual vendor's responsibility for the first year. The user organization prepared its own maintenance team to take charge thereafter. These approaches were clearly defined, not just described, and management retained the responsibility to see that they were observed.

25.7 Making the Commodity Software Choice

The technical, functional, and legal clauses we just reviewed are valid for all types of information systems purchases: for big computers and small computers, for interfaces and for communications devices, and for hardware and software. Still as far as the commodity software choices are concerned, more precision is required. To start with, one of the basic principles in software policy is to assure that *prototyping* (or, alternatively, system analysis and design) for DP, DB, DC, and end user functions is available to verify who will provide the applications packages, when exactly they should be available, and how much the packages will cost and/or the in-house programming work needed. A policy can also be established that in parallel to the selection and implementation procedures, the organization will train both the systems specialists and the end-user personnel. Policy also calls for assuring a fallback in case of delays.

A number of critical issues should characterize the choice of packages:

1. *Availability.* How long has the package been in general use? How many installations? Can we talk to current users?
2. *Hardware.* What is the minimum configuration the software will run on? Input-output specifications? Communications requirements?
3. *Flexibility.* Will the package run on different equipment or machine configurations? Can its functions grow? Is it modular? Can we purchase it one module at a time?
4. *Programming.* Is the package written in a modern and efficient language? Under which operating system has the package been designed? Under which OS does it currently run? Can it be ported?
5. *Support.* How much support will the vendor supply during installation? Will the vendor train systems professionals? End users?
6. *Maintenance.* Is maintenance regularly provided? What is the vendor's policy on new releases? Steady enhancements? How will we be notified about the ongoing work regarding new features and improvements of the package?

Documentation, costs, and current applications references are the other three major places on which management should focus significant interest prior to decision. For each, critical questions should be developed and made available throughout the organization.

Regarding documentation, the following questions should be asked: Does documentation include system- and run-level narrative descriptions? System logic and logic flow charts? Input-output and file descriptions? Communications protocols? File access? Preferred file organization? Operating instructions? Input preparation instructions? Prompts and self help?

The issue of cost should not be forgotten. Price alone is not enough. Pertinent queries include: Is the package available for purchase on a

LAN employment basis? What are stated conditions? Are there extra cost options and special features? How much will the vendor charge for training, installation, conversion, maintenance, and any modifications that might be necessary?

The answer to these questions helped to identify the quality of the software manufacturer, and of the field representatives, and also the product. It is most important prior to making a choice to find out the weaknesses. In the final application, these are going to be the most visible.

Chapter

26

LAN Applications Where Cost Benefit Really Counts

26.1 Introduction

Around 1980, when local area network installations got started, companies proceeded with one or two experimental LANs to help define for themselves what the new technology was all about. Atlantic Richfield, for example, installed a pilot project that linked 50 employees in its Los Angeles corporate headquarters. As the director of Arco's office support program suggested at the time: "People are collaborating more on documents; it is affecting the working style."

At the Transamerica Corporation offices, some 200 employees on three floors have been connected by LAN. The user organization looked forward to improved quality in the way people work. A similar reaction came from the Metropolitan Insurance Company, in New York: "With the minis," management pointed out, "clerks use some functions and not others because minicomputers are not user friendly; with each PC dedicated to one person, this has radically changed." The following jobs were the first to be selected for workstation implementation:

1. Data entry done at the local level. Metropolitan Insurance management found that this activity was significantly simplified. Specifically designed software and input devices helped the clerks enter the application for insurance, subsequently forwarding the file to the mainframe for processing.
2. Prospecting was made by sales agents using the PC. This integrated application involved client handling, report generating, and the evaluation of profit and loss.
3. New managerial functions have been implemented. They include a number of management information systems applications, inquiry, file verification, commission evaluation, premiums, electronic mail, and a cash quote system. With PCs and LANs, electronic mail started being used for communications, as a substitute for voice telephoning.
4. The application base was refined, advancing with PC installations at the agents. This is important. With minis, it would have been too costly to expand the network of intelligent machines to the agent level. The PC made this expansion not only feasible but, also, mandatory.

The message is that early PC and LAN implementations have had a dual goal. First, they improved over what was already done through other types of computers. Second, they created new applications landscapes which could be sustained at an affordable cost.

These continue to be LAN objectives. A third class has also been added as companies discovered the savings made possible through LAN implementation. It is the substitution of classical computer links by emphasizing the better cost effectiveness a local area network provides.

26.2 Making a Distinction Between Substitution and Innovation

Improved cost-benefit ratios may result in three ways: reducing the cost of what is already being done without degrading performance, improving the benefit through new applications domains, or, acting on cost and benefit at the same time. A basic management query is: "Can I do the same thing at lower cost? Or, keeping cost steady, can I improve the benefit which I derive?" These are the questions Digital Equipment Corp. asked itself when it decided to switch from DMR interfaces to Ethernet for VAX interconnection. A cost-evaluation study considered the same computer installation as well as communications links—but the type and cost of connectivity was radically changed from one situation to the other.

The typical local and remote DECnet installation of the early 1980s used ten DMR interfaces to interconnect two VAXs and two PDP 11s in a local area. There was also a link with two remote computers. The alternative solution replaced the ten DMRs with an Ethernet and four bus interface units (Deuna). The wide area interconnection was not altered. At the time this application was made, the costs were:

- 10 DMR at $4,400=$44,000
- 4 Deuna at $3,500=$14,000

This is a $30,000 difference between the old and the LAN approach, a cost ratio of 1:3.14. Accounting for interfaces and other supporting gear, the true cost difference is not 1:3 but 1:5. At the same time, the second solution is more elegant and more efficient—a good example on the substitution side of the local area networks equation.

A more complex interconnection situation is shown in Figure 26.1. This involved a variety of suppliers: IBM, DEC, Wang, Xerox, Hewlett-Packard, and Apple and a wide range of equipment, from small mainframes to departmental computers and personal workstations—including nonintelligent terminals and personal computers. As is common, in its early days this aggregate was much simpler. Complexity grew as the number of services increased and a communications-intense environment became the dominant feature. It included:

- Public telex network
- Mailway
- Word processing
- Electronic mail
- Private customers' worldwide mail network
- Telecom multiplexial switch
- Local mainframes
- Remote mainframes
- Other applications

Not only is the jungle of wires in Figure 26.1 confusing but also the whole system lacks robustness. Its functioning largely depends on one multiplexer. It was part of the telecommunications-office automation

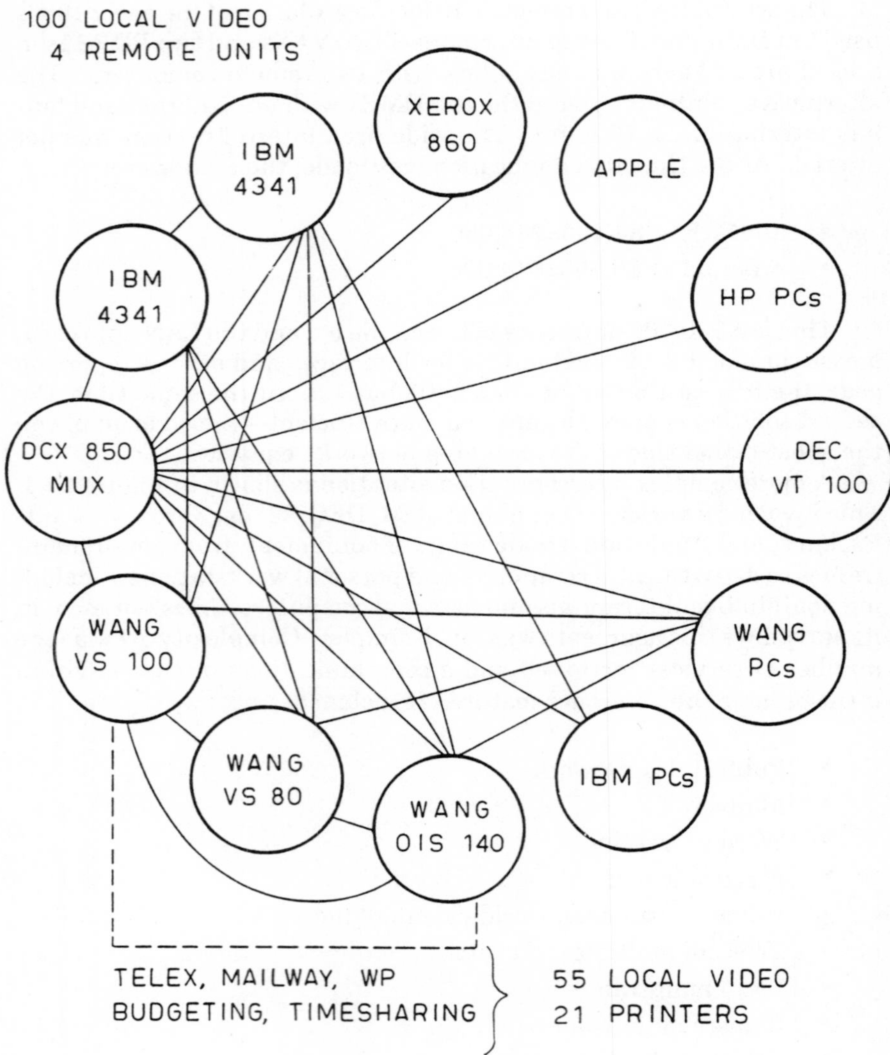

Figure 26.1 Complicated and ineffective interconnection prior to LAN implementation.

effort of a leading American bank prior to LAN implementation. It has been streamlined through a local area network application which simplifies the interconnection picture. Such streamlining is a prerequisite for a new range of applications, the crossing of new frontiers. Once complexity reaches a certain threshold, and Figure 26.1 shows what this means, it becomes virtually impossible to progress further. The wire jungle can be a major constraint. After streamlining, new perspectives open up. It becomes, for instance, possible to actively plan for the integration of voice, data, text, and image so that we would not need to change network design with the evolution of our applications environment.

There are major advantages in converting to multimedia solutions. In one project it was estimated that by integrating voice, image, text, and data, the resulting load would (about 85 percent voice and 12 percent data) be optimized. This project called for handling voice, text and data, and image at high speed on the same pipe, cross-country, with voice given preference. Economics of scale were behind this proposal. According to the projections which were made, the use of high technology in voice handling would have most likely saved some $75 million over 10 years for the company.

A whole infrastructure had to be created to support this system. There were prerequisites to be fulfilled. To do so, the requirements for managerial and professional workstations were clearly spelled out. They included:

1. Strategic consideration to establish goals, timetables, and budgets—in brief, the information systems plan.
2. Multipurpose operations to serve data processing and word processing needs, as well as electronic mail, time management, and document handling.
3. The ability to evolve the system to meet requirements, without modifying applications.
4. Modularity in terms of both physical and logical expansion.
5. Adaptability to the users' evolving needs toward multimedia, making their jobs easier and more productive.
6. Standardization of various logical and physical modules providing homogeneity, compatibility, and portability.
7. Online access to properly designed information center database(s), as well as public databases.

8. User-friendly interfaces, including prompting, help, and forgiveness.
9. On call assistance not only for training but also for timeout and other cases, which should be largely automated.
10. Transparent communications so that the user is unaffected by .the technique or routing used to accomplish a link (local or long haul).
11. Economic considerations to assure that sound investment and operational principles are observed, cost-benefit goals.
12. Steady review and reevaluation to assure actuality and chop the dead wood which invariably develops even in the best-designed system.

As the implementation of this strategy largely documented, the most important—but also most difficult—of the changes which had to be made was one designer's ideas.

26.3 LAN Capacity Planning

There are not many standards or references to guide the designer's hand in projecting what might be necessary in LAN capacity. In preceding chapters we have seen how and why a number of forecasts can go wrong:

- Asking the users about their projected data load practically leads nowhere. Such data load will greatly change with the power of the workstations which we put at their disposition and the applications they support.
- Starting on the premises that LAN capacity planning has lots in common with time-sharing may be nice—but we should recall that it took more than 10 years to understand how to tune a time-sharing system.
- Basing our projection on the LAN is an approach, though we should always remember that the single server with multiple applications on it is not the future. The future is multiple dedicated servers on a LAN.

A sound design principle is that the LAN should not be used as a bus for virtual disking. Core swapping should be the maximum acceptable load. Usage of transport facilities should mainly focus on message exchange. Leaving the information in place is another sound principle with myriaprocessors. It is also the right point at which to start dimensioning studies. Let's, however, notice that it affects the workstation and its storage media as much as it influences LAN decisions.

When the Aircraft Division of General Electric decided to interconnect its mainframes through a LAN, it was the file exchange among mainframes acting as database servers as well as between mainframes and the attached robots which set the stage for a LAN decision. These two factors were instrumental in the subsequent decision that the capacity of the LAN had to be increased by at least a factor of 5.

When a well-known financial institution decided to use a LAN as the kernel of its in-house communications system, the goal was established at the level of multimedia communications including telex. Subsequently, having found no LAN to satisfy such requirements, the first implementation was scaled down to what the market could offer. The overall design is shown in Figure 26.2.

Know-how is the cornerstone. LAN applications which are destined to be successful have to be studied case by case within their environment. We have to look with great care at the details. Ford found that with the same PC and the same application, people used different features, employed them in different ways, and got quite different results. The same is true with LAN implementations.

One of the main constraints today concerns capacity. But higher-capacity local area networks are coming. Fiber optics continue to expand rapidly. The technology's performance in long-distance telephone is moving toward 1.7 GBPS systems and above. New techniques offer still higher bandwidths. Recent attention focuses on industrial and LAN applications of fiber optics. Important progress can be seen in novel optoelectronic devices, passive optical components, and new types of fibers and cables. In fact, the impact of LAN and the local subscriber network is evident in developments such as transmitter-receiver technology and integrated optics for node connection.

Wireless LANs (satellite-based, dependable infrared) are also coming, but they probably will not change the vendor's protocols. The change is in media. The IEEE recommended standards are:

- 802.3, Ethernet/Starlan
- 802.4, token bus/BRB
- 802.5, token ring/BAB

But the number of interconnections may expand. A recent study

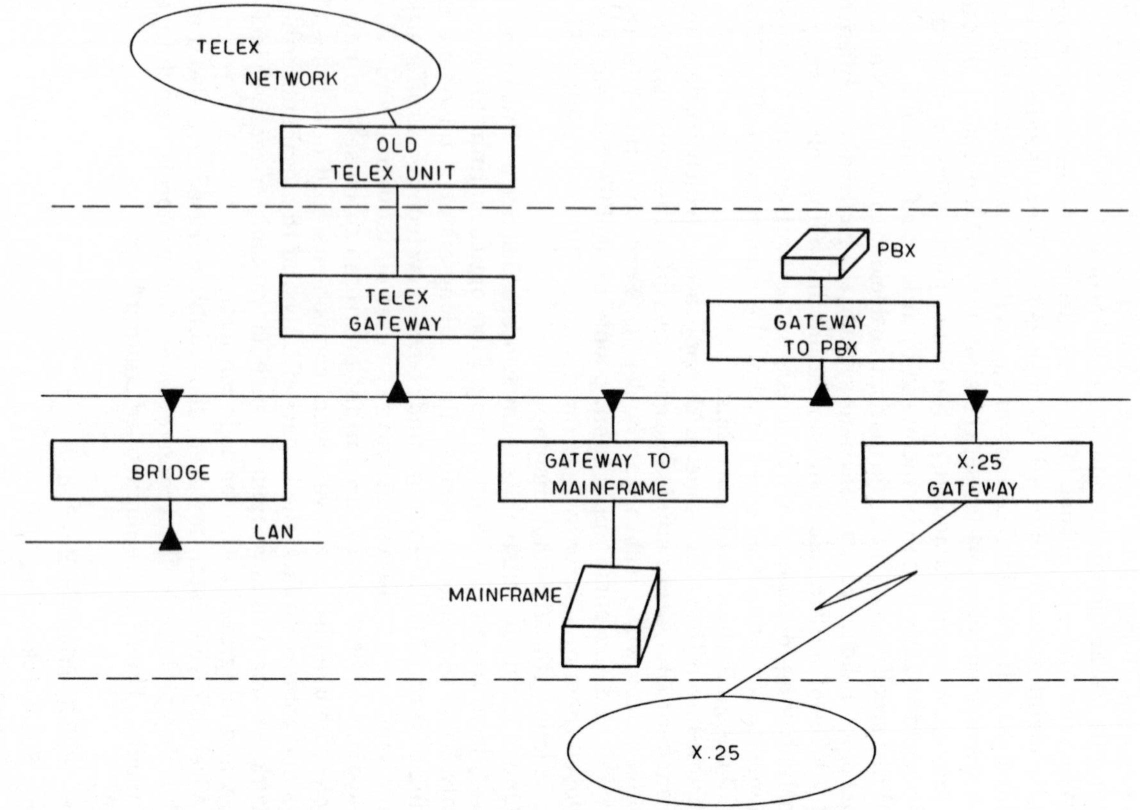

Figure 26.2 Layout of a system interpretating X25, telex, and local area networking.

demonstrated that most solutions serve a community of about 10 users. This is not an average, it is a mode—but it is indicative of a relatively low-level data load. Higher data loads are a characteristic of second-generation LAN implementations. These capitalize on acquired experience from the first-generation LAN, and the data load expands to meet and exceed available capacity at the local area network level.

Another lesson learned with second-generation LAN applications is that security is a major issue. The LAN cable can be easily tapped. There have also been lots of disturbances and interferences in a number of installations. By contrast, LAN reliability and availability has been good from the beginning. Precisely because of these considerations, local area networks show rapid advances particularly in widening applications. The trend to online operations sees to it that interconnection is a critical issue. Higher speeds and performances are sought after. Novel transmission technologies offer a wide range of interesting possibilities, stimulating discussion and a close examination of related issues.

When it comes to evaluating projected LAN data load and security requirements, we cannot afford to stereotype our conceptions. And we can even less afford to be sloppy and careless. If we wish to employ intelligent machines in an able manner, we must act with insight and foresight—which means with more intelligence.

26.4 LAN Availability

About 8 years ago, Brown University established Brunet, a broadband network by Sytek. The installation spans a campus of some 60 buildings. Operations-wide, it supports an impressive range of services: CAD, teleconferencing, shared access to special devices, WP, Teletex, educational TC, energy management, and security management. Prior to the implementation of a LAN solution, the university used a PBX to carry data and got a 25 percent per year escalation of costs. A year after the installation of the broadband LAN, the environment supported:

- 10 major hosts (mainframes)
- 30 minicomputers
- Over 500 terminals
- 100 plus personal computers belonging to the faculty

From the beginning of LAN operations, the students brought in their own personal computers, hooked up to the network, and worked online to the database. There are thousands of PCs working interactively today.

Brunet handles no voice, but gateways have been developed for X.25 and Ethernet. Figure 26.3 shows the network structure with the TV and satellite antennas, head end and four principle lines: north, south, east, and west. The head end includes pilot generators and a frequency

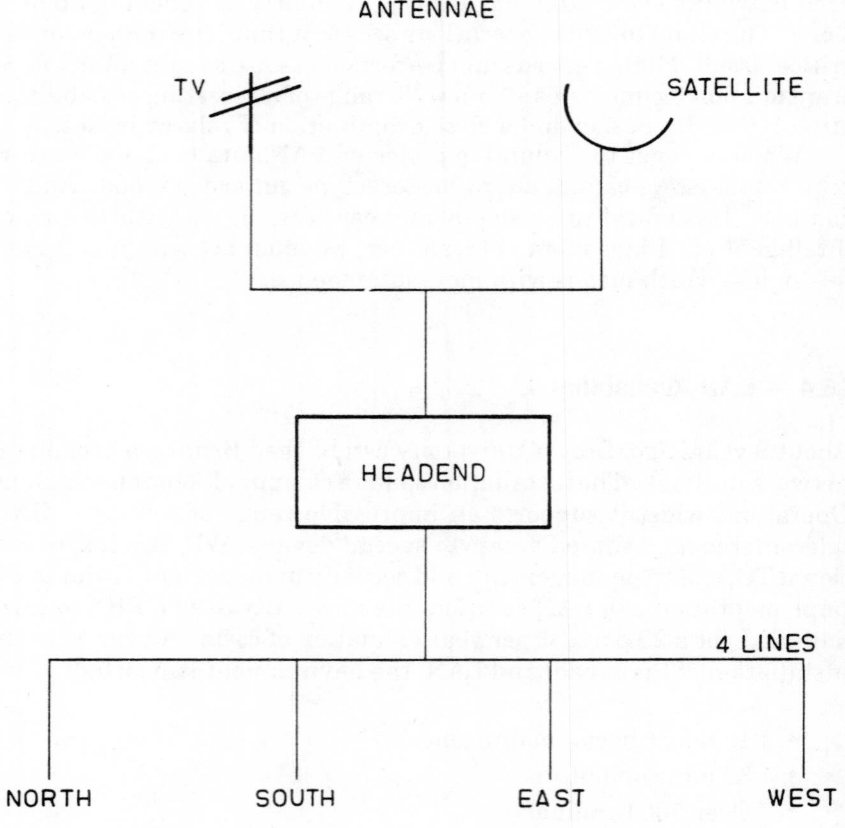

Figure 26.3 Network structure at Brown University including TV and satellite antennas.

translator. The cable does not need to be rigid the whole way through. The installed coaxial is an impressive:

7,500	m underground
350	m in tunnels
2,500	m inside buildings
10, 350	m long topology

There is a total of 20,700 m of cable, given the two wires in parallel. The following were the costs per connection at time of installation: terminals and PCs, $500; graphics WS, $2,000; hosts, $10,000. Attachment costs have become less expensive in the meantime. An approximate implementation budget for items other than transceivers and the attached gear at the time of installation was:

Survey and site preparation	$48,000
Coaxial cable	26,000
Conduit	15,000
Amplifiers	70,000
Head-end spares	15,000
Test and early maintenance	36,000

The information outlets cost of $26,000 for hardware and $20,000 for labor; this was to activate 1600 outlets in 20 different buildings—or about $29 per outlet.

Quite significantly, LAN maintenance is rather simple. It has been carried out by technicians testing amplifiers. Maintenance is eased or made more difficult depending on how good system planning is. Another interesting statistic is the budget the university established for the startup and yearly operations of Brunet:

- Startup budget $ 85,000
- Annual operations budget $150,000

Economics in telephone costs covered a good deal of the annual operations budget—while the obtained service more than compensated for the balance.

A key advantage has been in availability. As a result of a fire at the university's underground duct system, most campus telephones were out for 48 hours—some up to 1 week. The broadband coaxial cable was in operation within 45 minutes. This huge discrepancy in time to repair talks volumes in favor of the LAN. It also gives food for thought regarding installations which continue to be made in new office building, today. The fire at Brown was seven years ago. The lessons learned from it have not yet permeated the knowledge store of architects and building communications designers.

26.5 Cost Evaluation in a Small Business Environment

Part of what makes it so difficult to evaluate the opportunity of local area networks is the speed of innovation in the market place. Vendors are talking about taking advantage of transmissions possible with the new media to provide for video or graphics, not to mention combined voice and data capabilities. These are developments which typically interest the big firm, not so much the small business which has problems of its own to cope with. In this section we will see two applications of local area networks. One in the factory, the other in a commercial office.

The manager of a manufacturing company has been thinking of factory automation for some time. He did not think his firm was ready for robotics but saw advantages in networking, planning, and scheduling in inventory management and on the shop floor. A system analysis established that his factory would require 38 workstations: on the production floor, in the warehouse, in the staff departments, and for administrative and management purposes. Since the company offices were on the second floor of the factory building, the environment was noisy. Protected coaxial was the suggested solution. But one of the computer vendors opposed this plan, suggesting instead the installation of a small mainframe, multithreading the necessary terminals on it. Another vendor suggested a mincomputer installation as a better alternative, with nonintelligent terminals attached to each mini.

The factory manager asked his systems people to conduct a factual and documented study. They came up with four alternatives, evaluating cost and performance for each:

1. The small mainframe alternative was rejected outright as the most expensive and least reliable.
2. If the minicomputer line was followed, for response time reasons this would have called for 6 minis—with rather expensive interconnection problems and no major benefit over PC and LAN.
3. A mixed solution was also examined. It involved minis and PCs

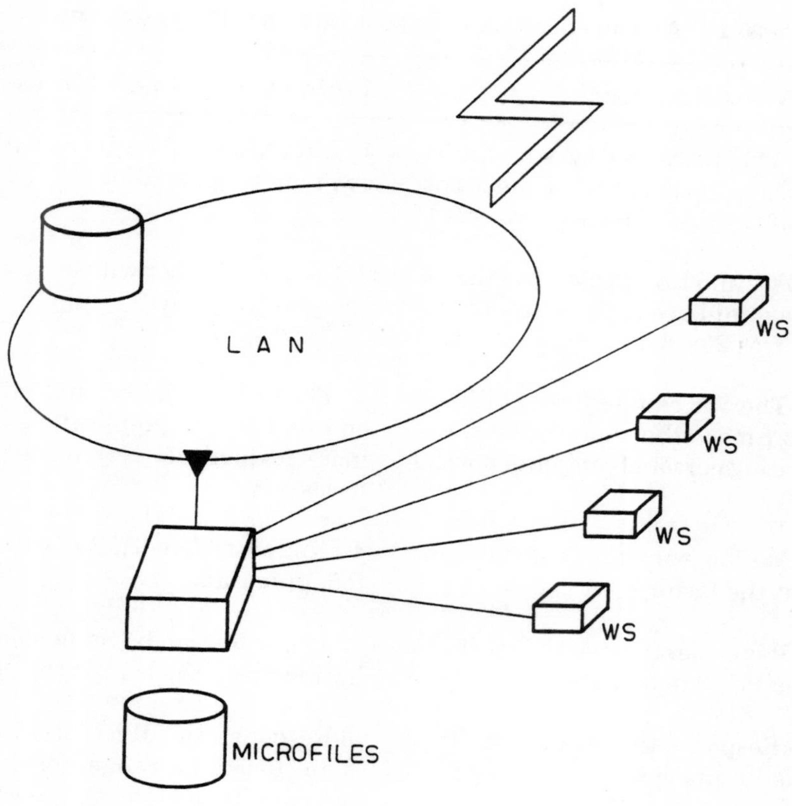

Figure 26.4 Workstation coupler attached to LAN, fileserver and gateway.

and fared better in functionality than solution No. 2 but ended at the upper level of price range. Figure 26.4 shows the concept of the suggested workstation coupler.

4. The fourth alternative considered LANs, PCs, and server stations. Three LANs could easily divide the 38 workstations and maintain a low response time.

Table 26.1 A Comparison LAN and Mini. Are They Really Alternatives?

LAN-based approach	*Minicomputer-run alternative*
1. The LAN can be simultaneously used for other functions than those currently projected.	1. Each mini will be dedicated to one type of application.
2. PCs and LANs cost a fraction of the mini-based approach (alternatives 2 and 3).	2. Costs are higher with out corresponding benefit.
3. The WS can perform at different times other applications, exploiting personal computer power.	3. For each mini, terminals ared, edicated to one application— or more expensive terminals are necessary.
4. Mailboxes can be used throughout the factory.	4. Not possible with the submitted proposals.
5. It is easier to attach hardcopy to the PC, if necessary.	5. Hardcopy can be implemented butincreases the load on the mini.
6. Response time is practically instantaneous	6. Response time fluctuates in the 3- to 10-seconds range, dependingon simultaneousterminal usage.

Alternative 4 was chosen. Because at most WSs there was both specialized and a general work, it was decided to choose PCs with hard disks. The analysts' reasons for discarding the minicomputer-run system are shown in Table 26.1.

Two supply sources were evaluated. The WS cost was practically the same. There was, however, a difference in the cost of servers and BIUs:

- The proposal by vendor A was $383,000 for the projected factory installation.
- The vendor B wanted $427,000 for the same system.

Following negotiations, vendor A offered a 30 percent reduction versus 20 percent from B.

Prior to commitment, a new requirement showed up. The small team of design engineers asked for two CAD workstations. The solution proposed by vendor B was the only one which could support them. Subsequently, the installation permitted an information center functionality as added value, with minimal cost. A server was added for the database. Some of the already installed WSs were used for page editing and access. Closed user groups were supported, limiting the visualization of file content to authorized parties. Management information and decision support applications took off.

The LAN proved to be versatile enough in running other applications, as well. A post-mortem evaluation documented that database efficiency was much greater than with mini-supported solutions.

A systems study for a wholesaler, involving LAN and workstations, elaborated two alternatives. The one manager and his five salespeople could have:

- 6 WSs on the basis of 1 person per PC
- 4 WSs on the basis of 2 salespeople per PC (with the manager having his own unit)

The first solution was preferred. Further, the local warehouse needed two WSs and the accounting office another two WSs. With the 1:1 solution this added up to ten WS plus one file server, printer, and gateway.

At the manager's request, secretarial work was not added in the first configuration since the three secretaries were already equipped with WSs. Subsequently, a cost-benefit evaluation demonstrated the wisdom of having the secretaries work online. Since sales office operations were not complex, it was decided that the WS could be of low cost. It was sufficient for the sales WSs to handle: order entry and inventory management. There was no reason for printers per WS, which helped keep the cost around $3,000. To this must be added a sharing of expenses for LAN installation, taps, BIU, file server, printer, and gateway.

Since all salespeople accessed the same files, it made no sense to provide microfiles at the WS level. However, to dimension the file server it was necessary to know the number of items in inventory for all four product lines. The statistics were as follows:

Products	*No. items*
• White	300 – 400
• Brown	200 – 300
• Lamps	1000 – 1500
• Specials	2000 – 2500
Total	3500 – 4700

As far as product files were concerned, what was needed has been only a fraction of a typical LAN file server. Nevertheless, more space was necessary for the billing operation.

Three vendors were asked to submit proposals; they ranged from $75,000 to $101,000, including:

- Workstations
- Servers
- Bus interface unit
- File server of 80 MB
- Printer
- Gateway

A major benefit was projected from direct online communications with clients and suppliers. The analysts underlined the need to remember that a LAN simply provides the means of communications. It does not guarantee it.

To assure communications, users must develop new ways of doing things, even new work patterns. This is a basic reason why installing a LAN can necessitate training and education activities over and above our efforts to show people how to use it.

Let's now examine benefits to the company from direct billing. $40 million per year is the billing level of the described operations. At 300 days per year, this amounts to about $130,000 per day. With online billing, the company expected to obtain a 5-day difference in value. With the prevailing 10 percent interest paid to banks, it amounts to a level of $120,000 per year. In less than 1 year the LAN and WS hardware expense was recovered. Software and training expenditures absorbed savings from another 4 1/2 months of operation.

26.6 A LAN Perspective Expended to Document Handling

This example concerns a large organization that decided to study the implementation of LAN and workstations. As a first goal, focus was placed primarily on managerial applications. This included spreadsheets and business graphics—online to information center facilities—but also time management and scheduling chores. It was decided that a LAN implementation should be projected around these main lines of interest. The bandwidth and type of the local area network studied was bound by these considerations. It documented that if it were only for secretarial functions a baseband solution (of up to 2.5 MBPS or, depending on architecture, 10 MBPS) might suffice. But the heavily managerial needs implied a broadband choice.

This set the stage for one of the most imaginative LAN implementations which have taken place, including a beginning of document handling capabilities to replace the movement of hard copy and microfiche through the office. However, the most significant part is the fact that provision of a broadband infrastructure made feasible, in 1987, scanning, filing, retrieval, manipulation, and flow of document images within the organization. The system consists of the local area network linking bit-mapped workstations and dedicated servers. One of the servers is attached to a large optical disk storage system. Software supports the substitution of documented images instead of physical paper. Figure 26.5 shows the configuration (it is FileNet). This optical disk-based image system was designed to perform well-defined repetitive tasks. The range of complexity of these tasks can vary widely depending on the required processing steps and the application.

The mechanics are based on the concept of decoupling information—in this case, the image from the paper which was formerly necessary for its use. A set of tasks can be defined for each type of document and for each specific workstation. The online optical disk-based library can support up to 70 million document images, which amounts to 4.2 terabytes. Software allows the user to employ windows on the workstation's bit-mapped display and invoke:

- Database query
- Image indexing
- Verification
- Annotation

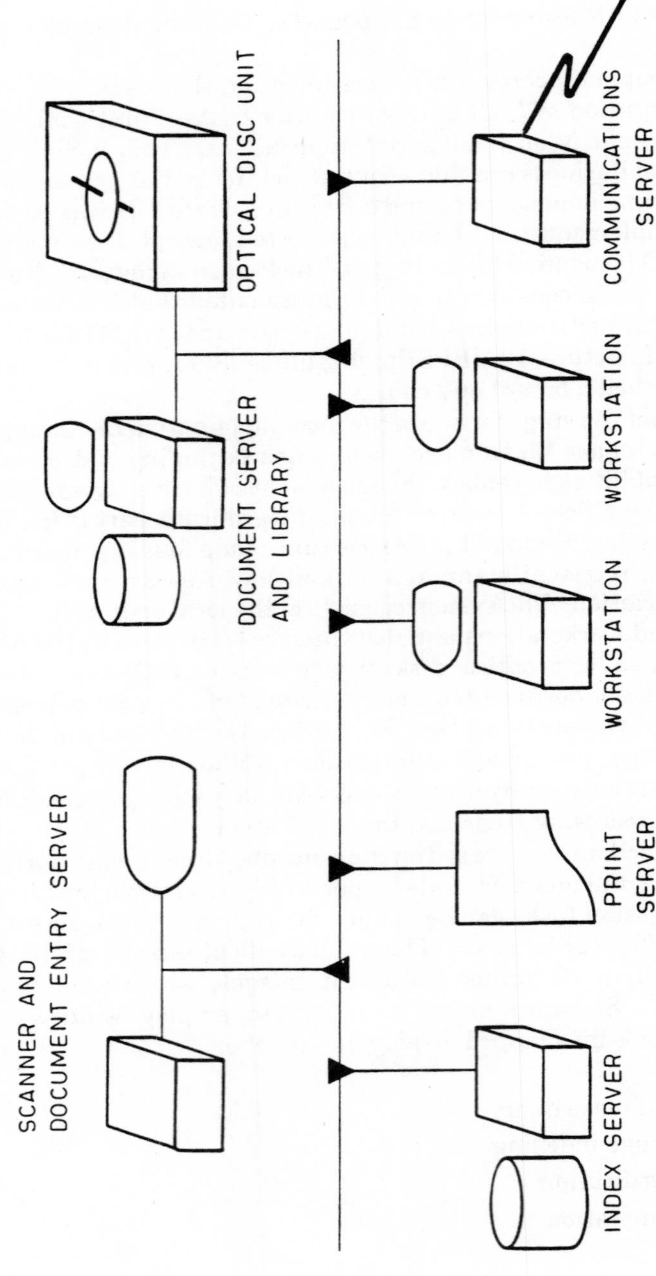

Figure 26.5 A LAN configuration including optical disk storage unit, document servers, index server, gateway, and many WS.

- Printing
- Word processing

Mainframe access is supported through terminal emulation windows.

Facilities and information required to perform office functions on digital paper images reside in one workstation along with access to a large image database. With this approach, management has automated tools to aid in controlling the flow of work in the office, while the clerical staff can work in parallel on the same application, if necessary. The optical disk drives are write once read many (WORM). They employ a 12-inch double-sided disk capable of storing approximately 2.6 billion bytes per cartridge. The library supports from one to four optical disk drives. Other peripherals attached to the document server include magnetic tape and magnetic disk drives.

Most network services on the LAN are provided from dedicated servers and a specialized set of application protocols used to obtain services from these devices. The application protocols address themselves to cache management, document handling, database query, batch entry, and queue management.

The cache protocol looks after storage and retrieval of objects from magnetic disk. The format and semantics of the bytes are unknown to the protocol which supports block-level access to objects. Therefore, either the entire object or some specific portion can be stored or retrieved. Objects residing on either magnetic or optical disk are assigned a unique binary document identifier when stored on the server and this value is returned to the calling client. The magnetic disk attached to the system is used to hold:

- Basic applications software
- The locator database which is responsible for mapping the document numbers to cartridges in the library
- Data being read from or written to optical disks

Among the servers in the system are document entry, index, print, and gateways:

- Document entry servers control the scanning, indexing, and verification tasks necessary to enter scanned paper images into the system.

- Index and print servers are responsible for supporting the database query and laser printing functions.
- Gateway servers assure both the internet routing and communications with other systems.

The software on the document server controls the optical disk jukebox and provides the optical storage filing function to workstations and servers attached to the LAN. This software works along with transport and application protocols which support access to the network services provided on the document server.

The other major issue facing management, as LAN experience accumulated and operations expanded, has been better solutions to communications. Here again, formats and protocols were the two pillars of the developing information system. Any network must define formats of information transferred between its nodes over links connecting them. And it must specify the protocols—hence, the rules—associated with the transfers. Formats and protocols are fundamental references in a functionally layered system, represented in the form of a meta-implementation. This means decomposable into components which are essentially protocol machines. The latter generate the valid output sequences in response to input sequences, subject to the associated rules for distinct information transfers. Meta-implementations resemble actual implementations in that they are defined in terms of a formal, executable notation using explicit data structures and having an underlying abstract machine environment. At this company, meta-implementations provided a concrete model for real implementations—which shows what a company can achieve after reaching the required level of expertise.

26.7 Designing Increasingly Powerful Workstations—Project Athena

The optical high-capacity storage file server addresses itself to the larger firm as do the design and availability of increasingly powerful workstations. Whether in America, Europe, or Japan, the current generation of WSs is taken only as a stepping stone toward the very high-capacity productivity that will be available (first hardware, then software) around 1990. At MIT, Project Athena is seen as a response to perceived problems of supporting managers and professionals.

The goal of Athena was to get away from centralized resources and associated high costs.* The project has three major areas:

1. Fostering innovation.
2. Developing a new architectural concept.
3. Implementing natural languages through artificial intelligence.

In order to foster innovation, Project Athena sponsors proposals from the MIT faculty, some 50 to 60 proposals per semester. Two-thirds are renewals, one-third are new projects. In 1987, 98 distinct projects were funded, about three-quarters of them having an impact on the MIT curriculums. One out of four was quite successful.

The overall goal is the development of a computer environment supportive of the 1990 educational perspective. Currently used equipment respond, to the prevailing hardware specifications, namely:

- 32-bit microprocessor with more than 1 MBPS of power
- *n* megabytes of central memory
- virtual address space
- local storage (magnetic and optical)
- high-resolution bit-map graphics
- pointer or selector (3-button mouse)
- LAN connection (with TCP/IP)

The specific aim is to put one of these WSs in front of every student, at total cost less than 10 percent of tuition per year. The not so clearly stated further aim is 5-MIPS, then 10-MIPS workstations. In the domain of managerial implementation, the top MIT project and offspring of Athena is X-Windows.

One of the basic premises of Project Athena is that both the system architecture and the operating system should have interactive, real time characteristics to facilitate multiple communication. An example is efficient document creation and editing, connected to interactive graphics. It is an architecture of eight layers, top to bottom:

1.. Pictures and image.

---

*The project was announced in 1983 with two partners: DEC and IBM.

2.. Drawings.
3. Properties of materials.
4. Structural drawings.
5. Construction codes.
6. Financial analysis.
7. Planning and evaluation (PERT) chart.
8. Geotechnical data.

Today, most existing architectures are rather weak in support of these areas. A new architecture will have to be exploited to incorporate them and allow advanced design features of the future. Part of this architectural solution is optical disk technology. In this specific MIT example, optical disks store pictures and image, thus serving the higher-up layer of the outlined structure.

The architecture under development supports secure direct access from all dedicated processors, enabling them to efficiently store, retrieve, or manipulate documents in their own storage (optical, magnetic) and in networked database servers. Currently available architectural functions are in the process of being greatly extended and enhanced. At the same time, natural language implementation through AI is a top-priority software project—including language translation. At MIT/Athena, there is a six-language support: English, Japanese, Russian, German, French, and Spanish. The project focuses on the ability to sustain a discourse in multiple languages. Other aims include:

- Reading foreign newspapers
- Menu-based 3-D presentation, such as navigation, to find an apartment
- Exercises to analyze voice spectograms

Some of the WS-based natural language subsystems are currently being pilot tested. The system goal is coherence, accommodating heterogeneous hardware, but having:

- One OS (Unix BSD). Different OS options have been examined and 4.3 BSD was chosen because it has valid functions. System V has been dropped because of inadequate support. MS DOS/Xenix was also eliminated.
- One DBMS (Ingres).

- Standard network protocols. TCP/IP is the current reference. No decision has yet been made on LU 6.2, DIA/DCA, or X.400. The ISO/OSI migration so far has not been defined, but will be so when the U.S. government supports OSI. However, Ingresnet is used for remote database access. This helps to immediately implement a distributed database environment.

Over 2000 WSs under Unix 4.3 BSD were planned to be on this network when the present text was written. Athena is also expected to go into business environments. With this in mind, a small set of languages has been chosen. C, Lisp, and Fortran were retained. Pascal was dropped. Since fourth-generation languages (4GL) are supported, those in the Ingres constellation are Quel, Equel, Vifred, RW, and ABF. Also important is the choice of a standardized data representation: graphics, equations, and vector fields. Project Athena adopted GKS as 2-D standard is not yet dedicated, but it should be before too long.

26.8 CASE—A Comprehensive Picture of Technological Change

Because of its multifunctional interests, Project Athena provides a comprehensive picture of the supporting services which will be necessary in the future for workstation implementation. The choices being made for it are valid and can serve as a frame of reference for the future. Two more references are in order:

1. User-oriented applications.
2. Consistent software development efforts.

Compound electronic documents and electronic publishing are the key for user orientation. The dual facility incorporates support for the seventh layer of ISO/OSI with desktop publishing systems.

Graphics operations were bypassed when large organizations and publishers spent millions to convert to electronic composition equipment. Until desktop publishing came along, it took hours after artists finished their work before a chart or graph was ready to print. While complex jobs such as camera-ready pages for books cannot yet be efficiently handled through desktop publishing, simpler applications can be handled. Using a low-cost graphics workstation, an artist can get camera-ready versions of charts and graphs from a LaserWriter printer in minutes. Once the chart is created, it can be stored electronically and updated when necessary. Currently available compound electronic document routines can create text, tables, maps, bar and pie charts, and other graphics illustrations. They can then be transmitted electronically to a similar WS. Some organizations use this procedure instead of expensive electronic composition systems.

The most recent high-technology issues at the software development side are:

- Application generators
- Computer-aided software engineering (CASE).

CASE, like CAD/CAM, is an ambiguous term. In its narrower sense, it usually refers to graphical aids for program design as opposed to the old programming and coding routines previous tools focused on. In its broader sense CASE refers to media which take graphics-based designs and output-finished programs. This is a technology under development. CASE increasingly incorporates expert system capabilities. Rule-based programming is potentially the greatest advance since the change from batch to online processing.

Until CASE becomes a mature technology, the application generator may have a few years of explosive growth. However, how successfully the computer vendors will adapt to the next stage of technology is an open question. Successful implementation will require a combination of foresight, training, momentum, product quality, and direction. Application generators, also known as application development systems, generate complete sets of programs without procedural code. They are a type of 4GL-oriented language and are usually associated with relational database management systems. Program code generators, report program generators, query languages, and screen design programs may be part of an offering. But there are also freestanding application generators. All are software productivity aids.

The major objective of application generators is to increase programmer productivity, for either professional programmers or end users. They help to:

1. Maintain a short learning curve.
2. Interface with the current systems and files.
3. Support both batch and online environments.
4. Provide adequate documentation.

As with all complex software, application generators must be selected systematically, matching the tools to specific application needs. Prototyping of applications is one of the more important uses of generators. Prototypes may be sample screens, functional models, or evolutionary systems. Other features of application generators include fast and ready implementation, agile use in prototyping, ease of maintenance, ability to impose standards, and an integrated development process that is transparent to the complex systems environment.

When the proper implementation perspective is maintained, application generators have specific application areas in which they are exceedingly useful. But there are also other areas in which they are not the most effective solution. They are superior for end-user programming of systems more complex than spreadsheets. They are inferior for production applications with complex file interactions. They are popular with end users because they can be used with relatively little training and require no support from professional programmers. They also produce lower error rates in the object program and are self-documenting and easy to modify. But application generators scarifice operating efficiency for general usefulness. End users do not care if the computer efficiency is good; they simply want the online systems benefits and the ability to prototype and modify at will—at the moment they need the service.

Advanced graphics for management use and powerful development tools come together in furthering technology implementation. The same is true of workstations and LAN technology. These are not subjects to be taken piecemeal. *We must know what we are doing throughout the whole breadth of the implementation. We must have a grand design and a strategic plan.*

As with all complex software, application generators must be selected systematically, matching the features to specific application needs. [illegible] is one of the more important features of generators. [illegible] may be [illegible] screens, [illegible] models, or [illegible] systems. [illegible] features of [illegible] generators include [illegible] and [illegible] management [illegible] of the complex systems [illegible].

[illegible] implementation [illegible] sometimes [illegible] specific [illegible] areas in which they are [illegible], but there are [illegible] in which they are not the most effective solution. [illegible] of systems [illegible] are [illegible] for [illegible] with complex [illegible]. They are popular with [illegible] because they can be used with relatively little training and require [illegible] from professional programmers. [illegible] often produce [illegible] and [illegible] the [illegible]. But application generators [illegible] operating [illegible] and [illegible] do not [illegible] computer [illegible] systems [illegible] modify [illegible] at the moment they need them.

[illegible] powerful [illegible] implementation [illegible] and [illegible] the [illegible] and a [illegible].

Index

Abort, 342
Access control, 390
Access protocol, 219
Adapter, 254
Administrator, 400
APPC, 310, 321
Advanced peer-to-peer networking (APPN), 305, 321, 322
Advanced program-to-program communication (APPC), 585
Aloha, 219
ANSI, 376
ANSI Data Description Committee, 485
ASCII, 264
AT+T, 73, 308, 334, 335
Analog signaling, 169
Apollo, 254
Applications Control Environment (ACE), 291, 292
Applications generators, 616
Applications packages, 516
Applications programs, 582
Architecture, 614
- unified, 7
Architectures, tightly coupled, 129
Arpanet, 244
Artificial intelligence, 11, 27, 109
AI constructs, 31, 241, 499
Asynchronous lines, 203
Automated Analytical Trading Group, 500
Automated shop floor, 75
Availability, 590

Backoff, 342
Bandwidth, 143, 154, 165, 167, 400
Bangor Punta Corporation, 501
Banking, 106
Bank of America, 100
Baseband, 120, 121, 136, 156, 168, 227-29, 231
Baseband and broadband, differences between, 170
Bit error rate (BER), 48
Boeing, 266
Broadband, 120, 121, 136, 156, 168, 227-29
231, 235, 236
Broadband local area network, 472
Bridge Communications, 334, 335
Bridges, 396
Brown University, 602
Brunet, 601, 602
Building wiring, 157
Bulk file transfer (BFT), 157
Burroughs, 85
Bus interface unit (BIU), 183, 185, 186, 191, 193,
195, 197, 202-06, 208, 222, 263, 325, 366, 567, 573

Cable television (CATV), 121, 156, 169, 177
Cabling system, 311, 318
Cache protocol, 611
Capacity, 165
CSMA, 70, 187, 219, 220
CSMA/CA, 191, 220
Carrier sensing multiple access and collision
detection (CSMA/CD), 64, 122-24, 203, 218
220, 222, 253, 343
Central processing unit (CPU), 119
Chemical Bank, 502, 503
Cincom, 458
Cipherlink, 459
Citibank, 96
Clarke, Arthur C., 66

Coaxial cable, 161, 333, 604
Collision detection, 206, 207
Collision resolution algorithm, 343
Command interpreter program, 490
Communications, 20, 32, 506
- any-to-any, 101
- multimedia, 24
- networks, modern, 46, 47, 484
- servers, 380, 395, 397, 399
- services, 358
- subsystem, 369
Component functionality, 103
Computer aide design (CAD), 73, 241
CAD/CAM, 96, 103
Computer aided software engineering (CASE), 616
Computer Corporation of America, 457
Computer literacy, 31
Computers and communications, 7, 11, 121
- architecture of, 44
COM, 83
Connection Machine, 32
Connectivity services, 322
CCITT, 207, 243, 470
CDC, 254, 288
Control software, 359
Control, span of, 96
Controlware interface attitudes, 401
Conte/Net, 191, 195
Corvus, 334
Cray, 254, 288
Cross-memory services, 256
Cullinet Software, 457
Cycle redundancy check (CRC), 340

Dai-Ichi Kanavo, 288
Data analyzers, 206
dBase, 552
Database, 527
Database access implementation, 515
Database administrator (DBA), 415, 474, 485
Database bandwidth, 132
Database computer (DBC), 259, 423
Database handlers, 490
Databases, 386
- distributed multimedia, 24
- global, 506
- local, 538
Database management systems (DBMS), 14, 36, 90, 134, 390, 557
Database management, distributed, 40
Database network, 484
Databasing, 491
Data communications, 491
Data conversion, 432
Data definitions, 414
Data dictionaries, user-definable, 38, 390, 413, 484, 485
Data encoding schemes, 206
Data entry, 594
Data exchange, 470
Data flows, 430
Data General, 254
Datagrams, 370
Data integrity measures, 438
Data link, 453
Data link protocols, 265
Data management requirements, 445
Data manipulation, 442
Data manipulation language, 488
Datapipe, 262
Datapoint's ARC, 164
Dataport boards, 254
Data processing, 491
Data redundancy, 446
Data resource development, 392
Data transport, 322
Decision, 97
Defer, 342
Demand assignment, 220
Department of Defense, 335
Design criteria, 119
Design experimentation, 410
Design guidelines, 365
Design semantics, 391
Device independence, 358, 489
Digital Equipment Corporation (DEC), 38, 222, 254, 288, 350, 521, 594
Decmail, 80
DECnet, 38, 132, 350, 595

Digital signaling, 169
Digital signaling processing, 110
Directory services, 322, 390
Direct access storage devices (DASD), 308
Distributed information system, 540
Documentation, 590
Document creation, 417
DCA, 328
DIA/DCA, 80
Down-line loading facility, 195
Driver service, 256
Dual-bus hypercubes, 221

Efficiency, 529
Electrical engineering business, 73
Electronic mail, 482, 483
Electronics Industry Association (EIA), 64,
177, 466, 467
End-user functions, 361, 492, 521
End-user-oriented approaches, 109
EMCS, 539
Engineering workstations, 107
Error notification, 438
Establishment Information System (EIS), 521, 522
Etherlink, 353
Etherlink board, 345, 347
Ethermail, 347
Ethernet, 38, 303, 304, 333, 334, 336, 337, 339,
340, 343, 344, 348, 351, 422, 594
Ethernet controller board, 339
Ethernet control procedure, 342
Ethernet packet structure, 340
Etherprint, 347, 353
Ethershare, 345, 347, 353
European Computer Manufacturers Association
(ECMA), 56
European Informatics Network (EIN), 435
Excelan, 335
Experimental engineering, 96
Expert systems, 27, 107

Factory automation, 74
FIPS (Federal Information Processing
Standard), 264
Fiber distributed data interface (FDDI), 229
Fiber optics transmission, 169
Fifth generation language (5GL), 361, 488
File allocation, 408
File and record selection, 411
File management, 425
File management statistics, 405
File management system (FMS), 433
File manager, 358
File manipulation, 455
FileNet, 609
File servers, 359, 382, 390, 395, 401-403,
408, 412, 418
File servers organization, 392
File server protocol structure, 423, 425
File structure conversion, 433
File transfer (FTS), 267, 428
File transfer model, 427
File transfer protocol, 421
File transfer setup menu, 423
First-in, first-out (FIFO), 381
Flat Concurrent Prolog, 130
Flat wire, 159
Flexibility, 590
Formatting, 456
Fourth generation Language (4GL), 36
416, 487, 488, 615
Forward error correction (FEC), 207
FEP, 483
Frequency division multiplexing (FDM), 20, 129, 164, 165
Fujitsu, 254

Gateways,13, 348, 396, 471, 473, 479, 480
Gateway server, 396
General Electric, 71, 75, 89, 281, 542, 599
General Mills, 84, 85, 89
General Motors, 71, 73, 80, 81, 89, 267
Giga instructions per second (GIPS), 134
Global Concatenation, 32

Global network management facility, 101
Graphics, advanced, 617
Graphics operations, 615
Guarded horn clauses (GHC), 130

Hminet, 430, 432, 435
Hammer and Company, 552
Hardware, 590
Harris, 254
Hartford Insurance, 564
Hewlett Packard, 254
Honeywell, 85, 254, 273, 281, 552
Host Database View, 264, 265
Hub, addressable, 209
Human window, 107
Hyperbus, 253, 254, 265
Hyperchannel, 77, 82-86, 253, 254, 257-59,
277, 301, 562, 564, 565
Hyperchannel B, 264, 265
Hypercubes, 32, 34

ICOT (Japanese New Generation Computer
Project), 481
Icons, 417
Imperial College, England, 130
Inference constructs, 29
Information age network, 50
Information Builders, 457
Information center, 505-507
Information elements (IE), 384, 385, 404
412, 417, 443
Information modeling tool, 428
Information systems, 125
Information transfer program, 326
Initialization, 256
Input-output processor (IOP), 262
IEEE 802, 42, 61, 64, 82, 166, 177, 199,
212, 215, 224, 226, 308
Integrated software, 493
Integration, 7, 37, 75
Integrity, 129
Integrity control, 391
Intel, 222
Intelligent user interfaces, 418
Intellink, 337
Interconnection mechanism, selection of, 367
Interlan, 335
IBM, 85, 254, 264, 273, 281, 288, 303-05,
308-11, 314, 318, 319, 322, 324, 327,
331, 501, 521, 524
IBM/PCM Block Multiplexer Channels, 280
ISDN, 45, 50-53
ISO/OSI, 12, 13, 22, 25, 31, 45, 46, 60, 61,
77, 101, 102, 214, 215, 245, 247,
263, 271, 273, 281, 289, 362, 371,
375, 397, 422, 435, 521, 538, 564
- seven leyers of, 56-60
Internet Protocol (IP), 244, 245
Internet working, 411
Intertask, 373
Intratask, 373

Knowledge bank (KB), 31, 506
Knowledge bank management system
(KBMS), 481

Line processor, 206
Line speed, 507
Link connection functions, 216
Links, 452
Local area networks (LANs), 4, 5, 36, 70,79,
83, 87, 115-17, 122, 123, 131, 135,
138, 140, 143-45, 150, 153, 155, 157,
165, 185, 324, 325, 358, 524, 526, 527,
531-33, 536-39, 545, 546, 553, 566,
583, 599, 607
LAN applications, second-generation, 601
LAN architectures, 357
LAN capacity, 598
LAN controller, 197, 198, 200
LAN design, 245, 246
LAN implementation, 141
LAN file server, 389
Local area network plant, 581
LAN maintenance, 603
LAN processors, 380
LAN software, 382

LAN processors, 380
LAN software, 382
Local and regional files, 394
Location independence, 489
Logical channels, 208
Logical link controls (LLC), 156, 187, 363
Loosely coupled information systems, 156
Low entry networking (LEN), 305, 306, 308

Mail and memogram service (MMS), 297
Mailway, 80
Main frames, 462, 465, 466
Mainframe access, 611
Mainframe business, 75
Maintainability, 15, 514
Maintenance, 590
MAP, 267-69, 538
Manufacturing requirements planning
(MRP), 74
Market study, 575
Martin Marietta Data Systems, 458
MIT, 539, 612
Masslink, 287
Massnet, 77, 268, 277, 278, 280, 289, 300, 353, 362
Massnet LAN software, 510
Masstor systems, 77, 86, 87, 278, 286-89,
300, 394, 511, 562, 565
McDonnell Douglas, 562, 565
Mean time between failures (MTBF), 105, 155
Mean time of system interrupt (MTOSI), 105,
284, 527
Mean time to repair (MTTR), 105, 155
MAC, 187, 199, 308, 363
MAC adapter, 200
Media access unit (MAU), 155, 156, 216, 363
Memory management, 255
Meshes, 34
Messages, 468
Message-based communications system, 369
Message exchange system, 446
Message Mailbox routines (MMS), 285
Message management, 442
Message systems, 368
Meta-implementations, 612
Metropolitan area network (MAN), 14, 162,
208, 521
Metropolitan Insurance Company, 593, 594
Microelectronics and Computer Development
Corp. (MCC), 29
Microfiles, 392
Migration paths, 103
Mitsubishi Research Institute (MIRI), 532, 533
Modules, functional, 403
Morgan Stanley, 487-89, 501
Multimedia, 29
Multimedia database (MDB), 30, 473, 508
Multimedia document solutions, 30
Multimedia solutions, 31, 597
Multimedia support systems,30
Multiple access methods, 221
MAP, 79, 80
Multiple file servers, 414
Microprocessors, 110
Multiprocessor organization, 139
Multicomputer service (MCS), 284
Multimainframe data processing, 259
MMS, 300
Myriaprocessor, 560, 580, 581
Myriaprocessor configuration table, 569
Myriaprocessor hardware directory, 569
MCS, 291-94, 296, 298, 299

Name strategy, 407
Nearest active upstream neighbor (NAUN), 63, 64
Netadm, 286
Netcon, 284
Netex, 254, 255, 259, 261, 268, 270, 353

Netex packages, 256
Netio, 286
Network addressable unit (NAU), 308
Network availability, 38, 438
Network-basic input-output system (NETBIOS), 585
Network concept, 12
Network control central (NCC), 13, 270, 329,
353, 565-67, 569
Network control functionality, 143
Network control functions, 183
Network data integrity, 39
Networking, 7
Networking functionality, 345
Network interconnection, host-level model of,
500, 565
Network integration, 39
Network management, 39, 101
Network, one logical, 13, 35
Network response time, 39
Network server, 345
Network service, 256
Network software, 365, 523
Network status information, 567
Networks, 5, 8, 11, 19, 24, 107
- global, 127
- intelligent, 109
- local, 115
- multimedia, 23
- twisted-pair, 120
Network Systems Corp. (NSC), 82
Network throughput, 153, 154
Netview, 329, 330, 565
Node definition, generic, 138
Nodes, 136, 138, 142, 216, 217
Nomura Securities, 532
Normalization, 43
North American Presentation Level Protocol (NA/PLP), 212
Northwestern Bell, 85, 87-90, 281

Office Document Architecture (ODA), 134, 215
Office document retrieval theory, 385
Omninet LAN, 159
Open vendor policy (OVP), 584, 585, 587
Operating system (OS), 353, 354, 356, 362,
363, 378, 552
OS, distributed, 354, 358
Operator interface, 256
Optical fiber, 162, 163

Packet broadcasting networks, 242
Packet selection, 340
Packet switching, 214
Pain Webber, 526
Parallel Prolog, 130
Passwords, 404
Performance measurements, 129
Peer-to-peer, 224
Perkin-Elmer, 254
Personal Computers (PCs), 451, 453, 462,
465, 466, 468, 531, 555, 560, 589
PC and mainframes, logical differences, 463
PC-to-mainframe communications, 467
PC-to-mainframe connection, 453
PC-to-mainframe connectivity, 452, 459
PC-to-mainframe link, 455, 460, 465
Personal computing, 579
Personal Decision Series (PDS), 264
Personal Sequential inference (PSI) engine, 481
Pipe commands, 448
Polling, 224
Portability, 514
Ports, 203
Prime, 254
Printed circuit board (PCB), 452
Printed server, 393, 394
PBX, 94, 125, 149-51, 153, 272
Process handling, 359
Process naming, 447
Productivity, 570
Product planning, 575
Programming, 590
Program simplification, 371
Project Athena, 383, 612, 613
Protocol, 122, 211, 212, 214, 215, 225, 242, 266, 367, 421, 422, 443,
540

Protocol-based file transfer service, 429
Protocol element, 430, 431
Protocol format, 430
Protocol shells, 273, 276
Protocol standards, 538
Protocol translator, 477
Prototype modeling, 229
Prototypes, 238, 239, 241
Prototyping, 103, 108, 239, 241, 242, 244
Pruning, 389

Quality databases, 568
Quality output, 395
Queries, 416, 445
Queue management, 193
Query tools, 418

Random access memory (RAM), 340
Reference database, 108
Reliability, 96, 416
Relational Technologies, 458
Relationships, 443
Resource-sharing machine, 131
Resource manager, 144
Response time, 231
Retransmit, 342
Retrieval process, 30
Reusability, 514
Ring, 148
Route selection, 322
Routing server, 396

St. Paul Insurance Companies, 560, 561, 566
Satellite Technology, 164
Security, 16
Security control, 237
Semaphores, 383, 449, 450
Servers, 375, 611, 612
Server station, 378
Service and Control Administration (SCA), 294, 298, 299
Session activation, 322, 323
Session service, 255
Siemens, 254
Signature recognition application, 502
Simplicity, 13
Single system view, 126
Slotted rings, 217
Small business system, 580
Software, 104, 609
Software-based communications features, 396
Software, status-reporting, 197
Spatial connectivity, 221
Standardization, 44
Standard software interface, 366
Star structures, 146
Star-type networks, 146
Sumitomo Bank, 533
Support, 590
SDLC, 179, 181
Synchronous lines, 203
Synchronization, 34
System architecture, 12, 27, 40, 41, 260,
361, 498
System application architecture (SAA), 304
System design, 406
System input service (SIS), 297
System integration, 13, 27, 71, 260, 545
System integration studies, 547, 549, 553
System Management Facility (SMF), 286
SNA, 306, 310, 319, 320
System output service (SOS), 297
System services control point (SSCP), 305
System software, 516
Sytek, 601

Tandem, 254
Task management, 256
Task queues, 195
Technical Office Protocol (TOP), 267-69
Telecommunications, 11, 20
Telecommunication network, 46, 47
Texas Instruments, 340
Text and data warehouse, 392
Throughput, 510, 527
TICOS, 191, 193
Tight coupling vs. loose coupling,

129
Time division multiplexing (TDM), 20, 151
Timer management, 255
Token passing, 64, 122-24, 217, 220, 222,
223, 312, 314
Tokens, 217
Toshiba, 107, 164
Trace facility, 255
Transamerica Corporation, 593
Transition plan, 49
Transfer protocol, 436
Transport service, 256
Transmit, 342
Twisted pair, 159

Uncertainty, 37
Uncertainty management, 30
Unisys, 254, 278
U.S. Department of Defense, 267
Univac, 85
Update mechanism, 487
User interface, 255
User request director, 255
Utility routines, 359

Value-added design, 110
Value-added function, 144
Value-added network (VAN), 562
Value-added solutions, 132
VLSI, 374, 376
Virtual terminal service, 411
Visual thinking, 108

Weitzman Institute of Science, 130
WYSIWYG, 214
Word processing, 75
Work area networks, 157
Workstation, 8, 38, 92, 536, 580, 584
- integrated, 546
- intelligent, 557
- managerial and professional, 597
- on line, 581

Xerox, 222, 334
Xerox 8000 Network, 201
Xerox Network Systems (XNS), 335, 336
X.75, 470, 471
X.25, 243, 244, 247, 470, 471
X.21, 249, 250